The
Zohar

by
Rav Shimon bar Yochai
From The Book of Avraham

with
The Sulam Commentary

by
Rav Yehuda Ashlag

The First Ever Unabridged
English Translation with Commentary

Published by
The Kabbalah Centre International Inc.
Dean Rav S. P. Berg Shlita

Edited and Compiled by
Rabbi Michael Berg

For the merit of
righteous and healthy children.
By the merit of the Zohar
righteous souls
shall descend to this world.

And
for the elevation of the souls
of my brother

Chaim ben Yosef

חיים בן יוסף

APPLYING THE POWER OF THE ZOHAR

The Zohar is a book of great mystical power and wisdom. It is Universally recognized as the definitive work on the Kabbalah – and it is also so Much more.

The Zohar is a wellspring of spiritual energy, a fountainhead of metaphysical power that not only reveals and explains, but literally brings blessing, protection, and well-being into the lives of all those who read or peruse its sacred texts. All that is required is worthy desire, the certainty of a trusting heart, and an open and receptive mind. Unlike other books, including the great spiritual texts of other traditions, The Zohar is written in a kind of code, through which metaphors, parables, and cryptic language at first conceal but ultimately reveal the forces of creation.

As electrical current is concealed in wire and cable before disclosing itself as an illuminated light bulb, the spiritual Light of the Creator is wrapped in allegory and symbolism throughout the Aramaic text of the Zohar. And while many books contain information and knowledge, the Zohar both expresses and embodies spiritual Light. The very letters on its pages have the power to bring spiritual wisdom and positive energy into every area of our lives.

As we visually scan the Aramaic texts and study the accompanying insights that appear in English, spiritual power is summoned from above – and worlds tremble as Light is sent forth in response.

It's primary purpose is not only to help us acquire wisdom, but to draw Light from the Upper Worlds and to bring sanctification into our lives. Indeed, the book itself is the most powerful of all tools for cleansing the soul and connecting to the Light of the Creator. As you open these pages, therefore, do not make understanding in the conventional sense your primary goal.

Although you may not have a knowledge of Aramaic, look first at the Aramaic text before reading the English. Do not be discouraged by difficulties with comprehension. Instead, open your heart to the spiritual transformation the Zohar is offering you.

Ultimately, the Zohar is an instrument for refining the individual soul – for removing darkness from the earth – and for bringing well being and blessing to our fellow man.

Its purpose is not only to make us intellectually wise, but to make us spiritually pure.

Glossary of Hebrew words

Torah

Also known as the Five Books of Moses, the Torah is considered to be the physical body of learning, whereas the Zohar is the internal soul. The literal stories of the Torah conceal countless hidden secrets. The Zohar is the Light that illuminates all of the Torah's sublime mysteries.

Beresheet	Genesis
Shemot	Exodus
Vayikra	Leviticus
Bemidbar	Numbers
Devarim	Deuteronomy

Prophets

Amos	Amos
Chagai	Haggai
Chavakuk	Habakkuk
Hoshea	Hosea
Malachi	Malachi
Melachim	Kings
Michah	Micah
Nachum	Nahum
Ovadyah	Obadiah
Shmuel	Samuel
Shoftim	Judges
Tzefanyah	Zephaniah
Yechezkel	Ezekiel
Yehoshua	Joshua
Yeshayah	Isaiah
Yirmeyah	Jeremiah
Yoel	Joel
Yonah	Jonah
Zecharyah	Zechariah

Writings

Daniel	Daniel
Divrei Hayamim	Chronicles
Eicha	Lamentations
Ester	Esther
Ezra	Ezra
Nechemiah	Nehemiah
Iyov	Job
Kohelet	Ecclesiastes
Mishlei	Proverbs
Rut	Ruth

Sir Hashirim	Songs of Songs
Tehilim	Psalms

The Ten Sfirot – Emanations

To conceal the blinding *Light* of the Upper World, and thus create a tiny point into which our universe would be born, ten *curtains* were fabricated. These ten *curtains* are called Ten Sfirot. Each successive Sfirah further reduces the emanation of *Light*, gradually dimming its brilliance to a level almost devoid of *Light* – our physical world known as *Malchut*. The only remnant of Light remaining in this darkened universe is a *pilot light* which sustains our existence. This Light is the life force of a human being and the force that gives birth to stars, sustains suns and sets everything from swirling galaxies to busy ant hills in motion. Moreover, the Ten Sfirot act like a prism, refracting the Light into many *colors* giving rise to the diversity of life and matter in our world.

The Ten Sfirot are as follows:

Keter	Crown
Chochmah	Wisdom
Binah	Understanding
Da'at	Knowledge
Zeir Anpin	Small Face,
	(includes the next six Sfirot):
Chesed	Mercy (Chassadim - plural)
Gvurah	Judgment (Gvurot - Plural)
Tiferet	Splendor
Netzach	Victory (Eternity)
Hod	Glory
Yesod	Foundation
Malchut	Kingdom

The Partzufim - Spiritual forms

One complete structure of the Ten Sfirot creates a *Partzuf* or Spiritual Form. Together, these forces are the building blocks of all reality. As water and sand combine to create cement, the Ten Sfirot

combine to produce a Spiritual Form [Partzuf]. Each of the Spiritual Forms below are therefore composed of one set of Ten Sfirot.

These Spiritual Forms are called:

Atik	Ancient
Atik Yomin	Ancient of Days
Atika Kadisha	Holy Ancient
Atik of Atikin	Anceint of Ancients
Aba	Father
Arich Anpin	Long Face
Ima	Mother
Nukva	Female
Tevunah	Intelligence
Yisrael Saba	Israel Grandfather
Zachar	Male

These names are not meant to be understood literally. Each represents a unique spiritual force and building block, producing a substructure and foundation for all the worlds make up reality.

The Five Worlds

All of the above Spiritual Forms [Partzufim] create one spiritual world. There are Five Worlds in total that compose all reality, therefore, five sets of the above Spiritual Forms are required.

Our physical world corresponds to the world of: Asiyah – Action

Adam Kadmon	Primordial Man
Atzilut	Emanation
Briyah	Creation
Yetzirah	Formation
Asiyah	Action

The Five Levels of the soul

Nefesh	First, Lowest level of Soul
Ruach	Second level of Soul
Neshamah	Third level of Soul
Chayah	Fourth level of Soul
Yechidah	Highest, fifth level of Soul

Names of God

As a single ray of white sunlight contains the seven colors of the spectrum, the one Light of the Creator embodies many diverse spiritual forces. These different forces are called *Names of God.* Each Name denotes a specific attribute and spiritual power. The Hebrew letters that compose these Names are the interface by which these varied Forces act upon our physical world. The most common Name of God is the Tetragrammaton (the four letters, *Yud Hei Vav Hei* יהוה.) Because of the enormous power that the Tetragrammaton transmits, we do not utter it aloud. When speaking of the Tetragrammaton, we use the term *Hashem* which means, *The Name.*

Adonai, El, Elohim, Hashem, Shadai, Eheyeh, Tzevaot, Yud Hei Vav Hei

People

Er	The son of Noach
Rabbi Elazar	The son of Rabbi Shimon bar Yochai
Rabbi Shimon bar Yochai	Author of the Zohar
Shem, Cham, Yefet	Noach's children
Shet	Seth
Ya'akov	Jacob
Yishai	Jesse (King David's father)
Yitzchak	Isaac
Yosef	Joseph
Yitro	Jethro
Yehuda	Judah

Angels

Angels are distinct energy components, part of a vast communication network running through the upper worlds. Each unique Angel is responsible for transmitting various forces of influence into our physical universe.

Adriel, Ahinael, Dumah (name of Angel in charge of the dead), Gabriel, Kadshiel, Kedumiel, Metatron, Michael, Rachmiel,

Glossary of Hebrew words

Raphael, Tahariel, Uriel

Nations

Nations actually represent the inner attributes and character traits of our individual self. The nation of Amalek refers to the doubt and uncertainty that dwells within us when we face hardship and obstacles. Moab represents the dual nature of man. Nefilim refers to the sparks of Light that we have defiled through our impure actions, and to the negative forces that lurk within the human soul as a result of our own wrongful deeds.

Amalek, Moab, Nefilim

General

Aba	Father
	Refers to the male principle and positive force in our universe. Correlates to the proton in an atom.
Arvit	The Evening prayer
Chayot	Animals
Chupah	Canopy (wedding ceremony)
Et	The
Avadon	Hell
Gehenom	Hell
Sheol	Hell
	The place a soul goes for purification upon leaving this world.
Ima	Mother
	The female principle and minus force in our universe. Correlates to the electron in an atom.
Kiddush	Blessing over the wine
Klipah	Shell (negativity)
Klipot	Shells (Plural)
Kriat Sh'ma	The Reading of the Sh'ma
Mashiach	Messiah
Minchah	The Afternoon prayer
Mishnah	Study
Mochin	Brain, Spiritual levels of Light
Moed	A designated time or holiday
Negev	The south of Israel
Nukva	Female

Partzuf	Face
Shacharit	The Morning prayer
Shamayim	Heavens (sky)
Shechinah	The Divine presence, The female aspect of the Creator
Tefilin	Phylacteries
The Dinur river	The river of fire
Tzadik	Righteous person
Zion	Another name for Jerusalem
Yisrael	The land of Israel
	The nation of Israel or an individual Israelite
Zohar	Splendor

The Hebrew vowels

Chirik אֽ, Cholam אֽ אֽ, Kamatz אֽ, Patach אֽ, Segol אֽ, Sh'va אֽ, Shuruk אֽ אֽ, Tzere אֽ.

The Twelve Tribes

Asher, Dan, Ephraim, Gad, Issachar, Judah, Levi, Menasheh, Naphtali, Reuben, Shimon, Zebulun

Jewish Holidays

Rosh Hashanah	The Jewish New Year
Yom Kippur	Day of Atonement
Sukkot	Holiday of the Booths
Shmini Atzeret	The day of Convocation
Simchat Torah	Holiday on which we dance with the Torah
Pesach	Passover
Shavout	Holiday of the Weeks

כרך טו

פרשת תזריע, מצורע, אחרי מות

Vol. XV

Tazria, Metzora, Acharei Mot

A Prayer from The Ari

To be recited before the study of the Zohar

Ruler of the universe, and Master of all masters, The Father of mercy and forgiveness, we thank You, our God and the God of our fathers, by bowing down and kneeling, that You brought us closer to Your Torah and Your holy work, and You enable us to take part in the secrets of Your holy Torah. How worthy are we that You grant us with such big favor, that is the reason we plead before You, that You will forgive and acquit all our sins, and that they should not bring separation between You and us.

And may it be your will before You, our God and the God of our fathers, that You will awaken and prepare our hearts to love and revere You, and may You listen to our utterances, and open our closed heart to the hidden studies of Your Torah, and may our study be pleasant before Your Place of Honor, as the aroma of sweet incense, and may You emanate to us Light from the source of our soul to all of our being. And, may the sparks of your holy servants, through which you revealed Your wisdom to the world, shine.

May their merit and the merit of their fathers, and the merit of their Torah, and holiness, support us so we shall not stumble through our study. And by their merit enlighten our eyes in our learning as it stated by King David, The Sweet Singer of Israel: "Open my eyes, so that I will see wonders from Your Torah" (Tehilim 119:18). Because from His mouth God gives wisdom and understanding.

"May the utterances of my mouth and the thoughts of my heart find favor before You, God, my Strength and my Redeemer" (Tehilim 19:15).

TAZRIA

Name of the articles

1. "By night on my bed"

A Synopsis
Rabbi Elazar explains that the title verse means that the children of Yisrael lay in the dust in exile, and beseeched God to take them out of it. Rabbi Yitzchak says that they asked God to join them so that He would gladden them and bless them in perfect joy.

1. וַיְדַבֵּר יְיָ׳ אֶל מֹשֶׁה לֵּאמֹר אִשָּׁה כִּי תַזְרִיעַ וְיָלְדָה זָכָר וְגוֹ׳. ר׳ אֶלְעָזָר פָּתַח, עַל מִשְׁכָּבִי בַּלֵּילוֹת בִּקַּשְׁתִּי וְגוֹ׳. עַל מִשְׁכָּבִי, בְּמִשְׁכָּבִי מִבָּעֵי לֵיהּ, מַהוּ עַל מִשְׁכָּבִי. אֶלָּא כְּנֶסֶת יִשְׂרָאֵל אָמְרָה קַמֵי קוּדְשָׁא בְּרִיךְ הוּא, וּבָעָאת מִנֵּיהּ עַל גָּלוּתָא, בְּגִין דְּהִיא יָתְבָא בֵּין שְׁאָר עַמִּין עִם בְּנָהָא, וּשְׁכִיבַת לְעַפְרָא, וְעַל דְּהִיא שְׁכִיבַת בְּאַרְעָא אָחֳרָא מְסָאֲבָא, אָמְרָה, עַל מִשְׁכָּבִי בָּעֵינָא, דְּשָׁכִיבְנָא בְּגָלוּתָא, וְעַל דָּא, בִּקַּשְׁתִּי אֶת שֶׁאָהֲבָה נַפְשִׁי וּלְאַפָּקָא לִי מִנֵּיהּ.

1. "And Hashem spoke to Moses saying, Speak to the children of Yisrael, saying, If a woman have conceived seed, and born a man child..." (Vayikra 12:2). Rabbi Elazar opened with, "By night on my bed I sought him whom my soul loves" (Shir Hashirim 3:1). HE ASKS, it says, "on my bed," while it should have said, "in my bed," why "on my bed"? AND HE ANSWERS, the Congregation of Yisrael spoke before the Holy One, blessed be He, and beseeched him concerning the exile, because she is sitting among the other nations with her children, and lying in the dust. And since she is lying in another, defiled land, she said, "on my bed" I beseech, since I am lying in exile, AND EXILE IS CALLED 'NIGHTS'. Therefore, "I sought him whom my soul loves," to take me out of it.

2. בִּקַּשְׁתִּיו וְלֹא מְצָאתִיו, דְּלָאו אָרְחֵיהּ לְאִזְדַּוְּוגָא בִּי אֶלָּא בְּהֵיכָלֵיהּ, קְרָאתִיו וְלֹא עָנָנִי. דְּהָא בֵּינֵי עַמִּין אָחֳרָנִין יָתִיבְנָא, וְקָלֵיהּ לָא שַׁמְעִין אֶלָּא בְּנוֹי. דִּכְתִיב, הֲשָׁמַע עָם קוֹל אֱלֹהִים וְגוֹ׳.

2. "I sought him, but found him not" (Ibid.) BECAUSE it is not His custom to join me save in His palace AND NOT IN EXILE. "I sought him, but I could not find him" (Shir Hashirim 5:6), since I dwelt among other nations, and

only His children hear His voice, as written, "Did ever people hear the voice of Elohim..." (Devarim 4:33).

3. רַבִּי יִצְחָק אָמַר, עַל מִשְׁכָּבִי בַּלֵּילוֹת. אָמְרָה כנ"י עַל מִשְׁכָּבִי אִתְרָעֲמְנָא קַמֵּיה, דִּיְהֵא מִזְדָּוֵוג עַמִּי לְמֶחֱדֵי לִי, וּלְבָרְכָא לִי, בְּחֶידוּ שְׁלִים. דְּהָכִי תָּנֵינָן דְּמִזְוּוּגָא דְּמַלְכָּא בכ"י, כַּמָּה צַדִּיקִים יַרְתּוּ יְרוּתַת אַחֲסַנְתָּא קַדִּישָׁא, וְכַמָּה בִּרְכָאן מִשְׁתַּכְּחֵי בְּעָלְמָא.

3. Rabbi Yitzchak said, "By night on my bed" said the Congregation of Yisrael, THE SHECHINAH. "on my bed" I complained before Him, NAMELY I ASKED HIM to join me to gladden me FROM THE LEFT COLUMN and bless me FROM THE RIGHT COLUMN in perfect joy FROM THE CENTRAL COLUMN. For we have learned that from the union of the King, ZEIR ANPIN, with the Congregation of Yisrael, many righteous people receive the inheritance of a holy portion, NAMELY SUPERNAL MOCHIN, and many blessings thus abide in the world.

2. "Who can find a woman of worth"

A Synopsis

A woman of worth and a virtuous woman is said to be the Congregation of Yisrael. "her price is far above rubies" means those lofty holy rubies that are the mysteries and inner meaning of the Torah. God may safely trust in the Congregation of Yisrael, which is why He put her in charge over the world. She bestows goodness on the world and not evil; the Tree of Life, Zeir Anpin, sends her life, that is Mochin from Binah, and shines upon her.

4. ר' אַבָּא הֲוָה אָזִיל לִכְפָר קַנְיָא, לִמְעָרְתָּא דְלוֹד. וַהֲווֹ עִמֵּיהּ ר' יוֹסֵי וְר' חִיָּיא. אָ"ר יוֹסֵי, כְּתִיב, אֵשֶׁת חַיִל עֲטֶרֶת בַּעְלָהּ וְגוֹ'. אֵשֶׁת חַיִל, דָא כ"י. וּכְרָקָב בְּעַצְמוֹתָיו מְבִישָׁה. אִלֵּין עַמִּין עכו"ם, דְקוּדְשָׁא בְּרִיךְ הוּא לָא יָכִיל לְמִסְבַּל לוֹן בְּעָלְמָא, כד"א, וָאָקוּץ בָּם. כְּהָנֵי קוֹצִין וְגוּבִין דְּדַחֲקִין לֵיהּ לב"נ וְלָא יָכִיל לְמִסְבַּל לוֹן. א"ר אַבָּא, הָכִי הוּא וַדַּאי, אֵשֶׁת חַיִל, דָא כ"י, דְּהִיא גְּבִירְתָּא מִכַּמָּה חַיָּילִין וְכַמָּה מַשְׁרְיָין דְּמִשְׁתַּכְּחֵי בְּעָלְמָא, עֲטֶרֶת בַּעְלָהּ, כד"א, עֲטֶרֶת תִּפְאֶרֶת, וְכֹלָּא חַד. עַד דַּהֲווֹ אָזְלֵי, א"ר אַבָּא כָּל חַד לֵימָא מִלָּה, בכ"י.

4. Rabbi Aba was walking to the cave of Lod in the village of Kanya with Rabbi Yosi and Rabbi Chiya. Rabbi Yosi said, it is written, "A virtuous woman is a crown to her husband" (Mishlei 12:4). The virtuous woman is the Congregation of Yisrael, THE SHECHINAH, while, "she that acts shamefully as a rottenness in his bones" (Ibid.) refers to the heathen nations, whom the Holy One, blessed be He, cannot tolerate in the world, as written, "therefore I abhorred (Heb. *akutz*) them" (Vayikra 20:23), like the thorns (Heb. *kotz*) and thistles that give pain to man so he cannot bear them. Rabbi Aba said, It is surely so, the "virtuous woman" is the Congregation of Yisrael, who is mistress over many armies and hosts OF ANGELS that abide in the world, NAMELY ALL THE DWELLERS IN BRIYAH, YETZIRAH AND ASIYAH THAT EXPAND FROM HER. "A VIRTUOUS WOMAN" MEANS BOTH A MISTRESS AND MASTER. "a crown to her husband" IS SIMILAR TO the words, "a crown of glory (lit. 'Tiferet')" (Yeshayah 62:3), and it is all the same, SINCE TIFERET IS THE HUSBAND OF THE SHECHINAH. While they were walking Rabbi Aba said, Let us each say something about the Congregation of Yisrael.

‎5. ר' אַבָּא פָּתַח וְאָמַר. אֵשֶׁת חַיִל מִי יִמְצָא, דָּא כ"י, דְּאִיהִי אֵשֶׁת‎
‎חַיִל, כְּמָה דְּאַמָרָן. מִי יִמְצָא, כד"א, אֲשֶׁר יִמְצָא אֶתְכֶם בְּאַחֲרִית‎
‎הַיָּמִים. מִי יִמְצָא, מַאן יִזְכֶּה לְמֶהֱוֵי בֵּהּ בִּשְׁלִימוּ, וּלְאִשְׁתַּכְּחָא עִמָּהּ‎
‎תָּדִיר.‎

5. Rabbi Aba opened with, "Who can find a woman of worth" (Mishlei 31:10). It is the Congregation of Yisrael, who is a woman of worth, like we said. "Who can find" resembles, "that which shall befall you in the last days" (Beresheet 49:1), WHICH MEANS THAT WHICH SHALL ARRIVE AND HAPPEN TO YOU. HERE TOO "Who can find" MEANS who will deserve TO ARRIVE AT IT and be in her to perfection and be with her always.

‎6. וְרָחוֹק מִפְּנִינִים מִכְרָהּ, מִכְרָהּ, מִקְחָהּ מִבְּעֵי לֵיהּ. אֶלָּא, לְכָל אִינוּן‎
‎דְּלָא אִתְדַּבְּקָן בָּהּ בִּשְׁלִימוּ, וְלָא שְׁלֵמִין בַּהֲדָהּ, הִיא מְכָרָה לוֹן‎
‎וְאַסְגְּרָא לוֹן בִּידָא דְּעַמְמִין אָחֲרָנִין. כד"א, וַיַּעַזְבוּ בְּנֵי יִשְׂרָאֵל אֶת יְיָ'‎
‎וַיִּמְכּוֹר אוֹתָם בְּיַד סִיסְרָא. וּכְדֵין כֻּלְּהוּ רְחִיקִין מֵאִלֵּין פְּנִינִים עִלָּאִין‎
‎קַדִּישִׁין, דְּלָא יְהֵא חוּלָקָא בְּהוּ. הה"ד וְרָחוֹק מִפְּנִינִים מִכְרָהּ.‎

6. "for her price (or: 'selling') is far above rubies" (Mishlei 31:10). HE ASKS, IT SAYS "her price," while it should have been 'her buying', WHICH MEANS IT IS MORE DIFFICULT TO BUY HER THAN RUBIES. WHY DID IT SAY "HER SELLING"? AND HE ANSWERS, since she sells all those who do not completely cleave to her or are whole towards her, and turns them over to the other nations, as you say, "And when they forgot Hashem their Elohim, He sold them into the hand of Sissra" (I Shmuel 12:9). Then they are all far from those lofty holy rubies, WHICH ARE THE MYSTERIES AND INNER MEANING OF THE TORAH, in which you shall have no part. This is the meaning of, "for her price is far above rubies."

‎7. ר' חִיָּיא פָּתַח קְרָא אֲבַתְרֵיהּ וְאָמַר, בָּטַח בָּהּ לֵב בַּעְלָהּ וְשָׁלָל לֹא‎
‎יֶחְסָר. בָּטַח בָּהּ לֵב בַּעְלָהּ, דָּא קוּדְשָׁא בְּרִיךְ הוּא, דִּבְגִינֵי כַּךְ מָנֵי לֵהּ‎
‎עַל עָלְמָא, לְאִתְדַּבְּרָא עָלַהּ, כָּל זִיּוּנִין דִּלֵיהּ אַפְקִיד בִּידָהָא, וְכָל אִינוּן‎

מַגִּיחֵי קְרָבָא, וְעַל דָּא, וְשָׁלָל לֹא יֶחְסָר.

7. Rabbi Chiya opened with the following verse, "The heart of her husband safely trusts in her, and he shall have no lack of gain" (Mishlei 31:11). "The heart of her husband safely trusts in her" refers to the Holy One, blessed be He, ZEIR ANPIN, who, for this reason, put her in charge over the world to be guided by her. All His armory He put in her hand and all the soldiers. Therefore, "he shall have no lack of gain."

ח. ר' יוֹסֵי פָּתַח קְרָא אֲבַתְרֵיה, וְאָמַר, גְּמָלַתְהוּ טוֹב וְלֹא רָע כָּל יְמֵי חַיֶּיהָ. גְּמָלַתְהוּ טוֹב, הִיא זְמִינַת טָב לְעָלְמָא, זְמִינַת טָב לְהֵיכָלָא דְּמַלְכָּא וְלִבְנֵי הֵיכָלֵיה. וְלֹא רָע. בְּגִין דִּכְתִיב, וְעֵץ הַדַּעַת טוֹב וָרָע, טוֹב אֵימָתַי, בְּזִמְנָא דְּאִינּוּן יְמֵי הַשָּׁמַיִם, נָהֲרִין עָלָה, וּמִזְדַּוְּוגָן עִמָּה כַּדְקָא יֵאוֹת, דְּאִינּוּן יְמֵי חַיֶּיהָ. בְּגִין דְּעֵץ הַחַיִּים, שָׁדַר לָה חַיִּים, וְנָהִיר לָה. וּבְהַהוּא זִמְנָא גְּמָלַתְהוּ טוֹב וְלֹא רָע. א"ר אַבָּא שַׁפִּיר הוּא, וְכֻלְּהוּ קְרָאֵי בִּכְנֶסֶת יִשְׂרָאֵל אִתְּמָרוּ.

8. Rabbi Yosi explained the following verse, "She will do him good and not evil all the days of her life" (Ibid. 12). "She will do him good" MEANS she bestows goodness upon the world and bestows goodness upon the King's palace and the household people. "and not evil" HAD TO BE MENTIONED due to the words, "and the Tree of Knowledge of Good and Evil" (Beresheet 2:9). MALCHUT IS CALLED THE TREE OF KNOWLEDGE OF GOOD AND EVIL BECAUSE IF ONE HAS MERIT IT IS GOOD, BUT IF ONE DOES NOT HAVE MERIT IT IS EVIL. IT THEREFORE SAYS, "AND NOT EVIL." When is it good AND NOT EVIL? When the days of heaven, THE SFIROT OF ZEIR ANPIN, shine upon her and unite with her properly. FOR THE DAYS OF HEAVEN are "the days of her life," because the Tree of Life, ZEIR ANPIN, sends her life, WHICH IS MOCHIN FROM BINAH, and shines upon her. At that time, "She will do him good and not evil." Rabbi Aba said, This is well, and all these verses refer to the Congregation of Yisrael.

3. If a woman conceives first she bears a male child

A Synopsis

Rabbi Yosi resolves some confusion over "If a woman have conceived seed" by saying that God distinguishes between a male and a female seed, and once He has seen it, He decides whether it will be male or female.

9. אִשָּׁה כִּי תַזְרִיעַ. תָּנֵינָן, אִשָּׁה מַזְרַעַת תְּחִלָּה יוֹלֶדֶת זָכָר. ר׳ אַחָא אָמַר, הָא תָּנֵינָן, דְּקוּדְשָׁא בְּרִיךְ הוּא גָּזַר עַל הַהִיא טִפָּה, אִי אִיהוּ דְכַר אִי אִיהִי נוּקְבָּא, וְאַתְּ אָמְרַת אִשָּׁה מַזְרַעַת תְּחִלָּה יוֹלֶדֶת זָכָר. א״ר יוֹסֵי, וַדַּאי קוּדְשָׁא בְּרִיךְ הוּא אַבְחִין בֵּין טִפָּה דִּדְכוּרָא וּבֵין טִפָּה דְנוּקְבָּא, וּבְגִין דְּאַבְחִין לֵיהּ, גָּזַר עֲלֵיהּ, אִי לֶהֱוֵי דְכַר אוֹ נוּקְבָּא.

9. "If a woman have conceived seed" (Vayikra 12:2). We learned that if a woman conceives first, she bears a male child. Rabbi Acha said that we learned that the Holy One, blessed be He, determines whether that drop will be male or female, yet you say that if a woman conceives first, she gives birth to a male child. IN THAT CASE, THERE IS NO NEED FOR THE DECISION OF THE HOLY ONE, BLESSED BE HE. Rabbi Yosi said, Surely the Holy One, blessed be He, distinguishes between a male drop and a female drop. Once He observed it, He decided whether it would be male or female.

10. א״ר אַחָא, וְיָלְדָה זָכָר, וְכִי כֵּיוָן דְּמַזְרַעַת יוֹלֶדֶת, דִּכְתִיב, וְיָלְדָה, הַאי קְרָא הָכִי מִבְּעֵי לֵיהּ, אִשָּׁה כִּי תַהַר וְיָלְדָה זָכָר. מַהוּ, כִּי תַזְרִיעַ וְיָלְדָה. אָמַר רַבִּי יוֹסֵי, אִתְּתָא, מִן יוֹמָא דְּאִתְעַבְּרַת עַד יוֹמָא דְּיוֹלֶדֶת לֵית לָהּ בְּפוּמָא, אֶלָּא יְלִידוּ דִּילָהּ אִי לֶהֱוֵי דְכַר, וְעַ״ד, אִשָּׁה כִּי תַזְרִיעַ וְיָלְדָה זָכָר.

10. Rabbi Acha said, "and born a man child" (Ibid.). Does she give birth once she conceives, that the verse says, "If a woman have conceived seed, and born a man child"? BUT IT DEPENDS UPON PREGNANCY, and the verse should have read, 'If a woman have been pregnant, and born a man child'. Why then, "have conceived seed, and born"? Rabbi Yosi said, From the day

THEY HAVE CONCEIVED, women talk of nothing except whether their baby will be male. Hence SCRIPTURE SAYS "If a woman have conceived seed, and born a man child."

4. "the earth is full of Your creatures"

A Synopsis
Rabbi Chizkiyah tells us that God does His deeds with wisdom, wisely sowing all the seeds so that each matures in its own time. "The earth is full" means that the earth has been filled by everything that flows from Binah.

11. אִשָּׁה כִּי תַזְרִיעַ. רִבִּי חִזְקִיָּה פָּתַח, מַה רַבּוּ מַעֲשֶׂיךָ יְיָ'. כַּמָּה סַגִּיאִין עוֹבָדוֹהִי דְּמַלְכָּא קַדִּישָׁא בְּעָלְמָא, מְתַל לב"נ דְּנָטִיל בִּידוֹהִי כַּמָּה מַקְטוֹרִין כַּחֲדָא, וְזַרַע לוֹן בְּזִמְנָא חֲדָא, וּלְבָתַר נָפִיק כָּל חַד וְחַד בִּלְחוֹדוֹי. כַּךְ קוּדְשָׁא בְּרִיךְ הוּא עָבִיד עוֹבָדוֹהִי בְּחָכְמָה, וּבְחָכְמָה נָטִיל כֹּלָּא כַּחֲדָא וְזַרַע לוֹן, וּלְבָתַר נָפְקוּ כָּל חַד וְחַד בְּזִמְנֵיהּ, הה"ד כֻּלָּם בְּחָכְמָה עָשִׂיתָ.

11. "If a woman have conceived seed" (Vayikra 12:2). Rabbi Chizkiyah opened with the verse, "Hashem, how manifold are Your works" (Tehilim 104:24). How many are the deeds of the Holy King in the world. This is likened to a man who took different kinds of seeds together and planted them at the same time. Afterwards each kind sprouts on its own. The Holy One, blessed be He, similarly does His deeds with wisdom, wisely taking everything together and planting them. Afterwards each comes out in its own time. This is the meaning of, "in wisdom have You made them all" (Ibid.).

12. אָמַר רִבִּי אַבָּא, מָה רַבּוּ מַעֲשֶׂיךָ יְיָ', כַּמָּה סַגִּיאִין אִינּוּן עוֹבָדוֹהִי דְּמַלְכָּא קַדִּישָׁא, וְכֻלְּהוּ, סְתִימִין בְּחָכְמָה, הה"ד כֻּלָּם בְּחָכְמָה עָשִׂיתָ. כֻּלְּהוּ בְּחָכְמָה כְּלִילָן, וְלָא נָפְקֵי לְבַר אֶלָּא בִּשְׁבִילִין יְדִיעָן, לְגַבֵּי בִּינָה. וּמִתַּמָּן, אִתְעֲבֵידוּ כֹּלָּא וְאִתְתְּקַנוּ, הה"ד וּבִתְבוּנָה יִתְכּוֹנָן. וְעַל דָּא כֻּלָּם בְּחָכְמָה עָשִׂיתָ, בְּבִינָה.

12. Rabbi Aba said, "Hashem, how manifold are Your works." How many are the deeds of the Holy deed. All, EVERYTHING EXISTENT THROUGHOUT THE WORLDS, is hidden with wisdom. Hence it says, "in wisdom have You made them all." They are all incorporated in wisdom and emerge only by

-10-

means of specific paths, THE 32 PATHS OF WISDOM to Binah. From there, FROM BINAH, everything is made and accomplished. Hence, "by understanding it is established" (Mishlei 24:3). It therefore says, "in wisdom have You made them all" in Binah, THROUGH BINAH.

13. מָלְאָה הָאָרֶץ, הָאָרֶץ: דָּא כ"י, דְּמִתַּמָּן אִתְמַלְיָא מִכֹּלָּא, כד"א כָּל הַנְּחָלִים הוֹלְכִים אֶל הַיָּם וְגוֹ'. קִנְיָנֶיךָ. דְּהִיא אַפִּיקַת לוֹן לְבָתַר, הה"ד אֵלֶּה תוֹלְדוֹת הַשָּׁמַיִם וְהָאָרֶץ בְּהִבָּרְאָם, בְּה' בְּרָאָם. בְּגִינֵי כָּךְ מָלְאָה הָאָרֶץ קִנְיָנֶיךָ.

13. "The earth is full" (Tehilim 104:24) : the earth is the Congregation of Yisrael, WHICH IS MALCHUT, which is filled of all things from there, FROM BINAH, as written, "All the rivers run into the sea…" (Kohelet 1:7). "Your creatures" were brought forth by MALCHUT afterwards, as written, "These are the generations of the heaven and of the earth when they were created (Heb. *behibr'am*)" (Beresheet 2:4), WHICH CAN BE CONSTRUED AS '*BEHEI BERA'AM* (HE CREATED THEM WITH HEI)'. IT IS MALCHUT, THE LAST HEI OF YUD HEI VAV HEI. For that reason, "the earth is full of Your creatures."

5. "Surely a man walks in an image"

A Synopsis

We learn that when a man and his wife are about to mate, God gives the spirit of the child who will be conceived to a minister, and tells him where it should go. God commands the spirit to be righteous, and then the spirit descends with an image. As long as he has that image with him, he exists in the world, but when it leaves him he dies. We read about the witchcraft described in the book of the sorcerers of Asmodeus, where they knew how to give over their images to the Other Side. We are told that one must never throw objects in his house because they are then of the other side. When that man who gave over his image to the other side dies, the evil spirit that was attached to his supernal image takes it away from him, so that it will never return. Before a soul is born it is shown the reward of good and evil, and the holy image stands by it; when it is born the image becomes part of it, and his life depends on it.

14. ת"ח, בְּשַׁעֲתָא דְּבַר נָשׁ אָתֵי לְאִתְקַדְּשָׁא לְאִזְדַּוְּוגָא בְּנוּקְבֵיהּ, בִּרְעוּתָא קַדִּישָׁא דִּילֵיהּ, אִתְּעַר עָלֵיהּ רוּחָא קַדִּישָׁא, כָּלִיל דְּכַר וְנוּקְבָּא. וְרָמִיז קוּדְשָׁא בְּרִיךְ הוּא לְחַד שְׁלוּחָא מְמָנָא עַל עִדּוּיֵיהוֹן דִּבְנֵי נָשָׁא, וּמְנֵי בִּידֵיהּ הַהוּא רוּחָא, וְאוֹדַע לֵיהּ, לְאָן אֲתַר יִפְקוֹד לֵיהּ. הֲדָא הוּא דִכְתִיב, וְהַלַּיְלָה אָמַר הוֹרָה גָּבֶר. הַלַּיְלָה אָמַר, לְהַהוּא מְמָנָא, הוֹרָה גָּבֶר מִפְּלַנְיָא, וְקוּדְשָׁא בְּרִיךְ הוּא אַפְקִיד לֵיהּ, לְהַהוּא רוּחָא, כָּל מַה דְּאַפְקִיד, וְהָא אוּקְמוּהָ.

14. Come and see, when man is about to be sanctified and mate with his wife with his holy will, a Holy Spirit is aroused upon him, included of male and female, SINCE HE IS BORN AND COMES FROM ZEIR ANPIN AND MALCHUT THAT ARE THE SECRET OF MALE AND FEMALE. The Holy One, blessed be He, indicates to a minister appointed over the conception of men and hands him that spirit and lets him know where to put it. That is the meaning of, "and the night which said, There is a man child conceived" (Iyov 3:2). THIS MEANS that the night, WHICH IS MALCHUT CALLED NIGHT, said to that minister, "There is a man child conceived" by so and so, SO HE WILL PUT THE SPIRIT THERE. And the Holy One, blessed be He, commands that spirit whatever He does, THAT IS, HE MAKES IT SWEAR TO BE RIGHTEOUS, ETC. This has already been explained.

15. כְּדֵין רוּחָא נַחְתָּא, וְחַד צוּלְמָא עִמֵּיה, הַהוּא דְּקָאֵים בְּדִיּוּקְנֵיה לְעֵילָּא, בְּהַהוּא צוּלְמָא אִתְבְּרֵי, בְּהַהוּא צוּלְמָא אָזִיל בְּהַאי עָלְמָא. הֲדָא הוּא דִּכְתִּיב, אַךְ בְּצֶלֶם יִתְהַלֶּךְ אִישׁ. בְּעוֹד דְּהַאי צוּלְמָא אִשְׁתְּכַח עִמֵּיה בַּר נָשׁ, קָאֵים בְּהַאי עָלְמָא, וּתְרֵין אִינּוּן דְּמִתְחַבְּרָן כַּחֲדָא, וּשְׁלֹמֹה מַלְכָּא אַזְהַר לִבְנֵי נָשָׁא וְאָמַר, עַד שֶׁיָּפוּחַ הַיּוֹם וְנָסוּ הַצְּלָלִים, תְּרֵי.

15. The spirit then descends with an image, the same IMAGE that assumes the supernal shape CALLED THE IMAGE OF ELOHIM. One is created with that image and walks about with it in this world. This is the meaning of, "Surely every man walks in a vain show (or: 'image')" (Tehilim 39:7). As long as that image is with him, man exists in this world, BUT IF THE IMAGE IS GONE FROM HIM HE DIES. These are two IMAGES (HEB. *tzelamim*) that join together. King Solomon warned people, saying, "Before the day cools, and the shadows (Heb. *tzelalim*) flee away" (Shir Hashirim 2:17), two of them.

16. וּבְסִפְרָא דְּחָרָשִׁין דְּאַשְׁמְדַאי, אַשְׁכַּחְנָא דְּאִינּוּן דְּבָעוּ לְחָרְשָׁא חָרָשִׁין מִסְטַר שְׂמָאלָא, וּלְאִתְדַּבְּקָא בְּהוּ, יְקוּם לִנְהוֹרָא דִּשְׁרָגָא, אוֹ בַּאֲתָר דְּיִתְחֲזוּן אִינּוּן צוּלְמִין דִּילֵיהּ, וְיֵימָא אִינּוּן מִלִּין דְּמִתְתַּקְנֵי לְאִינּוּן חָרָשִׁין, וְיִקְרֵי לוֹן, לְאִינּוּן סִטְרִין מְסָאֲבִין, בִּשְׁמָהָן מְסָאֲבִין דִּילְהוֹן, וְיַזְמִין צוּלְמִין דִּילֵיהּ לְאִינּוּן דְּקָאֲרֵי, וְיֵימָא דְּהוּא אִתְתַּקַּן בִּרְעוּתֵיהּ לְהוּ לְפִקּוּדַיְיהוּ, וְהַהוּא בַּר נָשׁ נָפַק מֵרְשׁוּ דְּמָארֵיהּ וּפִקְדּוֹנָא דִּילֵיהּ, יָהַב לְסִטַר מְסָאֲבָא.

16. In the book of the sorcerers of Asmodeus, I found that those who wish to perform witchcraft from the left side and be attached to them, must stand by candle light, or wherever his images are seen, THAT IS, BY THE LIGHT OF THE MOON, and say the words suitable for these enchantments and address those aspects of impurity using their names of impurity. One then hands over his images to those NAMES OF IMPURITY he summoned, and says he willingly sets them AT THEIR DISPOSAL and at their command. Man THEN leaves the domain of his Master, and his Master's deposit, NAMELY THE SOUL GIVEN TO HIM AS A DEPOSIT BY HIS MASTER HE gives to the aspects of impurity.

17. וּבְאִינּוּן מִלִּין דְּחָרָשִׁין דְּאִיהוּ יֵימָא, וְיִזְמִין לוֹן לְצוּלְמֵי, אִתְחַזּוּן תְּרֵין רוּחִין וּמִתְתַּקְּנִין בְּאִינּוּן צוּלְמִין דִּילֵיהּ, בְּחֵיזוּ דִּבְנֵי אֱנָשָׁא, וּמוֹדְעִין לֵיהּ מִלִּין לְאַבְאָשָׁא, וּמִלִּין לְאוֹטָבָא, לְזִמְנִין יְדִיעָן. וְאִלֵּין תְּרֵי רוּחִין, דְּלָא אִתְכְּלִילוּ בְּכְלָלָא דְּגוּפָא, הַשְׁתָּא אִתְכְּלִילָן בְּאִלֵּין צוּלְמִין, וּמִתְתַּקְּנָן בְּהוּ וּמוֹדְעִין לֵיהּ לְבַר נָשׁ מִלִּין לְאַבְאָשָׁא, וְדָא הוּא דְּנָפִיק מֵרְשׁוּתָא דְּמָארֵיהּ, וּפִקְדּוֹנָא דִּילֵיהּ, יָהִיב לִסְטַר מְסָאֲבָא.

17. By these words of witchcraft he uttered and by summoning HIS images, two spirits appear and settle in those images TO ASSUME human form. They tell him at specific times things to his own hurt and things to his own good. These two spirits that were not incorporated in a body, SINCE HE DID NOT HAVE TIME TO MAKE THEM BODIES BEFORE HE SANCTIFIED SHABBAT, are now incorporated in these images THAT MAN GAVE THEM. They settle in them and tell that man things to his own damage. Such a one left his Master's domain and gave his deposit, NAMELY HIS SOUL, to the side of defilement.

18. תָּא חֲזֵי, אָסִיר לֵיהּ לְבַר נָשׁ לְאַשְׁדָּאָה מָאנֵי דְּבֵיתָא, וּלְאַפְקְדָא לֵיהּ לְסִטְרָא אָחֳרָא, דְּלָא אִצְטְרִיךְ, אוֹ מִלָּה אָחֳרָא דִּכְוָותֵיהּ, דְּהָא כַּמָּה גַּרְדִּינֵי נִימוּסִין זְמִינִין לְהַהוּא מִלָּה לְקַבְּלָא לֵיהּ, וּמֵהַהוּא זִמְנָא, לָא שָׁארוּ עֲלֵיהּ בִּרְכָאן, דְּהָא מִסִּטְרָא אָחֳרָא הוּא. כ״שׁ מַאן דְּאַזְמִין בִּרְעוּתֵיהּ עַל הַהוּא טִיבוּ עִלָּאָה דִּילֵיהּ, לְאָחֳרָא וּלְסִטְרָא אָחֳרָא. דְּהָא, מֵהַהוּא דְּאַזְמִין לֵיהּ הֲוֵי.

18. Come and see, one must not throw the objects in his house or any other such thing IN HIS ANGER and thus deliver them to the Other Side. He must not DO SO because many litigants and persecutors await to receive that object. From that time on, no blessings dwell on it, because it is of the Other Side. This is more so for whoever willingly summons that supernal good, THAT IS, HIS IMAGE, to another and to the Other Side. Since he summons HIS IMAGE, he is his.

19. וְכַד קָרִיבוּ יוֹמִין דְּב״נ לְנָפְקָא מֵהַאי עָלְמָא, הַהוּא צוּלְמָא עִלָּאָה

דִּיהֲבֵי לֵיהּ, אַתְיָא הַהוּא רוּחָא בִּישָׁא דַּהֲוָה מִתְדַּבַּק בֵּיהּ בְּכָל יוֹמָא, וְנָטִיל לֵיהּ לְהַהוּא צוּלְמָא, וְאִתְתָּקַן בֵּיהּ וְאָזִיל לֵיהּ, וְלָא אִתְחֲזָר בֵּיהּ בב"נ לְעָלְמִין. כְּדֵין יִנְדַּע דְּהָא אִתְדַּחְיָא הוּא מִכֹּלָּא.

19. When the time draws near for man to depart from this world, the evil spirit that used to cleave daily to that supernal image that was given that man, and takes that image from him, it settles in it and walks away and THAT IMAGE will never return to that man. THAT MAN then realizes he is rejected in every sense.

20. תָּא חֲזֵי, בְּשַׁעֲתָא דְּנִשְׁמְתָא נַחְתָּא לְאַעֲלָא לֵיהּ בְּהַאי עָלְמָא, נַחְתָּא בְּגִנְתָּא דְּעֵדֶן דְּאַרְעָא, וְחָמָאת יְקָרָא דְּרוּחֵיהוֹן דְּצַדִּיקַיָּיא קַיְימִין שׁוּרִין שׁוּרִין. לְבָתַר אַזְלָא לַגֵּיהִנָּם, וְחָמָאת לְהוּ לְרַשִּׁיעַיָּיא דְּצַוְוחִין וַוי וַוי, וְלָא מְרַחֲמֵי עָלַיְיהוּ. וּבְכֹלָּא אַסְהִידוּ בָּהּ סַהֲדוּתָא, וְהַהוּא צוּלְמָא קַדִּישָׁא קַיְימָא עָלֵיהּ, עַד דְּנָפִיק לְעָלְמָא.

20. Come and see, when the soul descends to be ushered into this world, it first DESCENDS to the Garden of Eden where it beholds the glory of the spirits of the righteous that stand in rows. It then goes to Gehenom where it sees the wicked crying, 'Woe, woe,' but none has mercy upon them. It is given testimony about any thing. THE WICKED TESTIFY HOW THEY ARE PUNISHED FOR EVERY SIN AND THE RIGHTEOUS TESTIFY TO THE GOOD REWARD THEY RECEIVE FOR EACH PRECEPT. That holy image stands by it until it comes into this world.

21. כַּד נָפִיק לְעָלְמָא, אִזְדְּמַן הַהוּא צוּלְמָא לְגַבֵּיהּ, וְאִשְׁתְּתַף בַּהֲדֵיהּ, וְאִתְרַבֵּי עִמֵּיהּ. כְּמָה דְּאִתְּמַר, אַךְ בְּצֶלֶם יִתְהַלֶּךְ אִישׁ. וּבְהַהוּא צֶלֶם אִשְׁתְּתָפוּ יוֹמוֹי דְּבַר נָשׁ, וְתַלְיָין בֵּיהּ, הַהַ"ד, כִּי תְמוֹל אֲנַחְנוּ וְלֹא נֵדָע כִּי צֵל יָמֵינוּ עֲלֵי אָרֶץ. כִּי צֵל יָמֵינוּ וַדַּאי. וּמִן יוֹמָא דְּמִתְעַבְּרָא אִתְּתָא עַד יוֹמָא דְּאוֹלִידַת, לָא יַדְעִין בְּנֵי נָשָׁא עוֹבָדוֹי דְּקוּדְשָׁא בְּרִיךְ הוּא, כַּמָּה אִינוּן רַבְרְבִין, וְכַמָּה אִינוּן עִלָּאִין. הַהַ"ד, מַה רַבּוּ מַעֲשֶׂיךָ יְיָ' וְגוֹ'.

21. When it goes out into the world that image comes to it, joins it and grows with it, as said, "Surely every man walks in an image." Man's days join that image and depend on it, FOR ONCE IT IS GONE, MAN DEPARTS FROM THE WORLD. This is the meaning of, "for we are but of yesterday, and know nothing, because our days upon earth are a shadow" (Iyov 8:9). Assuredly, "our days upon earth are a shadow," AS OUR DAYS DEPEND ON THAT SHADOW. From the day a woman conceives until the day she gives birth, no men know the deeds of the Holy One, blessed be He, how great they are, how superior. This is the meaning of, "Hashem, how manifold are Your works" (Tehilim 104:24).

6. "and born a man child"

A Synopsis

Although the souls of male and female are supposed to come into this world together, ever since the sin of the first man and woman this has not been so. They are divided when they emerge from above into this world. If the man does not have enough merit, he never finds his soulmate, and if he marries another his children are impure. Rabbi Elazar says that thousands of souls emerge simultaneously into the world, but they are not considered Nefashot until they settle in the body and receive their illumination from Malchut, this takes 33 days. He talks about the blood of purification and the blood of circumcision.

22. תָּא חֲזֵי, כָּל רוּחִין דְּעָלְמָא כְּלִילָן דְּכַר וְנוּקְבָּא, וְכַד נָפְקִין, דְּכַר וְנוּקְבָּא נָפְקִין, וּלְבָתַר מִתְפָּרְשָׁן בְּאָרְחַיְיהוּ, אִי זָכֵי בַּר נָשׁ, לְבָתַר מִזְדַּוְּוגֵי כַּחֲדָא. וְהַיְינוּ בַּת זוּגוֹ, וּמִתְחַבְּרָן בְּזִוּוּגָא חַד בְּכֹלָּא, רוּחָא וְגוּפָא. דִּכְתִיב, תּוֹצֵא הָאָרֶץ נֶפֶשׁ חַיָּה לְמִינָהּ. מַאי לְמִינָהּ. הַהוּא רוּחָא דְּב"נ דְּנָפִיק זוּגֵיהּ דְּדָמֵי לֵיהּ.

22. Come and see, every spirit in the world incorporates male and female. When they emerge INTO THIS WORLD, they come out as male and female, and then divide according to their custom, THE SPIRIT OF THE MALE IS CLOTHED IN A MALE AND THE SPIRIT OF THE FEMALE IN A FEMALE. AFTERWARDS, if a man has merit, they join, he and his mate, and mate in a union in every sense, in spirit and bodily, as written, "Let the earth bring forth living creatures after their kind" (Beresheet 1:24). What is, "after their kind"? It is the spirit of the man that comes out with its mate that resembles it.

23. וּמַאי הָאָרֶץ, כד"א, רְקַמְתִּי בְּתַחְתִּיּוֹת אָרֶץ. וְהָא אוּקְמוּהָ. תּוֹצֵא הָאָרֶץ וַדַּאי, דְּהָא מִנָּהּ נָפְקִין נֶפֶשׁ חַיָּה, כְּמָה דְּאוֹקִימְנָא, דָּא רוּחֵיהּ דְּאָדָם קַדְמָאָה, הַיְינוּ דִּכְתִיב, וּמִפְּרִי הָעֵץ אֲשֶׁר בְּתוֹךְ הַגָּן. וּמִפְּרִי הָעֵץ, דָּא קוּדְשָׁא בְּרִיךְ הוּא, אֲשֶׁר בְּתוֹךְ הַגָּן, אֲשֶׁר בְּתוֹךְ הָאִשָּׁה, תָּנֵינָן, הַיְינוּ, אִשָּׁה כִּי תַזְרִיעַ וְיָלְדָה זָכָר, כְּתִיב. וְלָא כָּלִיל דְּכַר וְנוּקְבָּא, כְּפוּם אוֹרְחוֹי דְּעָלְמָא, דְּאִינוּן, גָּרְמוּ לֵיהּ, דְּלָא מִתְחַבְּרָן, כְּמָה

-17-

דְּנַפְקָן מִלְּעֵילָא זוּגוֹת.

23. HE ASKS, what is the earth IN THE VERSE, "LET THE EARTH BRING FORTH"? IT resembles the words, "and curiously wrought in the lowest parts of the earth" (Tehilim 139:15), WHICH IS MALCHUT. This has been explained. "Let the earth bring forth" as we explained it to refer to the spirit of the first man WHO EMERGED AND WAS BORN TO MALCHUT CALLED EARTH. This is the meaning of the words, "but of the fruit of the tree which is in the midst of the Garden" (Beresheet 3:3). "The fruit of the tree" refers to the Holy One, blessed be He, NAMELY ZEIR ANPIN CALLED THE TREE OF LIFE, WHOSE FRUIT IS THE SPIRIT OF THE FIRST MAN. "which is in the midst of the Garden," within the woman as we learned, WHO IS MALCHUT CALLED WOMAN AND CALLED GARDEN. FOR THE SPIRIT OF THE FIRST MAN CAME OUT FROM THE UNION OF ZEIR ANPIN AND MALCHUT. This is the meaning of, "If a woman have conceived seed, and born a man child" (Vayikra 12:2). THE WOMAN, MALCHUT BEARS THE SOULS. It is also written, "AND BORN A MAN CHILD," not included of male and female, as is the custom of the world, THAT THE SOULS ARE BORN MALE AND FEMALE. For THE LOWER BEINGS BY THEIR SINS cause MALCHUT THAT THE SOULS will not join MALE WITH FEMALE, as they come out from above as couples MALE AND FEMALE. HENCE IT IS WRITTEN, "AND BORN A MAN CHILD," SINCE IN THIS WORLD ONLY A MALE NOT INCLUDING A FEMALE APPEARS.

24. בְּגִין דְּאָדָם קַדְמָאָה, וְזִוּוּג דִּילֵיהּ, חָבוּ לְקוּדְשָׁא בְּרִיךְ הוּא, וְעַ"ד מִתְפָּרְשִׁין, כַּד נָפְקִין מִלְּעֵילָא, עַד דְּהֲוָה רַעֲוָא קַמֵּי קוּדְשָׁא בְּרִיךְ הוּא, אִי זָכָה ב"נ, יָהֲבִין לֵיהּ זוּגָתוֹ, וְאִי לָא, מַפְרִישִׁין לֵהּ מִנֵּיהּ, וְיָהֲבִין לֵהּ לְאָחֳרָא, מוֹלִידִין בְּנִין דְּלָא כַּדְקָא יֵאוֹת. וְעַ"ד כְּתִיב, לֹא יָדוֹן רוּחִי בָאָדָם. מַאי רוּחִי, רוּחוֹ מִבָּעֵי לֵיהּ, אִינּוּן תְּרֵין רוּחֵי, דְּנַפְקֵי זוּגוֹת, לָא יְדוּנוּן כַּחֲדָא, וְעַ"ד כְּתִיב, וְיָלְדָה זָכָר, וְלָא כָּלִיל דְּכַר וְנוּקְבָא, כְּפוּם אוֹרְחוֹי דְּעָלְמָא, דְּאִינּוּן גָּרְמוּ.

24. Since the first man and his mate EVE had sinned against the Holy One, blessed be He, MALE AND FEMALE are therefore divided when they emerge from above INTO THIS WORLD, THE SOUL OF THE MALE IS BORN ON ITS OWN AND THE SOUL OF THE FEMALE ON ITS OWN, until it will please the Holy One, blessed be He, if man gains merit, to give him his soulmate,

THAT IS, THE SOUL OF THE FEMALE THAT WAS INCORPORATED IN HIM ABOVE. Otherwise, she is separated from him and given to another, AND THEN they beget improper children. Hence it is written, "My spirit shall not always strive on account of man" (Beresheet 6:3). Why does it say "my spirit"? It should have said, 'his spirit' OF MAN. For there are two spirits emerging in twosomes. IT SHOULD RATHER BE PRONOUNCED 'SPIRITS'. THE VERSE SAYS they must not be striven after together, BECAUSE THEY COME OUT SEPARATELY. It is therefore written, "and born a man child," and not man and woman TOGETHER according to the ways of the world ABOVE, because of their deeds.

25. רִבִּי אֶלְעָזָר אָמַר לָאו הָכִי, דְּהָא כֹּלָּא, דְּכַר וְנוּקְבָּא כְּלִילָן כַּחֲדָא, וּמִתְפָּרְשָׁן לְבָתַר, אֲבָל וְיָלְדָה זָכָר, כְּלִילָן כַּחֲדָא מִסִּטְרָא דִּימִינָא, וְאִם נְקֵבָה תֵלֵד, כְּלִילָן בְּחַד נוּקְבָּא וּדְכַר מִסִּטְרָא שְׂמָאלָא, דְּשַׁלְטָא סְטָר שְׂמָאלָא עַל סְטָר יְמִינָא יַתִּיר, וּדְכוּרָא אִתְכַּפְיָא בִּימִינָא דְּלָא שַׁלְטָא, וּכְדֵין הַהוּא דְּכַר דְּנָפִיק מִגּוֹ נוּקְבָּא, מִסְטַר שְׂמָאלָא, כָּל אוֹרְחוֹי כְּנוּקְבָּא, אֲבָל דְּכַר דְּנָפִיק מִגּוֹ יְמִינָא, הוּא שַׁלְטָא, וְנוּקְבָּא דְּנָפְקָא מִנֵּיהּ אִתְכַּפְיָא, דְּהָא סְטָר שְׂמָאלָא לָא שַׁלְטָא, וְעַל דָּא וְיָלְדָה זָכָר כְּתִיב.

25. Rabbi Elazar said that it is not so THAT "AND BORN A MAN CHILD" MEANS HE IS BORN FROM MALCHUT INTO THIS WORLD AS A MAN WITHOUT A WOMAN. For male and female always come joined together, and are then divided AND COME AS MAN ALONE AND WOMAN ALONE. But "and born a man child" REFERS TO A MALE AND A FEMALE included together from the right side, WHICH IS CONSIDERED MALE. "But if she bear a female child" (Vayikra 12:5) MEANS they are included together as female and male from the left side, WHICH IS CONSIDERED FEMALE. Then the left side has more power over the right side, and the male on the right is subdued and has no power. The male that comes from the Nukva, MALCHUT, from Her left, always acts like a female AND IS THEREFORE CONSIDERED A FEMALE. But a male coming from the right side OF MALCHUT has power, and the female that emerges with him is subdued, since the left side has no power. Hence it is written of him, "and born a man child."

26. וְכַמָּה אֶלֶף וְרִבְבָן נָפְקֵי בְּזִמְנָא חֲדָא לְעָלְמָא. וּמִן יוֹמָא דְּאַפְקַת

לוֹן, לָא אִקְרוּן נַפְשָׁן, עַד דְּאִתְיַישְּׁבָן בְּגוּפָא. וְכַמָּה הוּא, ל"ג יָמִים. הַיְינוּ דִּכְתִּיב, וּשְׁלֹשִׁים יוֹם וּשְׁלֹשֶׁת יָמִים וְגו'. וְטָמְאָה שִׁבְעַת יָמִים, דְּהָא כָּל שִׁבְעַת יָמִים לָא עָאלִין רוּחִין לְגַבָּהּ, לְאִתְקַשְּׁרָא בָּהּ, וְכָל אִלֵּין שִׁבְעַת יָמִים, רוּחָא אָזְלָא בְּגוּפָא, לְאַשְׁכְּחָא אַתְרֵיהּ. וּכְדֵין כְּתִיב, וְהָיָה שִׁבְעַת יָמִים תַּחַת אִמּוֹ.

26. Thousands and myriads OF SOULS emerge simultaneously into the world. From the time she brought them forth they are not considered Nefashot UNTIL THEY RECEIVE THEIR ILLUMINATION FROM MALCHUT, until they settle in the body. This takes 33 days, as written, "thirty three days" (Vayikra 12:4). UNTIL THEN THE BODY IS INCOMPLETE FOR THE NEFESH TO SETTLE ON AND BE CLOTHED IN IT. "...then she shall be unclean seven days" (Ibid. 2), NAMELY THE NEFESH, for throughout those seven days no spirits enter her, MALCHUT, to be connected with her. And all those seven days, the spirit roams the body to find its place TO SETTLE IN. Then it is written, "it shall be seven days under its dam" (Vayikra 22:27), WHICH IS MALCHUT, AND HE IS UNDERNEATH HER AND CANNOT CONNECT WITH HER.

27. וּבְיוֹמָא תְּמִינָאָה, אִתְהַדְרוּ רוּחָא וְגוּפָא לְאִתְחֲזָאָה קָמֵי מַטְרוֹנִיתָא, וּלְאִתְקַשְּׁרָא בָּהּ, וּבִדְכוּרָא, בְּגוּפָא וּבְרוּחָא. וּשְׁלֹשִׁים יוֹם וּשְׁלֹשֶׁת יָמִים תֵּשֵׁב עַל דְּמֵי טָהֳרָה, לְאִתְיַישְּׁבָא רוּחָא בְּגוּפָא. וְג' יָמִים מַאי עֲבִידְתַּיְיהוּ. אֶלָּא שְׁלֹשֶׁת יָמִים דְּמִילָה, דְּרַבְיָא כָּאִיב, וְרוּחָא לָא שַׁרְיָא מָדוֹרֵיהּ בְּגוּפָא כִּשְׁאָר יוֹמִין, וְעַל דָּא וּשְׁלֹשִׁים יוֹם וּשְׁלֹשֶׁת יָמִים תֵּשֵׁב בִּדְמֵי טָהֳרָה.

27. On the eighth day the spirit and the body reappear before the Queen and connect with her and with the male, ZEIR ANPIN, in body and soul. "And she shall continue in the blood of her purifying for 33 days," IN ORDER for the spirit to settle in the body. HE ASKS, what is the purpose of the three days, AND ANSWERS, these are the three days after circumcision when the child suffers its pain, and the spirit does not dwell in the body as in other days. Hence "And she shall continue in the blood of her purifying for 33 days."

28. בִּדְמֵי טָהֳרָה בְּקַדְמֵיתָא, וּלְבָתַר יְמֵי טָהֳרָה. בִּדְמֵי טָהֳרָה, אִלֵּין, דְּמֵי מִילָה, דָּמָא בָּתַר דָּמָא דְּאָתֵי מֵרַבְיָא, וְקוּדְשָׁא בְּרִיךְ הוּא נָטִיר לְאִינּוּן דְּמֵי כָּל אִלֵּין יוֹמִין, הה"ד, תֵּשֵׁב בִּדְמֵי טָהֳרָה. טָהֳרָה סְתָם, וְלָא אַדְכִּיר ה"א בַּתְרָאָה, דְּלָא תֵּימָא תֵּימָא טָהֳרָה דְּמַטְרוֹנִיתָא, אֶלָּא טָהֳרָה סְתָם, דְּמֵי טָהֳרָה אִקְרוּן אִלֵּין דְּמֵי דַכְיָא.

28. HE ASKS, at first SCRIPTURE SAYS, "in the blood of her purifying" (Vayikra 12:5) and later "the days of her purifying" (Ibid. 6), AND ANSWERS, "the blood of her purifying" refers to the bloods of circumcision, blood and more blood coming from the child. The Holy One, blessed be He, keeps those bloods all these days. Hence it says, "And she shall continue in the blood of her purifying (Heb. *taharah*)." The word 'taharah' unspecified IS WRITTEN WITHOUT MAPPIQ (WHICH WOULD RENDER IT 'HER PURIFYING'), SO IT IS NOT PRONOUNCED WHEN READ. THIS INDICATES that the last Hei OF YUD HEI VAV HEI, WHICH IS MALCHUT, is not mentioned. SO you shall not say IT REFERS TO the purifying of the Matron, MALCHUT, THE MOTHER OF THE SOUL, but to purifying in general, SINCE unspecified "blood of her purifying" refers to pure bloods. THIS REFERS TO THE SOUL BORN TO HER. EVERY RISING AND CONNECTION SAID OF MALCHUT REFERS TO MALCHUT AS THE ROOT OF THAT SOUL.

29. בְּכָל קֹדֶשׁ לֹא תִגָּע וְאֶל הַמִּקְדָּשׁ וְגוֹ'. תָּא חֲזֵי, בְּכָל יוֹמָא וְיוֹמָא, כ"י, נַטְלָא מִבֵּי מַלְכָּא מְזוֹנָא לְרוּחֵיהוֹן דִּבְנֵי נָשָׁא, וְזָנַת לְהוּ בִּקְדוּשָׁה. בַּר לְהָנֵי, עַד דְּאִתְיַישְׁבָן בְּגוּפָא אִינּוּן רוּחִין, בָּתַר תְּלָתִין וּתְלַת יוֹמִין, אַשְׁגָּחַת עֲלַיְיהוּ כָּל יוֹמָא, דְּהָא רוּחִין מִתְקַשְּׁרָן בְּגוּפָא כִּשְׁאָר בְּנֵי עָלְמָא, כְּמָה דְּהִיא לָא שַׁרְיָא אֶלָּא בַּאֲתַר שְׁלִים, כַּךְ כָּל עוֹבָדוֹי כְּהַאי גַּוְונָא, עַד דְּאִשְׁתְּלִימוּ. בְּכָל קֹדֶשׁ לֹא תִגָּע, לְאַשְׁגָּחָא עֲלַיְיהוּ.

29. "she shall touch no hallowed thing, nor come in to the sanctuary" (Vayikra 12:4). Come and see, the Congregation of Yisrael, MALCHUT, daily takes food from the King's house for human spirits and nourishes them in holiness, except those SPIRITS DURING THE 33 DAYS OF PURIFYING, until those spirits settle in the body. After 33 days, she cares for them daily, since the spirits are then connected to the body like the rest of

the inhabitants of the world. As she, MALCHUT, dwells only on a wholesome place, likewise are her actions TOWARDS HUMAN SPIRITS until they are whole. THIS IS THE MEANING OF, "she shall touch no hallowed thing," WHICH MEANS for the purpose of taking care of souls. THAT MEANS SHE DOES NOT TOUCH HOLINESS TO RECEIVE FOOD FROM HOLINESS, WHICH IS ZEIR ANPIN, FOR THOSE SPIRITS.

7. "But if she bear a female child"

A Synopsis
Rabbi Elazar says that a female child comes from the left side, that has more power than the right. In order to let the spirit be clothed in a body, Malchut separates from Zeir Anpin.

30. וְאָם נְקֵבָה תֵלֵד. כְּמָה דְּאוֹקִימְנָא, דְּשַׁלְטָא סְטַר שְׂמָאלָא יַתִּיר וְאִתְכַּפְיָא יְמִינָא, וְעַל דָּא כֹּלָּא עַל חַד תְּרֵין, רְחִיקָא נוּקְבָא, מִדְּכוּרָא, לְאִתְקַשְׁרָא רוּחָא בְּגוּפָא, דְּהָא שְׂמָאלָא לָא אִתְיַישְׁבָא הָכִי כִּימִינָא, וְאִשְׁתְּכָחַת בְּתוּקְפָּא יַתִּיר.

30. "But if she bear a female child" (Vayikra 12:5), NAMELY as I interpreted, SINCE the left side has more power and the right is subdued before it. Hence it is all doubled. The Nukva, MALCHUT, is separated from the Male, ZEIR ANPIN, TO LET the spirit attach TO BE CLOTHED in a body, since the left does not settle in the body as well as the right, since it abides more in the strength OF GVUROT.

8. Circumcision and the foreskin

A Synopsis

Rabbi Elazar talks about the secret meaning of the circumcision on the eighth day, the sign of the holy covenant, Yesod. The foreskin is said to be the impure serpent, that must be banished from Yisrael, and after it is removed it is placed in dust since God made the serpent live in the dust. Everyone must offer a son as a peace offering, and the reason for the circumcision on the eighth day is that at least one Shabbat must have passed.

רעיא מהימנא

31. וּבַיּוֹם הַשְּׁמִינִי יִמּוֹל בְּשַׂר עָרְלָתוֹ. פִּקּוּדָא דָא, לְמִגְזַר לִתְמַנְיָא יוֹמִין גְּזִירוּ דְּקַיָּימָא קַדִּישָׁא. רָזָא עִלָּאָה, דִּכְתִיב, סוֹד יְיָ' לִירֵאָיו וּבְרִיתוֹ לְהוֹדִיעָם. לְמַאן, לְאִינוּן יִרְאָיו אִינוּן דַּחֲלֵי חַטָּאָה, דְּהָא רָזָא דְּקַיָּימָא קַדִּישָׁא לָא אִתְחֲזֵי לְגַלָּאָה בַּר לְהוּ. וְרָזָא דְּקַיָּימָא קַדִּישָׁא, הָא אוּקְמוּהָ וְאִתְּמַר בְּכַמָּה דּוּכְתִּין.

Ra'aya Meheimna (the Faithful Shepherd)

31. "And on the eighth day the flesh of his foreskin shall be circumcised" (Vayikra 12:3). That commandment IS to circumcise on the eighth day the circumcision of the holy covenant. It is a supernal secret, as written, "The secret of Hashem is with them that fear Him; and He will reveal to them His covenant" (Tehilim 25:14). To whom DOES HE REVEAL THE SECRET, WHICH IS THE COVENANT? To the fearful, who fear sin. For it is not suitable to reveal the secret of the holy covenant except for them. We have explained and learned the secret of the holy covenant in several places.

32. וְרָזָא דָּא, לַח' יוֹמִין, אִיהוּ חִיּוּבָא עַל עָלְמָא, לְכָל עַמָּא קַדִּישָׁא. דִּכְתִיב, וּבַיּוֹם הַשְּׁמִינִי יִמּוֹל בְּשַׂר עָרְלָתוֹ. יוֹם הַשְּׁמִינִי, דָּא הוּא אָת קַיָּימָא קַדִּישָׁא, וְאִיהוּ תְּמִינָאָה לְכָל דַּרְגִּין. וּגְזִירוּ דְּהַהוּא קַיָּימָא, לְאַעְבְּרָא הַהוּא עָרְלָה. מִקַּמֵּי בְּרִית.

32. This secret, WHICH IS on the eighth day, is a universal obligation to all the holy people, as written, "And on the eighth day the flesh of his foreskin

shall be circumcised." The eighth day is the sign of the holy covenant, NAMELY THE SFIRAH YESOD, which is the eighth among the Sfirot. IF YOU COUNT THE GRADES FROM CHOCHMAH DOWN, YESOD IS THE EIGHTH GRADE. KETER, THE SECRET OF THE ENDLESS LIGHT, IS NOT COUNTED. The purpose of the circumcision of the holy covenant IS to remove that foreskin, THE SECRET OF THE IMPURE SERPENT from before the covenant, THE HOLY YESOD.

33. דְּהָא בְּהַהוּא זִמְנָא דְּמִתְכַּנְּשֵׁי עַמָּא קַדִּישָׁא לְאַעְבְּרָא הַהוּא עָרְלָה מִקַּמֵּי בְּרִית, קוּדְשָׁא בְּרִיךְ הוּא כָּנִישׁ כָּל פָּמַלְיָא דִּילֵיהּ, וְאִתְגְּלֵי וַדַּאי לְאַעְבְּרָא לְהַהוּא עָרְלָה לְעֵילָא, מִקַּמֵּי בְּרִית קַיָּימָא קַדִּישָׁא. דְּהָא כָּל עוֹבָדִין דְּיִשְׂרָאֵל עַבְדִּין לְתַתָּא, מִתְעֲרֵי עוֹבָדָא לְעֵילָא. וּבְהַהוּא זִמְנָא אִתְדַחְיָיא הַהוּא עָרְלָה, מִכָּל עַמָּא קַדִּישָׁא לְעֵילָא. וּלְהַהוּא עָרְלָה מְתַקְּנֵי מָאנָא חֲדָא בְּעַפְרָא, לְאַשְׁרָאָה הַהוּא עָרְלָה בְּגַוֵּיהּ. בְּרָזָא דִכְתִיב, וְנָחָשׁ עָפָר לַחְמוֹ. וְעָפָר תֹּאכַל כָּל יְמֵי חַיֶּיךָ.

33. For when the holy nation gathers to remove that foreskin from before the covenant, the Holy One, blessed be He, gathers His retinue and reveals Himself so as to remove that foreskin above from before the sign of the holy covenant, YESOD. For all the deeds Yisrael do below rouse a deed above. THEREFORE at that time the foreskin, WHICH IS THE IMPURE SERPENT, is banished from before the whole holy nation above. A vessel with dust is prepared for that foreskin, to keep the foreskin, according to the secret of the verses, "and dust shall be the serpent's food" (Yeshayah 65:25), and, "and dust shall you eat all the days of your life" (Beresheet 3:14).

34. מִכָּאן, דְּלָא אִצְטְרִיךְ לְאַנְהֲגָא קְלָנָא בְּהַהוּא אֲתַר, אע"ג דִּמְעַבְּרֵי לֵיהּ מִקַּמֵּי הַאי בְּרִית, וְדוּכְתֵּיהּ, כַּד מִתְעַבְּרָא מֵהַאי בְּרִית, עַפְרָא אִיהוּ, דְּהָרֵי בָּתַר דְּהַהוּא נָחָשׁ אִתְעֲבַר מִקַּמֵּי אָדָם, קוּדְשָׁא בְּרִיךְ הוּא שַׁוֵּי לֵיהּ מָדוֹרֵיהּ בְּעָפָר, דִּכְתִיב וְעָפָר תֹּאכַל כָּל יְמֵי חַיֶּיךָ. וְכֵיוָן דְּקוּדְשָׁא בְּרִיךְ הוּא כַּד אַעְבַּר לֵיהּ מִקַּמֵּי אָדָם שַׁוֵּי מָדוֹרֵיהּ בְּעַפְרָא וְאַתְקִין לֵיהּ, כַּךְ בְּהַהוּא גַּוְונָא מַמָּשׁ, אֲנַן צְרִיכִין כַּד מְעַבְּרִין לַעֲרְלָה, לְאִתְתַקְּנָא לֵיהּ עַפְרָא, לְמֶהֱוִי בֵּיהּ מָדוֹרֵיהּ.

34. From this WE DERIVE that one must not act contemptuously towards that place, THE FORESKIN, even though it is removed from before the member of the covenant. It is placed, after being removed from that covenant, in the dust, since after the serpent was removed from man, the Holy One, blessed be He, made him dwell in dust, as written, "and dust shall you eat all the days of your life." Since the Holy One, blessed be He, made him dwell in dust and formed him so when He removed him from before men, so in the very same way, when we remove the foreskin, we should fix dust for it to dwell in.

35. כָּל בַּר נָשׁ אִצְטְרִיךְ לְקָרְבָא הַהוּא בְּרָא קָרְבָּנָא לְקוּדְשָׁא בְּרִיךְ הוּא, בְּחֶדְוָה, בִּרְעוּ דְלִבָּא, לְמֵיעַל לֵיהּ תְּחוֹת גַּדְפוֹי דִּשְׁכִינְתָּא, וְאִתְחֲשַׁב קַמֵּי קוּדְשָׁא בְּרִיךְ הוּא דְּאִיהוּ קָרְבְּנָא, שְׁלִים לְאִתְקַבְּלָא בְּרַעֲוָא.

35. Everyone has to offer a son as an offering to the Holy One, blessed be He gladly and willingly, to enter him under the wings of the Shechinah. This is considered before the Holy One, blessed be He as a peace offering and is willingly accepted.

36. וְקָרְבְּנָא דָא, כְּגַוְונָא דְקָרְבְּנָא דִּבְעִירָא, דָּא לַח' יוֹמִין, וְדָא לַח' יוֹמִין, דִּכְתִּיב, וּמִיּוֹם הַשְּׁמִינִי וָהָלְאָה יֵרָצֶה, בְּמַאי יֵרָצֶה. בְּמֶעְבַּר עֲלֵיהּ חַד שַׁבְּתָא, כֵּיוָן דְּאַעֲבַר עֲלֵיהּ חַד שַׁבְּתָא, כְּדֵין יֵרָצֶה דָּא לְקָרְבְּנָא, וְדָא לְקָרְבְּנָא. אֲמַאי. בְּגִין דְּאִתְדְּבַק וְאִזְדְּמַן לְגַבֵּי הַהוּא שַׁבְּת, רָזָא דִּבְרִית קַדִּישָׁא, וְעַל דָּא כֹּלָּא בְּרָזָא עִלָּאָה אִיהוּ.

ע"כ רעיא מהימנא

36. This offering resembles an offering from the cattle, as both occur on the eighth day, as written, "and from the eighth day and thenceforth it shall be accepted" (Vayikra 22:27). What makes it acceptable? IT IS because he already lived on Shabbat, BECAUSE IN EIGHT DAYS THERE MUST BE ONE SHABBAT. Once he underwent one Shabbat, the one shall be acceptable for an offering, THE ANIMAL, and the other shall be acceptable, THE CIRCUMCISED CHILD. The reason is that he cleaved and came to this

Shabbat, MALCHUT, the secret of the holy covenant, YESOD. THIS MEANS THAT YESOD EXISTS ON SHABBAT IN ITS ENTIRETY, AND HENCE THE CHILD RECEIVES ILLUMINATION FROM IT TO INSTITUTE HIS HOLY COVENANT. THE CATTLE SHALL ALSO BE ACCEPTABLE AS AN OFFERING, BECAUSE THE SACRIFICE UNITES YESOD AND MALCHUT, AND ONE SHOULD THEREFORE BE ESTABLISHED BY THE WHOLE YESOD ON SHABBAT DAY. Everything follows a supernal secret.

End of Ra'aya Meheimna (the Faithful Shepherd)

9. "Neither is there a rock like our Elohim"

A Synopsis

We learn from Rabbi Shimon that there are holy beings other than Elohim – angels, and the holy children of Yisrael, and yet they depend for their holiness on Elohim; He does not depend on theirs. We hear two explanations for the title verse, one of which compares the rock to the fetus God formed into which He blew the spirit of life. The other explanation says that the verse merely means that Elohim has power and dominion over everything.

37. אִשָּׁה כִּי תַזְרִיעַ וְיָלְדָה זָכָר וְגוֹ'. ר' יְהוּדָה פָּתַח, אֵין קָדוֹשׁ כַּיְיָ' כִּי אֵין בִּלְתֶּךָ וְאֵין צוּר בֵּאלֹהֵינוּ, הַאי קְרָא קַשְׁיָא, אֵין קָדוֹשׁ כַּיְיָ', מַשְׁמַע דְּאִיכָּא קָדוֹשׁ אָחֳרָא, בְּגִין דִּכְתִיב כַּיְיָ', וְאֵין צוּר בֵּאלֹהֵינוּ, מַשְׁמַע דְּאִיכָּא צוּר אָחֳרָא.

37. "If a woman have conceived seed, and born a man child" (Vayikra 12:2). Rabbi Yehuda opened with, "There is none holy as Hashem. For there is none beside You. Neither is there a rock like our Elohim" (I Shmuel 2:2). This is a difficult verse. IF IT IS WRITTEN, "There is none holy as Hashem" it would mean there is something else holy NEVERTHELESS, SOMEWHAT LESSER THAN HASHEM, as it says, "as Hashem." ALSO, "Neither is there a rock like our Elohim" means there is another rock SOMEWHAT LESSER THAN HASHEM.

38. אֶלָּא וַדַּאי, אֵין קָדוֹשׁ כַּיְיָ', דְּכַמָּה קַדִּישִׁין נִינְהוּ, קַדִּישִׁין לְעֵילָּא, דִּכְתִיב, וּמֵאֲמַר קַדִּישִׁין שְׁאֶלְתָּא. יִשְׂרָאֵל קַדִּישִׁין נִינְהוּ, דִּכְתִיב, קְדוֹשִׁים תִּהְיוּ. וְכֻלְּהוּ קַדִּישִׁין, וְלָאו קַדִּישִׁין כַּיְיָ'. ומ"ט. בְּגִין דִּכְתִיב, כִּי אֵין בִּלְתֶּךָ. מַאי, כִּי אֵין בִּלְתֶּךָ, אֶלָּא קְדוּשָׁה דְּקוּדְשָׁא ב"ה בִּלְתִּי קְדוּשָׁא דִּלְהוֹן, דְּהוּא לָא אִצְטְרִיךְ לִקְדוּשָׁה דִּלְהוֹן. אֲבָל אִינּוּן, לָאו אִינּוּן קַדִּישִׁין בִּלְתֶּךָ, וְדָא הוּא, כִּי אֵין בִּלְתֶּךָ, אֵין קְדוּשָׁה דִּלְהוֹן, בִּלְתֶּךָ.

38. HE ANSWERS, surely, "There is none holy as Hashem," since there are many holy beings. There are holy beings above, NAMELY ANGELS, as

-28-

written, "and the sentence by the word of the holy ones" (Daniel 4:14). Yisrael ALSO are holy, as written, "You shall be holy" (Vayikra 19:2). They are all holy, yet not as holy as Hashem. The reason is that it is written, "For there is none beside (or: 'without') You." It means that the holiness of the Holy One, blessed be He exists without their holiness OF THE ANGELS AND OF YISRAEL, since He is not in need of their holiness. But they are not holy without You, since without You they have no holiness.

39. וְאֵין צוּר כֵּאלֹהֵינוּ. כְּמָה דְּאוּקְמוּהָ, דְּקוּדְשָׁא בְּרִיךְ הוּא צָר צוּרָה בְּגוֹ צוּרָה, וְתָקִין לֵיהּ, וְנָפַח רוּחָא דְּחַיֵּי, וְאַפִּיק לֵיהּ לַאֲוִירָא דְּעָלְמָא, ד"א, וְאֵין צוּר כֵּאלֹהֵינוּ. אִית צוּר, דְּאִקְרֵי צוּר, הַבִּיטוּ אֶל צוּר חוּצַבְתֶּם. וְהִכִּיתָ בַצּוּר. הִנְנִי עוֹמֵד לְפָנֶיךָ שָׁם עַל הַצּוּר בְּחוֹרֵב. וְכֻלְּהוּ אִקְרוּן צוּר, וְאֵין צוּר כְּכֻלְּהוּ כֵּאלֹהֵינוּ, דִּילֵיהּ שׁוּלְטָנוּ וּמַלְכוּתָא עַל כֹּלָא.

39. "Neither is there a rock (Heb. *tzur*) like our Elohim" MEANS as explained that the Holy One, blessed be He shaped a form (Heb. *tzurah*) within a form, THAT IS, THE FORM OF THE FETUS IN THE FORM OF ITS MOTHER, improved it, blew into it the spirit of life and brought it out into the world. According to another explanation, "Neither is there a rock like our Elohim" means that there is a rock, which is called ONLY a rock, as written, "look to the rock from whence you are hewn" (Yeshayah 51:1), and, "and you shall smite the rock" (Shemot 17:6). They are all called 'rock' yet none is a rock like our Elohim, who has power and dominion over everything.

10. A star that struck another star three times

A Synopsis

Here we read the story of what happened at midnight as the rabbis rose to study the Torah. They see a star that strikes another star three times, and then they hear two sounds, one of which is a voice that tells of God entering the Garden of Eden to walk about with the righteous. The Congregation of Yisrael has united with God, and before dawn He holds out to her a thread of Chesed, just as the king held out the golden scepter to Esther.

40. רָבִּי חִיָּיא וְר' אֶחָא הֲוֹו יַתְבֵי לֵילְיָא חַד קַמֵּיה דְּרָבִּי אַבָּא. קָמוּ בְּפַלְגוּת לֵילְיָא לְמִלְעֵי בְּאוֹרַיְיתָא. עַד דְּנָפְקוּ לְבַר, חָמוּ חַד כֹּכְבָא דַּהֲוָה בָּטַשׁ ג' זִמְנֵי בְּכֹכְבָא אַחֲרָא וְסָתִים נְהוֹרֵיה. אַדְּהָכִי שָׁמְעוּ תְּרֵי קָלֵי בִּתְרֵי סִטְרֵי, קָלָא חַד לְסְטַר צָפוֹן לְעֵילָא, וְקָלָא חַד לְתַתָּא. וְהַהוּא קָלָא אַכְרִיז וְאָמַר, עוּלוּ וְאִתְכְּנִישׁוּ לְאַתְרַיְיכוּ, הַשְׁתָּא אִסְתַּמְרוּתָא דְּנוּקְבָּא פְּתִיחָא, קוּדְשָׁא בְּרִיךְ הוּא עָאל לְטַיְילָא בְּגִנְתָא, לְאִשְׁתַּעְשְׁעָא בְּצַדִּיקַיָּיא דִּי בְּגִנְתָא, אַעְבַּר הַהוּא קָלָא וְשָׁכִיךְ.

40. Rabbi Chiya and Rabbi Acha were sitting one night before Rabbi Aba. They rose at midnight to study Torah. As they were going out, they saw a star striking another star three times, masking its light. At the same time they heard two sounds from two directions, one from the north from above, and another from below. That sound BELOW proclaimed, 'Come and gather to your places, for just now the guarding over the Nukva, MALCHUT, has been released, for the Holy One, blessed be He, has entered the Garden to walk about and be delighted with the righteous therein'. That sound passed away and was silenced.

41(1). אַהֲדְרוּ ר' אֶחָא וְר' חִיָּיא, אָמְרוּ, הָא וַדַּאי עִדָּן רְעוּתָא, דְּאִתְעָרוּתָא דְּכ"י הוּא לְאִתְחַבְּרָא בְּמַלְכָּא קַדִּישָׁא, א"ר אֶחָא, וַדַּאי, לָא אִתְחַבְּרַת לָה כ"י בְּקוּדְשָׁא בְּרִיךְ הוּא אֶלָּא מִגּוֹ שִׁירָתָא, מִגּוֹ שְׁבָחָא דִּילָה לְגַבֵּיה.

41a. Rabbi Acha and Rabbi Chiya returned TO THE HOUSE and said, surely it is time of goodwill of the awakening of the Congregation of Yisrael to

unite with the Holy King, ZEIR ANPIN, THE CENTRAL COLUMN. Rabbi Acha said, surely the Congregation of Yisrael united with the Holy One, blessed be He, only by singing and by her praise for Him.

41(2). עַד דְּאָתֵי צַפְרָא, וְאוֹשִׁיט לָהּ מַלְכָּא חוּטָא דְחֶסֶד, וְרָזָא דְּמִלָּה כְּמָה דְּאַמְרֵינָן, וַיּוֹשֶׁט הַמֶּלֶךְ לְאֶסְתֵּר אֶת שַׁרְבִיט הַזָּהָב אֲשֶׁר בְּיָדוֹ וְגוֹ'. וְלָא תֵימָא דְּלָהּ בִּלְחוֹדָהָא אוֹשִׁיט לָהּ מַלְכָּא דָא, אֶלָּא לָהּ, וּלְכָל אִינוּן דְּמִתְחַבְּרָן בָּהּ. תָּא וְנִתְחַבֵּר כַּחֲדָא. יָתְבוּ.

41b. Before dawn, the King holds out to her a thread of Chesed, SINCE THEN THE CHOCHMAH IN HER IS CLOTHED IN CHESED AND ATTAINS COMPLETION. The secret of this is said in the verse, "and the king held out to Esther the golden scepter that was in his hand" (Ester 5:2). THE KING IS ZEIR ANPIN AND ESTER IS MALCHUT; THE GOLDEN SCEPTER IS THE THREAD OF CHESED, WHICH, WITH THE CLOTHING OF CHOCHMAH IN MALCHUT IN IT IS CALLED A GOLDEN SCEPTER. Do not say that the King holds out to her alone THE GOLDEN SCEPTER but to her and to all those who join her. Let us come together. They sat down.

11. "and He took one of his sides"

A Synopsis
Rabbi Shimon says that the first man was created male and female fastened together at their backs, but that later God severed them so they could be face to face. Because God blesses newlyweds with seven blessings, anyone who mates with another's wife destroys the union, and is not forgiven until he repents and dies.

42. פָּתַח רַבִּי אֲחָא וְאָמַר, וַיֹּאמֶר יְיָ׳ אֱלֹהִים לֹא טוֹב הֱיוֹת הָאָדָם לְבַדּוֹ וְגוֹ׳. אֲמַאי פָּתַח קְרָא הָכִי, אֶלָּא הָא אִתְּמַר, דְּעַל דָּא לָא כְּתִיב, כִּי טוֹב בַּשֵּׁנִי, בְּגִין דְּזַמִּין אָדָם לְאִתְפָּרְשָׁא, וּכְתִיב, לֹא טוֹב הֱיוֹת הָאָדָם לְבַדּוֹ.

42. Rabbi Aba opened with, "And Hashem Elohim said, It is not good that the man should be alone..." (Beresheet 2:18). HE ASKS, why did the verse speak this way, AND ANSWERS, that we learned that for this reason it is not written, "that it was good" about the second day, because man will be divided, THAT IS, A SIDE WILL BE DIVIDED FROM HIM TO BUILD THE WOMAN. It is also written, "it is not good that the man should be alone." FOR THAT REASON "THAT IT WAS GOOD" WAS NOT SAID IN RELATION TO THE SECOND DAY.

43. וְכִי לְבַדּוֹ הֲוָה, וְהָא כְּתִיב, זָכָר וּנְקֵבָה בְּרָאָם. וְתָנֵינָן אָדָם דּוּ פַּרְצוּפִין אִתְבְּרֵי, וְאַתְּ אָמְרַת, לֹא טוֹב הֱיוֹת הָאָדָם לְבַדּוֹ. אֶלָּא דְּלָא אִשְׁתְּדַל בְּנוּקְבֵּיה, וְלָא הֲוַת לֵיה, סָמֵךְ לָקֳבְלֵיה, בְּגִין דְּהֲוַת בְּסִטְרוֹי, וַהֲווֹ כַּחֲדָא מֵאֲחוֹרָא, וּכְדֵין הֲוָה הָאָדָם לְבַדּוֹ.

43. HE ASKS, was he alone? Yet it is written, "male and female He created them" (Beresheet 5:2). We learned that the first man was created double faced, THAT IS, A MALE AND A FEMALE FACES FASTENED AT THEIR BACKS. Yet you say, "it is not good that the man should be alone." HE ANSWERS, but he did not gain favor with his wife, and she was not a help to match him, but they were FASTENED together back to back. Then man was alone.

44. אֶעֱשֶׂה לּוֹ עֵזֶר כְּנֶגְדּוֹ. מַהוּ כְּנֶגְדּוֹ. לָקֳבֵל אַנְפּוֹי, לְאִתְדַּבְּקָא דָּא בְּדָא אַנְפִּין בְּאַנְפִּין, מָה עֲבַד קוּדְשָׁא בְּרִיךְ הוּא, נָסַר לֵיהּ וְנָטִיל נוּקְבָּא מִנֵּיהּ, הה"ד, וַיִּקַּח אַחַת מִצַּלְעוֹתָיו. מַהוּ אַחַת. דָּא נוּקְבָּא דִּילֵיהּ. כד"א, אַחַת הִיא יוֹנָתִי תַמָּתִי. וַיְבִיאֶהָ אֶל הָאָדָם, אַתְקִין לָהּ כְּכַלָּה וְאַיְיתֵי לָהּ לְמֶהֱוֵי לָהּ לָקֳבֵיל אַנְפּוֹי נְהִירִין אַנְפִּין בְּאַנְפִּין. וּבְעוֹד דַּהֲוָה מִתְדַּבְּקָא נוּקְבָּא בְּסִטְרוֹי, הֲוָה הָאָדָם לְבַדּוֹ. לְבָתַר, סְלִיקוּ תְּרֵין, וְקָמוּ שֶׁבַע כַּחֲדָא.

44. "I will make him a help to match him" (Beresheet 2:18). What is "to match him"? HE ANSWERS THAT IT MEANS facing him, so they will unite face to face. The Holy One, blessed be He, sawed him and took the female from him, as written, "and He took one of his sides" (Ibid. 21). What does 'one' refer to? It resembles the words, "My dove, my undefiled is but one" (Shir Hashirim 6:9). "…and brought her to the man" (Beresheet 2:22) MEANS He fixed her as a bride and brought her so she will face him and their faces would shine at each other's. As long as the woman was adjoined to his side, the man was alone. Afterwards two came out AND MATED, and seven emerged, NAMELY, CAIN WITH HIS TWIN SISTER, ABEL WITH HIS TWO TWIN SISTERS, WHICH MAKES FIVE. TOGETHER WITH ADAM AND EVE THEY ARE SEVEN.

45. ת"ח, בְּשַׁעֲתָא דְּאִתְתַּקָּנַת לְגַבֵּי אָדָם, קוּדְשָׁא בְּרִיךְ הוּא בְּרִיךְ לוֹן, הה"ד, וַיְבָרֶךְ אוֹתָם אֱלֹהִים. כְּחַזָּן דִּמְבָרֵךְ לְכַלָּה בְּשֶׁבַע בְּרָכוֹת. מִכָּאן אוֹלִיפְנָא, חָתָן וְכַלָּה, כֵּיוָן דְּאִתְבָּרְכָן בְּשֶׁבַע בְּרָכוֹת אִתְדַּבְּקָן כַּחֲדָא, כְּדוּגְמָא דִּלְעֵילָא.

45. Come and see, when EVE was made ready for Adam, the Holy One, blessed be He, blessed them. This is the meaning of, "And Elohim blessed them" (Beresheet 1:28), just as the cantor gives the bride seven blessings. From this we learned that once a bride and a groom are blessed with seven blessings, they are united as the likeness of above WHERE MALCHUT IS BLESSED WITH SEVEN BLESSINGS BY CHESED, GVURAH, TIFERET, NETZACH, HOD, YESOD AND MALCHUT OF ZEIR ANPIN.

46. וְעַל דָּא מַאן דְּאָתֵי לְאִתְחַבְּרָא בְּאִנְתּוּ דְּאָחֳרָא, הָא פָּגִים זוּוּגָא, דְּהָא זוּוּגָא דְּכ"י, בֵּיה בְּקוּדְשָׁא בְּרִיךְ הוּא בִּלְחוֹדוֹי, בְּזִמְנָא דְּאִיהוּ בְּרַחֲמֵי, וּבְזִמְנָא דְּאִיהוּ בְּדִינָא. ת"ח, מַאן דְּמִתְחַבֵּר בְּאִנְתּוּ דְּאָחֳרָא, כְּאִילּוּ מְשַׁקֵּר בֵּיה בְּקוּדְשָׁא בְּרִיךְ הוּא וּבכ"י, וְעַל דָּא קוּדְשָׁא בְּרִיךְ הוּא לָא מְכַפֵּר לֵיה בִּתְשׁוּבָה, וּתְשׁוּבָה תַּלְיָא עַד דְּיִסְתַּלַּק מֵעָלְמָא, הה"ד, אִם יְכוּפַּר הֶעָוֹן הַזֶּה לָכֶם עַד תְּמוּתוּן. וְאֵימָתַי, בְּשַׁעֲתָא דְּעָאל בִּתְשׁוּבָה לְהַהוּא עָלְמָא, וְאִית לֵיה לְקַבְּלָא עוֹנְשָׁא.

46. Therefore, whoever mates with another man's wife blemishes the union, because the Congregation of Yisrael unites with the Holy One, blessed be He, alone BOTH at the time when He is of Mercy AND when He is of Judgment. Come and see, whoever mates with another's wife, it is as if he is false to the Holy One, blessed be He, and the Congregation of Yisrael. For this reason the Holy One, blessed be He, does not forgive him through repentance, and repentance impends until he dies. This is the meaning of, "shall not be forgiven you till you die" (Yeshayah 22:14). When IS HE FORGIVEN? When he repents coming into that world, WHERE he needs to receive punishment. THEN HE IS FORGIVEN.

47. רַבִּי אֶלְעָזָר אָמַר, מַאן דִּמְשַׁקֵּר בכ"י, לָא יִתְקַבַּל בִּתְשׁוּבָה, עַד דְּיִתְדָּן בְּדִינָא דְּגֵיהִנָּם. כ"ש, מַאן דִּמְשַׁקֵּר בכ"י וּבְקוּדְשָׁא בְּרִיךְ הוּא. וכ"ש אִי אַטְרַח לֵיה לְקוּדְשָׁא בְּרִיךְ הוּא לְמֶעְבַּד דִּיּוּקְנָא דְּמַמְזֵר בְּאִנְתּוּ דְּאָחֳרָא, וְאַכְחִישׁ פּוּמְבֵי דְּמַלְכָּא.

47. Rabbi Elazar said, whoever is false to the Congregation of Yisrael BY MATING WITH ANOTHER MAN'S WIFE, HIS repentance is not accepted until he is punished in Gehenom. This is more true for whoever is false to the Congregation of Yisrael and the Holy One, blessed be He, and all the more so if he troubles the Holy One, blessed be He, to make the form of a bastard in another's wife, and is false to the King in public, openly.

12. "He who robs his father or his mother"

A Synopsis
Rabbi Chiya says that "his father" is God, "his mother" is the congregation of Yisrael, and the robbery is a man coveting a woman who is not his wife. Such a man blemishes above and blemishes below and blemishes his own soul.

48. ר' חִיָּיא פָּתַח וְאָמַר, גּוֹזֵל אָבִיו וְאִמּוֹ וְגוֹ'. אָבִיו, דָּא קוּדְשָׁא בְּרִיךְ הוּא. אִמּוֹ, דָּא כ"י. מַאי גּוֹזֵל. כד"א, גְּזֵלַת הֶעָנִי בְּבָתֵּיכֶם. וּמַאן אִיהוּ, מַאן דְּחָמִיד אִתְּתָא אָחֳרָא דְּלָאו אִיהִי בַּת זוּגֵיהּ.

48. Rabbi Chiya opened with the words, "He who robs his father or his mother…" (Mishlei 28:24). His father is the Holy One, blessed be He, and his mother is the Congregation of Yisrael. "robs" is as in the words, "the robbery of the poor is in your houses" (Yeshayah 3:14). What is THE ROBBERY? It is man coveting another woman, who is not his wife.

49. תַּמָּן תָּנֵינָן, כָּל הַנֶּהֱנֶה מִן הָעוֹלָם הַזֶּה בְּלֹא בְּרָכָה, כְּאִלּוּ גּוֹזֵל לְקוּדְשָׁא בְּרִיךְ הוּא וכ"י, דִּכְתִיב גּוֹזֵל אָבִיו וְאִמּוֹ וְגוֹ'. כָּל הַנֶּהֱנֶה מִן הָעוֹלָם הַזֶּה, כְּלָל דָּא, אִיהוּ אִינְתּוּ. מַאן דְּאִתְדַּבָּק בְּאִנְתּוּ לְמֶהֱנֵי מִנָּהּ, ואע"ג, דְּאִיהִי פְּנוּיָה, וְאַהֲנֵי מִנָּהּ בְּלָא בְּרָכָה, כְּאִלּוּ גּוֹזֵל קוּדְשָׁא בְּרִיךְ הוּא וּכְנֶסֶת יִשְׂרָאֵל. מ"ט, בְּגִין דְּזִוּוּגָא דִּלְהוֹן, בְּשֶׁבַע בְּרָכוֹת הוּא. וּמָה עַל פְּנוּיָה כָּךְ, מַאן דְּיִתְדַּבַּק בְּאִנְתּוּ דְאָחֳרָא, דְּקָאִים כְּגַוְונָא דִלְעֵילָא, בְּזִוּוּגָא דְז' בְּרָכוֹת, עַל אַחַת כַּמָּה וְכַמָּה.

49. We learned there that whoever derives any enjoyment from this world without blessing, it is as if he robs the Holy One, blessed be He, and the Congregation of Yisrael, as written, "He who robs his father or his mother, and says, It is no transgression; he is companion of a destroyer." Whoever enjoys anything of this world, THE WORDS 'WHOEVER ENJOYS' include a woman. Whoever joins a woman to enjoy her without a blessing, NAMELY WITHOUT THE SEVEN BLESSINGS BESTOWED ON THE BRIDE, it is as if HE robs the Holy One, blessed be He, and the Congregation of Yisrael. What is the reason thereof? Because they are united by means of the seven blessings

AND HE WHO DERIVES ENJOYMENT WITHOUT THEM BLEMISHES THE SUPERNAL SEVEN BLESSINGS. And if this is true to a single woman, it is all the more true for one who unites with another man's wife, who has the likeness of above by means of the seven blessings THROUGH HER HUSBAND, all the more so.

50. חָבֵר הוּא לְאִישׁ מַשְׁחִית, דָּא יָרָבְעָם, כְּמָה דְּאוּקְמוּהָ, וְאֹמֵר אֵין פָּשַׁע דְּאָמַר הָא פְּנוּיָה הִיא, אֲמַאי אָסוּר. בְּגִין דָּא גּוֹזֵל אָבִיו וְאִמּוֹ הֲוֵי. וְלֹא עוֹד אֶלָּא דְּחָבֵר הוּא לְאִישׁ מַשְׁחִית. מַאן הוּא אִישׁ מַשְׁחִית. דְּפָגִים דְּיוּקְנָא וְתִקוּנָא דִּלְעֵילָא. כ״ש מַאן דְּחָמִיד לְאִנְתּוּ דְּחַבְרֵיהּ לְאִתְדַּבְּקָא בָהּ, דְּפָגִים יַתִּיר. וְעַל דָּא אִתְפְּגִים הוּא לְעָלְמִין. אִישׁ מַשְׁחִית, דְּפָגִים לְעֵילָא, וּפָגִים לְתַתָּא, וּפָגִים לְנַפְשֵׁיהּ, דִּכְתִיב מַשְׁחִית, וּכְתִיב, מַשְׁחִית נַפְשׁוֹ הוּא יַעֲשֶׂנָּה.

50. "he is companion of a destroyer" (Mishlei 28:24) refers to Jeroboam, as was explained, who "says, It is no transgression" (Ibid.), saying, she is single, why should it be forbidden? Therefore, he "robs his father or his mother." Moreover, "he is companion of a destroyer." The destroyer is a man who blemishes the form and establishment of above, and all the more so whoever covets his neighbor's wife to cling to her, who blemishes even more. He is thus blemished forever. He is a destroyer because he blemishes above, blemishes below, and blemishes his soul, as written, "a destroyer," and, "he who does that destroys his soul" (Mishlei 6:32).

13. "Let me go, for the day breaks"

A Synopsis

Rabbi Shimon explains to Rabbi Aba that the angel prevailed over Jacob at night because he was from the side of judgment and night, but when daylight came his power was lessened and Jacob was able to overpower him. Jacob worried lest the angel should hold his usurpation of Esau's blessings against him, but the angel acknowledged that he had acquired the blessings rightfully, and he renamed Jacob Israel. Rabbi Shimon says that if the desire of Malchut is aroused first, drawing God to her with love and desire, she is filled from the right side, that is considered male, and she bears a boy child. God therefore decrees whether a boy or a girl shall be conceived. Desire should be prevalent first in the world, since in every sense people should desire God.

51. רִבִּי אַבָּא פָּתַח וְאָמַר, וַיֹּאמֶר שַׁלְּחֵנִי כִּי עָלָה הַשַּׁחַר וְגוֹ'. וַיֹּאמֶר שַׁלְּחֵנִי, וְכִי עָקוּד הֲוָה בִּידֵיה דְּיַעֲקֹב. אֶלָּא זַכָּאִין אִינּוּן צַדִּיקַיָּיא, דְּקוּדְשָׁא בְּ"ה חָס עַל יְקָרָא דִּלְהוֹן, וְלָא שָׁבִיק לוֹן לְעָלְמִין. הה"ד, לֹא יִתֵּן לְעוֹלָם מוֹט לַצַּדִּיק. וְהָא כְּתִיב, וַתֵּקַע כַּף יֶרֶךְ יַעֲקֹב.

51. Rabbi Aba opened with, "And he said, Let me go, for the day breaks" (Beresheet 32:27). HE ASKS, "And he said, Let me go." Was he a prisoner in Jacob's hands?! AND HE ANSWERS, happy are the righteous, that the Holy One, blessed be He, respects their honor and never leaves them. This is the meaning of, "He shall never suffer the righteous to be moved" (Tehilim 55:23). HE ASKS, yet it is written, "and the hollow of Jacob's thigh was put out of joint" (Beresheet 32:26)?

52. אֶלָּא לְדִידֵיהּ גָּבָה. וְהָא אִתְּמַר, כְּתִיב וְהוּא לָן בַּלַּיְלָה הַהוּא בַּמַּחֲנֶה. וּכְתִיב וַיִּקָּחֵם וַיַּעֲבִירֵם אֶת הַנַּחַל מַאי הֲוָה דַּעְתֵּיהּ דְּיַעֲקֹב, לְמֶעְבְּרָא לְהוֹן בְּנַחֲלָא בְּלֵילְיָא. אֶלָּא חָמָא מְקַטְרְגָא אָזִיל בֵּין מַשְׁרְיָיא דִּילֵיהּ, אָמַר יַעֲקֹב אַעֲבַר לְגִיסָא אָחֳרָא דְּנַהֲרָא, דִּלְמָא לָא יִשְׁתְּכַח עִרְבּוּבְיָא.

52. HE ANSWERS, the angel took from his own. We learned the words, "and he himself lodged that night in the camp" (Ibid. 22), and, "he took them, and

sent them over the wadi" (Ibid. 24). HE ASKS, what did Jacob have in mind to send them across the wadi at night, AND ANSWERS, he saw the persecutor walking among his camps. Jacob said to himself, I shall send them across the wadi. Perhaps confusion shall be avoided.

53. מַאי קָא חָמָא. חָמָא שַׁלְהוֹבָא דְּאֶשָּׁא מְלַהֲטָא, אַזְלָא וְטָאס בֵּין מַשְׁרְיָיתֵיה אָמַר יַעֲקֹב מוּטָב לְנַטְלָא מֵהָכָא, וְנַהֲרָא פָּסִיק בְּגַוַּון, וְלָא יִשְׁתְּכַח עִרְבּוּבְיָא. מִיָּד וַיִּקָּחֵם וַיַּעֲבִירֵם אֶת הַנָּחַל. וַיִּוָּתֵר יַעֲקֹב לְבַדּוֹ, מִכָּאן אוֹלִיפְנָא מַאן דְּאִשְׁתְּכַח בִּלְחוֹדוֹי בְּבֵיתָא בְּלֵילְיָא, אוֹ בִּימָמָא בְּבֵית מִיחֲדָא, כ״שׁ בְּלֵילְיָא, מַאי מִיחֲדָא. מִיחֲדָא מִשְּׁאָר בֵּיתִין. אוֹ מַאן דְּאָזִיל בִּלְחוֹדוֹי בְּלֵילְיָא יָכִיל לְאִתְזְקָא.

53. HE ASKS, what did he see? AND ANSWERS, he saw a flame of bright fire flying and sauntering among his camps. Jacob said to himself, it is better to take them from here ACROSS THE WADI, so the river may divide between them and thus there shall be no confusion, SINCE DEMONS CANNOT CROSS RIVERS. Immediately "he took them, and sent them over the wadi... And Jacob was left alone." SINCE JACOB PREVENTED HIM FROM HARMING THE CAMPS, "HE TOUCHED THE HOLLOW OF HIS THIGH; AND THE HOLLOW OF JACOB'S THIGH WAS PUT OUT OF JOINT." FOR HE TOOK FROM HIM WHAT WAS HIS OWN. From this we deduce about he who is at home alone at night or during the day in a certain house or more so at night IN A CERTAIN HOUSE. What is a certain house? IT IS unique and separate from other houses. Also whoever walks alone at night might come to harm.

54. תָּא חֲזֵי וַיִּוָּתֵר יַעֲקֹב לְבַדּוֹ, כְּדֵין וַיֵּאָבֵק אִישׁ עִמּוֹ וְגוֹ'. תָּנֵינָן מִסְּטְרָא דְּדִינָא קָא אָתֵי, וְשׁוּלְטָנֵיה בְּסְטַר לֵילְיָא. מַאי בְּסְטַר לֵילְיָא. לְאַעֲלָא בְּגָלוּתָא כֵּיוָן דְּסָלִיק נְהוֹרָא, תָּשַׁשׁ חֵילֵיה, וְאִתְגַּבַּר עֲלֵיה חֵילֵיה דְּיַעֲקֹב. דְּהָא מִסְּטְרָא דְּלֵילְיָא קָא אָתֵי, וּבְזִמְנָא דַּהֲוָה לֵילְיָא לָא הֲוָה יָכִיל בֵּיה יַעֲקֹב. כַּד סָלִיק נְהוֹרָא אִתְתְּקַף חֵילָא דְּיַעֲקֹב, וְאָחִיד בֵּיה, וְאִתְגַּבַּר עֲלֵיה. חָמָא לֵיה יַעֲקֹב דְּהָא שְׁלִיחָא הוּא.

54. Come and see, "And Jacob was left alone," and then, "there wrestled a man with him..." (Ibid. 25). We learned that THE ANGEL came from the

aspect of Judgment and his dominion was at the side of night. What is the side of night? IT MEANS HE IS APPOINTED to bring YISRAEL into exile, WHICH IS CONSIDERED NIGHT AND DARKNESS. Once light rose, his power diminished and Jacob overpowered him, because he came from the aspect of night. THEREFORE as long as it was night Jacob could not prevail against him, but once light rose Jacob's power grew, and he grabbed him and overpowered him. THEN Jacob knew he was an angel.

55. אָ"ל שְׁבוֹק לִי דְּלָא יָכִילְנָא לָךְ. מ"ט לָא יָכִיל לֵיהּ. בְּגִין דַּהֲוָה סָלִיק נְהוֹרָא, וְאִתְּבַּר חֵילָא דִּידֵיהּ, דִּכְתִיב בְּרָן יַחַד כֹּכְבֵי בֹקֶר וַיָּרִיעוּ כָּל בְּנֵי אֱלֹהִים. מַאי וַיָּרִיעוּ. דְּאִתְבָּרוּ כָּל אִינּוּן דְּאַתְיָין מִסִּטְרָא דְּדִינָא. כְּדֵין אִתְתָּקַּף יַעֲקֹב וְאָחִיד בֵּיהּ.

55. THE ANGEL said to him, release me, since I cannot prevail against you. Why could not he prevail against him? Because light rose and his power was broken, as written, "When the morning stars sang together, and all the sons of Elohim shouted for joy" (Iyov 38:7). What is "shouted"? IT MEANS all those of the aspect of Judgment were shattered, SINCE 'YARI'U (ENG. 'SHOUTED')' IS DERIVED FROM 'SHATTERED'. THE SONS OF ELOHIM ARE ALL THOSE COMING FROM THE ASPECT OF JUDGMENT CALLED ELOHIM. Jacob then grew strong and seized him.

56. אָמַר לֵיהּ שַׁלְּחֵנִי כִּי עָלָה הַשַּׁחַר, מָטָא זִמְנָא לְשַׁבְּחָא שְׁבָחָא דְּקוּדְשָׁא בְּרִיךְ הוּא, וּלְאִתְכַּנְּשָׁא. וַיֹּאמֶר לֹא אֲשַׁלֵּחֲךָ כִּי אִם בֵּרַכְתָּנִי, אִם תְּבָרְכֵנִי מִבָּעֵי לֵיהּ, מַאי אִם בֵּרַכְתָּנִי. אֶלָּא אָמַר לֵיהּ יַעֲקֹב, וַדַּאי אַבָּא בְּרִיךְ לִי אִינּוּן בִּרְכָאן דְּבָעָא לְבָרְכָא לְעֵשָׂו, וּמִסְתָּפֵינָא מִנָּךְ, עַל אִינּוּן בִּרְכָאן, אִי אוֹדִית עֲלַיְיהוּ, אִי לָאו, אוֹ תִּשְׁתְּכַח עֲלַי מְקַטְרְגָא בְּגִינֵיהוֹן.

56. He said to him, "And he said, Let me go, for the day breaks," NAMELY, the time has come to gather and sing the praise of the Holy One, blessed be He. "And he said to him, I will not let you go, unless you bless (lit. 'blessed') me" (Beresheet 32:27). HE ASKS, it should have said, 'unless you shall bless me'. Why is it written, "unless you blessed me" IN THE PAST TENSE? AND HE ANSWERS, Jacob said to him, my father gave me the

blessings he wished to confer upon Esau, and I fear you, whether you shall acknowledge these blessings or not, for you might denounce me because of them.

57. מִיַּד אָמַר לֵיהּ, וַיֹּאמֶר לֹא יַעֲקֹב יֵאָמֵר עוֹד שְׁמְךָ. מַאי קָאָמַר לֵיהּ, אֶלָּא הָכִי קָאָמַר לֵיהּ, לָאו בְּחַכִּימוּ, וְלָאו בְּעוֹקְבָא, רַוְוחַת לְאִינּוּן בִּרְכָאן, לָא יֵאָמֵר עוֹד שְׁמְךָ יַעֲקֹב, דְּהָא לָאו בְּעוֹקְבָא הֲוָה, כִּי אִם יִשְׂרָאֵל, יִשְׂרָאֵל וַדַּאי אוֹדֵי עֲלָךְ, וּמִנֵּיהּ נָפְקוּ בִּרְכָאן, בְּגִין דְּאַנְתְּ אָחִיד בֵּיהּ, וְעַל דָּא, אֲנָא וְכָל שְׁאַר אוּכְלוּסִין, אוֹדֵינָא עֲלַיְיהוּ.

57. Forthwith he told him, "And he said, Your name shall be called no more Jacob" (Ibid. 29). HE ASKS, what did he tell him? AND ANSWERS, he said, you have acquired these blessings neither by means of deceit nor by supplanting. HENCE "Your name shall be called no more Jacob," AS ESAU SAID, "IS NOT HE RIGHTLY NAMED JACOB? FOR HE HAS SUPPLANTED ME THESE TWO TIMES" (BERESHEET 27:36), for it did not occur through supplanting. "but Israel" (Beresheet 32:29): Israel, WHICH IS ZEIR ANPIN, from whom blessings come out, surely acknowledges you THAT THE BLESSINGS ARE YOURS, because you are attached to Him. Hence, I and the rest of the legions of angels acknowledge them that the blessings are yours.

58. כִּי שָׂרִיתָ עִם אֱלֹהִים וְעִם אֲנָשִׁים וַתּוּכָל, עִם אֱלֹהִים כָּל אִינּוּן דְּאַתְיָין מִסִּטְרָא דְּדִינָא קַשְׁיָא. וְעִם אֲנָשִׁים, דָּא עֵשָׂו וְאוּכְלוּסִין דִּילֵיהּ. וַתּוּכָל, יָכִילַת לְהוֹן, וְאִינּוּן לָא יַכְלִין לָךְ. וְלָא שָׁבִיק לֵיהּ יַעֲקֹב, עַד דְּאוֹדֵי לֵיהּ עַל אִינּוּן בִּרְכָאן, הה"ד וַיְבָרֶךְ אוֹתוֹ שָׁם.

58. "for you have contended with Elohim and with men, and have prevailed" (Ibid.). "with Elohim," namely, with all those coming from the aspect of harsh Judgment, "and with men" refers to Esau and his camps; "and have prevailed," you prevailed against them but not they against you. Jacob did not release him until he acknowledged these blessings. This is the meaning of, "And he blessed him there" (Ibid. 30).

59. ת"ח, בְּשַׁעֲתָא דְּסָלִיק נְהוֹרָא, אִתְכַּפְיָין כָּל אִינּוּן מָארֵי דְדִינִין, וְלָא מִשְׁתַּכְּחֵי, וכ"י מִשְׁתָּעֵי בֵּיהּ בְּקוּדְשָׁא בְּרִיךְ הוּא. וְהַהִיא שַׁעֲתָא

עִידָן דִּרְעֲוָא הוּא לְכֹלָּא, וְאוֹשִׁיט לָה מַלְכָּא וּלְכָל אִינּוּן דְּמִשְׁתַּכְּחֵי
עִמָּה, שַׁרְבִיטָא דְּחוּטָא דְּחֶסֶד, לְאִשְׁתַּכְּחָא בִּשְׁלִימוּ בְּמַלְכָּא קַדִּישָׁא,
וְהָא אִתְּמַר.

59. Come and see, when the light OF BINAH rises, all the litigants are
subdued and are not to be found, and the Congregation of Yisrael is talking
with the Holy One, blessed be He. That hour is a time of universal goodwill,
and the King holds out to her, TO MALCHUT, and to all those that are with
her, a scepter of the thread of Chesed, so as to be completely with the Holy
King. We already learned this.

60. תָּא חֲזֵי, בְּשַׁעֲתָא דְּקוּדְשָׁא בְּרִיךְ הוּא אִשְׁתְּכַח בָּה בכ"י, בְּאִינּוּן
זִמְנִין דְּאִשְׁתְּכַח עִמָּה, וְהִיא מַתְעָרַת רְעוּתָא לְגַבֵּיהּ בְּקַדְמֵיתָא,
וּמַשְׁכַאת לֵיהּ לְגַבָּהּ, בְּסַגִּיאוּת חֲבָתָא וְתִיאוּבְתָּא, כְּדֵין אִתְמַלְיָא
מִסִּטְרָא דִּימִינָא, וְכַמָּה אוּכְלוּסִין מִשְׁתַּכְּחֵי בְּסִטְרָא דִּימִינָא, בְּכֻלְּהוּ
עָלְמִין. וְכַד קוּדְשָׁא בְּרִיךְ הוּא אִתְּעַר חֲבִיבוּתָא וּרְעוּתָא בְּקַדְמֵיתָא,
וְהִיא אִתְּעָרַת לְבָתַר, וְלָאו בְּזִמְנָא דְּאִיהוּ אִתְּעַר, כְּדֵין כֹּלָּא בְּסִטְרָא
דְּנוּקְבָא אִשְׁתְּכַח, וּשְׂמָאלָא אִתְּעַר, וְכַמָּה אוּכְלוּסִין קַיְימֵי וּמִתְעָרֵי
בְּסִטְרָא דִּשְׂמָאלָא בְּכֻלְּהוּ עָלְמִין. כה"ג כְּתִיב, אִשָּׁה כִּי תַזְרִיעַ וְיָלְדָה
זָכָר וְגו'. מ"ט. תָּנֵינָן, עָלְמָא תַּתָּאָה כְּגַוְונָא דְּעָלְמָא עִלָּאָה אִשְׁתְּכַח,
וְדָא כְּדוּגְמָא דְּדָא.

60. Come and see, when the Holy One, blessed be He, is TOGETHER with
the Congregation of Yisrael, MALCHUT, whenever He is with her and she
rouses first a desire towards Him and draws Him to her with great love and
longing, MALCHUT is filled from the right side, WHICH IS CHASSADIM
THAT ARE CONSIDERED MALE. And many legions of angels abide in the
right side throughout the worlds. And when the Holy One, blessed be He, is
the first to rouse love and desire and MALCHUT is roused after, but not when
the Holy One, blessed be He, does, everything is considered female, WHICH
IS MALCHUT. The left is awakened and many legions are awakened on the
left side throughout the worlds. In the same manner it is written, "If a
woman have conceived seed, and born a man child" (Vayikra 12:2). THIS
MEANS THAT IF THE WOMAN HAS AN ORGASM FIRST SHE GIVES BIRTH TO

A BOY. The reason, we learned, IS BECAUSE the lower world is in the likeness of the upper world and the one resembles the other. JUST AS ABOVE, IF MALCHUT AWAKENS DESIRE FIRST, SHE IS FILLED FROM THE RIGHT SIDE, WHICH IS CONSIDERED MALE, SO IT IS BELOW.

61. וְעַל דָּא, קוּדְשָׁא בְּרִיךְ הוּא גָּזַר דְּכַר אוֹ נוּקְבָּא, לְאִשְׁתַּכְּחָא רְעוּתָא בְּעָלְמָא. וּבְכֹלָּא בָּעֵי ב"נ לְאִתְדַּבְּקָא רְעוּתָא לְעֵילָּא לְגַבֵּי קוּדְשָׁא בְּרִיךְ הוּא, לְאִשְׁתַּכְּחָא רַעֲוָון בְּעָלְמָא. זַכָּאָה חוּלָקֵיהוֹן דְּצַדִּיקַיָּיא, דְּאִינּוּן יַדְעִין לְאִדְבְּקָא רְעוּתְהוֹן לְגַבֵּי מַלְכָּא קַדִּישָׁא, עֲלַיְיהוּ כְּתִיב, וְאַתֶּם הַדְּבֵקִים בַּיְיָ' אֱלֹהֵיכֶם חַיִּים כֻּלְּכֶם הַיּוֹם.

61. The Holy One, blessed be He, therefore decrees whether it would be a boy or a girl, so that desire shall be prevalent FIRST in the world, WHICH IS MALCHUT. THEN THE WOMAN BELOW IS AWAKENED TO REACH AN ORGASM FIRST AND GIVES BIRTH TO A MALE BOY, FOR EVERYTHING DEPENDS ON WHAT IS ABOVE RATHER THAN BELOW. In every sense, man should have his desire cleave above to the Holy One, blessed be He, so desire shall be prevalent FIRST in the world, WHICH IS MALCHUT. THEN HIS WIFE SHALL BE THE FIRST TO REACH AN ORGASM AND GIVE BIRTH TO A MALE BOY. Happy is the lot of the righteous who know how to devote their desire to the Holy King. Of them it is written, "But you that did cleave to Hashem your Elohim are alive every one of you this day" (Devarim 4:4).

14. "Do not gaze upon me, because I am black"

A Synopsis

Rabbi Yehuda compares the title verse to the moon, that cannot be gazed upon because it is in darkness when in exile. When the sun shines it does so with six lights, or Sfirot, and when the sun is gone those six lights are gone. Yisrael was exiled because of punishment for sins, and was sentenced to keep the vineyards of other nations rather than keeping the vineyard of Yisrael itself.

62. אָדָם כִּי יִהְיֶה בְעוֹר בְּשָׂרוֹ שְׂאֵת אוֹ סַפַּחַת אוֹ בַהֶרֶת וְגוֹ'. רִבִּי יְהוּדָה פָּתַח וְאָמַר, אַל תִּרְאוּנִי שֶׁאֲנִי שְׁחַרְחֹרֶת שֶׁשְּׁזָפַתְנִי הַשָּׁמֶשׁ, הַאי קְרָא אִתְּמַר, אֲבָל בְּשַׁעְתָּא דְסִיהֲרָא אִתְכַּסְיָא בְּגָלוּתָא, הִיא אָמְרָה, אַל תִּרְאוּנִי. לָאו דְּאִיהִי פְּקִידַת דְּלָא לְמֶחֱמֵי לָה, אֶלָּא בְּגִין דְּאִיהִי חָמַת תִּיאוּבְתָּא דְיִשְׂרָאֵל לְגַבָּהּ, לְמֶחֱמֵי נְהוֹרָהָא, הִיא אַמְרַת אַל תִּרְאוּנִי, לָא תֵּיכְלוּן לְמֶחֱמֵי לִי. אַל תִּרְאוּנִי וַדַּאי. מ"ט. בְּגִין שֶׁאֲנִי שְׁחַרְחֹרֶת, בְּגִין דַּאֲנָא בְּקַדְרוּתָא.

62. "When a man shall have in the skin of his flesh a swelling, a scab, or bright spot…" (Vayikra 13:2). Rabbi Yehuda opened by saying, "Do not gaze upon me, because I am black (lit. 'blackish'), because the sun has scorched me" (Shir Hashirim 1:6). We have studied this verse, yet when the moon, WHICH IS MALCHUT, is concealed in exile, she says, "Do not gaze upon me." It is not that she orders not to look on her, but when she sees the yearning of Yisrael towards her, to behold her light, she says, "Do not gaze upon me," WHICH MEANS you cannot see me. "Do not gaze upon me" surely, because I am black, since I am in darkness.

63. מַאי שְׁחַרְחֹרֶת, שְׁחוֹרָה מִבָּעֵי לֵיהּ. אֶלָּא, תְּרֵין קַדְרוּתֵי, חַד שֶׁשְּׁזָפַתְנִי הַשָּׁמֶשׁ, דְּאִסְתַּלָּק מִנִּי שִׁמְשָׁא, לְאַנְהֲרָא לִי, וּלְאִסְתַּכְּלָא בִּי. וְחַד דִּבְנֵי אִמִּי נִחֲרוּ בִי.

63. HE ASKS, why does it say "blackish" when it should have said 'black'? HE ANSWERS, there are two kinds of darkness. One is that the sun has scorched me, WHICH MEANS the sun, WHICH IS ZEIR ANPIN, has gone away

from me, and the other is that "my mother's children were angry with me; they made me the keeper of the vineyards" (Ibid.).

64. שֶׁשֱׁזָפַתְנִי, שֶׁזָפַתְנִי מִבָּעֵי לֵיהּ. אֶלָּא רֶמֶז הוּא דְּקָא רָמִיז, בְּשֵׁשׁ. דְּכַד נַהֲרָא שִׁמְשָׁא בְּשֵׁשׁ נְהוֹרִין נָהִיר, וְכַד אִסְתַּלָּק, כָּל אִינּוּן שִׁית נְהוֹרִין אִסְתְּלָקוּ. בְּנֵי אִמִּי, אִלֵּין אִינּוּן דְּאַתְיָין מִסִּטְרָא דְּדִינָא קַשְׁיָא. נָחֲרוּ בִי, כד"א נָחַר גְּרוֹנִי, הה"ד עַל צַוָּארֵנוּ נִרְדַּפְנוּ דְּכַד הֲווֹ עַיְילִין יִשְׂרָאֵל בְּגָלוּתָא, הֲווֹ אַזְלֵי יְדַיְיהוּ מְהַדְקָן לַאֲחוֹרָא, וְרֵיחַיִין עַל צַוָּארֵיהוֹן, וְלָא יָכִילוּ לְאַפְתְּחָא פּוּמָא.

64. HE ASKS, IT SAYS, "because the sun has scorched me (Heb. *sheshezaftani*)," yet it should have said, 'the sun scorched me (Heb. *shezaftani*)'. HE ANSWERS, there is an allusion to six here, SINCE 'SHESHEZAFTANI' IS COMPOSED OF SHESH (ENG. 'SIX') ZAFTANI. For when the sun, ZEIR ANPIN, shines, it does so with six lights, NAMELY THE SIX SFIROT, CHESED, GVURAH, TIFERET, NETZACH, HOD AND YESOD. When it is gone, all these six lights are gone. "My mother's children" are all those coming from the aspect of harsh Judgment TO PUNISH FOR SINS. They "were angry (Heb. *nicharu*) with me" as in, "my throat is dried (Heb. *nichar*)" (Tehilim 69:4). This is what is meant by, "We are pursued to our necks" (Eichah 5:5), for when Yisrael reached exile, their hands were tied behind their backs and there was a millstone around their necks, so they could not speak. This is the meaning of, "were angry with me."

65. שָׂמוּנִי נוֹטֵרָה אֶת הַכְּרָמִים, לְמֵהַךְ בְּגָלוּתָא, לְנַטְרָא לִשְׁאַר עַמִּין בְּגִינֵיהוֹן דְּיִשְׂרָאֵל. כַּרְמִי שֶׁלִּי לֹא נָטָרְתִּי, דְּהָא לָא יָכִילְנָא לְנַטְרָא לְהוֹן כַּד בְּקַדְמֵיתָא. בְּקַדְמֵיתָא נְטִירְנָא כַּרְמִי שֶׁלִּי, וּמִנֵּיהּ אִתְנְטָרוּ שְׁאַר כַּרְמִין. הַשְׁתָּא נְטִירְנָא שְׁאַר כַּרְמִין בְּגִין כַּרְמִי שֶׁלִּי דִּלְהֱוֵי נָטִיר בֵּינַיְיהוּ.

65. "they made me the keeper of the vineyards," NAMELY, to go into exile and keep the other nations for the sake of Yisrael WHO ARE AMONG THEM IN EXILE. "but my own vineyard I have not kept" (Shir Hashirim 1:6), because I cannot keep them as before. At first, I kept my own vineyard,

NAMELY YISRAEL, and through it the other vineyards were kept, WHICH ARE THE OTHER NATIONS. Now I keep the other vineyards for the sake of my own vineyard, so it shall be kept among them.

15. "The earth is Hashem's, and the fullness thereof"

A Synopsis

Rabbi Yosi says we are not allowd to look at joyful things since the day the Temple was destroyed. The rabbis discuss the title verse, and they learn from Rabbi Shimon that all the Mochin come from the supernal river that flows out of Eden, and Malchut is established by them so that it can nourish the worlds. The main theme is that the world depends on righteousness.

66. רִבִּי חִיָּיא וְר' יוֹסֵי הֲווֹ אָזְלֵי בְּאוֹרְחָא, כַּד מָטוּ חַד בֵּי חַקְל, חָמוּ חַד דַּפְטִירָא דְּקִיטְפָא בֵּין אָרְחָא לִסְטַר יְמִינָא. א"ר יוֹסֵי, עֲטִיפָא דְּקוּטְרָא בְּעַיְינִין שְׁכִיחַ, לֵית לָן רְשׁוּ לְמֶחֱמֵי בְּחֶדְוָותָא, מִיּוֹמָא דְּאִתְחֲרִיב בֵּי מַקְדְּשָׁא.

66. Rabbi Chiya and Rabbi Yosi were walking along the way. When they reached a field they saw a balsam tree on the right side of the road. Rabbi Yosi said, enveloping smoke is in our eyes. We are not permitted to behold a joyful thing, SUCH AS A BALSAM TREE, since the day the Temple was destroyed.

67. פָּתַח וְאָמַר, לַיְיָ' הָאָרֶץ וּמְלוֹאָהּ תֵּבֵל וְיוֹשְׁבֵי בָהּ, כֵּיוָן דְּאָמַר לַיְיָ' הָאָרֶץ וּמְלוֹאָהּ, אֲמַאי תֵּבֵל וְיוֹשְׁבֵי בָהּ, וְכִי תֵּבֵל לָאו מִן אַרְעָא הוּא. אֶלָּא הָכִי קָאָמַר, לַיְיָ' הָאָרֶץ וּמְלוֹאָהּ, דָּא אַרְעָא קַדִּישָׁא, דְּאִקְרֵי אֶרֶץ הַחַיִּים. תֵּבֵל וְיוֹשְׁבֵי בָהּ, דָּא שְׁאָר אַרְעָאן, כד"א וְהוּא יִשְׁפּט תֵּבֵל בְּצֶדֶק, דְּתֵבֵל בְּצֶדֶק תַּלְיָא, וְכֹלָּא חַד מִלָּה.

67. He opened the discussion with, "The earth is Hashem's, and the fullness thereof; the world, and they that dwell in it" (Tehilim 24:1). HE ASKS, once saying, "The earth is Hashem's, and the fullness thereof," why REITERATE WITH "the world, and they that dwell in it," AND ANSWERS, this is what is meant. "The earth is Hashem's, and the fullness thereof" refers to the holy earth called the land of the living. "the world, and they that dwell in it" refers to other lands, as written, "And He will judge the world in righteousness" (Tehilim 9:9), since the world depends on righteousness. It all amounts to the same thing.

68. ר' חִיָּיא אָמַר, לַיְיָ' הָאָרֶץ וּמְלוֹאָהּ. הָאָרֶץ תֵּינַח, וּמְלוֹאָהּ מַאי
הִיא. אֶלָּא אִלֵּין נִשְׁמָתִין דְּצַדִּיקַיָּיא. תֵּבֵל וְיוֹשְׁבֵי בָהּ, תֵּבֵל: דָּא אַרְעָא
דִּלְתַתָּא. וְיוֹשְׁבֵי בָהּ: אִלֵּין אִינּוּן בְּנֵי נָשָׁא. אָמַר רִבִּי יוֹסֵי, אִי הָכִי
בְּמַאי אוֹקִימְנָא כִּי הוּא עַל יַמִּים יְסָדָהּ וְעַל נְהָרוֹת יְכוֹנְנֶהָ. אָמַר לֵיהּ
וַדַּאי הָכִי הוּא, דְּהַהִיא אֶרֶץ הַחַיִּים עַל יַמִּים יְסָדָהּ וְעַל נְהָרוֹת יְכוֹנְנֶהָ,
דְּכֻלְּהוּ נַפְקֵי מֵהַהוּא נָהָר עִלָּאָה דְּנָגִיד וְנָפִיק מֵעֵדֶן, וּבְהוּ אִתְתְּקָנַת
לְאִתְעַטְּרָא בְּמַלְכָּא קַדִּישָׁא, וּלְמֵיזָן עָלְמִין.

68. Rabbi Chiya said, "The earth is Hashem's, and the fullness thereof."
What are that specific land, MALCHUT, and the fullness thereof? HE
ANSWERS, these are the souls of the righteous IN MALCHUT. In "the world,
and they that dwell in it," the world is the lower earth IN THIS WORLD "and
they that dwell in it" are people. Rabbi Yosi said, if this is so THAT THE
EARTH MEANS MALCHUT, how are we to explain, "For He had founded it
upon the seas, and established it upon the floods" (Tehilim 24:2)? He said to
him, assuredly it is so, since the land of the living, MALCHUT, "He had
founded it upon the seas, and established it upon the floods." For they all,
ALL THE MOCHIN, come from that supernal river that comes out and flows
from Eden, WHICH IS BINAH, AND MALCHUT is established by them so as
to be crowned by the Holy King and nourish the worlds.

69. מִי יַעֲלֶה בְהַר יְיָ' וְגוֹ', נְקִי כַפַּיִם וּבַר לֵבָב אֲשֶׁר לֹא נָשָׂא לַשָּׁוְא
נַפְשִׁי וְגוֹ'. נַפְשׁוֹ כְּתִיב, מַהוּ נַפְשִׁי וְנַפְשׁוֹ. אֶלָּא כֹּלָּא חַד מִלָּה, כְּמָה
דְּאַתְּ אָמַר נִשְׁבַּע יְיָ' בְּנַפְשׁוֹ כַּאֲשֶׁר בִּלְבָבִי וּבְנַפְשִׁי יַעֲשֶׂה. וְדָוִד מַלְכָּא
אִתְאָחִיד בְּהַהוּא לֵב וּבְהַהוּא נֶפֶשׁ, וְעַל דָּא לֹא נָשָׂא לַשָּׁוְא נַפְשׁוֹ.

69. "Who shall ascend into the mountain of Hashem… He that has clean
hands, and a pure heart, who has not taken My name (lit. *Nefesh*) in vain"
(Ibid. 3-4). HE ASKS, it is spelled 'his Nefesh', yet is read "My Nefesh."
What are My Nefesh and his Nefesh MENTIONED IN THE VERSE? HE
ANSWERS, it is all the same thing, as written, "Hashem Elohim has sworn
by His Nefesh" (Amos 6:8), "that shall do according to that which is in My
heart and in My Nefesh" (I Shmuel 2:35). MY NEFESH IS MALCHUT. King
David united with that heart and Nefesh, NAMELY WITH MALCHUT. Hence it
says, "who has not taken his Nefesh in vain."

16. Sufferings of love

A Synopsis

We learn that God first punishes people for sins in places where others can not see, but if they continue to sin he marks them where it can be seen. A marked man who is talking to the rabbis threatens them with violence when his sons will come, but the rabbis reply that they must speak the words of Torah, otherwise they would be in contempt of God.

70. עַד דַּהֲווֹ אָזְלֵי, אַעֲרָעוּ בְּחַד בַּר נָשׁ, וְאַנְפּוֹי מַלְיָין מַכְתְּשִׁין, וַהֲוָה קָם מִתְּחוֹת אִילָנָא חַד, אִסְתְּכָּלוּ בֵּיהּ, וְחָמוּ אַנְפּוֹי סוּמָקִין בְּאִינוּן מַכְתְּשִׁין. א"ר חִיָּיא מַאן אַנְתְּ. אָ"ל יוּדָאי אֲנָא. א"ר יוֹסֵי חַטָּאָה הוּא, דְּאִי לָאו הָכִי, לָא אִתְרְשִׁימוּ אַנְפּוֹי בְּאִלֵּין מַרְעִין בִּישִׁין, וְאִלֵּין לָא אִקְרוּן יִסּוּרִין דְּאַהֲבָה. א"ר חִיָּיא הָכִי הוּא וַדַּאי, דְּיִסּוּרִין דְּאַהֲבָה מִתְחַפְּיָין אִינוּן מִבְּנֵי נָשָׁא.

70. While they were walking they chanced upon a man, whose face was full of wounds, who rose from underneath a tree. They looked at him and saw his face red because of the wounds. Rabbi Chiya said to him, who are you? He said, I am a Jew. Rabbi Yosi said, he is a sinner, for otherwise those evil wounds would not be marked on his face. And these are not considered sufferings of love. Rabbi Chiya said, it is surely so, because sufferings of love are hidden from people.

71. תָּא חֲזֵי, דִּכְתִּיב אָדָם כִּי יִהְיֶה בְעוֹר בְּשָׂרוֹ שְׂאֵת אוֹ סַפַּחַת אוֹ בַהֶרֶת. הָא ג' זִינִין הָכָא, וְכֻלְּהוּ אִקְרוּן נֶגַע צָרַעַת, הה"ד וְהָיָה בְעוֹר בְּשָׂרוֹ לְנֶגַע צָרָעַת. מַאי נֶגַע צָרָעַת. סְגִירוּ. סְגִירוּ בְּכֹלָּא, וּכְתִיב וְהוּבָא אֶל אַהֲרֹן הַכֹּהֵן וְגוֹ'. אֲבָל אִינוּן דְּיִתְחֲזוּן לְבַר כְּתִיב, וְרָאָהוּ הַכֹּהֵן וְטִמֵּא אוֹתוֹ. דְּהָא וַדַּאי אִינוּן דְּיִתְחֲזוּן לְבַר בִּבְנֵי נָשָׁא, מִסִּטְרָא דִּמְסָאֲבָא קָא אַתְיָין, וְלָאו יִסּוּרִין דְּאַהֲבָה נִינְהוּ.

71. Come and see, it is written, "When a man shall have in the skin of his flesh a swelling, a scab, or bright spot" (Vayikra 13:2). There are three kinds here, all considered the plague of leprosy. This is the meaning of,

-48-

"and it be in the skin of his flesh the plague of leprosy" (Ibid.). What is the plague of leprosy? IT MEANS 'CLOSED' IN THE ARAMAIC TRANSLATION, for it is closed in every respect, WHICH MEANS THE WOUND IS CLOSED AND CONCEALED FROM THE BEHOLDER. OF THIS it is written, "then he shall be brought to Aaron the priest..." (Ibid.). But in relation to those WOUNDS that are exposed, it is written, "the priest shall look on him, and pronounce him unclean" (Ibid. 3). For surely those seen from the outside to people come from the side of impurity and are not sufferings of love.

72. א"ר יוֹסֵי, מ"ל. א"ר חִיָּיא, דִּכְתִּיב טוֹבָה תּוֹכַחַת מְגוּלָּה מֵאַהֲבָה מְסוּתָּרֶת. אִי הַהִיא תּוֹכַחַת מֵאַהֲבָה, מְסוּתָּרֶת מִבְּנֵי נָשָׁא. כְּגַוְונָא דָא מַאן דְּאוֹכַח לְחַבְרֵיה בִּרְחִימוּתָא, בָּעֵי לְאַסְתָּרָא מִלּוֹי מִבְּנֵי נָשָׁא, דְּלָא יִכְסוֹף מִנַּיְיהוּ חַבְרֵיה, וְאִי מִלּוֹי אִינּוּן בְּאִתְגַּלְיָיא קָמֵי בְּנֵי נָשָׁא, לָאו אִינּוּן בִּרְחִימוּתָא.

72. Rabbi Yosi asked, whence do we know that? Rabbi Chiya said, from the words, "Open rebuke is better than hidden love" (Mishlei 27:5). THE MEANING OF "OPEN REBUKE IS BETTER" IS THAT if the rebuke is done with love it is hidden from people. So when one rebukes his neighbor with love, he must conceal his words from people, so his neighbor shall not be put to shame. If his words are public, they are not with love.

73. כָּךְ קוּדְשָׁא בְּרִיךְ הוּא כַּד אוֹכַח לב"נ, בְּכֹלָּא אוֹכַח בִּרְחִימוּתָא, בְּקַדְמֵיתָא מָחֵי לֵיה בְּגַרְמֵיה דִּלְגוֹ. אִי הָדַר בֵּיה, מוּטָב. וְאִי לָאו מָחֵי לֵיה תְּחוֹת תּוֹתְבֵיה, וְאִלֵּין אִקְרוּן יִסּוּרִין דְּאַהֲבָה, אִי הָדַר בֵּיה מוּטָב, וְאִי לָאו מָחֵי לֵיה בְּאִתְגַּלְיָיא בְּאַנְפּוֹי, קָמֵי כֹּלָּא, בְּגִין דְּיִסְתַּכְּלוּן בֵּיה, וְיִנְדְעוּן דְּהָא חַטָּאָה אִיהוּ, וְלָאו רְחִימָא דְּמָארֵיה הוּא.

73. The Holy One, blessed be He, does the same. When He rebukes man, He rebukes him always with love. At first He smites him in the internal part of the body. If he repents, it is well; otherwise, He smites him under his clothes. These are considered sufferings of love. If he repents, it is well. Otherwise, He smites him openly, in his face for everyone to see and know that he is a sinner, not beloved by his Master.

74. אָמַר לוֹן הַהוּא בַּר נָשׁ, בְּקִיטְרָא דְעֵיטָא חַד אֲתִיתוּן גַּבָּאי, וַדַּאי לָאו אַתּוּן אֶלָּא מֵאִינּוּן דְּדִיּוּרֵיהוֹן בְּבֵי רשב״י דְלָא דַּחֲלִין מִכֹּלָּא. אִי בְּנֵי דְאַתְיָין אֲבַתְרָאי יְקַטְרְגוּ בְּכוּ, אֵיךְ מְלַיְיכוּ בְּאִתְגַּלְיָיא. א״ל אוֹרַיְיתָא הָכִי הוּא, דִּכְתִּיב בְּרֹאשׁ הוֹמִיּוֹת תִּקְרָא בְּפִתְחֵי שְׁעָרִים בָּעִיר אֲמָרֶיהָ תֹאמֵר. וּמַה אִי בְּמִלֵּי דְאוֹרַיְיתָא אֲנָן דַּחֲלֵי מִקַּמָּךְ, הָא נִשְׁתְּכַח בִּכְסוּפָא קָמֵי קוּדְשָׁא בְּרִיךְ הוּא. וְלֹא עוֹד, אֶלָּא דְאוֹרַיְיתָא בָּעֵי צָחוּתָא. פָּתַח הַהוּא גַּבְרָא וְאָמַר מִי אֵל כָּמוֹךָ נוֹשֵׂא עָוֹן וְגוֹ'. אָרִים יְדוֹי וּבָכָה. אַדְּהָכִי מָטוֹן בְּנוֹי. אָמַר בְּרֵיהּ זְעֵירָא סִיַּיעְתָּא דִשְׁמַיָּא הָכָא.

74. That man said to them, you plot against me surely TO PUT ME TO SHAME. You must be of those who frequent the house of Rabbi Shimon, who fear nothing. If my sons, my descendants, SHALL COME, they will harm you. Why do you speak openly? YOU SHOULD FEAR MY SONS. They said to him, such is the Torah, as written, "she cries in the chief place of concourse, at the entrances of the gates. In the city she utters her words, saying" (Mishlei 1:21). If we fear you in words of Torah we shall be in contempt before the Holy One, blessed be He. Moreover, the Torah needs clarity, THAT IS, OPEN SPEECH. The man quoted, "Who is El like You, who pardons iniquity, and forgives the transgression" (Michah 7:18). In the meantime his sons arrived. His younger son said, help from heaven is here FOR MY FATHER.

17. "There is a just man who perishes in his righteousness"

A Synopsis

Rabbi Shimon says that King Solomon was the wisest of all men, and that during his time the moon was full. He saw everything. We learn that the righteous perish for the sins of the wicked when the world is full of wicked men and the moon is darkened.

75. פָּתַח וְאָמַר אֶת הַכֹּל רָאִיתִי בִּימֵי הֶבְלִי יֵשׁ צַדִּיק אוֹבֵד בְּצִדְקוֹ וְיֵשׁ רָשָׁע מַאֲרִיךְ בְּרָעָתוֹ. הַאי קְרָא אוֹלִיפְנָא בֵּי רִבִּי דּוֹסְתָּאי סָבָא, דַּהֲוָה אָמַר מִשְּׁמֵיהּ דְּרִבִּי יֵיסָא סָבָא. אֶת הַכֹּל רָאִיתִי בִּימֵי הֶבְלִי, וְכִי שְׁלֹמֹה מַלְכָּא דַּהֲוָה חַכִּים עַל כֹּלָּא, אֵיךְ אָמַר הָכִי דְּאִיהוּ חָמָא כֹּלָּא בְּזִמְנָא דְּאִיהוּ אָזִיל בַּחֲשׁוֹכֵי עָלְמָא דְּהָא כָּל מַאן דְּאִשְׁתָּדַל בַּחֲשׁוֹכֵי עָלְמָא, לָא חָמֵי מִדִי, וְלָא יָדַע מִדִי.

75. He opened with, "All things have I seen in the days of my vanity. There is a just man who perishes in his righteousness, and there is a wicked man who prolongs his life in his wickedness" (Kohelet 7:15). I have studied this verse with Rabbi Dustai Saba, who quoted Rabbi Yisa Saba. "All things have I seen in the days of my vanity." HE ASKS, how could King Solomon, the wisest man, speak so, that he saw everything, when he was treading the darkness of the world, THAT IS, IN THE DAYS OF HIS VANITY? For whoever is dealing with the darkness of the world sees nothing, and knows nothing.

76. אֶלָּא הָכִי אִתְּמַר, בְּיוֹמוֹי דִּשְׁלֹמֹה מַלְכָּא, קַיְימָא סִיהֲרָא בְּאַשְׁלְמוּתָא, וְאִתְחַכַּם שְׁלֹמֹה עַל כָּל בְּנֵי עָלְמָא, וּכְדֵין חָמָא כֹּלָּא, וְיָדַע כֹּלָּא. וּמַאי חָמָא. חָמָא כּ"ל, דְּלָא אַעֲדֵי מִן סִיהֲרָא. וַהֲוָה נָהִיר לֵהּ שִׁמְשָׁא. הה"ד אֶת הַכֹּל רָאִיתִי בִּימֵי הֶבְלִי. מַאן הֶבְלִי. דָּא סִיהֲרָא דְּאִתְכְּלִילַת מִן כֹּלָּא, מִן מַיָא וְאֵשָׁא וְרוּחָא כַּחֲדָא. כְּהֶבֶל דְּנָפִיק מִן פּוּמָא, דְּכָלִיל מִכֹּלָּא.

76. HE ANSWERS, we learned that during King Solomon's time the moon was full, and Solomon was the wisest among men. He then saw everything and knew everything. What did he see? He saw 'all', WHICH IS YESOD CALLED 'ALL', which never goes away from the moon, WHICH IS MALCHUT.

And the sun shone upon her. This is the meaning of, "All things have I seen in the days of my vanity." What is vanity (also: 'breath')? It is the moon, WHICH IS MALCHUT, which is included of all, of water, CHESED, fire, GVURAH, and wind, TIFERET, together, as a breath coming from the mouth includes all, WATER, WIND AND FIRE.

77. וְהוּא חָמָא כֹּ"ל, בְּהַהוּא הֶבֶל דִּילֵיהּ, דְּאָחִיד בֵּיהּ. יֵשׁ צַדִּיק אוֹבֵד בְּצִדְקוֹ, תָּ"ח, בְּזִמְנָא דְּאַסְגִּיאוּ זַכָּאִין בְּעָלְמָא, הַאי כֹּ"ל לָא לָא אַעֲדֵי מִן סִיהֲרָא לְעָלְמִין, וְהַאי כֹּ"ל נָטַל כָּל מְשַׁח וּרְבוּ וְחֶדוּ דִּלְעֵילָא, וְאִתְמְלֵי וְחַדֵּי וְרַבֵּי, בְּגִין לְאִזְדַּוְּוגָא בְּסִיהֲרָא, וְהוּא רָוַוח בְּגִינָהּ.

77. He saw 'all', YESOD, in that breath, MALCHUT, which is attached to it. "There is a just man who perishes in his righteousness." Come and see, when there are many righteous people in the world, 'all', WHICH IS YESOD, is never removed from the moon, MALCHUT. That 'all' receives ointment and strength and joy above, and becomes full, happy and elevated, in order to unite with the moon. It attains ALL THAT for her.

78. וּבְזִמְנָא דְּאַסְגִּיאוּ חַיָּיבִין בְּעָלְמָא, וְסִיהֲרָא אִתְחַשְּׁכַת, כְּדֵין צַדִּיק אוֹבֵד בְּצִדְקוֹ, צַדִּיק נֶאֱבַד לָא כְּתִיב, אֶלָּא צַדִּיק אוֹבֵד, דְּהָא לָא אִתְחֲזֵי בְּסִיהֲרָא, וְלָא נָטִיל מְשַׁח וּרְבוּ וְחֶדוּ לְמַלְיָא לָהּ, וּלְאִזְדַּוְּוגָא עִמָּהּ. וְעַ"ד צַדִּיק אוֹבֵד, בְּצִדְקוֹ, דָּא סִיהֲרָא, דִּבְגִין סִיהֲרָא דְּלָא אִשְׁתְּכַחַת לְאִזְדַּוְּוגָא עִמֵּיהּ, הוּא אָבִיד, דְּלָא שָׁאִיב מֶחֶדוּ כְּמָה דַּהֲוָה עָבֵיד. וּכְדֵין כָּל סְטַר שְׂמָאלָא אִתְּעַר, וְחַיָּיבִין מַאֲרִיכִין בְּשַׁלְוָה בְּעָלְמָא, הֲדָא הוּא דִּכְתִיב, וְיֵשׁ רָשָׁע מַאֲרִיךְ בְּרָעָתוֹ. מַאי בְּרָעָתוֹ בְּהַהוּא סְטַר דְּאִתְדַּבַּק בֵּיהּ.

78. When there are many wicked people in the world, and the moon is darkened, the Righteous, YESOD, "perishes in his righteousness." The righteous is not lost but loses. THIS IS BECAUSE he is not seen to the moon, THAT IS, DOES NOT BESTOW PLENTY UPON HER, or take ointment, strength and joy to fill her and unite with her. Hence the righteous loses ALL THAT "in his righteousness," which is the moon. Since the moon is not present to unite with him he loses and does not draw from the SUPERNAL joy, as he

used to. Then the whole left side stirs and the wicked live long and peacefully in the world. This is the meaning of, "and there is a wicked man who prolongs his life in his wickedness." What is "his wickedness"? It is that EVIL Side that cleaved to him.

79. תּוּ יֵשׁ צַדִּיק אוֹבֵד בְּצִדְקוֹ, דְּכַד חַיָּיבִין סַגִיאוּ בְּעָלְמָא, וְדִינָא תַּלְיָא צַדִּיק אוֹבֵד בְּצִדְקוֹ, אִיהוּ אִתְּפַּס בְּחוֹבַיְיהוּ, כְּגוֹן אַבָּא דְּאִתְּפַּס בְּחוֹבַיְיהוּ דִּבְנֵי מָאתֵיה, דַּהֲווֹ כֻּלְּהוּ חֲצִיפִין, וְהוּא לָא אַסְהִיד בְּהוּ וְלָא אַכְסִיף לְהוּ לְעָלְמִין, וּמָחֵי בִּידָן, דְּלָא נִתְגְּרֵי בְּהוּ בְּרַשִׁיעַיָּא. וַהֲוָה אָמַר לָן, לְדָוִד אַל תִּתְחַר בַּמְּרֵעִים אַל תְּקַנֵּא בְּעוֹשֵׂי עַוְלָה. אָמַר אֲבוּי, וַדַּאי קוּדְשָׁא בְּרִיךְ הוּא אַעֲנִישׁ לִי בְּדָא, דְּהָא הֲוָה רְשׁוּ בִּידִי לְמִחֱאָה בִּידַיְיהוּ, וְלָא עֲבָדִית, וְלָא אַכְסִיפְנָא לְהוּ, לָא בִּטְמִירוּ, וְלָא בְּאִתְגַּלְיָא.

79. Moreover, "There is a just man who perishes in his righteousness," because when there are many wicked people in the world, and punishment is suspended, "There is a just man who perishes in his righteousness," because he is punished for their sins like my father, who was punished for the sins of his town's people, who were all impudent. But he never admonished them or put them to shame. He stopped us from reproaching the wicked. He used to say to us, "Of David. Fret not yourself because of evil doers, nor be envious against the workers of iniquity" (Tehilim 37:1). His father said, Surely the Holy One, blessed be He, punished me this way, because I could have complained against them but I did not. I did not put them to shame, neither secretly nor openly.

18. "and breathed into his nostrils the breath of life"

A Synopsis

The second son of the marked man gives us this lesson. He says that man was born with two inclinations, the Good Inclination (corresponding to water) and the Evil Inclination (corresponding to fire). He says that the breath of life is the holy Neshamah that comes from Binah that produced the earth. The Neshamah has permission to ascend and speak before God. When a man sins or speaks evil, the Shechinah leaves him and an evil spirit comes to dwell on him, since holiness has departed from him. He is blemished everywhere, including in his flesh. People are also punished for omitting to speak good words when they should have, because this blemishes the speaking spirit.

80. תּוּ פָּתַח בְּרֵיהּ אָחֳרָא וְאָמַר, וַיִּיצֶר יְיָ' אֱלֹהִים אֶת הָאָדָם עָפָר מִן הָאֲדָמָה וְגוֹ'. וַיִּיצֶר יְיָ' אֱלֹהִים, בִּתְרֵי יוֹדִין, בִּתְרֵין יְצָרִין, יֵצֶר טוֹב וְיֵצֶר רָע, חַד לָקֳבֵל מַיָּא, וְחַד לָקֳבֵל אֶשָּׁא. יְיָ' אֱלֹהִים, שֵׁם מָלֵא. אֶת הָאָדָם, כָּלִיל דְּכַר וְנוּקְבָּא. עָפָר מִן הָאֲדָמָה, דָּא עַפְרָא דְּאַרְעָא קַדִּישָׁא, דְּמִתַּמָּן אִתְבְּרֵי, וְהוּא אֲתַר דְּבֵי מַקְדְּשָׁא.

80. His other son opened the discussion with the verse, "And Hashem Elohim formed man of the dust of the ground" (Beresheet 2:7). "And Hashem Elohim formed (Heb. *vayyitzer*)," 'VAYYITZER' IS SPELLED with two Yuds, TO INDICATE MAN WAS BORN with two inclinations, the Good Inclination and the Evil Inclination; one, THE GOOD INCLINATION, CORRESPONDS TO WATER, and one, THE EVIL INCLINATION, CORRESPONDS TO FIRE. Hashem Elohim is a full name. "the man" includes of male and female, SINCE THE (HEB. *ET*) ALLUDES TO THE FEMALE. "dust of the ground" is the dust of the holy land, whence he was created. It is the place of the Temple.

81. וַיִּפַּח בְּאַפָּיו נִשְׁמַת חַיִּים, דָּא נִשְׁמָתָא קַדִּישָׁא, דְּאִתְמְשָׁכָא מֵאִינּוּן חַיִּים דִּלְעֵילָּא. וַיְהִי הָאָדָם לְנֶפֶשׁ חַיָּה, אָדָם אִתְכְּלִיל בְּנַפְשָׁא קַדִּישָׁא, מֵחַיָּה עִלָּאָה. דְּאַפִּיקַת אַרְעָא דִּכְתִּיב תּוֹצֵא הָאָרֶץ נֶפֶשׁ חַיָּה, נֶפֶשׁ דְּהַהִיא חַיָּה עִלָּאָה.

81. "and breathed into his nostrils the breath (Heb. *Neshamah*) of life" (Ibid.). This is the holy Neshamah that is drawn from the supernal life, FROM BINAH. "and man became a living Nefesh" (Ibid.), since man includes a holy Nefesh from the supernal living creature, WHICH IS BINAH, that produced the earth, MALCHUT, as written, "Let the earth bring forth living creatures (lit. '*Nefesh*')" (Beresheet 1:24), the Nefesh of that supernal living creature BINAH.

82. ת״ח, בְּכָל זִמְנָא דְּהַאי נִשְׁמְתָא קַדִּישָׁא, אִתְדַּבְּקַת בֵּיה בְּבַר נָשׁ. רְחִימָא הוּא דְּמָארֵיה. כַּמָה נְטוּרִין נַטְרִין לֵיה מִכָּל סִטְרִין, רְשִׁימָא הוּא לְטָב לְעֵילָא וְתַתָּא, וּשְׁכִינְתָּא קַדִּישָׁא שַׁרְיָא עֲלוֹי.

82. Come and see, as long as that holy soul cleaves to man, he is beloved of his Master. He is well kept from every direction, he is marked for the good above and below and the holy Shechinah rests on him.

83. וּבְזִמְנָא דְּאִיהוּ אַסְטֵי אָרְחוֹי, שְׁכִינְתָּא אִסְתְּלָקַת מִנֵּיה, וְנִשְׁמְתָא קַדִּישָׁא לָא אִתְדַּבְּקַת בֵּיה. וּמִסְטְרָא דְּחִוְיָא בִּישָׁא תַּקִּיפָא, אִתְעַר רוּחָא חַד, דְּשָׁט וְאָזִיל בְּעָלְמָא, דְּלָא שַׁרְיָא אֶלָּא בַּאֲתַר דִּקְדוּשָׁה עִלָּאָה אִסְתְּלַק מִתַּמָּן. וּכְדֵין אִסְתְּאַב ב״נ, וְאִתְפְּגִים בְּבִשְׂרֵיה, בְּחֵיזוּ דְּאַנְפּוֹי בְּכֹלָּא.

83. When he deviates in his ways, the Shechinah is gone from him and the holy Neshamah does not cleave to him. From the side of the harsh serpent, a spirit is aroused that roams and walks the world, which rests only on a place supernal holiness has departed from, AND IT DWELLS ON THAT MAN. That man is then defiled and is blemished in his flesh, in everything, and in his countenance.

84. ות״ח, בְּגִין דְּהַאי נֶפֶשׁ חַיָּה אִיהִי קַדִּישָׁא עִלָּאָה, כַּד אַרְעָא קַדִּישָׁא מַשְׁכָא לָה, וְאִתְכְּלִילַת בְּגַוַּוה, כְּדֵין קָרֵינָן לָה נְשָׁמָה. וְדָא הִיא דְּסַלְקָא לְעֵילָא, וּמְמַלְלָא קָמֵי מַלְכָּא קַדִּישָׁא, וְעָיְילָא בְּכָל תַּרְעִין, וְלֵית דְּיִמְחֵי בִּידָהָא. וְעַל דָּא אִתְקְרֵי רוּחָא מְמַלְלָא, דְּהָא כָּל שְׁאָר

נַפְשָׁתָא לֵית לוֹן רְשׁוּ לְמַלְלָא קָמֵי מַלְכָּא, בַּר הַאי.

84. Come and see, since this living Nefesh is holy and supernal, NAMELY FROM BINAH, when the holy earth MALCHUT draws it and becomes a part within it, it is called Neshamah, SINCE THE LIGHT OF BINAH IS CALLED NESHAMAH. It is it that ascends and speaks before the Holy King and enters through all the gates with no one to detain it. It is therefore called 'a speaking spirit' IN THE ARAMAIC TRANSLATION, since every other Nefesh NOT FROM BINAH has no permission to speak before the King except this one FROM BINAH.

85. וְעַל דָּא אוֹרַיְיתָא אַכְרִיזַת וְאָמְרַת, נְצוֹר לְשׁוֹנְךָ מֵרָע וְגוֹ', וּכְתִיב שׁוֹמֵר פִּיו וּלְשׁוֹנוֹ וְגוֹ', בְּגִין דְּאִי שְׂפָוָותֵיה וְלִישָׁנֵיה מְמַלְלָן מִלִּין בִּישִׁין, אִינּוּן מִלִּין סַלְּקִין לְעֵילָא, וּבְשַׁעֲתָא דְּסַלְּקִין, כֹּלָּא מַכְרִיזִין וְאָמְרִין אִסְתְּלָקוּ מִסּוֹחֲרָנֵיה דְּמִלָּה בִּישָׁא דִּפְלַנְיָא, פְּנוּן אֲתָר לְאָרְחֵיה דְּחִוְיָא תַּקִּיפָא. כְּדֵין נִשְׁמָתָא קַדִּישָׁא אִתְעֲבָרָא מִנֵּיה וְאִסְתְּלָקַת, וְלָא יַכְלָא לְמַלְלָא, כד"א נֶאֱלַמְתִּי דוּמִיָּה הֶחֱשֵׁיתִי מִטּוֹב.

85. The Torah therefore proclaims, saying, "Keep your tongue from evil…" (Tehilim 34:14), and, "He who guards his mouth and his tongue…" (Mishlei 21: 23), since if his lips and tongue speak evil things, these things rise up, and when they do, everybody declares, 'Be gone from the proximity of the evil speech of so and so, give way to the path of the harsh serpent'. The holy Neshamah is then removed from him. It is gone and cannot speak, as it says, "I was dumb with silence, I held my peace, and had no comfort" (Tehilim 39:3).

86. וְהַהִיא נִשְׁמָתָא סַלְּקָא בְּכִסוּפָא, בְּעָאקוּ דְּכֹלָּא, וְלָא יָהֲבִין לָה אֲתָר כְּמִלְּקַדְּמִין. וְעַל דָּא כְּתִיב, שׁוֹמֵר פִּיו וּלְשׁוֹנוֹ שׁוֹמֵר מִצָּרוֹת נַפְשׁוֹ. נַפְשׁוֹ וַדַּאי הַהִיא דַּהֲוַת מְמַלְלָא, אִתְעֲבֵידַת מַשְׁתּוּקָא, בְּגִין מִלּוּלָא בִּישָׁא. וּכְדֵין חִוְיָא אִזְדְּמַן, דְּכֹלָּא לְאַתְרֵיה אִתְהַדָּר, וְכַד הַהִיא מִלָּה בִּישָׁא סַלְּקָא בְּאוֹרְחִין יְדִיעָן, וְשָׁארֵי קָמֵיה דְּחִוְיָא תַּקִּיפָא, כַּמָּה

רוּחִין מִתְעָרִין בְּעָלְמָא, וְרוּחָא נַחְתָּא מֵהַהוּא סִטְרָא, וְאַשְׁכַּח דְּהַהוּא בַּ"נ אִתְּעַר לֵיהּ בְּמִלָה בִּישָׁא, וְהָא רוּחָא מְמַלְלָא קַדִּישָׁא אִתְעַבְּרָא מִנֵּיהּ, כְּדֵין שַׁרְיָא עֲלוֹי וְסָאִיב לֵיהּ, וּכְדֵין הוּא סָגִיר.

86. That Neshamah rises in contempt, in trouble of every kind. It is not given place as before. Of this it is written, "He who guards his mouth and his tongue keeps his soul (Heb. *Nefesh*) from trouble." Surely his Nefesh, who used to speak, is not silent because of the evil words IT UTTERED. Then the serpent comes, since everything returned to its place, ITS ORIGINAL STATE, AS BEFORE HE ATTAINED A NESHAMAH. When the evil speech rises through certain paths and rests before the harsh serpent, many spirits are stirred in the world and a DEFILED spirit descends from that side OF THE SERPENT, and finds the man who roused it through evil speech and the speaking spirits removed from him. The DEFILED spirit defiles him, and he then becomes a leper.

87. כְּמָה דְעוֹנְשָׁא דְּהַאי בַּ"נ בְּגִין מִלָּה בִּישָׁא. כַּךְ עוֹנְשֵׁיהּ בְּגִין מִלָּה טָבָא, דְּקָאָתֵי לִידֵיהּ, וְיָכִיל לְמַלְּלָא, וְלָא מַלִּיל. בְּגִין דְּפָגִים לְהַהוּא רוּחָא מְמַלְּלָא, דְּהִיא אִתְתְּקָנַת לְמַלְּלָא לְעֵילָא, וּלְמַלְּלָא לְתַתָּא, וְכֹלָּא בִּקְדוּשָׁה. כ"ש אִי עַמָּא אַזְלִין בְּאוֹרְחָא עֲקִימָא, וְהוּא יָכִיל לְמַלְּלָא לְהוּ וּלְאוֹכָחָא לְהוּ, וְשָׁתִיק וְלָא מַלִּיל, כְּמָה דַאֲמֵינָא דִכְתִיב, נֶאֱלַמְתִּי דוּמִיָּה הֶחֱשֵׁיתִי מִטּוֹב וּכְאֵבִי נֶעְכָּר. נֶעְכָּר בְּמַכְתְּשִׁין דִּמְסָאֲבוּתָא, וְדָא הוּא דְּאָמַר דָּוִד מַלְכָּא אֱלֹקֵי בְּהַאי, וְאִתְפְּנֵי מִנֵּיהּ, דִּכְתִיב פְּנֵה אֵלַי וְחָנֵּנִי. מַהוּ פְּנֵה אֵלַי. כד"א וַיִּפֶן אַהֲרֹן. נַחְתּוּ ר' חִיָּיא וְר' יוֹסֵי, וְנָשְׁקוּהוּ. אִזְדַּוְּוגוּ כַּחֲדָא כָּל הַהוּא אוֹרְחָא, קָרָא רִבִּי חִיָּיא עֲלַיְיהוּ, וְאֹרַח צַדִּיקִים כְּאוֹר נֹגַהּ הוֹלֵךְ וָאוֹר עַד נְכוֹן הַיּוֹם.

87. Just as punishment is afflicted on man because of evil speech, so is he punished because he could have pronounced good words but did not. For he blemished that speaking spirit, which is composed so as to speak above and speak below, and everything is in holiness. It is even more true if the nation walks the crooked path and he can talk to them and reprove them yet he is silent and does not speak. As I said, IT IS SAID OF HIM, "I was dumb with silence, I held my peace, and had no comfort, and my pain was stirred up,"

stirred up by plagues of impurity. This is why it was said that King David was plagued WITH LEPROSY, AND THE HOLY ONE, BLESSED BE HE, turned away from him, as written THAT HE ASKED, "Turn You to me, and be gracious to me" (Tehilim 25:16), WHICH MEANS HE TURNED AWAY FROM HIM. What is "Turn You to me"? It resembles the words, "And Aaron looked (or: 'turned')" (Bemidbar 12:10). JUST AS THE LATTER VERSE ALLUDES TO LEPROSY, SO HERE IT ALLUDES TO LEPROSY. Rabbi Chiya and Rabbi Yosi alighted and kissed him. They went together all that way. Rabbi Chiya said of them, "But the path of just men is like the gleam of sunlight, that shines ever more brightly until the height of noonday" (Mishlei 4:18).

19. The plague of leprosy

A Synopsis

The priest knows all the types of plague, and whether the person is undergoing sufferings of love or is being rejected by God. One should consult his heart three times to lead it in the path of truth; it is evil that causes the plagues in the world. In Aramaic leprosy is translated as 'closing', because it closes off the supernal lights.

88. נֶגַע צָרַעַת כִּי תִהְיֶה בְּאָדָם וְהוּבָא אֶל הַכֹּהֵן. א"ר יוֹסֵי, הַאי נֶגַע, כָּל גַּוְונִין דִּילֵיהּ אִתְּעָרוּ בְּהוּ חַבְרַיָּיא, וְכַהֲנָא הֲוָה יָדַע בְּהוּ לְדַכְיָא וּלְמְסָאֲבָא, הֲוָה יָדַע, אִינּוּן דַּהֲווֹ יִסּוּרִין דִּרְחִימוּתָא, אוֹ אִינּוּן דְּאִשְׁתְּכָחוּ בְּמַאן דְּמָאִיס בֵּיהּ מָארֵיהּ וְרָחִיק בֵּיהּ, דְּהָא לְפוּם אָרְחוֹי דְּב"נ גָּרִים נֶגַע בְּעָלְמָא.

88. "When the plague of leprosy is in a man, then he shall be brought to the priest" (Vayikra 13:9). Rabbi Yosi said, the friends commented on all the colors of this plague. The priest knew whether to pronounce clean or unclean according to them. He knew if these are sufferings of love or those upon one whose Master rejects him and is far from him. For according to man's ways the plague is caused in the world.

89. כְּתִיב אַל תַּט לִבִּי לְדָבָר רָע לְהִתְעוֹלֵל עֲלִילוֹת בְּרֶשַׁע, מִכָּאן תְּנֵינָן בְּאָרְחָא דְּב"נ בָּעֵי לְמֵיהַךְ בָּהּ מַדְבְּרִין לֵיהּ. א"ר יִצְחָק, הַאי קְרָא קַשְׁיָא, וְכִי קוּדְשָׁא בְּרִיךְ הוּא אַסְטֵי לֵיהּ לְבַר נָשׁ לְמֵהַךְ בְּאֹרַח חַטָּאָה, וּלְמֶעְבַּד עוֹבָדִין בִּישִׁין, אִי הָכִי לֵית דִּינָא בְּעָלְמָא דָא, וְלָא בְּעָלְמָא דְּאָתֵי, וְאוֹרַיְיתָא לָא אִתְתָּקְנַת, דִּכְתִיב בָּהּ אִם תִּשְׁמַע וְאִם לֹא תִשְׁמַע.

89. It is written, "Incline not my heart to any evil thing, to practice wicked deeds with men who work iniquity" (Tehilim 141:4). From this we derive that a man is led in the way he wishes to walk. Rabbi Yitzchak, this verse is difficult. Does the Holy One, blessed be He, turn man to walk the path of sin and commit evil deeds, THAT HE SAYS, "INCLINE NOT MY HEART TO ANY EVIL THING"? In that case there is no justice in this world or in the

World to Come, and the Torah is imperfect, in which is written, "if you hearken" (Devarim 28:13), and, "if you will not hearken" (Ibid. 15), WHICH INDICATES THAT EVERYTHING DEPENDS ON MAN.

90. אֶלָּא דָּוִד אַזְהַר לְלִבֵּיהּ, לְדַבְּרָא לֵיהּ בְּאוֹרַח קְשׁוֹט, כד"א וַהֲשֵׁבוֹת אֶל לְבָבֶךָ. מַאי וַהֲשֵׁבוֹת. אֶלָּא זִמְנָא חַד, וּתְרֵין, וּתְלַת, לְאַהֲדָּרָא לְקַבְּלֵיהּ, וּלְדַבְּרָא, וּלְאַזְהֲרָא לֵיהּ. וְהָכִי קָאָמַר לֵיהּ, לִבִּי, אַל תַּט לִדְבַר רָע, דְּהָא דָּבָר רָע גָּרִים נֶגַע בְּעָלְמָא, וְדִינָא שַׁרְיָא בְּעָלְמָא, וְהַיְינוּ נֶגַע צָרַעַת.

90. AND HE ANSWERS, David admonished his heart, saying, "INCLINE NOT MY HEART TO ANY EVIL THING," so as to lead it in the path of truth, as written, "and consider it in your heart" (Devarim 4:39). What is consider? IT MEANS one should return to THE HEART once, twice and thrice to lead it IN THE PATH OF TRUTH and admonish it. He also said to it, "Incline not my heart to any evil thing," since an evil thing caused plagues in the world, so Judgment hovers about the world. This is the meaning of the plague of leprosy.

91. נֶגַע צָרַעַת, הָא אִתְּעֲרוּ חַבְרַיָּיא, אֲבָל צָרַעַת כְּתַרְגּוּמוֹ, א"ר יְהוּדָה, מַאי כְּתַרְגּוּמוֹ. סְגִירוּ, דְּסָגִיר וְלָא פָּתַח, וְכַד סָגִיר הוּא וְלָא פָּתַח, נֶגַע הוּא דְּאִקְרֵי. רַבִּי יוֹסֵי אָמַר, דְּלָא מִסְתַּפְּקִין אֲבָהָן, כָּל שֶׁכֵּן בְּנִין. וְהַיְינוּ דִּכְתִיב נֶגַע צָרַעַת כִּי תִהְיֶה בְּאָדָם, בְּאָדָם מַמָּשׁ, וּמִכָּאן נָחִית לְמַאן דְּנָחִית, אִשְׁתְּכַח נֶגַע לְכֹלָּא, מֵהַהוּא סְגִירוּ.

91. The friends spoke about the plague of leprosy, but leprosy IS EXPLAINED according to its Aramaic translation. Said Rabbi Yehuda, what is it translated into? It is 'closing', because it closes SUPERNAL LIGHTS and does not open up. When it closes and does not open, it is considered a plague. Rabbi Yosi said that the Patriarchs, CHESED, GVURAH AND TIFERET, are not nourished, THAT IS, THEY DO NOT RECEIVE LIGHT, and all the more so the children, NETZACH, HOD AND YESOD. This is the meaning of, "When the plague of leprosy is in a man," real man, NAMELY ZEIR ANPIN, THE SECRET OF YUD HEI VAV HEI FULLY SPELLED WITH

ALEPHS, WHICH HAS THE SAME NUMERICAL VALUE AS THAT OF ADAM (ENG. 'MAN'). From here it descends to whomever it descends to, NAMELY, TO LOWER MAN WHO CAUSED IT, AND CLOSES HIS LIGHT, so there is universal plague from the closing OF THE LIGHTS.

92. א"ר יִצְחָק, וַדַּאי דָּא הוּא רָזָא דְּמִלָּה, דִּכְתִיב נִאֵר מִקְדָּשׁוֹ. מ"ט. מִשּׁוּם דִּבְנֵי עָלְמָא גָּרְמוּ הַאי, דִּכְתִיב אֶת מִקְדַּשׁ יְיָ' טִמֵּא, טִמֵּא מַמָּשׁ. א"ר אֶלְעָזָר, טִמֵּא, מִשּׁוּם דְּאִסְתַּלָּקַת מַאן דְּאִסְתַּלָּק, וְחִוְיָא תַּקִּיפָא שַׁרְיָא, וְאָטִיל זוּהֲמָא, וְסָאִיב לְמַאן דְּסָאִיב, וְכֻלְּהוּ בְּגִין חוֹבֵי עָלְמָא.

92. Rabbi Yitzchak said, surely this is the inner meaning of the words, "He has abhorred His sanctuary" (Eichah 2:7), WHICH MEANS THE LIGHTS OF THE TEMPLE, WHICH IS MALCHUT, WERE SHUT. The reason is that the people in the world brought it about BY THEIR SINS, as written, "because he has defiled the sanctuary of Hashem" (Bemidbar 19:20), actually defiled. Rabbi Elazar said, he had defiled it because someone was gone, NAMELY ZEIR ANPIN, and the harsh serpent rests on it and injects filth and brings defilement to whomever it does. All this is due to the sins of the world.

20. "she eats, and wipes her mouth"

A Synopsis

We learn that because of man's evil tongue the serpent appears both above and below. The lights are closed when someone commits a sin and then says they have done nothing wrong.

93. תָּאנֵי, כַּד שָׁארֵי חִוְיָא לְאִתְגַּלָּאָה, מִסְתַּלְּקִין סָמְכִין וּבִנְיָינִין וּמִתְעַבְּרִין, וְאָתֵי חִוְיָא תַּקִּיפָא וְאָטִיל זוּהֲמָא, וּכְדֵין אִשְׁתְּכַח מַקְדְּשָׁא מְסָאָב, מַאן מַקְדְּשָׁא. כְּמָה דְאִתְּמַר וְנָתַתִּי נֶגַע צָרַעַת בְּבֵית אֶרֶץ אֲחוּזַּתְכֶם. וּכְתִיב וְהַנָּחָשׁ הָיָה עָרוּם מִכֹּל חַיַּת הַשָּׂדֶה אֲשֶׁר עָשָׂה יְיָ' אֱלֹהִים וַיֹּאמֶר אֶל הָאִשָּׁה. אֶל הָאִשָּׁה מַמָּשׁ, דְּאֲתַר מַקְדְּשָׁא אִתְאֲחִיד בְּגַוָּוהּ, וְהַיְינוּ אֶת מִקְדַּשׁ יְיָ' טִמֵּא בְּגִין חוֹבוֹי, מִשּׁוּם דְּאִתְגַּלְיָא חִוְיָא תַּקִּיפָא.

93. We learned that when the PRIMORDIAL serpent begins to be revealed, the supports, NETZACH AND HOD, and the edifices, THE MOCHIN, are gone and removed FROM MALCHUT, and the fierce serpent comes and injects filth, the Temple is considered defiled. What is the Temple? It is as we learned, "and I put the plague of leprosy in a house of the land of your possession" (Vayikra 14:34), and, "Now the serpent was craftier... And he said to the woman" (Beresheet 3:1), the actual woman, to which the place of the Temple is attached, WHICH IS MALCHUT. Hence, "because he has defiled the sanctuary of Hashem" (Bemidbar 19:20), by his sins, because THROUGH HIS SINS the fierce serpent is revealed.

94. מַאן חוֹבוֹי. דָּא לִישָׁנָא בִישָׁא, דְּבְגִין לִישָׁנָא בִישָׁא, חִוְיָא אִזְדַּמַּן, בֵּין לְעֵילָּא בֵּין לְתַתָּא, דִּכְתִיב וַיְשַׁלַּח יְיָ' בָּעָם אֶת הַנְּחָשִׁים הַשְּׂרָפִים. הַשּׂוֹרְפִים אוֹ הַשְּׂרוּפִים לָא כְּתִיב, אֶלָּא הַשְּׂרָפִים, מַאן שְׂרָפִים. דִּכְתִיב רָאשֵׁי תַנִּינִים תְּרֵי, חַד אִתְאֲחִיד לְעֵילָּא, וְחַד לְתַתָּא וּכְתִיב שְׂרָפִים עוֹמְדִים מִמַּעַל לוֹ, מִמַּעַל לוֹ וַדַּאי, כד"א לְהִתְיַצֵּב עַל יְיָ', וּכְדֵין סְגִירוּ בְּכֹלָּא, וְלֵית מַאן דְּפָתַח, וְעַל דָּא כְּתִיב כֵּן דֶּרֶךְ אִשָּׁה מְנָאָפֶת אָכְלָה וּמָחֲתָה פִיהָ וְגו', מַאי מְנָאָפֶת. מְנָאָפֶת מַמָּשׁ וַדַּאי, אָכְלָה וּמָחֲתָה פִיהָ וְאָמְרָה לֹא פָעַלְתִּי אָוֶן.

94. What are his sins? They are the evil tongue. For because of evil tongue, the PRIMORDIAL serpent appears both above and below, as written, "And Hashem sent venomous (Heb. *Seraphim*) serpents among the people" (Bemidbar 21:6). It is not spelled as '*sorfim* (Eng. 'burning')' or '*serufim* (Eng. 'burnt')', but rather Seraphim. Who are the Seraphim? HE ANSWERS, IT ALLUDES TO THE PRIMORDIAL SERPENT. THE REASON IT SAYS SERPENTS IN PLURAL IS THAT IT RESEMBLES the words, "the heads of the sea monsters" (Tehilim 74:13), two of them, one attached above and another attached below IN THIS WORLD. It is also written, "Seraphim stood above Him" (Yeshayah 6:2), above Him assuredly, NAMELY as in the verse, "to present themselves before (lit. 'above') Hashem" (Iyov 1:6), WHICH MEANS AGAINST HASHEM. FOR THE SONS OF ELOHIM ARE JUDGMENTS, AND HASHEM IS MERCY. HERE TOO, "ABOVE HIM" IS LIKE 'AGAINST HIM'. Then everything is closed, AS ALL THE LIGHTS ARE SHUT, and there is none to open, SINCE THEN THE SERPENT COMES AND INJECTS FILTH IN THE ROOT OF THE SOUL OF THE SINNER IN MALCHUT, WHICH IS CONSIDERED ADULTERY. Hence it is written, "Likewise the way of an adulterous woman; she eats, and wipes her mouth, and says, I have done nothing wrong" (Mishlei 30:20). What is adulterous? Actual ADULTEROUS surely, OF WHICH IT IS SAID, "she eats, and wipes her mouth, and says, I have done nothing wrong."

95. אָמַר רִבִּי חִיָּיא אָמַר ר׳ יִצְחָק, בִּרְעוּתָא דְּכֹלָּא לָא אִשְׁתְּכַח לְתַתָּא, אֶלָּא בְּגִין דְּאִשְׁתְּכַח לְעֵילָּא. וּלְעֵילָּא לָא אִשְׁתְּכַח, אֶלָּא כַּד אִשְׁתְּכַח לְתַתָּא בְּחוֹבֵי עָלְמָא, דְּיַלְפֵינָן דְּכֹלָּא תַּלְיָיא הַאי בְּהַאי, וְהַאי בְּהַאי.

95. Rabbi Chiya said in the name of Rabbi Yitzchak, by universal will, NAMELY THE SUPERNAL WILL, the serpent abides below only because he abides above. And he does not abide above except when he abides below due to the sins of the world, as we learned that everything is interdependent.

21. "wisdom excels folly"

A Synopsis

Rabbi Chiya wonders why Solomon says he saw that wisdom excels folly, since surely it must be obvious to everyone. We learn that no one was as wise as Solomon since he is named after the seven grades of wisdom, corresponding to seven Sfirot, and he actually spoke of seven vanities, or 'breaths'. The world is supported only by breath, since Rabbi Shimon taught that breath produces a sound by way of the wind and water in it, and the sound exists only by way of breath. In the same way that a man cannot exist without breath, the world cannot exist without the words of wisdom that Solomon said. And the breath by which the world endures comes from the breaths above. Wisdom is actually revealed by way of its opposite, folly, just as light would not be known without darkness, nor white without black, nor sweet without bitter, nor health without illness. God has made the one as well as the other.

96. וְאִישׁ כִּי יִמָּרֵט רֹאשׁוֹ וְגוֹ'. רַבִּי חִיָּיא פָּתַח וְאָמַר וְרָאִיתִי אָנִי שֶׁיֵּשׁ יִתְרוֹן לַחָכְמָה מִן הַסִּכְלוּת וְגוֹ', בְּכַמָּה אֲתָר אִסְתַּכַּלְנָא בְּמִלוֹי דִשְׁלֹמֹה מַלְכָּא, וְאַשְׁגַּחְנָא בְּחָכְמָתָא סַגִּיאָה דִילֵיהּ, וְאַסְתִּים מִלוֹי בְּגוֹ, לְגוֹ הֵיכְלָא קַדִּישָׁא. הַאי קְרָא אִית לְאִסְתַּכְּלָא בֵּיהּ, אֲמַאי אָמַר וְרָאִיתִי אָנִי, וְכִי שְׁאָר בְּנֵי עָלְמָא לָא יַדְעֵי וְלָא חָמָאן דָּא. אֲפִילוּ מַאן דְּלָא יָדַע חָכְמְתָא מִן יוֹמוֹי, וְלָא אַשְׁגַּח בָּהּ, יָדַע הַאי שֶׁיֵּשׁ יִתְרוֹן לַחָכְמָה מִן הַסִּכְלוּת כִּיתְרוֹן הָאוֹר מִן הַחֹשֶׁךְ. וְהוּא שַׁבַּח גַּרְמֵיהּ וְאָמַר רָאִיתִי אָנִי.

96. "And the man whose hair is fallen off his head" (Vayikra 13:40). Rabbi Chiya opened with, "Then I saw that wisdom excels folly..." (Kohelet 2:13). I have studied the words of King Solomon in different places, and observed his great wisdom, since he concealed the meaning of his words inside the holy sanctuary. This verse needs studying. Why did he say, "I saw"? Do not the rest of the people in the world know or see this? Even those who never knew wisdom or studied it know that "wisdom excels folly, as far as light excels darkness." Yet he praises himself and says, "Then I saw."

97. אֶלָּא הָכִי תָאנָא, מַאן חַכִּים כִּשְׁלֹמֹה דִּבְשִׁבְעָה דַרְגִּין דְּחָכְמָה אִתְקְרֵי כְּגַוְּונָא דִלְעֵילָא. שִׁיתָא יוֹמִין לְעֵילָא, שְׁבִיעָאָה עִלָּאָה עֲלַיְיהוּ.

שִׁיתָא יוֹמִין לְתַתָּא, שְׁבִיעָאָה עֲלַיְיהוּ. שִׁיתָא דַרְגִּין לְכוּרְסְיָיא, הוּא
עַל כּוּרְסְיָיא, דִּכְתִיב, וַיֵּשֶׁב שְׁלֹמֹה עַל כִּסֵּא יְיָ' לְמֶלֶךְ. שִׁבְעָה כִּתְרִין
דְּיוֹמִין לְעֵילָא, וּכְדֵין לָקֳבְלֵיהוֹן שִׁבְעָה שְׁמָהָן לִשְׁלֹמֹה. לְאִתְחֲזָאָה
בֵּיהּ חָכְמְתָא קַדִּישָׁא. וּבְג"כ אִתְקְרֵי שֶׁבַע שְׁמָהָן: שְׁלֹמֹה. יְדִידְיָה.
אָגוּר. בֶּן יָקֶה. לְמוּאֵל. אִיתִיאֵל, קֹהֶלֶת.

97. We learned that none is wise as Solomon who is named after the seven grades of wisdom, in the likeness of above, NAMELY, TO CORRESPOND TO CHESED, GVURAH, TIFERET, NETZACH, HOD, YESOD AND MALCHUT OF MALCHUT, THE SECRET OF LOWER CHOCHMAH, THE GRADE OF SOLOMON. For there are six days above, CHESED, GVURAH, TIFERET, NETZACH, HOD AND YESOD OF ZEIR ANPIN and a seventh above them, WHICH IS BINAH. There are seven days below IN MALCHUT, CHESED, GVURAH, TIFERET, NETZACH, HOD AND YESOD, and a seventh above them, WHICH IS BINAH. There are six steps to the throne OF SOLOMON and he is upon the throne, as written, "Then Solomon sat on the throne of Hashem as king" (I Divrei Hayamim 29:23). There are seven crowns of the days, NAMELY THE SEVEN SFIROT, CHESED, GVURAH, TIFERET, NETZACH, HOD, YESOD AND MALCHUT above and seven corresponding names to Solomon to indicate holy wisdom. Hence he had seven names, WHICH ARE Solomon, Yedidyah, Agur, ben Yaka, Lemuel, Itiel and Kohelet.

98. וְאָמַר שִׁבְעָה הֲבָלִים. וּמַה דְּאִיהוּ חָמָא לָא חָמָא ב"נ אָחֳרָא, וְכַד
כָּנַשׁ חָכְמְתָא וְאִסְתַּלַּק בְּדַרְגִּין דְּחָכְמְתָא, אִקְרֵי קֹהֶלֶת. וְשִׁבְעָה הֲבָלִין
אָמַר, לָקֳבֵיל ז' כִּתְרִין דִּלְעֵילָא, וְכָל הֶבֶל קָלָא אִתְעֲבֵיד מִנֵּיהּ, וְעָלְמָא
לָא מִתְקַיְּימָא אֶלָּא בַּהֶבֶל.

98. He spoke of seven vanities, NAMELY, "VANITY OF VANITIES, SAYS KOHELET, VANITY OF VANITIES; ALL IS VANITY" (KOHELET 1:2). THERE ARE THREE TIMES 'VANITY' AND TWICE 'VANITIES', WHICH ARE FOUR. TOGETHER THEY ARE SEVEN. He saw what no one else saw. And when he gathered wisdom and climbed the grade of wisdom he was called Kohelet. He spoke of seven vanities (also: 'breaths'), which correspond to the seven Sfirot above. And a sound is made of every breath, and the world is supported only by breath.

99. וְתָאנָא מִשְּׁמֵיהּ דר"ש, הֶבֶל אַפִּיק קָלָא בְּרוּחָא וּמַיָא דְּבֵיהּ, וְלֵית קָלָא אֶלָּא בַּהֶבֶל. וְתָאנָא בְּשִׁבְעָה הַבָלִין אִתְקַיְּימִין עֶלָּאִין וְתַתָּאִין. וְתָאנֵי ר' יִצְחָק, ת"ח, דְּעַל הֶבֶל מִתְקַיֵּים עָלְמָא, דְּאִלְמָּלֵא לָא הֲוָה הֶבֶל דְּנָפִיק מִפּוּמָא, לָא אִתְקַיֵּים ב"נ אֲפִילוּ שַׁעֲתָא חֲדָא.

99. We learned in the name of Rabbi Shimon, that breath produces a sound by the wind and water in it, and that sound exists only through breath. And we learned that by seven breaths the supernal and the lower beings exist. Rabbi Yitzchak taught, come and see that the world is supported by breath, for were no breath to come from man's mouth, it would not have been able to exist even a moment.

100. כְּגַוְונָא דָא אָמַר שְׁלֹמֹה מִלּוֹי, דְּעָלְמָא מִתְקַיְּימָא בְּהוּ, דְּהַאי הֶבֶל דְּמִתְקַיֵּים בֵּיהּ עָלְמָא. וְהַאי הֶבֶל דְּמִתְקַיֵּים בֵּיהּ עָלְמָא, מֵהַבָלִים דִּלְעֵילָא קָאָתֵי, הה"ד הֶבֶל הֲבָלִים, הֶבֶל מֵהֲבָלִים דִּלְעֵילָא. וְכָל מִלּוֹי הָכִי הֲווֹ. וּבַהֲבָלִים דִּלְעֵילָא כְּתִיב, כִּי עַל כָּל מוֹצָא פִי יְיָ' יִחְיֶה הָאָדָם. מַאי מוֹצָא פִי יְיָ'. דָּא הֲבָלִים דִּלְעֵילָא.

100. Similar to that THAT MAN CANNOT EXIST WITHOUT THE BREATH OF HIS MOUTH Solomon said his words upon which the world is supported. HE SAID that through breath the world endures. And the breath by which the world endures comes from the breaths above. This is the meaning of "Breath of breaths" (Kohelet 1:2), NAMELY a breath coming from the breaths above. All his words were in that strain. Of the supernal breaths it is written, "but by every word that proceeds out of the mouth of Hashem does man live" (Devarim 8:3). What is the "word that proceeds out of the mouth of Hashem"? It is the supernal breaths.

101. וְתַנְיָא, וְרָאִיתִי אָנִי שֶׁיֵּשׁ יִתְרוֹן לַחָכְמָה מִן הַסִּכְלוּת. מִן הַסִּכְלוּת מַמָּשׁ, אָתֵי תּוֹעַלְתָּא לְחָכְמְתָא, דְּאִלְמָּלֵא לָא אִשְׁתְּכַח שְׁטוּתָא בְּעָלְמָא, לָא אִשְׁתְּמוֹדְעָא חָכְמְתָא וּמִלּוֹי. וְתָאנָא חִיּוּבָא הוּא עַל ב"נ דְּאוֹלִיף חָכְמְתָא, לְמֵילַף זְעֵיר מִן שְׁטוּתָא, וּלְמִנְדַּע לָהּ. בְּגִין דְּאָתֵי תּוֹעַלְתָּא לְחָכְמְתָא בְּגִינֵיהּ. כְּמָה דְּאַתְיָא תּוֹעַלְתָּא לִנְהוֹרָא מֵחֲשׁוֹכָא,

דְּאִלְמָלֵא חֲשׁוֹכָא לָא אִשְׁתְּמוֹדַע נְהוֹרָא. וְלָא אַתְיָא תּוֹעַלְתָּא לְעָלְמָא מִנֵּיה.

101. We learned, "Then I saw that wisdom excels folly," wisdom excels through actual folly, for were there no folly in the world, wisdom and its matters would not be made known. We learned that one who studied wisdom must study some folly and know it, for this way wisdom excels, just as light excels through darkness, for were there no darkness, light would not be made known and the world would benefit by it.

102. תָּנָא שֶׁיֵּשׁ יִתְרוֹן לַחָכְמָה, לַחָכְמָה סְתָם. דְּאָמַר ר' שִׁמְעוֹן לְרַבִּי אַבָּא, תָּא חֲזֵי רָזָא דְּמִלָּה, לָא נָהִיר חָכְמְתָא דִּלְעֵילָּא, וְלָא אִתְנְהִיר, אֶלָּא בְּגִין שְׁטוּתָא דְּאִתְּעַר מֵאֲתַר אָחֳרָא, וְאִלְמָלֵא הַאי, נְהִירוּ וּרְבוּ סַגִּיא וְיַתִּיר לָא הֲוָה, וְלָא אִתְחַזְיָא תּוֹעַלְתָּא דְּחָכְמְתָא. וּבְגִין שְׁטוּתָא אִתְנְהִיר יַתִּיר, וּנְהִירִין לֵיה יַתִּיר, הה"ד שֶׁיֵּשׁ יִתְרוֹן לַחָכְמָה, לַחָכְמָה סְתָם, מִן הַסִּכְלוּת סְתָם. וְכָךְ לְתַתָּא, אִלְמָלֵא לָא הֲוָה שְׁטוּתָא שְׁכִיחַ בְּעָלְמָא, לָא הֲוֵי חָכְמְתָא שְׁכִיחַ בְּעָלְמָא.

102. We learned that wisdom excels, NAMELY wisdom in general, INCLUDING BOTH SUPERNAL WISDOM AND WORLDLY WISDOM. For, Rabbi Shimon said to Rabbi Aba, come and see the inner meaning of the matter. Supernal wisdom does not illuminate nor is it shone upon except for folly that was roused from a different place. Were it not for this FOLLY, there would be no expansion of light and greatness, and wisdom would not excel. For folly, WISDOM shone more and is shone more upon. This is the meaning of, "that wisdom excels," wisdom in general, BOTH ABOVE AND BELOW, more than folly in general, BOTH ABOVE AND BELOW. For this is the way below, were there no folly in the world, there would be no wisdom in the world.

103. וְהַיְינוּ דְּרַב הַמְנוּנָא סָבָא, כַּד הֲווֹ יַלְפִין מִנֵּיה חַבְרַיָּיא רָזֵי דְּחָכְמְתָא, הֲוָה מְסַדֵּר קַמַיְיהוּ פִּרְקָא דְּמִלֵּי דִּשְׁטוּתָא, בְּגִין דְּיֵיתֵי תּוֹעַלְתָּא לְחָכְמְתָא בְּגִינֵיה. הה"ד יָקָר מֵחָכְמָה וּמִכָּבוֹד סִכְלוּת מְעָט,

מִשּׁוּם דְּהִיא תִּקּוּנָא דְּחָכְמְתָא, וִיקָרָא דְּחָכְמְתָא. וְעַל דָּא כְּתִיב, וְלִבִּי נוֹהֵג בַּחָכְמָה וְלֶאֱחֹז בְּסִכְלוּת.

103. When the friends studied secrets of wisdom from Rav Hamnuna Saba, he used to teach them verses of folly, so that wisdom would excel for their sakes. This is the meaning of, "a little folly outweighs wisdom and honor" (Kohelet 10:1), because FOLLY is good for wisdom and the preciousness of wisdom. Hence it is written, "yet guiding my heart with wisdom; and to lay hold on folly" (Kohelet 2:3).

104. רַבִּי יוֹסֵי אָמַר יָקָר מֵחָכְמָה וּמִכָּבוֹד, כְּלוֹמַר יְקָרָא דְּחָכְמְתָא וְנוֹי דִּילָהּ, וִיקָרָא דִּכְבוֹד דִּלְעֵילָא, מַאי הִיא. סִכְלוּת מְעַט. זְעֵיר דִּשְׁטוּתָא אַחְזֵי וְגַלֵּי יְקָרָא דְּחָכְמְתָא וְכָבוֹד דִּלְעֵילָא, יַתִּיר מִכָּל אָרְחִין דְּעָלְמָא.

104. Rabbi Yosi said, "a little folly outweighs (Heb. *yakar*) wisdom and honor," namely, the preciousness (Heb. *yakar*) of wisdom and its beauty. And what is the preciousness of supernal honor, WHICH IS MALCHUT? It is a little folly, because a little folly discloses and reveals the preciousness of wisdom and honor of above more than any way in the world.

105. כִּיתְרוֹן הָאוֹר מִן הַחֹשֶׁךְ, תּוֹעַלְתָּא דִּנְהוֹרָא לָא אַתְיָא אֶלָּא מִן חֲשׁוֹכָא. תִּקּוּנָא דְּחִוְּורָא מַאי הִיא. אוּכָמָא, אִלְמָלֵא אוּכָמָא לָא אִשְׁתְּמוֹדַע חִוְּורָא, וּבְגִין אוּכָמָא, אִסְתָּלִיק חִוְּורָא וְאִתְיָקַר. אָמַר ר' יִצְחָק, מָשָׁל לְמָתוֹק בְּמַר, דְּלָא יָדַע אֵינָשׁ טַעֲמָא דִּמְתִיקָא, עַד דְּטָעִים מְרִירָא, מַאן עָבֵיד לְהַאי מְתִיקָא. הֲוֵי אוֹמֵר הַאי מְרִירָא. וְהַיְינוּ דִּכְתִיב גַּם אֶת זֶה לְעֻמַּת זֶה עָשָׂה זֶה הָאֱלֹהִים. וּכְתִיב טוֹב אֲשֶׁר תֶּאֱחֹז בָּזֶה וְגַם מִזֶּה אַל תַּנַּח יָדֶךָ.

105. "as far as light excels darkness" (Kohelet 2:13). For light excels only through darkness. What establishes white? Black, for were it not for black, white would not be comprehended. Since black exists, white is elevated and glorified. Rabbi Yitzchak said, this is like sweet and bitter. No one recognizes the sweet taste before he tastes bitter. What causes it to be sweet? Bitter. FOR OPPOSITES REVEAL EACH OTHER, LIKE WHITE AND

BLACK, LIGHT AND DARKNESS, THE SICK AND THE HEALTHY. FOR WERE THERE NO SICK PEOPLE IN THE WORLD, THE ADJECTIVE HEALTHY WOULD BE MEANINGLESS. This is the meaning of, "Elohim has made the one as well as the other" (Kohelet 7:14), and, "It is good that you should take hold of this; but do not withdraw your hand from that either" (Ibid. 18).

22. Man, person

A Synopsis

We learn that man has different names in different stages, but the greatest of these is Adam. In scripture it is often the word 'Adam' that is used rather than 'Ish' (person) or Enosh (human), for example, because it refers to man on the highest level. The name Adam includes the four faces of the Chariot, which is perfection. Everything that was created in the world exists for his sake. Once Adam was created, everything was completed above and below. The Hidden Book says that when Adam was created he descended in a holy supernal form and that two spirits came down with him, the right spirit is the holy Neshamah and the left spirit is the living Nefesh. It was due to his later sin that these two spirits were separated. We hear of how the demons and their offspring the plagues were created from the left hand spirit. The rabbis have a question about the nature of Ish, is it a perfect upright man or a man of judgment, since the word is used in both senses in scripture?

106. תָּאנָא בְּכַמָּה דַרְגִּין אִתְקְרֵי ב״נ: אָדָם, גֶּבֶר, אֱנוֹשׁ, אִישׁ. גָּדוֹל שֶׁבְּכֻלָּם אָדָם. דִּכְתִיב, וַיִּבְרָא אֱלֹהִים אֶת הָאָדָם בְּצַלְמוֹ. וּכְתִיב כִּי בְּצֶלֶם אֱלֹהִים עָשָׂה אֶת הָאָדָם. וְלָא כְּתִיב, גֶּבֶר, אֱנוֹשׁ, אִישׁ. א״ר יְהוּדָה, אִי הָכִי, וְהָא כְּתִיב אָדָם כִּי יַקְרִיב מִכֶּם קָרְבָּן לַיְיָ׳. מָאן בָּעֵי לְמִקְרַב קָרְבְּנָא. מָאן דְּאִיהוּ חַטָּאָה וּכְתִיב אָדָם.

106. We learned that man has names in different stages, FOR HE IS CALLED Adam (man), Gever (male man), Enosh (human), Ish (person). The greatest is Adam, as written, "So Elohim created man (Heb. *adam*) in His own image" (Beresheet 1:27), and, "for in the image of Elohim made He man (Heb. *adam*)" (Beresheet 9:6), instead of using Gever, Enosh or Ish. Rabbi Yehuda said, in that case, it is written, "If any man (Heb. *adam*) of you bring an offering to Hashem" (Vayikra 1:2). Who needs to bring an offering? Only whoever sins WHO IS OF A LESSER LEVEL. Nevertheless it is written, Adam.

107. אָמַר ר׳ יִצְחָק ת״ח, קִיּוּמָא דְּעָלְמָא דְּעֶלָּאִין וְתַתָּאִין, הוּא קָרְבְּנָא. נַיְיחָא דְּקוּדְשָׁא בְּרִיךְ הוּא. וּמָאן אִתְחֲזֵי לְמִקְרַב קַמֵּיהּ הַאי

נַיְיחָא, הֲוֵי אוֹמֵר הַאי אָדָם, דְּיַקִּירָא מִכֹּלָּא. אָ"ל אִי הָכִי, הָא כְּתִיב,
אָדָם כִּי יִהְיֶה בְּעוֹר בְּשָׂרוֹ וְגוֹ', וְהָיָה בְעוֹר בְּשָׂרוֹ לְנֶגַע צָרַעַת. אָמַר
לֵיהּ, לְהַאי בָּעֵי קוּדְשָׁא בְּרִיךְ הוּא לְדַכָּאָה יַתִּיר מִכֹּלָּא, דְּמַאן דְּאִיהוּ
בְּדַרְגָּא עִלָּאָה דְּכֻלְּהוּ, לָא לִיתִיב הָכֵי.

107. Rabbi Yitzchak said, come and see, the mainstay of the world, of the
upper and lower beings, is the sacrifice, which pleases the Holy One,
blessed be He. Who is worthy of offering before Him this pleasure? It is
Adam, the most precious, WHICH MEANS IT IS HIGHER THAN THE OTHER
THREE. He said to him, in that case it is written, "When a man (Heb. *adam*)
shall have in the skin of his flesh… and it be in the skin of his flesh the
plague of leprosy" (Vayikra 13:2), YET THE NAME ADAM IS USED. He said
to him, for this reason the Holy One, blessed be He, has to purify him more
than anyone ELSE, for whoever is on a superior level, THAT IS, THE ONE
CALLED ADAM, must not be that way UNPURIFIED.

108. וּבְגִין כַּךְ כְּתִיב בָּאָדָם, וְהוּבָא אֶל הַכֹּהֵן. וּבָא לָא כְּתִיב, אֶלָּא
וְהוּבָא, דְּכָל מַאן דְּחָמֵי לֵיהּ, אִתְחַיָּיב בֵּיהּ לְאַקְרוֹבֵי קַמֵּי כַּהֲנָא,
דְּדִיּוּקְנָא קַדִּישָׁא לָא לֵיתִיב הָכֵי. וּכְתִיב אִישׁ אוֹ אִשָּׁה כִּי יִהְיֶה בוֹ נֶגַע
וְגוֹ', וְאִישׁ אוֹ אִשָּׁה כִּי יִהְיֶה בְעוֹר בְּשָׂרָם בֶּהָרוֹת וְגוֹ', וְלָא כְּתִיב בְּהוּ
וְהוּבָא.

108. For this reason it is written of Adam, "He shall be brought to the
priest" (Vayikra 14:2). It is not written that he came TO THE PRIEST, but
that he was brought, WHICH INDICATES that whoever sees him has to
sacrifice him before the priest, so the holy form OF ADAM will not stay that
way. It is also written, "If a man (Heb. *ish*) or a woman have a plague…"
(Vayikra 13:29), and, "If a man (Heb. *ish*) or a woman have in the skin of
their flesh bright white spots" (Ibid. 38). Of them it does not say, "He shall
be brought," BUT IN RELATION TO ADAM ONLY, BECAUSE OF HIS VALUE.

109. אָמַר לֵיהּ, וְהָא כְּתִיב וְהָאִישׁ מֹשֶׁה, כִּי זֶה מֹשֶׁה הָאִישׁ, אֲמַאי
לָא אִקְרֵי אָדָם. אָמַר לֵיהּ מִשּׁוּם דְּאִקְרֵי עֶבֶד לְמַלְכָּא, דִּכְתִיב לֹא כֵן
עַבְדִּי מֹשֶׁה. מֹשֶׁה עַבְדִּי. וְאוּף הָכִי אִקְרֵי אִישׁ לְגַבֵּי אָדָם דִּלְעֵילָּא.

אָמַר לֵיהּ אִי הָכִי, וְהָא כְּתִיב יְיָ׳ אִישׁ מִלְחָמָה, וְלָא כְּתִיב אָדָם. אָ״ל סוֹד יְיָ׳ לִירֵאָיו. אָ״ל אִי הָכִי אֲנָא בֵּינַיְיהוּ יָתִיב בְּכֹלָּא, וּבַאֲתַר דָּא לָא זָכֵינָא.

109. He said to him, yet it is written, "Now the man (Heb. *ish*) Moses" (Bemidbar 12:3), and, "as for this Moses, the man (Heb. *ish*)" (Shemot 32:23). He answered, this is because he was considered the servant of the King, as written, "My servant Moses is not so" (Bemidbar 12:7), and, "Moses My servant" (Yehoshua 1:2). IN THE SAME WAY is *Ish* in relation to supernal Adam, WHICH IS ZEIR ANPIN, FULLY SPELLED WITH ALEPHS, WHICH AMOUNTS TO 'ADAM'. He said to him, if that is so, why then it is written, "Hashem is a man (Heb. *ish*) of war" (Shemot 15:3), instead of *Adam*? He said to him, "The counsel of Hashem is with them that fear Him" (Tehilim 25:14). He said to him, in that case, I dwell among them, WHICH MEANS THAT HE TOO IS ONE OF THOSE THAT FEAR HASHEM, yet I have not had the merit TO UNDERSTAND this paragraph.

110. אָ״ל זִיל לְרִבִּי אַבָּא, דַּאֲנָא אוֹלִיפְנָא מִנֵּיהּ עַל מְנָת דְּלָא לְגַלָּאָה. אָזַל לְגַבֵּי דְּרִבִּי אַבָּא, אַשְׁכְּחֵיהּ דַּהֲוָה דָּרִישׁ וְאָמַר, אֵימָתַי אִתְקְרֵי שְׁלֵימוּתָא דְּכֹלָּא, כַּד יָתִיב קוּדְשָׁא בְּרִיךְ הוּא בְּכוּרְסַיָּיא. וְעַד דְּלָא יָתִיב בְּכוּרְסַיָּיא, לָא אִשְׁתְּכַח שְׁלֵימוּתָא. דִּכְתִיב וְעַל דְּמוּת הַכִּסֵּא דְּמוּת כְּמַרְאֵה אָדָם עָלָיו מִלְמָעְלָה, מַשְׁמַע דִּכְתִיב אָדָם, דְּהוּא כְּלָלָא, וּשְׁלֵימוּתָא דְּכֹלָּא. אָמַר ר׳ יְהוּדָה, בְּרִיךְ רַחֲמָנָא דְּאַשְׁכַּחִית לָךְ בְּהַאי. אָ״ל אִי הָכִי הָא כְּתִיב יְיָ׳ אִישׁ מִלְחָמָה, וְלָא כְּתִיב אָדָם. אָ״ל יָאוּת שָׁאַלְתָּ.

110. He said to him, go to Rabbi Aba, since I learned from him but not in order to reveal. He went to Rabbi Aba and found him discoursing on the matter of when it is considered overall perfection – when the Holy One, blessed be He, sits on the throne, MALCHUT. Before He sits on the throne, BEFORE HE UNITES WITH MALCHUT, there is no perfection, as written, "and upon the likeness of the throne was the likeness as the appearance of a man (Adam) above upon it" (Yechezkel 1:26). The use of the word Adam WHEN HE SITS ON THE THRONE means HE IS IN PERFECTION, SINCE THE

NAME ADAM includes THE FOUR FACES OF THE CHARIOT, AS WRITTEN, "AS FOR THE LIKENESS OF THEIR FACES, THEY HAD THE FACE OF A MAN" (IBID. 10), which is perfection in every way. Rabbi Yehuda said TO HIM, blessed be the Merciful that I have found you discoursing on it. He said to him, in that case, it is written, "Hashem is a man (Heb. *ish*) of war," instead of Adam. He said, this is a good question.

111. ת״ח, הָתָם לָא אִשְׁתְּכַח שְׁלֵימוּתָא דְּכֹלָּא, וּבְגִינֵי כַּךְ אִקְרֵי אִישׁ. אֲבָל הָכָא, שְׁלֵימוּתָא דְּכֹלָּא, וּכְלָלָא דְּכֹלָּא, בְּגִין כַּךְ אִקְרֵי אָדָם. קָארֵי עֲלֵיהּ טוֹב לִי תוֹרַת פִּיךְ מֵאַלְפֵי זָהָב וָכָסֶף.

111. Come and see, there, ON THE SEA, there was no comprehensive perfection, BECAUSE HE EXECUTED JUSTICE ON EGYPT. Hence it is written *Ish*. But here, WHEN HE SITS UPON THE THRONE, there was comprehensive perfection, and the embodiment of everything. For this reason it is called Adam. RABBI YEHUDA recited over him, "The Torah of Your mouth is better to me than thousands in gold and silver" (Tehilim 119:72).

112. תוּ אָמַר לֵיהּ, כְּתִיב אָדָם וּבְהֵמָה, וְלָא כְּתִיב אִישׁ וּבְהֵמָה. אָמַר לֵיהּ וְלָא. וְהָכְתִיב לְמֵאִישׁ וְעַד בְּהֵמָה. אֲבָל מַה דִּכְתִיב אָדָם וּבְהֵמָה, כְּמָה דִּכְתִיב מִן הָאֶרֶז אֲשֶׁר בַּלְּבָנוֹן עַד הָאֵזוֹב אֲשֶׁר יוֹצֵא בַּקִּיר. אוֹרְחֵיהּ דִּקְרָא הוּא, דְּנָקִיט עִלָּאָה מִכֹּלְּהוּ, וְנָמִיךְ מִכֹּלְּהוּ. אוֹף הָכָא עִלָּאָה דְּכֹלָּא, אָדָם, וְנָמִיךְ מִכֹּלָּא בְּהֵמָה.

112. He said further, it is written, "man (Heb. *adam*) and beast" (Tehilim 36:7), and not, '*Ish* and beast', EVEN THOUGH THIS REFERS TO A LESSER DEGREE, SINCE IT LIKENS HIM TO A BEAST. He said to him, no, IT IS WRITTEN '*ISH*' as it is written, "neither against man (Heb. *ish*) or beast" (Shemot 11:7). But the words "man (Heb. *adam*) and beast" are similar to, "from the cedar tree that is in Lebanon to the hyssop that comes out of the wall" (I Melachim 5:13). For it is the style of the scripture to grasp the highest and lowliest. Here also, the highest is Adam and the lowest is the beast.

113. אָמַר לֵיהּ וְהָא וְהָא כְּתִיב וְאָדָם אַיִן לַעֲבוֹד אֶת הָאֲדָמָה. א״ל, תָּא

חֲזֵי, דְּכָל מַה דִּי בְּעָלְמָא לָא הֲוֵי אֶלָּא בְּגִינֵיהּ דְּאָדָם, וְכֻלְּהוּ בְּגִינֵיהּ
מִתְקַיְּימֵי, וְלָא אִתְחֲזִיאוּ בְּעָלְמָא, וְכֻלְּהוּ אִתְעַכְּבוּ עַד דְּיֵיתֵי הַהוּא
דְּאִקְרֵי אָדָם. הה"ד, וְכֹל שִׂיחַ הַשָּׂדֶה טֶרֶם יִהְיֶה בָאָרֶץ וְגו'. טֶרֶם: עַד
לָא, כְּתַרְגּוּמוֹ. מִשּׁוּם דְּדִיּוּקְנָא עִלָּאָה לָא אִתְחֲזֵי, הה"ד וְאָדָם אַיִן,
כְּלוֹמַר, כֻּלְּהוּ אִתְעַכְּבוּ בְּגִינֵיהּ דְּהַאי דִּיּוּקְנָא, עַד דְּאִתְחֲזֵי. ובג"כ לָא
אִתְבְּרֵי הַאי דִּיּוּקְנָא, אֶלָּא בְּדִיּוּקְנָא דְּאִתְחֲזֵי לֵיהּ, הה"ד וַיִּיצֶר יְיָ'
אֱלֹהִים אֶת הָאָדָם, בְּשֵׁם מָלֵא. כְּמָה דְּאוֹקִימְנָא, דְּאִיהוּ שְׁלֵימוּתָא
דְּכֹלָּא, וּכְלָלָא דְּכֹלָּא.

113. He said to him, yet it is written, "and there was not a man (Heb. *adam*) to till the ground" (Beresheet 2:5). WHAT IS THE SIGNIFICANCE OF MENTIONING THE NAME ADAM? He said to him, come and see, whatever is in the world was only for the sake of Adam, and everything exists for his sake. THEREFORE, they did not appear in the world and everything was held back, until the arrival of him that is called Adam. This is the meaning of, "And no plant of the field was yet in the earth" (Ibid.). "Yet" WAS TRANSLATED INTO 'not until', since the supernal form CALLED ADAM did not appear. This is the meaning of, "and there was not a man (Heb. *adam*) to till the ground." This means that everything was held until that form appeared. For that reason, that form, *ADAM*, was created solely with the shape appropriate for it. This is the meaning of, "And Hashem Elohim formed man" (Beresheet 2:7) with a complete name, as we explained THAT THE NAME ADAM comprises comprehensive perfection and encompassing wholeness.

114. תָּאנָא, בַּשִּׁשִּׁי נִבְרָא אָדָם, בְּשָׁעָה שֶׁנִּשְׁלַם הַכִּסֵּא. וְנִקְרָא כִּסֵּא,
דִּכְתִיב שֵׁשׁ מַעֲלוֹת לַכִּסֵּא. וּלְפִיכָךְ נִבְרָא הָאָדָם בַּשִּׁשִּׁי, שֶׁהוּא רָאוּי
לֵישֵׁב עַל הַכִּסֵּא. וְתָאנָא כֵּיוָן דְּנִבְרָא אָדָם אִתְתָּקַן כֹּלָּא, וְכָל מַה
דִּלְעֵילָּא וְתַתָּא, וְכֹלָּא אִתְכְּלִיל בְּאָדָם.

114. We learned that Adam was created on the sixth day, WHICH IS THE CHARIOT TO THE SUPERNAL MAN, ZEIR ANPIN, when the throne, WHICH IS MALCHUT, was completed, as written, "The throne had six steps" (I Melachim 10:19), WHICH ARE, CHESED, GVURAH, TIFERET, NETZACH,

HOD AND YESOD OF MALCHUT THAT IS CALLED THRONE. Therefore man was created on the sixth, WHEN THE SIX SFIROT, CHESED, GVURAH, TIFERET, NETZACH, HOD AND YESOD, REACHED COMPLETION, for he, SUPERNAL MAN, is worthy of sitting on the throne. We learned that once Adam was created, everything was completed, all that is above, NAMELY ZEIR ANPIN AND MALCHUT, and below, and all was included in Adam.

115. תַּנְיָא א"ר יוֹסֵי, כְּתִיב וּדְמוּת פְּנֵיהֶם פְּנֵי אָדָם, כְּלָלָא דְכֹלָא, וְכֹלָא כְּלִילָן בְּהַאי דִיוּקְנָא. א"ר יְהוּדָה וְהָא כְּתִיב וּפְנֵי אַרְיֵה אֶל הַיָּמִין לְאַרְבַּעְתָּם, וּפְנֵי שׁוֹר מֵהַשְּׂמֹאל לְאַרְבַּעְתָּן, אָמַר לֵיהּ כֹּלָּא אַפֵּי אָדָם הֲווֹ, וּבְהַהוּא דִיוּקְנָא דְאָדָם, אִתְחֲזִייָן כָּל גַּוְונִין וְכָל דִּיוּקְנִין. כְּמָה דְּתָנֵינָן אַנְפּוֹי אַנְפֵּי נִשְׁרָא, לָא דְּהוּא נִשְׁרָא, אֶלָּא דְאִתְחֲזֵי בְּדִיוּקְנָא דְאָדָם, מִשׁוּם דְּכָלִיל כָּל גַּוְונִין וְכָל דִּיוּקְנִין.

115. We learned: Rabbi Yosi said, it is written, "As for the likeness of their faces, they had the face of a man," WHICH MEANS THAT THE FACE OF MAN comprehends everything, and all THE THREE FACES, LION, OX AND EAGLE, are part of this form OF THE FACE OF MAN. Rabbi Yehuda said, yet it is written, "and they four had the face of a lion, on the right side. And they four had the face of an ox on the left side" (Yechezkel 1:10), SO THERE ARE ALSO THE FORMS OF A LION AND AN OX AS WELL. He said to him, they all had the face of a man, and in this form of man all the shades and forms were seen. As we learned, his face was the face of an eagle. Not that he is an eagle, but in the form of man THE FORM OF AN EAGLE could be seen, THOUGH ESSENTIALLY HE HAD THE FORM OF A MAN, since THE FACE OF MAN includes all aspects and shapes.

116. א"ר יִצְחָק, ת"ח, כָּל מַאן דְּאִיהוּ תְּחוֹת שׁוּלְטָנֵי דְאָדָם, אִתְקְרֵי אִישׁ. מִשׁוּם דְּאִתְתְּקַן בְּגַוְונָא דְאָדָם, מִדַּרְגָּא אָחֳרָא דַהֲוָה בֵּיהּ בְּקַדְמֵיתָא. דְּתַנְיָא בְּרָזָא עִלָּאָה בְּסִפְרָא דִּצְנִיעוּתָא, כַּד אִתְבְּרֵי אָדָם, נָחַת בְּדִיוּקְנָא קַדִּישָׁא עִלָּאָה, וְנַחְתּוּ עִמֵּיהּ תְּרֵין רוּחִין, מִתְּרֵין סִטְרִין, מִימִינָא וּמִשְּׂמָאלָא, כְּלָלָא דְאָדָם. וְרוּחָא דִּימִינָא, אִתְקְרֵי נִשְׁמָתָא קַדִּישָׁא, דִּכְתִיב וַיִּפַּח בְּאַפָּיו נִשְׁמַת חַיִּים. וְרוּחָא דִּשְׂמָאלָא, אִתְקְרֵי נֶפֶשׁ חַיָּה, וַהֲוָה אָזִיל וְנָחִית מֵעֵילָא לְתַתָּא, וְלָא אִתְיַישְׁבָא בַּהֲדֵי אָחֳרָא.

-75-

116. Rabbi Yitzchak said, come and see, whatever is under the power of man (Heb. *adam*) is called *Ish*, since he was established after the manner of Adam on a different grade than the latter had before. For we learned according to a high mystery of the Concealed Book that when Adam was created, he descended in a holy supernal form and two spirits came down with him on two sides, on the right and left, WHICH ARE the whole of man. The right spirit is called holy Neshamah, as written, "and breathed into his nostrils the breath (Heb. *Neshamah*) of life" (Beresheet 2:7). The spirit on the left is called living Nefesh. It gradually descended from above down TO THE GARDEN OF EDEN. AND THE NESHAMAH ON THE RIGHT did not settle with the other ON THE LEFT, WHICH MEANS THAT HE SINNED BY THE TREE OF KNOWLEDGE OF GOOD AND EVIL AND SEPARATED THE RIGHT FROM THE LEFT.

117. כַּד הֲוָה עָיֵיל שַׁבַּתָּא, וַהֲוָה חָב אָדָם, אִתְעָבֵידוּ מֵהַהוּא רוּחָא שְׂמָאלָא, בְּרַיָּין מִתְפַּשְּׁטָן בְּעָלְמָא, וְלָא אִסְתַּיָּימוּ גּוּפָא דִּלְהוֹן. וְאִתְחַבָּרוּ בְּהַאי גּוּפָא דְּאָדָם, בִּדְכוּרָא וְנוּקְבָּא, וְאִתְיְלִידוּ בְּעָלְמָא. וְאִלֵּין אִקְרוּן נִגְעֵי בְּנֵי אָדָם. תָּנָא, עִלָּאִין, מִנַּיְיהוּ דְּלָא אִתְדַּבָּקוּ לְתַתָּא, וְתַלְיָין בַּאֲוִירָא, וְשַׁמְעִין מַה דְּשַׁמְעִין מִלְעֵילָא. וּמִנַּיְיהוּ יָדְעִין אִינּוּן אָחֳרָנִין לְתַתָּא.

117. When Shabbat entered, and Adam had already sinned, creatures were formed from the left hand spirit, whose bodies were not completed, NAMELY DEMONS. They joined the body of Adam, the male and the female, EVE, and begot offspring in the world. They are called the plagues of men. We learned THAT THERE ARE supernal SPIRITS coming from those WHO WERE MADE FROM THE SPIRIT ON THE LEFT OF THE FIRST MAN. They are not attached below IN THIS WORLD, but are suspended in the air. They hear whatever they hear above, and from them other SPIRITS below IN THIS WORLD learn. THEY APPEAR TO PEOPLE IN THEIR DREAMS AND INFORM THEM.

118. תָּנָא, מִן בּוּצִינָא דְּקַרְדִּינוּתָא, נָפְקִין תְּלַת מְאָה וְעֶשְׂרִים וְחָמֵשׁ נִיצוֹצֵי, מִתְגַּלְפִין וּמִתְאַחֲדָן כַּחֲדָא מִסִּטְרָא דִּגְבוּרָה, דְּאִקְרוּן גְּבוּרוֹת, וּמִתְלַכְּדָן כַּחֲדָא, וְאִתְעָבֵידוּ חַד. וְכַד עַיְילִין אִלֵּין בְּגוּפָא, אִקְרֵי אִישׁ.

דָּא דְּתָנֵינָן אִישׁ תָּם וְיָשָׁר אִישׁ צַדִּיק, וְאִישׁ דְּהָכָא, אִישׁ מִלְחָמָה
כְּתִיב, דְּכֹלָּא סָלִיק דִּינָא, וְכֹלָּא חֲדָא. א"ר יְהוּדָה אֲמַאי. לָא הֲוָה
בִּידֵיהּ. אָתוּ שָׁאִילוּ קַמֵּיהּ דר"ש, אָמַר לוֹן, תּוּ קַשְׁיָא, דְּהָא תָּנֵינָן
כְּתִיב לְזֹאת יִקָּרֵא אִשָּׁה כִּי מֵאִישׁ לֻקֳחָה זֹאת, וְתָנֵינָן מַאן אִישׁ דָּא
חֶסֶד, וְהָכָא אַמְרִיתוּ דְּהוּא דִינָא.

118. We learned that 325 sparks come out of the hard spark. They are imprinted on and attached to the aspect of Gvurah and are called Gvurot. They converge and become one. When these enter the body, NAMELY ZEIR ANPIN CALLED BODY, it is called *Ish*. This we learned, that there is a perfect and upright man (Heb. *ish*), and a righteous man (Heb. *ish*). BUT the *Ish* here is a man of war, as written, NAMELY, "HASHEM IS A MAN (HEB. *ISH*) OF WAR" (SHEMOT 15:3), since He consists entirely of Judgment, and this all means the same thing. Rabbi Yehuda said, why DOES IT ALL MEAN THE SAME, SEEING THAT A PERFECT AND UPRIGHT *ISH* IS OF MERCY, WHILE *ISH* OF WAR IS JUDGMENT? He was unable TO ANSWER HIM. They came and asked Rabbi Shimon. He said to them, it is even more difficult. As we learned, it is written, "she shall be called Woman, because she was taken out of Man (Heb. *ish*)" (Beresheet 2:23). We learned that *Ish* is Chesed, but you said here that he is Judgment.

23. Holy and pure

A Synopsis

Rabbi Shimon explains that Ish is both mercy and judgment, and he tells how the presence and absence of hair on the head denote purity and impurity. The Levites are pure only when their hair is removed, because they come from the side of Judgment, and are Ish and not Adam. We learn about the purification by water, and are told that the supernal Ish, Zeir Anpin, is completed by washing in supernal Chesed. The rabbis also speak about a white reddish sore on a person, and the meaning of the white and the red. Lastly we hear that 'prayer' is actually the Congregation of Yisrael.

119. אֶלָּא הָכִי תָּאנָא, כֹּלָּא הוּא בְּחַד מַתְקְלָא סַלְקָא, וְכֹלָּא חַד. וּמִשּׁוּם דְּדִינֵי תַּתָּאֵי מִתְאַחֲדָן וּמִתְחַבְּרָן בְּשַׂעֲרוֹי דְּהַאי. אִקְרֵי הוּא דִּינָא קַשְׁיָא, וְכַד אִתְעֲבַּר מִנֵּיה שַׂעֲרָא דְּרֵישָׁא, אִתְבַּסַם, וְדִינִין דִּלְתַתָּא לָא אִזְדַמְּנוּ. ובג״כ אִקְרֵי טָהוֹר. דְּלָא אִקְרֵי טָהוֹר, אֶלָּא כַּד נָפִיק מִסִּטְרָא דִּמְסָאֲבָא, וְכַד נָפִיק מִן מְסָאֲבָא, אִקְרֵי טָהוֹר. דִּכְתִּיב, מִי יִתֵּן טָהוֹר מִטָּמֵא. מִטָּמֵא וַדַּאי, וְהָכָא כְּתִיב, וְאִישׁ כִּי יִמָּרֵט רֹאשׁוֹ קֵרֵחַ הוּא טָהוֹר הוּא.

119. We learned that everything eventually means the same and it is all the same, NAMELY, *ISH* IS BOTH CHESED AND JUDGMENT; since the Judgment of the lower join and unite with his hair, he is considered harsh Judgment. Once the hair of his head is removed, he is settled and the Judgments of the lower beings do not appear. This is why he is considered pure, since only that which comes out of the side of impurity is pure. When it comes out of the side of impurity it is considered pure, as written, "Who can bring a clean thing out of an unclean" (Iyov 14:4). Yet here it says, "And the man whose hair is fallen off his head, he is bald; yet is he clean" (Vayikra 13:40).

120. ות״ח, בְּרֵישָׁא דְּהַאי אִישׁ, בּוּצִינָא דְּקַרְדִּינוּתָא. ובג״כ גּוּלְגַּלְתָּא דְּרֵישָׁא דְּהַאי, סוּמָקָא כֹּלָּא כְּוַורְדָּא, וְשַׂעֲרֵי סוּמָקִי בְּגוֹ סוּמָקֵי, וְתַלְיָין מִנֵּיה כִּתְרִין תַּתָּאִין דִּלְתַתָּא, דְּמִתְעָרִין דִּינִין בְּעָלְמָא. וְכַד אִתְעֲבַר מִנֵּיה שַׂעֲרָא וְאִתְגְּלִישׁ, מֵחֶסֶד עִלָּאָה אִתְבַּסַם כֹּלָּא, וְאִתְקְרֵי טָהוֹר עַל

שְׁמֵיהּ.

120. Come and see, there is a hard spark upon the head of that man, and for that reason his skull is red as a rose and the hair is red within the redness OF THE SKULL. The lower Sfirot from below are suspended from him that rouse Judgments in the world. Once the hair is removed from him and he is bald, everything is firmly established by means of supernal Chesed, SINCE THE ILLUMINATION OF CHOCHMAH IN HIM IS ESTABLISHED THROUGH SUPERNAL CHESED, and he is named pure after him.

121. א"ר יְהוּדָה, אִי אִתְקְרֵי עַל שְׁמֵיהּ, קָדוֹשׁ אִתְקְרֵי, וְלֹא טָהוֹר. אָמַר לֵיהּ לָאו הָכִי, דְּקָדוֹשׁ לָא אִתְקְרֵי אֶלָּא כַּד תְּלֵי שַׂעֲרָא. דִּקְדוּשָׁה בְּשַׂעֲרָא תָּלֵי, דִּכְתִּיב קָדוֹשׁ יִהְיֶה גַּדֵּל פֶּרַע שְׂעַר רֹאשׁוֹ. וְהַאי אִקְרֵי טָהוֹר, מִסְטְרָא דְּתַלְיָין לְתַתָּא מִנֵּיהּ, וּבְגִינֵי כָּךְ אִתְעֲבָר מִנֵּיהּ שַׂעֲרָא, וְאִתְדַּכְיָא.

121. Rabbi Yehuda said, if he is named after him, he should be called holy, not pure. He said to him, it is not so, since he is considered holy only when the hairs on his head are hanging, since holiness comes from the hair, as written, "he shall be holy, and shall let the locks of the hair of his head grow" (Bemidbar 6:5). This ISH is considered pure from the aspect of those that come down from him, THE IMPURE EXTERNAL FORCES THAT WERE REMOVED WITH THE REMOVAL OF HIS HAIR. For that reason, once the hairs were removed from him, he is purified.

122. וְתָא חֲזֵי כָּל מַאן דְּאִיהוּ מִסְטְרָא דְּדִינָא, וְדִינִין מִתְאַחֲדִין בֵּיהּ, לָא אִתְדְּכֵי, עַד דְּאִתְעֲבָר מִנֵּיהּ שַׂעֲרָא, וּמִדְּאִתְעֲבָר מִנֵּיהּ שַׂעֲרָא אִתְדְּכֵי. וְאִי תֵּימָא אָדָם. לָאו הָכִי, דְּהָא הוּא שְׁלֵימוּתָא דְּכֹלָּא, וְרַחֲמֵי אִשְׁתְּכָחוּ בֵּיהּ. בְּגִין כָּךְ לָאו הָכִי דְּכֻלְּהוּ קְדוּשָׁאן וְקַדִּישִׁין אִתְיַיחֲדוּ בֵּיהּ. אֲבָל הַאי, הוּא דִּינָא, וְדִינֵי אִתְאַחֲדָן בֵּיהּ, לָא אִתְבְּסַם עַד דְּאִתְעֲבָר מִנֵּיהּ שַׂעֲרָא.

122. Come and see, whoever is from the aspect of Judgment, and Judgments cleave to him, is purified only when his hair is removed. Once his hair is

removed he is purified. As for Adam, it is not so, because complete perfection and mercy abide in him, so it is not true, since all that is holy and the holy ones are united in him. But as for that WHO IS CALLED *ISH* AND NOT ADAM, he is THEN of Judgment and Judgments are attached to him, NAMELY TO HIS HAIR. THEREFORE he is not firmly established until his hair is removed.

123. ת״ח, דְּהָא לֵיוָאֵי דְּאָתוּ מֵהַאי סִטְרָא דְּדִינָא, לָא מִתְדַּכְּאָן עַד דְּאִתְעֲבָרוּ מִנְּהוֹן שַׂעֲרָא, דִּכְתִיב וְכֹה תַעֲשֶׂה לָהֶם לְטַהֲרָם הַזֵּה עֲלֵיהֶם מֵי חַטָּאת וְהֶעֱבִירוּ תַעַר עַל כָּל בְּשָׂרָם וְגוֹ'. וּבְגִין דְּיִתְבַּסְּמוּן יַתִּיר, בָּעֵי כַּהֲנָא דְּאָתָא מִסִּטְרָא דְּחֶסֶד עִלָּאָה, לְאַרְמָא לוֹן, דִּכְתִיב וְהֵנִיף אַהֲרֹן אֶת הַלְוִיִּם תְּנוּפָה לִפְנֵי יְיָ'. כְּמָה דְּאִיהוּ לְהַאי אִישׁ דִּלְעֵילָא, דְּכַד בָּעֵי לְאִתְבַּסְּמָא יַתִּיר, אִתְגַּלְיָיא בֵּיהּ חֶסֶד עִלָּאָה, וְאִתְבְּסַם. וּמְבַסֵּם הוּא, לְתַתָּא.

123. Come and see, the Levites come from this side of Judgment. They are purified only when their hair is removed, as written, "And thus shall you do to them, to cleanse them: Sprinkle water of purifying on them, and let them shave all their flesh" (Bemidbar 8:7). And in order for them to be more established, the priest that comes from the aspect of supernal Chesed should offer them, as written, "and Aaron shall offer the Levites before Hashem for an offering" (Ibid. 11), IN ORDER TO INCLUDE THE ILLUMINATION OF CHOCHMAH IN THEM IN CHASSADIM OF THE PRIEST, the same as with the *Ish* above. When he needs to be more established, supernal Chesed THAT CLOTHES CHOCHMAH is revealed in him and he is more established. ALSO he establishes CHESED below IN THE LEVITES.

124. וְהַאי אִישׁ בִּכְלָלָא דְּאָדָם הוּא. וְכַד בָּעֵי קוּדְשָׁא בְּרִיךְ הוּא לְאַגָּחָא קְרָבָא, בְּהַאי אִישׁ אַגַּח בְּהוּ קְרָבָא, דִּכְתִיב יְיָ' אִישׁ מִלְחָמָה, בְּהַאי אִישׁ מַמָּשׁ. וְלָא אַגַּח בְּהוּ קְרָבָא, עַד דְּאַעֲבָּר לֵיהּ שַׂעֲרָא דְּרֵישָׁא, בְּגִין דְּיִשְׁתַּכְלְלוּן מִשְּׁלְשׁוּלַיְיהוֹן, וְיִתְבְּרוּן כָּל אִינוּן כִּתְרִין דְּמִתְאַחֲדָן בְּשַׂעֲרֵי. הה״ד בַּיּוֹם הַהוּא יְגַלַּח יְיָ' וְגוֹ'. בְּעֶבְרֵי נָהָר בְּמֶלֶךְ אַשּׁוּר אֶת הָרֹאשׁ וְשַׂעַר הָרַגְלָיִם וְגַם אֶת הַזָּקָן תִּסְפֶּה.

124. That *Ish* is included in Adam. When the Holy One, blessed be He, wishes to wage war, He does so with that *Ish*, as written, "Hashem is a man (Heb. *ish*) of war" (Shemot 15:3), NAMELY with this very *Ish*. He does not wage war with them, until He removes the hair of his head, so that all the crowns FROM THE OUTER ASPECT THAT ARE HANGING AND clinging to the hairs OF ZEIR ANPIN FROM THE ASPECT OF *ISH* will be taken away from their hanging AND ATTACHMENT. This is the meaning of, "On the same day shall Hashem shave... with them beyond the river with the king of Assyria the head, and the hair of the legs. And it shall also sweep away the beard" (Yeshayah 7:20). THAT MEANS THAT IN ORDER TO OVERTHROW THE KING OF ASSYRIA, HE WILL SHAVE ALL THE HAIR OF THE HIGHER BEINGS TO WHICH THEY ARE ATTACHED.

125. תָּאנָא, וְכֹה תַעֲשֶׂה לָהֶם לְטַהֲרָם. מַאי וְכֹה. כְּגַוְונָא דִּלְעֵילָּא, הַזֶּה עֲלֵיהֶם מֵי חַטָּאת, שִׁיּוּרֵי טַלָּא דִּבְדוֹלְחָא הָכָא מֵי חַטָּאת, דְּאִינּוּן שִׁיּוּרֵי טַלָּא. לְזִמְנָא דְּאָתֵי כְּתִיב, וְזָרַקְתִּי עֲלֵיכֶם מַיִם טְהוֹרִים. וְכִבְּסוּ בִגְדֵיהֶם, כְּגַוְונָא דִּלְעֵילָּא, דְּתִקּוּנוֹי דְּהַאי אִישׁ אִתְּסָחָן בְּחֶסֶד עִלָּאָה וְאִתְדַּכֵּי מִכֹּלָא.

125. We learned: "And thus shall you do to them, to cleanse them" (Bemidbar 8:7). What is 'thus'? IT MEANS it bears the semblance of above. "Sprinkle water of purifying on them," NAMELY the residue of crystal dew. Here there is water of purifying, which is the residue of dew. In the future to come it is written, "Then will I sprinkle clean water upon you, and you shall be clean" (Yechezkel 36:25). "and let them wash their clothes, and so make themselves clean" (Bemidbar 8:7) bears the semblance of the higher, ZEIR ANPIN, for that *Ish* is completed by washing in supernal Chesed and purifies in every respect. HERE TOO, "LET THEM WASH THEIR CLOTHES" WITH CHESED THAT IS CALLED WATER.

126. וְתָנֵינָן, אֲמַאי כְּתִיב בְּתַעַר וְלֹא בְּמִסְפָּרַיִם. אֶלָּא מִשׁוּם דְּיִתְעֲבַר שַׂעֲרָא בְּשָׁרְשׁוֹי, וְיִתְעַבְרוּן מִנֵּיהּ דִּינִין תַּתָּאִין מִשּׁוּלְשׁוּלֵיהוֹן. וּלְזִמְנָא דְּיִתְכַּשְׁרוּן עוֹבָדִין לְתַתָּא, זַמִּין קוּדְשָׁא בְּרִיךְ הוּא שַׂעֲרָא דָּא לְאַעְבְּרָא לֵיהּ, וּלְמִגְלְשֵׁיהּ בְּגִין דְּלָא יִצְמַח וְיִרְבֶּה, דִּכְתִיב כִּי יִמְרֹט כִּי יְמָרֵט רֹאשׁוֹ.

126. We learned the reason why it is written that they shave rather than cut. HE ANSWERS, this is so that the hairs would be removed from their roots, SINCE SHAVING REMOVES THE HAIR FROM THE ROOT, and the lower Judgments will be removed from their hold ON HIS HAIR. When the deeds of the lower beings are upright, the Holy One, blessed be He, will remove these hairs and shave them off, so they will not grow and increase, as written, "whose hair is fallen off his head" (Vayikra 13:40).

127. א"ר יִצְחָק, רַב מִכָּל לֵיוָאֵי, קֹרַח הֲוָא, דְּעַבְדֵיה קוּדְשָׁא בְּרִיךְ הוּא לְתַתָּא, כְּגַוְונָא דִּלְעֵילָא, וְקַרְיֵיה קֹרַח. אֵימָתַי. בְּשַׁעְתָּא דְּגָלִישׁ בְּגִינֵיה לְהַאי אִישׁ, דִּכְתִּיב קֹרֵחַ הוּא.

127. Rabbi Yitzchak said, the greatest of all the Levites is Korah, whom the Holy One, blessed be He, made below as a likeness of *Ish* above and called him Korah. When DID HE CALL HIM KORAH? When He made bald the *Ish* ABOVE, as written, "A MAN (*ISH*) WHOSE HAIR IS FALLEN OFF HIS HEAD, he is bald."

128. וְכַד חָמָא קֹרַח רֵישֵׁיה בְּלָא שַׂעֲרָא, וְחָמָא לְאַהֲרֹן מִתְקַשֵּׁט בְּקִשׁוּטֵי מַלְכִין, אִתְזַלְזַל בְּעֵינֵיה וְקַנֵּא לְאַהֲרֹן. א"ל קוּדְשָׁא בְּרִיךְ הוּא, אֲנָא עֲבָדִית לָךְ כְּגַוְונָא דִּלְעֵילָא, לָא בָּעָאת לְאַעֲלָאָה בְּעֶלָּאִין, חוּת לְתַתָּא וַהֲוֵי בְּתַתָּאִין. דִּכְתִּיב וְיָרְדוּ חַיִּים שְׁאוֹלָה. מַאי אִיהוּ שְׁאוֹל. גֵּיהִנָּם. דְּתַמָּן צַוְוחִין חַיָּיבִין, וְלֵית מַאן דִּמְרַחֲמֵי עֲלַיְיהוּ. וּזְמִינִין אִינוּן לְאַחֲיָיא וּלְאַעֲלָא, כַּד יִתְעַר קוּדְשָׁא בְּרִיךְ הוּא לְעַמֵּיה, וּלְאַחֲיָיא לְהוּ. דִּכְתִּיב, יְיָ' מֵמִית וּמְחַיֶּה מוֹרִיד שְׁאוֹל וַיָּעַל.

128. When Korah saw his head hairless and saw Aaron bedeck himself with royal adornments, he felt himself slighted and was jealous of Aaron. The Holy One, blessed be He, said to him, 'I made you resemble the higher, yet you do not wish to ascend among the higher. Go down and be among the lower, as written, "and they go down alive into Sheol"' (Bemidbar 16:30). What is Sheol? It is Gehenom, where the wicked cry out but there is no one to have pity on them. They will be resurrected and rise FROM GEHENOM when the Holy One, blessed be He, will rouse His people and revive them,

as written, "Hashem kills, and gives life. He brings down to Sheol, and brings up" (I Shmuel 2:6).

129. וְאִם מִפְּאַת פָּנָיו יִמָּרֵט רֹאשׁוֹ. תָּאנָא, אִית פָּנִים וְאִית פָּנִים, וּמַאן פָּנִים הַלָּלוּ. אִלֵּין אִינּוּן דְּאִקְרוּן פָּנִים שֶׁל זַעַם. וְכָל אִלֵּין דְּתַלְיָין מֵאִינּוּן פָּנִים חֲצִיפִין, כֻּלְּהוּ תַּקִּיפִין. כֻּלְּהוּ דְּלָא מְרַחֲמֵי, וְכַד אִתְעֲבַר שַׂעֲרָא מִסִּטְרָא דְּאִינּוּן פָּנִים, מִתְעַבְּרָן כֻּלְּהוּ וְאִתְּבָּרוּ.

129. "And he whose hair is fallen off from the part of his head toward his face" (Vayikra 13:41). We learned that there is face and there is face. What is the face IN THE VERSE, "AND HE WHOSE HAIR IS FALLEN..."? It is called a wrathful face, since all that derives from that impudent face is harsh without mercy. When the hair is removed from the part of the head towards the face, all THE EXTERNAL FORCES HANGING FROM THEM are removed and subdued.

130. דְּתַנְיָא, כָּל אִינּוּן דְּתַלְיָין מִשַּׂעֲרָא דְּרֵישָׁא, אִינּוּן עִלָּאִין עַל אַחֲרָנִין, וְלָא חֲצִיפִין כְּוָותַיְיהוּ. וְכָל אִינּוּן דְּתַלְיָין מִסִּטְרָא דְּשַׂעֲרָא דְּאִינּוּן פָּנִים, כֻּלְּהוּ חֲצִיפִין וְתַקִּיפִין, וּבְג"כ אַנְפּוֹי מִתְלַהֲטָן כְּאֶשָּׁא, מִשּׁוּם נִיצוֹצָא דְּבוּצִינָא דְּקַרְדִּינוּתָא. וּבְהַאי כְּתִיב, פְּנֵי יְיָ' חִלְּקָם. פְּנֵי יְיָ' בְּעוֹשֵׂי רָע.

130. We learned that all those EXTERNAL FORCES coming from the hair of the head are superior to others and not as impudent. All those coming from the side of the hair towards the IMPUDENT face are all powerful and impudent. For that reason his face is burning like fire, because of the hard spark IN IT. Of this it is written, "The anger (lit. 'face') of Hashem has divided them" (Eichah 4:16), and, "The face of Hashem is against those who do evil" (Tehilim 34:17).

24. "A white reddish sore"

131. א"ר יִצְחָק מַהוּ נֶגַע לָבָן אֲדַמְדָּם. נֶגַע מַמָּשׁ הוּא, אִי חִוָּרָא אִתְחֲזֵי, וְסוּמָקָא לָא אִתְעֲבַר. מַשְׁמַע דִּכְתִיב לָבָן אֲדַמְדָּם. א"ר יוֹסֵי, דְּחִוָּרָא לָא אִתְחֲזֵי אֶלָּא בְּסוּמָקָא, כְּגַוְונָא חִוָּרָא וְסוּמָקָא. רַבִּי יִצְחָק אָמַר, אע"ג דְּחִוָּרָא אִתְחֲזֵי, אִי סוּמָקָא לָא אָזִיל, נֶגַע הוּא. דִּכְתִיב אִם יִהְיוּ חֲטָאֵיכֶם כַּשָּׁנִים כַּשֶּׁלֶג יַלְבִּינוּ. וְכַד אִתְחַוָּור, כֹּלָּא רַחֲמֵי אִשְׁתְּכָחוּ, וְדִינִין לָא אִשְׁתְּכָחוּ.

131. Rabbi Yitzchak said, what is "a white reddish sore" (Vayikra 13:42), and answers that it is an actual sore if the white is exposed and the redness does not go away. This is derived from the words, "white reddish," AS BOTH ARE SEEN. Rabbi Yosi said, "WHITE REDDISH" MEANS the white is seen only with the red, as white and red TOGETHER. Rabbi Yitzchak said THAT THE MEANING IS AS WAS SAID ABOVE. Even though the white appears, if the red does not disappear, it is a sore, as written, "though your sins be like scarlet, they shall be as white as snow" (Yeshayah 1:18). For when it turns completely white, there is Mercy, and no Judgment.

132. תָּאנֵי רִבִּי אַבָּא, כְּתִיב נֶגַע הוּא, וּכְתִיב נֶגַע הִיא. חַד דְּכַר וְחַד נוּקְבָּא. אֶלָּא כַּד נוּקְבָּא, אִסְתְּאָבַת בְּגִין חוֹבֵי תַּתָּאֵי, כְּתִיב נֶגַע הִיא. וְכַד דְּכַר לָא אִתְדְּכֵי בְּגִין חוֹבֵי תַּתָּאֵי, כְּתִיב נֶגַע הוּא.

132. We learned that Rabbi Aba taught, it is written NOW "it is a sore" in the masculine, and NOW "it is a sore" in the feminine. AND HE ANSWERS, when the female, MALCHUT, is defiled because of the iniquities of the lower beings, it is written "it is a sore" IN THE FEMININE. When the male, WHICH IS ZEIR ANPIN ON THE LEVEL OF ISH, is not purified because of the iniquities of the lower beings, it is written, "it is a sore" IN THE MASCULINE.

133. וְאִשְׁתְּמוֹדְעָן מִלִּין אִלֵּין לְגַבֵּי כַּהֲנָא, דִּינִין דְּאָתוּ מֵהַאי, וְדִינִין דְּאָתוּ מֵהַאי. וְאִשְׁתְּמוֹדְעָן קָרְבְּנֵי דְּבַעְיָין לְקָרְבָּא, דִּכְתִיב זָכָר תָּמִים. וּכְתִיב נְקֵבָה תְּמִימָה יְבִיאֶנָּה, דְּהָא אִשְׁתְּמוֹדְעָן מִלֵּי, מַאן אָתוּ דִּינִין,

-84-

וּמֵאָן אִינּוּן חוֹבֵי. דְּאִתְאַחֲדָן בְּהַאי אוֹ בְּהַאי. וְעַל דָּא כְּתִיב, זִבְחֵי
אֱלֹהִים רוּחַ נִשְׁבָּרָה. לְאַפָּקָא שְׁאָר קָרְבָּנִין דְּלָא כְּתִיב רוּחַ נִשְׁבָּרָה,
דְּאִינּוּן שְׁלָמָא לְעָלְמָא, וְחֶדְוָה דְּעִלָּאִין וְתַתָּאִין.

133. The priest ascertains whether the Judgments come from the one, ZEIR ANPIN, or the other, MALCHUT, and learns about the offerings that need to be brought as written, "a male without blemish" (Vayikra 4:23), or, "he shall bring it a female without blemish" (Ibid. 32). For THE PRIEST finds out whence the Judgments came and whence the iniquities; whether they are attached to this, THE MALE, or that, THE FEMALE. Hence it is written IN RELATION TO THE SACRIFICES, "the sacrifices of Elohim are a broken spirit" (Tehilim 51:19), excluding the other sacrifices, of which it is not written, "a broken spirit," since they are peace in the world and the joy of the higher and lower beings.

134. וְאִם יִרְאֶנָּה הַכֹּהֵן. תָּאנֵי רִבִּי יוֹסֵי, כְּתִיב שׁוֹמֵעַ תְּפִלָּה עָדֶיךָ וְגוֹ'.
שׁוֹמֵעַ תְּפִלָּה, דָּא קוּדְשָׁא בְּרִיךְ הוּא. ר' חִזְקִיָּה אָמַר, שׁוֹמֵעַ תְּפִלָּה,
שׁוֹמֵעַ תְּפִלּוֹת מִבָּעֵי לֵיהּ, מַהוּ שׁוֹמֵעַ תְּפִלָּה. אֶלָּא תְּפִלָּה, דָּא כ"י,
דְּאִיהִי תְּפִלָּה, דִּכְתִיב וַאֲנִי תְּפִלָּה וְדָוִד בְּגִין כנ"י קָאָמַר לָהּ. וּמַה
דְּאָמַר וַאֲנִי תְּפִלָּה, כֹּלָּא חַד, וְעַל דָּא שׁוֹמֵעַ תְּפִלָּה, וְדָא תְּפִלָּה שֶׁל יָד,
דִּכְתִיב עַל יָדְכָה בְּהֵ"א.

134. "But if the priest look on it" (Vayikra 13:21). Rabbi Yosi taught, it is written, "O You that hear prayer, to You…" (Tehilim 65:3). "You that hear prayer" refers to the Holy One, blessed be He, NAMELY ZEIR ANPIN. Rabbi Chizkiyah said, "You that hear prayer": it should have said 'prayers'. Wherefore is it "hear prayer"? AND HE ANSWERS, prayer is the Congregation of Yisrael, NAMELY MALCHUT, which is CALLED prayer, as written, "while I have nothing but (or: 'I am') prayer" (Tehilim 109:4). David said that for the sake of the Congregation of Yisrael, and as for his worlds, "I am prayer," it has the same meaning, SINCE MALCHUT IS CALLED BOTH 'I' AND 'PRAYER'. Regarding this IT IS SAID, "You that hear prayer (Heb. *tfilah*)," WHICH IS MALCHUT. This is the hand Tefilin (or Tfilah), of which it is written, "upon your hand" (Shemot 13:16) spelled with Hei IN THE END, AN INDICATION OF MALCHUT.

25. "He shall be brought to the priest"

A Synopsis

The question arises to whom a person should be brought when he has a pain or a plague or an affliction; the 'priest' is said to be God, who can purify the afflicted. And the priest below knows how to rekindle the light when leprosy has closed off the supernal light and stopped the supernal goodness from descending into the world.

135. עָדֶיךָ כָּל בָּשָׂר יָבוֹאוּ. בְּשַׁעְתָא דְגוּפָא שַׁרְיָא בְּצַעֲרָא, בְּמַרְעִין בְּמַכְתָּשִׁין. כד"א וּבָשָׂר כִּי יִהְיֶה בְעוֹרוֹ. אֶת הַנֶּגַע בְּעוֹר הַבָּשָׂר. הַבָּשָׂר הַחַי. ובג"כ לָא כְּתִיב, כָּל רוּחַ יָבֹאוּ, אֶלָּא כָּל בָּשָׂר יָבֹאוּ. מַהוּ עָדֶיךָ. אֶלָּא כְּמָה דְאִתְּמַר, וְהוּבָא אֶל הַכֹּהֵן, דָא הוּא קוּדְשָׁא בְּרִיךְ הוּא. הה"ד, וְאִם יִרְאֶנָּה הַכֹּהֵן. ת"ח, בַּאֲתַר חַד אַהֲרֹן הַכֹּהֵן, וּבְאַתְרָא אָחֳרָא הַכֹּהֵן סְתָם, וְדָא קוּדְשָׁא בְּרִיךְ הוּא.

135. "To You shall all flesh come" (Tehilim 65:3), NAMELY, when the body is in pain, afflictions and plagues, as written, "Or if there be any flesh, in the skin" (Vayikra 13:24), "the plague in the skin of the flesh" (Ibid. 3), and, "the raw flesh" (Ibid. 15). Hence it is not written, 'To You shall all spirit come', but rather, "To You shall all flesh come." What is "to You"? It is as we learned that "he shall be brought to the priest" (Ibid. 9) refers to the Holy One, blessed be He. This is the meaning of, "But if the priest look on it" (Ibid. 21). Come and see, at one place IT IS WRITTEN, "Aaron the priest," while at another just "the priest," NOT MENTIONING AARON. In that case it is the Holy One, blessed be He.

136. א"ר יִצְחָק, וְהָא כְּתִיב נֶגַע צָרַעַת כִּי תִהְיֶה בְּאָדָם וְהוּבָא אֶל הַכֹּהֵן, אִי הָכִי דָא קוּדְשָׁא בְּרִיךְ הוּא. א"ל אִין. בְּגִין דְּבֵיהּ תַּלְיָא כָּל דַּכְיוּתָא וְכָל קְדוּשָׁה. א"ל, אִי הָכִי, אֲמַאי וְהוּבָא, וְהוּעֲלָה מִבָּעֵי לֵיהּ. א"ל, כד"א וְהוּבָא אֶת בַּדָּיו בַּטַּבָּעוֹת, דְּעָיֵיל דָא בְּגוֹ דָא. אוּף הָכָא וְהוּבָא, דְיִכָּנְסוּן לֵיהּ לְכַהֲנָא, לְדַכָּאָה לֵיהּ וְיֵעֲלוּן מִלָּה קַמֵּיהּ.

136. Rabbi Yitzchak said, yet it is written, "When the plague of leprosy is in a man, then he shall be brought to the priest" (Ibid. 9). Is that the Holy One, blessed be He? He said to him, yes, IT IS THE HOLY ONE, BLESSED BE HE, since all matters of purity and holiness come from the Holy One, blessed be He. He said to him, in that case, why IS IT SAID, "he shall be brought"? It should have said, 'raised'. FOR ASCENSION, NOT BRINGING, PERTAINS TO THE HOLY ONE, BLESSED BE HE. He said to him, this resembles the words, "And the poles shall be put into the rings" (Shemot 27:7), WHICH MEANS putting them into each other. Here too, "be brought" MEANS he is brought to the Holy One, blessed be He that is called a priest in order to purify him, like bringing the matter before Him.

137. א"ר יִצְחָק, הָכִי תָּנֵינָן, נֶגַע צָרַעַת. נֶגַע הוּא דִּינָא תַּקִּיפָא שַׁרְיָא בְּעָלְמָא. צָרַעַת: סְגִירוּ. כד"א, סְגִירוּ דִּנְהוֹרָא עִלָּאָה. סְגִירוּ דְּטִיבוּ עִלָּאָה, דְּלָא נָחִית לְעָלְמָא. כִּי תִהְיֶה בְּאָדָם, בְּאָדָם סְתָם. וְהוּבָא אֶל הַכֹּהֵן. דָּא כֹּהֵן דִּלְתַתָּא, דְּהוּא אִתְתָּקַן לְמִפְתַּח הַהוּא סְגִירוּ, וּלְאַדְלָקָא בּוֹצִינַיָא דְּיִשְׁתַּכְחוּ עַל יְדוֹי בִּרְכָן לְעֵילָּא וּלְתַתָּא. וְיִתְעֲבָר וְיִסְתַּלַּק הַהוּא נֶגַע, וְיִשְׁרֵי נְהִירוּ דְּרַחֲמֵי עַל כֹּלָּא, ובג"כ וְהוּבָא אֶל הַכֹּהֵן.

137. Rabbi Yitzchak said, we learned that in "a plague of leprosy," plague MEANS harsh Judgment that rests over the world. Leprosy MEANS closing, as we learned, which is a closing of the supernal light, shutting the supernal goodness from descending into the world. It "is in a man": man in general ALLUDES BOTH TO MAN ABOVE AND MAN BELOW. "he shall be brought to the priest," NAMELY the priest below, who is knowledgeable in opening that closing and kindling the lamps, WHICH ARE THE SFIROT, so that through him there will be blessings above and below, that plague shall be removed and gone, and the light of mercy will dwell on everything. For that reason, "he shall be brought to the priest."

26. "and be holy"

A Synopsis

We learn here of the proper time for mating for those who study the Torah, and that is midnight on Shabbat when God walks with the righteous in the Garden of Eden. People are holy only by association with their God; if they draw away from Him they lose their holiness and draw upon themselves souls from the side of the Evil Inclination. The priest can recognize peoples' sins by the blemishes that show they come from the Other Side.

138. אָמַר רִבִּי אַבָּא, חֲמֵינָא לְאִינְהוּ בְּנֵי עָלְמָא, דְּלָא מַשְׁגִּחָן, וְלָא יַדְעִין בִּיקָרָא דְּמָארֵיהוֹן, כְּתִיב בְּהוּ בְּיִשְׂרָאֵל, אֲשֶׁר הִבְדַּלְתִּי אֶתְכֶם מִן הָעַמִּים לִהְיוֹת לִי. וּכְתִיב, וְהִתְקַדִּשְׁתֶּם וִהְיִיתֶם קְדוֹשִׁים כִּי קָדוֹשׁ אָנִי יְיָ'. אִי אִינּוּן מִתְרַחֲקָן, אָן הוּא קְדוּשָׁה דִּלְהוֹן, הָא רְעוּתָא דִּלְהוֹן אִתְרַחֲקַת מִנֵּיה. וּקְרָא אַכְרִיז וְאָמַר, אַל תִּהְיוּ כְּסוּס כְּפֶרֶד אֵין הָבִין, בַּמָּה אִתְפָּרְשָׁן בְּנֵי נָשָׁא מִסּוּס וָפֶרֶד, בִּקְדוּשָׁה דְּגַרְמַיְיהוּ, לְאִשְׁתַּכְּחָא שְׁלֵימִין וּרְשִׁימִין מִכֹּלָּא.

138. Rabbi Aba said, I see that the people in the world do not observe or know the glory of their Master. It is written, of Yisrael, "and have separated you from the peoples, that you should be Mine" (Vayikra 20:26), and, "Sanctify yourselves therefore, and be holy, for I am Hashem your Elohim" (Ibid. 7). But if they draw far FROM THE HOLY ONE, BLESSED BE HE, where is their holiness, if their wish is distanced from Him? The verse declares, "Be not like the horse, or the mule, which have no understanding" (Tehilim 32:9). For people are different from a horse and a mule only by their holiness, so as to be whole and distinguished more than everything.

139. וְעַ"ד זוּוּגָא דִּבְנֵי נָשָׁא הוּא בְּזִמְנִין יְדִיעָן, לְכַוְּונָא רְעוּתָא לְאִתְדַּבְּקָא בֵּיה בְּקוּדְשָׁא בְּרִיךְ הוּא. וְהָא אִתְּעָרוּ, בְּפַלְגוּת לֵילְיָא קוּדְשָׁא בְּרִיךְ הוּא עָאל בְּגִנְתָא דְּעֵדֶן, לְאִשְׁתַּעְשְׁעָא עִם צַדִּיקַיָּיא, וְכִ"י מְשַׁבְּחַת לֵיה לְקוּדְשָׁא בְּרִיךְ הוּא, וְהִיא שַׁעֲתָא דִּרְעוּתָא לְאִתְדַּבְּקָא בְּהוּ.

139. Therefore people mate at specific times so as to direct their will to cleave to the Holy One, blessed be He. It has been remarked that at midnight the Holy One, blessed be He, enters the Garden of Eden to delight Himself with the righteous, and the Congregation of Yisrael, WHICH IS MALCHUT, praises the Holy One, blessed be He. It is a favorable time to cleave to them, TO THE HOLY ONE, BLESSED BE HE AND HIS SHECHINAH.

140. וְחַבְרַיָּיא דְּמִשְׁתַּדְּלֵי בְּאוֹרַיְיתָא, מִשְׁתַּתְּפֵי בָּהּ בכנ"י, לְשַׁבְּחָא לְמַלְכָּא קַדִּישָׁא, וְאִתְעַסְּקָן בְּאוֹרַיְיתָא, שְׁאָר בְּנֵי נָשָׁא כְּדֵין עִידָן רְעוּתָא לְאִתְקַדְּשָׁא בִּקְדוּשָׁה דְּקוּדְשָׁא בְּרִיךְ הוּא, וּלְכַוְּונָא רְעוּתָא לְאִתְדַּבְּקָא בֵּיהּ. וְאִינּוּן חַבְרַיָּיא דְּמִשְׁתַּדְּלֵי בְּאוֹרַיְיתָא זִוּוּגָא דִּלְהוֹן בְּשַׁעֲתָא דְּזִוּוּגָא אַחֲרָא אִשְׁתְּכַח, וְהַאי מְשַׁבְּת לְשַׁבְּת לְכַוְּונָא רְעוּתָא לְאִתְדַּבְּקָא בֵּיהּ בְּקוּדְשָׁא בְּרִיךְ הוּא וּבִכְנֶסֶת יִשְׂרָאֵל, דְּהוּא עִידָן רְעוּתָא דְּמִתְבָּרְכָן כֹּלָּא עִלָּאֵי וְתַתָּאֵי.

140. The friends who are engaged in Torah unite with the Congregation of Yisrael in praising the Holy One, blessed be He, and they are occupied with the Torah. For other people it is a favorable time to be sanctified with the holiness of the Holy One, blessed be He, NAMELY BY MATING, and direct their wishes to cleave to Him. The friends who are occupied with the Torah, the time for them to mate is when another, SUPERNAL union takes place. This occurs on Shabbat, so as to direct one's desire to cleave to the Holy One, blessed be He and the Congregation of Yisrael. For it is a time of goodwill when everything, the higher and lower, are blessed.

141. אִי בְּנֵי נָשָׁא אִתְרַחֲקוּ מִנֵּיהּ, וְעַבְדָן כִּבְעִירֵי, אָן הוּא קְדוּשָׁה דִּלְהוֹן, לְאִשְׁתַּכְּחָא קַדִּישִׁין. אָן אִינּוּן נַפְשָׁאן קַדִּישִׁין דְּמַשְׁכָן מֵעֵילָּא. וּשְׁלֹמֹה מַלְכָּא צָוַוח וְאָמַר, גַּם בְּלֹא דַעַת נֶפֶשׁ לֹא טוֹב. גַּם בְּלֹא דַעַת, מַאן הוּא דַעַת. דָּא קוּדְשָׁא בְּרִיךְ הוּא. נֶפֶשׁ לֹא טוֹב, דָּא הוּא נֶפֶשׁ, דְּאִינּוּן מַשְׁכִין בְּעוֹבָדַיְיהוּ, לֹא טוֹב, דְּהָא מִסִּטְרָא אַחֲרָא אִתְמַשְּׁכָאן עֲלַיְיהוּ נַפְשָׁתָא דְּלָאו אִיהוּ טוֹב, בְּגִין דְּלָא מְכַוְּונֵי לְבַיְיהוּ לְקוּדְשָׁא בְּרִיךְ הוּא.

-89-

141. If people keep away from the Holy One, blessed be He and conduct themselves like animals, where is their holiness to make them holy? Where are their holy souls, which they draw from above? King Solomon cries out, saying, "Also, that the soul be without knowledge is not good" (Mishlei 19:2). In, "without knowledge," knowledge refers to the Holy One, blessed be He. "...the soul...is not good" refers to the soul they draw by their deed. It is "not good" since that soul comes to them from the Other Side, which is not good, since they do not direct their heart towards the Holy One, blessed be He.

142. מַאן דְּאִתְלָהִיט בְּיֵצֶר הָרָע, בְּלָא רְעוּתָא וְכַוָּונָה דְּלִבָּא לְקוּדְשָׁא בְּרִיךְ הוּא. מִסִּטְרָא דְּיֵצֶר הָרָע אִתְמְשַׁךְ עָלֵיהּ נַפְשָׁא, דְּלָאו אִיהִי טוֹב, הה"ד גַּם בְּלָא דַעַת נֶפֶשׁ לֹא טוֹב וְאָץ בְּרַגְלַיִם חוֹטֵא. מַאן דְּאִיהוּ אָץ בְּרַגְלַיִם וְדָחֵי שַׁעֲתָא בְּלָא רְעוּתָא קַדִּישָׁא, חוֹטֵא. חוֹטֵא וַדַּאי, בְּכֹלָּא.

142. Whoever gets hot with the Evil Inclination, without directing his desire and heart toward the Holy One, blessed be He, THEN a soul that is not good is drawn upon him from the side of the Evil Inclination. This is the meaning of, "Also, that the soul be without knowledge is not good." "and he that hastens with his feet sins" (Ibid.). Whoever hastens with the feet and precipitates matters, THAT IS, DOES NOT WAIT UNTIL THE TIME IS PROPER, BUT IS without a holy wish, sins. Assuredly he sins in every way.

143. וְעַל דָּא שַׁרְיָין מַכְתְּשִׁין בִּישִׁין בִּבְנֵי נָשָׁא, וְאַסְהִידוּ בְּאַנְפַּיְיהוּ בַּחֲצִיפוּתָא דִּלְהוֹן, לְאַחֲזָאָה דְּהָא קוּדְשָׁא בְּרִיךְ הוּא מָאִיס בְּהוּ, וְלָאו דַּעְתֵּיהּ בְּהוֹן, עַד דְּאִינּוּן זַכָּאן וּמַכְשְׁרָאן עוֹבְדַיְיהוּ כְּמִלְּקַדְמִין, וּמִתְבָּרְכָן. וְע"ד אִשְׁתְּמוֹדְעָן מַכְתְּשִׁין לְגַבֵּי כַּהֲנָא, אִינּוּן דְּאַתְיָין מִסִּטְרָא דִּמְסָאֲבָא, וְאִינּוּן דְּאַתְיָין מִסִּטְרָא אַחֲרָא.

143. For that reason evil plagues dwell in people and testify on their faces to their impudence, to show that the Holy One, blessed be He, rejects them and does not pay attention to them until they are worthy and better their deeds as before. For that reason the priest recognizes that the plagues come from the side of impurity and that they come from the Other Side.

27. Plagues of houses

A Synopsis

We learn that when Yisrael came into the land of Canaan, they demolished the houses that had plague in them, and then found treasures hidden there. Rabbi Shimon talks about how the words uttered over a work in progress bring the spirit of holiness or the spirit of defilement over it. By breaking down the contaminated houses, the land was sanctified as before and the spirit of impurity was removed. Then Yisrael dwelled in holiness with the Shechinah among them.

144. כְּגַוְונָא דָּא כְּתִיב, כִּי תָבֹאוּ אֶל אֶרֶץ כְּנַעַן וְגו', וְנָתַתִּי נֶגַע צָרַעַת בְּבֵית אֶרֶץ אֲחוּזַּתְכֶם. וְכִי אֲגַר טַב הוּא, דְּיִשְׁתְּכַח בְּאִינּוּן דְּזַכָּאן לְמֵיעַל בְּאַרְעָא. אֶלָּא הָא אוּקְמוּהָ לְאַשְׁכְּחָא מַטְמוֹנִין דְּאַטְמִירָן בְּבֵיתַיְיהוּ, וּלְאַהֲנָאָה לוֹן לְיִשְׂרָאֵל.

144. Similarly, it is written, "When you come into the land of Canaan...and I put the plague of leprosy in the house of the land of your possession" (Vayikra 14:34). HE ASKS, what is the good reward in finding PLAGUES IN THE HOUSES OF those of were worthy of entering the land? AND HE ANSWERS, it has been explained that it is THAT AFTER THEY WILL DEMOLISH THE CONTAMINATED HOUSES, they will find treasures THE CANAANITES have hidden in their houses and Yisrael will benefit from them.

145. אֲבָל ת"ח, זַכָּאִין אִינּוּן יִשְׂרָאֵל, דְּאִינּוּן מִתְדַּבְּקָן בֵּיהּ בְּקוּדְשָׁא בְּרִיךְ הוּא, וְקוּדְשָׁא בְּרִיךְ הוּא רָחִים לְהוּ, דִּכְתִיב אָהַבְתִּי אֶתְכֶם אָמַר יְיָ'. וּמִגּוֹ רְחִימוּתָא דִּילֵיהּ, אָעֵיל לְהוּ לְאַרְעָא קַדִּישָׁא, לְאַשְׁרָאָה שְׁכִינְתֵּיהּ בֵּינַיְיהוּ, וּלְמֶהֱוֵי דִּיּוּרֵיהּ עִמְּהוֹן, וְיִשְׂרָאֵל דְּיִשְׁתַּכְּחוּן קַדִּישִׁין עַל כָּל בְּנֵי עָלְמָא.

145. Yet come and see, happy are Yisrael to be cleaving to the Holy One, blessed be He. And the Holy One, blessed be He loves them as written, "I have loved you, says Hashem" (Malachi 1:2). In His love, He brought them into the holy land, to cause His Shechinah to rest among them and to dwell among them, so that Yisrael will be holier than all the inhabitants of the world.

146. ת״ח, כְּתִיב וְכָל הַנָּשִׁים אֲשֶׁר נָשָׂא לִבָּן וְגוֹ׳. בְּשַׁעֲתָא דַּהֲווֹ עַבְדִּין עֲבִידְתָּא, הֲווֹ אַמְרֵי, דָּא לְמַקְדְּשָׁא. דָּא לְמַשְׁכְּנָא. דָּא לְפָרוֹכְתָּא. וְכֵן כָּל אִינּוּן אוּמָנִין בְּגִין דְּיִשְׁרֵי קְדוּשָׁה עַל יְדַיְיהוּ, וְאִתְקַדַּשׁ הַהוּא עֲבִידְתָּא. וְכַד סָלִיק לְאַתְרֵיה, בִּקְדוּשָׁה סָלִיק.

146. Come and see, it is written, "And all the women whose heart stirred them…" (Shemot 35:26), THAT IS, when they were doing their work they used to say, this is for the Temple, this is for the tabernacle, that is for the curtain. All the craftsmen DID the same, so that holiness shall dwell on their efforts and that workmanship shall be sanctified. When they brought it to its place it turned into AND WAS IN holiness.

147. כְּגַוְונָא דָּא מַאן דְּעָבֵיד עֲבִידְתָּא לע״ז, אוֹ לִסְטְרָא אָחֳרָא, דְּלָא קַדִּישָׁא. כֵּיוָן דְּאִדְכַּר לֵיה עַל הַהוּא עֲבִידְתָּא, הָא רוּחַ מְסָאֲבָא שַׁרְיָא עֲלוֹי, וְכַד סָלִיק עֲבִידְתָּא, בִּמְסָאֲבָא סָלִיק. כְּנַעֲנִים פַּלְחֵי לע״ז אִינְהוּ, וּמִתְדַּבְּקָן כֻּלְּהוּ כַּחֲדָא בְּרוּחַ מְסָאֲבָא בע״ז, וַהֲווֹ בִּנְיָין בָּנְיָין לְפַרְצוּפַיְיהוּ וּלְגִעוּלַיְיהוּ לִסְטַר מְסָאֲבָא לע״ז, וְכַד שָׁרָאן לְמִבְנֵי, הֲווֹ אַמְרֵי מִלָּה, וְכֵיוָן דְּאִתְדְּכַר בְּפוּמַיְיהוּ, סָלִיק עֲלֵיה רוּחַ מְסָאֲבָא. כַּד אִסְתָּלִיק עֲבִידְתָּא, בְּרוּחַ מְסָאֲבָא אִסְתָּלִיק.

147. In the same way, whoever creates something for idol worship or for another, unholy side, once he mentions it in regard to that work, the spirit of defilement dwells on it. As the work progresses, it does so in impurity. The Canaanites were idol worshippers and used to build edifices for sculptures of their faces and for their abominations on the side of impurity, for the purpose of idol worship. When they started building, they used to say something. Once it was uttered, the spirit of impurity rose over the building. As the work progressed, it did so by the spirit of impurity.

148. כֵּיוָן דְּעָאלוּ יִשְׂרָאֵל לְאַרְעָא, בָּעָא קוּדְשָׁא בְּרִיךְ הוּא לְדַכְּאָה לוֹן, וּלְקַדְּשָׁא לוֹן אַרְעָא, וּלְאַפְנָאָה אֲתַר לִשְׁכִינְתָּא דְּלָא תִּשְׁרֵי שְׁכִינְתָּא גּוֹ מְסָאֲבָא. וְעַ״ד בְּהַהוּא נֶגַע צָרַעַת, הֲווֹ סָתְרִין בִּנְיָינִין

דְּאָעִין וַאֲבָנִין דְּאִתְעֲבֵידוּ בִּמְסָאֲבוּ.

148. Once they entered the land of Yisrael, the Holy One, blessed be He, wanted to purify and sanctify the land for them, and make room for the Shechinah, so that the Shechinah will not dwell on an impure place. Hence, by that plague of leprosy they would demolish the buildings of wood and stone made in impurity.

149. ת"ח, אִי עוֹבָדָא דָא הֲוָה לְאַשְׁכְּחָא מַטְמוֹנִין בִּלְחוֹדוֹי, יְהַדְרוּן אֲבָנִין לְבָתַר כְּמָה דְּאִינּוּן לְאַתְרַיְיהוּ, וְעַפְרָא לְאַתְרֵיהּ. אֲבָל קְרָא כְּתִיב, וְחִלְּצוּ אֶת הָאֲבָנִים. וּכְתִיב וְעָפָר אַחֵר יִקַּח. בְּגִין דְּיִתְעֲבַר רוּחַ מְסָאֲבָא, וְיִתְפְּנֵי וְיִתְקַדַּשׁ הַשָּׁתָא כְּמִלְּקַדְמִין, וְיִשְׁתְּכְחוּ יִשְׂרָאֵל בִּקְדוּשָׁה, וּבְדִיּוּרָא קַדִּישָׁא, לְמִשְׁרֵי בֵּינַיְיהוּ שְׁכִינְתָּא.

149. Come and see, if this action OF BREAKING DOWN THE CONTAMINATED HOUSES was done for the sake of finding treasures alone, they would have to return the stones back into place as they were and ALSO TO RETURN the dust to its place. Yet scripture says, "they take away the stones" (Vayikra 14:40), and, "he shall take other mortar" (Ibid. 42). Thus the spirit of impurity will be removed and taken out, and THE LAND shall be sanctified as before and Yisrael will dwell in holiness, in holy habitation, so the Shechinah will dwell among them.

28. "Woe to him that builds his house by unrighteousness"

A Synopsis

We are told that whoever builds a building must start by saying that he is doing it for the worship of God, and then the peace of heaven will rest on it. Anyone who builds a house dedicated to the other side will be punished by that house before he dies, and others who live in it may come to harm. God marked the houses in Canaan by the plague so that Yisrael would know which houses were cursed.

150. וְעַל דָּא מַאן דְּבָנֵי בִּנְיָן כַּד שָׁארֵי לְמִבְנֵי, בָּעֵי לְאַדְכְּרָא בְּפוּמֵיהּ, דְּהָא לְפוּלְחָנָא דְּקוּדְשָׁא בְּרִיךְ הוּא הוּא בָּנֵי. בְּגִין דִּכְתִיב הוֹי בּוֹנֶה בֵיתוֹ בְּלֹא צֶדֶק וְגוֹ', וּכְדֵין סִיַּיעְתָּא דִּשְׁמַיָּא שָׁארֵי עֲלוֹי, וְקוּדְשָׁא בְּרִיךְ הוּא זַמִין עֲלֵיהּ קְדוּשָׁתָא, וְקָארֵי עֲלֵיהּ שָׁלוֹם, הה"ד וְיָדַעְתָּ כִּי שָׁלוֹם אָהֳלֶךָ וְגוֹ'. מַהוּ וּפָקַדְתָּ נָוְךָ, הָא אוּקְמוּהָ, אֲבָל וּפָקַדְתָּ, לְאַפְקְדָא מִלָּה בְּפוּמָא כַּד אִיהוּ בָּנֵי. וּכְדֵין וְלֹא תֶחֱטָא כְּתִיב. וְאִי לָאו הָא זַמִין לְבֵיתֵיהּ סִטְרָא אָחֳרָא.

150. Therefore, whoever builds a building, before starting, should utter by mouth that he does so for the worship of the Holy One, blessed be He, since it is written, "Woe to him that builds his house by unrighteousness" (Yirmeyah 22:13). Then help from heaven rests on it, ON THE HOUSE, and the Holy One, blessed be He, readies His sanctity upon it and calls it peace. This is the meaning of, "And you shall know that your tent is at peace; AND YOU SHALL VISIT YOUR HABITATION, AND MISS (OR: 'SIN') NOTHING" (Iyov 5:24). What is meant by, "and you shall visit your habitation"? It has been explained, yet, "visit" MEANS to visit by mouth when building, NAMELY, TO SAY WITH HIS MOUTH THAT HE BUILDS IT TO SERVE THE HOLY ONE, BLESSED BE HE. Then it is written, "and sin nothing." Otherwise, the Other Side is ready TO DWELL on his house.

151. כ"ש, מַאן דְּבָנֵי וּרְעוּתֵיהּ בְּגַוְונָא אָחֳרָא, בְּגִין דִּמְיַחֵד בֵּיתָא לְסִטְרָא אָחֳרָא, לְאַסְתַּאֲבָא בֵּיהּ. הָא וַדַּאי שַׁרְיָא בֵּיהּ רוּחַ מְסָאֲבָא, וְלָא נָפִיק הַהוּא ב"נ מֵעָלְמָא, עַד דְּאִתְעֲנַשׁ בְּהַהוּא בֵּיתָא, וּמַאן דְּדָיְיר בֵּיהּ, יָכִיל לְאִתְזְקָא, דְּהָא הַהוּא דִּירָה רוּחַ מְסָאֲבָא שַׁרְיָא בֵּיהּ, וְאָזִיק מַאן דְּאִשְׁתְּכַח בֵּיהּ.

151. This is more so for whoever builds with his wish directed in a different way, in dedicating his house to the other side to be defiled by it. Surely the spirit of defilement rests on that man and he is punished by that house before he dies. Whoever lives in it may come to harm, since the spirit of defilement rests in that abode and harms whoever is in it.

152. וְאִי תֵּימָא בְּמַה יְדִיעַ. כְּגוֹן דְּאִתְּזַק בְּהַהוּא בֵּיתָא, הַהוּא דְּבָנֵי לָהּ, אוֹ אַנְשֵׁי בֵּיתֵיהּ, אוֹ בְּנִזְקֵי דְּגוּפָא, אוֹ בְּנִזְקֵי מָמוֹנָא, הוּא וּתְרֵין אָחֳרָנִין אֲבַתְרֵיהּ. הָא וַדַּאי יַעֲרוֹק ב"נ לְטוּרָא, וְלָא יָדוּר בֵּיהּ. יָדוּר בְּטִיחֲלָא דְּעַפְרָא, וְלָא יָדוּר בֵּיהּ.

152. You may ask, how is it made known WHETHER THE BUILDER DREW ON IT THE SPIRIT OF DEFILEMENT? If whoever built it came to harm in that house, or any of his household, whether in body or finance, AND ALSO two NEIGHBORS after him WHO DWELT THERE. One should run into the mountain rather than live in it, dwell in an earthen cave rather than live in it.

153. וּבְגִין כַּךְ, קוּדְשָׁא בְּרִיךְ הוּא חָס עָלַיְיהוּ דְּיִשְׂרָאֵל, דְּאִינּוּן לָא יַדְעִין מִלָּה בְּכָל אִינּוּן בָּתֵּי. וְהוּא אָמַר, אַתּוּן לָא יַדְעִין, אֲנָא יְדַעְנָא, וְאַרְשִׁימְנָא לוֹן בְּנִגְעָא. נֶגַע דְּיַיר בְּבֵיתָא, הָא נֶגַע אָחֳרָא תַּקִּיפָא, דְּיַפִּיק לֵיהּ, וְיַעֲבַּר לֵיהּ מִן עָלְמָא. וּכְדֵין וְנָתַץ אֶת הַבַּיִת אֶת אֲבָנָיו וְאֶת עֵצָיו. כֵּיוָן דְּאָזִיל לֵיהּ, מַאי טַעֲמָא וְנָתַץ אֶת הַבַּיִת. אֶלָּא בְּכָל זִמְנָא דְּהַהוּא בִּנְיָן לֶהֱוֵי קַיָּים, דִּילֵיהּ הוּא, וְיָכִיל לְאַהֲדָרָא.

153. For that reason, the Holy One, blessed be He, took pity on Yisrael, who did not know at all about those houses THEY FOUND IN THE LAND, WHETHER THE SPIRIT OF IMPURITY WAS THERE OR NOT. The Holy One, blessed be He, said, even if you do not know, I do know and I shall mark them by a plague. If a plague rests in the house, WHICH IS THE OTHER SIDE, behold another powerful plague THAT I SENT THERE to take it out and destroy it. Then, "And he shall break down the house, the stones of it, and its timber" (Vayikra 14:45). HE ASKS, once THE PLAGUE is gone BECAUSE OF THE OTHER PLAGUE THAT BROUGHT IT OUT, why "break down the house," SEEING THAT THE OTHER SIDE HAS ALREADY LEFT?

HE ANSWERS, as long as the house stands, it is his, OF THE OTHER SIDE, who can return.

29. "And he shall break down the house"

A Synopsis

Rabbi Yosi once entered a house, and then heard a voice saying he would be harmed; he left in fear. Rabbi Chiya wonders why the idol worshippers who live in that house are not harmed, and Rabbi Yosi says it is because they are all from the other side and it will not harm them. We also learn that the wicked can dwell safely in a house that was built on righteousness.

154. הַאי בְּאַרְעָא קַדִּישָׁא, כ"ש בְּאַרְעָא אָחֳרָא, דִּזְמִינָא רוּחַ מְסָאֲבָא יַתִּיר, וְיָכִיל ב"נ לְאִתְזְקָא. א"ר אֶלְעָזָר, וכ"ש דְּאִקְרֵי בְּקִלְפּוֹי דְּחַבְרוֹי אָחֳרָנִין, לְאִשְׁתַּכְּחָא תַּמָּן, וַאֲפִילוּ טוּרְפֵי דְּקַסְפְּתָא לָא מַעְבְּרָן לֵיה מֵהַהוּא בֵּיתָא, ובג"כ הַאי קְרָא אַכְרִיז וְאָמַר, הוֹי בּוֹנֶה בֵיתוֹ בְּלֹא צֶדֶק. הוֹי וַדַּאי קָאָמְרֵי כָּל יוֹמָא בְּהַהִיא בֵּיתָא.

154. This applies to the holy land and all the more so to other lands, where the spirit of impurity is more prevalent IN THOSE HOUSES and people might come to harm FROM IT. Rabbi Elazar said, moreover, THE SPIRIT OF IMPURITY THAT IS THERE calls to its other friends and Klipot to be there. Even knocking on vessels, WHICH WAS DONE TO EXORCISE SPIRITS AND DEMONS FROM A PLACE does not remove THE DEMONS from that house. For that reason scripture says, "Woe to him that builds his house by unrighteousness" (Yirmeyah 22:13). THE DWELLERS in this house surely recite THIS VERSE daily.

155. ר' יוֹסֵי עָאל חַד יוֹמָא בְּחַד בֵּיתָא, מָטָא בְּסִפְּתָא, עָאל לְגוֹ. שָׁמַע חַד קָלָא דְּאָמַר, אִתְכְּנָשׁוּ עוּלוּ, הָא חַד פְּלוּגְתָּא דִּילָן. סִיפָתוּ וְנַנְזִיק לֵיה עַד לָא יִנְפּוֹק, אָמְרוּ, לָא נֵיכוּל אֶלָּא אִי דִּיּוּרֵיה הָכָא. נָפַק ר' יוֹסֵי וְדָחִיל. אָמַר, וַדַּאי מַאן דְּאַעְבַּר עַל מִלּוֹי דְּחַבְרַיָּיא, אִתְחַיָּיב בְּנַפְשֵׁיה.

155. One day Rabbi Yosi entered a certain house. He reached the threshold, COMPOSED HIMSELF, and entered into the house. He heard a voice saying, Gather round, here is one of our dissenters. Let us take him and harm him before he leaves. They said to it, we cannot HARM HIM unless he lived here.

Rabbi Yosi went out in fear. He said, surely whoever transgresses the words of the friends risks his life.

156. אָ"ל ר' חִיָּיא, וְהָא גּוֹיִם וּשְׁאָר בְּנֵי נָשָׁא דַּיְירֵי בְּגַוֵּיה, וְאִשְׁתְּלִימוּ. אָ"ל, אִינּוּן מִסְּטְרַיְיהוּ קָא אַתְיָין, אֲבָל מַאן דְּדָחִיל חַטָּאָה, יָכִיל לְאִתְזְקָא. וַאֲפִילוּ אִינּוּן, אִי יְעַכְּבוּ דִּיּוּרֵיהוֹן בֵּיה, לָא יִפְקוּן בִּשְׁלָם. אָ"ל, וְהָא כְּתִיב בָּתֵּיהֶם שָׁלוֹם מִפָּחַד. אָ"ל כְּגוֹן דַּהֲוָה מֵאָחֳרָא, וְאִתְבְּנֵי מִצֶּדֶק. וּקְרָא הָכִי הוּא, בָּתֵּיהֶם שָׁלוֹם מִפָּחַד, כְּשֶׁבָּתֵּיהֶם שָׁלוֹם מִפָּחַד שֵׁבֶט אֱלוֹהַּ לָא שַׁרְיָא עֲלֵיהֶם.

156. Rabbi Chiya said to him, but idol worshippers and other people live in that house, yet they are well, UNHARMED. He said to him, they come from their side AND ARE THEREFORE NOT HARMED BY THEM. But whoever fears sin might come to harm. Even they, if they continue to live in it, do not leave in peace. He said to him, yet it is written, "Their houses are safe without fear" (Iyov 21:9). He said to him, this means THE HOUSE came from another who built it in righteousness, AND THE WICKED TOOK IT AND DWELT IN IT. The verse is as follows, "Their houses are safe without fear," namely, when "Their houses are safe without fear," BECAUSE THEY WERE BUILT ON RIGHTEOUSNESS, THEN the rod of Eloha is not upon them.

30. The plague and the spirit of defilement are opposites

A Synopsis

We are told that when the plague enters a house the spirit of defilement appears and they fight each other. The priest is then told about the plague, and he comes and demolishes the house. Rabbi Yehuda says that Yisrael received wealth twice, once when they left Egypt and again when they entered the land, by breaking down the contaminated houses. Lastly, Rabbi Yosi talks about the bright white spot that is sometimes found in the flesh of a person, and Rabbi Yitzchak says there are 300 arguments that may be derived from the intensely bright spot.

157. וּבָא אֲשֶׁר לוֹ הַבַּיִת וְהִגִּיד וְגוֹ'. וְהִגִּיד, וַיֹּאמֶר מִבָּעֵי לֵיהּ, אוֹ וַיְדַבֵּר, מַהוּ וְהִגִּיד. אֶלָּא בְּכָל אֲתַר מִלָּה דְּחָכְמְתָא הוּא, וְהָא אוּקְמוּהָ. כְּנֶגַע נִרְאָה לִי בַּבַּיִת, כְּנֶגַע, נֶגַע מִבָּעֵי לֵיהּ. נִרְאָה לִי, יֵשׁ לִי מִבָּעֵי לֵיהּ. דְּהָא כְּתִיב, וְנָתַתִּי נֶגַע צָרַעַת בְּבֵית אֶרֶץ אֲחֻזַּתְכֶם, דְּיִתְחֲזֵי לְכֹלָּא. אֲמַאי כְּנֶגַע נִרְאָה לִי.

157. "and he that owns the house shall come and tell" (Vayikra 14:35). HE ASKS, IT SAYS, "and tell." It should have said, 'said', or 'speak'. Why "tell"? AND HE ANSWERS, this always alludes to a matter of wisdom, and it has been explained. "It seems to me there is as it were a plague in the house" (Ibid.). HE SAYS, "as it were a plague" should have been just "a plague." HE SAYS, "It seems to me there is" should have been 'there is', as written, "I put the plague of leprosy in a house of the land of your possession" (Ibid. 34), WHICH MEANS it will be visible to everyone. Why DOES HE SAY, "It seems to me there is as it were a plague"?

158. אֶלָּא בְּשַׁעֲתָא דְּהַאי עָיֵיל, אָחֳרָא אִתְגַּלְיָא. וּמְקַטְרְגָא דָּא בְּדָא. וְעַ"ד נִרְאָה לִי, הַהוּא דְּאִתְכַּסֵּי אִתְגַּלְיָא, וּדְאִתְגַּלְיָא אִתְכַּסֵּי, וּלְבָתַר מִתְחֲזֵי לֵיהּ בְּדִיּוּקְנָא דְּהַהוּא נֶגַע דְּבֵיתָא, וְאִתְכַּסְיָא אָחֳרָא. וְעַל דָּא וְהִגִּיד לַכֹּהֵן, דְּמִלָּה דְּחָכְמְתָא הִיא.

158. AND HE ANSWERS, when the one, THE PLAGUE, enters THE HOUSE, the other appears, THE SPIRIT OF DEFILEMENT THAT RESIDED IN THE

HOUSE, and they fight each other. Hence HE SAID, "It seems to me," FOR IT WAS SEEN TO ME AT FIRST. For the one hidden, THE SPIRIT OF DEFILEMENT THAT USED TO HIDE UPON THE COMING OF THE PLAGUE, was exposed, and the one exposed, THE PLAGUE, hid. Later it assumed a form as that plague WAS SEEN in the house and the other was hidden, THE SPIRIT OF DEFILEMENT. Hence IT IS WRITTEN, "tell the priest" (Ibid. 35), for it is a matter of wisdom, AS TELLING INDICATES WISDOM.

159. וּכְדֵין אָתֵי כַּהֲנָא, וְיִרְמוּן בֵּיתָא, וְיִנְתְּצוּן לֵיהּ אַבְנִין וְאָעִין וְכֹלָּא. כֵּיוָן דְּאִנְתְּצָן וְאִתְדְּכָן כֹּלָּא, מִתְבָּרְכָאן, כְּדֵין כְּתִיב, וּבָתִּים טוֹבִים תִּבְנֶה וְיָשָׁבְתָּ. אִלֵּין אִקְּרוּן טוֹבִים, דְּהָא קַדְמָאֵי לָאו אִינוּן טוֹבִים, וְלָאו בִּכְלָלָא דִּקְדוּשָׁה וְדַכְיוּ נִינְהוּ.

159. The priest then comes, and they demolish the house and break it down, the wood, stones and the rest. Once they broke it and were purified in every way, they are blessed. Then it is written, "and have built goodly houses, and dwelt in them" (Devarim 8:12), WHICH MEANS THEY WILL BUILD THEM RIGHTEOUSLY. These are called goodly houses, because the earlier ones were not good, not pertaining to the holy and the pure.

160. א"ר יְהוּדָה, אִי הָכִי בְּמַאי מוּקְמֵינָן קְרָא דִּכְתִיב, וּבָתִּים מְלֵאִים כָּל טוּב אֲשֶׁר לֹא מִלֵּאתָ. אִי רוּחַ מְסָאֲבָא שַׁרְיָא בְּגַוַּויְיהוּ הֵיךְ מְלֵאִים כָּל טוּב. א"ר אֶלְעָזָר, מְלֵאִים כָּל טוּב: בְּמָמוֹנָא, בְּכַסְפָּא, וּבְדַהֲבָא, וּבְכֹלָּא. כד"א כִּי טוּב כָּל אֶרֶץ מִצְרַיִם. וא"ר יְהוּדָה, וְהָא כָּל בָּתֵּי דְּמִצְרָאֵי, מַלְיָין חַרְשִׁין וְטַעֲוָון הֲווֹ. אֶלָּא בְּגִין עוּתְרָא דְּאַרְעָא אִתְּמַר. אוּף הָכָא בְּגִין עוּתְרָא וּמָמוֹנָא הוּא.

160. Rabbi Yehuda said, in that case, how can we explain the verse, "houses full of all good things, which you did not fill" (Devarim 6:11). If the spirit of defilement rests in them, how can they be filled with goodness? Rabbi Elazar said, they are filled with good things, money, silver and gold and everything, as written, "for the good of all the land of Egypt" (Beresheet 45:20). Rabbi Yehuda also said, yet all the houses in Egypt were filled with witchcraft and items of idolatry. HOW CAN THE VERSE SAY "FOR THE

GOOD OF ALL THE LAND OF EGYPT"? It was said, "FOR THE GOOD..." because of the wealth of the land. Here too, due to the wealth and money IT SPEAKS OF "HOUSES FULL OF ALL GOOD THINGS."

161. תְּרֵין עוּתְרִין נַטְלוּ יִשְׂרָאֵל, חַד כַּד נָפְקוּ מִגָּלוּתָא דְמִצְרַיִם. וְחַד כַּד עָאלוּ לְאַרְעָא. ר' שִׁמְעוֹן אָמַר, כָּל דָּא וַדַּאי הֲוָה לְאִתְקַדְּשָׁא אַרְעָא, וּלְאַעְבְּרָא רוּחַ מִסְאֲבָא מֵאַרְעָא, וּמִגּוֹ יִשְׂרָאֵל. וְכַד בֵּיתָא הֲוָה נָתִיץ, הֲוָה אִשְׁתְּכַח בָּה מָמוֹנָא, לְמִבְנֵי לֵיהּ, וּלְמַלְיָא בֵּיתֵיהּ, בְּגִין דְּלָא יִצְטַעֵר עַל בֵּיתָא, וְיִשְׁרוּן בְּדִיּוּרָא דִקְדוּשָׁה.

161. Yisrael received two TIMES wealth, once when they left Egypt and one when they entered the land, BY BREAKING DOWN THE CONTAMINATED HOUSES. Rabbi Shimon said, the purpose of all these PLAGUES IN THE HOUSES was to sanctify the land and remove the spirit of defilement from the land and from Yisrael. IN ADDITION, when one broke down a house, he would find a treasure in it SUFFICIENT to rebuild and fill his house, so he will not be sorry for the house THAT WAS BROKEN DOWN, and they will dwell in a holy habitation.

162. וְאִישׁ אוֹ אִשָּׁה כִּי יִהְיֶה בְעוֹר וְגוֹ'. ר' יוֹסֵי אָמַר, בְּסִילְתָּא דְמוּקְפֵי בְּבַהֶרֶת עַזָּה, חֵיזוּ תְּנֵינָא, וּבְחֵיזוּ אִתְדָּן, בְּאִינוּן גַּוְונִין. א"ר יִצְחָק ש' טַעֲמֵי אִית מַאן דְּגָרִיס בְּבַהֶרֶת עַזָּה. וְכֻלְּהוּ אוֹלִיפְנָא מֵהָכָא, בַּר חֵיזוּר חַד סָאִיב, סָהֲדָא חַד. תְּרֵין, תְּרֵי סַהֲדֵי, וְדָכֵי. מִכָּאן וּלְהָלְאָה, אֲפִילוּ מֵאָה כִּתְרֵי, וּתְרֵי כְּמֵאָה. וְדָא אוֹלִיפְנָא לְבָתַר דִּכְתִיב, לֹא יָקוּם עֵד אֶחָד בְּאִישׁ וְגוֹ', עַל פִּי שְׁנַיִם עֵדִים וְגוֹ'.

162. "If a man also or a woman have in the skin of their flesh bright white spots" (Vayikra 13:38). Rabbi Yosi said, we learned that the excessive acidity in the intensely bright spot, OF WHICH 300 AGREED-UPON LAWS WERE RECITED, follows its appearance. And its appearance is judged in these MANY ways. Rabbi Yitzchak said, one may derive 300 arguments from the intensely bright spot. I have learned them all from my father, excepting THE ONE when there is one BLACK hair, ONE IS STILL impure BECAUSE it is one witness. Two BLACK HAIRS are two witnesses and so one is pure. More

than that, even a hundred HAIRS are like two, and the two HAIRS are as a hundred. Thus I have learned this afterwards FROM THE WORDS, "One witness shall not rise up against a man... at the mouth of two witnesses..." (Devarim 19:15).

31. The white color and the red color

A Synopsis

Rabbi Chizkiyah says that the sore is considered a sore when the white that indicates Chesed does not remain as it is but turns red that indicates judgment. It is written that Esau came out ``````red at birth, so judgments dwell in him. If the sore began red and turned white, it is becoming purified; if it began white and turned red it begins to be defiled. The priest can recognize all these things. Rabbi Yehuda and Rabbi Yitzchak talk about why Elisha obtained a double portion of Elijah's spirit.

163. ר' חִזְקִיָּה הֲוָה יָתִיב קַמֵּיהּ דְּרַבִּי שִׁמְעוֹן, אָמַר, כְּתִיב נֶגַע לָבָן אֲדַמְדָּם, כְּדֵין הוּא נֶגַע, דְּהָא חִוָּורָא לָא קָאֵים בְּעֵינֵיהּ. פָּתַח ר"ש וְאָמַר, כְּתִיב אִם יִהְיוּ חֲטָאֵיכֶם כַּשָּׁנִים וְגו', זַכָּאִין אִינּוּן יִשְׂרָאֵל, דְּקוּדְשָׁא בְּרִיךְ הוּא בָּעֵי לְדַכְּאָה לוֹן בְּכֹלָּא, בְּגִין דְּלָא יִשְׁתַּכְּחוּן בְּדִינָא קַמֵּיהּ. וּמָארֵיהוֹן דְּדִינָא לָא יִשְׁלְטוּן בְּהוֹן, דְּהָא כֹּלָּא אָזִיל בָּתַר זִינֵיהּ. סוּמָקָא לְסוּמָקָא, וְחִוָּורָא לְחִוָּורָא. יְמִינָא לִימִינָא, וּשְׂמָאלָא לִשְׂמָאלָא.

163. Rabbi Chizkiyah was sitting before Rabbi Shimon. He said, it is written, "a white reddish sore" (Vayikra 13:42). It is considered a sore when the white THAT INDICATES CHESED does not remain as it is BUT TURNS RED THAT INDICATES JUDGMENT. Rabbi Shimon opened with the words, "though your sins be like scarlet, they shall be as white as snow" (Yeshayah 1:18). Happy are Yisrael, whom the Holy One, blessed be He, wishes to purify completely, so they will not be in a state of Judgment before Him, and so the administrators of Judgments will have no power over them. For everything follows its own kind; red FOLLOWS JUDGMENTS, THE SECRET OF red, and white FOLLOWS CHESED, THE SECRET OF white; the right, WHICH IS WHITE to the right, WHICH IS CHESED, and the left, WHICH IS RED to the left, WHICH IS JUDGMENT.

164. בְּעֵשָׂו כְּתִיב, וַיֵּצֵא הָרִאשׁוֹן אַדְמוֹנִי, וְעַל דָּא שַׁרְיָא בֵּיהּ זִינֵיהּ. וְאִי תֵּימָא אַדְמוֹנִי כְּתִיב בְּעֵשָׂו. וּכְתִיב בֵּיהּ בְּדָוִד, וַיְבִיאֵהוּ וְהוּא אַדְמוֹנִי. אֶלָּא דָּא מִזּוֹהֲמָא דְּדַהֲבָא אִתְעֲבִיד, וְדָא בְּזוֹהֲרָא דְּדַהֲבָא אִתְדְּבַק, בְּעֵשָׂו כְּתִיב בֵּיהּ, אַדְמוֹנִי כֻּלּוֹ כְּאַדֶּרֶת שֵׂעָר, בְּזוֹהֲמָא

דְּהֲתוּכָא נָפַק. בֵּיהּ כְּתִיב בְּדָוִד, עִם יְפֵה עֵינַיִם וְטוֹב רֹאִי.

164. It is written, of Esau, "And the first came out red" (Beresheet 25:25). Hence its own kind dwells in him, NAMELY JUDGMENTS, THE SECRET OF RED. You may say that red applies to Esau, yet it is written of David, "Now he was ruddy" (I Shmuel 16:12). HE ANSWERS, the one, ESAU, was made of the dross of gold, WHICH IS HARSH JUDGMENTS; the other, DAVID, was attached to the brightness of gold, WHICH IS THE LEFT OF BINAH THAT IS CALLED GOLD, AND IS MERCY. It is written of Esau, "red, all over like a hairy garment," WHICH MEANS he came out of the dross REMAINING from the melting OF GOLD. It is written of David, "with fine eyes, and good looking" (Ibid.), WHICH ALLUDES TO THE ILLUMINATION OF CHOCHMAH CALLED EYES AND ALSO CALLED SIGHT THAT IS DRAWN FROM THE LEFT COLUMN OF BINAH, INCLUDED WITHIN THE RIGHT IN IT.

165. ת"ח, מ"ט. גַּוְונָא חִוָּורָא אִשְׁתְּמוֹדַע, וְגַוְונָא סוּמָקָא אִשְׁתְּמוֹדַע, סוּמָקָא בְּקַדְמֵיתָא, וְהָא אִתְחֲזֵי בֵּיהּ חִוָּורָא, הָא דַכְיוּתָא אִתְיְילִיד בֵּיהּ, וְשָׁארֵי לְאִתְדַּכְּאָה. חִוָּורָא בְּקַדְמֵיתָא, וְאִתְחֲזֵי בֵּיהּ סוּמָקָא, הָא שָׁארֵי לְאִסְתַּאֲבָא, וּכְתִיב וְטִמְּאוֹ הַכֹּהֵן, דְּהָא אִתְיְילִיד בֵּיהּ סוּמָקָא, לְאִסְתַּאֲבָא. וְכַהֲנָא הֲוָה יָדַע בְּכָל אִינּוּן גַּוְונִין. וּלְזִמְנִין דְּאִתְחֲזֵי בֵּיהּ גַּוְונָא דְּדַכְיוּתָא, וְיַסְגַר לֵיהּ לְמֶחֱמֵי אִי אִתְיְילִיד בֵּיהּ גַּוְונָא אָחֳרָא. וְאִי לָא, מַדְכֵּי לֵיהּ, הַה"ד וְטִהֲרוֹ הַכֹּהֵן וְגוֹ'.

165. Come and see, what is the reason A WHITE REDDISH SORE IS IMPURE? If the white color is known TO BE CHESED and the red color TO BE JUDGMENT, THEN if it was FIRST red, AND NOW white appears in it, then purity emerges and it begins to be purified. But if it was white at first and the red appears in it NOW it begins to be defiled. It is also written, "and the priest shall pronounce him unclean" (Vayikra 13:11). The priest recognized all these appearances. Sometimes the appearance of purity is seen, so he will quarantine him to see whether another appearance will emerge. Otherwise, he pronounces him clean, as written, "the priest shall pronounce him clean" (Ibid. 6).

166. רַבִּי יִצְחָק וְר' יְהוּדָה הֲווֹ אָזְלֵי בְּאָרְחָא, אָמַר רַבִּי יְהוּדָה, כְּתִיב

וְצָרַעַת נַעֲמָן תִּדְבַּק בְּךָ וּבְזַרְעֲךָ לְעוֹלָם וְגוֹ', אִי הוּא חָטָא בְּנוֹי אֲמַאי יִלְקוֹן. אָ"ל, אֱלִישָׁע יַתִּיר מִשְּׁאָר נְבִיאֵי חָמָא. חָמָא דְּלָא נָפִיק מִגֵּחֲזִי בְּרָא דִּמְעַלְיָא, וְעַ"ד לָיֵיט לְכֻלְּהוּ.

166. Rabbi Yitzchak and Rabbi Yehuda were walking along the way. Rabbi Yehuda said, it is written, "So let the disease of Na'aman cleave to you, and to your seed for ever" (II Melachim 5:27). HE ASKS, if he sinned, why shall his children be stricken? He said to him, Elisha saw deeper than the other prophets. He saw that no worthy son will come from Gehazi, and he therefore cursed him.

167. וְלֹא עוֹד, אֶלָּא אָ"ל, אֲנָא פּוּלְחָנָא בְּשִׁמּוּשָׁא עִלָּאָה לְגַבֵּי אֵלִיָּהוּ, וְזָכֵינָא בִּתְרֵין חוּלָקִין, דְּהָא פְּלַחְנָא לֵיהּ בִּקְשׁוֹט, וְאַנְתְּ רָשָׁע פְּגִימַת לִי, אוֹמֵית לְשִׁקְרָא, וַחֲמִידַת, הָא עָבַרְתְּ עַל אוֹרַיְיתָא כֹּלָּא, וּמַאן דְּאַעֲבָר עַל דָּא, מִית הוּא לְעָלְמָא דְּאָתֵי. אֲבָל בְּגִין דְּפַלַחַת לִי, שִׁמּוּשָׁא דִּילָךְ לָא לֶהֱוֵי לְמַגָּנָא, תֶּהֱוֵי מִיתָה דִּילָךְ בְּעָלְמָא דֵּין, וּבְעָלְמָא דְּאָתֵי לָא. וּבְגִין כָּךְ, וְצָרַעַת נַעֲמָן תִּדְבַּק בְּךָ וּבְזַרְעֲךָ.

167. He also told him, I did a superior service by Elijah and attained two portions, NAMELY, HE ATTAINED A DOUBLE PORTION OF THE SPIRIT OF ELIJAH, since I served him in truth. But you are wicked. You injured me by swearing falsely and coveting NA'AMAN'S GIFT. So you have transgressed the whole Torah. But since you served me, your service will not be in vain and your death shall be in this world but not in the World to Come. For that reason, "So let the disease of Na'aman cleave to you, and to your seed."

32. "She seeks wool, and flax"

A Synopsis
We learn that the power of the plague that comes from a highest place has power over everything, both wool and linen.

168. א"ר יוֹסֵי, בֶּגֶד הַצֶּמֶר אוֹ הַפִּשְׁתִּים אֲמַאי. א"ר יִצְחָק, בְּכֹלָא שַׁרְיָא, וּבְכֹלָא שַׁלְטָא. וְאִית כְּגַוְונָא דָּא דִכְתִּיב, דָּרְשָׁה צֶמֶר וּפִשְׁתִּים. וּבְגִינֵי כָּךְ, שׁוּלְטָנֵיהּ דְּהַהוּא נֶגַע דְּנָפִיק מֵאֲתַר עִלָּאָה, דָּא שַׁלְטָא בְּכֹלָא, בִּתְרֵי גַּוְונֵי, בְּצֶמֶר וּבְפִשְׁתִּים. וּבְגִין כָּךְ, זֹאת תּוֹרַת נֶגַע הַצָּרַעַת בֶּגֶד הַצֶּמֶר אוֹ הַפִּשְׁתִּים.

168. Rabbi Yosi said, why mention a woolen garment or linen garment? IT SHOULD HAVE SPOKEN PLAINLY OF A GARMENT. Rabbi Yitzchak said, THE VERSE TEACHES US THAT THE PLAGUE dwells everywhere and has power over everything, SINCE WOOL COMES FROM BINAH, AND LINEN FROM MALCHUT AND THE PLAGUE HAS POWER OVER BOTH. There is a likeness, as written, "She seeks wool, and flax" (Mishlei 31:13), WHICH TEACHES US THAT MALCHUT MAKES USE OF BOTH. For that reason IT TEACHES US HERE that the power of the plague that comes from a highest place has power over everything, NAMELY the two kinds, wool and linen. For that reason THE VERSE SAYS, "This is the Torah of the plague of leprosy in a garment of woolen or linen" (Vayikra 13:59).

33. "Woe to him that builds his house by unrighteousness," part two

A Synopsis

Rabbi Yitzchak follows a man with a load tied on his shoulders into a cave. Inside the cave he sees the man entering a hole in the ground and disappearing, so the Rabbi is afraid and leaves the cave. Rabbi Yehuda tells him that God has saved him from a cave of lepers and sorcerers that do witchcraft with black serpents. The rabbis encounter a man who is taking his son to the cave for healing; the son was harmed by a spirit in their house. We learn that the first to receive a house owns it forever, whether it be the spirit of holiness or the spirit of defilement. If the defiled house is destroyed it should be rebuilt slightly farther away with new materials, and it should be dedicated to the Holy Name. We now hear that the man who took his son to the cave for healing left his son for a moment, during which time the boy was hit on the head by a smoky column of fire and killed. Rabbi Elazar says that a man should speak the Holy Name over everything he does so that the Other Side will not dwell on it.

169. רִבִּי יִצְחָק הֲוָה אָזִיל לְקַטְפוּרֵי דַּאֲבוֹי. חָמָא חַד בַּ״נ, דְּסָאטֵי בְּקוּטְרָא דְּמָטוּלָא אֲכַתְפוֹי. אָמַר לֵיה, שׁוּרְטָא דְּקִישְׁטָא בְּכַתְפָךְ אֲמַאי, לָא אָמַר לֵיה מִדִי. אָזַל אֲבַתְרֵיה, חָמָא דְּעַיֵיל בִּמְעַרְתָּא חֲדָא, עָאל אֲבַתְרֵיה, חָמָא קְטוּרָא דִּתְנָנָא דַּהֲוָה סָלִיק מִתְּחוֹת אַרְעָא, וְעָאל הַהוּא בַּר נָשׁ בְּנוּקְבָּא חַד, וְאִתְכַּסְיָא מִנֵּיה. דָּחִיל רִבִּי יִצְחָק, וְנָפַק לְפוּם מְעַרְתָּא.

169. Rabbi Yitzchak was going to his father's vineyard. He saw a man turning FROM THE ROAD with a load tied to his shoulder. He asked him, what is the rope that adorns your shoulders for, THAT IS, WHY DID YOU TIE THE LOAD TO YOUR SHOULDERS? He did not answer at all. He followed him and saw him entering a cave, so he entered after him. He saw a column of smoke rising from beneath the ground and the man entering a hole and disappearing from his sight. Rabbi Yitzchak was afraid and went out to the mouth of the cave.

170. עַד דַּהֲוָה יָתִיב, אַעְבְּרוּ ר׳ יְהוּדָה וְרִבִּי חִזְקִיָּה, חָמָא לוֹן, וְקָרִיב גַּבֵּיהוֹן, סָח לוֹן עוֹבָדָא. א״ר יְהוּדָה, בְּרִיךְ רַחֲמָנָא דְּשֵׁזָבָךְ. הַאי

מְעַרְתָּא דְּסָגִּיר, דְּסָרוֹנְיָא הִיא, וְכָל יַתְבֵי הַהִיא קַרְתָּא, חַרְשִׁין אִינּוּן, וְאַתְיָין לְמַדְבְּרָא לְחַוְוְיָין אוּכָמִין, דְּאִינּוּן בְּנֵי עֲשַׂר שְׁנִין, אוֹ יַתִּיר, לְמֶעְבַּד חֲרָשִׁין, וְלָא מְנַטְּרָא מִנַּיְיהוּ, וְאִתְעָבֵידוּ סְגִירִין וְכָל זַיְינֵי חֲרָשִׁין דִּלְהוֹן בְּהַאי מְעַרְתָּא אִינּוּן.

170. While he was sitting, Rabbi Yehuda and Rabbi Chizkiyah passed by. When he saw them he approached them and told them what happened. Rabbi Yehuda said, blessed is the Merciful who saved you. This is a cave of lepers from the city of Srunya. All the inhabitants of that city are sorcerers that go to the desert to seek black serpents, which are at least ten years old, in order to do witchcraft. They did not take care of themselves so became lepers. The different kinds of witchcraft are done in that cave.

171. אָזְלוּ, עַד דַּהֲווֹ אָזְלֵי, אִעַרְעֲרוּ בְּחַד בַּר נָשׁ דַּהֲוָה אָתֵי, וּבְרֵיהּ דַּהֲוָה מְרַע, קָטִיר עַל חֲמָרָא. אָמְרוּ לֵיהּ מַאן אַתְּ. אָמַר לְהוּ יוּדָאי, וְדָא הוּא בְּרִי דְּאִיהוּ קָטִיר עַל חֲמָרָא. אָמְרוּ לֵיהּ, אֲמַאי הוּא קָטִיר. אָמַר לוֹן דִּיּוּרִי הוּא בְּחַד כְּפַר, דְּאִיהוּ מִבְּנֵי רוֹמָאֵי, וְהַאי בְּרִי הֲוָה אוֹלִיף אוֹרַיְיתָא בְּכָל יוֹמָא, וַהֲוָה אַהְדָּר לְבֵיתָא, וְלָעֵי לוֹן לְאִינּוּן מִלִּין. וְג' שְׁנִין הֲוָה דִּיּוּרִי בְּהַהוּא בֵּיתָא, וְלָא חֲמֵינָא מִדִּי. וְהַשְׁתָּא יוֹמָא חַד עָאל בְּרִי לְבֵיתָא לְאַהְדָּרָא מִלִּין, אַעֲבַר חַד רוּחָא קַמֵּיהּ, וְנָזִיק לֵיהּ, אַעֲקַם פּוּמֵיהּ וְעֵינוֹי, וִידוֹי אִתְעַקָּמוּ, וְלָא יָכִיל לְמַלָּלָא. וְאַתֵינָא לְגַבֵּי מְעַרְתָּא דְּסָגִּירוּ דְּסָרוֹנְיָא דִּלְמָא יַלְפוּן לִי מִלָּה דְּאַסְוָותָא.

171. They walked on. While they were walking they met a man coming with his sick child on a donkey. They asked him, who are you? He said to them, I am a Jew, and this is my son bound upon the donkey. They asked him why he was bound, and he said to them, I dwell in a certain village that belongs to the citizens of Rome. This my son used to study Torah daily and return home to learn these matters. I dwelt in this house for three years and saw nothing. Now, one day my son went home to repeat the things HE LEARNED, when a spirit passed before him and harmed him. His mouth, eyes and hands became contorted and he cannot speak. Now I come to the lepers' cave of Srunya. They may teach me some healing.

172. אָמַר לֵיהּ רִבִּי יְהוּדָה, וּבַהַהוּא בֵּיתָא יְדַעַת מִן קַדְמַת דְּנָא,
דְּאִתְנְזַק בֵּיהּ ב"נ אָחֳרָא. אָמַר לֵיהּ יְדַעְנָא, דְּהָא מִכַּמָה יוֹמִין אִתְנְזַק
בֵּיהּ חַד ב"נ, וַהֲווֹ אַמְרֵי דְּמַרְעָא הֲוָה, וּמִנַּיְיהוּ אַמְרֵי דְּרוּחָא דְּבֵיתָא,
וּלְבָתַר עָאלוּ בֵּיהּ כַּמָה בְּנֵי נָשָׁא, וְלָא אִתְנְזִיקוּ. אָמְרוּ, הַיְינוּ דְּאָמְרֵי
חַבְרַיָּיא, וַוי לְאִינוּן דְּעַבְרִין עַל מִלַּיְיהוּ.

172. Rabbi Yehuda said, do you know of anyone else who came to harm in
that house before? He said that he knew that some time ago another man
came to harm. Some said it is a disease while others said the spirit in that
house HURT HIM. Later a few people came into that house but were not hurt.
RABBI YEHUDA AND RABBI CHIZKIYAH said, that is, the friends said, THAT
A HOUSE BUILT NOT WITH RIGHTEOUSNESS, THE SPIRIT OF DEFILEMENT
THAT HARMS ITS DWELLERS RESTS IN IT. Woe to those who transgress
their words.

173. פָּתַח ר' יְהוּדָה וְאָמַר, הוֹי בּוֹנֶה בֵיתוֹ בְּלֹא צֶדֶק, דְּהָא בְּכָל אֲתַר
דְּאִשְׁתְּכַח בֵּיהּ צֶדֶק, כָּל רוּחִין וְכָל מַזִּיקֵי עָלְמָא עַרְקֵי מִנֵּיהּ, וְלָא
מִשְׁתַּכְּחֵי קַמֵּיהּ. וְעִם כָּל דָּא, מַאן דְּאַקְדִּים וְנָטִיל אֲתַר, אָחִיד בֵּיהּ.
אָמַר לֵיהּ רִבִּי חִזְקִיָּה, אִי הָכִי שָׁקִיל שְׁמָא קַדִּישָׁא כְּרוּחַ מִסְאֲבָא.

173. Rabbi Yehuda opened the discussion with, "Woe to him that builds his
house by unrighteousness" (Yirmeyah 22:13). Wherever there is
righteousness, MALCHUT, all the spirits and demons in the world flee that
place and do not stay before it. Nevertheless, whoever is the first to take that
place, acquires it. IF MALCHUT OF HOLINESS IS THE FIRST TO RECEIVE
THAT PLACE, HOLINESS SECURES IT, BUT IF THE OTHER SIDE IS THE
FIRST TO RECEIVE THAT PLACE, IT SECURES IT. Rabbi Chizkiyah said to
him, in that case the Holy Name is equal to the spirit of defilement,
ACCORDING TO YOUR WORDS THAT WHOEVER IS THE FIRST SECURES IT.

174. אָמַר לֵיהּ, לָאו הָכִי, אֶלָּא שְׁמָא קַדִּישָׁא לָא שַׁרְיָא בַּאֲתַר
מִסְאֲבָא, וּבְגִין כָּךְ, אִי שְׁמָא קַדִּישָׁא נָטִיל אֲתַר מִקַּדְמַת דְּנָא, כָּל
רוּחִין וְכָל מַזִּיקִין דְּעָלְמָא לָא יַכְלִין לְאִתְחֲזָאָה בֵּיהּ, כָּל שֶׁכֵּן לְקָרְבָא

בַּהֲדֵיהּ. אִי רוּחַ מִסְאֲבָא קָדִים, נָטִיל אֲתַר. שְׁמָא קַדִּישָׁא לָא שַׁרְיָא בֵּיהּ, דְּהָא לָאו אַתְרֵיהּ.

174. He said to him, it is not so, but the Holy Name, MALCHUT, does not dwell on a place of defilement, for the reason that if the Holy Name is the first to receive that place, none of the spirits and demons of the world can be seen there, not to mention approaching it. But if the spirit of defilement is the first, it takes that place, and the Holy Name does not dwell in it, since it is not its place.

175. וְכַד הֲוָה נָחִית נֶגַע צָרַעַת, הֲוָה מַדְכֵּי אַתְרָא, וְאַפִּיק לְרוּחַ מִסְאֲבָא מֵאַתְרֵיהּ, וּלְבָתַר מְנַתְּצֵי בֵּיתָא, אֲבָנִין וְאָעִין וְכֹלָּא, וּבָנֵי לָהּ כְּמִלְּקַדְמִין, בְּסִטְרָא קַדִּישָׁא בְּצֶדֶק, דְּדָכִיר לֵיהּ לִשְׁמָא קַדִּישָׁא, וְלִשְׁרֵי עֲלֵיהּ קְדוּשָׁה, וְעִם כָּל דָּא בְּעַפְרָא אָחֳרָא, וְיַרְחִיק בֵּיתָא מֵאַתְרֵיהּ, מִיְּסוֹדָא קַדְמָאָה תְּרֵי טְפָחִים.

175. When the plague of leprosy descended UPON THAT HOUSE, it would purify that place and bring out the spirit of defilement from its place. Later, that house was broken down together with its wood, stones and everything, and rebuilt through the holy side and in righteousness, by mentioning the Holy Name and causing holiness to rest on it. Nevertheless ONE SHOULD BUILD IT using a different earth and build it two hand-breadths away.

176. הַשְׁתָּא דְּלָא אִתְחֲזֵי, וְלָא נָחִית מַאן דִּמְקַטְרֵג בֵּיהּ בְּהַהוּא רוּחַ מִסְאֲבָא, לְאַפְּקָא לֵיהּ מֵאַתְרֵיהּ, מַאי תַּקַנְתֵּיהּ. אִי יָכִיל לְנַפְּקָא מֵהַאי בֵּיתָא שַׁפִּיר. וְאִי לָאו יִבְנֶה לֵיהּ כְּמִלְּקַדְמִין, בַּאֲבָנִין אָחֳרָנִין, וְאָעִין וְכֹלָּא, וְיַפִּיק וְיַרְחִיק לֵיהּ מֵאֲתַר קַדְמָאָה, וְיִבְנֵי לֵיהּ עַל שְׁמָא קַדִּישָׁא.

176. Now that nothing appears or descends to fight the spirit of holiness to uproot it from its place, SINCE THERE ARE NO PLAGUES NOW, what is to be done IN A HOUSE WHERE THE SPIRIT OF DEFILEMENT WAS THE FIRST TO DWELL? HE ANSWERS, if one can take it out ON HIS OWN from the house, it is well. Otherwise, he should rebuild it using different stones, wood, etc., and pull it away from its first location and dedicate its building to the Holy Name.

177. וְעַכ"ד, לָא נָפִיק הַהוּא רוּחָא מִן אֲתַר קַדְמָאָה, בְּגִין דִּקְדוּשָׁה לָא שַׁרְיָא עַל אֲתַר מְסָאֲבָא. א"ר יִצְחָק לָמָה לֵיהּ לְאַטְרְחָא כּוּלֵי הַאי, בְּזִמְנָא דָא כְּתִיב, מְעֻוָּת לֹא יוּכַל לִתְקוֹן וְגו'. מִיּוֹמָא דְּאִתְחָרַב בֵּי מַקְדְּשָׁא, לָא אִשְׁתְּכַח אַסְוָותָא בְּעָלְמָא, בְּגִינֵי כָּךְ בָּעֵי ב"נ לְאִזְדַּהֲרָא, כִּי הֵיכִי דִּלְהֱוֵי נָטִיר.

177. With all that, the spirit of defilement does not leave its first place and holiness does not dwell on a defiled place. Rabbi Yitzchak said, why should one bother so IN DEMOLISHING THE HOUSE AND REBUILDING IT IN A DIFFERENT LOCATION, these days WHEN THERE ARE NO PLAGUES? It is written, "That which is crooked cannot be made straight" (Kohelet 1:15), FOR ever since the Temple was destroyed, AND THERE ARE NO PLAGUES, there is no remedy. For that reason one should be careful to be guarded FROM THE SPIRIT OF DEFILEMENT, THAT IS, THAT IT WILL NO LONGER DWELL IN THAT HOUSE.

178. אַמְרֵי נֵזִיל בַּהֲדֵי הַאי ב"נ וְנֶחֱמֵי. א"ר יִצְחָק, אָסִיר לָן. אִי הֲוָה אָזִיל לְגַבֵּי גַּבְרָא רַבָּא דְּחִיל חַטָּאָה, כְּגוֹן נַעֲמָן לְגַבֵּי אֱלִישָׁע, נֵזִיל אֲבַתְרֵיהּ. הַשְׁתָּא דְּאִיהוּ אָזִיל לְגַבֵּי רְחִיקֵי עָלְמָא, רְחִיקֵי אוֹרַיְיתָא, גַּעֲלֵי מִכֹּלָּא, אָסִיר לָן לְאִתְחֲזָאָה קַמַּיְיהוּ. בְּרִיךְ רַחֲמָנָא דִּי שֵׁזִיב לָן מִנַּיְיהוּ. וְהַאי ב"נ אָסִיר לֵיהּ. א"ר יְהוּדָה, וְהָא תָּנֵינַן בְּכֹל מִתְרַפְּאִין, חוּץ מֵעֲצֵי אֲשֵׁרָה וְכו'. אָמַר לֵיהּ, וְדָא ע"ז אִיהוּ, וְלָא עוֹד, אֶלָּא דְּהָא כְּתִיב לֹא יִמָּצֵא בְךָ מַעֲבִיר בְּנוֹ וּבִתּוֹ בָּאֵשׁ וְגו'. אַזְלוּ לְאָרְחַיְיהוּ.

178. They said, let us go with that man TO THE LEPERS' CAVE, and see. Rabbi Yitzchak said, we must not. Had he gone to receive remedy from a great sin-fearing man, like Na'aman, who went to Elisha, we would follow. But now that he goes to those who are distant from the world, THE LEPERS AND THE SORCERERS, distant from the Torah, abominable in every respect, we must not appear before them. Blessed is the Merciful who saved us from them, and a man is forbidden TO RECEIVE REMEDY FROM THEM. Rabbi Yehuda said, yet we learned that everything is good for remedy excepting the woods of the Ashera. He said to him, this is idolatry AND SO IS FORBIDDEN. Moreover, it is written, "There must not be found among you

-111-

anyone that makes his son or his daughter to pass through the fire" (Devarim 18:10). They went on their way.

179. אָזַל הַהוּא בַּ"נ לְהַהִיא מְעַרְתָּא, הוּא וּבְרֵיה, שָׁרֵי לֵיה בִּמְעַרְתָּא. עַד דְּנָפַק אֲבוֹי לְקַטְרָא לַחֲמָרֵיה, נָפַק קִיטוּרָא דְאֶשָּׁא, וּמָחָא לֵיה בְּרֵישָׁא, וְקַטְלֵיה. אַדְהֲכִי עָאל אֲבוֹי, וְאַשְׁכְּחֵיה מִית. נָטַל לֵיה וְלַחֲמָרֵיה, וְאָזַל לֵיה. וְאַשְׁכַּח לְהוּ לְבָתַר יוֹמָא חַד, לְרִ' יִצְחָק, וּלְרִ' יְהוּדָה, וְרַבִּי חִזְקִיָּה, דַּהֲווֹ אַזְלֵי. בָּכָה קַמַּיְיהוּ, וְסָח לוֹן עוֹבָדָא. אָמַר רַבִּי יִצְחָק, וְלָא זִמְנִין סַגִּיאִין אֲמֵינָא לָךְ, דְּאָסִיר לְמֵיהַךְ תַּמָּן. בְּרִיךְ רַחֲמָנָא, דִּי כָל מַעֲבָדוֹהִי קְשׁוֹט, וְאָרְחָתֵיה דִין. זַכָּאִין אִינּוּן צַדִּיקַיָּיא, דְּאַזְלִין בְּאֹרַח קְשׁוֹט, בְּעָלְמָא דֵּין, וּבְעָלְמָא דְאָתֵי, וַעֲלַיְיהוּ כְּתִיב, וְאֹרַח צַדִּיקִים כְּאוֹר נֹגַהּ וְגוֹ'.

179. That man went to that cave with his son, and left him in there. As his father went out to fasten his donkey, a smoky column of fire came out and struck HIS SON on his head, killing him. When his father entered, he found him dead. He took him and his donkey and went his way. Another day after that he found Rabbi Yitzchak, Rabbi Yehuda and Rabbi Chizkiyah walking. He wept before them and told them what happened. Rabbi Yitzchak said, did I not tell you many times it is forbidden to go there? Blessed is the Merciful, all of whose deeds are true and whose ways are just. Happy are the righteous, who walk the path of truth in this world and in the World to Come. Of them it is written, "But the path of just men is like the gleam of sunlight..." (Mishlei 4:18).

180. א"ר אֶלְעָזָר, בְּכָל עוֹבָדוֹי דְּבַ"נ, לִבְעֵי לֵיה דִּלְהֱווֹן כֻּלְּהוּ לִשְׁמָא קַדִּישָׁא. מַאי לִשְׁמָא קַדִּישָׁא. לְאַדְכְּרָא בְּפוּמֵיה שְׁמָא קַדִּישָׁא עַל כָּל מַה דְּאִיהוּ עָבֵיד, דְּכֹלָּא הוּא לְפוּלְחָנֵיה, וְלָא יִשְׁרֵי עֲלוֹי סִטְרָא אָחֳרָא. בְּגִין דְּאִיהוּ זַמִּין תְּדִירָא לְגַבֵּי בְּנֵי נָשָׁא, וְיָכִיל לְאַשְׁרָאָה עַל הַהוּא עֲבִידְתָּא. וְעַל דָּא, הַשְׁתֵּי אוֹ הָעֶרֶב הֲוָה אִסְתָּאַב, וְשַׁרְיָא עֲלֵיה רוּחַ מְסָאֲבָא. וּמַה בְּהַאי כָּךְ, מַאן דְּפָקִיד מְלוֹי לְסִטְרָא אָחֳרָא דְּלָא אִצְטְרִיךְ, עאכ"ו. ובג"כ כְּתִיב וְנִשְׁמַרְתָּ מִכָּל דָּבָר רָע.

180. Rabbi Elazar said, in whatever man does, everything needs to be dedicated to His Holy Name. What does this mean? IT MEANS he should utter with his mouth the Holy Name over anything he does, so that everything will be for His service and the Other Side will not dwell on it. For THE OTHER SIDE is always ready against men and might dwell on the deed one performs. For that reason, the warp and woof would be defiled and the spirit of defilement dwelt on it. And if this is so, THE SPIRIT OF DEFILEMENT DWELLS much more when one commands his words to the Other Side BY SWEARING, ETC., for he must not DO SO. For that reason it is written, "then keep you from every evil thing" (Devarim 23:10).

34. "Say, I pray you, you are my sister"

A Synopsis

We learn that Abraham told his wife to say she was his sister because he was counting on her merit; whoever merits a prudent wife merits everything. Abraham saw an angel who said he would protect her, so he had no fear for his wife but some fear for himself. Sarai ordered the angel to strike Pharaoh ten times with ten plagues. Rabbi Aba talks about the difference between the redemption from Egypt, that occurred on one day from one king and one kingdom, and the final redemption that will be from all the kings of the world – everyone shall acknowledge God's reign and glorify Him. Then the Patriarchs will be resurrected with joy, and they will see the redemption of their children as before.

181. רִבִּי אֶלְעָזָר הֲוָה אָזִיל לְמֶחֱמֵי לַאֲבוּי וַהֲוָה עִמֵּיה רִבִּי אַבָּא. א״ר אַבָּא נֵימָא מִלִּין דְּאוֹרַיְיתָא וְנֵזִיל. פָּתַח רִבִּי אֶלְעָזָר וְאָמַר, אִמְרִי נָא אֲחוֹתִי אַתְּ, הַאי קְרָא קַשְׁיָא. וְכִי אַבְרָהָם דְּאִיהוּ דָּחִיל חַטָּאָה, רְחִימוּ דְּקוּדְשָׁא בְּרִיךְ הוּא, הֲוָה אָמַר הָכִי עַל אִתְּתֵיה, בְּגִין דְּיוֹטְבִין לֵיה. אֶלָּא אַבְרָהָם, אע״ג דַּהֲוָה דָּחִיל חַטָּאָה, לָא סָמִיךְ עַל זְכוּתָא דִּילֵיה, וְלָא בָּעָא מִן קוּדְשָׁא בְּרִיךְ הוּא לְאַפָּקָא זְכוּתֵיה, אֶלָּא עַל זְכוּתָא דְּאִתְּתֵיה, דְּיִרְוַוח בְּגִינָהּ מָמוֹנָא דִּשְׁאָר עַמִּין, דְּהָא מָמוֹנָא בְּאִתְּתֵיה זָכֵי לֵיה ב״נ, הה״ד בַּיִת וָהוֹן נַחֲלַת אָבוֹת וּמֵיְיָ׳ אִשָּׁה מַשְׂכָּלֶת. מָאן דְּזָכֵי בְּאִשָּׁה מַשְׂכָּלֶת, זוֹכֶה בְּכֹלָּא. וּכְתִיב, בָּטַח בָּהּ לֵב בַּעֲלָהּ וְשָׁלָל לֹא יֶחְסָר.

181. Rabbi Elazar went to see his father, accompanied by Rabbi Aba. Rabbi Aba said, let us speak words of Torah as we walk. Rabbi Elazar started with, "Say, I pray you, you are my sister" (Beresheet 12:13). This is a difficult verse. Could it be that Abraham, who feared sin and was the friend of the Holy One, blessed be He, would speak so about his wife so as to derive benefit from it? HE ANSWERS, even though Abraham was sin-fearing, he did not count on his own merit and did not wish the Holy One, blessed be He, to deduct from his merit, but COUNTED on his wife's merit, that through her he will gain money from other nations. For man attains money through his wife, as written, "House and riches are the

inheritance of fathers, but a prudent wife is from Hashem" (Mishlei 19:14). Whoever merits a prudent wife merits everything. It is also written, "The heart of her husband safely trusts in her, and he shall have no lack of gain" (Mishlei 31:11).

182. וְאַבְרָהָם הֲוָה אָזִיל בְּגִינָהּ, לְמֵיכַל שְׁלָלָא מִשְּׁאַר עַמִּין, וְסָמִיךְ עַל זְכוּתָא דִּילָהּ, דְּלָא יֵכְלוּן לְאַעְנְשָׁא לֵיהּ, וּלְחַיְיבָא בָּהּ. וּבְגִינֵי כַּךְ לָא יָהִיב מִדִּי לְמֵימַר אֲחוֹתִי הִיא. וְלָא עוֹד, אֶלָּא דְּחָמָא חַד מַלְאָכָא אָזִיל קַמָּהּ, וְאָמַר לֵיהּ לְאַבְרָהָם, לָא תִּדְחַל מִנָּהּ, קוּדְשָׁא בְּרִיךְ הוּא שָׁדַר לִי, לְאַפָּקָא לֵהּ מָמוֹנָא דִּשְׁאַר עַמִּין, וּלְנַטְרָא לָהּ מִכֹּלָּא. וּכְדֵין לָא דָּחִיל אַבְרָהָם מֵאִתְּתֵיהּ, אֶלָּא מִנֵּיהּ, דְּלָא חָמָא עִמֵּיהּ מַלְאָכָא, אֶלָּא עִמָּהּ. אָמַר הָא הִיא מִתְנַטְרָא, וַאֲנָא לָא נְטִירְנָא. וּבְגִינֵי כַּךְ אָמַר, אִמְרִי נָא אֲחוֹתִי אַתְּ וְגוֹ'.

182. Abraham, through her merit, went to consume the gain of the other nations, AS IN, "AND HE SHALL HAVE NO LACK OF GAIN." He counted on her merit that they will be unable to punish him or make advances on her. For that reason he gave THEM nothing by saying, "She is my sister" (Beresheet 12:19). Moreover, he saw an angel walking before her, who said to Abraham, Do not worry for her. The Holy One, blessed be He, sent me to take money from the other nations and keep her from anything. Abraham then had no fear for his wife but for himself, because he saw the angel not with him but with his wife. He said to himself, so she is kept but I am not. For that reason he said, "Say, I pray you, you are my sister."

183. יִיטַב לִי, וְיֵיטִיבוּ לִי מִבָּעֵי לֵיהּ, דִּכְתִּיב וְהָיָה כִּי יִרְאוּ אוֹתָךְ הַמִּצְרִים וְאָמְרוּ אִשְׁתּוֹ זֹאת, וְעַ"ד יֵיטִיבוּ לִי מִבָּעֵי לֵיהּ. אֶלָּא יִיטַב לִי, דָּא דְּאָזִיל קַמָּךְ. יִיטַב לִי בְּהַאי עָלְמָא קוּדְשָׁא בְּרִיךְ הוּא בְּמָמוֹנָא. וְחָיְתָה נַפְשִׁי בְּהַהוּא עָלְמָא בִּגְלָלֵךְ, דְּלָא תִּסְטֵי מִן אוֹרְחָא דִּקְשׁוֹט, דְּאִי אַזְכֵּי בְּגִינָךְ בְּמָמוֹנָא בְּהַאי עָלְמָא, וְתִסְטֵי אַנְתְּ בְּאוֹרְחָא, הָא מִיתָא זְמִינָא בְּהַהוּא עָלְמָא, אֶלָּא תִּסְתַּמֵּר, דְּתִחֵי נַפְשִׁי בְּהַהוּא עָלְמָא בִּגְלָלֵךְ.

183. "that it may be well with me" (Ibid. 13). HE ASKS, it should have said, 'they may do well', since they said, "therefore it shall come to pass, when

the Egyptians shall see you, that they shall say, This is his wife" (Ibid. 12). Hence it should have said, 'they may do well'. HE ANSWERS, "it may be (or: 'do') well" refers to him that walks before you, NAMELY THE ANGEL. The Holy One, blessed be He, may do well with me in this world, "and my soul shall live" (Ibid. 13) in that world, "because of you" (Ibid.), if you turn not from the path of truth. For if I gain money because of you in this world and you turn from the way, I shall deserve death in that world. So beware that my soul shall live in that world for your sake.

184. וּבְגִין דְּהַהוּא מַלְאָכָא אָזִיל קַמָּה לְנַטְרָא לָהּ, מַה כְּתִיב. וַיְנַגַּע יְיָ' אֶת פַּרְעֹה וְגוֹ', עַל דְּבַר שָׂרַי וַדַּאי, דַּהֲוַת אָמְרַת לְמַלְאָכָא מְחֵי, וְהוּא מְחֵי. וְעַ"ד לָא דָּחִיל אַבְרָהָם מִנָּהּ כְּלוּם, דְּהָא הִיא מִתְנַטְרָא. וּמַה דְּדָחִיל, מִגַּרְמֵיהּ דָּחִיל, דְּלָא חָמָא עִמֵּיהּ נְטוּרָא הָכִי.

184. Because of the angel that was walking before her to keep her, it is written, "And Hashem plagued Pharaoh...because of Sarai" (Ibid. 17); "because of Sarai" surely, NAMELY BECAUSE OF HER WORDS. She would say to the angel, 'strike', and he struck. Abraham therefore had no fear for her, since she was protected. The reason he feared for himself was because he saw nothing guarding him.

185. ת"ח, עֶשֶׂר זִמְנִין פְּקִידַת שָׂרָה לְמַלְאָכָא, לְמַחָאָה לְפַרְעֹה. וּבְעֶשֶׂר מַכְתְּשִׁין אַלְקֵי. סִימָנָא עַבְדַת שָׂרָה לִבְנָהָא בַּתְרָאָה בְּמִצְרַיִם.

185. Come and see, ten times did Sarai command the angel to strike Pharaoh, and he was smitten with ten plagues. FOR Sarai made a sign for her descendants after her in Egypt, NAMELY, THAT THE EGYPTIANS WILL BE SMITTEN BY TEN PLAGUES, BEFORE THEY WILL BE REDEEMED FROM THEIR POWER.

186. ר' אַבָּא פָּתַח, כִּימֵי צֵאתְךָ מֵאֶרֶץ מִצְרַיִם אַרְאֶנּוּ נִפְלָאוֹת. זַמִּין קוּדְשָׁא בְּרִיךְ הוּא לְאַחֲזָאָה פוּרְקָנָא לִבְנוֹי, כְּאִינוּן יוֹמִין דְּשַׁלַּח קוּדְשָׁא בְּרִיךְ הוּא לְאַפָּקָא לְיִשְׂרָאֵל, וְאַחֲזֵי אִינוּן מַכְתְּשִׁין בְּמִצְרָאֵי, וְאַלְקֵי לוֹן בְּגִינֵיהוֹן דְּיִשְׂרָאֵל. תָּא חֲזֵי, מַה בֵּין פוּרְקָנָא דָּא, לְפוּרְקָנָא דְּמִצְרַיִם. פּוּרְקָנָא דְּמִצְרַיִם הֲוָה בְּחַד מַלְכָּא, וּבְמַלְכוּ חֲדָא. הָכָא, בְּכָל

מַלְכִין דְּעָלְמָא, וּכְדֵין יִתְיָיקַר קוּדְשָׁא בְּרִיךְ הוּא בְּכָל עָלְמָא, וְיִנְדְעוּן
כֹּלָּא שׁוּלְטָנוּ דְקוּדְשָׁא בְּרִיךְ הוּא, וְכֻלְּהוּ יִלְקוּן בְּמַכְתָּשִׁין עִלָּאִין, עַל
חַד תְּרֵין, בְּגִין דְּיִסָּרְבוּן כֻּלְּהוּ בְּיִשְׂרָאֵל.

186. Rabbi Aba opened with, "As in the days of your coming out of the land of Egypt I will show him marvelous things" (Michah 7:15). The Holy One, blessed be He, will display redemption for His children as in the days when the Holy One, blessed be He, sent to take Yisrael out OF EGYPT, and showed all those plagues in Egypt and smote them because of Yisrael. Come and see the difference between this redemption AT THE END OF DAYS and the redemption from Egypt. The redemption from Egypt occurred on one day, from one king and one kingdom. Here it will be from all the kings of the world. Then the Holy One, blessed be He, will be glorified over the whole world and everyone will acknowledge the reign of the Holy One, blessed be He, and everyone will be smitten with celestial plagues, twice for each one, because they all were reluctant TO RELEASE Yisrael.

187. וּכְדֵין יִתְגְּלֵי שׁוּלְטָנֵיה דְּקוּדְשָׁא בְּרִיךְ הוּא, דִּכְתִּיב וְהָיָה יְיָ'
לְמֶלֶךְ עַל כָּל הָאָרֶץ. וּכְדֵין כֻּלְּהוּ יִתְנַדְּבוּן בְּהוּ בְּיִשְׂרָאֵל לְקוּדְשָׁא
בְּרִיךְ הוּא, הה"ד, וְהֵבִיאוּ אֶת כָּל אֲחֵיכֶם וְגו'. כְּדֵין קַיְימִין אֲבָהָן
בְּחֶדְוָה, לְמֶחֱמֵי פּוּרְקָנָא דִּבְנַיְיהוּ כְּמִלְּקַדְמִין. הה"ד, כִּימֵי צֵאתְךָ
מֵאֶרֶץ מִצְרָיִם אַרְאֶנּוּ נִפְלָאוֹת.

187. The reign of the Holy One, blessed be He, will be then revealed as written, "And Hashem shall be king over all the earth" (Zecharyah 14:9). The nations will then be prompted to bring Yisrael to the Holy One, blessed be He. This is the meaning of, "And they shall bring all your brethren" (Yeshayah 66:20). Then the Patriarchs will resurrect joyfully to behold the redemption of their children as before. This is the meaning of, "As in the days of your coming out of the land of Egypt I will show him marvelous things."

אָמֵן כֵּן יְהִי רָצוֹן

Amen, so will be desired.

METZORA

❧❧

Names of the articles

1. "That you may know that there is judgment"

A Synopsis

Rabbi Aba begins by reminding us that it is only those who study the Torah and abide by all her ways that are protected by guardian angels and have the Shechinah rest on them. He says that the sword in "be afraid of the sword" is the evil tongue of the serpent. God has a sword with which he punishes the wicked, and anyone who speaks with the evil tongue will be punished with it. Rabbi Elazar says that people do not try to understand God's will even though the supernal Announcer speaks to them every day.

1. וַיְדַבֵּר יְיָ׳ אֶל מֹשֶׁה לֵאמֹר. זֹאת תִּהְיֶה תּוֹרַת הַמְצוֹרָע בְּיוֹם טָהֳרָתוֹ וְגוֹ׳. ר׳ אַבָּא פָּתַח, גּוּרוּ לָכֶם מִפְּנֵי חֶרֶב כִּי חֵמָה עֲוֹנוֹת חָרֶב לְמַעַן תֵּדְעוּן שַׁדּוּן. שַׁדּוּן, שַׁדִּין כְּתִיב. כַּמָּה אִית לוֹן לִבְנֵי נָשָׁא לְאִסְתַּמְּרָא אָרְחַיְיהוּ וּלְדַחֲלָא מְקַמֵּי קוּדְשָׁא בְּרִיךְ הוּא, דְּלָא יִסְטֵי מֵאָרְחָא דְּכַשְׁרָא, וְלָא יַעֲבוֹר עַל פִּתְגָּמֵי אוֹרַיְיתָא, וְלָא יִתְנְשֵׁי מִנָּה.

1. "And Hashem spoke to Moses, saying: 'This shall be the Torah of the leper in the day of his cleansing'" (Vayikra 14:1-2). Rabbi Aba opened the discussion with the verse: "Be afraid of the sword: for wrath brings the punishments of the sword that you may know that there is judgment (Heb. *shadun*)" (Iyov 19:29). It is PRONOUNCED, "*shadun*," but spelled *shedin* (lit. 'demons'). Observe in how many ways people should guard their way, fear the Holy One, blessed be He, and not depart from the right way, and people should neither transgress the laws of the Torah nor ever leave her.

2. דְּכָל מַאן דְּלָא לָעֵי בְּאוֹרַיְיתָא, וְלָא יִשְׁתְּדַל בָּה, נְזִיפָא הוּא מְקוּדְשָׁא בְּרִיךְ הוּא, רְחִיקָא הוּא מִנֵּיה, לָא שַׁרְיָא שְׁכִינְתָּא עֲמֵיה. וְאִינּוּן נְטוּרִין, דְּאַזְלִין עֲמֵיה, אִסְתְּלָקוּ מִנֵּיה, וְלֹא עוֹד אֶלָּא דְּמַכְרְזֵי קָמֵיה וְאַמְרֵי, אִסְתְּלָקוּ סוֹחֲרָנֵיה דִּפְלַנְיָא, דְּלָא חָשׁ עַל יְקָרָא דְּמָארֵיה. וַוי לֵיה, דְּהָא שַׁבְקוּהוּ עִלָּאִין וְתַתָּאִין. לֵית לֵיה חוּלָקָא בְּאָרְחָא דְּחַיֵּי.

2. He who does not learn the Torah and does not strive by her is scorned by the Holy One, blessed be He. The Shechinah does not rest upon him and the guardian ANGELS who accompany him TO PROTECT HIM depart from him.

Moreover they stand before him proclaiming: 'Withdraw from this man, for he does not honor his Master'. Woe to him, for he is abandoned by the upper and lower beings and has no part in the way of the living.

3. וְכַד אִיהוּ אִשְׁתְּדַל בְּפוּלְחָנָא דְּמָארֵיה, וְלָעֵי בְּאוֹרַיְיתָא, כַּמָה נְטוּרִין זְמִינִין לְקַבְּלֵיהּ לְנַטְרָא לֵיהּ, וּשְׁכִינְתָּא שַׁרְיָא עָלֵיהּ, וְכֹלָּא מַכְרְזֵי קַמֵּיה וְאַמְרֵי, הָבוּ יְקָרָא לְדִיּוּקְנָא דְּמַלְכָּא, הָבוּ יְקָרָא לִבְרֵיהּ דְּמַלְכָּא, אִתְנְטִיר הוּא בְּעָלְמָא דֵין וּבְעָלְמָא דְּאָתֵי, זַכָּאָה חוּלָקֵיה.

3. When man makes an effort in serving his Master and learns the Torah, many guards are there to protect him. The Shechinah also rests upon him and everyone proclaims: 'Honor the image of the King! Honor the son of the King! He is protected in this world and the World to Come! Blessed be he!'

4. ת״ח, בְּלִישָׁנָא בִּישָׁא דְּאָמַר נָחָשׁ לְאִתְּתָא, גְּרִים לְאִתְּתָא, וּלְאָדָם, לְמִגְזַר עֲלַיְיהוּ מִיתָה, וְעַל כָּל עָלְמָא בְּלִישָׁנָא בִּישָׁא כְּתִיב, וּלְשׁוֹנָם חֶרֶב חַדָּה. בְּגִ״כ, גּוּרוּ לָכֶם מִפְּנֵי חָרֶב, מִפְּנֵי לִישָׁנָא בִּישָׁא. כִּי חֵמָה עֲוֹנוֹת חָרֶב. מַאי כִּי חֵמָה עֲוֹנוֹת חָרֶב. דָּא חֶרֶב לַיְיָ׳, דְּתָנָן, חֶרֶב אִית לֵיהּ לְקוּדְשָׁא בְּרִיךְ הוּא, דְּבֵיהּ דָּאִין לְחַיָּיבַיָּא. הה״ד חֶרֶב לַיְיָ׳ מָלְאָה דָם. וְחַרְבִּי תֹּאכַל בָּשָׂר. וּבג״כ גּוּרוּ לָכֶם מִפְּנֵי חֶרֶב כִּי חֵמָה עֲוֹנוֹת חָרֶב לְמַעַן תֵּדְעוּן שַׁדּוּן, שַׁדִּין כְּתִיב. בְּגִין דְּתֵדְעוּן דְּהָכִי אִתְדָּן, מַאן דְּאִית לֵיהּ חֶרֶב בְּלִישָׁנֵיהּ, אִזְדְּמַן לֵיהּ חֶרֶב דְּשָׁצֵי כֹּלָּא, הה״ד זֹאת תִּהְיֶה תּוֹרַת הַמְּצוֹרָע.

4. Come and behold: the evil tongue of the Serpent, with which he spoke to the woman, brought death upon the man, the woman, and the whole world. Thus, it is written: "And their tongue a sharp sword" (Tehilim 57:5), referring to the evil tongue. Therefore, "be afraid of the sword," NAMELY the evil tongue. What does the following verse mean? "For wrath brings the punishments of the sword." This is "the sword of Hashem," for as we learned, the Holy One, blessed be He, has a sword with which He punishes the wicked, as it is written: "the sword of Hashem is filled with blood"

(Yeshayah 34:6). It is also written: "My sword shall devour flesh," (Devarim 32:42) FOR THIS IS THE ASPECT OF JUDGMENT WITHIN MALCHUT. Therefore, "be afraid of the sword for wrath brings the punishments of the sword that you may know that there is judgment," WHICH MEANS that you know it has been so decreed, and THAT ANYONE who has a sword in his tongue – NAMELY, HE WHO SPEAKS WITH THE EVIL TONGUE – is punished with the sword that destroys all, FOR THIS IS MALCHUT FROM THE SIDE OF JUDGMENT. This is the meaning of: "This shall be the Torah of the leper"; THAT IS, MALCHUT FROM THE ASPECT OF JUDGMENT, WHICH IS CALLED 'THIS', JUDGES THE LEPER FOR HIS EVIL TONGUE, BECAUSE PLAGUES COME FROM THE EVIL TONGUE.

5. רִבִּי אֶלְעָזָר פָּתַח, וְכַצִּפֳּרִים הָאֲחוּזוֹת בַּפָּח כָּהֵם יוּקָשִׁים בְּנֵי הָאָדָם. הַאי קְרָא הָא אִתְּמַר. אֲבָל ת"ח, בְּנֵי נָשָׁא לָא יַדְעִין, וְלָא שַׁמְעִין, וְלָא מִסְתַּכְּלֵי בִּרְעוּתָא דְּמָארֵיהוֹן, וְכָרוֹזָא כָּל יוֹמָא קָארֵי קַמַיְיהוּ, וְלֵית מָאן דְּצָיֵית לֵיהּ, וְלֵית מַאן דְּיִתְּעַר רוּחֵיהּ לְפוּלְחָנָא דְּמָארֵיהּ.

5. Rabbi Elazar cited the verse: "Like the birds that are caught in the snare, so are the sons of men snared in an evil time" (Kohelet 9:12). Although we have already learned this verse, come and behold: people are not aware of their Master's desire and do not listen to it, nor do they look to it. The supernal announcer goes before them every day to awaken them, but no one is there to listen to him and no one awakens his spirit to worship his Master.

2. When night comes

A Synopsis

We read about what happens when night falls and people go to sleep, and are told that at midnight God goes into the Garden of Eden to walk with the righteous. Those who are awake study the Torah and praise God until morning, at which time the angels all praise Him and lovingkindness is drawn to the Congregation of Yisrael. Anyone who does not wake up to worship God will come to judgment in the end.

‎6. בְּשַׁעֲתָא דְּרָמַשׁ לֵילְיָא, וְתַרְעִין סְתִימִין, אִתְּעַר נוּקְבָּא דִּתְהוֹמָא רַבָּא, וְכַמָּה חֲבִילֵי טְרִיקִין מִשְׁתַּכְּחֵי בְּעָלְמָא. כְּדֵין אָפִיל קוּדְשָׁא בְּרִיךְ הוּא שֵׁינָתָא עַל כָּל בְּנֵי עָלְמָא, וַאֲפִילוּ עַל כָּל דִּי בְּהוֹן אִתְּעָרוּתָא דְּחַיֵּי, וְאִינּוּן שָׁאטָן בְּעָלְמָא, וּמוֹדְעִין לְהוּ לִבְנֵי נָשָׁא, מִלִּין, מִנְּהוֹן כְּדִיבָן, וּמִנְּהוֹן קְשׁוֹט, וּבְנֵי נָשָׁא אִתְקַטְרוּ בְּשֵׁינָתָא.

6. When the night falls and the gates are closed, a chasm in the great abyss is opened and many battalions of demons present in the world. Then, the Holy One, blessed be He, casts sleep upon all human beings in the world AND CASTS SLEEP even upon those who are awake, NAMELY THE RIGHTEOUS. AND THE SPIRITS go around the world and inform people of different matters IN THEIR DREAMS, part of which is false and part of which is truth. People are thus linked with them in their sleep.

‎7. כַּד אִתְּעַר רוּחָא דְּצָפוֹן, וְאִתְפְּלִיג לֵילְיָא, שַׁלְהוֹבָא נָפְקָא וּבָטַשׁ תְּחוֹת גַּדְפוֹי דְּתַרְנְגוֹלָא, וְקָרֵי, וְקוּדְשָׁא בְּרִיךְ הוּא עָאל בְּגִנְתָּא דְּעֵדֶן לְאִשְׁתַּעְשְׁעָא עִם צַדִּיקַיָּא. וּכְדֵין כָּרוֹזָא נָפִיק וְקָרֵי, וְכָל בְּנֵי עָלְמָא מִתְעָרֵי בְּעַרְסַיְיהוּ, אִינּוּן דִּי בְּהוֹן אִתְּעָרוּתָא דְּחַיֵּי, קַיְימִין לְפוּלְחָנָא דְּמָארֵיהוֹן, וְעַסְקֵי בְּאוֹרַיְיתָא וּבְשִׁבְחָא דְּקוּדְשָׁא בְּרִיךְ הוּא עַד דְּאָתֵי צַפְרָא.

7. When the north wind is awakened at midnight, a flame comes out and slaps the rooster's wings and it cries. Then, the Holy One, blessed be He, comes into the Garden of Eden to delight Himself with the righteous. An

announcer comes out and proclaims, and all people awaken in their beds. Those who are awake stand by their beds to worship their Master. They learn Torah and praise the Holy One, blessed be He, until the morning comes.

8. כַּד אָתֵי צַפְרָא, כָּל חַיָּילִין וּמַשִׁרְיָין דִּלְעֵילָּא מְשַׁבְּחָן לֵיהּ לְקוּדְשָׁא בְּ"ה. הַהַ"ד בְּרָן יַחַד כֹּכְבֵי בֹקֶר וְגוֹ'. כְּדֵין כַּמָה תַּרְעִין אִתְפְּתָחוּ לְכָל סִטְרִין. וְתַרְעָא דְאַבְרָהָם, אִתְפְּתַח בָּהּ בִּכְנֶסֶת יִשְׂרָאֵל, לְזַמְּנָא לְכָל בְּנֵי עָלְמָא, הֲדָא הוּא דִכְתִיב, וַיִּטַּע אֶשֶׁל בִּבְאֵר שָׁבַע.

8. When the morning comes, all the battalions of angels above praise the Holy One, blessed be He, as it is written: "When the morning stars sang together" (Iyov 38:7). Many gates are then opened on all sides and the gate of Abraham, THE SECRET OF CHESED, is opened to the Congregation of Yisrael, WHICH IS MALCHUT, and invites all the people of the world TO ENJOY THE CHASSADIM, as it is written: "And Abraham planted a tamarisk in Beer-Sheva" (Beresheet 21:33). MALCHUT IS CALLED 'BEER-SHEVA', AND ABRAHAM PLANTED A TREE OF CHESED THERE.

9. וּמַאן דְּלָא יִתְּעַר רוּחֵיהּ בְּפוּלְחָנָא דְמָרֵיהּ, בְּהֵיךְ אַנְפִּין יְקוּם קָמֵי מַלְכָּא, כַּד יִתְּעֲרוּן עָלֵיהּ בְּדִינָא, וְיִתְפְּשׁוּן לֵיהּ בְּקוֹלָרָא, וְלָא יִשְׁתְּכַח עָלֵיהּ זְכוּתָא לְאִשְׁתְּזָבָא, כְּדֵין כְּתִיב, וְכַצִפֳּרִים הָאֲחֻזוֹת בַּפָּח כָּהֵם יוּקָשִׁים בְּנֵי אָדָם. וְעַד לָא יִנְפּוֹק בַּ"נ מֵהַאי עָלְמָא, בְּכַמָה דִינִין אִתְדָּן נַפְשָׁא עִם גּוּפָא, עַד לָא יִתְפָּרְשׁוּן דָּא מִן דָּא, וְלֵית מַאן דְּיַשְׁגַּח.

9. How will a man who does not wake up to worship his Master come before the King when Judgment is brought against him? He will be fettered in chains, MEANING THAT HE WILL BE IMPRISONED AND BROUGHT TO TRIAL, and no merit will be there to save him. Then he will be "like the birds that are caught in the snare, so are the sons of men snared in an evil time" (Kohelet 9:12). Thus, before man departs from this world, both the body and the soul suffer many chastisements before they are separated from each other, and no one is there to care ABOUT IT.

3. The punishments of the soul and body

A Synopsis
Rabbi Elazar says that when the time comes for the soul to leave
the body, it sees the Shechinah and goes toward Her with joy, but
if the person was not righteous the Shechinah leaves the soul to
mourn, separated from its body and from the Shechinah.
Afterwards both soul and body are punished and then purified.

10. בְּהַהוּא זִמְנָא דְמָטָא שַׁעֲתָא לְאִתְפָּרְשָׁא, לָא נָפְקָא נַפְשָׁא מִן
גּוּפָא, עַד דְּאִתְגְּלֵי עֲלֵיה שְׁכִינְתָּא, וְנַפְשָׁא, מִגּוֹ חֶדְוָתָא וַחֲבִיבוּתָא
דִשְׁכִינְתָּא, נָפְקָא מִגּוּפָא לְקַבְּלָהָא. אִי זַכָּאָה הוּא, מִתְקְשַׁר בָּה
וְאִתְדַּבָּק בָּה. וְאִי לָאו, שְׁכִינְתָּא אַזְלָא, וְהִיא אִשְׁתְּאָרַת, וְאָזְלַת
וּמִתְאַבְּלָא עַל פְּרִישׁוּתָא דְגוּפָא. מַתְלָא אָמְרֵי. שׁוּנְרָא מֵאֶשָׁא לָא
מִתְפְּרְשָׁא, חַדְדֵי לְסַכִּינָא, אַזְלָא אֲבַתְרֵיה.

10. When that time comes, WHEN THE SOUL must depart FROM THE BODY,
the soul does not leave the body until the Shechinah shows Herself to it.
Then it goes out from the body in joy and love of the Shechinah to meet
Her. If a man is righteous, he cleaves and bonds himself to Her. If not, the
Shechinah departs FROM HIM and his soul is left behind, mourning over its
separation from the body. It is similar to what is said about the cat which
will not be driven away from the fire: 'Sharpen Your knife and it shall
follow you', FOR IT WILL THINK THAT YOU ARE GOING TO CUT MEAT, AND
SO IT WILL BE DRIVEN AWAY FROM THE FIRE. THUS, THE SOUL DOES
NOT WANT TO SEPARATE FROM THE BODY BUT WHEN THE SHECHINAH
SHOWS HERSELF TO IT, IT LEAVES THE BODY.

11. לְבָתַר אִתְדָּנוּ תַּרְוַויְיהוּ עַל יְדוֹי דְדוּמָה. גּוּפָא אִתְּדָן בְּקִבְרָא עַד
דְּתָב לְעַפְרָא, וְנַפְשָׁא בְּאֶשָׁא דְּגֵיהִנָּם בְּכַמָּה דִינִין, עַד הַהוּא זִמְנָא
דְּאִתְגְּזַר עֲלָה לְקַבְּלָא עוֹנָשָׁא. בָּתַר דְּקַבִּילַת עוֹנָשָׁא, וּמָטֵי זִמְנָא
לְאִתְדַּכָּאָה, כְּדֵין אִסְתְּלָקָא מִגֵּיהִנָּם, וְאִתְלַבְּנַת מֵחוֹבָהָא כְּפַרְזְלָא
דְּאִתְלָבַּן בְּנוּרָא, וְסַלְקִין עִמָּה, עַד דְּעָאלַת לְגִנְתָּא דְּעֵדֶן דִּלְתַתָּא,
וְאִסְתַּחֵי תַּמָּן בְּאִינּוּן מַיָּא, וְאִסְתַּחֵי בְּבוּסְמִין דְּתַמָּן. כד"א, מְקֻטֶּרֶת מֹר

וּלְבָנָה. וְקַיְּימָא תַּמָּן עַד זִמְנָא דְּאִתְגְּזַר עֲלֵיהּ לְאִתְרַחֲקָא מֵאֲתַר דְּיַתְבִין בֵּיהּ צַדִּיקַיָּא.

11. Afterwards, both the soul and the body are punished by the hand of THE ANGEL Dumah. The body is sentenced to the grave until it returns to dust, and the soul IS SENTENCED to the fire of Gehenom in several trials until its time comes to be punished. After being punished, the time comes for it to be purified. The soul comes out of Gehenom and is cleansed of its sins like an iron whitened in the fire. ANGELS ascend with it until it arrives at the Lower Garden of Eden, where it is cleansed in the water and perfumed with its spices, as written: "Perfumed with myrrh and frankincense" (Shir Hashirim 3:6). It stays there until that time is over when it must be far from the righteous IN THE UPPER GARDEN OF EDEN.

12. וְכַד מָטָא זִמְנָא לְסַלְּקָא, כְּדֵין סַלְּקִין עִמָּהּ, דַּרְגָּא בָּתַר דַּרְגָּא, עַד דְּאִתְקְרִיבַת כְּקוּרְבְּנָא עַל מַדְבְּחָא. הה"ד, זֹאת תִּהְיֶה תּוֹרַת הַמְּצוֹרָע בְּיוֹם טָהֳרָתוֹ וְהוּבָא אֶל הַכֹּהֵן, כַּהֲנָא עִלָּאָה דִּלְעֵילָא, הַאי נַפְשָׁא דְּלָא אִסְתְּאָבַת כ"כ, בְּהַאי עָלְמָא, הַאי אִית לָהּ תַּקַנְתָּא, כְּגַוְונָא דָּא. וְאִי לָאו, מְעֻוָּות לֹא יָכוֹל לִתְקוֹן וְגוֹ'.

12. When the time comes for it to ascend TO THE UPPER GARDEN OF EDEN, it ascends stage after stage until it is brought as a sacrifice on the altar, MEANING IT IS BROUGHT TO THE NUKVA OF MALCHUT, WHICH IS CALLED AN ALTAR. This is the meaning of, "This shall be the Torah of the leper; in the day of his cleansing he shall be brought to the priest" (Vayikra 14:2), NAMELY the supernal Priest above, WHO IS THE ANGEL MICHAEL. This is the fate of a soul that has not been defiled much in this world and that can still be healed, AS IT IS SAID ABOVE. Otherwise, "THAT WHICH IS crooked cannot be made straight" (Kohelet 1:15).

13. זֹאת תִּהְיֶה תּוֹרַת הַמְּצוֹרָע. ר' יִצְחָק פָּתַח, וְזָרַח הַשֶּׁמֶשׁ וּבָא הַשֶּׁמֶשׁ וְגוֹ'. הַאי קְרָא אִתְּמַר, וְאוֹקִימְנָא לֵיהּ בְּנִשְׁמָתָא דְּב"נ, בְּשַׁעֲתָא דְּהִיא קַיְּימָא עִמֵּיהּ דְּב"נ בְּהַאי עָלְמָא, כְּדֵין, וְזָרַח הַשֶּׁמֶשׁ. וּבָא הַשֶּׁמֶשׁ, בְּזִמְנָא דְּנָפִיק ב"נ מֵהַאי עָלְמָא, וְאִשְׁתְּכַח בִּתְשׁוּבָה, כְּדֵין אֶל

מְקוֹמוֹ שׁוֹאֵף זוֹרֵחַ הוּא שָׁם, אִי זַכָּאָה אִיהוּ, כד"א, וּבָא הַשֶּׁמֶשׁ וְטָהֵר, וְאַחַר יֹאכַל מִן הַקֳּדָשִׁים.

13. "This shall be the Torah of the leper." Rabbi Yitzchak opened the discussion with the verse: "the sun also rises and the sun also goes down" (Kohelet 1:5). We have learned this verse and explained that it speaks of the soul of a man. When the soul is with man, then "the sun also rises". However, "the sun goes down," REFERS to the time when he departs from the world. If he is in a state of repentance, then it "hastens to its place where it rises again" (Ibid.). If he is righteous, it is written: "And when the sun goes down he shall be clean" (Vayikra 22:7), MEANING THAT WHEN "THE SUN GOES DOWN," HE DEPARTS FROM THIS WORLD. HE IS PURE AND HE "shall afterwards eat of the holy things" (Ibid.).

4. He who speaks with an evil tongue

A Synopsis

Rabbi Yitzchak says that God pardons everything except an evil tongue; one who speaks evil, intending to defile another, is defiled himself. Because of the sins of Yisrael, the Other Side was awakened in Jerusalem and it was abandoned by God. Rabbi Yehuda says that the word Metzora, meaning 'leper', includes the words Mozi Ra, meaning 'speaks evil', and we learn that the prayers of one who speaks evil never come before God until he repents; then he will be cleansed.

14. ת״ח, כָּל חוֹבֵי עָלְמָא, קוּדְשָׁא בְּרִיךְ הוּא מְכַפֵּר עָלַיְיהוּ, בִּתְשׁוּבָה, בַּר מֵהַהוּא לִישָׁנָא בִּישָׁא, דְּאַפִּיק שׁוּם בִּישׁ עַל חַבְרֵיה. וְהָא אוּקְמוּהָ, דִּכְתִיב, זֹאת תִּהְיֶה תּוֹרַת הַמְצוֹרָע, זֹאת הִיא תּוֹרָתוֹ שֶׁל מוֹצִיא שֵׁם רָע. רִבִּי חִיָּיא אָמַר, כָּל מַאן דְּאַפִּיק לִישָׁנָא בִּישָׁא, אִסְתָּאֲבָן לֵיה כָּל שַׁיְיפוֹי, וְיִתְחֲזֵי לְסַגְרָא, בְּגִין דְּהַהִיא מִלָּה בִּישָׁא סַלְקָא וְאִתְּעַר רוּחָא מְסָאֲבָא עֲלוֹי וְאִסְתָּאַב, אָתֵי לְאִסְתָּאֲבָא מְסָאֲבִין לֵיה, בְּמִלָּה דִּלְתַתָּא אִתְּעַר מִלָּה אָחֲרָא.

14. Come and behold: the Holy One, blessed be He, grants pardons for all the sins of the world, save the evil tongue, for this man speaks evil of another, as written: "This shall be the Torah of the leper (Heb. *metzora*)" (Vayikra 14:2). THAT IS, he speaks evil of his friend, SINCE "*METZORA*" IS SPELLED WITH THE SAME LETTERS AS THE WORDS, *MOTZI RA* (LIT. 'SPREADS EVIL'). Rabbi Chiya said: If someone spreads an evil name, all his limbs become defiled and he should be shut out, for his evil speech rises aloft and calls down an unclean Spirit on him, and he is defiled. He who intends to defile is defiled; by the deed below another one is roused.

15. פָּתַח וְאָמַר, אֵיכָה הָיְתָה לְזוֹנָה קִרְיָה נֶאֱמָנָה וְגוֹ'. מַאן דַּהֲוַת מְהֵימְנָא לְבַעֲלָהּ, אַהֲדָרַת לְזוֹנָה. מְלֵאֲתִי מִשְׁפָּט, מִשְׁפָּט, וַדַּאי דָּא קוּדְשָׁא בְּרִיךְ הוּא, צֶדֶק, דָּא כ״י, וּבְגִין דְּאִתְּעָרַת מִלָּה אָחֲרָא, אִסְתְּלַק מִנָּהּ קוּדְשָׁא בְּרִיךְ הוּא, וְשַׁרְיָא בָּהּ רוּחָא דִּקְטוּלֵי. הה״ד וְעַתָּה מְרַצְּחִים. וּמַה יְרוּשְׁלֵם קַרְתָּא קַדִּישָׁא כָּךְ, שְׁאָר בְּנֵי נָשָׁא עאכ״ו.

הה"ד, זֹאת תִּהְיֶה תּוֹרַת הַמְּצֹרָע.

15. He opened the discussion, saying: "How is the faithful city become a harlot" (Yeshayah 1:21), MEANING HOW can she, who was faithful to her husband, become a harlot? "It was full of judgment (or: justice)" (Ibid.). Justice is the Holy One, blessed be He, and righteousness is the Congregation of Yisrael, NAMELY MALCHUT. Because another aspect was awakened – THE OTHER SIDE WAS AWAKENED BECAUSE OF THE SINS OF YISRAEL – the Holy One, blessed be He, called 'Justice', departs from her, NAMELY, FROM MALCHUT THAT IS CALLED 'RIGHTEOUSNESS'. A spirit of murderers abides in her, as it is written: "But now murderers" (Ibid.). If that was the fate of Jerusalem, the Holy City, how much more so must that be the fate of ordinary men, as it is written: "This shall be the Torah of the leper."

16. רִבִּי יְהוּדָה אָמַר, זֹאת תִּהְיֶה וַדַּאי לְקַבְּלֵיהּ לְאִתְפָּרְעָא מִנֵּיהּ, דְּהַהוּא מוֹצִיא שֵׁם רָע, בְּיוֹם טָהֳרָתוֹ וְהוּבָא אֶל הַכֹּהֵן, מַאי קָמ"ל. מַשְׁמַע, מַאן דְּאִית לֵיהּ לִישָׁנָא בִּישָׁא צְלוֹתֵיהּ לָא עָאלַת קַמֵּי קוּדְשָׁא בְּרִיךְ הוּא, דְּהָא אִתְּעַר עֲלֵיהּ רוּחָא מְסָאֲבָא. כֵּיוָן דְּאָהֲדַר בִּתְשׁוּבָה וְקַבִּיל עֲלֵיהּ תְּשׁוּבָה, מַה כְּתִיב, בְּיוֹם טָהֳרָתוֹ וְהוּבָא אֶל הַכֹּהֵן וְגוֹ' וְרָאָה הַכֹּהֵן וְגוֹ'.

16. Rabbi Yehuda opened the discussion saying: "This," MALCHUT, shall confront him, the one who spread the evil speech, to punish the man who speaks evil, FOR THE WORD METZORA (LIT. 'A LEPER') INCLUDES THE WORDS MOZI RA, THAT IS, 'SPEAKS EVIL'. "In the day of his cleansing he shall be brought to the priest" (Vayikra 14:2). We learn from this verse that the prayer of the man who has an evil tongue does not come before the Holy One, blessed be He, for the Evil Spirit abides with him. However, if he repents, then "in the day of his cleansing he shall be brought to the priest... and the priest shall look..." (Ibid. 2-3).

17. וְצִוָּה הַכֹּהֵן וְלָקַח לַמִּטַּהֵר שְׁתֵּי צִפֳּרִים חַיּוֹת. ר' יִצְחָק וְר' יוֹסֵי הֲווֹ שְׁכִיחֵי קַמֵּיהּ דְּר"שׁ. יוֹמָא חַד אָ"ל, עֵץ אֶרֶז הָא יְדִיעַ, כְּד"א, מִן הָאֶרֶז אֲשֶׁר בַּלְּבָנוֹן, דְּהָא הַהוּא עֵץ אֶרֶז, לָא אִשְׁתְּרְשָׁן נְטִיעוֹי אֶלָּא בַּלְּבָנוֹן,

וְהָא אִתְּמַר. אֵזוֹב לְמָה, וּמַאי הוּא.

17. "Then shall the priest command to take for him to be cleansed two live clean birds" (Vayikra 14:4). Rabbi Yitzchak and Rabbi Yosi were staying with Rabbi Shimon. One day, he said to them: It is known that a cedar tree IS TIFERET, for it is written, "From the cedar tree that is in Lebanon" (I Melachim 5:13). That cedar, WHICH IS TIFERET, can strike roots only in Lebanon, WHICH IS BINAH, and we have already learned this. BUT what is the point of the "hyssop that comes out of the wall" (Ibid.)?

5. "Two clean, live birds"

A Synopsis
Rabbi Shimon says that when a man comes with repentance to be purified, God and the Shechinah return to him.

‎18. פָּתַח וְאָמַר, וְלָקַח לַמְּטַהֵר שְׁתֵּי צִפֳּרִים חַיּוֹת טְהוֹרוֹת וְעֵץ אֶרֶז וּשְׁנִי תוֹלַעַת וְאֵזוֹב. ת״ח, ב״נ דְּמִשְׁתַּדֵּל בְּפוּלְחָנָא דְּמָארֵיהּ, וְאִשְׁתְּדַל בְּאוֹרַיְיתָא, קוּדְשָׁא בְּרִיךְ הוּא שָׁארֵי עֲלוֹי וּשְׁכִינְתָּא אִשְׁתַּתְּפָא בַּהֲדֵיהּ. כֵּיוָן דְּב״נ אָתֵי לְאִסְתַּאֲבָא, שְׁכִינְתָּא אִסְתַּלְּקַת מִנֵּיהּ, קוּדְשָׁא בְּרִיךְ הוּא אִתְרְחִיק מִנֵּיהּ, וְכָל סִטְרָא דִּקְדוּשָׁה דְּמָארֵיהּ מְרַחֲקִין מִנֵּיהּ, וְשָׁארֵי עֲלֵיהּ רוּחַ מִסְאֲבָא וְכָל סִטְרָא דִּמְסָאֲבָא, אָתֵי לְאִתְדַּכְּאָה מְסַיְּיעִין לֵיהּ. בָּתַר דְּאִתְדָּכֵי וְאַהְדַּר בִּתְשׁוּבָה, הַהוּא דְּאִסְתַּלָּק מִנֵּיהּ אַהְדָּר, וְשָׁארֵי עֲלוֹי.

18. He opened the discussion, saying: "Then shall the priest command to take for him to be cleansed two clean, live birds, and cedar wood, and scarlet and hyssop" (Vayikra 14:4). Come and behold: when a man worships his Master and studies the Torah, the Holy One, blessed be He, rests upon him and the Shechinah joins with him. When a man is defiled, the Shechinah departs from him and the Holy One, blessed be He, draws away from him. All the sides of his Master's Holiness draw away from him and the Defiled Spirit rests upon him, as do all the sides of Impurity. When a man comes to purify himself, he is assisted. Then after he was purified and after repenting all that departed from him, NAMELY THE HOLY ONE, BLESSED BE HE, AND HIS SHECHINAH, return to him and rest upon him.

‎19. ת״ח, כְּתִיב וְלָקַח לַמְּטַהֵר שְׁתֵּי צִפֳּרִים חַיּוֹת טְהוֹרוֹת. כֵּיוָן דְּאָמַר, שְׁתֵּי צִפֳּרִים, לָא יְדַעְנָא דְּאִינּוּן חַיּוֹת, אֶלָּא, הָא אוּקְמוּהָ, אֲבָל חַיּוֹת, חַיּוֹת מַמָּשׁ. כד״א וָאֵרֶא הַחַיּוֹת, לָקֳבֵל אֲתַר דְּיַנְקֵי מִנַּיְיהוּ נְבִיאֵי מְהֵימְנֵי, וְעֵץ אֶרֶז הָא אִתְּמַר, וּשְׁנִי תוֹלַעַת, סְטַר סוּמָקָא דִּגְבוּרָה דְּאִשְׁתַּתָּף בַּהֲדֵיהּ בְּקַדְמֵיתָא. וְאֵזוֹב, דָּא ו׳ זְעֵירָא, דְּיָנִיק לֵיהּ לכ״י, ובג״כ, עֵץ אֶרֶז וְאֵזוֹב, אַזְלָן כַּחֲדָא, וְעַל דָּא ו׳ ו׳ כַּחֲדָא אִשְׁתְּכָחוּ, חַד

עִלָאָה, וְחַד זְעֵירָא, וְקַרְיָין לוֹן, ו' עִלָאָה, ו' תַּתָּאָה. וְכֻלְּהוּ אַהֲדְרוּ
לְשַׁרְיָא עֲלוֹי בְּגִין דְּהָא אִתְדְּכֵי, לָקֲבֵל אִלֵּין, לְתַתָּא, עֵץ אֶרֶז וְאֵזוֹב
וּשְׁנִי תוֹלַעַת אִשְׁתְּכָחוּ בְּדַכְיוּתָא דָּא, וְתַלְיָין מֵאִלֵּין עִלָּאִין.

19. Come and behold: it is written, "Then shall the priest command to take for him to be cleansed two clean, live birds..." HE ASKS: Do I not know that when it says, "two birds," it means that they are "live"? WHY IS "LIVE" WRITTEN? HE ANSWERS: It was already explained that "live" MEANS actually living, as written, "I beheld the living creatures" (Yechezkel 1:15), WHICH corresponds to the place from which the true prophets draw inspiration, NAMELY NETZACH AND HOD, CALLED 'LOWER LIVING CREATURES'. In regards to, "A cedar wood," we have already learned THAT THIS IS TIFERET, and "scarlet" is the red side of Gvurah OF THE SHECHINAH, which associated with him at first. "Hyssop" is the small *Vav*, WHICH IS YESOD, that gives sustenance to the Congregation of Yisrael, THE SHECHINAH. Therefore, "cedar wood and hyssop," WHICH ARE TIFERET AND YESOD, go together, MEANING THAT THEY ARE CONSIDERED AS ONE. Therefore, *Vav* and *Vav* are together as one WHEN IT IS UTTERED IN THE NAME YUD HEI VAV HEI, SINCE *VAV* IS PRONOUNCED *VAV*. One IS above, NAMELY TIFERET, and the other IS smaller, NAMELY YESOD, and they are called the upper *Vav* and the lower *Vav*. All of them – THE HOLY ONE, BLESSED BE HE, WHO IS TIFERET AND YESOD AND THE SHECHINAH – return and rest upon him AS BEFORE, for he is purified. Corresponding to those THAT RETURN TO HIM, WHICH ARE TIFERET AND YESOD AND THE SHECHINAH, are "cedar wood and hyssop and scarlet" below, which pertain to that purification, which come down from THE SFIROT above.

6. "And happy are those who hold her fast"

A Synopsis

From Rabbi Yehuda we learn that the Torah is a "Tree of Life"; Torah means 'showing' – it reveals all that is hidden and unknown. Those people who help support students of the Torah with their money are blessed. Those who hold on to the Torah are worthy of having prophets as their descendants.

20. ר' יְהוּדָה וְר' יִצְחָק הֲוֹו אַזְלֵי בְּאָרְחָא. יָתְבוּ בְּהַהוּא בֵּי חַקְלָא וְצַלּוּ. בָּתַר דְּסַיְּימוּ צְלוֹתָא קָמוּ וְאַזְלוּ. פָּתַח ר' יְהוּדָה בְּמִלֵּי דְאוֹרַיְיתָא. וְאָמַר, עֵץ חַיִּים הִיא לַמַּחֲזִיקִים בָּה וְתוֹמְכֶיהָ מְאוּשָׁר. עֵץ חַיִּים, דָּא אוֹרַיְיתָא, דְּאִיהִי אִילָנָא עִלָּאָה רַבָּא וְתַקִּיף. תּוֹרָה, אֲמַאי אִקְרֵי תּוֹרָה. בְּגִין דְּאוֹרֵי וְגַלֵּי בְּמָה דַּהֲוָה סָתִים דְּלָא אִתְיְדַע. חַיִּים, דְּכָל חַיִּים דִּלְעֵילָא בָּהּ אִתְכְּלִילוּ, וּמִנָּהּ נָפְקִין. לַמַּחֲזִיקִים בָּהּ, לְאִינּוּן דְּאַחֲדִין בָּהּ, דְּמַאן דְּאָחִיד בְּאוֹרַיְיתָא אָחִיד בְּכֹלָּא, אָחִיד לְעֵילָא וְתַתָּא. וְתוֹמְכֶיהָ מְאוּשָׁר, מַאן תּוֹמְכֶיהָ. אִלֵּין אִינּוּן דְּמַטִילִין מְלָאי, לְכִיסָן שֶׁל ת"ח, כְּמָה דְאוּקְמוּהָ.

20. Rabbi Yehuda and Rabbi Yitzchak were once on their way together. They stopped at a certain field to pray and then continued along. Rabbi Yehuda commenced a discourse on the Torah and said: "She is a Tree of Life to those who lay hold on her and happy are those who hold her fast" (Mishlei 3:18). "A Tree of Life" is the Torah, which is a great and mighty tree. It is called Torah (lit. 'showing'), for it shows and reveals all that was hidden and unknown. IT IS CALLED 'Life', for all life above is contained in it and issues from it. "Those who lay hold on her" are those who are attached to her above and below. "Happy are those who hold her fast," are those who throw their fill, THEIR PROFIT OF MERCHANDISE, into the purses of students of the Torah, AND THEY BECOME WORTHY OF A PART IN THEIR PROFIT, as explained.

21. וְתוֹמְכֶיהָ, זָכֵי לִנְבִיאֵי מְהֵימְנֵי דְּיִפְּקוּן מִנֵּיהּ. מְאוּשָׁר, אַל תִּקְרֵי מְאוּשָׁר, אֶלָּא מֵרֹאשׁוֹ, אִינּוּן תַּמְכִין לְאוֹרַיְיתָא, מֵרֹאשׁוֹ וְעַד סוֹפוֹ. מֵרֹאשׁוֹ, דָּא רֵישָׁא דְּכֹלָּא דְּאִקְרֵי רֹאשׁ, דִּכְתִּיב, מֵעוֹלָם נִסַּכְתִּי מֵרֹאשׁ.

וְרֹאשׁ דָּא חָכְמָה, דְּאִיהִי רֵישָׁא לְכָל גּוּפָא, וְגוּפָא אִתְפְּשָׁט בֵּיהּ עַד
סִיּוּמָא דְּשִׁית סִטְרִין, וְתוֹמְכֵיהָ, כד"א, שׁוֹקָיו עַמּוּדֵי שֵׁשׁ. דְּאִינּוּן
דְּמַטִּילִין מִלָּאי לְכִיסָן שֶׁל ת"ח אִינּוּן תַּמְכִין לְאוֹרַיְיתָא מֵרֵישָׁא עַד
סִיּוּמָא דְּגוּפָא, וְכָל מְהֵימְנוּתָא, בֵּיהּ תַּלְיָא, וְאִתְּמַךְ. וְזָכֵי לִבְנִין
דְּיִתְחֲזוּן לִנְבִיאֵי מְהֵימְנֵי.

21. "Those who hold her fast," MEANS that they become worthy of producing CHILDREN WORTHY OF BEING faithful prophets, FOR THE TORAH ALLUDES TO TIFERET, WHICH IS THE BODY OF ZEIR ANPIN. NETZACH AND HOD, WHICH ARE THE SECRET OF THE PROPHETS, ARE LIKE THE LEGS WHO HOLD THE TIFERET, THE TORAH, AS THE LEGS HOLD THE BODY. THEREFORE, THOSE WHO HOLD THE TORAH ARE WORTHY OF HAVING PROPHETS AS DESCENDANTS. "Happy (Heb. me'ushar)" should be pronounced merosho, meaning literally 'from his head', HAVING THE SAME LETTERS AS MEUSHAR – FOR NETZACH AND HOD support the Torah, WHICH IS ZEIR ANPIN, from the top all the way down LIKE THE LEGS SUPPORT THE BODY FROM THE TOP ALL THE WAY DOWN. The meaning of 'from his head' is the head of all, called 'head', as it is written: "I was set up from everlasting from the beginning (Heb. merosh)" (Mishlei 8:23). This beginning (lit. 'head') is Chochmah, for it is the head of the whole body, WHICH IS TIFERET, and the body spreads in it to the end of the six directions – WHICH ARE CHESED, GVURAH, TIFERET, NETZACH, HOD AND YESOD. Those "who hold her fast" ARE as written: "His legs are pillars of marble" (Shir Hashirim 5:15), WHICH ARE NETZACH AND HOD. Those who put their sales profits into the pockets of students of the Torah become pillars of the Torah from its head to the body's end, WHICH IS YESOD. All the Faith, WHICH IS MALCHUT, depends on THE BODY, WHICH IS THE TORAH, and it is supported and merits sons who are fit to be faithful prophets.

7. The best man of the King and the best man of the Queen

A Synopsis

Rabbi Shimon explains to Rabbi Yitzchak that Moses is greater than Aaron because Moses is the King's best man and Aaron is the Queen's best man; Aaron's duty as high priest is to bring Malchut to perfection. Rabbi Yehuda says that God draws the wicked toward Him so they will repent; if they do not, he destroys them even from the World to Come. And yet if they want to be purified they are helped and brought to peace.

22. רִבִּי יִצְחָק פָּתַח, וַיִּקְרָא אֶל מֹשֶׁה וַיְדַבֵּר יְיָ' אֵלָיו מֵאֹהֶל מוֹעֵד לֵאמֹר. וַיִּקְרָא אָלֶף זְעֵירָא, אֲמַאי. אֶלָּא בְּגִין לְאַחֲזָאָה מַאן הוּא הַהוּא דְּקָרָא, הַהוּא דִּשָׁרֵי בְּמַקְדְּשָׁא, וּכְדֵין זַמִּין לְמֹשֶׁה, כְּמַאן דְּזַמִּין אוּשְׁפִּיזָא. הָכָא א' זְעֵירָא, הָתָם א' רַבְּתָא, אָדָם שֵׁת אֱנוֹשׁ. דָּא שְׁלִימוּ דְּכֹלָּא.

22. Rabbi Yitzchak opened the discussion with the verse: "And Hashem called to Moses, and spoke to him out of the tent of meeting, saying" (Vayikra 1:1). HE ASKS: Why is the word "called" (Heb. *vaikra*) SPELLED WITH a small Aleph? HE ANSWERS: The one who abides in the sanctuary, WHICH IS MALCHUT, is the one who called MOSES and invited Moses TO APPEAR BEFORE HER as one invites a guest. Here, IT IS WRITTEN with a small Aleph and in another verse, "Adam, Seth, Enosh" (Divrei Hayamim 1:1) is WRITTEN a big one, FOR A BIG ALEPH IS BINAH, which is the perfection of all. SMALL LETTERS ARE IN MALCHUT AND THE BIG ONES ARE IN BINAH.

23. תָּ"ח, מַה בֵּין מֹשֶׁה לְאַהֲרֹן, הֵי מִנַּיְיהוּ עִלָּאָה. אֶלָּא מֹשֶׁה עִלָּאָה, מֹשֶׁה שׁוֹשְׁבִינָא דְּמַלְכָּא, אַהֲרֹן שׁוֹשְׁבִינָא דְּמַטְרוֹנִיתָא. מָתַל לְמַלְכָּא דַּהֲוָ"ל מַטְרוֹנִיתָא עִלָּאָה. מָה עֲבַד. יָהַב לָהּ שׁוֹשְׁבִינָא לְתַקְּנָא לָהּ וּלְאִסְתַּכְּלָא בְּמִלֵּי דְּבֵיתָא. וְעַ"ד, כַּד עָיֵיל שׁוֹשְׁבִינָא דָּא לְמַלְכָּא, לָא עָיֵיל אֶלָּא עִם מַטְרוֹנִיתָא, הה"ד, בְּזֹאת יָבֹא אַהֲרֹן וְגוֹ'.

23. Come and behold: there is a difference between Moses and Aaron. Which one is superior? HE ANSWERS: Moses is greater, FOR Moses is the

King's best man and Aaron is the Queen's best man. This is like a king who gave his exalted queen a best man to attend to her and her house so that the companion would never appear before the king without the queen. Thus, it is written about Aaron: "Thus (lit. 'with this') (Heb. *zot*) shall Aaron come into the holy place" (Vayikra 16:3), THAT IS, WITH MALCHUT, CALLED 'ZOT', AS HER BEST MAN.

24. מֹשֶׁה שׁוּשְׁבִינָא לְמַלְכָּא, בְּג"כ אִזְדְּמַן כְּאוּשְׁפִּיזָא, וּלְבָתַר, וַיְדַבֵּר יְיָ' אֵלָיו. אַהֲרֹן הוּא שׁוּשְׁבִינָא לְמַטְרוֹנִיתָא, וְכָל מִלּוֹי הֲווֹ, לְפַיְּיסָא לְמַלְכָּא בְּמַטְרוֹנִיתָא, וְיִתְפַּיֵּיס מַלְכָּא בַּהֲדָהּ. וְעַ"ד בְּגִין דְּאִיהוּ, שׁוּשְׁבִינָא לָהּ שַׁוֵּי מָדוֹרֵיהּ בַּהֲדָהּ, לְתַקְּנָא בֵּיתָא וּלְעַיְינָא תָּדִיר בְּמִלֵּי דְּבֵיתָא. וְעַ"ד אִתְתָּקַן כְּגַוְונָא דִּלְעֵילָּא, וְאִקְרֵי כֹּהֵן גָּדוֹל. מ"ל. דִּכְתִיב אַתָּה כֹהֵן לְעוֹלָם עַל דִּבְרָתִי מַלְכִּי צֶדֶק.

24. Moses WAS the best man of the King. Therefore, he was invited to MALCHUT as a guest, WHICH IS THE SECRET OF THE SMALL ALEPH IN THE WORD VAYIKRA (LIT. 'CALLED'). Then "Hashem spoke to him." Aaron was the best man of the Queen, NAMELY MALCHUT, and all his discourse was for the purpose of the King making pleasing to the Queen, so that the King would be pleased with Her. AARON, who is the best man of the Queen, made a dwelling with Her to attend to her house. He was perfected for this after the supernal model, AS CHESED OF ZEIR ANPIN, and was called a "High Priest." Whence do we know that? It is written: "You shall be a priest forever, after the manner of Melchizedek," (Tehilim 110:4) MEANING THAT "A PRIEST FOREVER" IS CHESED, AND HIS DUTY IS TO BRING MALCHUT, WHICH IS CALLED 'MELCHIZEDEK', TO PERFECTION.

25. וּבְג"כ כָּל מַה דְּאִצְטְרִיךְ מִבֵּי מַלְכָּא, נָטִיל, וְלֵית מַאן דִּימְחֵי בִּידֵיהּ. וְעַ"ד הוּא קָאִים לְדַכְּאָה לְכָל אִינּוּן דְּעָאלִין לְבֵי מַטְרוֹנִיתָא, בְּגִין דְּלָא יִשְׁתְּכַח מְסָאֲבָא בְּאִינּוּן בְּנֵי הֵיכָלָא. וּבְג"כ כְּתִיב, וְלָקַח לַמִּטַּהֵר שְׁתֵּי צִפֳּרִים וְגוֹ'.

25. Therefore, he took everything he needed from the residence of the King. And he had to purify all those coming to the house of the Queen, so that

there would be none who were unclean among those who entered the sanctuary. Hence, it is written: "Then shall the priest command to take for him to be cleansed two clean, live birds" (Vayikra 14:4).

26. רִבִּי יְהוּדָה פָּתַח וְאָמַר, יוֹשֵׁב בַּשָּׁמַיִם יִשְׂחָק יְיָ' יִלְעַג לָמוֹ. יוֹשֵׁב בַּשָּׁמַיִם יִשְׂחָק, דָּא יִצְחָק דְּאָתֵי מִסִּטְרָא דְּחַמְרָא, נָהִיר בְּקַדְמֵיתָא, וְחַיֵּיךָ, וּלְבָתַר זָעִים וְתָרִיךָ. הה"ד יוֹשֵׁב בַּשָּׁמַיִם וְלָא כְּתִיב, יוֹשֵׁב שָׁמַיִם. יִשְׂחָק, נָהִיר וְחַיֵּיךָ. וְעַל דָּא דִּינָא נָהִיר וְחַיֵּיךָ, לְהוּ לְרַשִׁיעַיָּיא.

26. Rabbi Yehuda opened the discussion with the verse: "He who sits in the heavens laughs, Hashem has them in derision" (Tehilim 2:4). "He who sits in the heavens laughs" is "Isaac (lit. 'he will laugh')," who comes from the side of wine, that first smiles and laughs and then rages and bewilders. Hence, it says "who sits in the heavens," and it is not written, 'who sits (in) heaven', FOR HEAVEN IS ZEIR ANPIN, WHICH INCLUDES CHESED, GVURAH, TIFERET, NETZACH, HOD AND YESOD. WERE IT WRITTEN 'WHO SITS (IN) HEAVEN', I WOULD SAY IT IS ZEIR ANPIN, BUT IT IS WRITTEN: "HE WHO SITS IN THE HEAVENS," THAT IS, IN ONE SIDE OF THE HEAVEN, WHICH IS GVURAH AND THE ATTRIBUTE OF ISAAC. Isaac laughs, THAT IS, laughs and illuminates, and therefore the Judgment illuminates and laughs upon the wicked.

27. וּלְבָתַר מַה כְּתִיב, אָז יְדַבֵּר אֵלֵימוֹ בְּאַפּוֹ וּבַחֲרוֹנוֹ יְבַהֲלֵמוֹ. וְכַךְ אָרְחֵי דְּחַיָּיבַיָּא, קוּדְשָׁא בְּרִיךְ הוּא נָהִיר לְהוּ בְּהַאי עָלְמָא, וְנָהִיר לוֹן אַנְפִּין כְּחַמְרָא, דְּנָהִיר בְּקַדְמֵיתָא, וּלְבָתַר זָעִים וְקָטִיל. וְקוּדְשָׁא בְּרִיךְ הוּא מָשִׁיךְ לוֹן לְחַיָּיבַיָּא, אִי יְהַדְרוּן לְקַבְלֵיה, יָאוּת, וְאִי לָא שָׂצֵי לוֹן מֵהַהוּא עָלְמָא דְּאָתֵי, וְלֵית לוֹן בֵּיה חוּלָקָא, וְיִשְׁתֵּצוּן מִכֹּלָא. אַתּוּן לְאִתְדַּכְּאָה, מְסַיְיעִין לוֹן. וְקוּדְשָׁא בְּרִיךְ הוּא מְדַכֵּי לוֹן וְקָרִיב לוֹן לְגַבֵּיה, וְקָארִי עֲלַיְיהוּ שָׁלוֹם. הֲדָא הוּא דִּכְתִּיב שָׁלוֹם שָׁלוֹם לָרָחוֹק וְלַקָּרוֹב וְגו'.

27. Then it is written: "Then shall He speak to them in His wrath, and terrify them in His burning anger" (Tehilim 2:5). Such is the way for the wicked. The Holy One, blessed be He, at first shines on them and shows them favor,

as the wine sheds light at first, and then rages and kills. The Holy One, blessed be He, draws the wicked to Him, SO THEY WILL REPENT. If they turn to Him, all is well. If they do not turn to Him, He destroys them and removes them from the World to Come. They have no share in it and they are lost to everything. If they desire to be purified, they are helped. The Holy One, blessed be He, purifies them and brings them close to Him and calls peace upon them, as written: "Peace, peace, both for far and near says Hashem" (Yeshayah 57:19).

8. "And if a woman has an issue of her blood"

A Synopsis

Rabbi Chiya talks about the day that God will punish the wicked and take final vengeance on those who oppressed the children of Yisrael. Rabbi Shimon says that the wicked cause these judgments to be brought to the world before their time. Yet God adds judgments only to the extent that the world is able to bear them. In the time to come God will remove the Unclean Spirit from the world altogether.

28. וְאִשָּׁה כִּי יָזוּב זוֹב דָּמָהּ יָמִים רַבִּים בְּלֹא עֶת נִדָּתָהּ וְגוֹ'. ר' חִיָּיא פָּתַח וְאָמַר, הִנֵּה יוֹם בָּא לַיְיָ' וְחֻלַּק שְׁלָלֵךְ בְּקִרְבֵּךְ. הַאי קְרָא הָכִי מִבְּעֵי לֵיהּ, הִנֵּה יוֹם יָבֹא, מַאי, הִנֵּה יוֹם בָּא. אֶלָּא שֶׁכְּבָר בָּא, עַד לָא אִבְרֵי עָלְמָא, וְהוּא יוֹם דְּבֵיהּ יַעֲבִיד דִּינָא לְחַיָּיבַיָּא. וְהוּא יוֹם דְּבֵיהּ יִתְפְּרַע קוּדְשָׁא בְּרִיךְ הוּא מֵאִינוּן דְּעָקוּן לוֹן לְיִשְׂרָאֵל. הַאי יוֹם בָּא וְקָאִים קַמֵּי קוּדְשָׁא בְּרִיךְ הוּא, וְתָבַע מִנֵּיהּ לְמֶעְבַּד דִּינָא וּלְשֵׁיצָאָה עכו"ם, וְאִתְיְהִיב לֵיהּ רְשׁוּ, כד"א וְאָסַפְתִּי אֶת כָּל הַגּוֹיִם אֶל יְרוּשָׁלַם לַמִּלְחָמָה וְגוֹ'.

28. "And if a woman has an issue of her blood for many days not in the time of her menstruation..." (Vayikra 15:25). Rabbi Chiya opened the discourse on the verse: "Behold, the day of Hashem comes when Your spoil shall be divided in the midst of you" (Zecharyah 14:1). This verse should have been written, 'Behold the day...will come'. Why is it written: "the day comes (also: 'came')"? HE ANSWERS: This day has come before the creation of the world, MEANING MALCHUT OUT OF WHICH ALL JUDGMENTS COME. On this day, the Holy One, blessed be He, will punish the wicked and take vengeance on those that afflict Yisrael. That day comes and stands before the Holy One, blessed be He, and calls upon Him to execute judgment and to destroy the heathens. It receives permission, as written: "For I will gather all the nations against Jerusalem to battle" (Ibid. 2).

29. רִבִּי יִצְחָק אָמַר, תְּרֵין יוֹמִין אִינוּן לְקוּדְשָׁא בְּרִיךְ הוּא, חַד שָׁארִי עִמֵּיהּ, וְחַד אָתֵי לְקַמֵּיהּ, וּבְאִלֵּין עָבֵיד קוּדְשָׁא בְּרִיךְ הוּא קְרָבִין בְּכֹלָּא. וְכַד הַאי יוֹמָא, אָתֵי לְאַגָּחָא קְרָבָא, אִזְדְּוַּג בְּהַהוּא יוֹמָא אָחֳרָא, וְנָטִיל

זַיְינִין עַל זַיְינֵיהּ, וְאָגַח קְרָבָא בְּכֹלָא, בְּאִינוּן רָאמִין וּנְמוּכִין. הה"ד כִּי יוֹם לַיְיָ' צְבָאוֹת, עַל כָּל גֵּאֶה וָרָם וְעַל כָּל נִשָּׂא וְשָׁפֵל.

29. Rabbi Yitzchak said: The Holy One, blessed be He, has two days, one that stays with Him, NAMELY GVURAH, and one that comes before Him, NAMELY MALCHUT. And with these, He makes war on all. When that day, MALCHUT, comes to make war, it unites with the other day, WHICH IS GVURAH OF ZEIR ANPIN. It takes the arms OF GVURAH OF ZEIR ANPIN and supplements ITS OWN arms, "for the day of Hashem, Tzva'ot shall be upon every one that is proud and lofty, and upon every one that is lifted up that he shall be brought low" (Yeshayah 2:12).

30. רִבִּי שִׁמְעוֹן אָמַר, וְאִשָּׁה כִּי יָזוּב זוֹב דָּמָהּ וְגוֹ'. הַיְינוּ דִכְתִּיב, חֶרֶב לַיְיָ' מָלְאָה דָם. מָלְאָה דָם וַדַּאי, דִּכְתִּיב כִּי יָזוּב זוֹב דָּמָהּ יָמִים רַבִּים. בְּלֹא עֵת נִדָּתָהּ, הַיְינוּ דִכְתִּיב, וַיִּשְׁקוֹד יְיָ' עַל הָרָעָה וַיְבִיאֶהָ עָלֵינוּ. דְּתָנֵינָן, קוּדְשָׁא בְּרִיךְ הוּא אַקְדִּים פּוּרְעָנוּתָא לְעָלְמָא, חַיָּיבַיָּא מְקַדְּמִין פּוּרְעָנוּתָא בְּחוֹבֵיהוֹן לְמֵיתֵי לְעָלְמָא, אוֹ כִּי תָזוּב עַל נִדָּתָהּ. הַיְינוּ וְיָסַפְתִּי לְיַסְּרָה אֶתְכֶם, מַהוּ וְיָסַפְתִּי לְיַסְּרָה. אוֹסִיף דִּינָא עַל דִּינָא, וְאֶתֵּן דָּמָא עַל דָּמָא, יַתִּיר עַל מַה דְּאִית בְּהַהוּא חֶרֶב לַיְיָ' מָלְאָה דָם.

30. Rabbi Shimon cited the verse: "And if a woman has an issue of her blood." This verse has the same meaning as the following: "The sword of Hashem is filled with blood" (Yeshayah 34:6). MALCHUT IS CALLED 'A SWORD' AND ALSO 'A WOMAN', for assuredly she "is filled with blood," THAT IS, JUDGMENTS, as written: "an issue of her blood many days not in the time of her menstruation." This has the same meaning as the verse: "Therefore, Hashem has watched over the evil and brought it upon us," (Daniel 9:14) for we have learned that by their sins, the wicked cause the Holy One, blessed be He, to bring punishments to the world BEFORE THEIR TIME, AND THAT IS THE SECRET OF "NOT IN THE TIME OF HER MENSTRUATION." "Or if it run beyond the time of her menstruation" (Vayikra 15:25), NAMELY, "then I will punish you...more" (Vayikra 26:18). What is the meaning of "punish you...more"? THIS MEANS I will increase more and more Judgments and add blood to blood, more than there is in "the sword of Hashem is filled with blood." THAT IS, THERE ARE MORE

JUDGMENTS THAN THERE ALREADY ARE IN MALCHUT HERSELF, FOR
THIS IS THE SECRET OF: "IF IT RUN BEYOND THE TIME OF HER
MENSTRUATION." THAT IS, MORE JUDGMENTS WILL RUN BEYOND
THOSE OF HER MENSTRUATION; WHICH ARE, HER OWN JUDGMENTS.

31. כְּתִיב, לֹא אוֹסִיף לְקַלֵּל עוֹד אֶת הָאֲדָמָה בַּעֲבוּר הָאָדָם. מַהוּ לֹא
אוֹסִיף. אֶלָּא, לָא אֶתֵּן עוֹד תּוֹסֶפֶת לְהַהוּא חֶרֶב, אֶלָּא כְּגַוְונָא דְּיָכִיל
עָלְמָא לְמִסְבַּל. וְהָא כְּתִיב וְיָסַפְתִּי. אֶלָּא לְיַסְּרָה כְּתִיב, וְלָא לְשֵׁיצָאָה.
הה"ד, אוֹ כִי תָזוּב עַל נִדָּתָהּ.

31. It is written: "I will not again curse the ground any more for man's sake"
(Beresheet 8:21), MEANING I will not again add JUDGMENTS to this sword,
WHICH IS MALCHUT, but only to the extent that the world is able to sustain.
HE ASKS: It is written "more," MEANING THAT HE WILL SUPPLEMENT
JUDGMENTS TO MALCHUT. HE ANSWERS: Yet it is written, "I will punish
you MORE," not 'destroy', WHICH MEANS HE GIVES MORE ONLY TO THE
EXTENT THAT THE WORLD WILL BE ABLE TO SUFFER. Therefore, it is
written: "If it run beyond the time of her menstruation," SHE WILL HAVE
MORE JUDGMENTS THAN SHE HAS OF HER OWN.

32. כָּל יְמֵי זוֹב טוּמְאָתָהּ. מַהוּ כָּל יְמֵי זוֹב טוּמְאָתָהּ. אֶלָּא חַיָּיבַיָּא
מְסָאֲבִין בְּחוֹבֵיהוֹן לְגַרְמֵיהוֹן, וּמְסָאֲבִין לַאֲתַר אָחֳרָא, כד"א, כִּי אֶת
מִקְדַּשׁ יְיָ' טִמֵּא. וְאִתְּעַר רוּחַ מְסָאֲבָא עֲלַיְיהוּ. וּלְזִמְנָא דְּאָתֵי, זַמִּין
קוּדְשָׁא בְּרִיךְ הוּא לְדַכְּאָה לְהוּ לְיִשְׂרָאֵל וּלְאַעְבְּרָא לְהַהוּא רוּחָא
מְסָאֲבָא מֵעָלְמָא. דִּכְתִּיב, לֹא יוֹסִיף יָבֹא בָךְ עוֹד עָרֵל וְטָמֵא. וּכְתִיב
וְאֶת רוּחַ הַטּוּמְאָה אַעֲבִיר מִן הָאָרֶץ. מִן הָאָרֶץ וַדַּאי.

32. "All the days of the issue of her uncleanness" (Vayikra 15:25). What are
"the days of the issue of her uncleanness"? HE ANSWERS: The wicked
pollute BOTH themselves and another place with their sins, as it is written:
"Because he has defiled the sanctuary of Hashem" (Bemidbar 19:20). An
Unclean Spirit is awakened against them. In the time to come, the Holy
One, blessed be He, will purify Yisrael and remove that Unclean Spirit from
the world, as written: "For henceforth there shall no more come into you the

uncircumcised and unclean" (Yeshayah 52:1), and: "And also I will cause the Unclean Spirit to pass out of the land" (Zecharyah 13:2); out of the land indeed.

9. "In the day of prosperity be joyful"

A Synopsis

Rabbi Elazar says that when a man is prosperous he should show himself in public and give kindness to everyone else; then kindness from above rests on him. But in times of adversity he should not show himself in case the Judgment that is looming everywhere should fall on him too. Many swords hang from the highest sword of judgment, and whoever meets them is harmed.

33. ר' חִזְקִיָּה הֲוָה יָתִיב קַמֵּיה דְּר' אֶלְעָזָר, לֵילְיָא חַד קָמוּ בְּפַלְגוּת לֵילְיָא לְמִלְעֵי בְּאוֹרַיְיתָא. פָּתַח רִבִּי אֶלְעָזָר וְאָמַר, בְּיוֹם טוֹבָה הֱיֵה בְטוֹב וְגוֹ' גַּם אֶת זֶה לְעוּמַת זֶה עָשָׂה הָאֱלֹהִים וְגוֹ'. בְּיוֹם טוֹבָה הֱיֵה בְטוֹב, בְּזִמְנָא דְּאַסְגֵּי קוּדְשָׁא בְּרִיךְ הוּא חֶסֶד בְּעָלְמָא, בָּעֵי בַּר נָשׁ לְמֵיהַךְ בְּשׁוּקֵי וּלְאִתְחֲזָאָה קַמֵּי כֹּלָּא, דְּהָא כַּד שָׁארֵי טִיבוּתָא דְּקוּדְשָׁא בְּרִיךְ הוּא בְּעָלְמָא, בְּכֹלָּא שָׁארֵי, וּבְכֹלָּא עָבֵיד טִיבוּ וְאַסְגֵּי לֵיה בְּעָלְמָא. וּבְג"כ, יִתְחֲזֵי ב"נ בְּאִתְגַּלְיָא בְּשׁוּקֵי, וְיַעֲבֵיד טִיבוּ דְּלִשְׁרֵי עֲלֵיה טִיבוּ אָחֳרָא. הֲדָא הוּא דִכְתִיב בְּיוֹם טוֹבָה הֱיֵה בְטוֹב. הֱיֵה בְטוֹב וַדַּאי.

33. Rabbi Chizkiyah was studying with Rabbi Elazar. One night, they rose at midnight to study the Torah and Rabbi Elazar discoursed on the following verse: "In the day of prosperity be joyful...Elohim has made the one as well as the other..." (Kohelet 7:14). "In the day of prosperity be joyful," MEANS THAT when the Holy One, blessed be He, lavishes kindness on the world, a man should go to the marketplace and show himself before everyone. The Chesed of the Holy One, blessed be He, rests upon all, for He shows kindness to everybody and increases it in the world. Therefore, a man should show himself in public, and he should do kindness so that another Chesed FROM ABOVE will rest upon him, as it is written: "In the day of prosperity be joyful." He will indeed be joyful.

34. וּבְיוֹם רָעָה רְאֵה. לָא כְּתִיב וּבְיוֹם רָעָה הֱיֵה בְרַע, אֶלָּא, בְּיוֹם רָעָה רְאֵה. דְּהָא בְּשַׁעֲתָא דְּדִינָא תַּלְיָא בְּעָלְמָא, לָא לִבְעֵי לֵיה לְאֵינִישׁ לְאִתְחֲזָאָה בְּשׁוּקָא וּלְמֵיהַךְ יְחִידָאָה בְּעָלְמָא. דְּהָא כַּד דִּינָא שַׁרְיָא

בְּעָלְמָא, עַל כֹּלָא שָׁאֲרֵי. וּמַאן דְּפָגַע בֵּיהּ, וְאָעְרַע קַמֵּיהּ, יִתְדָּן בְּהַהוּא
דִּינָא. וּכְדֵין כְּתִיב, וְיֵשׁ נִסְפֶּה בְּלֹא מִשְׁפָּט. דְּהָא מִשְׁפָּט אִסְתַּלָּק
מִצֶּדֶק, וְלָא שַׁרְיָין דָּא בְּדָא עַל עָלְמָא. וְעַל דָּא רְאֵה. רְאֵה וַהֲוֵי נָטִיר,
אַשְׁגַּח וְעַיֵּין לְכָל סְטָר. וַהֲוֵי יָדַע, דִּבְכֻלְּהוּ שַׁרְיָא דִּינָא, וְלָא תִּפּוּק
לְבַר, וְלָא תִּתְחֲזֵי בְּשׁוּקָא, בְּגִין דְּלָא יִשְׁרֵי עֲלָךְ. מַ"ט. בְּגִין דְּגַם אֶת זֶה
לְעֻמַּת זֶה עָשָׂה הָאֱלֹהִים. כְּמָה דְּכַד שָׁאֲרֵי טִיבוּ בְּעָלְמָא שָׁאֲרֵי עַל
כֹּלָא, כָּךְ, כַּד שַׁרְיָא דִּינָא בְּעָלְמָא שָׁאֲרֵי עַל כֹּלָא, וּמַאן דְּאָעְרַע בֵּיהּ
אִתְפַּס.

34. "But in the day of adversity consider" (Ibid.). It is not written: 'In the day of adversity be sad', AS IT IS WRITTEN, "IN THE DAY OF PROSPERITY BE JOYFUL," but rather, "in the day of adversity consider," MEANING at the time that Judgment looms over the world, a man should not show himself in the marketplace and should not walk alone. When Judgment looms over the world, it looms over all, and whoever meets THE DESTRUCTIVE ANGEL is sentenced by that Judgment, as it is written: "Sometimes ruin comes for want of justice" (Mishlei 13:23). This is because justice, WHICH IS ZEIR ANPIN, departs from righteousness, WHICH IS MALCHUT, and they do not dwell within one another, AND HAVE NO INFLUENCE on the world. Therefore, IT IS WRITTEN, "consider," NAMELY consider and be vigilant and watchful on every side and know that Judgment abides everywhere. Do not show yourself abroad so that JUDGMENT shall not rest upon you. The reason is that, "Elohim has made the one as well as the other." Thus, at the time that kindness rests upon the world, it rests all over. Also, when Judgment looms over the world, it looms over all. He who chances upon it WILL BE caught.

35. ת"ח, כַּד דִּינָא שַׁרְיָא בְּעָלְמָא, כַּמָּה סַיְיפִין תַּלְיָין, דְּנַפְקֵי מֵהַהוּא
חֶרֶב עִלָּאָה, וְזַקְפִין רֵישָׁא וְחָמָן דְּהָא הַהוּא חֶרֶב עִלָּאָה סוּמָקָא,
מַלְיָיא דָּמָא בְּכָל סִטְרִין, כְּדֵין גְּזָרִין נִימוּסִין. וְכַמָּה סַיְיפַיָּא אִתְּעָרוּ,
כד"א, אִישׁ חַרְבּוֹ עַל יְרֵכוֹ. וּכְתִיב, וְחַרְבּוֹ שְׁלוּפָה בְּיָדוֹ. וְכֻלְּהוּ
מִשְׁתַּכְּחֵי לְמֶעְבַּד דִּינָא. וּמַאן דְּיְעְרַע בְּהוּ אִתְּזַק. כְּתִיב, הִנֵּה נָא מָצָא
עַבְדְּךָ חֵן בְּעֵינֶיךָ וַתַּגְדֵּל חַסְדְּךָ וְגוֹ'. מַ"ט, בְּגִין דִּבְכָל אֲתַר דְּדִינָא

שַׁרְיָא בְּכֹלָּא שַׁרְיָא, בֵּין בְּמָתָא בֵּין בְּמַדְבְּרָא וּבְסְחָרָנָא דְּמָתָא.

35. Come and behold: at the time that Judgment looms over the world, many swords, NAMELY LITIGANTS, are suspended from that highest sword. They lift up their heads and see that the highest sword, NAMELY THE SIDE OF JUDGMENT OF MALCHUT, is red and bloody on all sides, THAT IS, WITH JUDGMENTS. Then they decree punishments and all SORTS OF swords are aroused, as written: "Every man has his sword upon his thigh" (Shir Hashirim 3:8), and, "With his sword drawn in his hands" (Yehoshua 5:13). All those swords are ready to punish, and whoever meets them is harmed. It is written: "Behold now Your servant has found favor in Your sight and You have magnified Your mercy which You have shown to me in saving my life; I CANNOT ESCAPE TO THE MOUNTAIN" (Beresheet 19:19). The reason that HE (LOT) WAS AFRAID TO ESCAPE TO THE MOUNTAIN was that Judgment looms over all, in towns, deserts and around the city.

10. "Set me as a seal upon Your heart"

A Synopsis

Rabbi Elazar talks about the Tefilin and their meaning in terms of the seal mentioned in the title verse. When the Tefilin are placed both on the arm and on the heart, man makes himself perfect. The topic turns to the time of death when it is so hard for the soul to leave the body; it is just as hard for Yisrael to separate from God, so great is their love for Him. We hear that the two lowest grades of Gehenom are Sheol and Ruin. It is said that "jealousy is as cruel as Sheol", and this is because it is as hard to escape from Sheol as it is for the jealous person to leave his beloved. When the Congregation of Yisrael is jealous for God, her flame sets the world on fire.

36. תּוּ פָּתַח וְאָמַר, שִׂימֵנִי כַחוֹתָם עַל לִבֶּךָ וְגוֹ'. שִׂימֵנִי כַחוֹתָם, כְּנֶסֶת יִשְׂרָאֵל אָמְרָה דָא לְקוּדְשָׁא בְּרִיךְ הוּא. שִׂימֵנִי כַחוֹתָם, מַאן הוּא חוֹתָם. דָא חוֹתָם דְּגוּשְׁפַּנְקָא דִקְשׁוֹט. כַחוֹתָם עַל לִבֶּךָ, דָא חוֹתָם שֶׁל תְּפִלִּין, דְּאָנַח ב"נ עַל לִבֵּיהּ. כַחוֹתָם עַל זְרוֹעֶךָ, דָּא יַד כֵּהָה, דְּמַנַּח בְּהַהוּא זְרוֹעַ, וּמַנוּ יִצְחָק. וְכ"י קָאָמַר שִׂימֵנִי כַחוֹתָם, חוֹתָם מִבְּעֵי לֵיהּ, מַאי כַחוֹתָם. כְּאִינּוּן תְּפִלִּין דְּרֵישָׁא, דְּאָתֵי שְׁבָחָא לְכָל גּוּפָא. וְעַל דָּא תְּפִלִּין בִּזְרוֹעַ, עַל הַלֵּב, וּבְדָא אִשְׁתְּכַח בַּר נָשׁ שְׁלִים כְּגַוְונָא דִּלְעֵילָּא.

36. Rabbi Elazar further discussed the verse: "Set me as a seal upon Your heart" (Shir Hashirim 8:6). The Congregation of Yisrael, WHICH IS MALCHUT, asked the Holy One, blessed be He, to "set me as a seal." "A seal" is the ring seal of Truth. "As a seal upon Your heart" is the seal of the Tefilin that a man places on his heart. "As a seal upon the arm" (Ibid.) is a dark hand, NAMELY MALCHUT which he places on the arm. What is it? It is Isaac, THE LEFT SIDE OF ZEIR ANPIN. The Congregation of Yisrael says, "Set me as a seal," but should say, 'set me a seal' and not "as a seal." HE EXPLAINS THAT "AS A SEAL" means as the head Tefilin, CALLED "A SEAL," whence gain, NAMELY THE MOCHIN, comes to the whole body. Therefore, the Tefilin is placed both on the arm and on the heart. By so doing, a man makes himself perfect, after the supernal model.

37. כִּי עַזָּה כַמָּוֶת אַהֲבָה. מַאי כִּי עַזָּה כַמָּוֶת. אֶלָּא לָא אִשְׁתְּכַח

קַשְׁיוּתָא בְּעָלְמָא, כְּמָה דִּפְרִישׁוּ דְנַפְשָׁא מִגּוּפָא, כַּד בַּעְיָין לְאִתְפָּרְשָׁא. כָּךְ אַהֲבַת כְּנֶסֶת יִשְׂרָאֵל לְקוּדְשָׁא בְּרִיךְ הוּא, דְּלָא אִתְפָּרְשָׁן לְעָלְמִין. וּבג"כ תְּפִלָּה שֶׁל יַד, אִתְקַשְׁרָא בִּזְרוֹעַ, לְקַיְּימָא דִכְתִיב, שְׂמֹאלוֹ תַּחַת לְרֹאשִׁי.

37. "For love is strong as death" (Shir Hashirim 8:6). HE ASKS: What is "love is strong as death"? HE ANSWERS: There is nothing so hard in the world as the departure of the soul from the body AT THE TIME OF DEATH when they must separate. Such is the love of Yisrael for the Holy One, blessed be He, that they should never separate. Therefore, the hand Tefilin, WHICH IS MALCHUT, combines with that on the arm, WHICH IS THE LEFT SIDE OF ZEIR ANPIN, and fulfills that which is written: "His left hand is under my head" (Shir Hashirim 2:6).

38. קָשָׁה כִשְׁאוֹל קִנְאָה. בְּכָל דַּרְגִּין דְּגֵיהִנָּם, לָא אִית קַשְׁיָא כִּשְׁאוֹל, דְּנָחִית לְתַתָּא מִנַּיְיהוּ, בַּר הַהוּא דַּרְגָּא דְּאִקְרֵי אֲבַדּוֹן, וְדָא וְדָא אִשְׁתָּתְּפוּ כַּחֲדָא. וְדָא קַשְׁיָא לְהוּ לְחַיָּיבַיָּא מִכֹּלָּא. כָּךְ, קָשָׁה כִשְׁאוֹל קִנְאָה, דְּלֵית קִנְאָה אֶלָּא בִּרְחִימוּתָא, וּמִגּוֹ רְחִימוּתָא אָתֵי קִנְאָה, וּמַאן דְּקַנֵּי לְהַהוּא דְּרָחִים יַתִּיר, קַשְׁיָא לֵיהּ לְאִתְפָּרְשָׁא מִנֵּיהּ מֵהַהוּא דַּרְגָּא דְּאִקְרֵי שְׁאוֹל, דְּאִיהוּ קַשְׁיָא מִכָּל דַּרְגִּין דְּגֵיהִנָּם.

38. "Jealousy is as cruel as Sheol" (Shir Hashirim 8:6). Of all the grades of Gehenom, there is no PLACE MORE harsh than Sheol, for it descends down BELOW ALL THE GRADES except the one called 'Ruin', WHICH IS EVEN FURTHER BELOW SHEOL. Both of them are combined and they are harder on the wicked than all the others. Thus, "jealousy is as cruel as Sheol," for jealousy comes only out of love, and out of love comes jealousy. HE WHO IS JEALOUS BECAUSE OF HAVING SO LITTLE LOVE IS LIKE ONE WHO IS JEALOUS OF HIS WIFE. Whoever is extremely jealous of a beloved one finds it more difficult to depart from him than from the level called Sheol, the harshest and most difficult level in Gehenom.

39. רְשָׁפֶיהָ רִשְׁפֵּי אֵשׁ שַׁלְהֶבֶת יָהּ. וּמַאן אִיהוּ שַׁלְהֶבֶת יָהּ, דָּא אֶשָׁא

דְּנָפִיק מִגּוֹ שׁוֹפָר, כָּלִיל מֵרוּחָא וּמַיָא. וּמִגּוֹ הַהוּא שַׁלְהוֹבָא כַּד
מִתְלַהֲטָא בכ״י, אוֹקִיד עָלְמָא בְּשַׁלְהֲבוּתָא בְּקִנְאָה דְּקוּדְשָׁא בְּרִיךְ
הוּא, וּבְשַׁעֲתָא דְּהִיא מְקַנְּאָה לֵיהּ, וַוי דְּאַעְרַע בְּשַׁלְהוֹבִיתָא, דְּאִיהוּ
יִתּוֹקַד בְּהוּ.

39. "The coals thereof are coals of fire which have a most vehement flame" (Ibid.). HE ASKS: What does "coals of fire" mean? HE ANSWERS: This is the fire that issues from the Shofar compounded of air and water, MEANING THE ILLUMINATION OF THE CHOCHMAH THAT ISSUES FROM THE LEFT SIDE, THE SECRET OF THE FIRE OF THE BINAH THAT IS CALLED 'SHOFAR'. FOR THAT FIRE, WHICH IS THE LEFT SIDE, ALSO INCLUDES TWO SIDES: THE CENTRAL SIDE, WHICH IS CALLED 'AIR', AND THE RIGHT SIDE, WHICH IS CALLED 'WATER'. That flame which burns in the Congregation of Yisrael, WHICH IS MALCHUT, then sets the world on fire when she is jealous for the Holy One, blessed be He. Woe to he who crosses the path of that flame, for it will burn them.

11. "Cannot quench love"

A Synopsis
Rabbi Elazar gives us two interpretations of "many waters" that cannot quench love. He talks about all the illuminations of the Mochin that God gives Yisrael because they love Him. He tells how a man should put on the hand Tefilin in order to combine Chochmah with Chassadim.

40. תּוּ פָּתַח וְאָמַר. מַיִם רַבִּים לֹא יוּכְלוּ לְכַבּוֹת וְגו'. מַיִם רַבִּים דָּא דְּרוֹעָא יְמִינָא, דְּבָעֵי לְקַשְּׁרָא בֵּיהּ קִשְׁרָא דִּתְפִלָּה עַל דְּרוֹעָא שְׂמָאלָא, לְקַיְּימָא וִימִינוֹ תְּחַבְּקֵנִי. ד"א, מַיִם רַבִּים, דָּא הוּא נָהָר עִלָּאָה, דְּמִנֵּיהּ נָפְקִין נַהֲרִין לְכָל עֵבָר, וְכֻלְּהוּ נַגְדִּין וְאִתְמַשְּׁכָן מִנֵּיהּ. כד"א, מִקּוֹלוֹת מַיִם רַבִּים. מֵאִינּוּן קוֹלוֹת דְּמַיִם רַבִּים, דְּנַפְקָן וְאִתְמַשְּׁכָן מִנֵּיהּ. וּנְהָרוֹת, כד"א, נָשְׂאוּ נְהָרוֹת וְגו'.

40. Rabbi Elazar cited more verses and said: "Many waters cannot quench love nor can the floods drown it" (Shir Hashirim 8:7). "Many waters," refers to the right arm, WHICH IS CHESED, with which one should bind the Tefilin on the left hand to carry out that which is written in the verse: "And His right hand embraces me" (Shir Hashirim 2:6). FOR THERE IS NO ILLUMINATION OF CHOCHMAH OF THE LEFT SIDE UNLESS IT IS COMBINED WITH THE CHASSADIM OF THE RIGHT SIDE. There is also another explanation. "Many waters" refers to the supernal river, WHICH IS BINAH, from which issue lights in every direction, TO THE RIGHT SIDE AND TO THE LEFT. All of them flow and emerge from it, as written: "Than the noise of many waters" (Tehilim 93:4), MEANING from "the noise of many waters," WHICH ARE THE SEVEN SFIROT OF ZEIR ANPIN, SEVEN VOICES that come out and flow FROM THE SUPERNAL RIVER, WHICH IS BINAH. "The floods" ARE THE SFIROT OF ZEIR ANPIN, as written: "The floods have lifted up their voice, the floods lift up their roaring" (Tehilim 93:3), NAMELY, THE SFIROT OF ZEIR ANPIN.

41. אִם יִתֵּן אִישׁ אֶת כָּל הוֹן בֵּיתוֹ בָּאַהֲבָה, דִּרְחִים כ"י לְקוּדְשָׁא בְּרִיךְ הוּא, יָבוּזוּ לוֹ. בּוֹז יָבוּזוּ לוֹ, יָבוּז מִבָּעֵי לֵיהּ, מַאי יָבוּזוּ לוֹ. אֶלָּא, אִם יִתֵּן אִישׁ, דָּא קוּדְשָׁא בְּרִיךְ הוּא. אֶת כָּל הוֹן בֵּיתוֹ, כד"א כָּל הוֹן יָקָר

וְנָעִים. בְּאַהֲבָה, דְּכ"י לְגַבֵּיהּ, וְלָא לְאִתְקַשְּׁרָא בַּהֲדָהּ, בּוֹז יָבוּזוּ לוֹ, כָּל אִינּוּן אוּכְלוּסִין וְכָל אִינּוּן מַשְׁרְיָין דִּלְעֵילָּא, לְהַהוּא הוֹן יָקָר, דְּהָא לֵית רְעוּתָא לְכֻלְּהוּ אֶלָּא בְּשַׁעֲתָא דְּכ"י מִתְקַשְּׁרָא בֵּיהּ בְּקוּדְשָׁא בְּרִיךְ הוּא, וּמִתְעַטְּרָא בַּהֲדֵיהּ, כְּדֵין כָּל אִינּוּן אוּכְלוּסִין, וְכָל אִינּוּן מַשְׁרְיָין, וְכֻלְּהוּ עָלְמִין כֻּלְּהוּ בְּחֶדוּ, בִּנְהִירוּ, בְּבִרְכָאן, וְעַל דָּא אָמַר שְׂמֹאלוֹ תַּחַת לְרֹאשִׁי וִימִינוֹ תְּחַבְּקֵנִי.

41. "If a man would give all the substance of his house for love..." (Shir Hashirim 8:7) – with which the Congregation of Yisrael love the Holy One, blessed be He – "It would be utterly scorned (lit. 'they will scorn him')" (Ibid.). HE ASKS: IT IS WRITTEN that "they will scorn him." It should have been written, 'He will scorn him'. What does "they" mean? HE EXPLAINS THAT, "If a man would give," is the Holy One, blessed be He, and, "all the substance of his house," IS ALL THE ILLUMINATIONS OF THE MOCHIN HE HAS, as written: "filled with all precious and pleasant riches" (Mishlei 24:4). "For love," IS THE LOVE of the Congregation of Yisrael for Him, WHICH IS THE LOVE OF THE RIGHT SIDE – NAMELY, THE UNREVEALED CHASSADIM. Yet, He will not be united with her, NAMELY, WITH THE LOWER CHOCHMAH IN HER, BY POURING ON HER NOT THE ILLUMINATION OF CHOCHMAH, BUT THE UNREVEALED CHASSADIM, WHICH ARE "ALL THE SUBSTANCE OF HIS HOUSE." Then, "they will scorn him"; all those battalions and legions above WILL SCORN those "precious and pleasant riches," WHICH ARE CHASSADIM, for they do not desire them, except when the Congregation of Yisrael associate with the Holy One, blessed be He. She is crowned with Him, FOR HE SPREADS CHOCHMAH UPON HER AND THAT CHOCHMAH IN HER IS CLOTHED IN HIS CHASSADIM. Then all the battalions and all the worlds are full of joy, light and blessings, as it is written: "His left hand is under my head," FOR IT IS THE SECRET OF THE ILLUMINATION OF CHOCHMAH. "And His right hand embraces me" IS THE SECRET OF THE UNITY OF CHOCHMAH WITH CHASSADIM.

42(1). מַאן דְּאָנַח תְּפִלִּין, כַּד מָנַח תְּפִלָּה שֶׁל יַד, בָּעֵי לְאוֹשָׁטָא דְּרוֹעָא שְׂמָאלָא, לְקַבְּלָה לָהּ לְכ"י, וּלְקַשְּׁרָא קִשְׁרָא עִם יְמִינָא, בְּגִין לְחַבְּקָא לָהּ, לְקַיְימָא דִּכְתִּיב, שְׂמֹאלוֹ תַּחַת לְרֹאשִׁי וִימִינוֹ תְּחַבְּקֵנִי. לְאִתְחֲזָאָה בַּר נָשׁ כְּגַוְונָא דִּלְעֵילָּא, וּלְאִתְעַטְּרָא בְּכֹלָּא, וּכְדֵין ב"נ שְׁלִים בְּכֹלָּא,

בִּקְדוּשָׁה עִלָּאָה. וְקוּדְשָׁא בְּרִיךְ הוּא קָארֵי עָלֵיהּ, יִשְׂרָאֵל אֲשֶׁר בְּךָ אֶתְפָּאָר.

42a. When a man puts Tefilin on his hand, he should stretch out his left hand, ON WHICH CHOCHMAH IS POURED, to receive the Congregation of Yisrael, WHICH IS MALCHUT. He should make a tie with his right HAND and embrace her WITH THE CHASSADIM OF THE RIGHT, SO THAT CHOCHMAH WILL BE COMBINED WITH CHASSADIM to fulfill that which is written in the verse: "His left hand is under my head and His right hand embraces me," so as to copy the supernal model and be adorned in everything, WITH BOTH CHOCHMAH AND CHASSADIM. That man is then whole in everything, in the supernal sanctity, and the Holy One, blessed be He, calls him: "Yisrael in whom I will be glorified" (Yeshayah 49:3).

A Synopsis
We hear of the seven days of Sukkot, and the numbers seven and seventy are emphasized.

תוספתא

42(2). בּוֹז יָבוּזוּ לוֹ. מַאי בּוֹז. יוֹמָא תִּנְיָינָא וְיוֹמָא שְׁתִיתָאָה וְיוֹמָא שְׁבִיעָאָה דְּסוּכּוֹת, דִּבְהוֹן הֲווֹ מְנַסְּכֵי מַיִם וְיַיִן. דְּז' יוֹמִין דְּסוּכּוֹת, בְּהוֹן הֲווֹ מַקְרִיבִין יִשְׂרָאֵל, ע' פָּרִים, לְכַפָּרָא עַל שַׁבְעִין מְמָנָן, בְּגִין דְּלָא יִשְׁתְּאַר עָלְמָא חָרוּב מִנַּיְיהוּ, הה"ד וּבַחֲמִשָּׁה עָשָׂר יוֹם וְגוֹ' וְהִקְרַבְתֶּם עוֹלָה אִשֵּׁה וְגוֹ'.

ע"כ תוספתא.

Tosefta (Addendum)

42b. "It would be utterly scorned (Heb. *buz*)" (Shir Hashirim 8:7). What is 'buz'? IT IS THE INITIALS OF Bet (= 2), the second day, Vav (= 6), the sixth day, and Zayin (= 7) the seventh day of Sukkot (the Holiday of Booths), on which water and wine were poured, FOR WATER IS THE SECRET OF CHASSADIM AND WINE IS THE SECRET OF CHOCHMAH. During the seven days of Sukkot, Yisrael sacrificed seventy bulls to atone for the seventy

SUPERNAL MINISTERS who are in charge of THE SEVENTY NATIONS. THIS IS THE SECRET OF THE ILLUMINATION OF THE LEFT. THE NATIONS HAVE ONLY THE ILLUMINATION OF THE LEFT, AND YISRAEL DID THIS in order to prevent the destruction of the world by them. Hence, it is written: "And on the fifteenth day...you shall offer a burnt offering, a sacrifice made by fire" (Bemidbar 29:12-13).

End of Tosefta (Addendum)

12. "Hear the right"

A Synopsis

Rabbi Chizkiyah says that the children of Yisrael are so beloved by God that whenever Malchut comes before Him, He is ready to receive her. We learn that every word of prayer ascends through the firmaments to a place that tests how genuine it is; if the prayer is genuine it is brought before God to be fulfilled, but if it is not it invokes an alien spirit from the Other Side. Rabbi Elazar says that everyone who studies the Torah at night and then comes to praise God in the morning will be happy.

43. רְבִּי חִזְקִיָּה פָּתַח וְאָמַר, שִׁמְעָה יְיָ' צֶדֶק וְגו'. כַּמָּה חֲבִיבָה כְּנֶסֶ"י קַמֵי קוּדְשָׁא בְּרִיךְ הוּא, דִּבְכָל זִמְנָא דְּכ"י, אָתַת לְקַמֵּיה דְּקוּדְשָׁא בְּרִיךְ הוּא, קוּדְשָׁא בְּרִיךְ הוּא אִזְדְּמַן לְקַבְּלָהּ. הה"ד שִׁמְעָה יְיָ' צֶדֶק הַקְשִׁיבָה רִנָּתִי הַאֲזִינָה תְפִלָּתִי. אָמַר דָּוִד, אֲנָא אִתְקַטַרְנָא בכ"י. כְּמָה דְּהִיא אִשְׁתְּכַחַת לְקַמָּךְ, אֲנָא נָמֵי הָכִי אִשְׁתַּכַּחְנָא. וּבְגִין כָּךְ שִׁמְעָה יְיָ' צֶדֶק, בְּקַדְמֵיתָא, וּלְבָתַר, הַקְשִׁיבָה רִנָּתִי הַאֲזִינָה תְפִלָּתִי.

43. Rabbi Chizkiyah cited the verse: "Hear the right, Hashem, attend to my cry..." (Tehilim 17:1). The Congregation of Yisrael is so beloved by the Holy One, blessed be He, that whenever she, MALCHUT, comes before Him, He is ready to receive her, as written: "Hear the right, O Master, attend to my cry, give ear to my prayer." David said: 'I am linked with the Congregation of Yisrael, being before You as she is.' Therefore, "hear the right, Hashem," first, WHICH IS MALCHUT, CALLED 'RIGHTEOUSNESS', and afterwards, "attend to my cry, give ear to my prayer."

44. בְּלֹא שִׂפְתֵי מִרְמָה. מַאי בְּלֹא שִׂפְתֵי מִרְמָה. אֶלָּא הָכִי תָּנֵינָן. כָּל מִלָּה וּמִלָּה דִּצְלוֹתָא, דְּאַפִּיק ב"נ מִפּוּמֵיה, סַלְקָא לְעֵילָא וּבָקְעָא רְקִיעִין, וְעָאלַת לַאֲתַר דְּעָאלַת, תַּמָּן אִתְבְּחָנַת הַהִיא מִלָּה, אִי הִיא מִלָּה דְּכַשְׁרָא אִי לָא, אִי אִיהִי מִלָּה דְּכַשְׁרָא עָאלִין לָהּ קַמֵי מַלְכָּא קַדִּישָׁא לְמֶעְבַּד רְעוּתָהּ. וְאִי לָאו, סָאטִין לָהּ לְבַר, וְאִתְעַר בְּהַהִיא מִלָּה רוּחָא אָחֳרָא.

44. "From lips without deceit" (Ibid.). HE ASKS: What does that verse mean? HE ANSWERS: We have learned that every word of prayer that issues from a man's mouth ascends aloft through all the firmaments to a place that tests whether it is genuine or not. If it is genuine, then it is brought before the Holy King to be fulfilled, but if not he is driven away and an alien spirit FROM THE OTHER SIDE is evoked by it.

45. ות"ח, כְּתִיב בֵּיה בְּיוֹסֵף, עִנּוּ בַכֶּבֶל רַגְלוֹ וְגוֹ'. עַד אֵימָתַי, עִנּוּ בַכֶּבֶל רַגְלוֹ. עַד עֵת בֹּא דְבָרוֹ אִמְרַת יְיָ' צְרָפָתְהוּ. עַד עֵת בֹּא דְבָרוֹ דְמַאן. אֶלָּא עַד עֵת בֹּא דְבָרוֹ דְיוֹסֵף, וְאִתְבְּחִין הַהִיא מִלָּה, הה"ד, אִמְרַת יְיָ' צְרָפָתְהוּ. כְּדֵין, שָׁלַח מֶלֶךְ וַיַּתִּירֵהוּ מוֹשֵׁל עַמִּים וַיְפַתְּחֵהוּ. אַדְהָכִי הֲוָה אָתָא צַפְרָא.

45. Come and behold: it is written of Joseph, "Whose foot they hurt with fetters" (Tehilim 105:18). They hurt his foot with fetters "until the time that his word came to pass, the word of Hashem had tested him" (Ibid. 19). HE ASKS: To whose word does it refer in that verse: "Until the time that his word came"? HE ANSWERS: The words of Joseph's PRAYER came to heaven and were tested TO DISCOVER IF THEY WERE GENUINE, AS WRITTEN: "The word of Hashem had tested him," MEANING THAT HIS WORDS WERE TESTED AND PURIFIED. Then, "the king sent and loosed him, and the ruler of the people let him go free" (Ibid. 20). Meanwhile, morning had arrived.

46. א"ר אֶלְעָזָר, כְּתִיב, וְהָיְתָה נֶפֶשׁ אֲדוֹנִי צְרוּרָה בִּצְרוֹר הַחַיִּים. נֶפֶשׁ אֲדֹנִי, סְתָם. כד"א, אֲשֶׁר לֹא נָשָׂא לַשָּׁוְא נַפְשִׁי, הָא עִידָנָא בְּצַפְרָא לְאִתְקַשְּׁרָא כ"י וּלְאִתְחַבְּרָא בְּבַעְלָה, זַכָּאִין אִינוּן צַדִּיקַיָּא דְּמִשְׁתַּדְּלִין בְּאוֹרַיְיתָא בְּלֵילְיָא, וְאָתָאן לְאִתְקַשְּׁרָא בֵּיה בְּקוּדְשָׁא בְּרִיךְ הוּא ובכ"י. עָלַיְיהוּ כְּתִיב, יִשְׂמַח אָבִיךְ וְאִמֶּךָ וְתָגֵל יוֹלַדְתֶּךָ.

46. Rabbi Elazar cited that verse and said: It is written, "Yet the soul (Nefesh) of my Master shall be bound in the bond of life with Hashem your Elohim" (I Shmuel 25:29). "The soul of my Master" is unspecified and has the same reference as in the verse: "Who has not taken My Name (Nefesh)

in vain" (Tehilim 24:4), meaning the morning is the proper time for the Congregation of Yisrael, WHICH IS MALCHUT CALLED 'NEFESH', to unite with her husband, ZEIR ANPIN. THEREFORE, happy are the righteous who study the Torah by night and then come IN THE MORNING to unite with the Holy One, blessed be He, and the Congregation of Yisrael. Of them, it is written: "Let your father and your mother be glad, and let her who bore you rejoice" (Mishlei 23:25).

13. There are two spirits

A Synopsis

We read about the Strange Spirit and the Spirit of Defilement that descend to earth whenever men are defiled below. Rabbi Elazar talks about when the plague of leprosy is sent to a house and how the house can be purified. He tells how a man who wants to defile himself is defiled by bringing upon himself a second Spirit of Uncleanness; he must be destroyed for the world to be purified.

47. א"ר אֶלְעָזָר כְּתִיב, וְהִזַּרְתֶּם אֶת בְּנֵי יִשְׂרָאֵל מִטֻּמְאָתָם וְגוֹ' בְּטַמְּאָם אֶת מִשְׁכָּנִי אֲשֶׁר בְּתוֹכָם. וְהִזַּרְתֶּם, כְּהַאי זָר, דְּאִיהוּ זָר מִכֻּלְּהוּ, וְלָא אִתְחַבָּר בְּמָה דְּלֵיתֵיהּ דִּילֵיהּ.

47. Rabbi Elazar cited that verse: "Thus shall you separate the children of Yisrael from their uncleanness...when they defile My tabernacle that is among them" (Vayikra 15:31). "Thus shall you separate" MEANS like a stranger who is a stranger to everyone and is not bonded with that which is not his.

48. ות"ח, בְּשַׁעֲתָא דְּמִסְתַּאֲבִין בְּנֵי נָשָׁא לְתַתָּא, מְסָאֲבִין לוֹן בְּכֹלָּא, וְהָא אִתְּמַר. אֲבָל, בְּשַׁעֲתָא דְּרוּחַ מְסָאֲבָא אִתְּעַר לְתַתָּא, אִתְּעַר רוּחַ זָר, רוּחַ מְסָאֲבָא דִּלְתַתָּא, אִתְּעַר רוּחַ מְסָאֲבָא אָחֳרָא, וְאִתְיְהִיב לֵיהּ רְשׁוּתָא לְנַחְתָּא לְעָלְמָא. מַאי רְשׁוּתָא, רְשׁוּתָא דִּקְדוּשָׁה דַּהֲוָה נָחִית וּמָחֵי בֵּיהּ, לָא אִשְׁתְּכַח, וְאִסְתְּלַק, וּכְדֵין אִתְגַּלְיָיא דִּינָא, לְקַבְּלֵיהוֹן דְּחַיָּיבִין, וְאוֹסִיף דִּינָא עַל דִּינֵיהּ, וּכְדֵין, תְּרֵין רוּחִין מִשְׁתַּכְּחִין בְּעָלְמָא, חַד, רוּחָא דְּדִינָא, וְחַד, רוּחָא דִּמְסָאֲבָא.

48. HE EXPLAINS HIS WORDS: Come and behold: When men are defiled below, they are defiled in every respect, as we have already learned. When the Unclean Spirit is roused below, BY DRAWING THE ILLUMINATION OF THE LEFT SIDE FROM ABOVE DOWNWARDS, a strange spirit arises, FOR the Unclean Spirit below rouses another unclean spirit. It obtains permission to go down to the world. HE ASKS: What kind of permission DOES IT OBTAIN? HE ANSWERS: The same permission of Holiness that formerly

ALWAYS came down and prevented THAT STRANGE SPIRIT FROM RULING. This spirit is no longer there BECAUSE OF THE UNCLEAN SPIRIT. For when it leaves, the Judgment, WHICH IS THE STRANGE SPIRIT, is revealed and confronts the sinners and augments Judgment. THEN THERE ARE two harmful spirits in the world, one is the spirit of Judgment NAMELY THE STRANGE SPIRIT and the Spirit of Defilement.

49. א״ר אֶלְעָזָר, אִצְטְרִיכְנָא הָכָא לְמֵימַר מִלָּה דְּאוֹלִיפְנָא מֵאַבָּא. תָּ״ח, הָכָא יַלְפִינָן מִנֶּגַע דְּבֵיתָא. דְּכַד רוּחָא מְסָאֲבָא שַׁרְיָא בְּבֵיתָא וְקוּדְשָׁא בְּרִיךְ הוּא בָּעֵי לְדַכְּאָה לֵיהּ, שָׁדַר נֶגַע צָרַעַת בְּבֵיתָא, לְקַטְרְגָא דָּא בְּדָא, וְהַהוּא נֶגַע לָא אַעְדֵּי מִבֵּיתָא, וְאע״ג דְּרוּח מְסָאֲבָא אִסְתְּלַק מֵהַהוּא בֵּיתָא, עַד דְּיִנְתְּצוּן בֵּיתָא, אֲבָנִין וְאָעִין וְכֹלָּא, כְּדֵין אִתְדְּכֵי אַתְרָא.

49. Rabbi Elazar said: Here I must say something that I have learned from my father. Come and behold: see what we learned here in relation to the plague in the house. When the Unclean Spirit rests upon a house and the Holy One, blessed be He, wants to purify that house, He sends a plague of leprosy there in order to make them denounce each other – THE SPIRIT OF THE PLAGUE FIGHTS THAT ONE OF THE UNCLEANNESS. Although the Unclean Spirit is gone from the house, that plague does not depart from the house AFTER OVERPOWERING THE SPIRIT OF DEFILEMENT until the house is shattered, stones, timbers, and all. Only then is the place purified.

50. כְּהַאי גַּוְונָא, מַאן דְּאִסְתְּאָב וְאִתְּעַר רוּחָא מְסָאֲבָא וְשָׁארֵי עֲלוֹי, כַּד בָּעֵי קוּדְשָׁא בְּרִיךְ הוּא לְדַכְּאָה עָלְמָא, אִתְּעַר רוּחַ דִּינָא תַּקִּיפָא, וְאִשְׁתְּכַח בְּעָלְמָא וְשַׁרְיָא עַל הַהוּא רוּחָא מְסָאֲבָא, וּמְקַטְרְגֵי דָּא בְּדָא, עַד דְּיִתְעֲבַר מֵעָלְמָא, וְהַהוּא רוּחָא דִּינָא תַּקִּיפָא, לָא אִסְתְּלַק מֵאַתְרֵיהּ עַד דְּיִנְתֵּץ אֲתַר, שַׁיְיפִין וְגַרְמִין וְכֹלָּא, כְּדֵין אִתְדְּכֵי עָלְמָא וְאִתְעַבְּרוּ מִנֵּיהּ רוּחִין מְסָאֲבִין, וְעָלְמָא אִשְׁתְּכַח בְּדַכְיוּ.

50. When a man is defiled and arouses the Unclean Spirit to rest upon him and the Holy One, blessed be He, wants to purify the world, He arouses AGAINST HIM a spirit of Stern Judgment that remains in the world and rests

upon that Unclean Spirit. They fight each other until He removes THE UNCLEAN SPIRIT from the world. That spirit of harsh Judgment OF THE PLAGUE THAT IT CAUSED TO DEPART FROM THE WORLD does not depart from the place until it is completely shattered, NAMELY THE BODY, the limbs, the bones and everything. Only then is the world purified; the Unclean Spirits are removed, and the world is in a state of cleanliness.

51. וְעַל דָּא תָּנֵינָן, אָתָא לְאִסְתַּאֲבָא מְסָאֲבִין לֵיהּ וַדַּאי. וַוי לֵיהּ לב"ן כַּד שָׁארִי עֲלֵיהּ רוּחַ מְסָאֲבָא, וְאִשְׁתְּכַח בֵּיהּ בְּעָלְמָא, דְּוַדַּאי לִינְדַע, דְּקוּדְשָׁא ב"ה בָּעֵי לְבַעֲרָא לֵיהּ מִן עָלְמָא. זַכָּאִין אִינוּן צַדִּיקַיָּא דְּכֻלְּהוּ קַדִּישִׁין, וְאִשְׁתְּכָחוּ בִּקְדוּשָׁה קַמֵּי מַלְכָּא קַדִּישָׁא, וְשַׁרְיָא עֲלַיְיהוּ רוּחַ קַדִּישָׁא, בְּהַאי עָלְמָא וּבְעָלְמָא דְּאָתֵי. כֵּיוָן דְּאָתָא צַפְרָא קָמוּ אַזְלוּ.

51. Therefore, we have learned that when a man wants to defile himself, he is indeed defiled, FOR THE SECOND SPIRIT OF UNCLEANNESS REMOVES THE FIRST ONE, AS IT IS SAID ABOVE. Woe to the man upon whom rests an Unclean Spirit that dwells with him in the world, for it is well known that the Holy One, blessed be He, desires to remove it from the world; THEREFORE, HE DEFILES HIM MORE, AS SAID. Happy are the righteous who are Holy and appear before the Holy King in their Holiness, and upon whom a Spirit of Holiness rests in this world and in the World to Come. When the morning came, they went on their way.

14. "And angels of Elohim met him"

A Synopsis

Rabbi Elazar says that during the time that Jacob lived with Laban God did not speak to him, until he was about to leave; then angels met and accompanied him on his trip. Both the angels of judgment and angels of mercy combined with him; Jacob is the Central Column that combines them both. The angels rescued him from the hands of Esau.

52. עַד דַּהֲווֹ אָזְלֵי, פָּתַח רבי אֶלְעָזָר וְאָמַר, וְיַעֲקֹב הָלַךְ לְדַרְכּוֹ וַיִּפְגְּעוּ בוֹ מַלְאֲכֵי אֱלֹהִים. וְיַעֲקֹב הָלַךְ לְדַרְכּוֹ, דַּהֲוָה אָזִיל לְקַבֵּל אֲבוּהִי. ת״ח, כָּל זִמְנָא, דְּיַעֲקֹב אִשְׁתְּכַח לְגַבֵּיה דְּלָבָן לָא מַלִּיל עִמֵּיה קוּדְשָׁא בְּרִיךְ הוּא, וְאִי תֵימָא, וְהָא כְּתִיב, וַיֹּאמֶר יְיָ' אֶל יַעֲקֹב שׁוּב אֶל אֶרֶץ אֲבוֹתֶיךָ וּלְמוֹלַדְתֶּךָ וְגו'. הַאי בְּסוֹפָא הֲוָה, בְּזִמְנָא דְּבָעָא לְאִתְפָּרְשָׁא מִלָּבָן וְכַד אִתְפְּרַשׁ מִנֵּיה, אָתוּ לְקָבְלֵיה אִינּוּן מַלְאֲכֵי וְאוֹזְפוּהוּ בְּאוֹרְחָא.

52. On their way, Rabbi Elazar opened the discussion, saying: "And Jacob went on his way, and angels of Elohim met him" (Beresheet 32:2). "And Jacob went on his way," MEANING that he was going towards his father. Come and behold: all the time that Jacob was with Laban, the Holy One, blessed be He, did not speak with him. Although it is written: "And Hashem said to Jacob, 'Return to the land of your fathers and to your kindred'" (Beresheet 31:3), this was only at the very end, when he was about to depart from Laban. After leaving him, the angels came and met him and accompanied him on his way.

53. ת״ח, כְּתִיב, וַיִּפְגְּעוּ בוֹ. וַיִּפְגַּע בְּמַלְאֲכֵי אֱלֹהִים מִבָּעֵי לֵיה, מַאי בוֹ. אֶלָּא אִינְהוּ אָתוּ לְאִתְכַּלְּלָא בֵּיה. מַאי לְאִתְכַּלְּלָא בֵּיה. אֶלָּא אִינּוּן מִסִּטְרָא דִּגְבוּרָה קָאַתְיָין, דִּכְתִּיב מַלְאֲכֵי אֱלֹהִים, וְחָמָא מִסִּטְרָא אַחֲרָא מַלְאֲכֵי דְרַחֲמֵי, וְאִתְכְּלָלוּ בֵּיה רַחֲמֵי וְדִינָא.

53. Come and behold: it is written, "met him," but it should have said, 'He met angels of Elohim', SINCE IT WAS JACOB WHO MET THEM. What is the meaning of, "met him"? HE EXPLAINS: They came to combine with him. HE asks: What does this mean? HE ANSWERS: They came from the side of

Gvurah, as written, "Angels of Elohim," AND GVURAH IS CALLED
"ELOHIM." JACOB saw Angels of Mercy coming from another side. Then
both the ANGELS OF Judgment and THOSE OF Mercy combined with him,
FOR JACOB IS REFERRED TO AS THE CENTRAL COLUMN, WHICH
INCLUDES WITHIN IT THE LEFT AND THE RIGHT, MERCY AND
JUDGMENT.

54. ת״ח, בְּקַדְמֵיתָא, מַחֲנֵה אֱלֹהִים, זֶה חַד. לְבָתַר וַיִּקְרָא שֵׁם הַמָּקוֹם
הַהוּא מַחֲנָיִם, תְּרֵי. חַד מִסִּטְרָא דְּדִינָא וְחַד מִסִּטְרָא דְּרַחֲמֵי, מַלְאָכִין
מֵהַאי גִּיסָא, וּמַלְאָכִין מֵהַאי גִּיסָא, וְעַל דָּא כְּתִיב, וַיִּפְגְּעוּ בוֹ. בּוֹ,
דַּיְיקָא. וַיֹּאמֶר יַעֲקֹב כַּאֲשֶׁר רָאָם, רָאָה אוֹתָם מִבָּעֵי לֵיהּ, מַאי רָאָם.
אֶלָּא חָמָא לוֹן כְּלִילָן כַּחֲדָא, מִתְדַּבְּקָן דָּא בְּדָא, מִתְחַבְּרָן דָּא בְּדָא,
וְעַל דָּא כְּתִיב רָאָם, וְכֻלְּהוּ אָתוּ לְאוֹזְפָא לֵיהּ וּלְשֵׁיזָבָא לֵיהּ מִידָא
דְּעֵשָׂו.

54. Come and behold: at first IT IS WRITTEN, "Elohim's camp" (Beresheet
32:3), which is one, and afterwards IT IS WRITTEN, "He called the name of
that place *Mahanayim* (lit. 'two camps')" (Ibid.), which is two CAMPS. BUT
IT WAS PREVIOUSLY EXPLAINED THAT one CAMP was from the side of
Judgment and one was from the side of Mercy. There were angels of BOTH
THE LEFT and RIGHT sides, FOR JACOB IS THE CENTRAL COLUMN AND
INCLUDES BOTH OF THEM. Therefore, it is written: "met him," BEING THE
CENTRAL COLUMN. "And when Jacob saw them (Heb. *ra'am*)" (Ibid.). HE
ASKS: Why is it written, "*ra'am*" as one word, which is not usually used. It
should have been written, '*ra'ah otam*', meaning that he saw them, as it is
used in Hebrew. The reason for this is that he saw THE ANGELS OF MERCY
AND JUDGMENT cleaved together and bonded to each other. Therefore, it is
written, "*ra'am*," TO INSTRUCT THAT THEY WERE COMBINED, and all of
them came to accompany him and rescue him from the hands of Esau.

15. "And the first came out red"

A Synopsis

Because Isaac came from the side of stern Judgment, Esau came out with the red color of the side of Judgment. Jacob was from the second drop of sperm, that was from the side of Mercy and included both the right and the left. Esau came out from the dross of gold because at the time of Esau's conception Isaac's thoughts had been centered on ending the stern Judgment. It is important therefore for a man to concentrate his thoughts on the desire of God during the time he mates so that his descendants will be holy. Isaac's intention at the moment of Jacob's conception was connected with the mighty tree, Zeir Anpin, the Central Column. From this point of view, Jacob is regarded as the firstborn, and Esau not as important. We hear that one day the walls of Jerusalem will reach as high as the Throne of God, and the light of the moon will be as the light of the sun, and the light of the sun will be seven times as bright as it is now.

55. כְּתִיב בֵּיה בְּעֵשָׂו, וַיֵּצֵא הָרִאשׁוֹן אַדְמוֹנִי. וַיֵּצֵא הָרִאשׁוֹן, אִי תֵּימָא, דְּיַעֲקֹב טִפָּה קַדְמָאָה הֲוָה, לָאו הָכֵי, דְּהָא כְּתִיב, וַיֵּצֵא הָרִאשׁוֹן, וְלָא כְּתִיב, וַיֵּצֵא רִאשׁוֹן. וּבְגִין דְּיִצְחָק אָתֵי מִסִּטְרָא דְּדִינָא קַשְׁיָא, נָפַק עֵשָׂו אַדְמוֹנִי, סוּמָקָא. דְּאִי יַעֲקֹב הֲוָה בּוּכְרָא, הַהִיא טִפָּה קַדְמָאָה נָפְקָא הָכִי סוּמָקָא. אֲבָל טִפָּה תִּנְיָינָא הֲוָה, וּבְגִין כַּךְ לָא נָפְקָא הָכֵי, דְּהָא מִסִּטְרָא דְּרַחֲמֵי הֲוַת הַהִיא טִפָּה, מֵהַאי גִּיסָא וּמֵהַאי גִּיסָא.

55. It is written of Esau: "And the first came out red" (Beresheet 25:25). "And the first," FOR HE IS CALLED 'FIRST'. It is not so that Jacob was the first drop OF THE SEED AND ESAU WAS THE FIRST TO COME FORTH TO THE WORLD, for it is written: "And the first," NAMELY, THE FIRST AT THE TIME OF PROCREATION. It is not written, 'first', WITHOUT THE DEFINITE ARTICLE HEI, FOR THEN YOU MIGHT SAY THAT HE IS ONLY THE FIRST TO COME FORTH AND NOT THE FIRST OF THE SEED. Because Isaac came from the side of the Stern Judgment, BEING OF THE LEFT SIDE OF ZEIR ANPIN, Esau "came out red," NAMELY, WITH THE RED COLOR OF THE SIDE OF GVURAH. If Jacob was the first IN THE INSEMINATION, THAT IS, IF THE FIRST DROP OF SPERM WAS JACOB'S, then he would have been red, for the first drop LOOKS red AND JACOB WAS NOT RED. Thus, JACOB

was from the second drop of sperm and he did not come out so RED, for that drop OF SPERM came from the side of Mercy and INCLUDED this side and that side, BOTH THE RIGHT AND THE LEFT.

56. וְטִפָּה דְּעֵשָׂו לָא הֲוַת כְּטִפָּה דְיַעֲקֹב, דְּדָא שְׁלִים וְדָא לָא שְׁלִים. וּבְהַהִיא שַׁעֲתָא, יִצְחָק הֲוָה מְכַוֵּון בְּסִיּוּמָא דְּדִינָא קַשְׁיָא, דְּאַפִּיק בְּסִטְרוֹי, בִּגְלִיפוֹי טְהִירִין בְּשַׁיְיפוֹי, וּבְגִין כָּךְ עֵשָׂו, זוּהֲמָא דְּאִתְהַתִּיךְ מִדַּהֲבָא.

56. The drop of sperm of Esau was not like that of Jacob, for that one was complete and the other was not. At the time OF THE INSEMINATION OF ESAU, Isaac's thoughts were centered on ending the Stern Judgment, MEANING AT THE END OF THE LEFT SIDE WHERE THE DROSS OF GOLD, NAMELY THE KLIPOT, STARTS. For he produced from his own side, the LEFT, lights imprinted on the limbs OF ESAU. Hence, Esau WAS filth, NAMELY the dross which was melted out of gold.

57. וְעַל דָּא תָּנֵינָן, דְּבָעֵי ב"נ לְכַוְונָא בְּהַהִיא שַׁעֲתָא, בִּרְעוּתָא דְּמָארֵיה, בְּגִין דְּיִפּוּק בְּנִין קַדִּישִׁין לְעָלְמָא. וְאִי תֵּימָא, יִצְחָק לָא אִתְכַּוֵּון. לָאו הָכִי, אֶלָּא אִתְכַּוֵּון בִּקְדוּשָׁה, וְאִתְכַּוֵּון בְּסִיּוּמָא דְּהַהוּא אֲתַר, וְאִשְׁתְּכַח כַּד נָפַק הַהִיא טִפָּה קַדְמָאָה, בְּהַהוּא אֲתַר מַמָּשׁ, וְעַל דָּא כְּתִיב, כֻּלּוֹ כְּאַדֶּרֶת שֵׂעָר.

57. Therefore, we have learned that at the time OF MATING, a man should meditate on the desire of his Master so that his descendants will be holy. You might say that Isaac did not meditate ON HOLINESS. This is not so, for he centered his thoughts on Holiness and meditate on the end of the place OF THE LEFT SIDE, WHERE THE KLIPOT START BUT WHICH PERTAINS TO HOLINESS. When the first drop of the sperm came out, IT WAS exactly at that point. Therefore, it is written: "all over like a hairy garment" (Ibid.), NAMELY JUDGMENTS WHICH ARE CALLED 'HAIR'.

58. תָּא חֲזֵי, דָּוִד בְּשַׁפִּירוּ דְּסוּמָקָא נָפַק, וְאִתְאֲחַד בִּקְדוּשָׁה דְּמָארֵיה. וְעַל דָּא כְּתִיב, וְהוּא אַדְמוֹנִי עִם יְפֵה עֵינַיִם וְטוֹב רֹאִי. אֲבָל יַעֲקֹב

בּוּכְרָא הֲוָה מִנֵּיהּ דְּעֵשָׂו, לָא מִטִּפָּה, אֶלָּא דְּכַוָּונָה דִּרְעוּתָא, בְּאִילָנָא
עִלָּאָה רַבְרְבָא וְתַקִּיף, וְעֵשָׂו בְּהַהוּא אֲתַר דְּסִיּוּמָא דְּכֹלָּא, וּבְגִין כָּךְ
כְּתִיב, הִנֵּה קָטֹן נְתַתִּיךְ בַּגּוֹיִם בָּזוּי אַתָּה מְאֹד.

58. Come and behold: of David, IT IS WRITTEN THAT HE WAS "RUDDY," FOR he was created from the beauty of the red COLOR, WHICH IS THE LEFT SIDE OF BINAH AND WHICH ILLUMINATES MALCHUT. He was linked with his Master's sanctity. Therefore, it is written: "Now he was ruddy with fine eyes and good looking" (I Shmuel 16:12). THE SAME CANNOT BE SAID OF ESAU, FOR HE WAS CREATED FROM THE DROSS OF GOLD, WHICH BEGINS AT THE END OF THE LEFT SIDE, AS SAID. Indeed, Jacob was the firstborn, BEFORE Esau, not through the drop OF SPERM but because the intention DURING MATING was connected with the huge and mighty tree, NAMELY ZEIR ANPIN, THE CENTRAL COLUMN. Esau CAME FROM THE DIRECTING OF DESIRE, at the place which is the ending of all, NAMELY, THE PLACE WHERE HOLINESS ENDS, FOR THERE THE KLIPOT BEGIN. FROM THAT ASPECT, JACOB IS REGARDED AS THE FIRSTBORN AND THE FIRST, AND ESAU WAS SMALLER THAN HIM. Therefore, it is written: "Behold, I will make you small among all the nations; you are greatly despised" (Ovadyah 1:2).

59. רִבִּי יְהוּדָה הֲוָה מַתְנֵי הָכֵי. עֵשָׂו נִקְרָא רִאשׁוֹן, דִּכְתִיב, וַיֵּצֵא
הָרִאשׁוֹן אַדְמוֹנִי כֻּלּוֹ. וְקוּדְשָׁא בְּרִיךְ הוּא אִקְרֵי רִאשׁוֹן, דִּכְתִיב אֲנִי
רִאשׁוֹן וַאֲנִי אַחֲרוֹן וְאֶת אַחֲרוֹנִים אֲנִי הוּא. וְזַמִּין לְאִתְפָּרְעָא רִאשׁוֹן
מֵרִאשׁוֹן. וּלְמִבְנֵי רִאשׁוֹן, דִּכְתִיב, כִּסֵּא כָבוֹד מָרוֹם מֵרִאשׁוֹן. וּלְזִמְנָא
דְּאָתֵי כְּתִיב, רִאשׁוֹן לְצִיּוֹן הִנֵּה הִנָּם וְלִירוּשָׁלַם מְבַשֵּׂר אֶתֵּן.

59. Rabbi Yehuda taught that Esau is called "first," as it is written: "And the first came out red." The Holy One, blessed be He, is called "first" as it is written: "I am the first and I am the last" (Yeshayah 44:6), "and with the last, I am he" (Yeshayah 41:4). The "first" will one day punish the "first," meaning THE HOLY ONE, BLESSED BE HE, WILL PUNISH ESAU and build THE TEMPLE, WHICH IS CALLED 'first', as written: "A glorious throne exalted from the beginning (lit. 'first')" (Yirmeyah 17:12). Of the days to come, it is written: "A harbinger (lit. 'first') to Zion will I give, behold, behold them, and to Jerusalem a messenger of good tidings" (Yeshayah 41:27).

60. תָּאנָא, זְמִינָא יְרוּשָׁלַם, לְמֶהֱוֵי שׁוּרָהָא לְעֵילָא וּלְאִתְקָרְבָא עַד כּוּרְסֵי יְקָרָא דְּמַלְכָּא. הה"ד בָּעֵת הַהִיא יִקְרְאוּ לִירוּשָׁלַם כִּסֵּא יְיָ'. כְּדֵין כְּתִיב, וְהָיָה אוֹר הַלְּבָנָה כְּאוֹר הַחַמָּה וְאוֹר הַחַמָּה יִהְיֶה שִׁבְעָתַיִם. כְּדֵין בַּיּוֹם הַהוּא יִהְיֶה יְיָ' אֶחָד וּשְׁמוֹ אֶחָד.

60. We have learned that one day the walls of Jerusalem will reach on high to the Throne of the King, as it is written: "At that time they shall call Jerusalem the Throne of Hashem" (Yirmeyah 3:17). Then, "the light of the moon shall be as the light of the sun, and the light of the sun shall be sevenfold" (Yeshayah 30:26). FOR THE LIGHT OF MALCHUT, WHICH IS CALLED 'THE MOON', WILL BE AS THE LIGHT OF ZEIR ANPIN, WHICH IS CALLED 'THE SUN', AND THE LIGHT OF THE SUN, WHICH IS ZEIR ANPIN, WILL BE SEVENFOLD MORE THAN IT IS NOW. Then, "on that day, Hashem shall be One and His Name One" (Zecharyah 14:9).

ברוך אדני לעולם אמן ואמן. יתברך אדני לעולם אמן ואמן.

Blessed be Hashem forever and ever. Amen and Amen. Hashem will reign forever and ever. Amen and Amen.

16. "Two young deers"

A Synopsis

Rabbi Elazar and Rabbi Yosi hear a voice coming from a cave that speaks about two young deers and says they are the holy camp that Jacob met on his way. The voice then says that those two were Abraham and Isaac. Rabbi Elazar sees his father's image, and it says that the voice is a mouth which speaks great things. Rabbi Shimon also says that the souls of the righteous, who are holy angels, come to the righteous to save them. Although Isaac was alive when he was about to be sacrificed on the altar, his soul was taken to the Throne of God, after which time his eyes were dim.

תוֹסֶפְתָּא

61. רִבִּי אֶלְעָזָר, וְר' יוֹסֵי חָמוּי, הֲווֹ אָזְלֵי מֵאוּשָׁא לְלוּד. א"ר יוֹסֵי לְר' אֶלְעָזָר, אֶפְשָׁר שַׁמַעַת מֵאָבוּךְ מַאי דִּכְתִּיב, וְיַעֲקֹב הָלַךְ לְדַרְכּוֹ וְגוֹ'. א"ל לָא יְדַעֲנָא. עַד דַּהֲווֹ אָזְלֵי מָטוּ לִמְעַרְתָּא דְּלוּד. שָׁמְעוּ הַהוּא קָלָא דְּאָמַר, תְּרֵי עוּזְלִין דְּאַיַלְתָּא עָבְדוּ קַמַאי רְעוּתָא דְּנִיחָא לִי. וְאִינּוּן הֲווֹ מַשְׁרְיָיתָא קַדִּישָׁא דְּעָרַע יַעֲקֹב קַמֵּיה. אִתְרְגִישׁ ר' אֶלְעָזָר, וְאִסְתָּעַר בְּנַפְשׁוֹי, וְאָמַר, מָרֵיה דְּעָלְמָא כָּךְ אוֹרְחוֹי, טַב לָן דְּלָא נִשְׁמַע, שְׁמַעֲנָא וְלָא יְדַעֲנָא.

Tosefta (Addendum)

61. Rabbi Elazar and Rabbi Yosi his father-in-law were on their way from Osha to Lod. Rabbi Yosi asked Rabbi Elazar whether he had heard from his father an explanation of the verse written of Jacob: "And Jacob went on his way and angels of Elohim met him" (Beresheet 32:2). He latter replied that he did not know. When they arrived at the cave of Lod, they heard a voice that said: 'Two young deers have pleased me by fulfilling My desire; these are the holy camp that Jacob met on his way'. Those words made Rabbi Elazar very excited, and he then said: Master of the Universe, such are His ways, for it is better for us not to hear. I hear yet do not comprehend.

62. אִתְרְחִישׁ לֵיה נִיסָא, וְשָׁמַע הַהוּא קָלָא דְּאָמַר, אַבְרָהָם וְיִצְחָק הֲווֹ,

נָפַל עַל אַנְפּוֹי וְחָמָא דְּיוּקְנָא דַּאֲבוֹי, אָ"ל, אַבָּא, שְׁאִילְנָא וַאֲתִיבוּנָא,
דְּאַבְרָהָם וְיִצְחָק הֲווֹ, דְּעָרְעוּ לְיַעֲקֹב כַּד אִשְׁתְּזִיב מִלָּבָן. אָ"ל בְּרִי, פּוּק
פִּסְקָךְ, וְסַב סְבָתֶךְ, פּוּם מְמַלֵּל רַבְרְבָן הֲוָה. וְלָא דָא הִיא בִּלְחוֹדוֹי,
אֶלָּא לְכָל צַדִּיקַיָּא נִשְׁמָתְהוֹן דְּצַדִּיקַיָּא מְעַרְעִין קַדְמוֹהִי לְשֵׁיזָבוּתֵיהּ,
וְאִינּוּן מַלְאֲכֵיא קַדִּישֵׁי עִלָּאֵי.

62. Then a miracle happened to him and again he heard the same voice saying to him that those two were Abraham and Isaac. Then he fell to his face and his father's image appeared before him. He said to him: Father, I have asked ABOUT THE TWO DEERS, and was answered that they were Abraham and Isaac; they met Jacob when he was saved from Laban. He said to him: 'Son, release that which was cut off and accept your NEW source. It was a mouth which speaks greatly.' Furthermore, the souls of the righteous, who are holy supernal angels, come to all the righteous to save them.

63. וַת"ח, יִצְחָק קַיְּים הֲוָה בְּהַהִיא שַׁעֲתָא, אֲבָל נִשְׁמָתֵיהּ קַדִּישָׁא
אִתְנְסִיבַת בְּכוּרְסְיָא יְקָרָא דְּמָארֵיהּ, כַּד אִתְעֲקַד עַל גַּבֵּי מַדְבְּחָא.
וּמִכְּדֵין אַסְתְּמוּ עֵינוֹי מֵחֵיזוּ. הַיְינוּ דִּכְתִּיב, לוּלֵא וְגוֹ' וּפַחַד יִצְחָק הָיָה
לִי.

ע"כ תוספתא

63. Come and behold: Isaac was alive at that time, but his holy soul was taken to the Throne of his Master when he was to be sacrificed on the altar. After that, his eyes were dim, as it is written: "Were it not that...the fear of Isaac had been with me" (Beresheet 31:42).

End of Tosefta (Addendum)

ACHAREI MOT

Names of the article

1. "After the death of the two sons of Aaron"

A Synopsis

Rabbi Yehuda and Rabbi Shimon discuss the words 'spoke' and 'said' in "Hashem spoke to Moses" and "Hashem said to Moses" and we learn that they are from two levels, judgment and mercy, but nevertheless are from the same source, that is Zeir Anpin. Rabbi Yitzchak says that one verse says to serve Hashem in fear and another says to come before him with singing, and that these two verses seem contradictory. Rabbi Shimon says that if one shows awe and reverence, he will then deserve the joy and singing. One should not rejoice too much over worldly matters, so that he wil be able to perform the precepts with gladness. We are told that fear of God is the beginning of service to Him. We read of the several reasons that Nadab and Abihu died while giving the offering, and that they were still under the authority of Aaron at the time. Rabbi Chiya tells how he encountered two men studying the Torah in a cleft in the mountain, and of how they were discussing poems and psalms and songs, and speaking about the sons of Korah who did not die. They say that every time a righteous person dies it brings forgiveness for the sins of the whole generation. The memory of the two sons of Aaron serves as atonement for Yisrael while they are in exile, because Nadab and Abihu are each considered equal to the seventy members of the Sanhedrin who served before Moses.

1. וַיְדַבֵּר יְיָ' אֶל מֹשֶׁה אַחֲרֵי מוֹת שְׁנֵי בְּנֵי אַהֲרֹן וְגוֹ'. וַיֹּאמֶר יְיָ' אֶל מֹשֶׁה. רְבִּי יְהוּדָה אָמַר, כֵּיוָן דִּכְתִּיב וַיְדַבֵּר יְיָ' אֶל מֹשֶׁה, אֲמַאי זִמְנָא אָחֳרָא וַיֹּאמֶר יְיָ' אֶל מֹשֶׁה דַּבֵּר אֶל אַהֲרֹן אָחִיךָ, דְּהָא בְּמִלּוּלָא קַדְמָאָה סַגֵּי. אֶלָּא הָכִי תָּנֵינָן, כְּתִיב, וַיִּקְרָא אֶל מֹשֶׁה וַיְדַבֵּר יְיָ' אֵלָיו. וּכְתִיב, וְאֶל מֹשֶׁה אָמַר עֲלֵה אֶל יְיָ'. וְהָא אוּקְמוּהָ מִלָּה, דְּהָכָא דַּרְגָּא חַד. וּלְבָתַר, דַּרְגָּא אָחֳרָא. אוּף הָכָא, וַיְדַבֵּר יְיָ' אֶל מֹשֶׁה דַּרְגָּא חַד. וּלְבָתַר וַיֹּאמֶר יְיָ' אֶל מֹשֶׁה דַּבֵּר אֶל אַהֲרֹן אָחִיךָ, דַּרְגָּא אָחֳרָא. וְכֹלָּא, בְּחַד מַתְקְלָא סַלְקָא, וּמִן שָׁרְשָׁא חַד כֹּלָּא אִתְחַבָּר.

1. "And Hashem spoke to Moses after the death of the two sons of Aaron... and Hashem said to Moses" (Vayikra 16:1). Rabbi Yehuda comments: Since the verse says, "And Hashem spoke to Moses," what need is there to repeat

"and Hashem said to Moses, Speak to your brother Aaron..."? The first statement should have sufficed. HE ANSWERS: We learn that it is written, "And Hashem (lit. 'He') called to Moses and (lit. 'Hashem') spoke to him" (Vayikra 1:1) and also, "And He said to Moses, Come up to Hashem" (Shemot 24:1). It has already been established that the discourse here, NAMELY "AND HE CALLED TO MOSES" OR "AND HE SAID TO MOSES" represents one level, NAMELY MALCHUT. Afterwards, the words, "AND HASHEM SPOKE TO HIM" OR "COME UP TO HASHEM" represent another level, NAMELY ZEIR ANPIN. Here too in our text, "And Hashem spoke to Moses" represents one level, NAMELY THE LEVEL OF JUDGMENT REFERRED TO AS 'SPEAKING', and afterwards the verse, "And Hashem said to Moses, Speak to your brother Aaron" represents another level, NAMELY THE QUALITY OF MERCY REFERRED TO AS 'SAYING'. IN BOTH INSTANCES THE NAME YUD HEI VAV HEI IS MENTIONED, which reveals that they carry one equal scale and all are joined from one source. THIS MEANS THAT BOTH LEVELS, JUDGMENT AND MERCY, ARE OF ONE SCALE FROM ONE SOURCE, WHICH IS ZEIR ANPIN REFERRED TO AS YUD HEI VAV HEI.

2. אַחֲרֵי מוֹת שְׁנֵי בְּנֵי אַהֲרֹן. רִבִּי יִצְחָק פָּתַח, עִבְדוּ אֶת יְיָ' בְּיִרְאָה וְגִילוּ בִּרְעָדָה. וּכְתִיב, עִבְדוּ אֶת יְיָ' בְּשִׂמְחָה בָּאוּ לְפָנָיו בִּרְנָנָה. הָנֵי קְרָאֵי קַשְׁיָין אֲהַדְדֵי, אֶלָּא הָכִי תָּאנָא, עִבְדוּ אֶת יְיָ' בְּיִרְאָה. דְּכָל פּוּלְחָנָא דְּבָעֵי ב"נ לְמִפְלַח קַמֵּי מָארֵיה, בְּקַדְמֵיתָא בָּעֵי יִרְאָה, לְדַחֲלָא מִנֵּיהּ, וּבְגִין דַּחֲלָא דְּמָארֵיהּ, יִשְׁתְּכַח לְבָתַר דְּיַעֲבֵיד בְּחֶדְוָותָא פִּקּוּדֵי אוֹרַיְיתָא. וְעַל דָּא כְּתִיב, מָה יְיָ' אֱלֹהֶיךָ שׁוֹאֵל מֵעִמָּךְ כִּי אִם לְיִרְאָה.

2. "After the death of the two sons of Aaron": Rabbi Yitzchak opened the discussion saying, "Serve Hashem in fear, and rejoice with trembling" (Tehilim 2:11). It is also written, "Serve Hashem with gladness: come before Him with singing" (Tehilim 100:2). These verses appear to contradict one another, as ONE SAYS TO SERVE IN FEAR AND TREBLING WHILE THE OTHER SAYS WITH GLADNESS AND SINGING. HE ANSWERS: We have learned that "serve Hashem in fear" means that one must first show fear and awe in every act he wishes to perform before his Master. As a result of this reverence before his Master, he will merit to serve with joy the commandments of the Torah. Therefore, it is written, "What does Hashem your Elohim require of you, but to fear" (Devarim 10:12). THROUGH FEAR, HE WILL MERIT IT ALL.

‫3. וְגִילוּ בִּרְעָדָה. דְּאָסִיר לֵיהּ לב"נ לְמֶחְדֵי יַתִּיר בְּעָלְמָא דֵין. הַאי‬
‫בְּמִלֵּי דְעָלְמָא, אֲבָל בְּמִלֵּי דְאוֹרַיְיתָא וּבְפִקּוּדֵי דְאוֹרַיְיתָא, בָּעֵי לְמֶחְדֵּי.‬
‫לְבָתַר, יִשְׁתְּכַּח בַּר נָשׁ דְּיַעֲבִיד בְּחֶדְוָותָא פִּקוּדֵי אוֹרַיְיתָא. דִּכְתִיב,‬
‫עִבְדוּ אֶת יְיָ' בְּשִׂמְחָה.‬

3. "And rejoice with trembling," MEANING that man must not overly rejoice in this world, referring only to worldly matters, but one must rejoice in the matters of Torah and the performance of precepts. Then, AS ONE WILL REFRAIN FROM REJOICING IN MUNDANE MATTERS, man will find himself able to perform Torah and precepts with happiness, as is written, "Serve Hashem with gladness."

‫4. ר' אַבָּא אָמַר, עִבְדוּ אֶת יְיָ' בְּיִרְאָה. רָזָא דְּמִלָּה הוּא, עִבְדוּ אֶת יְיָ'‬
‫בְּיִרְאָה, מַה יִרְאָה הָכָא. אֶלָּא כְּמָה דְאוּקִימְנָא, דִּכְתִיב, יִרְאַת יְיָ'‬
‫רֵאשִׁית דָּעַת, וּכְתִיב, רֵאשִׁית חָכְמָה יִרְאַת יְיָ'. יִרְאַת יְיָ', קוּדְשָׁא בְּרִיךְ‬
‫הוּא הָכִי אִקְרֵי. ר' אֶלְעָזָר אָמַר, עִבְדוּ אֶת יְיָ' בְּיִרְאָה, מַאן דְּבָעֵי‬
‫לְמֶעְבַּד פּוּלְחָנָא דְּמָארֵיהּ, מֵאן אֲתַר שָׁארֵי, וּבְאָן אֲתַר יְכַוֵּין פּוּלְחָנָא‬
‫לְיַחֲדָא שְׁמָא דְּמָארֵיהּ. הָדַר וְאָמַר בְּיִרְאָה, בְּיִרְאָה הוּא שֵׁירוּתָא,‬
‫מִתַּתָּא לְעֵילָא.‬

4. Rabbi Aba said, "Serve Hashem in fear": What fear is meant here? IN OTHER WORDS, WHAT IS THE EXPLANATION IN THIS CONTEXT OF FEAR? HE ANSWERS: As we have established, it is written, "The fear of Hashem is the beginning of knowledge" (Mishlei 1:7) and "the fear of Hashem is the beginning of wisdom" (Tehilim 111:10), so the Holy One, blessed be He, is referred to in this name, "Fear of Hashem," NAMELY MALCHUT. Rabbi Elazar said: IN EXPLANATION OF RABBI ABA'S WORDS, "Serve Hashem in fear," MEANING he who wishes to perform the service of his Master, from what point should he begin and to which area should he aim his service in order to unify the name of his Master? He repeats his words "with fear," because fear, WHICH IS MALCHUT, is the start OF SERVICE going from below upwards, AS THE FIRST SFIRAH GOING FROM BELOW UPWARDS IS MALCHUT.

‫5. ת"ח, מַה כְּתִיב הָכָא אַחֲרֵי מוֹת, וּלְבָתַר דַּבֵּר אֶל אַהֲרֹן אָחִיךָ וְגוֹ'‬

בְּזֹאת יָבֹא אַהֲרֹן, אֶלָּא מִכָּאן, שֵׁירוּתָא לְאַזְהָרָא לְכַהֲנֵי, כָּל מַאן,
דְּבַעְיָין לְאִזְדַהֲרָא בְּהַאי זֹאת, וְדָא הִיא יִרְאַת יְיָ'.

5. Come and see: It is written: here, "After the death" and later, "Speak to Aaron your brother...Thus shall Aaron come." (Vayikra 16:2-3). WHAT CONNECTION IS THERE BETWEEN "AFTER THE DEATH OF" TO THE VERSE, "THUS (LIT. 'WITH THIS') SHALL AARON COME"? HE ANSWERS: FROM THE DEATH OF THE SONS OF AARON commences the warning to each of the priests that they must be mindful of *Zot* (Eng. 'this' fem.), which is the fear of Hashem, WHICH IS MALCHUT. FOR THE DEATHS OF THE SONS OF AARON WERE AS A RESULT OF THEIR NEGLIGENCE IN RELATION TO MALCHUT.

6. דָּבָר אַחֵר. אַחֲרֵי מוֹת שְׁנֵי בְּנֵי אַהֲרֹן. ר' יוֹסֵי אָמַר, אַחֲרֵי מוֹת נָדָב
וַאֲבִיהוּא, מִבָּעֵי לֵיהּ, מ"ט שְׁנֵי בְּנֵי אַהֲרֹן, וְהָא יְדִיעַ דִּבְנוֹי הֲווֹ. אֶלָּא
הָכִי תָּאנָא, דְּעַד כָּאן לָאו בִּרְשׁוּתַיְיהוּ קַיְּימֵי, אֶלָּא בִּרְשׁוּתָא דְּאֲבוּהוֹן,
ובג"כ, בְּקָרְבָתָם לִפְנֵי יְיָ' וַיָּמוּתוּ, דְּאִינּוּן דָּחֲקוּ שַׁעֲתָא בְּחַיֵּי דְּאֲבוּהוֹן,
וְכֹלָּא הֲוָה, בְּגִין הַהוּא חוֹבָא דְּעָבְדוּ, דִּכְתִּיב בְּהַקְרִיבָם אֵשׁ זָרָה.
דְּתַנְיָא, בְּאֲתַר חַד, כְּתִיב בְּהַקְרִיבָם אֵשׁ זָרָה, וּבְאֲתַר חַד כְּתִיב,
בְּקָרְבָתָם לִפְנֵי יְיָ'. וְהַאי וְהַאי הֲוָה, ובג"כ כְּתִיב הָכָא בְּנֵי אַהֲרֹן,
וּכְתִיב בְּקָרְבָתָם.

6. Another explanation for, "After the death of the two sons of Aaron." Rabbi Yosi said: It should have read, 'After the death of Nadab and Abihu', so what is the reason THAT IT SAYS, "The two sons of Aaron"? It is obvious that they were his sons. HE ANSWERS: We have learned that until that time they were not adults but still under the authority of their father; CONSEQUENTLY, THE VERSE REFERS TO THEM AS THE SONS OF AARON. Hence, "when they came near before Hashem, and died" (Vayikra 16:1), they were rushing the time OF OFFERING INCENSE during the lifetime of their father, AS IS INDICATED LATER, and there was more, MEANING OTHER CAUSES PRECIPITATED THEIR DEATH. ALSO, because of the sin they committed "when they offered a foreign fire" (Bemidbar 3:4) as we learned, in one place it is written, "When they offered a foreign fire," AND FOR THIS REASON THEY DIED. In another place, it is written, "When they came near

before Hashem," THEY DIED BECAUSE THEY SACRIFICED, BECAUSE THEY RUSHED THE TIME TO BURN INCENSE DURING THE LIFETIME OF THEIR FATHER, AS MENTIONED ABOVE. THIS MEANS THE COMBINATION OF both matters CAUSED THEIR DEATHS, so it is written: here, "The two sons of Aaron" TO TEACH THAT THEY WERE STILL UNDER THE AUTHORITY OF AARON, AS DECLARED ABOVE. It is written, "When they came near," FOR THE DEATH WAS AS A RESULT OF THEIR APPROACH BEFORE HASHEM, DURING THE LIFETIME OF THEIR FATHER.

7. א"ר חִיָּיא, יוֹמָא חַד הֲוֵינָא אָזִיל בְּאָרְחָא, לְמֵיהַךְ גַּבֵּי דְּרִבִּי שִׁמְעוֹן, לְמֵילַף מִנֵּיהּ פַּרְשָׁתָּא דְּפִסְחָא. עַרְעִית בְּחַד טוּרָא, וַחֲמֵינָא בְּקִיעִין גּוּמִּין בְּחַד טִינָרָא, וּתְרֵין גּוּבְרִין בָּהּ. עַד דַּהֲוֵינָא אָזִיל, שְׁמַעְנָא קָלָא דְּאִינּוּן גּוּבְרִין, וַהֲווֹ אַמְרִין, שִׁיר מִזְמוֹר לִבְנֵי קֹרַח גָּדוֹל יְיָ' וּמְהֻלָּל מְאֹד וְגוֹ'. מַאי שִׁיר מִזְמוֹר. אֶלָּא הָכִי תָּאנָא מִשְּׁמֵיהּ דר' שִׁמְעוֹן, שִׁיר דְּאִיהוּ כָּפוּל, שִׁיר דְּאִיהוּ מְשׁוּבָּח מִשְּׁאַר שִׁירִין, וְעַל דְּאִיהוּ מְשׁוּבָּח מִשְּׁאַר שִׁירִין, תְּרֵין זִמְנִין אִתְּמַר בֵּיהּ שִׁירָתָא, וְכֵן מִזְמוֹר שִׁיר לְיוֹם הַשַּׁבָּת. כה"ג, שִׁיר הַשִּׁירִים אֲשֶׁר לִשְׁלֹמֹה, שִׁירָתָא לְעֵילָא מִן שִׁירָתָא.

7. Rabbi Chiya said: One day I was traveling to Rabbi Shimon to be taught by him the laws of the Pesach (Passover). I encountered a mountain and I saw clefts and cavities in one rock, and two men were in there. As I approached, I heard the voices of these people who were saying, "A song, a psalm for the sons of Korah, Great is Hashem and highly to be praised..." (Tehilim 48:1-2). Wherefore "A song, a psalm"? HE ANSWERS: Thus do we learn on behalf of Rabbi Shimon: The song is two-fold, NAMELY A SONG AND A PSALM, and since it is a better song than other songs, it is named "song" twice. Similarly, "A psalm, a poem for the Shabbat day" (Tehilim 92:1), MEANING THAT IT IS MORE PRAISEWORTHY THAN OTHER SONGS. In the same fashion, "the song of songs which is Solomon's" (Shir Hashirim 1:1), INDICATING a song that stands above all other songs.

8. שִׁיר מִזְמוֹר, שִׁירָתָא דְּקוּדְשָׁא בְּרִיךְ הוּא, דְּקָא מְזַמְּרֵי בְּנֵי קֹרַח עַל אִינּוּן דְּיַתְבֵי, עַל פִּתְחָא דְּגֵיהִנָּם. וּמַאן אִינּוּן, אֲחוּהוֹן דְּאִינּוּן דְּיַתְבֵי

בְּתַרְעֵי דְּגֵיהִנָּם. וְעַ"ד, שִׁירָתָא דָּא בְּיוֹם שֵׁנִי אִתְּמַר. קָרִיבְנָא גַּבַּיְיהוּ,
אֲמֵינָא לְהוּ, מַאי עֶסְקַיְיכוּ בַּאֲתַר דָּא. אָמְרוּ מְזַבְּנֵי אֲנָן, וּתְרֵי יוֹמֵי
בְּשַׁבַּתָּא, בְּדִילְנָא מִישׁוּבָא וְנַעֲסֵק בְּאוֹרַיְיתָא. בְּגִין דְּלָא שַׁבְקִין לָן בְּנֵי
נָשָׁא, כָּל יוֹמָא וְיוֹמָא. אֲמֵינָא זַכָּאָה חוּלָקֵיכוֹן.

8. ALSO HERE, WHERE IT IS WRITTEN, "A song, a psalm," THIS SONG IS
SUPERIOR TO OTHERS. It is a song describing the Holy One, blessed be He,
which the sons of Korah were singing about those who were dwelling in the
doorway of Gehenom. Who were THE SONS OF KORAH? They were the
brothers of those residing at the gates of Gehenom, AS THE HOLY SAGES
COMMENT ON THE VERSE, "THE SONS OF KORAH DID NOT DIE"
(BEMIDBAR 26:11), BUT A PLACE WAS SET FOR THEM IN GEHENOM. As
a result, this song was recited on Monday IN THE TEMPLE. I approached
them and said to them: What are you doing in this place? They replied: We
are merchants, but twice weekly we leave our community to study Torah
here because IN THE SETTLEMENT, WE ARE DISTURBED EACH DAY by
people and they do not allow us TO STUDY TORAH. I replied to them: How
fortunate is your lot.

9. תּוּ פָּתְחוּ וְאָמְרוּ. בְּכָל זִמְנָא דְּצַדִּיקַיָּא מִסְתַּלְּקֵי מֵעָלְמָא, דִּינָא
אִסְתַּלָּק מֵעָלְמָא, וּמִיתַתְהוֹן דְּצַדִּיקַיָּא מְכַפְּרֶת עַל חוֹבֵי דָּרָא. וְעַל דָּא
פָּרְשָׁתָא דִּבְנֵי אַהֲרֹן, בְּיוֹמָא דְּכִפּוּרֵי קָרֵינָן לָהּ, לְמֶהֱוֵי כַּפָּרָה לְחוֹבֵיהוֹן
דְּיִשְׂרָאֵל. אָמַר קוּדְשָׁא בְּרִיךְ הוּא, אִתְעַסְּקוּ בְּמִיתַתְהוֹן דְּצַדִּיקַיָּא
אִלֵּין, וְיִתְחֲשַׁב לְכוּ כְּאִילוּ אַתּוּן מְקָרְבִין קָרְבָּנִין בְּהַאי יוֹמָא לְכַפְּרָא
עֲלַיְיכוּ. דְּתָנֵינָן, כָּל זִמְנָא דְּיִשְׂרָאֵל יְהוֹן בְּגָלוּתָא, וְלָא יִקְרְבוּן קָרְבָּנִין
בְּהַאי יוֹמָא, וְאִינּוּן תְּרֵין שְׂעִירִין לָא יַכְלִין לְקָרְבָא, יְהֵא לְהוּ דּוּכְרָנָא,
דִּתְרֵי בְּנֵי אַהֲרֹן, וְיִתְכַּפַּר עֲלַיְיהוּ.

9. Furthermore, they said: Every time that the righteous depart this world,
there is likewise annulled from this world all the harsh decrees, and the
death of the righteous brings forgiveness for the sins of the generation.
Therefore, we read the portion dealing with the sons of Aaron on Yom
Kippur (Day of Atonement) to bring forgiveness for the sins of Yisrael. The
Holy One, blessed be He, says, 'Contemplate the death of these pious ones,

and it will be accredited for you, as if you offered sacrifice this day to attain forgiveness'. We have learned that as long as Yisrael will be in exile and neither be able to offer offerings on this day nor will they be able to offer the two goats, they will at least have the memory of the two sons of Aaron. Thus, it will serve as atonement for them.

10. דְּהָכִי אוֹלִיפְנָא, דִּכְתִיב וְאֵלֶּה שְׁמוֹת בְּנֵי אַהֲרֹן הַכֹּהֲנִים וְגוֹ'. וּכְתִיב, הַבְּכֹר נָדָב וַאֲבִיהוּא אֶלְעָזָר וְאִתָּמָר. וְאֶלְעָזָר וְאִתָּמָר מִבָּעֵי לֵיהּ, מַהוּ אֶלְעָזָר וְאִתָּמָר. אֶלָּא שָׁקוּל הֲוָה אֲבִיהוּא כִּתְרֵי אֲחוֹי. וְנָדָב כְּכֻלְּהוּ.

10. We have learned that it is written, "These are the names of the sons of Aaron, the priests" (Bemidbar 3:3) and also, "Nadab the firstborn, and Abihu, Elazar and Itamar" (Ibid. 2). HE QUESTIONS: It should read: 'And Elazar and Itamar' JUST LIKE IT SAYS "AND ABIHU," so why write "Elazar and Itamar"? WHY DELETE THE CONNECTING 'AND' (VAV) FROM ELAZAR? HE ANSWERS: Abihu was equal to his two brothers. The VERSE EQUATES ABIHU TO ELAZAR AND ITAMAR, and Nadab is equal to all the others.

11. וְאִית דְּמַתְנֵי הַבְּכֹר נָדָב, דָּא בִּלְחוֹדוֹי, וַאֲבִיהוּא בִּלְחוֹדוֹי, וְכָל חַד אִתְחֲשִׁיב בְּעֵינֵיהּ, כִּתְרַוְיְיהוּ, כְּאֶלְעָזָר וְאִתָּמָר. אֲבָל נָדָב וַאֲבִיהוּא בִּלְחוֹדַיְיהוּ, שְׁקוּלִין הֲווֹ לָקֳבֵל שַׁבְעִין סַנְהֶדְרִין, דַּהֲווֹ מְשַׁמְּשִׁין קַמֵּי מֹשֶׁה. וּבְגִין כָּךְ, מִיתָתְהוֹן מְכַפְּרָא עַל יִשְׂרָאֵל. וְעַל דָּא כְּתִיב, וַאֲחֵיכֶם כָּל בֵּית יִשְׂרָאֵל יִבְכּוּ אֶת הַשְּׂרֵפָה. וְאָמַר ר' שִׁמְעוֹן, הַבְּכֹר נָדָב, כְּלוֹמַר, הַהוּא, דְּכָל שְׁבָחָא וִיקָרָא דִּילֵיהּ. נָדָב וַאֲבִיהוּא, עַל אַחַת כַּמָּה וְכַמָּה, דְּהָנֵי תְּרֵי, לָא אִשְׁתְּכָחוּ כְּוָתַיְיהוּ בְּיִשְׂרָאֵל.

11. The firstborn Nadab stands on his own merits and Abihu rests on his own, AND FOLLOWING THEM ELAZAR AND ITAMAR ARE READ AS JOINED TOGETHER TO TEACH that each one OF NADAB AND ABIHU are considered in the eyes OF SCRIPTURE as both Elazar and Itamar TOGETHER. But BOTH Nadab and Abihu by themselves are each considered equal to the seventy members of the Sanhedrin who served before Moses. For this reason, their

deaths atoned for Yisrael. Therefore, it is written, "But let your brethren, the whole house of Yisrael bewail the burning" (Vayikra 10:6). Rabbi Shimon said: THEREFORE THE VERSE SPECIFIES "Nadab the firstborn," meaning he is the one that all acclaim and praise are his. How much more so with Nadab and Abihu TOGETHER, because these two have no equal among all Yisrael.

2. "Jacob, who redeemed Abraham"

A Synopsis

We learn that Jacob redeemed Abraham just because God saw that Jacob would descend from Abraham. Rabbi Chizkiyah questions why Hananiah, Mishael and Azariah (who threw themselves into a burning fire) are referred to as descendants of Jacob, when in fact they were the descendants of Judah. Rabbi Shimon explains that is because in their time of danger they referred to Jacob, and God took note of this and protected them, and those who had ridiculed the name of Jacob were killed by the flame.

12. וַיְדַבֵּר יְיָ' אֶל מֹשֶׁה אַחֲרֵי מוֹת שְׁנֵי בְּנֵי אַהֲרֹן. רִבִּי חִזְקִיָּה פָּתַח וְאָמַר, לָכֵן כֹּה אָמַר יְיָ' אֶל בֵּית יַעֲקֹב אֲשֶׁר פָּדָה אֶת אַבְרָהָם וְגוֹ'. הַאי קְרָא קַשְׁיָא, לָכֵן כֹּה אָמַר יְיָ' אֲשֶׁר פָּדָה אֶת אַבְרָהָם מִבָּעֵי לֵיהּ. מַאי, כֹּה אָמַר יְיָ' אֶל בֵּית יַעֲקֹב אֲשֶׁר פָּדָה אֶת אַבְרָהָם.

12. "And Hashem spoke to Moses after the death of the two sons of Aaron" (Vayikra 16:1): Rabbi Chizkiyah opened the discussion saying, "Therefore, thus says Hashem concerning the house of Jacob, who redeemed Abraham..." (Yeshayah 29:22). This verse is troublesome. It should read, 'Therefore, thus says Hashem, who redeemed Abraham'. Why does it say "Therefore, thus says Hashem concerning the house of Jacob, who redeemed Abraham"?

13. אֶלָּא הָא אוּקְמוּהָ וְהָא אִתְּמַר, דְּיַעֲקֹב פָּדָה אֶת אַבְרָהָם וַדַּאי. דִּבְהַהִיא שַׁעֲתָא דְּנָפַל בְּגוֹ נוּרָא דְּכַשְׂדָּאֵי, דָּנוּ דִּינֵיהּ קַמֵּי קוּדְשָׁא בְּרִיךְ הוּא, בְּגִין מַאי יִשְׁתְּזִיב הַאי, זְכוּת אַבְהָן לֵית לֵיהּ. א"ל, יִשְׁתְּזֵיב בְּגִין בְּנוֹי, דְּהָכִי תַּנְיָא, בְּרָא מְזַכֵּי אַבָּא. אָמְרוּ, הָא יִשְׁמָעֵאל דְּנָפִיק מִנֵּיהּ. אָמַר קוּדְשָׁא בְּרִיךְ הוּא, הָא יִצְחָק, דְּיוֹשִׁיט קְדָלֵיהּ עַל גַּבֵּי מַדְבְּחָא. אָמְרוּ, הָא עֵשָׂו דְּנָפִיק מִנֵּיהּ. אָמַר, הָא יַעֲקֹב, דְּאִיהוּ כֻּרְסַיָּא שְׁלֵימָתָא, וְכָל בְּנוֹהִי שְׁלֵימִין קַמָּאי. אָמְרוּ, הָא וַדַּאי בִּזְכוּתָא דָּא יִשְׁתְּזִיב אַבְרָהָם הה"ד אֲשֶׁר פָּדָה אֶת אַבְרָהָם.

13. We have already learned that Jacob surely redeemed Abraham. At the time that ABRAHAM fell into THE FURNACE OF the Chaldeans' fire, his fate was being decided before the Holy One, blessed be He. In what merit should this one be saved as he lacks ancestral merits? THE HOLY ONE, BLESSED BE HE, said TO THE COURT ON HIGH: 'He should be saved because of his sons.' As we have learned, a son can bring merits for his father. The others replied: But Ishmael will descend from him. The Holy One, blessed be He, replied, 'But Isaac WILL DESCEND FROM HIM, who will extend his throat FOR THE SACRIFICE on the altar'. The others said: But Esau will derive from Isaac. THE HOLY ONE, BLESSED BE HE, said, 'But Jacob will DESCEND FROM HIM, who is a whole throne, and all his sons are perfect before Me.' They concurred by saying: Surely for this merit, Abraham shall be rescued. Such is the meaning of, "who redeemed Abraham."

14. לֹא עַתָּה יֵבוֹשׁ יַעֲקֹב וְלֹא עַתָּה פָּנָיו יֶחֱוָרוּ כִּי בִרְאוֹתוֹ יְלָדָיו מַעֲשֵׂה יָדַי בְּקִרְבּוֹ יַקְדִּישׁוּ שְׁמִי. מַאן אִינּוּן יְלָדָיו מַעֲשֵׂה וְגוֹ'. אִלֵּין אִינּוּן, חֲנַנְיָה מִישָׁאֵל וַעֲזַרְיָה. בְּנֵי יְהוּדָה אִקְרוּן, ובג"כ לֹא עַתָּה יֵבוֹשׁ יְהוּדָה מִבָּעֵי לֵיהּ, מַאי לֹא עַתָּה מַאי בָּעֵי הָכָא יַעֲקֹב, וְהָא כְּתִיב, וַיְהִי בָהֶם מִבְּנֵי יְהוּדָה דָּנִיֵּאל חֲנַנְיָה מִישָׁאֵל וַעֲזַרְיָה. בְּנֵי יְהוּדָה אִקְרוּן, ובג"כ לֹא עַתָּה יֵבוֹשׁ יְהוּדָה מִבָּעֵי לֵיהּ, מַאי לֹא עַתָּה יֵבוֹשׁ יַעֲקֹב.

14. IT IS WRITTEN, "Jacob shall not now be ashamed, neither shall his face now grow pale; when he sees his children, the work of My hands, in the midst of him, sanctifying My name" (Yeshayah 29:22-23). HE QUESTIONS: Who are "his children, the work of My hands"? HE ANSWERS: They are Hananiah, Mishael, and Azariah, WHO THREW THEMSELVES INTO A BURNING FIRE TO SANCTIFY MY NAME. HE QUESTIONS, "Jacob shall not now be ashamed": What is Jacob doing here? For it is written, "These were among the descendants of Judah: Daniel, Hananiah, Mishael, and Azariah" (Daniel 1:6). NOTE, they are referred to as scions of Judah. As a result, it should read: 'Judah shall not now be ashamed'. Why then does it state, "Jacob shall not now be ashamed"?

15. אֶלָּא הָכִי תָּנֵינָן. בְּהַאי שַׁעֲתָא דְּאִתְכַּפְיָתוּ, לְמִנְפַּל בְּנוּרָא, כָּל חַד אָרִים קַלֵיהּ וְאָמַר, גַּבֵּי כָּל אִינּוּן עַמִּין וּמַלְכִין וְאָפַרְכַיָּא, חֲנַנְיָה אָמַר,

יְיָ' לִי לֹא אִירָא מַה יַּעֲשֶׂה לִי אָדָם יְיָ' לִי בְּעוֹזְרָי וַאֲנִי אֶרְאֶה בְּשׂוֹנְאָי
טוֹב לַחֲסוֹת בַּייָ' וְגוֹ'. מִישָׁאֵל פָּתַח וְאָמַר, וְאַתָּה אַל תִּירָא עַבְדִּי יַעֲקֹב
נְאֻם יְיָ' וְגוֹ' כִּי אִתְּךָ אֲנִי נְאֻם יְיָ' לְהוֹשִׁיעֶךָ כִּי אֶעֱשֶׂה וְגוֹ'. בְּהַהִיא
שַׁעֲתָא, דְּשַׁמְעוּ כֻּלְּהוּ שְׁמָא דְּיַעֲקֹב. תַּוְּוהוּ וְחַיְיכוּ בְּלֵצָנוּתָא. עֲזַרְיָה
פָּתַח וְאָמַר, שְׁמַע יִשְׂרָאֵל יְיָ' אֱלֹהֵינוּ יְיָ' אֶחָד.

15. HE ANSWERS: We have learned at the time they bound HANANIAH, MISHAEL AND AZARIAH in order to cast them into fire, each raised his voice and spoke before all the gathered nations, kings and nobles. Hananiah said, "Hashem is with me, I will not fear: what can man do to me? Hashem takes my part with those who help me: therefore I shall gaze upon those who hate me. It is better to take refuge in Hashem..." (Tehilim 118:6-8). Mishael said, "Therefore fear you not, My servant Jacob, says Hashem...For I am with you, says Hashem, to help you, for I will make a full end of all the nations" (Yirmeyah 30:10-11). At that moment, when THE NATIONS AND THE NOBLES heard the name Jacob, they were disgusted and began mockingly to laugh, BECAUSE HE PUT HIS TRUST IN JACOB. Azariah commenced to proclaim, "Hear O' Yisrael, Hashem our Elohim; Hashem is One" (Devarim 6:4).

16. הה"ד, זֶה יֹאמַר לַייָ' אָנִי וְגוֹ'. זֶה יֹאמַר לה' אָנִי, דָּא חֲנַנְיָה, וְזֶה
יִקְרָא בְּשֵׁם יַעֲקֹב, דָּא מִישָׁאֵל, וְזֶה יִכְתּוֹב יָדוֹ לַייָ' וּבְשֵׁם יִשְׂרָאֵל יְכַנֶּה,
דָּא עֲזַרְיָה, בֵּיהּ שַׁעֲתָא כָּנַשׁ קוּדְשָׁא בְּרִיךְ הוּא פָּמַלְיָא דִּילֵיהּ, אָמַר
לוֹן, בְּמַאן מִלָּה, מֵאִינּוּן מִלִּין דְּאָמְרוּ אִלֵּין תְּלָתָא, אֲשֵׁזִיב לוֹן. פָּתְחוּ
וְאָמְרוּ, וְיֵדְעוּ כִּי אַתָּה שִׁמְךָ יְיָ' לְבַדֶּךָ עֶלְיוֹן עַל כָּל הָאָרֶץ.

16. This is what is written, "One shall say, I am Hashem's..." (Yeshayah 44:5). "One shall say, I am Hashem's" refers to Hananiah, WHO DECLARED THAT "HASHEM TAKES MY PART..." "And another shall call himself by the name of Jacob" (Ibid.): This is Mishael, WHO SAID, "FEAR YOU NOT, O MY SERVANT JACOB." "And another shall subscribe with his hand to Hashem, and surname himself by the name of Yisrael" (Ibid.). This is Azariah, WHO SAID, "HEAR O' YISRAEL..." At that moment, the Holy One, blessed be He, assembled His heavenly council, NAMELY THE ANGELS, and said to them, 'For which word among the words that these three uttered, should I save them?' They replied, "That they may know that You alone,

whose name is Hashem, are the most high over all the earth" (Tehilim 83:19), MEANING SAVE THEM, BECAUSE THEY TRUSTED IN HASHEM.

17. בָּה שַׁעֲתָא אָמַר קוּדְשָׁא בְּרִיךְ הוּא לְכוּרְסְיָיא, כּוּרְסְיָיא דִילִי, בְּמַאן מִלָּה מֵאִינוּן מִלִּין, אַשְׁזִיב לְאִינּוּן צַדִּיקַיָּיא. אָמַר לֵיהּ, בְּהַאי מִלָּה דְּכֻלְּהוּ חַיְיכִין בָּהּ, אַשְׁזִיב לוֹן לֹא עַתָּה יֵבוֹשׁ יַעֲקֹב וְלֹא עַתָּה פָּנָיו יֶחֱוָרוּ. כְּמָה דְּקָאֵים יַעֲקֹב לְגַבֵּי דְּאַבְרָהָם בְּנוּרָא, יְקוּם הַשְׁתָּא לְגַבֵּי אִלֵּין, הַהָ״ד, כֹּה אָמַר יְיָ׳ אֶל בֵּית יַעֲקֹב אֲשֶׁר פָּדָה אֶת אַבְרָהָם לֹא עַתָּה יֵבוֹשׁ יַעֲקֹב וְגוֹ׳. מֵהַאי כְּסוּפָא דִּלֵצָנוּתָא.

17. At that hour, the Holy One, blessed be He, said to the throne, WHICH IS MALCHUT, 'My throne, for which word, among all the words THEY UTTERED, should I save these righteous men?' It replied: For the word that all the others mocked, I would save them, NAMELY THE MERIT OF JACOB, "Jacob shall not now be ashamed, neither shall his face now grow pale," SO THEY WILL SEE THAT THEY WERE SAVED IN HIS MERIT. Just as THE MERIT OF Jacob stood fast when Abraham was cast into the fire, now it will stand fast for these – NAMELY HANANIAH, MISHAEL AND AZARIAH. This is what is written, "Thus says Hashem concerning the house of Jacob, who redeemed Abraham, Jacob shall not now be ashamed..." namely by the contempt and the mockery with which THE NATIONS AND NOBLES RIDICULED HIM.

18. תָּנָא, כֻּלְּהוּ דַּהֲווֹ חַיְיכִין מִמִּלָּה דָא, אִתּוֹקְדוּ בְּהַהוּא נוּרָא, וְקָטַל לוֹן שְׁבִיבָא דְּנוּרָא. מַאן שֵׁזִיב לְאַלֵּין. עַל דַּהֲווֹ מְצַלָּן קַמֵּי קוּדְשָׁא בְּרִיךְ הוּא וּמְיַחֲדָן שְׁמֵיהּ כַּדְקָא יֵאוֹת, וְעַל דִּמְיַחֲדָן שְׁמֵיהּ כַּדְקָא יֵאוֹת, אִשְׁתְּזִיבוּ מֵהַהוּא נוּרָא יָקִידְתָּא.

18. We have learned that all those who ridiculed this word, NAMELY "JACOB," were consumed by that fire, and a spark of flame killed them. Who saved Hananiah, Mishael and Azariah? HE DID, because they prayed before the Holy One, blessed be He, Hashem, and unified His Name properly. Because they unified His Name properly, they were saved from that consuming fire.

3. Nadab and Abihu

A Synopsis
Rabbi Shimon says that in a way Nadab and Abihu died twice, once before God when offering the sacrifice, and once because they left no children, as someone who does not merit children is considered as though dead. We learn that Nadab and Abihu died physically but did not die spiritually because they were reincarnated in Pinchas. The reason they were reincarnated together in one body was because they had not married and so were only considered a half body each. Their sin was later corrected by Pinchas' action in slaying the foreign woman. The two sons of Aaron and Zimri had essentially committed the same sin, that is, bringing near something that was far from holiness. Rabbi Shimon talks about the covenant of peace. We learn that Rabbi Yosi had said that people have their sins forgiven when they feel compassion for afflictions visited upon the just; therefore during Yom Kippur people read about the death of the two sons of Aaron, and they feel distress for them so that their own sins are forgiven. Also, they are reassured that their own children will not die during their lifetimes.

19. תְּרֵי בְּנֵי אַהֲרֹן קְרִיבוּ אֶשָּׁא נוּכְרָאָה, דְּלָא אִתְיַחֲדוּ שְׁמֵיה כַּדְקָא יֵאוֹת, וְאִתּוֹקָדוּ בְּנוּרָא. רַבִּי יִצְחָק אָמַר, כְּתִיב, אַחֲרֵי מוֹת. וּכְתִיב וַיָּמוּתוּ. כֵּיוָן דְּאָמַר אַחֲרֵי מוֹת שְׁנֵי בְּנֵי אַהֲרֹן, לָא יְדַעְנָא, דְּהָא וַיָּמוּתוּ. אֶלָּא הָכִי תָּנֵינָן, תְּרֵי מִיתוֹת הֲווֹ, חַד לִפְנֵי יְיָ' וְחַד, דְּלָא הֲווֹ לְהוּ בְּנִין, דְּכָל מַאן דְּלָא זָכֵי לִבְנִין מִית הוּא. בְּגִין כָּךְ, אַחֲרֵי מוֹת, וַיָּמוּתוּ.

19. The two sons of Aaron offered a foreign fire, as they did not unify His Name properly and, therefore, were consumed in fire. Rabbi Yitzchak stated that it is written, "After the death" and it is later written, "and died" IN THE SAME VERSE. If it states "after the death of the two sons of Aaron" (Vayikra 16:1), wouldn't I know that they died? HE ANSWERS: We are taught that there were two deaths, one before Hashem and one because they left no children, for one who does not merit children is CONSIDERED dead. For this reason, it is written, "After the death...and died"; NAMELY, "AFTER THE DEATH" IS TO BE UNDERSTOOD LITERALLY AND "AND DIED" REFERS TO THEIR NOT HAVING CHILDREN.

20. רִבִּי אַבָּא אָמַר, מַאי דִכְתִּיב, וַיָּמָת נָדָב וַאֲבִיהוּא לִפְנֵי יְיָ׳ בְּהַקְרִיבָם אֵשׁ זָרָה לִפְנֵי יְיָ׳ בְּמִדְבַּר סִינַי וּבָנִים לֹא הָיוּ לָהֶם וַיְכַהֵן אֶלְעָזָר וְאִתָּמָר. מַאי דָא לְגַבֵּי דָא, דִכְתִּיב, וּבָנִים לֹא הָיוּ לָהֶם, וַיְכַהֵן אֶלְעָזָר וְאִתָּמָר. אֶלָּא רָזָא דְמִלְתָא. הַאי דְאָמֵינָא, וַיָמוּתוּ, דְּלָא הֲווֹ לְהוּ בְּנִין. וְהָכִי הוּא וַדַּאי. אֲבָל לָא כִּשְׁאָר בְּנֵי עָלְמָא, אע״ג דְלָא אַנְסִיבוּ, דְהָא אִלֵּין לָא מִיתוּ אֶלָּא מִיתַת גַּרְמֵיהוֹן, אֲבָל מִיתַת נַפְשֵׁהוֹן לָא מִיתוּ.

20. Rabbi Aba said that it is written, "And Nadab and Abihu died before Hashem, when they offered a foreign fire before Hashem in the wilderness of Sinai, and they had no children: and Elazar and Itamar ministered in the priest's office" (Bemidbar 3:4). HE QUESTIONS: What connection does one have with the other in saying, "And they had no children: and Elazar and Itamar ministered in the priest's office"? DID THE LATTER INHERIT THE PRIESTHOOD FROM NADAB AND ABIHU BECAUSE THEY WERE CHILDLESS? HE ANSWERS: This is what I have said THAT they died because they had no children AND WERE CONSIDERED AS IF DEAD. This is definite, but not like other people even though they did not marry, for they died only a physical death and not a spiritual one.

21. מנ״ל, דִכְתִּיב, וְאֶלְעָזָר בֶּן אַהֲרֹן לָקַח לוֹ מִבְּנוֹת פּוּטִיאֵל לוֹ לְאִשָּׁה וַתֵּלֶד לוֹ אֶת פִּנְחָס אֵלֶּה רָאשֵׁי אֲבוֹת הַלְוִיִם לְמִשְׁפְּחוֹתָם. אֵלֶּה, וְהָא פִּנְחָס בִּלְחוֹדוֹי הֲוָה. וּכְתִיב, רָאשֵׁי אֲבוֹת הַלְוִיִם, בְּג״כ, מִיתַת גַּרְמֵיהוֹן מִיתוּ, מִיתַת נַפְשֵׁהוֹן לָא מִיתוּ. א״ר אֶלְעָזָר וַדַּאי מַשְׁמַע אֵלֶּה, וּמַשְׁמַע רָאשֵׁי.

21. From where do we know THAT THEY DID NOT DIE A SPIRITUAL DEATH? For it is written, "And Elazar, son of Aaron took him one of the daughters of Putiel to wife; and she bore him Pinchas: these are the heads of the fathers of the Levites according to their families" (Shemot 6:25). HE QUESTIONS: IT SAYS "these," yet Pinchas alone is mentioned, and it says, "heads of the fathers of the Levites" OF PINCHAS ALONE. THIS IS BECAUSE NADAB AND ABIHU WERE REINCARNATED IN PINCHAS;

THEREFORE, THE VERSE READS OF HIM, "THESE ARE THE HEADS," A PLURAL EXPRESSION. According to this, their deaths were physical not spiritual, as THEY WERE REINCARNATED IN PINCHAS. Rabbi Elazar said: THIS IS SO and it is understood WHEN IT IS WRITTEN ABOUT HIM, "These," A PLURAL EXPRESSION. It is likewise inherent WHEN IT IS WRITTEN ABOUT HIM, "Heads," A PLURAL EXPRESSION.

22. וּבג"כ כְּתִיב, פִּנְחָס בֶּן אֶלְעָזָר בֶּן אַהֲרֹן הַכֹּהֵן וּכְתִיב וּפִנְחָס בֶּן אֶלְעָזָר בֶּן אַהֲרֹן הַכֹּהֵן הָיָה כֹהֵן בַּיָּמִים הָהֵם, פִּנְחָס בֶּן אֶלְעָזָר הַכֹּהֵן מִבָּעֵי לֵיה, אֶלָּא בְּכָל אֲתַר דְּאָתָא פִּנְחָס בֶּן אַהֲרֹן הַכֹּהֵן כְּתִיב, וְאֶלְעָזָר לָא כְּתִיב אֶלָּא אֶלְעָזָר הַכֹּהֵן. דִּכְתִיב וְלִפְנֵי אֶלְעָזָר הַכֹּהֵן. וַיֹּאמֶר אֶלְעָזָר הַכֹּהֵן וְגוֹ'. וְעַל דָּא מִיתַת גַּרְמֵיהוֹן מִיתוּ, מִיתַת נַפְשַׁהוֹן לָא מִיתוּ.

22. Due to this, it is written, "Pinchas, the son of Elazar, the son of Aaron the priest" (Bemidbar 25:7) and also it is written, "And Pinchas son of Elazar, son of Aaron" (Shoftim 20:28) was a priest in those days. It should simply read: 'Pinchas, the son of Elazar the priest'; WHY MENTION "SON OF AARON THE PRIEST"? He wished to tell us that whenever Pinchas is mentioned, IT IS WRITTEN, "son of Aaron the priest." BUT WITH REGARD TO ELAZAR, it is only written, "Elazar the priest" AND NO MENTION OF SON OF AARON, as we find written, "Before Elazar the priest" (Bemidbar 27:21) or "And Elazar the priest said" (Bemidbar 31:21). THIS IS DUE TO THE FACT THAT NADAB AND ABIHU, SONS OF AARON, WERE REINCARNATED IN PINCHAS; THEREFORE, THE VERSE MENTIONS 'SON OF AARON' REGARDING HIM. Consequently, their deaths were physical but spiritually they did not die, AS THEY WERE REINCARNATED IN PINCHAS.

23. וְתָנֵינָן בְּרָזָא דְּמַתְנִיתִין, תְּרֵי זוּג, פֶּן חָס. וְהָא אִתְּמַר, יוֹ"ד זְעֵירָא בֵּינֵי אַתְוָון דְּפִנְחָס. דְּהַאי יוֹ"ד כָּלִיל תְּרֵי כַּחֲדָא, וְדָא הוּא רָזָא דְּמִלָּה, וְהָא אִתְּמַר.

23. We have learned from the secret of the Mishnah THAT THE NAME PINCHAS IS FORMED FROM two NAMES, WHICH CONSTITUTE a pair, Pin

and Chas. Indeed, Pinchas is spelled with a small Yud-PE YUD NUN CAF SAMECH-for the Yud incorporates the two together. This is the profound explanation that we have already been taught.

24. ר' אֶלְעָזָר שָׁאִיל לַאֲבוּי, א"ל, וְהָא תְּרֵי אִינּוּן וּתְרֵי הֲווֹ, אֲמַאי לָא אִשְׁתְּכָחוּ תְּרֵי. א"ל, תְּרֵי פַּלְגֵי גּוּפָא הֲווֹ, דְּהָא לָא אַנְסִיבוּ, וּבג"כ, בְּחַד אִתְכְּלִילוּ, דִּכְתִּיב, וַתֵּלֶד לוֹ אֶת פִּנְחָס אֵלֶּה רָאשֵׁי וְגוֹ'.

24. Rabbi Elazar inquired of his father: Behold, NADAB AND ABIHU were two individuals, why were there not two, MEANING WHY WERE THEY NOT REINCARNATED INTO TWO PEOPLE, BUT ONLY IN PINCHAS? He replied: Each was a half body because they did not marry, AND ONE WHO DOES NOT MARRY IS CONSIDERED A HALF PERSON. For this reason, the two are incorporated in one, as it is written, "And she bore him Pinchas: these are the heads."

25. וְיוֹ"ד דְּפִנְחָס, לָא אִתְיְיהִיב בֵּיהּ לְחַבְּרָא אַתְוָון, אֶלָּא בְּשַׁעֲתָא דְּקַנֵּי לְקוּדְשָׁא בְּרִיךְ הוּא, וְאָתָא לְיַשְּׁרָא עֲקִימָא, דְּחָמָא דְּהַאי אֶת בְּרִית קַדִּישָׁא, עָיֵיל זִמְרִי בִּרְשׁוּתָא אָחֳרָא. וּבְמָה דְּאִתְעֲקַם בְּקַדְמֵיתָא, אִתְתָּקַן הָכָא. בְּנוּכְרָאָה אִתְעַקַם בְּקַדְמֵיתָא, דִּכְתִּיב, בְּהַקְרִיבָם אֵשׁ זָרָה, הָכָא בְּנוּכְרָאָה, אִתְתָּקַן, כְּמָה דִּכְתִּיב, וּבָעַל בַּת אֵל נֵכָר. מַה לְהַלָּן אֵשׁ זָרָה, אַף כָּאן נָמֵי אִשָּׁה זָרָה.

25. The Yud in Pinchas was put in him to enjoin the letters only when he has been zealous for the Holy One, blessed be He, and came to straighten that which was crooked upon seeing the sign of the member of the holy covenant that Zimri inserted into another territory. NADAB AND ABIHU were corrected here from their earlier deviation, for NADAB AND ABIHU deviated in a foreign female, as it is written, "When they offered a foreign fire" (Bemidbar 3:4). They were corrected through the foreign woman THAT PINCHAS SLEW, as it is written, "And has married the daughter of a strange El" (Malachi 2:11). Just as in the first case there was a foreign fire, here too was a foreign woman.

26. מַאי אִתְחֲזֵי הָכָא. אֶלָּא בְּקַדְמֵיתָא רְחִיקָא קָרִיבוּ, דִּכְתִּיב,

בְּהַקְרִיבָם אֵשׁ זָרָה. אוף הָכָא זִמְרִי, הֲוָה קָרִיב רְחִיקָא, שְׁמָא דְמַלְכָּא, הֲוָה קָרִיב גַּבֵּי רְחִיקָא, מִיַּד, וַיַּרְא פִּנְחָס בֶּן אֶלְעָזָר בֶּן אַהֲרֹן הַכֹּהֵן וַיָּקָם מִתּוֹךְ הָעֵדָה. הָכָא אַתְקִין עֲקִימָא דְקַדְמֵיתָא, כְּדֵין אִתְיְיהִיב יו"ד בִּשְׁמֵיהּ לְחַבְּרָא אַתְוָון כַּחֲדָא, וְאִתְבְּשַׂר בִּשְׁלוֹם, דִּכְתִּיב, לָכֵן אֱמוֹר הִנְנִי נוֹתֵן לוֹ אֶת בְּרִיתִי שָׁלוֹם. בְּרִיתִי מַמָּשׁ.

26. HE QUESTIONS: What is apparent here, MEANING WHAT IS THE CONNECTION BETWEEN A FOREIGN FIRE TO A FOREIGN WOMAN? HE ANSWERS: At the beginning, they brought near TO THE HOLINESS something that was far removed FROM HOLINESS AND DEFILED THE HOLINESS, as is written, "When they offered a foreign fire." Here too, Zimri COMMITTED THE VERY SAME SIN in that he brought near THAT which was far FROM HOLINESS – NAMELY, THE FOREIGN WOMAN TO THE HOLINESS – BECAUSE he brought near the name of the King, THE SIGN OF THE HOLY COVENANT, to the distant one – NAMELY, THE FOREIGN WOMAN. Immediately, "When Pinchas, the son of Elazar, the son of Aaron the priest, saw it, he rose up from among the congregation" (Bemidbar 25:7). At this point, he corrected the earlier crookedness. Then the Yud was added to his name to enjoin the letters together, THE SECRET OF YESOD THAT CONNECTS ZEIR ANPIN WITH MALCHUT. Thus, he was promised peace, WHICH IS YESOD REFERRED TO AS PEACE, as it is written, "Wherefore say, Behold, I give to him My covenant of peace" (Ibid. 12), My very covenant, NAMELY YESOD.

27. מַאי שָׁלוֹם הָכָא, אֶלָּא בְּהַהוּא כִּתְרָא, חָבוּ בְּקַדְמֵיתָא, בְּהַהוּא כִּתְרָא, אִתְּעָרוּ קְטָטוּתָא בְּקַדְמֵיתָא, וְהַשְׁתָּא דְּאִתְתָּקַן, כְּתִיב הִנְנִי נוֹתֵן לוֹ אֶת בְּרִיתִי שָׁלוֹם. בְּרִיתִי מַמָּשׁ, תְּהֵא עִמֵּיהּ בִּשְׁלוֹם, וּבְגִין כַּךְ, אִתְיְיהִיב יו"ד זְעֵירָא בִּשְׁמֵיהּ, דְּהָא מֵאַתְוָון זְעֵירָאן הִיא, לְאַתְחֲזָאָה דְּהָא אִתְתָּקַן מַה דְּאִתְעַקָּם בְּקַדְמֵיתָא, וְהָא אַשְׁלִימַת עִמֵּיהּ. אָתָא ר' אֶלְעָזָר וְנָשִׁיק יְדוֹי. אָמַר, בְּרִיךְ רַחֲמָנָא דְּשָׁאִילְנָא הַאי מִלָּה, וְלָא אִתְאֲבִיד מִנָּאי.

27. HE ASKS: What is this 'peace' we speak of here WHEN IT SAYS, "BEHOLD, I GIVE TO HIM MY COVENANT OF PEACE"? HE ANSWERS: At

first they sinned against this Sfirah, YESOD, BY OFFERING FOREIGN FIRE, AS EARLIER MENTIONED. They damaged this Sfirah in instigating a quarrel BETWEEN ZEIR ANPIN AND MALCHUT, AS WRITTEN ABOVE. Now that it is corrected, it is written, "Behold I give him My covenant of peace," My actual covenant, NAMELY THE SFIRAH OF YESOD WHICH GOES BY THE NAME COVENANT. It will be at peace with him, NAMELY THE PEACE BETWEEN ZEIR ANPIN AND MALCHUT. For this reason, a small Yud was added to his name, WHICH HINTS AT YESOD, which is of the small letters to show that what was earlier crooked has already been corrected, MEANING THAT YESOD WHICH WAS CURVED EARLIER HAS BEEN STRAIGHTENED, AS WAS SAID BEFORE, and now MALCHUT is perfected through YESOD. Rabbi Elazar kissed his hands and said: Blessed is the Merciful One for allowing me to ask this thing so it should not get lost from me.

28. תָּאנָא א״ר יוֹסֵי, בְּהַאי יוֹמָא דְּכִפּוּרֵי, אִתְתְּקַן לְמִקְרֵי פַּרְשָׁתָא דָּא, לְכַפְּרָא לְיִשְׂרָאֵל בְּגָלוּתָא, בְּגִין דָּא, סִדְרָא דְּיוֹמָא דָּא, הָכָא אִתְסְדַּר, וּבְגִין דְּמִיתַתְהוֹן דִּבְנֵי אַהֲרֹן, מְכַפְּרָא עַל יִשְׂרָאֵל.

28. We have learned that Rabbi Yosi said: It was established to read this chapter OF THE SONS OF AARON on this day of Yom Kippur, in order to bring atonement for Yisrael in exile WHO ARE UNABLE TO OFFER SACRIFICES. For this reason the order OF SACRIFICES for this day, YOM KIPPUR, was established here IN THE PORTION ABOUT THE SONS OF AARON, AND RECITING IT COMES IN PLACE OF SACRIFICE. FURTHERMORE, the deaths of the sons of Aaron atone for Yisrael.

29. מִכָּאן אוֹלִיפְנָא, כָּל הַהוּא ב״נ דְּיִסוּרֵי דְּמָארֵיה אַתְיָין עֲלֵיה, כַּפָּרָה דְּחוֹבוֹי אִינוּן. וְכָל מַאן דְּמִצְטָעַר עַל יִסוּרֵיהוֹן דְּצַדִּיקַיָּא, מַעֲבִירִין חוֹבַיָּיא דִּלְהוֹן מֵעָלְמָא. וְעַ״ד בְּיוֹמָא דָּא, קוֹרִין, אַחֲרֵי מוֹת שְׁנֵי בְּנֵי אַהֲרֹן, דְּיִשְׁמְעוּן עַמָּא, וְיִצְטַעֲרוּן עַל אֲבוּדְהוֹן דְּצַדִּיקַיָּא, וְיִתְכַּפֵּר לְהוֹן חוֹבַיְיהוּ. וְכָל דְּמִצְטָעַר עַל אֲבוּדְהוֹן דְּצַדִּיקַיָּא, אוֹ אָחִית דִּמְעִין עֲלַיְיהוּ, קוּדְשָׁא בְּרִיךְ הוּא מַכְרִיז עֲלֵיה וְאוֹמֵר, וְסָר עֲוֹנֶךָ וְחַטָּאתְךָ תְּכוּפָּר. וְלֹא עוֹד, אֶלָּא דְּלָא יְמוּתוּן בְּנוֹי בְּיוֹמוֹי. וַעֲלֵיה כְּתִיב, יִרְאֶה זֶרַע יַאֲרִיךְ יָמִים וְגוֹ'.

29. We also learn from here that every person who has affliction visited upon him from his Master, they serve as atonement for sins. All who have distress for affliction brought upon the just will have their sins pass away from this world. For this reason, on this day, YOM KIPPUR, we read about, "After the death of the two sons of Aaron" so that the congregation listens and feels distress for the pious who were lost and thus the congregation have their sins forgiven. Of him, who feels sorrow for the righteous who perished, or sheds tears for them, the Holy One, blessed be He, announces, "And your iniquity is taken away, and your sin is purged" (Yeshayah 6:7). Furthermore, he is reassured that his children will not die during his lifetime and it is written about him, "He shall see his seed, he shall prolong his days" (Yeshayah 53:10).

4. "All the rivers run into the sea"

A Synopsis

Rabbi Shimon wonders how people can ignore the wishes of God for so long, and says that no one lends his ear or wakens his heart. He says that in later generations people will have forgotten the Torah entirely; there will never be another generation like Rabbi Shimon's until the generation in the time of the coming of Messiah, when knowledge will reawaken in the world again. We read about the river, Binah, in which the roots of the Tree of Life are spread. We read of the Sfirot that come forth from this river and the anointing oil that replenishes the Garden of Eden. These streams flow down to the righteous and join together in the sea of wisdom, Malchut. When the wicked interfere, the blessings of these streams are not felt, and judgment is awakened in the world instead of peace. Then people can be blessed only through the priest.

30. וַיֹּאמֶר יְיָ' אֶל מֹשֶׁה דַּבֵּר אֶל אַהֲרֹן אָחִיךְ וְאַל יָבֹא בְכָל עֵת אֶל הַקֹּדֶשׁ וְגוֹ' ר״ש פָּתַח וְאָמַר, כָּל הַנְּחָלִים הוֹלְכִים אֶל הַיָּם וְהַיָּם אֵינֶנּוּ מָלֵא וְגוֹ'. אָמַר רִבִּי שִׁמְעוֹן, תַּוּוּהְנָא עַל בְּנֵי עָלְמָא, דְּהָא לֵית לְהוּ עַיְינִין לְמֶחֱזֵי, וְלִבָּא לְאַשְׁגְּחָא, וְלָא יַדְעִין, וְלָא שַׁוְיָין לִבַּיְיהוּ לְאִסְתַּכְּלָא בִּרְעוּתָא דְמָארֵיהוֹן, הֵיךְ נַיְימִין, וְלָא מִתְעָרֵי מִשְׁנָתַיְיהוּ, עַד לָא יֵיתֵי הַהוּא יוֹמָא דְּחָפֵי עֲלַיְיהוּ חֲשׁוֹכָא וְקַבְלָא, וְיִתְבַּע הַהוּא מָארֵיהּ דְּפִקְדוֹנָא, חוּשְׁבְּנָא מִנַּיְיהוּ.

30. "And Hashem said to Moses, Speak to Aaron your brother, that he come not at all times into the holy place" (Vayikra 16:2). Rabbi Shimon said, "All the rivers run into the sea; yet the sea is not full..." (Kohelet 1:7). Rabbi Shimon said: I wonder about people, that they have no eyes to see, no heart to observe, they do not know, or pay attention to the wishes of their Master. How asleep they are and do not awaken before the day will come when thick darkness will cover them; the owner of the deposit will demand his due accounting from them.

31. וְכָרוֹזָא כָּל יוֹמָא קָארֵי עֲלַיְיהוּ, וְנִשְׁמָתְהוֹן, אַסְהִידַת בְּהוֹן בְּכָל יוֹמָא וְלֵילְיָא, אוֹרַיְיתָא רָאמַת קָלִין לְכָל עֵבָר, מַכְרֶזֶת וְאוֹמֶרֶת, עַד

מָתַי פְּתָאִים תְּאֵהֲבוּ פֶתִי מִי פֶתִי יָסוּר הֵנָה חֲסַר לֵב אָמְרָה לוֹ. לְכוּ
לַחֲמוּ בְלַחְמִי וּשְׁתוּ בְּיַיִן מָסָכְתִּי. וְלֵית מַאן דְּיַרְכִּין אוּדְנֵיהּ, וְלֵית מַאן
דְּיִתְּעַר לְבֵּיהּ.

31. An announcement is called out about them daily and their soul testifies within them day and night. The Torah raises its voice in all directions and says, "How long, fools, will you love foolishness" (Mishlei 1:22.). "Whoever is a fool, let him turn in here: as for him that lacks understanding, she says to him, Come, eat of my bread, and drink of the wine which I have mixed" (Mishlei 9:4-5). No one lends his ear or wakens his heart.

32. ת"ח, זְמִינִין דָּרֵי בַּתְרָאֵי דְיֵיתוּן, דְּיִתְנְשֵׁי אוֹרַיְיתָא מִבֵּינַיְיהוּ,
וְחַכִּימֵי לִבָּא יִתְכַּנְּשׁוּן לְאַתְרַיְיהוּ, וְלָא יִשְׁתְּכַּח מַאן דְּסָגִיר וּפָתַח. וַוי
לְהַהוּא דָּרָא. וּמִכָּאן וּלְהָלְאָה, לָא יְהֵא דָּרָא כְּדָרָא דָא, עַד דָּרָא דְיֵיתֵי
מַלְכָּא מְשִׁיחָא, וּמַנְדְּעָא יִתְּעַר בְּעָלְמָא, דִּכְתִיב, כִּי כֻלָּם יֵדְעוּ אוֹתִי
לְמִקְטַנָּם וְעַד גְּדוֹלָם.

32. Come and see: Later generations will come when Torah will be forgotten among them, the wise will gather in their own place and there won't be found anyone who can begin to explain and finalize THE TORAH. Woe to that generation. From here on, there will not be a generation like the present one until the generation in the time of King Messiah, when knowledge will awaken in the world, as it is written, "For they shall all know Me, from the lowest of them to the greatest of them" (Yirmeyah 31:33).

33. ת"ח, כְּתִיב, וְנָהָר יוֹצֵא מֵעֵדֶן. וְתָנֵינָן, מַה שְּׁמֵיהּ דְּהַהוּא נָהָר.
אוֹקִימְנָא יוּבַל שְׁמֵיהּ, דִּכְתִיב, וְעַל יוּבַל יְשַׁלַּח שָׁרָשָׁיו. וּבְסִפְרָא דְּרַב
הַמְנוּנָא סָבָא, חַיִּים שְׁמֵיהּ, דְּמִתַּמָּן נָפְקִין חַיִּים לְעָלְמָא, וְאִינּוּן אִקְרוּן
חַיֵּי מַלְכָּא. וְהָא אוֹקִימְנָא, הַהוּא אִילָנָא רַבָּא וְתַקִּיפָא, דִּמְזוֹן לְכֹלָּא
בֵּיהּ. אִקְרֵי עֵץ חַיִּים. אִילָנָא דְּנָטַע שָׁרְשׁוֹי בְּאִינּוּן חַיִּים, וְכֹלָּא הוּא
שַׁפִּיר.

33. It is written, "And a river went out of Eden" (Beresheet 2:10). We have learned the name of this river. We established that its name is Yuval,

NAMELY BINAH, as it is written, "And that spreads out its roots by the river (Heb. *yuval*)" (Yirmeyah 17:8). In the book of Rabbi Hamnuna Saba (the elder), IT SAYS that its name is life, NAMELY BINAH, whence life comes to the world, which is referred to as the life of the King. We established that it is that great and strong tree, WHICH IS ZEIR ANPIN, that feeds all and is called the Tree of Life, MEANING the tree that has planted its roots in that life ABOVE, NAMELY BINAH. And all is appropriate.

34. וְתָאנָא, הַהוּא נָהָר אַפִּיק נַחֲלִין עֲמִיקִין, בְּמִשַׁח רְבוּת, לְאַשְׁקָאָה גִּנְתָּא, וּלְרַוָּואָה אִילָנִין וּנְטִיעִין, דִּכְתִיב יִשְׂבְּעוּ עֲצֵי יְיָ' אַרְזֵי לְבָנוֹן אֲשֶׁר נָטָע, וְאִינּוּן נַחֲלִין, נַגְדִּין וְאִתְמַשְׁכָן וּמִתְכַּנְּשִׁין בִּתְרֵין סַמְכִין וְאִינּוּן בְּרַיְיתֵי קַרְיָינָן לְהוּ, יָכִי"ן וּבוֹעַ"ז, וְשַׁפִּיר. וּמִתַּמָּן נָפְקִין כָּל אִינּוּן נַחֲלִין, וְשַׁרְיָין לוֹן בְּחַד דַּרְגָּא דְּאִקְרֵי צַדִּיק, דִּכְתִיב, וְצַדִּיק יְסוֹד עוֹלָם. וְכֻלְּהוּ אַזְלִין וּמִתְכַּנְּשִׁין לְהַהוּא אֲתָר דְּאִקְרֵי יָם, וְהוּא יַמָּא דְּחָכְמְתָא, הה"ד, כָּל הַנְּחָלִים הוֹלְכִים אֶל הַיָּם וְגו'.

34. We have learned that this river gave forth deep streams, WHICH REPRESENT THE THREE SFIROT – CHESED, GVURAH AND TIFERET OF ZEIR ANPIN – with the anointing oil to replenish the Garden of Eden, WHICH IS MALCHUT, and water the trees and plants, NAMELY THE SFIROT OF MALCHUT. Of this, it is written, "The trees of Hashem have their fill; the cedars of Lebanon, which He has planted" (Tehilim 104:16). These streams, NAMELY CHESED, GVURAH AND TIFERET, flow and continue on and join two pillars that the Baraithas refer to as Yachin and Boaz, NAMELY NETZACH AND HOD. These NAMES are appropriate. From there, NETZACH AND HOD come out all these streams, NAMELY CHESED, GVURAH AND TIFERET, and rest in a certain level referred to as Righteous, NAMELY YESOD, as is written, "But the righteous is an everlasting foundation (Heb. *yesod*)" (Mishlei 10:25). All together they join in that level referred to as "sea" that is the sea of wisdom, NAMELY MALCHUT. This is the meaning of the verse, "All the rivers run into the sea" (Kohelet 1:7).

35. וְאִי תֵּימָא, דְּהָא מָטוּ לַאֲתָר דָּא, וּפַסְקִין, וְלָא תַּיְיבִין, לְבָתַר כְּתִיב, אֶל מְקוֹם שֶׁהַנְּחָלִים הוֹלְכִים שָׁם הֵם שָׁבִים לָלֶכֶת, בְּגִין דְּהַהוּא

נַהֲרָא לָא פָּסִיק לְעָלְמִין. הֵם שָׁבִים, לְאָן אֲתַר שָׁבִים, לְאִינּוּן תְּרֵין
קַיְימִין, נֶצַח וְהוֹד. לָלֶכֶת, בְּהַאי צַדִּיק, לְאַשְׁכְּחָא בִּרְכָאן וְחִידוּ. וְהַיְינוּ
רָזָא דִּתְנֵינָן, לִוְיָתָן זֶה יָצַרְתָּ לְשַׂחֶק בּוֹ, דָּא צַדִּיק.

35. If you should say that when the streams reach this spot, NAMELY
MALCHUT, they stop and don't come back, yet immediately following that,
it says, "To the place where the rivers flow, thither they return (lit. 'return to
go')" (Ibid.), for the river never stops its waters. "They return": To where do
THEY return? HE ANSWERS: They "return" to the two pillars, Netzach and
Hod. They "go" to this Righteous, WHICH IS YESOD, to seek out blessings
and joy. This is the secret of what we learned, "This is the Leviathan, whom
You have made to play therein" (Tehilim 104:26). It is the righteous.

36. כֻּלָּם אֵלֶיךָ יְשַׂבֵּרוּן לָתֵת אָכְלָם בְּעִתּוֹ. מַאן עִתּוֹ. דָּא מַטְרוֹנִיתָא,
דְּאִקְרֵי עִתּוֹ דְּצַדִּיק, וּבג"כ כֻּלְּהוּ מְחַכָּאן לְהַאי עִתּוֹ, כֻּלְּהוּ דְּאִתְזְנָן
לְתַתָּא, מֵאֲתַר דָּא אִתְזְנָן, וְרָזָא דָּא אוֹקִימְנָא, עֵינֵי כֹל אֵלֶיךָ יְשַׂבֵּרוּ
וְגו' כְּמָה דְּאוֹקִימְנָא.

36. "These wait all upon You: that You may give them their food in due
season" (Ibid. 27). What is meant by "in due season"? This is the Matron,
NAMELY MALCHUT, known as the time of the Righteous, WHICH IS YESOD.
For this reason, all look up to this "due season," all that are sustained here
below. They are fed from this source, AS THE LOWER BEINGS RECEIVE
ONLY FROM MALCHUT. This secret meaning was established in, "These
wait all upon You..." as we have established.

37. ת"ח, בְּשַׁעֲתָא דְּהַאי כֹּל, מְבַסֵּם לְעִתּוֹ, וּמִתְחַבְּרָא עִמֵּיהּ, כֻּלְּהוּ
עָלְמִין בְּחֵידוּ, כֻּלְּהוּ עָלְמִין בְּבִרְכָאן, כְּדֵין שְׁלָמָא אִשְׁתְּכַח בְּעִלָּאֵי
וְתַתָּאֵי. וְכַד גָּרְמִין חַיָּיבֵי עָלְמָא, דְּתַמָּן לָא אִשְׁתְּכָחוּ בִּרְכָאן דְּאִינּוּן
נַחֲלֵי, וְיָנְקָא, הַאי עֵת, מִסִּטְרָא אָחֳרָא, כְּדֵין דִּינִין מִתְעָרִין בְּעָלְמָא,
וּשְׁלָמָא לָא אִשְׁתְּכַח. וְכַד בָּעָאן בְּנֵי עָלְמָא לְאִתְבָּרְכָא, לָא יַכְלִין אֶלָּא
עַל יְדָא דְּכַהֲנָא, בְּגִין דְּיִתְעַר כִּתְרָא דִּילֵיהּ, וְיִתְבָּרַךְ מַטְרוֹנִיתָא,
וְיִשְׁתְּכָחוּ בִּרְכָאן בְּכֻלְּהוּ עָלְמִין.

37. Come and see: When this "all," WHICH IS YESOD, KNOWN AS "*KOL* (LIT. 'ALL')," perfumes "due season," WHICH IS MALCHUT, which joins with him, all the world rejoices in blessings and peace is found among the upper and lower beings. However, when the wicked cause, that blessings of these streams are not present – NAMELY, CHESED, GVURAH AND TIFERET OF ZEIR ANPIN, and this season receives nourishment from another side, NAMELY JUDGMENT, then Judgments are awakened in the world and there is no peace. When people want to be blessed, they can do so only through the priest, who could arouse his Sfirah, WHICH IS CHESED. Thus, the Matron, WHO IS MALCHUT, is blessed and the blessings will prevail throughout the worlds.

5. "That he come not at all times into the holy place"

A Synopsis

We learn that God told Moses that he should speak to his brother, Aaron, since Aaron was given the blessings for above and below. There are times when one may go before God and ask petitions, because it is a time of goodwill; there are other times when harsh decrees are aroused and blessings are not forthcoming. Sometimes judgments are present but impending, held over the world to frighten it. We learn that these cycles occur in the year, in the week, in the day and even in the hour. Rabbi Shimon says that things are good in their due season. Analyzing the scripture, "That he come not at all times into the holy place," Rabbi Shimon tells his son that God was admonishing Aaron not to make the same mistake that his sons did, so that he will not damage this time that is Malchut. He also says that incense is the most praiseworthy of all sacrifices, because incense in Aramaic means 'connecting'.

38. תָּאנָא, בְּהַהִיא שַׁעֲתָא, בָּעָא מֹשֶׁה קָמֵי קוּדְשָׁא בְּרִיךְ הוּא, מִלָּה דָא, אָמַר לֵיהּ, אִי בְּנֵי עָלְמָא יְתוּבוּן קַמָּךְ, עַל יְדֵי דְּמַאן מִתְבָּרְכָאן. א״ל קוּדְשָׁא בְּרִיךְ הוּא, וְלִי אַתְּ אוֹמֵר, דַּבֵּר אֶל אַהֲרֹן אָחִיךְ, דְּהָא בִּידֵיהּ מְסִירָאן בִּרְכָאן לְעֵילָּא וְתַתָּא.

38. We have learned that AFTER THE DEATHS OF THE SONS OF AARON, Moses was seeking from the Holy One, blessed be He, this matter, WHICH IS CHESED. MOSES said to Him: If people return in repentance to You, by whom will they be blessed? The Holy One, blessed be He, replied: 'You are speaking to Me? "Speak to Aaron your brother," for in his hands are given the blessings for above and below', FOR HE IS THE CHARIOT FOR CHESED, AS MENTIONED ABOVE.

39. וַיֹּאמֶר יְיָ' אֶל מֹשֶׁה דַּבֵּר אֶל אַהֲרֹן אָחִיךְ וְאַל יָבֹא בְכָל עֵת אֶל הַקֹּדֶשׁ וְגוֹ'. אָמַר רִבִּי אַבָּא, זִמְנִין אִית קָמֵי קוּדְשָׁא בְּרִיךְ הוּא, לְאִשְׁתַּכְּחָא רַעֲוָון, וּלְאִשְׁתַּכְּחָא בִּרְכָאן, וּלְמִתְבַּע בָּעוּתֵי, וְזִמְנִין, דְּרַעֲוָון לָא אִשְׁתַּכְּחוּ, וּבִרְכָאן לָא מִזְדַּמְּנָן, וְדִינִין קַשְׁיִין מִתְעָרִין בְּעָלְמָא. וְזִמְנִין דְּדִינָא תָּלֵי. תָּא חֲזֵי, זִמְנִין אִית בְּשַׁתָּא, דִּרְעוּתָא

אִשְׁתְּכַח. וְזִמְנִין אִית בְּשַׁתָּא, דְּדִינָא אִשְׁתְּכַח. וְזִמְנִין אִית בְּשַׁתָּא,
דְּדִינָא אִשְׁתְּכַח וְתַלְיָא. זִמְנִין אִית בְּיַרְחֵי, דְּרַעֲוָא אִשְׁתְּכַח בְּהוּ. וְזִמְנִין
אִית בְּיַרְחֵי, דְּדִינִין אִשְׁתְּכָחוּ, וְתַלְיָין עַל כֹּלָא.

39. "And Hashem said to Moses, Speak to Aaron your brother, that he come not at all times into the holy place" (Vayikra 16:2). Rabbi Aba said: There are times before the Holy One, blessed be He, when His goodwill is found, blessings are available and one may ask petitions. There are other times when His graciousness is unavailable, blessings are not forthcoming and harsh decrees are aroused in the world. There are times when Judgment is impending. There are times during the year when graciousness is present and there are times during the year when decrees are present. There are other times when Judgment is present but is impending, MEANING TO SAY THE JUDGMENT IS HELD IN ABEYANCE TO FRIGHTEN THE WORLD, BUT IT IS NOT YET IN EFFECT. There are also times during the month when graciousness is to be found and times when Judgments are present and impending over everything.

40. זִמְנִין אִית בְּשָׁבוּעֵי, דְּרַעֲוָון מִשְׁתַּכְּחָן, וְזִמְנִין אִית בְּשָׁבוּעֵי, דְּדִינִין
מִשְׁתַּכְּחָן בְּעָלְמָא. וְזִמְנִין אִית בְּיוֹמֵי, דְּרַעֲווא אִשְׁתְּכַח בְּעָלְמָא וְעָלְמָא
אִתְבַּסְּמָא. וְזִמְנִין אִית בְּיוֹמֵי דְּדִינִין תַּלְיָין וּמִשְׁתַּכְּחָן, וַאֲפִילוּ בְּשַׁעֲתֵי.
וְעַל דָּא כְּתִיב, וְעֵת לְכָל חֵפֶץ וְגוֹ'. וּכְתִיב, וַאֲנִי תְפִלָּתִי לְךָ וְגוֹ'.
וּכְתִיב, דִּרְשׁוּ יְיָ' בְּהִמָּצְאוֹ. וּכְתִיב, לָמָה יְיָ' תַּעֲמוֹד בְּרָחוֹק תַּעְלִים
לְעִתּוֹת בַּצָּרָה. וּכְתִיב, מֵרָחוֹק יְיָ' נִרְאָה לִי. וְזִמְנִין דְּאִיהוּ קָרוֹב,
דִּכְתִיב, קָרוֹב יְיָ' לְכָל קוֹרְאָיו. בְּג"כ, וְאַל יָבֹא בְכָל עֵת אֶל הַקֹּדֶשׁ וְגוֹ'.

40. There are times during the week when graciousness abounds and there are times during the week when decrees are in the world. There are times during the day when graciousness prevails and the world is pampered. There are times during the day when the Judgments are impending and are present. Even during the hour, THERE ARE VARIOUS TIMES. Consequently, it is written, "And a time for every purpose" (Kohelet 3:1). It is also written, "But as for me, let my prayer be to You, Hashem, in an acceptable time" (Tehilim 69:14) and "Seek Hashem while He may be found" (Yeshayah 55:6). Another verse reads, "Why stand You afar off, Hashem? Why hide

You Yourself in times of trouble?" (Tehilim 10:1) and another verse reads, "From afar Hashem appeared to me" (Yirmeyah 31:2). At other times, He is close as it is written, "Hashem is near to all those who call upon Him" (Tehilim 145:18). Due to this, it is written, "that he will not come at all times into the holy place..."

41. רַבִּי שִׁמְעוֹן אָמַר, הָא אוֹקִימְנָא. מִלָּה בְּעִתּוֹ, וְהָכִי הוּא וַדַּאי, וְהָכָא אָתָא קוּדְשָׁא בְּרִיךְ הוּא לְאַזְהָרָא לְאַהֲרֹן, דְּלָא יִטְעֵי בְּהַהוּא חוֹבָא, דְּטָעוּ בְּנוֹי, דְּהָא הַאי עֵת יְדִיעָא, בְּג"כ לָא יִטְעֵי לְחַבְּרָא עֵת אָחֳרָא, לְגַבֵּי מַלְכָּא. הה"ד, וְאַל יָבֹא בְכָל עֵת אֶל הַקֹּדֶשׁ. כְּלוֹמַר, אַף עַל גַּב דְּיֶחֱמֵי עִידָן, דְּאִתְמְסַר בִּידָא אָחֳרָא, לְאִתְנָהֲגָא עָלְמָא, וְיִתְמְסַר בִּידוֹי לְיַיחֵד בֵּיהּ לְקָרְבָא לֵיהּ לְקוּדְשָׁא, דְּהָא אֲנָא וּשְׁמִי חַד הוּא. וּבְגִינֵי כַּךְ, וְאַל יָבֹא בְכָל עֵת אֶל הַקֹּדֶשׁ. וְאִי בָּעֵי לְמִנְדַּע בַּמָּה יֵיעוּל. בְּזֹאת. בְּזֹאת יָבֹא אַהֲרֹן אֶל הַקֹּדֶשׁ. דְּהַאי זֹאת, הִיא עֵת דַּאֲחִידַת בִּשְׁמִי, בְּהַאי י', דִּרְשִׁימָא בִּשְׁמִי, יֵיעוּל אֶל הַקֹּדֶשׁ. וְאַל יָבֹא בְכָל עֵת.

41. Rabbi Shimon said: We have ascertained that something in its due season IS EXCELLENT. This is sure. At this point, the Holy One, blessed be He, came to warn Aaron not to err with the same sin with which his sons erred. This due season is well known TO BE MALCHUT. For this reason, he must not err by joining a different time to the King. This is the meaning of the verse, "That he come not at all times into the holy place." Even when he will see that the time is given over to another, NAMELY THE OTHER SIDE, to run the world, IT SHOULD BE given over to its hands in order to enjoin and bring the world near to holiness, as I and My Name are one, SINCE EVEN THE OTHER SIDE SERVES ONLY ME. For this reason, "that he come not at all times (or: 'with every time') into the holy place." If he wishes to know with what he should approach, the answer is with *zot* (Eng. 'this' fem.), WHICH IS MALCHUT OF HOLINESS, "With this (Heb. *zot* fem.) shall Aaron come into the holy place" (Vayikra 16:3). This *zot* is the time that holds to My name through Yud, WHICH IS YESOD, that is imprinted in My name AND WITH IT he may come into the holy place, not at all times, but "he come not at all times."

42. תָּאנָא אָמַר ר' יוֹסֵי כְּתִיב אֶת הַכֹּל עָשָׂה יָפֶה בְעִתּוֹ הַאי מִלָּה

אוֹקְמָה בּוּצִינָא קַדִּישָׁא וְהָכִי הוּא דְּתָנֵינָא אֶת הַכֹּל עָשָׂה יָפֶה בְעִתּוֹ וְהָכִי הוּא וַדַּאי. אֶת הַכֹּל וַדַּאי. עָשָׂה יָפֶה בְעִתּוֹ, דָּא בְּדָא, וְלָא יִתְעָרְבוּן אָחֳרָנִין בֵּינַיְיהוּ. בְּעִתּוֹ מַמָּשׁ, וְלָא בְּאָחֳרָא. בְּגִינֵי כָּךְ, אַזְהָרוּתָא לְאַהֲרֹן, וְאַל יָבֹא בְכָל עֵת אֶל הַקֹּדֶשׁ. אֲבָל בְּמָה יֵיעוּל. בְּזֹאת, כְּמָה דְּאוֹקִימְנָא, דִּכְתִיב בְּזֹאת יָבֹא אַהֲרֹן אֶל הַקֹּדֶשׁ.

42. Rabbi Yosi said that it is written, "He has made every thing beautiful in its time" (Kohelet 3:11). This matter was explained by the holy luminary, and it is so that we learned that "He has made every thing beautiful in its time." Assuredly everything, WHICH IS YESOD NAMED ALL, He did in its time REFERS TO MALCHUT CALLED TIME, one with another, and no other thing may come between them. It is literally "in its time," MEANING MALCHUT and not in another. For this reason, it is a warning to Aaron "that he come not at all times into the holy place." With what may he enter? With *Zot*, MEANING MALCHUT CALLED *ZOT*, as we established from the verse, "Thus (with *zot*) shall Aaron come into the holy place" (Vayikra 16:3).

43. רבִּי אֶלְעָזָר הֲוָה יָתִיב קַמֵּי אֲבוּהָ, אָמַר לֵיהּ, כְּתִיב בִּכְנִישְׁתָּא דְּקֹרַח, וַיֹּאבְדוּ מִתּוֹךְ הַקָּהָל, מַאי וַיֹּאבְדוּ. אֶלָּא כְּמָה דִּכְתִיב, וְהַאֲבַדְתִּי אֶת הַנֶּפֶשׁ הַהִיא מִקֶּרֶב עַמָּהּ. א"ר שִׁמְעוֹן, שָׁאנֵי אִינּוּן בְּנֵי אַהֲרֹן, דְּלָא כְּתִיב בְּהוּ אֲבֵדָה, כְּאִינּוּן דִּכְנִישְׁתָּא דְּקֹרַח, דִּכְתִיב בְּהוּ, וַיֹּאבְדוּ מִתּוֹךְ הַקָּהָל. וּכְתִיב, הֵן גָּוַעְנוּ אָבַדְנוּ כֻּלָּנוּ אָבַדְנוּ. לְאַכְלָלָא אִינּוּן דְּאַקְרִיבוּ קְטֹרֶת בּוּסְמִין, מָאתָן וְחַמְשִׁין, דְּאִתְאֲבִידוּ וַדַּאי, וְאִלֵּין לָא אִתְאֲבִידוּ.

43. Rabbi Elazar was sitting before his father. He said to him that it is written about the congregation of Korah, "And they perished from among the congregation" (Bemidbar 16:33). What is meant by "and they perished"? It is similar to that which is written, "The same person will I destroy from among his people" (Vayikra 23:30). Rabbi Shimon said that the sons of Aaron are different THAN THE CONGREGATION OF KORAH, because 'perish' is not written about them, as it does about the congregation of Korah, where it is written, "And they perished from among the congregation." It is also written, "Behold, we die, we perish, we all perish"

(Bemidbar 17:27), which included the 250 people who offered the incense. THEY surely perished; however, THE SONS OF AARON did not perish.

44. א״ל כְּתִיב, וְאַל יָבֹא בְכָל עֵת אֶל הַקֹּדֶשׁ. וּכְתִיב, בְּזֹאת יָבֹא אַהֲרֹן אֶל הַקֹּדֶשׁ. כֵּיוָן דְּאָמַר, וְאַל יָבֹא בְכָל עֵת, אֲמַאי לָא כְּתִיב, בְּמָה זִמְנָא יֵיעוּל. א״ל אֶלְעָזָר, הָא אִתְּמַר, וּמִלָּה חַד הוּא, וְזִמְנָא חַד הוּא הֲוֹו יַדְעֵי כַּהֲנֵי. אֲבָל עַל מַה דְּחָאבוּ בְּנוֹי, בָּעָא לְאַזְהָרָא הָכָא, וְהָא אִתְּמַר. א״ל, וַאֲנָא הָכִי סָבִירְנָא, וּבְגִין לְאִתְיַישְׁבָא מִלָּה בְּעֵינָא.

44. He replies that it is written, "That he come not at all times into the holy place." Another verse reads, "Thus (Heb. with *zot*) shall Aaron come into the holy place." HE QUESTIONS: If the verse stated "that he will not come at all times," why doesn't it write at what time he may come? IT SHOULD READ THAT ON THE TENTH OF THE MONTH, HE SHALL COME INTO THE HOLY PLACE, BUT INSTEAD IT SAYS, "THUS SHALL AARON COME INTO THE HOLY PLACE," YET GIVES NO EXPLICIT TIME. He said to him: Elazar, we learned that it is the same word and same time, FOR TIME AND *ZOT* ARE THE SAME WORD, NAMELY BOTH ARE NAMES OF MALCHUT, which the priests knew. But in relation to his sons sinning, the Holy One, blessed be He, wanted to admonish here, NAMELY, THAT HE SHOULD NOT DAMAGE THIS TIME WHICH IS MALCHUT AS HIS SONS DID. We have already learned this. He replied: I also thought so, but I wanted TO HEAR THIS FROM YOU in order to reconcile this matter.

45. א״ל, אֶלְעָזָר בְּרִי ת״ח, כָּל קׇרְבְּנִין וְכָל עִלָוָון, נַיְיחָא הוּא דְּקוּדְשָׁא בְּרִיךְ הוּא, אֲבָל לָא הֲוָה נַיְיחָא, כְּמָה דְּהַאי קְטֹרֶת, דִּקְטֹרֶת מְעַלְיָא מִכֹּלָּא. וּבג״כ, הֲווֹ מַעֲלִין לֵיהּ לְגוֹ בְּגוֹ, בִּלְחִישׁוּ. וְהָא אִתְּמַר. ובג״כ, לָא אִתְעֲנָשׁוּ כָּל בְּנֵי נָשָׁא בִּשְׁאָר קׇרְבְּנִין וְעִלָוָון כְּמוֹ בַּקְּטֹרֶת, דְּכָל פּוּלְחָנָא דְּקוּדְשָׁא בְּרִיךְ הוּא, הָכָא אִתְקְטַר וְאִתְקְשַׁר יַתִּיר מִכֹּלָּא. וְע״ד אִקְרֵי קְטֹרֶת. וְהָא אִתְּמַר, שֶׁמֶן וּקְטֹרֶת יְשַׂמַּח לֵב.

45. He said to him: Elazar, my son, come and see that all sacrifices and burnt offerings bring gratification to the Holy One, blessed be He. But there is no truer gratification BEFORE HIM than the incense, for the incense is the

most praiseworthy. This is the reason that it is offered in the innermost chambers, NAMELY THE HOLY OF HOLIES, silently. We have learned that. For this reason people were not punished for other kinds of sacrifices and burnt offerings as for incense, because in the whole of the service of the Holy One, blessed be He, this is the most joined and connected. That is why it is called incense, BECAUSE INCENSE IN ARAMAIC MEANS CONNECTING, so it says, "Ointment and incense rejoice the heart" (Mishlei 27:9).

6. "Therefore do the virgins love you"

A Synopsis

Rabbi Shimon tells how the fragrance of the incense rises and joins with the flow of the holy ointment (the Sfirah of Zeir Anpin); they waken each other and are then good for illumination. The oil is then poured down from level to level to Malchut and thence to all the worlds. The Congregation of Yisrael is like the incense and Zeir Anpin is like the ointment.

46. פָּתַח ר' שִׁמְעוֹן וְדָרַשׁ, לְרֵיחַ שְׁמָנֶיךָ טוֹבִים וְגוֹ'. הַאי קְרָא אִסְתַּכַּלְנָא בֵּיהּ, וְהָכִי הוּא. לְרֵיחַ, מַאי רֵיחַ. רֵיחַ דִּקְטֹרֶת דְּאִיהוּ דְּקִיקָא וּמֵעַלְיָא וּפְנִימָאָה מִכֹּלָּא, וְכַד סָלִיק הַהוּא רֵיחַ לְאִתְקַשְּׁרָא, בְּהַהוּא מְשַׁח רְבוּת דְּנַחֲלֵי מַבּוּעָא, אִתְּעָרוּ דָּא בְּדָא וְאִתְקְטָרוּ כַּחֲדָא. וּכְדֵין אִינּוּן מִשְׁחָן טָבָאן לְאַנְהָרָא. כד"א, לְרֵיחַ שְׁמָנֶיךָ טוֹבִים.

46. Rabbi Shimon opened the discussion saying, "Your ointments are fragrant..." (Shir Hashirim 1:3). I have closely studied this verse and this is the explanation: What is meant by "fragrant"? IT MEANS THAT the fragrance of the incense is subtle and finer, more interior than anything else. When this fragrance rises to join with the anointing oil of the fountain streams, WHICH ARE THE SFIROT OF ZEIR ANPIN, they wake one another and connect together. Then these ointments are good for illumination, as the verse says, "Your ointments are fragrant (lit. 'good for fragrance)."

47. וּכְדֵין אִתְרַק מִשְׁחָא מִדַּרְגָּא לְדַרְגָּא, בְּאִינּוּן דַּרְגִּין דְּאִקְרוּן שְׁמָא קַדִּישָׁא, הה"ד, שֶׁמֶן תּוּרַק שְׁמֶךָ עַל כֵּן עֲלָמוֹת אֲהֵבוּךָ. מַאי עֲלָמוֹת. כְּמָה דְּאוֹקִימְנָא עוֹלָמוֹת, עוֹלָמוֹת מַמָּשׁ, ד"א עַל כֵּן עֲלָמוֹת אֲהֵבוּךָ. כד"א, עַל עֲלָמוֹת שִׁיר. וְכֹלָּא חַד.

47. The oil was then poured from level to level among the levels that are called the Holy Name, WHICH IS MALCHUT, and the verse then reads, "For your flowing oil you are renowned: therefore do the virgins love you" (Ibid.). What is meant by "virgins" (Heb. alamot)? It is worlds (Heb. olamot), as we mentioned, actual worlds. INASMUCH AS THE OIL POURS TO MALCHUT CALLED NAME, ALL WORLDS RECEIVE FROM HER. Another

explanation for *alamot* is as written, "A song to Alamot" (Tehilim 46:1), MEANING GRADES REPRESENTING ASPECTS OF CHASSADIM THAT IS REFERRED TO AS ALOMOT, DERIVED FROM THE WORD *HE'ALEM* (LIT. 'HIDDEN'). It all comes to the same thing. THE WORD *OLAMOT* (LIT. 'WORLDS') ALSO COMES FROM THEIR BEING CONCEALED

48. וּבְסִפְרָא דְּרַב הַמְנוּנָא סַבָא כְּתִיב, מַאי עוֹלָמוֹת. כְּמָה דְאַתְּ אָמַר, וַתִּתֵּן טֶרֶף לְבֵיתָה וְחֹק לְנַעֲרוֹתֶיהָ. נַעֲרוֹתֶיהָ הָנֵי עֲלָמוֹת, אֲהֵבוּךָ, לְבָרְכָא שְׁמָךְ, וּלְזַמְּרָא קַמָּךְ, וּמִתַּמָּן אִשְׁתַּכְּחָן בִּרְכָאן בְּכֻלְּהוּ תַּתָּאֵי, וּמִתְבָּרְכִין עִלָּאִין וְתַתָּאִין.

48. In the book of Rabbi Hamnuna Saba, it is written: what is the meaning of 'worlds (Heb. *olamot*)'? It is according to the verse, "She rises also while it is yet night, and gives food to her household, and a portion to her maidens" (Mishlei 31:15). THIS IS THE SECRET OF THE SEVEN CHAMBERS OF BRIYAH, WHICH SERVICE MALCHUT AND ARE REFERRED TO AS MAIDENS. These maidens ARE "the virgins (Heb. *alamot*) love you," to bless Your name and to sing praises before You. From there, there are blessings among all the lower beings, and the upper and lower beings are blessed.

49. ד"א ע"כ עֲלָמוֹת אֲהֵבוּךָ. שַׁפִּיר הוּא מַאן דְּאָמַר. עַל מָוֶת אֲהֵבוּךָ, דְּהָא בְּמִלָּה דָא מָארֵיהוֹן דְּדִינִין אִתְבַּסְּמָן, וּבְגִין דְּהַאי קְטֹרֶת, אִתְקְטַר בְּמִשְׁחָא דִלְעֵילָא יַתִּיר, אִתְחֲשַׁב קַמֵּיה דְּקוּדְשָׁא בְּרִיךְ הוּא, מִכָּל קָרְבְּנִין וְעָלָוָן. אָמְרָה כ"י, אֲנָא כִּקְטֹרֶת, וְאַנְתְּ כְּמִשְׁחָא, מָשְׁכֵנִי אַחֲרֶיךָ נָרוּצָה וְגוֹ'. נָרוּצָה: כד"א, עַל כֵּן עֲלָמוֹת אֲהֵבוּךָ. אֲנָא וְכָל אוּכְלוּסִין, דְּהָא כֻּלְּהוּ בִּי אֲחִידָן, וְעַל דָּא מָשְׁכֵנִי, דְּהָא בִּי תַּלְיָין.

49. Another explanation for "the virgins (Heb. *alamot*) love you": It is fine to read this verse as: 'over death (Heb. *al mavet*) they love you', for with this, NAMELY OIL WHICH DENOTES CHASSADIM, the harsh prosecutors embalm themselves, AS 'ALAMOT' IS SPELLED WITH THE SAME LETTERS AS 'AL MAVET'. For incense, SIGNIFYING THE ILLUMINATION OF CHOCHMAH, joins with the higher level ointment, WHICH IS CHASSADIM, and is held in high esteem before the Holy One, blessed be He, more than all

sacrifices and burnt offerings. The Congregation of Yisrael said: I am like the incense, DENOTING MALCHUT, AS MALCHUT IS THE SECRET MEANING OF LOWER CHOCHMAH, and You, DENOTING ZEIR ANPIN, are like ointment, DENOTING CHASSADIM. THEREFORE, "Draw me, we will run after you" (Shir Hashirim 1:4). "We will run" IS A PLURAL EXPRESSION, as in, "therefore do the virgins love you," THAT IS, I and all my troops, who all hold onto me. Hence, "draw me," as they are all dependent on me.

50. הֱבִיאַנִי הַמֶּלֶךְ חֲדָרָיו. אִם יֵיעוּל לִי מַלְכָּא בְּאִדָרוֹי, נָגִילָה וְנִשְׂמְחָה בָּךְ, אֲנָא וְכֻלְהוּ אוּכְלוּסִין. תָּאנָא. כֻּלְהוּ אוּכְלוּסִין, בְּשַׁעֲתָא דִכְנֶסֶת יִשְׂרָאֵל חַדָאת וּמִתְבָּרְכָא, כֻּלְהוּ חַדָאן, וְדִינָא לָא שַׁרְיָא כְּדֵין בְּעָלְמָא. וְעַל דָּא כְּתִיב, יִשְׂמְחוּ הַשָׁמַיִם וְתָגֵל הָאָרֶץ.

50. "The king has brought me into his chambers" (Ibid.): If the King will bring me into His chambers, then "we will be glad and rejoice in you" (Ibid.), meaning I and all the troops. We have learned that all the forces rejoice when the Congregation of Yisrael is joyous and blessed, and harsh decrees do not transpire in the world. Hence, it says, "Let the heavens rejoice, and let the earth be glad" (Tehilim 96:11).

7. "For I appear in the cloud upon the ark cover"

A Synopsis

Rabbi Yehuda brings up various verses where a cloud or a storm of wind are mentioned. Speaking about the cloud upon the ark cover, he says that this is the place where the cherubs, Metatron and Sandalphon, rested, and that a miracle occurred three times a day when the Shechinah revealed herself in their wings. Rabbi Shimon tells what song the cherubs sang when the Shechinah came down.

51. כִּי בֶּעָנָן אֵרָאֶה עַל הַכַּפֹּרֶת. א"ר יְהוּדָה, זַכָּאִין אִינּוּן צַדִּיקַיָּא, דְּקוּדְשָׁא בְּרִיךְ הוּא בָּעֵי בִּיקָרֵיהוֹן. וְתָנֵינָא, מֶלֶךְ בָּשָׂר וָדָם, אִי ב"נ רָכִיב עַל סוּסְיָא דִּילֵיהּ, בַּר קַטָלָא הוּא, קוּדְשָׁא בְּרִיךְ הוּא אַרְכִּיב אֵלִיָּהוּ עַל דִּילֵיהּ, דִּכְתִיב, וַיַּעַל אֵלִיָּהוּ בַּסְּעָרָה הַשָּׁמָיִם וְגוֹ'. הָכָא מַאי כְּתִיב, וְלֹא יָמוּת כִּי בֶּעָנָן אֵרָאֶה עַל הַכַּפֹּרֶת. וְקוּדְשָׁא בְּרִיךְ הוּא עָיֵילֵיהּ לְמֹשֶׁה בֵּיהּ, הה"ד, וַיָּבֹא מֹשֶׁה בְּתוֹךְ הֶעָנָן, בְּתוֹךְ הֶעָנָן מַמָּשׁ, כִּי בֶּעָנָן אֵרָאֶה עַל הַכַּפֹּרֶת. הה"ד, וּבָרָא יְיָ' עַל כָּל מְכוֹן הַר צִיּוֹן וְעַל מִקְרָאֶיהָ עָנָן יוֹמָם וְעָשָׁן. וּכְתִיב, כִּי עֲנַן יְיָ' עַל הַמִּשְׁכָּן יוֹמָם.

51. "For I appear in the cloud upon the ark cover" (Vayikra 16:2). Rabbi Yehuda said: Fortunate are the righteous, whom the Holy One, blessed be He, delights to honor. We have learned about a king of flesh and blood, that if someone rides on his horse, he has committed a capital offense. However, the Holy One, blessed be He, placed Elijah on His own, as is written, "And Elijah went up by a storm of wind into heaven" (II Melachim 2:11) AND IT IS WRITTEN, "HASHEM ANSWERED JOB OUT OF THE STORM" (IYOV 38:1). It is written: here "that he die not: for I appear in the cloud upon the ark cover." The Holy One, blessed be He, brought Moses into the cloud, as it says, "And Moses went into the midst of the cloud" (Shemot 24:18), meaning into the midst of the cloud, DENOTING MALCHUT. IT IS WITHIN THE SAME CLOUD, OF WHICH IT SAYS, "For I appear in the cloud upon the ark cover." This is the meaning of, "And Hashem will create upon every dwelling place of Mount Zion and upon its assemblies, a cloud and smoke by day" (Yeshayah 4:5), "For the cloud of Hashem was upon the tabernacle by day" (Shemot 40:38). ALL THESE CLOUDS HINT AT MALCHUT.

52. וְתָאנָא, הַאי דִּכְתִּיב, וַיֵּרֶד יְיָ' בֶּעָנָן. בֶּעָנָן אֶרָאֶה עַל הַכַּפֹּרֶת. תָּאנָא, אֲתַר דַּהֲווֹ שָׁרָאן אִינּוּן כְּרוּבֵי, כְּמָה דְּאוֹקִימְנָא, כְּרוּבִים עַל אֵת הֲווֹ יַתְבִין. וְתָאנָא, ג' זִמְנִין בְּיוֹמָא אִתְרְחִישׁ נִיסָא, בְּגַדְפַּיְיהוּ. בְּשַׁעֲתָא דְּאִתְגְּלֵי עָלַיְיהוּ קְדוּשָׁה דְּמַלְכָּא, אִינּוּן מִגַּרְמַיְיהוּ סַלְקִין גַּדְפַּיְיהוּ, וּפַרְסִין לוֹן, וְחַפְיָין עַל כַּפֹּרְתָּא. לְבָתַר קַמְטִין גַּדְפַּיְיהוּ, וְנֶאֶחָזִין בְּגוּפַיְיהוּ כד"א וְהָיוּ הַכְּרוּבִים פּוֹרְשֵׂי כְנָפַיִם לְמַעְלָה, פּוֹרְשֵׂי וְלָא פְּרוּשֵׂי. סוֹכְכִים וְלָא סְכוּכִים. דָּא בָּאַת הֲווֹ קַיְימֵי וְחַדָּאן בִּשְׁכִינְתָּא.

52. We have learned that it is written, "And Hashem descended in the cloud" (Shemot 34:5) and "I appear in the cloud upon the ark cover." We have learned that this is the place, NAMELY MALCHUT, where the Cherubs rested, WHO ARE METATRON AND SANDALPHON, as we learned. The Cherubs were in place by means of a miracle (Heb. *nes*), MEANING UPON MALCHUT THAT IS CALLED *NES*. We have learned that three times daily – THE SECRET MEANING OF THE THREE COLUMNS – a miracle (Heb. *nes*) occurred, MEANING THAT THE SHECHINAH REVEALED HERSELF in their wings. At the moment when the sanctity of the King revealed itself upon them, they raised their wings of their own accord, spread them, and covered over the ark cover. Afterwards, they closed their wings and held them against their bodies, as the verse says, "And the Cherubs shall stretch out their wings on high" (Shemot 25:20). The verse uses the term "stretch out," MEANING AT TIMES THEY WOULD SPREAD AND AT TIMES CLOSE. The verse does not read 'stretched out', WHICH WOULD BE CORRECT WERE THEY PASSIVE; IN THE SAME WAY, 'overspreading' instead of 'were overspread'. This is WHAT THEY SAID, 'they were erect by means of a miracle and were rejoicing in the Shechinah'.

53. א"ר אַבָּא, מַה בָּעָא הָכָא, כִּי בֶּעָנָן אֶרָאֶה עַל הַכַּפֹּרֶת. וּכְתִיב בְּזֹאת יָבֹא אַהֲרֹן, וְהָא כַּהֲנָא לָא חָמֵי לִשְׁכִינְתָּא בְּשַׁעֲתָא כַּד הֲוָה עָאל. אֶלָּא עֲנָנָא הֲוָה נָחִית, וְכַד הֲוָה נָחִית מָטָא עַל הַאי כַּפֹּרֶת, וּמִתְעָרִין גַּדְפַּיְיהוּ דִכְרוּבִין, וְאַקְשֵׁי לְהוּ וְאַמְרֵי שִׁירָתָא.

53. Rabbi Aba said: What does THE VERSE wish to say with the statement, "I appear in the cloud upon the ark cover," WHICH MEANS THAT PRIEST

SEES THE SHECHINAH? ALSO, in the verse, "Thus (with *zot*) shall Aaron come," WHICH IS THE SHECHINAH IS REFERRED TO AS *ZOT*. Behold, the priest did not see the Shechinah when he entered THE HOLY OF HOLIES. HE ANSWERS: The cloud, WHICH IS THE SHECHINAH, would come down. In coming down, it reached the covering of the ark, the wings of the Cherubs would stir and the Cherubs would strike with their wings and sing a song. FROM THIS, THE PRIEST WOULD REALIZE THAT THE SHECHINAH WAS NOW APPEARING. THIS IS WHAT IS MEANT BY, "I APPEAR IN THE CLOUD UPON THE ARK COVER."

54. וּמַה שִׁירָתָא אַמְרֵי כִּי גָדוֹל יְיָ' וּמְהֻלָּל מְאֹד נוֹרָא הוּא עַל כָּל אֱלֹהִים. הַאי כַּד סַלְקֵי גַּדְפַּיְיהוּ. בְּשַׁעֲתָא דְּפַרְסִין לְהוּ אַמְרֵי, כִּי כָּל אֱלֹהֵי הָעַמִּים אֱלִילִים וַיְיָ' שָׁמַיִם עָשָׂה. כַּד חַפְיָין עַל כַּפּוֹרְתָּא, אַמְרֵי, לִפְנֵי יְיָ' כִּי בָא לִשְׁפּוֹט הָאָרֶץ יִשְׁפּוֹט תֵּבֵל בְּצֶדֶק וְעַמִּים בְּמֵישָׁרִים.

54. HE QUESTIONS: What song did they sing? HE ANSWERS, "For Hashem is great, and greatly to be praised: He is to be feared above all Elohim" (Tehilim 96:4). THEY SAID this when they raised their wings, WHICH IS THE ASPECT OF THE RIGHT COLUMN, MEANING CHESED TERMED "GREAT." When they spread them, they would say, "For all the Elohim of the nations are idols: but Hashem made the heavens" (Ibid. 5). THIS IS THE ASPECT OF THE LEFT COLUMN THAT SUBDUES THE ENTIRE OTHER SIDE. When they covered the ark cover, they would say, "Before Hashem; for He comes to judge the earth: with righteousness shall He judge the world, and the people with equity" (Tehilim 98:9). THIS IS THE ASPECT OF THE CENTRAL COLUMN DENOTING TIFERET, REFERRED TO AS JUSTICE.

8. "And their faces shall look one to another"

A Synopsis

Rabbi Shimon says that when the priest heard the voices of the Cherubs he placed the incense in the right place and had the correct intent, so that the blessings should flow to all. The wings of the cherubs were moving up and down, singing and covering the ark. We learn that the Cherubs are male and female, which establishes equity. Rabbi Yitzchak says that whenever there are not both female and male present, one is not worthy to look at the Shechinah.

55. וְקַלְהוֹן הֲוָה שָׁמַע כַּהֲנָא בְּמַקְדְּשָׁא, כְּדֵין שַׁוֵּי קְטֹרֶת בְּאַתְרֵיהּ, וְאִתְכְּוָון בְּמָה דְאִתְכַּוָּון, בְּגִין דְיִתְבְּרַךְ כֹּלָא. וְגַדְפֵי כְּרוּבַיָּיא, סַלְּקִין וְנַחְתִּין, וְזַמְרֵי שִׁירָתָא, מְחַפְּיָין לְכַפּוּרְתָּא וְסַלְּקֵי לְהוּ. הה"ד סוֹכְכִים סוֹכְכִים. דַיְיקָא ומנ"ל דְקַלְהוֹן אִשְׁתְּמַע, כד"א וָאֶשְׁמַע אֶת קוֹל וְגוֹ'.

55. When the priest heard their voices in the Temple, he placed the incense in its right place and meditated on something, in order that the blessing should flow to all. The wings of the Cherubs were moving up and down, singing and covering the ark. Then they would raise them. This is the meaning of "overspreading." "Overspreading" is precise. Where do we derive that their voices were heard? NAMELY from the verse, "I heard the noise of their wings" (Yechezkel 1:24).

56. א"ר יוֹסֵי, וְעַמִּים בְּמֵישָׁרִים. מַהוּ בְּמֵישָׁרִים. כד"א, מֵישָׁרִים אֲהֵבוּךָ, לְאַכְלְלָא תְּרֵין כְּרוּבִין, דְכַר וְנוּקְבָּא, מֵישָׁרִים וַדַּאי. וְעַל דָּא, וְעַמִּים בְּמֵישָׁרִים.

56. Rabbi Yosi said, "and the people with equity (Heb. *meisharim*)" (Tehilim 98:9): What is meant by *Meisharim*? HE ANSWERS: As the verse says, "sincerely (Heb. *meisharim*) they love you" (Shir Hashirim 1:4). THE SHECHINAH includes BY THIS the two Cherubs, METATRON AND SANDALPHON, who are assuredly called "*meisharim*," and IT SAYS about this, "And the people with equity (Heb. *meisharim*)." BEFORE THIS, IT IS WRITTEN, "WITH RIGHTEOUSNESS SHALL HE JUDGE THE WORLD"

(Tehilim 98:9) AND "JUDGE" REFERS TO ZEIR ANPIN, WHILE "RIGHTEOUSNESS" DENOTES MALCHUT. LATER, THE VERSE INCLUDES ALSO THE CHERUBS AND THUS SAYS, "AND THE PEOPLE WITH EQUITY."

57. וּכְתִיב, וַיִּשְׁמַע אֶת הַקּוֹל מִדַּבֵּר אֵלָיו מִבֵּין שְׁנֵי הַכְּרוּבִים וַיְדַבֵּר אֵלָיו. ר' יִצְחָק אָמַר, מִכָּאן אוֹלִיפְנָא דִּבְכָל אֲתַר דְּלָא אִשְׁתְּכַח דְּכַר וְנוּקְבָּא, לָאו כְּדַאי לְמֶחֱמֵי אַפֵּי שְׁכִינְתָּא. הה"ד, יֵשְׁבוּ יְשָׁרִים אֶת פָּנֶיךָ, וְתָנֵינָן, כְּתִיב, צַדִּיק וְיָשָׁר הוּא, דְּכַר וְנוּקְבָּא, אוּף הָכָא כְּרוּבִים דְּכַר וְנוּקְבָּא. וְעֲלַיְיהוּ כְּתִיב, אַתָּה כּוֹנַנְתָּ מֵישָׁרִים. וְעַמִּים בְּמֵישָׁרִים. וּבְגִינֵי כָּךְ, וּפְנֵיהֶם אִישׁ אֶל אָחִיו, וְהָא אוֹקִימְנָא.

57. It is written, "Then he heard the voice speaking to him from off the covering that was upon the ark of Testimony, from between the two Cherubs: and it spoke to him" (Bemidbar 7:89). Rabbi Yitzchak said: From here, we learned that whenever there are not both male and female present, one is not worthy to behold the presence of the Shechinah. THEREFORE, HE HEARD THE VOICE SPEAKING ONLY FROM BETWEEN THE TWO CHERUBS. This is the intent of the verse, "The upright (Heb. *yesharim*) shall dwell in Your presence" (Tehilim 140:14), MEANING THE CHERUBS REFERRED TO AS *MEISHARIM*. We have learned that there is a verse, "Just and right is He" (Devarim 32:4), DENOTING male and female. "JUST" REFERS TO THE MALE, MEANING YESOD, AND "RIGHT" REFERS TO THE FEMALE, MEANING MALCHUT. Here also, the Cherubs are male and female, as it is written of them, "You have established equity (Heb. *meisharim* in plural)" (Tehilim 99:4) AND ALSO "the people with equity (Heb. *meisharim*)," AS MENTIONED ABOVE. For this reason, "And their faces shall look one to another" (Shemot 25:20), THE SECRET OF FACE TO FACE UNION, as we have established.

9. "Behold, how good and how pleasant"

A Synopsis

Rabbi Shimon talks about "how good and how pleasant it is for brothers to dwell together in unity," explaining that it means male and female turned toward one another. He says that righteousness and justice go together, otherwise things are not well with the world. The rabbis had been complaining because rain was needed, and Rabbi Shimon says that is because male does not reside within the female, but everything is about to return to its proper place and there will soon be rain. then they talk about the interpretations of "I am black, but comely" and the following verses. Returning to the title verse, we hear that it refers to the friends, who fear God and speak about Him to one another, and have peace and brotherly love.

58. תַּנְיָא א"ר יוֹסֵי, זִמְנָא חֲדָא, הֲוָה צְרִיכָא עַלְמָא לְמִטְרָא, אָתוּ לְקַמֵּיה דר"ש, ר' יֵיסָא וְרִבִּי חִזְקִיָּה וּשְׁאָר חַבְרַיָּיא. אַשְׁכְּחוּהוּ דַּהֲוָה אָזִיל לְמֶחֱמֵי, לְר' פִּנְחָס בֶּן יָאִיר, הוּא ור"א בְּרֵיה. כֵּיוָן דְּחָמָא לוֹן, פָּתַח וְאָמַר, שִׁיר הַמַּעֲלוֹת הִנֵּה מַה טּוֹב וּמַה נָּעִים שֶׁבֶת אַחִים גַּם יָחַד. מַאי שֶׁבֶת אַחִים גַּם יָחַד.

58. We have learned that Rabbi Yosi said, once the world needed rain. Rabbi Yesa, Rabbi Chizkiyah and other friends came before Rabbi Shimon. They found him and his son going to see Rabbi Pinchas ben Yair. When he saw them, he said, "A poem of ascent of David. Behold, how good and how pleasant it is for brothers to dwell together in unity" (Tehilim 133:1). HE QUESTIONS: What is meant by "brothers to dwell together in unity"?

59. כד"א, וּפְנֵיהֶם אִישׁ אֶל אָחִיו, בְּשַׁעֲתָא דַּהֲווֹ חַד בְּחַד מַשְׁגִּיחִין אַנְפִּין בְּאַנְפִּין, כְּתִיב, מַה טוֹב וּמַה נָּעִים. וְכַד מְהַדַּר דְּכוּרָא אַנְפּוֹי מִן נוּקְבָּא, וַוי לְעָלְמָא. כְּדֵין כְּתִיב, וְיֵשׁ נִסְפֶּה בְּלֹא מִשְׁפָּט. בְּלֹא מִשְׁפָּט וַדַּאי, וּכְתִיב, צֶדֶק וּמִשְׁפָּט מְכוֹן כִּסְאֶךָ, דְּלָא אָזִיל דָּא בְּלָא דָא, וְכַד מִשְׁפָּט, מִתְרַחֵק מִצֶּדֶק, וַוי לְעָלְמָא.

59. HE ANSWERS: THIS IS as is said, "And their faces shall look one to another (lit. 'man to his brother')" (Shemot 25:20), BROTHERS MEANING

MALE AND FEMALE, for the time that ZEIR ANPIN AND MALCHUT faced each other, it is written, "How good and how pleasant." However, when the male turns his face away from the female, woe is to the world. Then it is written, "But sometimes ruin comes for want of justice" (Mishlei 13:23) and assuredly without justice, MEANING WITHOUT ZEIR ANPIN CALLED JUSTICE, WHO DOES NOT LOOK OR GIVE ABUNDANCE TO THE FEMALE CALLED RIGHTEOUSNESS. The verse, "Righteousness and justice are the foundation of Your throne" (Tehilim 89:15) means that one does not go without the other. When justice, WHICH IS ZEIR ANPIN, moves afar from righteousness, WHICH IS MALCHUT, woe is to the world.

60. וְהַשְׁתָּא חֲמֵינָא, דְּאַתוּן אֲתִיתוּן, עַל דִּדְכוּרָא לָא שַׁרְיָא בְּנוּקְבָּא, אֲמַר, אִי לְדָא אֲתִיתוּן גַּבַּאי תִּיבוּ. דְּהַאי יוֹמָא אִסְתַּכַּלְנָא, דְּיִתְהַדָר כֹּלָּא לְמִשְׁרֵי אַנְפִּין בְּאַנְפִּין. וְאִי לְאוֹרַיְיתָא אֲתִיתוּן, שָׁרוּ גַּבַּאי. אָמְרוּ לֵיהּ, לְכֹלָּא, קָא אֲתֵינָא לְגַבֵּי דְּמַר, יִשְׁתְּמִיט חַד מִינָן, לְבַשְׂרָא לַאֲחָנָא, שְׁאַר חַבְרַיָּיא, וַאֲנָן נֵתִיב לְקַמֵּיהּ דְּמַר.

60. I see that you have come now because the Male does not reside within the Female AND, AS A RESULT, THERE IS NO RAIN IN THE WORLD. He said, If you have come to me for this reason, then go back, as this day I have seen that everything will return to be face to face AND THERE WILL BE NO LACK OF ABUNDANCE OF RAIN IN THE WORLD. However, if you have come here to study Torah, then stay with me. They replied to him: We came to our master for both of them, FOR RAINFALL AND FOR STUDY OF TORAH. Allow one of us to report to our brethren ABOUT THE SALVATION OF RAIN, while we, and the other friends with us, will remain with our master.

61. עַד דַּהֲווֹ אַזְלֵי, פָּתַח וְאָמַר, שְׁחוֹרָה אֲנִי וְנָאוָה בְּנוֹת יְרוּשָׁלַים וְגוֹ'. אָמְרָה כְּנֶסֶת יִשְׂרָאֵל קָמֵי קוּדְשָׁא בְּרִיךְ הוּא, שְׁחוֹרָה אֲנִי בְּגָלוּתָא, וְנָאוָה אֲנִי בְּפִקּוּדֵי אוֹרַיְיתָא, דְּאע״ג דְּיִשְׂרָאֵל בְּגָלוּתָא לָא שַׁבְקֵי לוֹן. כְּאָהֳלֵי קֵדָר, דְּאִינוּן בְּנֵי קְטוּרָה, דְּאִתְקַדְּרוּ אַנְפַּיְיהוּ תְּדִירָא, וְעִם כָּל דָּא כִּירִיעוֹת שְׁלֹמֹה, כְּהַהוּא שְׁמַיָא חִזוּ לְמִדְכֵּי, דִּכְתִיב, נוֹטֶה שָׁמַיִם כַּיְרִיעָה.

61. As they were walking, he said, "I am black, but comely, O daughters of Jerusalem..." (Shir Hashirim 1:5). The Congregation of Yisrael said before the Holy One, blessed be He: I may be black in exile but I am comely with the commandments of the Torah. Even though Yisrael are in exile, they do not forsake THE PRECEPTS. "Like the tents of Kedar" (Ibid.), MEANING EVEN THOUGH I AM like the children of Keturah, whose faces are always black, still I am like "the curtains of Solomon" (Ibid.), MEANING like the view of heaven for purity, as it is written, "Who stretches out the heavens like a curtain" (Tehilim 104:2). SOLOMON (HEB. *SHLOMO*) IS THE HOLY ONE, BLESSED BE HE, THE KING OF PEACE (HEB. *SHALOM*).

62. אַל תִּרְאוּנִי שֶׁאֲנִי שְׁחַרְחוֹרֶת. מ"ט אַל תִּרְאוּנִי, בְּגִין שֶׁאֲנִי שְׁחַרְחוֹרֶת. שֶׁשְּׁזָפַתְנִי הַשָּׁמֶשׁ, דְּלָא אִסְתָּכַּל בִּי שִׁמְשָׁא, לְאַנְהָרָא לִי כַּדְקָא יֵאוֹת. יִשְׂרָאֵל מַה אִינּוּן אַמְרִין. בְּנֵי אִמִּי נִחֲרוּ בִי. מַאן אִינּוּן בְּנֵי אִמִּי, אִלֵּין רַבְרְבִין מְמָנָן תְּרִיסִין עַל שְׁאָר עַמִּין.

62. "Do not look upon me, because I am black" (Shir Hashirim 1:6), MEANING what is the reason you should not look upon me? Because I am black AND THEREFORE YOU CANNOT SEE ME. "Because the sun has scorched me" (Ibid.), MEANING the sun did not look at me, REFERRING TO ZEIR ANPIN, to properly shed light upon me. What do Yisrael say to this? "My mother's children were angry with me" (Ibid.). Who are the children of my mother? These are appointed ministers who protect the other nations.

63. ד"א, בְּנֵי אִמִּי מַמָּשׁ. כד"א, הִשְׁלִיךְ מִשָּׁמַיִם אֶרֶץ וְגוֹ'. וְכַד הִשְׁלִיךְ מִשָּׁמַיִם אֶרֶץ, שָׂמוּנִי נוֹטֵרָה אֶת הַכְּרָמִים. מ"ט. דְּכַרְמִי שֶׁלִּי לֹא נָטָרְתִּי. וְתָנֵינָן, בְּנֵי אִמִּי וַדַּאי אִסְתְּכְּמוּ עָלַי, כְּלוֹמַר, כַּד אִתְעֲדֵי אֶרֶץ, מִשָּׁמַיִם, כְּמָה דְּאוּקִימְנָא, דִּכְתִּיב, וַתֵּתַצַּב אֲחוֹתוֹ מֵרָחוֹק.

63. Another explanation is that THE SHECHINAH SPOKE literally OF "my mother's children," REFERRING TO THE SFIROT OF ZEIR ANPIN, THE CHILDREN OF BINAH WHO IS THE MOTHER OF THE SHECHINAH, as the verse says, "And cast down from heaven (to) earth..." (Eichah 2:1). So when ZEIR ANPIN threw from heaven the earth, MEANING THE SHECHINAH, "they made me the keeper of the vineyards" (Shir Hashirim 1:6),

REFERRING TO THE NATIONS OF THE WORLD. SHE HAS TO POUR ABUNDANCE TO THE NATIONS OF THE WORLD SO THAT YISRAEL WILL DRAW SUSTENANCE FROM THEM. What is the reason? BECAUSE "my own vineyard," NAMELY YISRAEL, "I have not kept" (Ibid.), BECAUSE THEY SINNED. We thus learn that "the children of my mother," NAMELY THE SFIROT OF ZEIR ANPIN, agreed against me, TO DISTANCE ME, meaning the earth was removed with this, REFERRING TO MALCHUT, from heaven, DENOTING ZEIR ANPIN. We established that it is written, "And his sister stood afar off" (Shemot 2:4). THE SHECHINAH, CALLED THE SISTER OF ZEIR ANPIN, STOOD FROM A DISTANCE, MEANING ZEIR ANPIN HAD CAUSED HER TO STAND AT A DISTANCE.

64. וְהָכָא אִתְּמַר וַדַּאי, הִנֵּה מַה טוֹב וּמַה נָּעִים שֶׁבֶת אַחִים גַּם יָחַד. וּבְהוּ אוֹקִימְנָא, גַּם יָחַד. כד"א. כד"א גַּם זֹאת בִּהְיוֹתָם, שֶׁבֶת אַחִים בִּכְלַל, כֵּיוָן דִּכְתִּיב, גַּם, לְאַכְלְלָא כָּל אִינוּן דִּלְעֵילָא, דְּכָל שׁוּלְטָנוּתָא בְּהַהוּא אֲתַר אִשְׁתְּכַח.

64. IN CONTRAST TO WHAT IS WRITTEN, "AND HIS SISTER STOOD AFAR OFF," it is surely said, "Behold, how good and how pleasant it is for brothers to dwell together (Heb. gam) in unity" WHEN MALCHUT, WHICH IS THE SISTER OF ZEIR ANPIN, STANDS NOT AT A DISTANCE BUT TOGETHER. Regarding them, ZEIR ANPIN AND MALCHUT, we have explained "also together" the same way as "And yet (Heb. gam) for all that (Heb. zot fem.)" (Vayikra 26:44), GAM BEING THE SECRET OF MALCHUT CALLED ZOT. SIMILARLY, "GAM IN UNITY" REFERS TO MALCHUT. IN TRUTH, it would have been included in the brothers sitting together AND THERE WOULD BE NO NEED TO INSCRIBE THE WORD GAM. Since "Gam (Eng. 'also')" is written it is meant to include all of those higher above ZEIR ANPIN AND MALCHUT; THAT IS, THEY ARE YISRAEL–SABA AND TEVUNAH. For the whole reign is now in that place – YISRAEL–SABA AND TEVUNAH.

65. ד"א. הִנֵּה מַה טוֹב וּמַה נָּעִים וְגוֹ'. אִלֵּין אִינוּן חַבְרַיָּיא, בְּשַׁעֲתָא דְּאִינּוּן יַתְבִין כַּחֲדָא, וְלָא מִתְפָּרְשָׁן דָּא מִן דָּא. בְּקַדְמֵיתָא אִתְחֲזוּן גּוּבְרֵי מַגִּיחֵי קְרָבָא, דְּבָעוּ לְקַטְלָא דָּא לְדָא. לְבָתַר, אִתְהַדְרוּ

בְּרְחִימוּתָא דְּאַחֲוָה. קוּדְשָׁא בְּרִיךְ הוּא מַהוּ אוֹמֵר, הִנֵּה מַה טּוֹב וּמַה נָּעִים שֶׁבֶת אַחִים גַּם יָחַד. גַּם, לְאַכְלְלָא עִמְּהוֹן שְׁכִינְתָּא. וְלֹא עוֹד, אֶלָּא קוּדְשָׁא בְּרִיךְ הוּא אָצִית לְמִלּוּלַיְיהוּ, וְנִיחָא לֵיהּ וְחַדֵּי בְּהוּ. הה"ד אָז נִדְבְּרוּ יִרְאֵי יְיָ' אִישׁ אֶל רֵעֵהוּ וַיַּקְשֵׁב יְיָ' וַיִּשְׁמָע וַיִּכָּתֵב סֵפֶר זִכָּרוֹן לְפָנָיו וְגוֹ'.

65. Another explanation for, "Behold, how good and how pleasant..." These are the friends, when they sit together and don't sit apart from one another. At first they appear as people at war with each other, wanting to kill one another. Afterwards, they return to each other in brotherly love. What does the Holy One, blessed be He, say ABOUT THEM? "Behold how good and pleasant it is for brothers to dwell together (Heb. *gam*, Eng. 'also') in unity." The word *gam* comes to include the Shechinah. Moreover, the Holy One, blessed be He, pays attention to what they say, and has enjoyment and rejoices with them. This is the essence of the verse, "Then they who feared Hashem spoke to one another: and Hashem hearkened, and heard it, and a book of remembrance was written before Him..." (Malachi 3:16).

66. וְאַתּוּן חַבְרַיָּיא דְּהָכָא, כְּמָה דַּהֲוֵיתוֹן בַּחֲבִיבוּתָא בִּרְחִימוּתָא, מִקַּדְמַת דְּנָא, הָכִי נָמֵי, מִכָּאן וּלְהָלְאָה לָא תִּתְפָּרְשׁוּן דָּא מִן דָּא, עַד דְּקוּדְשָׁא בְּרִיךְ הוּא יַחֲדֵי עִמְּכוֹן, וְיִקְרֵי עֲלַיְיכוּ שָׁלָם. וְיִשְׁתְּכַח בְּגִינֵיכוֹן שְׁלָמָא בְּעָלְמָא. הה"ד לְמַעַן אַחַי וְרֵעַי אֲדַבְּרָה נָא שָׁלוֹם בָּךְ.

66. My friends, just as you have had affection for each other until now, do not part from one another from now on until the Holy One, blessed be He, rejoices with you. He will call peace upon you and, for your merits, peace will prevail in the world. This is the meaning of the verse, "For my brethren and friends' sakes, I will now say, Peace be within you" (Tehilim 122:8).

67. אָזְלוּ. עַד דַּהֲווֹ אַזְלֵי, מָטוּ לְבֵי רַבִּי פִּנְחָס בֶּן יָאִיר. נָפַק רַבִּי פִּנְחָס, וּנְשָׁקֵיהּ. אָמַר, זָכֵינָא לְנַשְּׁקָא שְׁכִינְתָּא. זַכָּאָה חוּלָקִי אַתְקִין לְהוּ טִיקְלֵי דְּעַרְסֵי, קַפְטוֹרֵי דְּקִילְטָא. אָמַר רַבִּי שִׁמְעוֹן, אוֹרַיְיתָא לָא בָּעֵי הָכִי, אַעֲבַר לְהוֹן, וְיָתִיבוּ. א"ר פִּנְחָס, עַד לָא נֵיכוּל, נִשְׁמַע מִמָּארֵיהּ

דְּאוֹרַיְיתָא מִלָּה. דְּהָא ר"ש כָּל מִלּוֹי בְּאִתְגַּלְיָיא אִינּוּן, אִיהוּ גַּבְרָא
דְּלָא דָּחִיל מֵעֵילָּא וּמִתַּתָּא, לְמֵימַר לוֹן, לָא דָּחִיל מֵעֵילָּא, דְּהָא
קוּדְשָׁא בְּרִיךְ הוּא אִסְתָּכַּם בֵּיהּ, לָא דָּחִיל מִתַּתָּא, כְּאַרְיֵה דְּלָא דָּחִיל
מִבְּנֵי עָנָא. אָמַר רִבִּי שִׁמְעוֹן לְרִבִּי אֶלְעָזָר בְּרֵיהּ, אֶלְעָזָר קוּם בְּקִיּוּמָךְ,
וְאֵימָא מִלָּה חַדְתָּא, לְגַבֵּי דְּרִבִּי פִּנְחָס וּשְׁאָר חַבְרַיָּיא.

67. They went. As they were going, they reached the home of Rabbi Pinchas ben Yair. Rabbi Pinchas ben Yair came out, kissed RABBI SHIMON, and said: I have earned the right to kiss the Shechinah. How fortunate is my lot. He set up for them expensive bed sheets. Rabbi Shimon said: The Torah does not require this. He removed THE SPREADS and they sat down. Rabbi Pinchas said: Before we eat, we will hear a discourse from the master of Torah, as all the words of Rabbi Shimon are open as a revelation. He is a man who need not be afraid from above or below of preaching them. He fears not what is above, as the Holy One, blessed be He, agrees with him. He is also not fearful of those below, just as a lion fears not the flock of sheep. Rabbi Shimon said to Rabbi Elazar, his son: Elazar, stand where you are and recite a novel Torah interpretation before Rabbi Pinchas and the other friends.

10. "After the death of the two sons of Aaron"

A Synopsis
We learn from Rabbi Shimon that God wished only Aaron to deal with the sweet incense, for Aaron increased peace in the world; when his sons offered the incense during their father's lifetime, they made a great mistake.

68. קָם ר׳ אֶלְעָזָר פָּתַח וְאָמַר, וַיְדַבֵּר יְיָ׳ אֶל מֹשֶׁה אַחֲרֵי מוֹת שְׁנֵי בְּנֵי אַהֲרֹן וְגוֹ׳. הַאי קְרָא אִית לְאִסְתַּכְּלָא בֵּיה, דְּאִתְחֲזֵי דְּיַתִּירָא אִיהוּ. דְּהָא כְּתִיב בַּתְרֵיה, וַיֹּאמֶר יְיָ׳ אֶל מֹשֶׁה דַּבֵּר אֶל אַהֲרֹן אָחִיךְ. מִכָּאן שֵׁירוּתָא דְּפָרְשָׁתָא, הַאי קְרָא דִּלְעֵילָא, מַאי הוּא, דִּכְתִיב, וַיְדַבֵּר יְיָ׳ אֶל מֹשֶׁה. מַאי הוּא דְּאָמַר לֵיה, וּלְבָתַר וַיֹּאמֶר יְיָ׳ אֶל מֹשֶׁה.

68. Rabbi Elazar rose and opened the discussion saying, "And Hashem spoke to Moses after the death of the two sons of Aaron..." (Vayikra 16:1). This verse needs introspection, for it appears that it is superfluous, as it writes afterwards, "And Hashem said to Moses, Speak to Aaron your brother." Now WE SHOULD ASK, if at the beginning of the portion, in the first verse it says, "And Hashem spoke to Moses," what did He say to him, SEEING THAT afterwards it is written, "And Hashem said to Moses"?

69. אֶלָּא בְּשַׁעֲתָא דְּקוּדְשָׁא בְּרִיךְ הוּא יָהַב קְטֹרֶת בּוּסְמִין לְאַהֲרֹן, בָּעָא, דְּלָא יִשְׁתַּמֵּשׁ בֵּיה בְּחַיָּיוֹי ב״נ אָחֳרָא. מ״ט. בְּגִין דְּאַהֲרֹן אַסְגֵּי שְׁלָמָא בְּעָלְמָא. א״ל קוּדְשָׁא בְּרִיךְ הוּא, אַתְּ בָּעֵי לְאַסְגָּאָה שְׁלָמָא בְּעָלְמָא, עַל יְדָךְ יִסְגֵּי שְׁלָמָא לְעֵילָא, הָא קְטֹרֶת בּוּסְמִין, יְהֵא מָסוּר בִּידָךְ מִכָּאן וּלְהָלְאָה, וּבְחַיֶּיךְ לָא יִשְׁתַּמֵּשׁ בֵּיה ב״נ אָחֳרָא. נָדָב וַאֲבִיהוּא אַקְדִּימוּ בְּחַיֵּי דַּאֲבוּהוֹן, לְאַקְרָבָא מַה דְּלָא אִתְמְסַר לְהוּ. וּמִלָּה דָּא, גָּרִים לְהוֹן דְּטָעוּ בֵּיה.

69. HE ANSWERS: At the time when the Holy One, blessed be He, gave the sweet incense to Aaron, He wanted no one else to deal with this during his lifetime. For what reason? Because Aaron increased peace in the world. The Holy One, blessed be He, said to him: 'Since you wish to increase peace in

the world, peace will multiply above through you. The sweet incense will be transmitted to you from now on, AS INCENSE INCREASES PEACE ABOVE, and during your life, no one else will be permitted to deal with it.' During their father's lifetime, Nadab and Abihu hastened to offer that which was not given to them, and this matter caused them to make a mistake BY OFFERING A FOREIGN FIRE.

70. וְתָאנָא, מֹשֶׁה הֲוָה מְהַרְהֵר, מַאן גָּרַם לוֹן טָעוּתָא דָא, וַהֲוָה עָצִיב. מַה כְּתִיב, וַיְדַבֵּר יְיָ׳ אֶל מֹשֶׁה אַחֲרֵי מוֹת שְׁנֵי בְּנֵי אַהֲרֹן. וּמַה אָמַר לֵיהּ, בְּקָרְבָתָם לִפְנֵי יְיָ׳ וַיָּמוּתוּ. בְּהַקְרִיבָם לָא כְּתִיב, אֶלָּא בְּקָרְבָתָם. א״ל קוּדְשָׁא בְּרִיךְ הוּא לְמֹשֶׁה, דָּא גַּרְמָא לְהוּ, דְּדַחֲקוּ שַׁעֲתָא בְּחַיֵּי אֲבוּהוֹן, וְטָעוּ בָהּ, וְהַיְינוּ דִכְתִיב, אֲשֶׁר לֹא צִוָּה אוֹתָם, אוֹתָם לֹא צִוָּה, אֲבָל לְאַהֲרֹן צִוָּה. וּמַה תְּרֵין בְּנֵי אַהֲרֹן, עַל דְּדָחִיקוּ שַׁעֲתָא בְּחַיֵּי אֲבוּהוֹן גָּרְמוּ לְגַרְמַיְיהוּ כָּל כַּךְ, אֲנָא לְגַבֵּי אַבָּא וְרִבִּי פִּנְחָס וּשְׁאָר חַבְרַיָּיא, עַל אַחַת כַּמָּה וְכַמָּה. אָתָא רִבִּי פִּנְחָס נְשָׁקֵיהּ וּבָרְכֵיהּ.

70. We have learned Moses was pondering who caused them to make this mistake OF OFFERING FOREIGN FIRE, and was sad. It is written, "And Hashem spoke to Moses after the death of the two sons of Aaron." What did He say to him? "When they came near before Hashem, and died" (Vayikra 16:1) It is not written: 'offered', but "came near." The Holy One, blessed be He, said to Moses, 'This is what caused them this, for they hurried the hour TO OFFER INCENSE during the lifetime of their father.' They erred in this, IN OFFERING FOREIGN FIRE, so the verse says, "Which He commanded them not" (Vayikra 10:1). They were not commanded to OFFER, for only Aaron did He command. SO THE EXPLANATION OF THE VERSE, "AND OFFERED FOREIGN FIRE BEFORE HASHEM" (IBID.) IS THAT THEY ERRED IN THIS BECAUSE "HE COMMANDED THEM NOT" TO OFFER INCENSE BUT HE COMMANDED AARON ALONE. And if the two sons of Aaron, by rushing the time during their father's lifetime, brought all this on themselves, this is all the more true for me, in relation to my father and Rabbi Pinchas and the other friends. I AM NOT PERMITTED TO RUSH THE HOUR AND SAY NOVEL TORAH INTERPRETATIONS IN THEIR STEAD. Rabbi Pinchas came forth, and kissed and blessed him.

11. "Sixty valiant men"

A Synopsis

Rabbi Shimon tells us that the name Solomon (Shlomo) refers to Zeir Anpin, to whom the peace (shalom) belongs. We read about Malchut's aspect of harsh judgment and the fire guards and Metatron on whose side is the mighty bright sword and on whose other side are burning coals. The sword is received from the place called 'fear', and night is the time for judgment. We read about the many creature aspects of the flow of Mochin, about the archangels and the crocodiles and the four shapes of the faces that appear. We read about large faces and small faces, about the judgments named hair, and many other wonders. In the end we learn that the priest needs to meditate on sublime matters, to bring holiness to the proper place and to expel the Other Side. If people knew the judgment that could come upon them they would pay more attention to their deeds and stop sinning. We are reminded that God has a covenant with those who study the Torah.

71. רִבִּי שִׁמְעוֹן פָּתַח וְאָמַר, הִנֵּה מִטָּתוֹ שֶׁלִּשְׁלֹמֹה שִׁשִּׁים גִּבּוֹרִים סָבִיב לָהּ וְגוֹ'. הִנֵּה מִטָּתוֹ שֶׁלִּשְׁלֹמֹה, מַאי מִטָּתוֹ. דָּא כּוּרְסֵי יְקָרָא דְּמַלְכָּא, דִּכְתִּיב בֵּיהּ, בָּטַח בָּהּ לֵב בַּעְלָהּ. שֶׁלִּשְׁלֹמֹה, מַלְכָּא דִּי שְׁלָמָא כֹּלָּא דִּילֵיהּ הוּא. שִׁשִּׁים גִּבּוֹרִים סָבִיב לָהּ, דְּאִתְאַחֲדָן בְּסִטְרָהָא מְדִינָא קַשְׁיָא, וְאִקְרוּן, שִׁתִּין פּוּלְסֵי דְּנוּרָא, דְּהַהוּא נַעַר, אִתְלְבַּשׁ בְּהוּ.

71. Rabbi Shimon opened the discussion saying, "Behold the bed of Solomon sixty valiant men are round about it..." (Shir Hashirim 3:7). "Behold the bed of Solomon": What is meant by "his litter"? It refers to the throne of glory of the King, NAMELY MALCHUT CALLED BED. It is written about it, "The heart of her husband safely trusts in her" (Mishlei 31:11) and Solomon (Heb. *Shlomo*) REFERS TO the King that the peace (Heb. *shalom*) is His, REFERRING TO ZEIR ANPIN. "Sixty valiant men are round about it": They are attached to MALCHUT'S aspect of harsh Judgment and are connoted as sixty fire guards, MEANING SIXTY GUARDIANS FROM FIRE. That youth, MEANING METATRON, clothes himself with them.

72. מִימִינֵיהּ, שִׁנָּנָא דְּחַרְבָּא תַּקִּיפָא, מִשְּׂמָאלֵיהּ גּוּמְרֵי דְּנוּרָא תַּקִּיפָא, דְּמִתְאַחֲדָא בְּגְלִיפוֹי, בְּשַׁבְעִין אֶלֶף לַהֲטֵי נוּרָא דְּאַכְלָא, וְאִינּוּן שִׁתִּין

מְזַיְּינֵי זִיּוּנֵי קַשְׁיָין, מֵאִינּוּן גְּבוּרָן תַּקִיפָן, דְּהַהִיא גְּבוּרָה עִלָּאָה דְּקוּדְשָׁא בְּרִיךְ הוּא. הה"ד מִגִּבּוֹרֵי יִשְׂרָאֵל.

72. On the right side OF METATRON is the mighty bright sword, and on the left are strong burning coals that enjoin his imprints with 70,000 flames of consuming fire. They are sixty mighty ones heavily armed with the mighty Gvurot of supernal Gvurah of the Holy One, blessed be He, NAMELY ZEIR ANPIN. This is what is meant by, "Of the mighty ones of Yisrael" (Shir Hashirim 3:7), NAMELY GVURAH OF ZEIR ANPIN REFERRED TO AS YISRAEL.

73. וְתָאנָא, בְּהַאי עַרְסָא, מַה כְּתִיב בָּהּ, וַתָּקָם בְּעוֹד לַיְלָה, כַּד יַנְקָא מִסִּטְרָא דְּדִינָא. וַתִּתֵּן טֶרֶף לְבֵיתָהּ. מַאי טֶרֶף, כד"א וְטָרַף וְאֵין מַצִּיל. הה"ד כֻּלָּם אֲחוּזֵי חֶרֶב מְלוּמְּדֵי מִלְחָמָה, זְמִינִין בְּכָל אֲתַר לְמֶעְבַּד דִּינָא, וְאִקְרוּן מָארֵי דִיבָבָא וִילָלָה.

73. We have learned that this bed, REFERRING TO MALCHUT, it is written regarding it, "She rises also while it is yet night" (Mishlei 31:15). When she nurtures from the side of Judgment, MEANING WHEN MALCHUT RISES TO POUR THE ABUNDANCE OF THE ILLUMINATION OF CHOCHMAH, IT IS NIGHT, MEANING JUDGMENT, SINCE HER CHOCHMAH IS GIVEN ONLY WITH JUDGMENTS. AS EARLIER MENTIONED, "RISING" REFERS TO THE ILLUMINATION OF CHOCHMAH. "And gives food (Heb. *teref*) to her household" (Ibid.): What is meant by "*teref*"? It is the same as in, "And tears down (Heb. *taraf*) in pieces, and none can deliver" (Michah 5:7), NAMELY THE JUDGMENTS ATTACHED TO THIS CHOCHMAH FROM WHICH THERE IS NO SAVING. This is what is meant by, "All girt with swords, and expert in war" (Shir Hashirim 3:8). They are ready to execute Judgment everywhere and are called wailers and moaners.

74. אִישׁ חַרְבּוֹ עַל יְרֵכוֹ. כד"א, חֲגוֹר חַרְבְּךָ עַל יָרֵךְ גִּבּוֹר. מִפַּחַד בַּלֵּילוֹת. הָא אוּקְמוּהָ, מִפַּחְדָּהּ דְּגֵיהִנָּם וְכוּ' אֲבָל מִפַּחַד בַּלֵּילוֹת, כְּלוֹמַר, כָּל דָּא מָאן אֲתַר נַטְלִין, מֵהַהוּא אֲתַר דְּאִקְרֵי פַּחַד, כד"א וּפַחַד יִצְחָק הָיָה לִי. וַיִּשָּׁבַע יַעֲקֹב בְּפַחַד אָבִיו יִצְחָק. בַּלֵּילוֹת, בְּזִמְנִין דְּאִינּוּן מִתְפַּקְּדִין לְמֶעְבַּד דִּינָא.

74. "Every man has his sword upon his thigh" (Ibid.): It is as you say, "Gird your sword upon your thigh, O mighty one" (Tehilim 45:4). THE SECRET MEANING OF THE SWORD HAS ALREADY BEEN EXPLAINED, "because of the fear by nights" (Shir Hashirim 3:8), they explained it as the fear of Gehenom. Yet, "because of the fear by nights" is saying where they receive it from – from fear, from the place called fear, as the verse says, "And the fear of Isaac, had been with me" (Beresheet 31:42), WHICH IS GVURAH OF ZEIR ANPIN, THE LEFT COLUMN KNOWN AS ISAAC. Just as this verse reads, "And Jacob swore by the fear of his father Isaac" (Ibid. 53), "by nights" REFERS TO those times designated for Judgments to be done, AS NIGHT IS THE TIME FOR JUDGMENT.

75. וְתָאנָא, כְּתִיב זָמְמָה שָׂדֶה וַתִּקָּחֵהוּ. הה"ד, וְכָל חַיַּת הַשָּׂדֶה יְשַׂחֲקוּ שָׁם. וְעַל דָּא כְּתִיב, זֶה הַיָּם גָּדוֹל וּרְחַב יָדַיִם וְגוֹ' שָׁם אֳנִיּוֹת יְהַלֵּכוּן וְגוֹ' כד"א. הָיְתָה כָּאֳנִיּוֹת סוֹחֵר מִמֶּרְחָק תָּבִיא לַחְמָהּ. מִמֶּרְחָק וַדַּאי. מֵרֵישָׁא דְמוֹחָא, וּמֵעֵילָא דְּרֵישָׁא, תָּבִיא לַחְמָהּ. עַל יְדָא דְּצַדִּיק, כַּד מִזְדַּוְּוגָן כְּחַד, כְּדֵין חֵידוּ בְּכֹלָּא. הה"ד, לִוְיָתָן זֶה יָצַרְתָּ לְשַׂחֶק בּוֹ.

75. We have learned that it is written, "She considers a field, and buys it" (Mishlei 31:16). This is like what is written, "Where all the wild beasts (lit. 'beasts of the field') play" (Iyov 40:20), WHICH REFERS TO THE ASPECT OF JUDGMENT OF MALCHUT, WHOSE SECRET IS NIGHT AS MENTIONED EARLIER, AND IS ALSO REFERRED TO AS FIELD. "THE WILD BEASTS" REFLECTS THE SECRET OF YESOD, AND "PLAY" REFERS TO MATING, and about this is written, "So is this great and wide sea...There go the ships; there are the Leviathan, whom You have made to play therein" (Tehilim 104:25-26). LEVIATHAN IS THE SECRET OF YESOD, "TO PLAY" ALLUDES TO UNION, AS IT IS WRITTEN, "AND, BEHOLD, ISAAC WAS SPORTING WITH HIS WIFE" (BERESHEET 26:8). This is as the verse, "She is like the merchant ships: she brings her bread from afar" (Mishlei 31:14); "from afar" surely. FOR "HER BREAD," WHICH IS THE SECRET ILLUMINATION OF CHOCHMAH, DOES NOT SHED LIGHT SAVE FROM "AFAR," MEANING IT DOES SO WITH JUDGMENTS THAT REMOVE THE EXTERNAL FORCES FAR AWAY SO THEY WOULD NOT NURTURE FROM THIS GREAT LIGHT. THIS IS THE SECRET OF, "HASHEM APPEARED TO ME FROM AFAR" (YIRMEYAH 31:2). AND THE SECRET OF THE UNION PERTAINS TO NIGHT AND TO THE FIELD, AS MENTIONED EARLIER, AS IT BRINGS HER LIGHT from the brain

inside the head, NAMELY CHOCHMAH, and from that which is above the head, NAMELY THE BLESSED ENDLESS LIGHT. THEREFORE, SHE NEEDS PROTECTION FROM EXTERNAL FORCES. "She brings her bread," NAMELY through the means of the righteous man, DENOTING YESOD. When they join together, there is universal joy. This is the meaning of the verse, "There are the dolphins (Heb. *Leviathan*) who you have made to play therein," THE LEVIATHAN BEING YESOD, WHILE "TO PLAY" REFERS TO MATING, AS EARLIER MENTIONED.

76. תָּאנָא, אֶלֶף וַחֲמֵשׁ מְאָה, מָארֵי תְּרִיסִין, מָארֵי דְשׁוּלְטָנוּתָא, אִתְאַחֲדָן מֵהַאי סִטְרָא, דְּאִינּוּן גִּיבָּרִין. בִּידוֹי דְּהַהוּא דְּאִקְרֵי נַעַר, אַרְבַּע מַפְתְּחִין רַבְרְבָן. תַּנִּינַיָּיא אַזְלִין תְּחוֹת סְפִינָה, דְּהָא יַמָּא רַבָּא, לְאַרְבַּע זְוְיָין. דָּא אָזִיל לְסִטְרָא דָא, וְדָא אָזִיל לְסִטְרָא דָא. וְכֵן כֻּלְּהוּ. אַרְבַּע חֵיוּוּ דְאַנְפִּין אִתְחַזְיָין בְּהוּ, וְכַד אִתְכְּלִילָן בְּחַד, כְּתִיב, וּדְמוּת פְּנֵיהֶם פְּנֵי אָדָם, פְּנֵיהֶם דְּכֹלָּא.

76. We have learned that 1,500 sword-bearers wielding authority are linked to the side of these SIXTY mighty ones. In the hands of the one known as the youth, NAMELY METATRON, are four large keys, REFERRING TO FOUR ANGELS – MICHAEL, GABRIEL, URIEL AND REPHAEL. THEY ARE REFERRED TO AS LARGE KEYS, BECAUSE THEY CAUSE THE MOCHIN OF GREATNESS TO FLOW TO THOSE BELOW. Crocodiles, NAMELY THE GRADES OF CHOCHMAH, move under the ship, WHICH IS MALCHUT, THAT IS, IN BRIYAH, of the great sea, BINAH, FROM WHICH MALCHUT RECEIVES HER LIGHT, to HER four corners. The one moves to this side, SOUTH, and the other moves to this side, NORTH, and it is so with all of them, ALSO EASTWARD AND WESTWARD, WHICH ARE THE SECRET OF CHESED, GVURAH, TIFERET AND MALCHUT. The four shapes of the face appear in them, MEANING IN THESE CROCODILES, AND ARE LION, OX, EAGLE AND MAN, FOR THEY ARE DRAWN FROM THE THREE COLUMNS AND MALCHUT THAT RECEIVES THEM, WHICH IS THE FACE OF A MAN. When they are joined within the one WHICH IS MALCHUT, it is written, "As for the likeness of their faces, they had the face of a man" (Yechezkel 1:10). THIS MEANS the face of all of them, NAMELY THE THREE SHAPES OF LION, OX, EAGLE, RECEIVES A HUMAN FACE LIKE MALCHUT WHEN ALL ARE INCLUDED IN IT.

77. אַפֵּי רַבְרְבֵי, וְאַפֵּי זוּטְרֵי, כְּלִילָן כְּחַד לְעֵילָא, תְּרֵי סַלְקִין וְשָׁאטִין, וּתְרֵין מַגְרוֹפִין בִּידַיְיהוּ. אֶלֶף טוּרִין סַלְקִין וְעָאלִין בְּכָל יוֹמָא, מִשַּׁקְיוּ דְּהַהוּא יַמָּא, לְבָתַר, אִתְעֲקָרוּ מִנָּהּ, וְסַלְקִין לְיַמָּא אָחֳרָא.

77. Large faces REPRESENT THE MOCHIN OF GREATNESS and small faces, MEANING MOCHIN OF SMALLNESS, join together above, IN ZEIR ANPIN AND MALCHUT. Two, MEANING THE TWO COLUMNS – RIGHT AND CENTRAL – rise and wander with two shovels in their hands. A thousand mountains rise and arrive daily TO DRAW NOURISHMENT from the potions of that sea, NAMELY BINAH, AS THE LIGHT OF CHOCHMAH ALSO KNOWN AS A THOUSAND MOUNTAINS IS DRAWN THROUGH BINAH ALONE. Afterwards, they are pulled away from it, FROM BINAH, and move into the other sea, NAMELY MALCHUT.

78. לֵית חוּשְׁבָּנָא לְאִינוּן דְּאִתְאַחֲדָן בְּשַׂעֲרָתָא, תְּרֵין בְּנִין יַנְקִין כָּל יוֹמָא, דְּאִקְרוּן מְאַלְּלֵי אַרְעָא. וְדָא הוּא רָזָא דְּסִפְרָא דִּצְנִיעוּתָא, דִּכְתִיב, וַיִּשְׁלַח יְהוֹשֻׁעַ בֶּן נוּן מִן הַשִּׁטִּים שְׁנַיִם אֲנָשִׁים מְרַגְּלִים חֶרֶשׁ לֵאמֹר. וְאִלֵּין, יַנְקִין מִתְּחוֹת סִטְרֵי אֶבְרָהָא, תְּרֵין בְּנָות בִּתְחוֹת רַגְלָהָא, וְעַל דָּא כְּתִיב, וַיִּרְאוּ בְּנֵי הָאֱלֹהִים אֶת בְּנוֹת הָאָדָם. וְאִלֵּין מִתְאַחֲדָן בְּטוּפְרֵי דְּהַהִיא עַרְסָא, וְדָא הוּא דְּתָנֵינָן, דִּכְתִיב, אָז תָּבֹאנָה שְׁתַּיִם נָשִׁים זוֹנוֹת אֶל הַמֶּלֶךְ. אָז תָּבֹאנָה, וְלָא מִקַּדְמַת דְּנָא, וּבְזִמְנָא דְּיִשְׂרָאֵל לְתַתָּא, אַהֲדְרוּן קָדָל מִבָּתַר קוּדְשָׁא בְּרִיךְ הוּא, מַאי כְּתִיב, עַמִּי נוֹגְשָׂיו מְעוֹלֵל וְנָשִׁים מָשְׁלוּ בוֹ. וַדַּאי.

78. There is no count to those holding on to the hair OF MALCHUT, MEANING THE JUDGMENTS THEREIN NAMED HAIR. Two sons suckle daily FROM MALCHUT called the spies of the earth and this is the secret written in the Hidden Book (Heb. Safra Det'zeniuta) AT THE END OF TRUMAH, "And Joshua the son of Nun sent out of Shitim two men to spy secretly, saying" (Yehoshua 2:1). These TWO SONS nurturing from under the sides of the wings OF MALCHUT ARE THE SECRET OF CHESED AND GVURAH. Now two daughters, WHOSE SECRET IS TWO HARLOTS, are under the feet OF MALCHUT, MEANING NETZACH AND HOD OF MALCHUT. Therefore, it is written ABOUT THEM, "And the sons of Elohim saw the daughters of men"

(Beresheet 6:2). They, THE SONS AND DAUGHTERS OF THE KLIPAH, hold on to the nails of that bed, NAMELY MALCHUT, AS HER NAILS MEAN THE BACK PART OF THE FINGERS OF THE HANDS AND FEET. This is what the verse teaches us, "Then came there two women, that were harlots, to the king" (I Melachim 3:16), "Then came" but not before. And when Yisrael are down, turning their backs on the Holy One, blessed be He, it is written, "As for My people, children are their oppressors, and women rule over them" (Yeshayah 3:12), surely REFERRING TO THE TWO WOMEN MENTIONED ABOVE.

79. בִּידָא שְׂמָאלָא, שַׁבְעִין עַנְפִין, דְּמִגַּדְּלִין בֵּין נוּנֵי יַמָּא, כֻּלְּהוּ סוּמָקֵי כְּווֹרְדָּא. וְעֵילָא מִנְהוֹן, עַנְפָּא חַד סוּמָקָא יַתִּיר, דָּא סָלִיק וְנָחִית. וְכֻלְּהוּ אִתְחַפְיָין בְּשַׂעֲרָהָא.

79. In the left hand, MEANING FROM THE LEFT COLUMN OF MALCHUT, seventy branches COME OUT, WHO ARE THE SEVENTY CHIEFTAINS OF THE WORLD NATIONS, who are raised among the fish of the sea, REPRESENTING THE LEVELS OF THE ILLUMINATION OF CHOCHMAH OF THE LEFT, REFERRED TO AS FISH. THE SEA MEANS MALCHUT. All of them are red like a rose, BECAUSE OF THE JUDGMENTS WITHIN THEM, AS THE JUDGMENTS OF THE LEFT ARE RED. Above them, one branch is extremely red. THAT IS THE HARSHEST JUDGMENT OF ALL, NAMELY SAMAEL. It goes up and down, MEANING ATTRACTS CHOCHMAH FROM ABOVE DOWNWARD. IT IS HE WHO RODE ON THE SERPENT AND ENTICED ADAM TO DRAW CHOCHMAH FROM ABOVE DOWNWARD, WHICH IS THE SECRET OF THE TREE OF KNOWLEDGE OF GOOD AND EVIL. All of them are covered with hair OF MALCHUT, MEANING HER JUDGMENTS REFFERED TO AS HAIRS.

80. מָארֵי דְּלִישָׁנָא בִּישָׁא. כַּד נָחִית חִוְיָא. אִתְעָבֵיד מְקַפֵּץ עַל טוּרִין, מְדַלְגָא עַל טְנָרֵי. עַד דְּיִשְׁכַּח טַרְפָּא, דְּאָחִיד בְּטוּפְרֵי וְיֵיכוּל. כְּדֵין שָׁכִיךְ, וְאִתְחַזָר לִישַׁנֵיה לְטָב. זַכָּאִין אִינּוּן יִשְׂרָאֵל, דִּמְזַמְּנִין לֵיה טַרְפֵּיה. אַהֲדָר לְאַתְרֵיה, עַיֵיל בְּנוּקְבָּא דִּתְהוֹמָא רַבָּא.

80. When the chief slanderer, THE SERPENT, descends, it begins to jump over the hills and skip over the mountains until there is prey seized by the

nails, which it eats. Then it becomes calm and its tongue speaks well, MEANING THAT ITS SLANDERING TALK ENDS AND BECOMES GOOD TALK. Fortunate are Yisrael who prepare food for it, and THE SERPENT returns to its place and enters the hole of the great abyss.

81. כַּד סַלְקִין מָארֵי דְרוֹמְחִין וְסַיְיפִין, דְּלֵית לוֹן חוּשְׁבָּנָא, סוֹחֲרָנַיְיהוּ דְּאִינּוּן שִׁתִּין עִלָּאִין, דְּסוּחֲרָנֵיה דְּהַאי עַרְסָא, אֶלֶף אַלְפִין, וְרִבּוֹא רִבְוָון, קַיְימִין בְּכָל סִטְרָא דְּהַאי עַרְסָא לְעֵילָּא. וּמִנֵּיה אִתְזָנָן, כֻּלְּהוּ מְקַמֵיה יְקוּמוּן.

81. When the countless spearmen and swordsmen rise around these supernal sixty MIGHTY MEN THAT STEM FROM THE LEFT COLUMN, who circle the bed, NAMELY MALCHUT, AND THE LEFT JOINS THE RIGHT BECAUSE OF THEM, THEN thousands upon thousands and tens of ten thousands stand along all sides of THAT supernal bed. From it, THE BED WHICH IS MALCHUT, they are sustained and all rise in its presence, IN ACCORDANCE WITH THE VERSE, "SHE RISES ALSO WHILE IT IS YET NIGHT" (MISHLEI 31:15).

82. מִתְּחוֹת כֻּלְּהוּ, נָפְקִין כַּמָּה אֶלֶף וְרִבְבָן, דְּלֵית לוֹן חוּשְׁבָּנָא, וְנַחְתִּין וְשָׁאטִין בְּעָלְמָא, עַד דְּתַקְעֵי מָארֵי שׁוֹפָרָא, וּמִתְכַּנְּשֵׁי. וְהָנֵי בְּזוּהֲמָא דְטוּפְרֵי אֲחִידָן.

82. Underneath all of them, MEANING BELOW ALL LEVELS OF HOLINESS MENTIONED BEFORE, many thousands and tens of thousands OF KLIPOT come out, IN ACCORDANCE WITH THE SECRET MEANING OF THE VERSE, "A THOUSAND SHALL FALL AT YOUR SIDE, AND TEN THOUSAND AT YOUR RIGHT HAND: BUT IT SHALL NOT COME NEAR YOU" (TEHILIM 91:7). They come down and wander through the world until the Shofar blowers blow, THAT IS THE SECRET OF UNITY OF THE THREE COLUMNS – KNOWN AS FIRE, WATER AND AIR – THAT ARE INCLUDED IN THE SOUND EMANATING FROM THE SHOFAR. Then they reassemble and hold to the scum found in the nails, NAMELY IN THE REFUSE MATTER OF THE ILLUMINATION OF THE BACK SIDE KNOWN AS NAILS, AS MENTIONED ABOVE.

83. דָּא עַרְסָא כָּלִיל לוֹן, דָּא עַרְסָא, רַגְלוֹהִי אֲחִידָן בְּאַרְבַּע סִטְרֵי

עָלְמָא, כֹּלָא עָאלִין בִּכְלָלָא, דְּאִשְׁתְּכַח לְעֵילָא, וְאִשְׁתְּכַח לְתַתָּא, בַּשָּׁמַיִם מִמַּעַל, וְעַל הָאָרֶץ מִתָּחַת, וְעַל דָּא כְּתִיב הִנֵּה. מַאי הִנֵּה. בְּגִין דִּזְמִינָא לְכֹלָא לְעֵילָא וְתַתָּא. וּרְשׁוּמָא הַאי עַרְסָא מִכֹּלָא, אֲדֹנָ"י אִתְקְרֵי, רִבּוֹנָא דְּכֹלָא, רְשִׁימָא בֵּין חַיָּילָהָא.

83. This bed, NAMELY MALCHUT, includes them, NAMELY ALL THOSE LEVELS MENTIONED ABOVE. This bed's legs link to the four directions of the world, MEANING IT CONTAINS IN IT THE FOUR SFIROT OF CHESED, GVURAH, TIFERET AND MALCHUT – WHICH IS THE SECRET OF THREE COLUMNS AND MALCHUT THAT RECEIVES THEM. Everything is counted, BOTH what there is above, NAMELY THE GRADES OF ZEIR ANPIN, AND what is below, NAMELY HER OWN GRADES. THIS IS THE SECRET OF "in heaven above," NAMELY ZEIR ANPIN, "and upon the earth beneath" (Devarim 4:39), NAMELY MALCHUT, KNOWN AS EARTH. Therefore, it is written, "Behold," MEANING "BEHOLD THE BED OF SOLOMON." What is meant by "Behold"? It means it is ready TO SHED LIGHT to all above and below, and this bed is impressed by all. It is called Adonai, which means master (Heb. *adon*) over all, marked among its armies.

84. בְּג"כ, כַּהֲנָא בָּעֵי לְכַוְּונָא מִלֵּי דִּלְעֵילָא, לְיַחֲדָא שְׁמָא קַדִּישָׁא מֵאֲתַר דְּבָעֵי לְיַחֲדָא, וְעַל דָּא תָּנֵינָן, כְּתִיב, בְּזֹאת יָבֹא אַהֲרֹן אֶל הַקֹּדֶשׁ, בְּהַאי בָּעֵי לְקָרְבָא קְדוּשָׁה לְאַתְרֵיהּ, מֵהַאי אֲתַר, בָּעֵי בַּר נָשׁ לְדַחֲלָא מִקַּמֵּי קוּדְשָׁא בְּרִיךְ הוּא. וְעַל דָּא כְּתִיב, לוּ חָכְמוּ יַשְׂכִּילוּ זֹאת מִיַּד יָבִינוּ לְאַחֲרִיתָם. כְּלוֹמַר, אִי יִסְתַּכְּלוּן בְּנֵי נָשָׁא בְּעוֹנְשָׁא, הֵיךְ אֲחִידַת זֹאת בֵּין חַיָּילָהָא, וְהֵיךְ אִתְמַנוּ קַמָּהּ כָּל אִינוּן בְּנֵי חַיָּילִין, וַאֲחִידָן בְּפוּלְחָנָא לְאִתְפָּרְעָא מִן חַיָּיבַיָּא, מִיַּד יָבִינוּ לְאַחֲרִיתָם, וְיִסְתַּמְּרוּן עוֹבָדֵיהוֹן, וְלָא יְחוּבוּן קַמֵּי מַלְכָּא קַדִּישָׁא.

84. Because of this, the priest needs to meditate upon sublime matters, to unify the Holy Name from that place that requires unity, MEANING TO DRAW IN THE ILLUMINATION OF CHOCHMAH ONLY TO MALCHUT. Therefore, we learned that it is written, "Thus (with *zot*) shall Aaron come into the holy place" (Vayikra 16:3). Through *zot*, DENOTING MALCHUT, he needs to bring holiness near its place AND TO EXPEL THE OTHER SIDE,

WHICH DESIRES TO DRAW FROM HER THE ILLUMINATION OF CHOCHMAH
FROM ABOVE DOWNWARD. From this place, FROM MALCHUT, man needs
to fear the Holy One, blessed be He, MEANING THAT WITH THE
ILLUMINATION OF CHOCHMAH THAT IS REVEALED AT MALCHUT HARSH
JUDGMENTS THAT PUNISH THE WICKED AND MOVE THE OTHER SIDE
FAR AWAY ARE ALSO REVEALED. AS A RESULT, ONE FEARS HER. About
this, it is written, "O that they were wise, that they understood this (Heb.
zot)" (Devarim 32:29). Immediately, "they would consider their latter end"
(Ibid.). This means that if people would look at the penalty AND SEE how
ZOT, NAMELY MALCHUT, is united together with her hosts, MEANING SHE
GIVES LIGHT TO THEM ONLY FROM THE ASPECT OF BELOW UPWARDS,
and how all these members of the hosts, who are attached to her to serve her
were appointed before her to punish and repay the wicked, WHO WISH TO
DRAW DOWN HER LIGHT FROM ABOVE DOWNWARDS, immediately "they
will understand their latter end" and pay attention to their deeds and not sin
before the Holy King.

85. תּוּ אָמַר ר"ש, כָּל ב"נ דְּזָכֵי לְמֵילַף אוֹרַיְיתָא, וְנָטִיל לָהּ לְהַאי
זֹאת. הַאי זֹאת נְטִירַת לֵיהּ, וְגָזַר עִמֵּיהּ קַיָּימָא עַל קַיָּימָא דִּילֵיהּ, דְּלָא
יִתְעֲדֵי מִנֵּיהּ, וּמִן בְּנוֹהִי וּמִן בְּנֵי בְּנוֹהִי לְעָלְמִין. הה"ד, וַאֲנִי זֹאת
בְּרִיתִי אוֹתָם וְגוֹ'. יָתְבוּ לְמֵיכַל. עַד דְּאָכְלוּ, אר"ש לְחַבְרַיָּיא, כָּל חַד
וְחַד לֵימָא מִלָּה חַדְתָּא דְּאוֹרַיְיתָא. עַל פָּתוֹרָא, לְקַמֵּיהּ דר' פִּנְחָס.

85. Rabbi Shimon said further, this *Zot* keeps everyone who merits to learn
Torah and keep *Zot*, NAMELY MALCHUT, and makes another covenant with
him, in addition to the existing covenant, that she will not part from him,
from his children or grandchildren eternally. This is the meaning of the
verse, "As for me, this is My covenant with them..." (Yeshayah 59:21).
They sat down to eat. As they were eating, Rabbi Shimon said to his friends:
Each one of you should say some new thoughts of the Torah at the table in
the presence of Rabbi Pinchas.

12. "The tongue of the learned"

A Synopsis

Rabbi Chizkiyah tells us how lucky Yisrael are that God chose them for His own and called them holy, and that it was because they merited the Torah. We read about the flow of holiness or Chochmah from the highest all the way to Malchut, and that when the secrets of Torah come out of her she is called 'the holy tongue'. We then learn of the flow that results in 'the tongue of the learned' that goes out to awaken the sublime holy ones. God gave this tongue to Rabbi Shimon and raised him higher and higher to the upper worlds.

86. פָּתַח ר' חִזְקִיָּה וְאָמַר, יְיָ' אֱלֹהִים נָתַן לִי לְשׁוֹן לִמּוּדִים לָדַעַת לָעוּת אֶת יָעֵף דָּבָר וְגוֹ'. זַכָּאִין אִינּוּן יִשְׂרָאֵל, דְּקוּדְשָׁא בְּרִיךְ הוּא אִתְרְעֵי בְּהוּ מִכָּל שְׁאָר עַמִּין, וּקְרָאָן, קֹדֶשׁ. דִּכְתִּיב. קֹדֶשׁ יִשְׂרָאֵל לַיְיָ'. וְיָהִיב לְהוּ חוּלָק, לְאִתְאַחֲדָא בִּשְׁמָא קַדִּישָׁא. וּבְמָה אֲחִידוּ יִשְׂרָאֵל בִּשְׁמָא קַדִּישָׁא. בְּגִין דְּזָכוּ בְּאוֹרַיְיתָא, דְּכָל מַאן דְּזָכֵי בְּאוֹרַיְיתָא זָכֵי בֵּיהּ בְּקוּדְשָׁא בְּרִיךְ הוּא.

86. Rabbi Chizkiyah opened the discussion saying, "Hashem Elohim has given me the tongue of the learned, that I should know to sustain him that weary" (Yeshayah 50:4). How fortunate are Yisrael that the Holy One, blessed be He, chose them from among all nations and called them "holy," as is written, "Yisrael is holy to Hashem" (Yirmeyah 2:3). He gave them a share to maintain the Holy Name. With what right can they hold on to the Holy Name? It is because they merited the Torah, as anyone who merits Torah merits his portion in the Holy One, blessed be He.

87. וְתָנֵינָן קַמֵּיהּ דְּמַר, מַאי קֹדֶשׁ. שְׁלִימוּתָא דְּכֹלָּא דְּאִקְרֵי חָכְמָה עִלָּאָה, וּמֵהַאי אֲתַר נָגִיד מְשַׁח רְבוּת קַדִּישָׁא בִּשְׁבִילִין יְדִיעָן, לַאֲתַר דְּאִקְרֵי בִּינָה עִלָּאָה, וּמִתַּמָּן נַפְקִין מְבוּעִין וְנַחֲלִין לְכָל עֵבֶר, עַד דְּמָטוּ לְהַאי זֹאת. וְהַאי זֹאת כַּד מִתְבָּרְכָא, אִקְרֵי קֹדֶשׁ, וְאִקְרֵי חָכְמָה, וּקְרָאן לֵיהּ רוּחַ הַקֹּדֶשׁ. כְּלוֹמַר, רוּחַ, מֵהַהוּא קֹדֶשׁ דִּלְעֵילָּא. וְכַד נַפְקִין וּמִתְעָרִין מִנֵּהּ רָזֵי אוֹרַיְיתָא, כְּדֵין אִתְקְרֵי לְשׁוֹן הַקֹּדֶשׁ.

87. We have learned before my master what is Holiness – It is perfection of all called the highly sublime Chochmah, WHICH IS THE SECRET OF SUPERNAL ABA AND IMA. From this place flows the holy anointing oil through known paths to the place called supernal Binah, THE SECRET OF YISRAEL–SABA AND TEVUNAH. From there flow streams and fountains in every direction, MEANING BOTH TO CHOCHMAH AND TO CHASSADIM until they reach this *zot* (Eng. 'this'), NAMELY MALCHUT. When blessed, this *zot* is called holiness and is called Chochmah and we call her the Spirit of the Holiness, meaning spirit, NAMELY THE SIX ENDS, from this holiness of higher above, MEANING THE SIX EXTREMITIES OF CHOCHMAH. When the secrets of Torah exit and stir from her, she is then called 'the holy tongue'.

88. וּבְשַׁעֲתָא דְּנָגִיד הַהוּא רְבוּת קַדִּישָׁא, לְאִינּוּן תְּרֵי קַיְימִין, דְּאִקְרוּן לְמוּדֵי ה', וְאִקְרוּן צְבָאוֹת, אִתְכְּנַשׁ תַּמָּן, וְכַד נָפִיק מִתַּמָּן, בְּהַהוּא דַּרְגָּא דְּאִקְרֵי יְסוֹד, לְהַהוּא חָכְמָה זְעֵירָא, כְּדֵין אִתְקְרֵי לָשׁוֹן לִמּוּדִים. וְנָפִיק לְאִתְּעָרָא לְאִינּוּן קַדִּישֵׁי עֶלְיוֹנִים. כְּדֵין כְּתִיב, יְיָ' אֱלֹהִים נָתַן לִי לְשׁוֹן לִמּוּדִים. וְלָמָּה. לָדַעַת לָעוּת אֶת יָעֵף דָּבָר. וְקוּדְשָׁא בְּרִיךְ הוּא יָהִיב הַאי לְבוּצִינָא קַדִּישָׁא, ר"ש. וְעוֹד דְּסָלִיק לֵיהּ לְעֵילָּא, לְעֵילָּא בְּג"כ, כָּל מִלּוֹי בְּאִתְגַּלְּיָיא אִתְּמָרוּ, וְלָא אִתְכַּסְיָין. עֲלֵיהּ כְּתִיב, פֶּה אֶל פֶּה אֲדַבֶּר בּוֹ וּמַרְאֶה וְלֹא בְחִידוֹת.

88. When the anointing oil flows to these two pillars, referred to as "students of Hashem" (Yeshayah 54:13), and are called Tzevaot, NAMELY NETZACH AND HOD, it gathers there. When it exits from there through that level called Yesod AND ARRIVES at the smaller Chochmah THAT IS MALCHUT, KNOWN AS THE SMALL CHOCHMAH BECAUSE IT CONTAINS ONLY SIX CORNERS OF CHOCHMAH AS EXPLAINED EARLIER, it is called the 'tongue of the learned'. FROM HER, it goes out to awaken the sublime holy beings. At that point, it is written, "Hashem Elohim has given me the tongue of the learned." Why? "That I should know how to sustain him that weary." The Holy One, blessed be He, gave this to the holy luminary, Rabbi Shimon. Furthermore, he raised him higher and higher TO UPPER WORLDS. For this reason, all his words are said manifestly, and are not concealed. About him, it is written, "With him I speak mouth to mouth, manifestly, and not in dark speeches" (Bemidbar 12:8).

13. The moon in its fullness

A Synopsis

Rabbi Yesa says that during Solomon's days the moon was full, and God gave wisdom and knowledge to Solomon. Reading that there was peace between Solomon and Hiram, Rabbi Shimon says that Hiram had announced himself to be a deity until Solomon persuaded him otherwise with his wisdom. We learn that all those who study the Torah at night have their images carved above before God, who pays attention to them.

89. פָּתַח רְבִּי יֵיסָא וְאָמַר, וַיְיָ' נָתַן חָכְמָה לִשְׁלֹמֹה כַּאֲשֶׁר דִּבֶּר לוֹ וַיְהִי שָׁלוֹם בֵּין חִירָם וּבֵין שְׁלֹמֹה וְגוֹ'. וַיְיָ' נָתַן חָכְמָה לִשְׁלֹמֹה, דָּא הוּא דְּתָנֵינָן, בְּיוֹמֵי דִּשְׁלֹמֹה מַלְכָּא, קַיְימָא סִיהֲרָא בְּאַשְׁלָמוּתָא, כַּאֲשֶׁר דִּבֶּר לוֹ, כְּמָה דְּאִתְּמַר לֵיהּ, הַחָכְמָה וְהַמַּדָּע נָתוּן לָךְ.

89. Rabbi Yesa opened the discussion saying, "And Hashem gave Solomon wisdom, as he promised him: and there was peace between Hiram and Solomon..." (I Melachim 5:26). "And Hashem gave Solomon wisdom": This is what we learned that during the days of King Solomon, the moon, DENOTING MALCHUT, remained in its fullness; THEN MALCHUT IS CALLED CHOCHMAH, AS MENTIONED. And He gave it to Solomon "as he promised him," MEANING as was said to him, "Wisdom and knowledge are granted to you" (II Divrei Hayamim 1:12).

90. וַיְהִי שָׁלוֹם בֵּין חִירָם וּבֵין שְׁלֹמֹה. וְכִי מַה בֵּין הַאי לְהַאי. אֶלָּא הָכִי תָּנֵינָן, וַיְיָ' נָתַן חָכְמָה לִשְׁלֹמֹה. וְהַאי חָכְמָה בְּמַאי אוֹקִים לָהּ. אָמַר ר' יוֹסֵי, אוֹקִים לָהּ בְּהַאי, דִּשְׁלֹמֹה עֲבַד דְּנָחִית לְחִירָם מֵהַהוּא דַּרְגָּא, דַּהֲוָה אָמַר, מוֹשַׁב אֱלֹהִים יָשַׁבְתִּי וְגוֹ', דְּתַנְיָא, חִירָם מֶלֶךְ צוֹר עֲבַד גַּרְמֵיהּ אֱלוֹהַּ. בָּתַר דִּשְׁלֹמֹה אָתָא, עֲבַד לֵיהּ בְּחָכְמָתֵיהּ, דְּנָחִית מֵהַהוּא עֵיטָא, וְאוֹדֵי לֵיהּ לִשְׁלֹמֹה. ובג"כ, וַיְהִי שָׁלוֹם בֵּין חִירָם וּבֵין שְׁלֹמֹה.

90. "And there was peace between Hiram and Solomon": HE ASKS: What is THE CONNECTION between them? HE ANSWERS: We have learned that

"Hashem gave Solomon wisdom." How did he establish this wisdom? Rabbi Yosi said: This is how he established this wisdom. Solomon caused Hiram to descend from that level where he said, "I sit in the seat of Elohim" (Yechezkel 28:2). We have learned that Hiram, King of Tyre, announced himself a deity, MEANING HE WAS DEVOTED TO OTHER ELOHIM WHO DRAW CHOCHMAH FROM ABOVE DOWNWARD, AS MENTIONED, AND BEHAVED LIKE THEM. Afterwards, SOLOMON came and, with his wisdom, caused Hiram to depart from this counsel OF OTHER ELOHIM. Thus, he thanked Solomon for this. For this reason, "there was peace between Hiram and Solomon."

91. וְתָנֵינָן, א״ר יִצְחָק א״ר יְהוּדָה, דְּשָׁדַר לֵיהּ, חַד שֵׁידָא, וְנָחִית לְיַד שִׁבְעָה מָדוֹרִין דְּגֵיהִנָּם וְסַלְקֵיהּ, וְשָׁדַר לֵיהּ פִּתְקִין בְּכָל יוֹמָא וְיוֹמָא בִּידֵיהּ, עַד דְּאָהֲדַר, וְאוֹדֵי לֵיהּ לִשְׁלֹמֹה. וְתָנֵינָן. שְׁלֹמֹה יָרִית לָהּ לְסִיהֲרָא, בְּכָל סִטְרוֹי. בְּג״כ, בְּכֹלָּא שַׁלִּיט בְּחָכְמָתֵיהּ. וְר״ש בֶּן יוֹחַאי, שַׁלִּיט בְּחָכְמָתֵיהּ עַל כָּל בְּנֵי עָלְמָא, כָּל אִינּוּן דְּסַלְּקִין בְּדַרְגּוֹי, לָא סַלְּקִין אֶלָּא לְאַשְׁלְמָא עִמֵּיהּ.

91. We have learned that Rabbi Yitzchak said in the name of Rabbi Yehuda: SOLOMON sent TO HIRAM a demon that lowered him to the seven chambers of Gehenom, and then raised him up. Then, he sent him letters daily until he repented FROM HIS DEEDS, and thanked Solomon ABOUT THIS. We have learned that Solomon inherited the moon, DENOTING MALCHUT, in all its aspects, BOTH CHOCHMAH AND CHASSADIM, for he ruled over all this with his wisdom. Rabbi Shimon bar Yochai ruled with his wisdom over mankind, and all those that rise to his level only rise to perfect MALCHUT with him.

92. פָּתַח ר׳ יוֹסֵי וְאָמַר, יוֹנָתִי בְּחַגְוֵי הַסֶּלַע בַּסֵּתֶר הַמַּדְרֵגָה וְגוֹ׳. יוֹנָתִי, דָּא כ״י, מַה יוֹנָה לָא שַׁבְקַת בֶּן זוּגָּהּ לְעָלְמִין, כָּךְ כ״י לָא שַׁבְקַת לְקוּדְשָׁא בְּרִיךְ הוּא לְעָלְמִין. בְּחַגְוֵי הַסֶּלַע, אִלֵּין ת״ח, דְּלָא מִשְׁתַּכְּחֵי בְּנַיְיחָא בְּעָלְמָא דֵּין. בַּסֵּתֶר הַמַּדְרֵגָה, אִלֵּין ת״ח, הַצְּנוּעִין, דִּבְהוֹן חֲסִידִין דַּחֲלֵי קוּדְשָׁא בְּרִיךְ הוּא, דִּשְׁכִינְתָּא לָא אַעֲדֵי מִנַּיְיהוּ לְעָלְמִין. כְּדֵין, קוּדְשָׁא בְּרִיךְ הוּא מַתְבַּע הוּא בְּגִינַיְיהוּ לכ״י, וְאָמַר, הַרְאִינִי אֶת

מַרְאַיִךְ הַשְׁמִיעִנִי אֶת קוֹלֵךְ כִּי קוֹלֵךְ עָרֵב, דְּלֵית קָלָא מִשְׁתְּמַע לְעֵילָא,
אֶלָּא קָלָא דְּאִינוּן דְּמִתְעַסְּקֵי בְּאוֹרַיְיתָא.

92. Rabbi Yosi said, "My dove, who is in the clefts of the rock, in the secret places of the cliff" (Shir Hashirim 2:14). "My dove" refers to the Congregation of Yisrael, DENOTING MALCHUT. Just as a dove never forsakes her mate, so the Congregation of Yisrael never forsakes the Holy One, blessed be He. "In the clefts of the rock": These are the Torah scholars that find no peace in this world, AND ARE HIDING, SO TO SPEAK, IN THE CRACKS OF THE ROCK FROM THEIR ENEMIES. "In the secret places of the cliff": These are the modest scholars WHO CONCEAL THEIR LEVEL FROM PEOPLE. Among them are the pious who fear the Holy One, blessed be He, from whom the Shechinah never departs. Then, the Holy One, blessed be He, demands from the Congregation of Yisrael on behalf of the pious and says, "Let me see your countenance, let me hear your voice; for sweet is your voice" (Ibid.), for no voice is heard above except the voice of those who toil in the Torah.

93. וְתָאנָא, כָּל אִינוּן דְּמִתְעַסְּקֵי בְּאוֹרַיְיתָא, בְּלֵילְיָא, דְּיוּקְנֵיהוֹן
אִתְחַקַּק לְעֵילָא קַמֵּי קוּדְשָׁא בְּרִיךְ הוּא, וְקוּדְשָׁא בְּרִיךְ הוּא מִשְׁתַּעְשַׁע
בְּהוּ כּוּלֵיה יוֹמָא, וּמִסְתְּכַל בְּהוּ. וְהַהוּא קָלָא, סָלִיק וּבָקַע כָּל אִינוּן
רְקִיעִין, עַד דְּסָלִיק קַמֵּי קוּדְשָׁא בְּרִיךְ הוּא. כְּדֵין כְּתִיב, כִּי קוֹלֵךְ עָרֵב
וּמַרְאֵךְ נָאוֶה. וְהַשְׁתָּא קוּדְשָׁא בְּרִיךְ הוּא חָקַק דְּיוּקְנָא דר"ש לְעֵילָא
וְקָלֵיה לְעֵילָא לְעֵילָא סַלְקָא, וּמִתְעַטְּרָא בְּכִתְרָא קַדִּישָׁא, עַד דְּקוּדְשָׁא
בְּרִיךְ הוּא מִתְעַטַּר בֵּיה בְּכֻלְּהוּ עָלְמִין. וּמִשְׁתְּבַח בֵּיה. עֲלֵיה כְּתִיב,
וַיֹּאמֶר לִי עַבְדִּי אָתָּה יִשְׂרָאֵל אֲשֶׁר בְּךָ אֶתְפָּאָר.

93. We have learned that all those that toil in Torah at night have their images carved above before the Holy One, blessed be He. The Holy One, blessed be He, enjoys Himself with them all day and pays attention to them. That voice rises and penetrates all firmaments until it arises before the Holy One, blessed be He. Then the verse writes, "For sweet is your voice, and your countenance is comely" (Ibid.). Now the Holy One, blessed be He, has carved the image of Rabbi Shimon on high, whose voice rises higher and higher and is crowned with the holy crown until the Holy One, blessed be

He, crowns him throughout the worlds and commends him. About him, it is written, "And said to Me, You are My servant, Yisrael, in whom I will be glorified" (Yeshayah 49:3).

14. The souls until their descent to the world

A Synopsis

Rabbi Chiya tells us that everything and everyone that exists now and that will exist in the future existed before the world began. Some souls are distanced from God before birth and also in this lifetime, although they may repent later and get back their saintly part. Rabbi Chiya says that the two sons of Aaron were righteous, and he can not understand how God could have wished them to perish considering their own merits, their ancestral merits and the merits of Moses. Rabbi Shimon says that God made sure their souls were not lost, and Pinchas had already been born to house their souls. He also tells us that righteous souls are prepared above and given names before ever they come to this world.

94. פָּתַח רִבִּי חִיָּיא וְאָמַר, מַה שֶׁהָיָה כְּבָר הוּא וַאֲשֶׁר לִהְיוֹת וְגוֹ'. מַה שֶׁהָיָה כְּבָר, הַיְינוּ דְּתָנֵינָן, עַד לָא בָּרָא קוּדְשָׁא בְּרִיךְ הוּא הַאי עָלְמָא, הֲוָה בָּארֵי עָלְמִין וְחָרִיב לוֹן, עַד דְּקוּדְשָׁא בְּרִיךְ הוּא סָלִיק בִּרְעוּתֵיה, לְמִבְרֵי הַאי עָלְמָא, וְאַמְלִיךְ בְּאוֹרַיְיתָא. כְּדֵין אִתְתָּקַן הוּא בְּתִקּוּנוֹי, וְאִתְעַטָּר בְּעִטְרוֹי, וּבָרָא הַאי עָלְמָא, וְכָל מַאי דְּאִשְׁתְּכַח בְּהַאי עָלְמָא, הָא הֲוָה קָמֵיה, וְאִתְתָּקַן קָמֵיה.

94. Rabbi Chiya said, "That which is, already has been; and that which is to be has already been..." (Kohelet 3:15). "That which is, already has been." We have learned that before the Holy One, blessed be He, created this world, He created worlds and destroyed them – THIS IS THE SECRET OF THE BREAKING OF THE VESSELS – until it entered the will of the Holy One, blessed be He, to create this world. First, He took counsel with the Torah, THE SECRET OF THE CENTRAL COLUMN, then He put on His adornments and was crowned with His crowns and created this world. All that is found in this world was there before Him, AT THE TIME OF CREATION, and was prepared before Him.

95. וְתָאנָא, כָּל אִינוּן דַּבְרֵי עָלְמָא, דְּאִשְׁתְּכָחוּ בְּכָל דָּרָא וְדָרָא, עַד לָא יֵיתוּן לְעָלְמָא, הָא הֲווֹ קַיְימֵי קָמֵיה בְּדִיּוּקְנַיְיהוֹן. אֲפִילוּ כָּל אִינוּן נִשְׁמָתִין דִּבְנֵי נָשָׁא, עַד לָא יֵחֲתוּן לְעָלְמָא, כֻּלְּהוּ גְּלִיפִין קָמֵיה

בִּרְקִיעָא, בְּהַהוּא דִּיּוּקְנָא מַמָּשׁ, דְּאִינוּן בְּהַאי עָלְמָא. וְכָל מַה דְּאוֹלְפִין בְּהַאי עָלְמָא, כֹּלָּא יָדְעוּ עַד לָא יֵיתוּן לְעָלְמָא. וְתָנֵינָא, הַאי בְּאִינוּן זַכָּאֵי קְשׁוֹט.

95. We have learned that all leaders of every generation were present before the Holy One, blessed be He, in their forms before they came to the world. Furthermore, before they came into the world, all human souls were carved before Him in the heavens with the same forms literally as they are in this world. All that these souls learn in this world, they already knew before coming to this world. We have learned that all this holds true with the people of true piety.

96. וְכָל אִינוּן דְּלָא מִשְׁתַּכְּחִין זַכָּאִין בְּהַאי עָלְמָא, אֲפִילוּ תַּמָּן, מִתְרַחֲקִין מִקַּמֵּי קוּדְשָׁא בְּרִיךְ הוּא, וְעָאלִין בְּנוּקְבָּא דִּתְהוֹמָא רַבָּא, וְדַחֲקִין שַׁעֲתָא, וְנַחְתִּין לְעָלְמָא. וְהָהִיא נִשְׁמָתָא דִּלְהוֹן, הָא אוֹלִיפְנָא, כְּמָה דְּאִינוּן קְשֵׁי קְדָל בְּהַאי עָלְמָא, כַּךְ הֲווֹ עַד לָא יֵיתוּן לְעָלְמָא. וְהַהוּא חוּלָקָא קַדִּישָׁא דְּיָהַב לוֹן רָמָאן לֵיה, וְאָזְלִין וְשָׁאטִין וְאִסְתַּאֲבוּן, בְּהַהוּא נוּקְבָּא דִּתְהוֹמָא רַבָּא, וְנַטְלֵי חוּלָקֵיהוֹן מִתַּמָּן, וְדַחֲקִין שַׁעֲתָא וְנַחְתֵּי לְעָלְמָא. אִי זָכֵי לְבָתַר, וְתָב בְּתִיּוּבְתָּא קַמֵּי מָארֵיה, הוּא נָטִיל הַהוּא חוּלָקָא דִּילֵיה מַמָּשׁ, הה"ד, מַה שֶׁהָיָה כְּבָר הוּא וַאֲשֶׁר לִהְיוֹת וְגוֹ' כְּבָר הָיָה.

96. All of these that are not found to be just in this world, even there ABOVE BEFORE COMING TO THE WORLD, distance themselves from the presence of the Holy One, blessed be He. They enter the chasm of the great abyss and hurry to descend to this world. And we learned that their souls are stiff necked in this world, as they were before coming to this world. They throw away the saintly part that THE HOLY ONE, BLESSED BE HE, gave to them FROM THE SIDE OF HOLINESS and go wander about and become impure in that chasm of the great abyss. They take their share there, precipitate the hour and descend to earth. If a man later gains merit and repents before his Master, he will receive back his own portion, NAMELY, THE HOLY PORTION THAT HE THREW UPWARD, AS MENTIONED. This is the meaning of the verse, "That which is, already has been; and that which is to be has already been..."

97. ת״ח בְּנֵי אַהֲרֹן לָא אִשְׁתְּכָחוּ בְּיִשְׂרָאֵל כְּוָותַיְיהוּ, בַּר מֹשֶׁה וְאַהֲרֹן, וְאִינּוּן אִקְרוּן אֲצִילֵי בְּנֵי יִשְׂרָאֵל. וְעַל דְּטָעוּ קָמֵי מַלְכָּא קַדִּישָׁא, מִיתוּ. וְכִי קוּדְשָׁא בְּרִיךְ הוּא בָּעָא לְאוֹבָדָא לוֹן, וְהָא תָּנֵינָן בְּרָזָא דְּמַתְנִיתִין, דְּקוּדְשָׁא בְּרִיךְ הוּא עָבַד חֶסֶד בְּכֹלָּא, וַאֲפִילוּ בְּרַשִׁיעֵי עָלְמָא לָא בָּעֵי לְאוֹבָדָא לוֹן. וְהָנֵי זַכָּאֵי קְשׁוֹט ס״ד דְּאִינּוּן אִתְאֲבִידוּ מֵעָלְמָא, זְכוּתָא דִּלְהוֹן אָן הוּא. זְכוּתָא דַּאֲבוּהוֹן אָן הוּא. זְכוּתָא דְּמֹשֶׁה הָכִי נָמֵי. וְאִינּוּן הֵיךְ אִתְאֲבִידוּ.

97. Come and see that the sons of Aaron had no equal in Yisrael, except for Moses and Aaron. They were called "the nobles of the children of Yisrael" (Shemot 24:11) and they died because they erred before the Holy King. HE QUESTIONS: Did the Holy One, blessed be He, wish that they should perish? Did we not learn in the secret of the Mishnah that the Holy One, blessed be He, does kindness with everyone, and even evildoers He does not wish to cause to perish. But these most saintly ones, NADAB AND ABIHU, will it enter your mind that they should perish from the world? Where were their merits, the merits of their ancestors and also the merit of Moses? How could they have perished?

98. אֶלָּא הָכִי אוֹלִיפְנָא מִבּוּצִינָא קַדִּישָׁא, דְּקוּדְשָׁא בְּרִיךְ הוּא חַס עַל יְקָרָא דִּלְהוֹן, וְאִתּוֹקַד גַּרְמֵיהוֹן לְגוֹ, וְנִשְׁמָתֵהוֹן לָא אִתְאֲבִידוּ, וְהָא אוֹקִימְנָא. ות״ח עַד לָא מִיתוּ בְּנֵי אַהֲרֹן כְּתִיב, וְאֶלְעָזָר בֶּן אַהֲרֹן לָקַח לוֹ וְגוֹ', אִקְרֵי שְׁמֵיהּ פִּנְחָס, דַּהֲוָה זַמִּין לְאִתְתַּקְּנָא עֲקִימָא, הה״ד וַאֲשֶׁר לִהְיוֹת כְּבָר הָיָה.

98. HE ANSWERS: We have learned from the holy luminary that the Holy One, blessed be He, concerned Himself with their honor, so inwardly their bodies were tinged with fire, but their soul was not lost, as we have already established. Come and see that even before the deaths of Aaron's sons, it is written, "And Elazar, Aaron's son took of the daughters of Putiel to wife; AND SHE BORE HIM PINCHAS" (Shemot 6:25). He was called Pinchas because he was destined to straighten that which is crooked, MEANING TO CORRECT THE DAMAGE OF NADAB AND ABIHU, AS EXPLAINED EARLIER, EVEN THOUGH NADAB AND ABIHU HAD NOT YET DIED. This is the essence of the verse, "And that which is to be has already been."

99. וְתָאנָא, כֻּלְּהוּ זַכָּאֵי קְשׁוֹט, עַד לָא יֵיתוּן לְעָלְמָא, כֻּלְּהוּ אִתְּתְקָנוּ לְעֵילָא, וְאִקְרוּן בִּשְׁמָהָן. וְר"ש בֶּן יוֹחָאי, מִן יוֹמָא דְּבָרָא קוּדְשָׁא בְּרִיךְ הוּא עָלְמָא, הֲוָה אִזְדְּמַן קַמֵּי קוּדְשָׁא בְּרִיךְ הוּא, וְאִשְׁתְּכַח עֲמֵיהּ. וְקוּדְשָׁא בְּרִיךְ הוּא קָרֵי לֵיהּ בִּשְׁמֵיהּ, זַכָּאָה חוּלָקֵיהּ לְעֵילָא וְתַתָּא, עֲלֵיהּ כְּתִיב יִשְׂמַח אָבִיךָ וְאִמֶּךָ, אָבִיךָ: דָּא קוּדְשָׁא בְּרִיךְ הוּא. וְאִמֶּךָ: דָּא כ"י.

99. We have learned that before coming to the world, all the true pious people were prepared above and were given names. From the day that the Holy One, blessed be He, created the world, even Rabbi Shimon bar Yochai was prepared and came before the Holy One, blessed be He. The Holy One, blessed be He, called him by his name. How fortunate is his lot above and below. About him, is addressed the verse, "Let your father and your mother be glad" (Mishlei 23:25). "Your father" is the Holy One, blessed be He, and "your Mother" is the Congregation of Yisrael.

15. "While the King was reclining at his board"

A Synopsis

Rabbi Aba opens by saying that the title verse means that Yisrael emitted a wonderful fragrance when they stood at Mount Sinai to receive the Torah. While Moses went up to receive the tablets, Yisrael deserted their wonderful fragrance and turned to the golden calf. Rabbi Aba explains the verses from the esoteric point of view, telling us about the flow of wisdom and understanding down from the highest realms and culminating in the union of Zeir Anpin and Malchut; this brings blessings to every level.

١٠٠. פָּתַח ר' אַבָּא וְאָמַר עַד שֶׁהַמֶּלֶךְ בִּמְסִבּוֹ נִרְדִּי נָתַן רֵיחוֹ. הַאי קְרָא אוּקְמוּהָ חַבְרַיָּיא, בְּשַׁעֲתָא דְקוּדְשָׁא בְּרִיךְ הוּא אִשְׁתְּכַח וְזַמִּין בְּטוּרָא דְסִינַי, לְמֵיהַב אוֹרַיְיתָא לְיִשְׂרָאֵל, נִרְדִּי נָתַן רֵיחוֹ, יִשְׂרָאֵל יָהֲבוּ וּסְלִיקוּ רֵיחָא טַב, דְּקָאֵים וְאָגֵין עָלַיְיהוּ לְדָרֵי דָרִין. וְאָמְרוּ, כָּל אֲשֶׁר דִּבֶּר יְיָ' נַעֲשֶׂה וְנִשְׁמָע. ד"א עַד שֶׁהַמֶּלֶךְ בִּמְסִבּוֹ, בְּעוֹד דְּסָלִיק מֹשֶׁה לְקַבְּלָא אוֹרַיְיתָא מְקוּדְשָׁא בְּרִיךְ הוּא, וְאִתְחֲקַק בִּתְרֵי לוּחֵי אֲבָנִין, יִשְׂרָאֵל שָׁבְקוּ הַהוּא רֵיחָא טָבָא דַּהֲוָה מִתְעַטֵּר עָלַיְיהוּ, וְאָמְרוּ לָעֵגֶל, אֵלֶּה אֱלֹהֶיךָ יִשְׂרָאֵל.

100. Rabbi Aba opened the discussion with the verse, "While the king was reclining at his board, my nard sent forth its fragrance" (Shir Hashirim 1:12). This verse has been explained by the friends. When the Holy One, blessed be He, was ready and present on Mount Sinai to give Torah to Yisrael, "my nard sent forth its fragrance," as Yisrael emitted a wonderful fragrance that has shielded them for countless generations. This was what they said then, "All that Hashem has said will we do, and obey" (Shemot 24:7). Another explanation of, "While the King was reclining at his board": While Moses went up to receive the Torah from the Holy One, blessed be He, which was engraved within the two tablets of stone, Yisrael deserted that wonderful fragrance that crowned them and said to the golden calf, "These are your Elohim, Yisrael" (Shemot 32:4).

١٠١. הַשְׁתָּא הַאי קְרָא בְּרָזָא דְחָכְמְתָא הוּא, ת"ח, כְּתִיב וְנָהָר יוֹצֵא מֵעֵדֶן לְהַשְׁקוֹת אֶת הַגָּן, הַאי נָהֲרָא אִתְפְּשַׁט בְּסִטְרוֹי, בְּשַׁעֲתָא

דְּמִזְדַּוֵּוג עִמֵּיהּ בְּזִוּוּגָא שְׁלִים, הַאי עֵדֶן בְּהַהוּא נָתִיב, דְּלָא אִתְיָידַע
לְעֵילָּא וְתַתָּא, כד"א נָתִיב לֹא יְדָעוֹ עָיִט. וְאִשְׁתְּכָחוּ בִּרְעוּתָא דְּלָא
מִתְפָּרְשָׁן תְּדִירָא חַד מֵחַד. כְּדֵין נָפְקִין מַבּוּעִין וּנְחָלִין, וּמְעַטְּרִין לְבֵן
קַדִּישָׁא, בְּכָל אִינּוּן כִּתְרִין, כְּדֵין כְּתִיב בַּעֲטָרָה שֶׁעִטְּרָה לּוֹ אִמּוֹ.
וּבְהַהִיא שַׁעֲתָא יָרִית הַהוּא בֵּן אַחֲסַנְתָּא דַּאֲבוֹי וְאִמֵּיהּ, כְּדֵין הוּא
אִשְׁתַּעֲשַׁע, בְּהַהוּא עִנּוּגָא וְתַפְנוּקָא.

101. Now, LET US EXPLAIN this verse from the standpoint of the secret of wisdom. Come and see, "And a river went out of Eden to water the garden" (Beresheet 2:10). This river, DENOTING BINAH, spreads on all sides when this Eden, NAMELY CHOCHMAH, joins with it in complete union in this path not known above or below, DENOTING YESOD OF CHOCHMAH, as in the verse, "There is a path which no bird of prey knows" (Iyov 28:7). Thus, CHOCHMAH AND BINAH desire not to part from one another. Then fountains and streams exit FROM THEM, DENOTING THE MOCHIN OF ZEIR ANPIN, and crown the holy son, ZEIR ANPIN THE SON OF YUD HEI, with all these crowns, DENOTING MOCHIN. It is then written, "With the crown with which his mother crowned him" (Shir Hashirim 3:11), DENOTING MOCHIN ALSO KNOWN AS CROWN. At that time, that son ZEIR ANPIN will inherit the inheritance of his father and mother, NAMELY THE MOCHIN THAT EXUDES FROM THE UNION OF CHOCHMAH AND BINAH THAT ARE REFERRED TO AS ABA AND IMA. Then, He will delight in pleasures and delight

102. וְתָאנָא, בְּשַׁעֲתָא דְּמַלְכָּא עִלָּאָה בְּתַפְנוּקֵי מַלְכִין, יָתִיב בְּעִטְרוֹי,
כְּדֵין כְּתִיב עַד שֶׁהַמֶּלֶךְ בִּמְסִבּוֹ נִרְדִּי נָתַן רֵיחוֹ. דָּא יְסוֹד דְּאַפִּיק בִּרְכָּאן
לְאִזְדַּוְּוגָא מַלְכָּא קַדִּישָׁא בְּמַטְרוֹנִיתָא. וּכְדֵין אִתְיַיהֲבוּ בִּרְכָּאן בְּכֻלְּהוּ
עָלְמִין, וּמִתְבָּרְכָן עִלָּאִין וְתַתָּאִין. וְהַשְׁתָּא הָא בּוּצִינָא קַדִּישָׁא מִתְעַטֵּר
בְּעִטְרוֹי דְּהַאי דַּרְגָּא, וְהוּא וְחַבְרַיָּיא סְלִיקוּ תּוּשְׁבְּחָן מִתַּתָּא לְעֵילָּא,
וְהִיא מִתְעַטְּרָא בְּאִינּוּן תּוּשְׁבְּחָן. הַשְׁתָּא אִית לְאַפָּקָא בִּרְכָּאן לְכֻלְּהוּ
חַבְרַיָּיא מֵעֵילָּא לְתַתָּא, בְּהַאי דַּרְגָּא קַדִּישָׁא, ור' אֶלְעָזָר בְּרֵיהּ לֵימָא
מֵאִינּוּן מִלִּין מְעַלְּיָין דְּאוֹלִיף מֵאֲבוֹי.

102. We have learned that when the supernal King, NAMELY ZEIR ANPIN, with delicacies fit for kings sits crowned, it is written, "While the king was reclining at his board, my nard sent forth its fragrance." "MY NARD" refers to Yesod that emits blessings so that the holy King, ZEIR ANPIN, joins with the Queen, NAMELY MALCHUT. Then blessings are given to the worlds and those in the upper and lower worlds are blessed. Now the holy luminary is crowned by this level, MEANING THE MOCHIN OF ZEIR ANPIN FROM ABA AND IMA, ALSO KNOWN AS CROWNS. He and the friends lift up the praise from below upward, NAMELY FROM MAYIM NUKVIN (FEMALE WATERS), and MALCHUT crowns herself with these praises AS SHE JOINS WITH ZEIR ANPIN. Now there are blessings to pour from above downward to all friends of this MENTIONED level. Rabbi Elazar, his son, should now say some of the praiseworthy words he heard from his father.

16. "And behold a well in the field"

A Synopsis

Rabbi Elazar talks about "the well that the princes dug out," saying that the well is filled with blessings from Netzach, Hod and Yesod; the well sustains everyone above and below. The great stone that was rolled over the well's mouth refers to harsh judgment, that is removed when the blessings flow through the Sfirot. In a similar way, God poured blessings on the generation of Rabbi Shimon.

103. פָּתַח ר' אֶלְעָזָר וְאָמַר, וַיַּרְא וְהִנֵּה בְאֵר בַּשָּׂדֶה וְגוֹ'. וְנֶאֶסְפוּ שָׁמָּה כָל הָעֲדָרִים וְגוֹ'. הָנֵי קְרָאֵי אִית לְאִסְתַּכְּלָא בְּהוּ, וּבְרָזָא דְחָכְמְתָא אִינּוּן, דְּאוֹלִיפְנָא מֵאַבָּא, וְהָכִי אוֹלִיפְנָא, וַיַּרְא וְהִנֵּה בְאֵר בַּשָּׂדֶה, מַאן בְּאֵר. דָּא הוּא דִכְתִיב, בְּאֵר חֲפָרוּהָ שָׂרִים כָּרוּהָ נְדִיבֵי הָעָם. וְהִנֵּה שָׁם שְׁלֹשָׁה עֶדְרֵי צֹאן רוֹבְצִים עָלֶיהָ, אִלֵּין אִינּוּן נֶצַח הוֹד יְסוֹד, דְּאִלֵּין אִינּוּן רְבִיעִין עֲלָהּ, וְקַיְימִין עֲלָהּ, וּמֵאִלֵּין אִתְמַלְיָא בִּרְכָאן הַהִיא בְּאֵר.

103. Rabbi Elazar opened the discussion saying, "And he looked, and behold a well in the field...And there were all the flocks gathered" (Beresheet 29:2-3). These verses need to be examined, as they contain the secret of wisdom that I learned from my father. So I learned, "And he looked, and behold a well in the field." What is the "well"? It is the one mentioned in "the well that the princes dug out, that the nobles of the people delved" (Bemidbar 21:18), MEANING MALCHUT THAT IS EMBELLISHED FROM ABA AND IMA REFERRED TO AS PRINCES. "And, lo, there were three flocks of sheep lying by it" (Beresheet 29:2): These represent Netzach, Hod and Yesod, which rest by it and stand over it. From them the well was filled with blessings.

104. כִּי מִן הַבְּאֵר הַהִיא יַשְׁקוּ הָעֲדָרִים, דְּהָא מִן הַאי בְּאֵר אִתְּזָנוּ עִלָּאִין וְתַתָּאִין, וּמִתְבָּרְכָאן כֻּלְּהוּ כַּחֲדָא. וְהָאֶבֶן גְּדוֹלָה עַל פִּי הַבְּאֵר, דָּא הוּא דִּינָא קַשְׁיָא, דְּקַיְימָא עֲלָהּ מִסִּטְרָא אָחֳרָא לְיַנְקָא מִינָהּ. וְנֶאֶסְפוּ שָׁמָּה כָל הָעֲדָרִים, אִלֵּין אִינּוּן שִׁית כִּתְרֵי מַלְכָּא, דְּמִתְכַּנְּשֵׁי כֻּלְּהוּ, וְנַגְדֵי בִּרְכָאן מֵרֵישָׁא דְמַלְכָּא, וּמְרִיקָן בָּהּ. וְכַד אִתְחַבְּרָאן כֻּלְּהוּ כַּחֲדָא לְאַרְקָא בָּהּ, כְּתִיב וְגָלְלוּ אֶת הָאֶבֶן מֵעַל פִּי הַבְּאֵר, מְגַנְדְרִין

לְהַהוּא דִּינָא קַשְׁיָא, וּמְעַבְּרָן לֵיהּ מִינָהּ.

104. "For out of that well they watered the flocks" (Ibid.), because all are sustained from that well, higher and lower beings, and together they are blessed. "And a great stone was upon the well's mouth" (Ibid.) refers to the harsh Judgment THAT IS KNOWN AS THE GREAT ROCK, which stands upon it from the Other Side to suckle from it. "And there were all the flocks gathered": These are the six Sfirot of the King, ZEIR ANPIN – NAMELY CHESED, GVURAH, TIFERET, NETZACH, HOD AND YESOD – which all assemble and draw blessings from the head of the King, NAMELY FROM THE THREE FIRST SFIROT OF ZEIR ANPIN KNOWN AS HEAD. They pour into it and, when they all merge together and feed into it, it is written, "And they rolled the stone from the well's mouth" (Ibid. 3), meaning they roll away the harsh Judgment, KNOWN AS A STONE, and remove it.

105. וְהִשְׁקוּ אֶת הַצֹּאן, מְרִיקִין בִּרְכָאן מֵהַהִיא בְּאֵר, לְעֶלָאִין וְתַתָּאִין לְבָתַר וְהֵשִׁיבוּ אֶת הָאֶבֶן עַל פִּי הַבְּאֵר לִמְקוֹמָהּ. תָּב הַהוּא דִּינָא לְאַתְרֵיהּ, בְּגִין דְּאִצְטְרִיךְ לֵיהּ לְבַשְׂמָא עָלְמָא, וּלְתַקְּנָא עָלְמָא. וְהַשְׁתָּא הָא קוּדְשָׁא בְּרִיךְ הוּא אָרִיק עֲלַיְיכוּ בִּרְכָאן, מִמַּבּוּעָא דְּנַחֲלָא, וּמִנַּיְיכוּ כָּל בְּנֵי דָּרָא מִתְבָּרְכִין. זַכָּאָה חוּלָקֵיכוֹן בְּעָלְמָא דֵין, וּבְעָלְמָא דְּאָתֵי עֲלַיְיכוּ כְּתִיב, וְכָל בָּנַיְךְ לִמוּדֵי יְיָ׳ וְרַב שָׁלוֹם בָּנַיְךְ.

105. "And watered the sheep" (Ibid.), MEANING they pour out blessings from this well to the higher and lower levels. Afterwards, they "put the stone back upon the well's mouth" (Ibid.), MEANING the Judgment returns to its position. It is because it is needed in order to bring fragrance and correction to the world. Now, the Holy One, blessed be He, has poured upon you blessings from the springs of the fountain stream and from you are blessed all the members of your generation. How fortunate is your share in this world and in the World to Come. About you, it is written, "And all your children shall be taught of Hashem; and great shall be the peace of your children" (Yeshayah 54:13).

17. "The twelve...and this"

A Synopsis

Rabbi Shimon tells how the Torah is crowned with the thirteen attributes of mercy, and the knot of Faith is tied with those thirteen attributes. Jacob blessed his sons in the name of the faith according to the blessing of each attribute. Rabbi Shimon says that Rabbi Pinchas ben Yair binds the highest knot, the knot of holiness, the knot of Faith.

106. פָּתַח ר"ש וְאָמַר, יַעְלְזוּ חֲסִידִים בְּכָבוֹד יְרַנְּנוּ עַל מִשְׁכְּבוֹתָם וְגוֹ', תָּאנָא בִּי"ג מְכִילָן, אִתְקְשַׁר קִשְׁרָא דִּמְהֵימְנוּתָא, לְאִשְׁתַּכְּחָא בִּרְכָאן לְכֹלָּא. וְכָל מְהֵימְנוּתָא דְּקוּדְשָׁא בְּרִיךְ הוּא בִּתְלָתָא אַסְתִּימוּ. וְעַל הַאי, בִּי"ג מְכִילָן, אוֹרַיְיתָא מִתְעַטְּרָא, כְּמָה דְּאוֹקִימְנָא מִק"ו וּמִג"ש וְכוּ', וְכַמָּה זִמְנִין אוֹקִימְנָא הַאי. וּשְׁמָא קַדִּישָׁא בְּהַאי מִתְעַטְּרָא.

106. Rabbi Shimon opened the discussion saying, "Let the pious be joyful in glory: let them sing aloud upon their beds" (Tehilim 149:5). We have learned that the knot of Faith, NAMELY MALCHUT, is tied with the thirteen attributes OF MERCY so that blessings are to be available for all. The entire Faith of the Holy One, blessed be He, is enclosed in three, NAMELY THREE COLUMNS, THE SECRET OF THIRTEEN, AS THEY ENLIGHTEN EACH OF FOUR SFIROT – CHESED, GVURAH, TIFERET AND MALCHUT WITHIN IT. NOW, THREE TIMES FOUR EQUALS TWELVE AND, TOGETHER WITH MALCHUT THAT CONTAINS THEM, THERE ARE THIRTEEN. Consequently, the Torah is crowned with the thirteen attributes, as we have established IN THE BARAITHA OF RABBI YISHMAEL, namely using the arguments of an inference from minor to major and comparison by analogy. We have explained this several times. The Holy Name, NAMELY MALCHUT, is crowned with this.

107. ת"ח, בְּהַהִיא שַׁעֲתָא דְּבָעָא יַעֲקֹב, דְּיִתְבָּרְכוּן בְּנוֹי בִּשְׁמָא דִּמְהֵימְנוּתָא. מַה כְּתִיב, כָּל אֵלֶּה שִׁבְטֵי יִשְׂרָאֵל שְׁנֵים עָשָׂר וְזֹאת, הָא תְּלֵיסַר, דְּאִשְׁתַּתַּף עִמְּהוֹן שְׁכִינְתָּא, וְאִתְקָיְימוּ בִּרְכָאן. וְהַיְינוּ דִכְתִיב, אִישׁ אֲשֶׁר כְּבִרְכָתוֹ בֵּרַךְ אוֹתָם. מַאי כְּבִרְכָתוֹ. בְּהַהוּא דּוּגְמָא דִּלְעֵילָא, כְּבִרְכָתוֹ דְּכָל מְכִילָא וּמְכִילָא.

107. Come and see that when Jacob wished his sons to be blessed in the name of the Faith, it is written, "All these are the twelve tribes of Yisrael: and this (Heb. *zot* fem.) IS THAT WHICH THEIR FATHER SPOKE TO THEM" (Beresheet 49:28). TWELVE AND *ZOT* are thirteen, since the Shechinah, CALLED *ZOT*, participated with them and the blessings were fulfilled. This is the meaning of the verse, "Every one according to his blessing he blessed them" (Ibid.). What is meant by "according to his blessing"? MEANING according to the resemblance to that which is above, THE THIRTEEN ATTRIBUTES OF MERCY, NAMELY according to the blessing of each attribute.

108. וְתָאנָא, כָּל אִינּוּן מְכִילִין סַלְקִין, וּמִתְעַטְּרִין וְנַיְיחִין בְּרֵישָׁא חֲדָא, וְתַמָּן מִתְעַטְּרָא רֵישָׁא דְּמַלְכָּא, הַהוּא דְּאִקְרֵי בְּדַרְגָּא עִלָּאָה דַּחֲסִידוּת. וְחֲסִידִים, יַרְתִּין כָּל הַהוּא כָּבוֹד דִּלְעֵילָּא, דִּכְתִּיב יַעְלְזוּ חֲסִידִים בְּכָבוֹד, בְּהַאי עָלְמָא. יְרַנְּנוּ עַל מִשְׁכְּבוֹתָם בְּעָלְמָא דְּאָתֵי. רוֹמְמוֹת אֵל בִּגְרוֹנָם, דְּיַדְעִין לְקַשְּׁרָא קִשְׁרָא דִּמְהֵימְנוּתָא כַּדְקָא יֵאוֹת, וּכְדֵין חֶרֶב פִּיפִיּוֹת בְּיָדָם. מַאן חֶרֶב פִּיפִיּוֹת. דָּא הוּא חֶרֶב לה', חַרְבָּא דְּקוּדְשָׁא בְּרִיךְ הוּא. פִּיפִיּוֹת: לְהַיטָא בִּתְרֵין דִּינִין. וְלָמָּה. לַעֲשׂוֹת נְקָמָה בַּגּוֹיִם וְגוֹ'.

108. We have learned that all these attributes OF MALCHUT rise and become crowned and rest in a head OF ZEIR ANPIN. There is crowned the head of the King, He that is called by the highest level of Piety, NAMELY ZEIR ANPIN, WHOSE CHESED CONVERTS TO CHOCHMAH. The pious ones THAT CLING TO ZEIR ANPIN inherit all that glory of above, WHICH IS MALCHUT WITH HER THIRTEEN ATTRIBUTES, as is written, "Let the pious be joyful in glory," NAMELY in this world, DENOTING MALCHUT. "Let them sing aloud upon their beds," MEANING in the World to Come, DENOTING BINAH. "The high praises of El are in their mouths" (Tehilim 149:6), MEANING they know to bind the bond of Faith properly, AS MALCHUT IS CALLED EL. Then "and a two-edged sword in their hand" (Ibid.). What is "a two-edged sword"? This is Hashem's sword, DENOTING MALCHUT FROM THE ASPECT OF JUDGMENT, REFERRED TO AS SWORD. "Two-edged sword" implies that it flames with two Judgments, NAMELY JUDGMENTS OF LEFT AND JUDGMENTS OF THE CURTAIN. For what purpose is all this? It is "to execute vengeance upon the nations..." (Ibid.)

109. וְהָא ר' פִּנְחָס בֶּן יָאִיר, כִּתְרָא דְחֶסֶד, רֵישָׁא עִלָּאָה. בְּג"כ כְּבוֹד
דִלְעֵילָא יָרִית, וְהוּא קָשִׁיר קִשְׁרָא עִלָּאָה, קִשְׁרָא קַדִּישָׁא, קִשְׁרָא
דִמְהֵימְנוּתָא. זַכָּאָה חוּלָקֵיה בְּעָלְמָא דֵין וּבְעָלְמָא דְּאָתֵי. עַל הַאי
פָּתוֹרָא אִתְּמַר, זֶה הַשֻּׁלְחָן אֲשֶׁר לִפְנֵי יְיָ'. קָם ר' פִּנְחָס, וְנָשִׁיק לֵיה,
וּבָרִיךְ לֵיה, וְנָשִׁיק לר' אֶלְעָזָר, וּלְכֻלְּהוּ חַבְרַיָּיא, וּבָרִיךְ לוֹן, נָטַל כַּסָּא
וּבָרִיךְ.

109. Behold, here is Rabbi Pinchas ben Yair, who is Sfirah of Chesed, a supernal head OF ZEIR ANPIN, MEANING THAT HIS CHESED HAS BECOME CHOCHMAH, WHICH IS HEAD. For this reason, he inherits the glory of most High and binds the highest knot, the knot of holiness, the knot of Faith, MEANING THE UNITY OF ZEIR ANPIN WITH MALCHUT. How fortunate is his share in this world and in the World to Come. About this table is said, "This is the table that is before Hashem" (Yechezkel 41:22). Rabbi Pinchas rose and kissed him and blessed him. He kissed Rabbi Elazar and all the friends and blessed them. He then took the cup and said a blessing.

18. "You prepare a table before me"

A Synopsis
We read of how the scholars spend all day speaking about the Torah and rejoicing in it and in each other.

110. פָּתַח וְאָמַר, תַּעֲרוֹךְ לְפָנַי שֻׁלְחָן נֶגֶד צוֹרְרָי וְגוֹ', יָתְבוּ תַּמָּן, כָּל הַהוּא יוֹמָא, וַהֲווֹ חַבְרַיָּא כֻּלְּהוּ חַדָּן בְּמִלֵּי דְאוֹרַיְיתָא, וְחֶדְוָותָא דר״ש הֲוָה סַגִּי. נָטַל ר׳ פִּנְחָס לר׳ אֶלְעָזָר, וְלָא שַׁבְקֵיה כָּל הַהוּא יוֹמָא וְכָל לֵילְיָא, וַהֲוָה חַדֵי עִמֵּיה, קָרָא עָלֵיה, אָז תִּתְעַנַּג עַל יְיָ', כָּל חֶדְוָותָא וְעֲנוּגָא יַתִּירָא דָא דְחוּלָקִי הוּא, זְמִינִין בְּהַהוּא עָלְמָא לְאַכְרְזָא עָלַי, זַכָּאָה חוּלָקָךְ ר׳ פִּנְחָס, דְּאַנְתְּ זָכִית לְכָל הַאי, שָׁלוֹם לָךְ וְשָׁלוֹם לְעוֹזְרֶךְ כִּי עֲזָרְךָ אֱלֹהֶיךָ. אַשְׁכִּימוּ לְמֵיזַל, קָם ר׳ פִּנְחָס וְאָחִיד בֵּיה בר׳ אֶלְעָזָר, וְלָא שַׁבְקֵיה לְמֵיהַךְ. אוֹזִיף ר׳ פִּנְחָס לר״ש וּבַרְכֵיה, וּלְכֻלְּהוּ חַבְרַיָּיא. עַד דַּהֲווֹ אַזְלֵי אָמַר לְהוּ ר׳ שִׁמְעוֹן לְחַבְרַיָּיא, עֵת לַעֲשׂוֹת לַיְיָ'.

110. He opened the discussion saying, "You prepare a table before me in the presence of my enemies" (Tehilim 23:5). They sat there all day long. The friends were rejoicing with words of Torah and the joy of Rabbi Shimon was great. Rabbi Pinchas took hold of Rabbi Elazar and did not leave him all that day and night, and rejoiced with him. He referred to a verse about him, "Then you shall delight yourself in Hashem" (Yeshayah 58:14). All this great joy and pleasure are in my portion, AS RABBI ELAZAR WAS HIS DAUGHTER'S SON. Sometime in the future, they will in that world announce about me: Fortunate is your lot, Rabbi Pinchas, that you have merited all this and "peace, peace be to you, and peace to your helpers; for your Elohim helps you" (I Divrei Hayamim 12:19). They rose to depart. Rabbi Pinchas rose, held onto Rabbi Elazar and did not let him leave. Rabbi Pinchas escorted Rabbi Shimon and blessed him and all the scholars. As they were departing, Rabbi Shimon said to the friends, "It is time to act for Hashem" (Tehilim 119:126).

19. "And Aaron shall cast lots upon the two goats"

A Synopsis

Rabbi Aba wonders what the "lots" in the title verse were for. Rabbi Shimon begins his explanation by talking about why Shimon was the brother chosen by Joseph to be taken away and bound. Shimon was from the aspect of harsh judgment, and he had allied himself with Levi who was also from the side of judgment. We learn of two spirits who pursue judgment, and who spy on the land every day. We are reminded how Yisrael is beloved of God above all other nations, and that God gave them one day a year to purify themselves so that they will rule over all the prosecutors and spirits. Rabbi Shimon says that one of the goats in the title verse was for Hashem and one for Azazel. If both goats had been for Azazel the world would not have been able to bear it. The goat cannot slander the children of Yisrael on Yom Kippur because it finds them doing good deeds, and in fact it becomes their defender. As a result of the sacrifice of the goat, judgment no longer rules over Yisrael.

111. אָתָא רִבִּי אַבָּא וְשָׁאִיל, כְּתִיב וְנָתַן אַהֲרֹן עַל שְׁנֵי הַשְּׂעִירִים גּוֹרָלוֹת וְגוֹ'. הָנֵי עַדְבִין לָמָה. וְאַהֲרֹן לָמָה לֵיהּ לְמֵיהַב עַדְבִין. וּפָרְשָׁתָא דָּא לָמָה. וְהָא אוֹלִיפְנָא קַמֵּי דְּמָר סִדְרָא דְּיוֹמָא, וְהַאי בְּעֵינָא לְמִנְדַּע.

111. It is written, "And Aaron shall cast lots upon the two goats..." (Vayikra 16:8). Rabbi Aba came and asked: What where those lots for? Why did it require Aaron to place the lots? What is this Torah portion for? I have learned before my master the order OF THE YOM KIPPUR service, and also this matter I wish to know.

112. פָּתַח ר"ש וְאָמַר, וַיִּקַּח מֵאִתָּם אֶת שִׁמְעוֹן וַיֶּאֱסֹר אֹתוֹ לְעֵינֵיהֶם. וְכִי מַה חָמָא יוֹסֵף לְמֵיסַב לְשִׁמְעוֹן עִמֵּיהּ יַתִּיר מֵאֲחוֹהִי. אֶלָּא, אָמַר יוֹסֵף, בְּכָל אֲתַר שִׁמְעוֹן פְּתִיחוּתָא דְּדִינָא אִיהוּ, וְהַהִיא שַׁעֲתָא דַּאֲזִילְנָא מֵאַבָּא לְגַבַּיְיהוּ דְּאָחַי, שִׁמְעוֹן פָּתַח בְּקַדְמֵיתָא בְּדִינָא, הה"ד וַיֹּאמְרוּ אִישׁ אֶל אָחִיו הִנֵּה בַּעַל הַחֲלוֹמוֹת הַלָּזֶה בָּא וְעַתָּה לְכוּ וְגוֹ'.

לְבָתַר בִּשְׁכֶם, וַיִּקְחוּ שְׁנֵי בְנֵי יַעֲקֹב שִׁמְעוֹן וְלֵוִי, כֻּלְּהוּ בְּדִינָא הֲווֹ. טַב לְמֵיסַב דָּא, וְלָא יִתְעַר קַטְטוּתָא בְּכֻלְּהוּ שִׁבְטִין.

112. Rabbi Shimon opened the discussion saying, "And took from them Simeon, and bound him before their eyes" (Beresheet 42:24). He questions: For what reason did Joseph see fit to take Simeon with him rather than any one of the OTHER brothers? HE ANSWERS: Joseph said that Simeon always was the opening for Judgment. When I left my father to go to my brothers, Simeon first began the Judgment, as the verse says, "And they said one to another, Behold, this dreamer comes. Come now therefore..." (Beresheet 37:19). Later in Shechem, "that two sons of Jacob, Simeon and Levi..." (Beresheet 34:25). All these actions pertain to Judgment. THEREFORE, it is better to take this one and not allow him to arouse quarreling among all the tribes.

113. וְתָנֵינָן, מַאי קָא חָמָא שִׁמְעוֹן לְאִזְדַּוְּוגָא בְּלֵוִי יַתִּיר מִכֹּלָּא. וְהָא רְאוּבֵן הֲוָה אֲחוּהָ וְסָמִיךְ לֵיהּ, אֶלָּא שִׁמְעוֹן חָמָא וְיָדַע דְּלֵוִי מִסִּטְרָא דְּדִינָא קָא אָתֵי, וְשִׁמְעוֹן מִסִּטְרָא דְּדִינָא קַשְׁיָא יַתִּיר אִתְאֲחָד. אָמַר נִתְעָרַב חַד בְּחַד וַאֲנָן נֶחֱרִיב עָלְמָא. מָה עָבֵד קוּדְשָׁא בְּרִיךְ הוּא, נָטַל לֵיהּ לְחוּלָקֵיהּ לְלֵוִי, אָמַר מִכָּאן וּלְהָלְאָה שִׁמְעוֹן לֵיתִיב בְּקוּפְטִירָא בַּהֲדֵיהּ בִּלְחוֹדוֹי.

113. We have learned, what did Simeon see in attaching himself to Levi more than to the others? Reuben was also his brother and close to him, JUST AS LEVI, SO WHY DID HE NOT STICK WITH REUBEN? HE ANSWERS: Simeon saw and realized that Levi was of the aspect of Judgment and Simeon was caught up with even harsher Judgment, so he said: Let us join one with the other and we could destroy the world. What did the Holy One, blessed be He, do? He took Levi aside to His place and said, 'From this point on, let Simeon stay bound with ropes alone.'

114. תָּאנָא בְּסִטְרָא דְּאִימָא, תְּרֵין גַּרְדִּינֵי טְהִירִין אִתְאַחֲדָן בִּידָא שְׂמָאלָא, וְהָא אוֹקִימְנָא דְּאִינּוּן מְאַלְּלֵי אַרְעָא בְּכָל יוֹמָא וְיוֹמָא, וְהַיְינוּ רָזָא דִּכְתִיב שְׁנַיִם אֲנָשִׁים מְרַגְּלִים.

114. We have learned that from the aspect of Ima there are two spirits who pursue Judgment attached to the left hand. We have established that they daily spy on (or 'from the feet of') the land, NAMELY MALCHUT, MEANING THEY NOURISH FROM NETZACH, HOD, YESOD OF MALCHUT, REFERRED TO AS FEET. This is the secret of, "two men to spy" (Yehoshua 2:1).

115. וְתָאנָא, זַכָּאָה חוּלְקֵיהוֹן דְּיִשְׂרָאֵל יַתִּיר מִכָּל עַמִּין עע״ז דְּקוּדְשָׁא בְּרִיךְ הוּא בָּעֵי לְדַכְּאָה לְהוּ, וּלְרַחֲמָא עָלַיְיהוּ, דְּאִינּוּן חוּלְקֵיהּ וְעַדְבֵיהּ, הה״ד כִּי חֵלֶק יְיָ׳ עַמּוֹ וְגוֹ׳, וּכְתִיב יַרְכִּיבֵהוּ עַל בָּמֳתֵי אָרֶץ. עַל בָּמֳתֵי אָרֶץ דַּיְיקָא. דְּהָא אִינּוּן אִתְאַחֲדָן לְעֵילָּא לְעֵילָּא. וְע״ד קוּדְשָׁא בְּרִיךְ הוּא רְחִימוּתָא דִּילֵיהּ אִתְדְּבָק בְּהוּ, הה״ד אָהַבְתִּי אֶתְכֶם אָמַר יְיָ׳, וּכְתִיב כִּי מֵאַהֲבַת יְיָ׳ אֶתְכֶם וְגוֹ׳, וּמִגּוֹ רְחִימוּתָא יַתִּירָא דִּרְחִים לְהוּ, יָהַב לוֹן יוֹמָא חַד בְּשַׁתָּא לְדַכְּאָה לְהוּ, וּלְזַכָּאָה לְהוּ מִכָּל חוֹבֵיהוֹן, דִּכְתִּיב כִּי בַיּוֹם הַזֶּה וְגוֹ׳. בְּגִין דִּיהוֹן זַכָּאִין בְּעָלְמָא דֵּין, וּבְעָלְמָא דְּאָתֵי, וְלָא יִשְׁתְּכַּח בְּהוּ חוֹבָא. וְע״ד בְּיוֹמָא דָּא, מִתְעַטְּרִין יִשְׂרָאֵל, וְשַׁלְּטִין עַל כֻּלְּהוּ גַּרְדִּינִין, וְעַל כֻּלְּהוּ טְהִירִין.

115. We have learned that Yisrael has a more fortunate share than the idolatrous nations, as the Holy One, blessed be He, desired to purify them and have mercy for them as they are His portion and inheritance. It is written, "For Hashem's portion is His people..." (Devarim 32:9) and "He made him ride on the high places of the earth" (Ibid. 13). "On the high places" exactly, as they join up higher and higher WITH ZEIR ANPIN. Therefore, the love of the Holy One, blessed be He, is clinging to them, as it is written, "'I have loved you', says Hashem" (Malachi 1:2) and, "But because Hashem loved you" (Devarim 7:8). From this excessive love, He gave them one day during the year to purify them and clear them from their sins, as is written, "for on that day..." (Vayikra 16:30). This was in order that they may be meritorious in this world and in the World to Come, and that no sin may be found in them. Consequently on this day, Yisrael are crowned and rule over the prosecutors and all spirits.

116. תָּאנָא וְנָתַן אַהֲרֹן עַל שְׁנֵי הַשְּׂעִירִים גּוֹרָלוֹת. וְנָתַן אַהֲרֹן, בְּגִין דְּאָתֵי מִסִּטְרָא דְּחֶסֶד. עַל שְׁנֵי הַשְּׂעִירִים, עַל דַּיְיקָא, בְּגִין דְּתִתְבְּסַם

מַטְרוֹנִיתָא. גּוֹרָל אֶחָד לַיְיָ׳ וְגוֹרָל לַעֲזָאזֵל וְהָא תְּרֵין שְׂעִירִין אִינּוּן, אֲמַאי חַד לַיְיָ׳. אֶלָּא אָמַר קוּדְשָׁא בְּרִיךְ הוּא, יֵתִיב הַאי גַּבָּאי, וְחַד יֵזִיל וְיְשׁוּט בְּעָלְמָא, דְּאִלְמָלֵי תַּרְוַויְיהוּ מִזְדַּוְּוגָן, לָא יָכִיל עָלְמָא לְמִסְבָּל.

116. We have learned that "And Aaron shall cast lots upon the two goats." "Aaron shall cast," WHY ONLY AARON? Because he stems from the aspect of Chesed, AND THUS IS ABLE TO PERFECT MALCHUT WITH CHASSADIM. "Upon the two goats": BEHOLD "upon" is to be understood precisely, HINTING ABOUT MALCHUT WHICH IS ABOVE THE TWO GOATS, so as to give fragrance to the Matron, DENOTING MALCHUT. "One lot for Hashem, and the other lot for Azazel" (Vayikra 16:8). HE QUESTIONS: These two goats SYMBOLIZE JUDGMENTS, so why should one of them be for Hashem? HE ANSWERS: The Holy One, blessed be He, said, 'Let one GOAT stay with Me and let the other wander around in the world, for if both joined together, the world would not be able to bear it.'

117. נָפַק הַאי, אָזִיל וְשָׁאט בְּעָלְמָא, וְאַשְׁכַּח לְהוּ לְיִשְׂרָאֵל, בְּכַמָּה פּוּלְחָנִין, בְּכַמָּה דַּרְגִּין, בְּכַמָּה נִמּוּסִין טָבָן, לָא יָכִיל לְהוּ, כֻּלְּהוּ שְׁלָמָא בֵּינַיְיהוּ, לָא יָכִיל לְמֵיעָל בְּהוּ בְּדַלְטוֹרָא. הַאי שְׂעִירָא שַׁלְחִין לֵיהּ בְּמַטּוּלָא דְּכָל חוֹבַיְיהוּ דְּיִשְׂרָאֵל.

117. This GOAT comes out and roams around the world. It finds Yisrael performing various kinds of worship on various levels and a variety of good practices and it can not overcome them. Among them all, peace reigns and the goat can not commence to slander them, MEANING TO INSTIGATE AGAINST THEM. This goat is sent with the burden of all the sins of Yisrael.

118. תָּאנָא, כַּמָּה חֲבִילֵי טְרִיקִין מִזְדַּמְּנָן, דְּאִינּוּן תְּחוֹת יְדֵיהּ, וּמְמָנָן לְאַלְלָא אַרְעָא, עַל כָּל אִינּוּן דְּעָבְרִין עַל פִּתְגָּמֵי אוֹרַיְיתָא. וְהַהוּא יוֹמָא, לָא שְׁכִיחַ דַּלְטוֹרָא לְמַלְּלָא בְּהוּ בְּיִשְׂרָאֵל. כַּד מָטָא הַאי שְׂעִירָא לְגַבֵּי טוּרָא, כַּמָּה חֶידוּ עַל חֶידוּ מִתְבַּסְּמִין כֻּלְּהוּ בֵּיהּ. וְהַהוּא גַּרְדִּינָא דְּנָפִיק, אַהֲדַר וְאָמַר תּוּשְׁבַּחְתָּא דְּיִשְׂרָאֵל, קַטֵיגוֹרָא אִתְעֲבֵיד סַנֵּיגוֹרָא.

-247-

118. We have learned that numerous bands of demons are ready under the authority OF THIS GOAT, prepared to spy out the land against all those transgressing the Torah, but on that day, YOM KIPPUR, it is unable to find words of slander against Yisrael. When this goat OF AZAZEL arrives at the mountain, multiple joys burst forth from it to all. Even he who pursued Judgment that emerged, NAMELY THE SUPERNAL GOAT, recants and speaks praise of Yisrael. The prosecutor has become the defense attorney, MEANING THE SLANDERER HAS NOW BECOME THE CHAMPION SPOKESMAN FOR YISRAEL.

119. וְת"ח, לָאו דָּא בִּלְחוֹדוֹי הוּא, אֶלָּא בְּכָל אֲתַר דְּבַעְיָין יִשְׂרָאֵל לְאִתְדַּכְּאָה מֵחוֹבַיְיהוּ, קוּדְשָׁא בְּרִיךְ הוּא יָהִיב לוֹן עֵיטָא לְקַשְׁרָא מָארֵי דְּדִינָא, וּלְבַסְּמָא לְהוּ בְּאִינוּן קָרְבְּנִין וְעָלָוָון, דִּקְרֵבִין קָמֵי קוּדְשָׁא בְּרִיךְ הוּא, וּכְדֵין לָא יַכְלִין לְאַבְאָשָׁא. וְהַהוּא יוֹמָא יַתִּיר עַל כֹּלָּא, כְּמָה דִּמְבַסְּמִין יִשְׂרָאֵל לְתַתָּא לְכֹלָּא, הָכִי מְבַסְּמִין לְכָל אִינוּן דְּאִית לְהוּ דַּלְטוֹרָא וְכֹלָּא קָרְבְּנָא הוּא וּפוּלְחָנָא דְּקוּדְשָׁא בְּרִיךְ הוּא.

119. Come and see not only this alone, but everywhere that Yisrael need to cleanse themselves their sin, the Holy One, blessed be He, gives them a plan to bind the accusers, SO THEY WILL NOT ACCUSE. It is also to pacify them through the means of sacrifices and burnt offerings that they offer before the Holy One, blessed be He. From then on, they are unable to cause harm and on that day, YOM KIPPUR, more than any other day, just as Yisrael below plead everyone delight, THROUGH THE TWO GOATS, so they all accusers. All of this is as a result of the sacrifice and the service of the Holy One, blessed be He.

120. תָּאנָא, בְּהַהִיא שַׁעֲתָא דִּכְתִיב, וְלָקַח אַהֲרֹן אֶת שְׁנֵי הַשְּׂעִירִים וְגוֹ', מִתְעָרִין אִינוּן בְּהַהוּא יוֹמָא לְעֵילָא, וּבַעְיָין לְשַׁלְטָאָה וּלְמֵיפָּק בְּעָלְמָא. כֵּיוָן דְּכַהֲנָא מְקָרֵב אִלֵּין לְתַתָּא, מִתְקָרְבִין אִינוּן לְעֵילָא. כְּדֵין עַדְבִין סַלְקִין בְּכָל סִטְרִין, כַּהֲנָא יָהַב עַדְבִין לְתַתָּא, כַּהֲנָא יָהִיב עַדְבִין לְעֵילָא. כְּמָה דְּחַד אִשְׁתְּאַר בֵּיה בְּקוּדְשָׁא בְּרִיךְ הוּא לְתַתָּא. וְחַד אַפְּקִין לֵיה לְהַהוּא מַדְבְּרָא, הָכִי נָמֵי לְעֵילָא, חַד אִשְׁתְּאַר בֵּיה

בְּקוּדְשָׁא בְּרִיךְ הוּא, וְחַד נָפִיק וְשָׁט בְּעָלְמָא, לְהַהוּא מַדְבְּרָא עִלָּאָה, וְחַד בְּחַד מִתְקַשָּׁר.

120. We have learned that at that time it is written that Aaron "shall take the two goats..." (Vayikra 16:7), these TWO GOATS are stirred up that very day above. They wish TO JOIN TOGETHER, AS MENTIONED, to rule and to set out into the world. When the priest offers the two goats down below in the Temple, they are offered above, and when the lots are spread in every direction, the priest casts lots down below. Then the priest, WHO IS CHESED, casts the lots on high. Just as one remains with the Holy One, blessed be He, REFERRING TO THE ONE GOAT ALLOTTED TO HASHEM, below, and one, NAMELY THE GOAT OF AZAZEL, is brought out to the desert, so it is on high. One remains with the Holy One, blessed be He, IN THE CENTRAL COLUMN, and one goes out and wanders in the world into the desert on high, MEANING THE JUDGMENTS THAT BECOME REVEALED WITH THE EMERGENCE OF CHOCHMAH, WHICH ARE CONSIDERED OF THE ASPECT OF DESERT AND FOREBODING WILDERNESS. The one joins with another, MEANING THEY SHED LIGHT ONE UPON THE OTHER.

121. כְּתִיב וְסָמַךְ אַהֲרֹן אֶת שְׁתֵּי יָדָיו עַל רֹאשׁ הַשָּׂעִיר הַחַי וְהִתְוַדָּה עָלָיו וְגוֹ'. בְּג"כ וְסָמַךְ אַהֲרֹן אֶת שְׁתֵּי יָדָיו, דְּקוּדְשָׁא בְּרִיךְ הוּא יִסְתְּכַם עַל יְדוֹי. עַל רֹאשׁ הַשָּׂעִיר הַחַי, הַחַי דַּיְיקָא, לְאַכְלְלָא הַהוּא דִּלְעֵילָּא.

121. It is written, "And Aaron shall lay both his two hands on the head of the live goat, and confess over him..." (Ibid. 21). Hence it is written, "And Aaron shall lay both his two hands," WHICH ARE THE SECRET OF THE RIGHT AND LEFT COLUMNS so that the Holy One, blessed be He, THE CENTRAL COLUMN, will harmonize his hands. In "On the head of the live goat," "the live" is precise, AS IT COMES to include the goat above.

122. וְהִתְוַדָּה עָלָיו אֶת כָּל עֲוֹנוֹת, כְּמָה דִּכְתִיב וְהִתְוַדָּה אֲשֶׁר חָטָא עָלֶיהָ. וְאוֹקִימְנָא עָלֶיהָ, דְּאִתְדְּכֵי ב"נ וְאִשְׁתְּאַר עָלֶיהָ כָּל הַהוּא חוֹבָא. אוֹף הָכִי וְהִתְוַדָּה עָלָיו, בָּתַר דְּאוֹדֵי כַּהֲנָא בְּגִינַיְיהוּ דְּיִשְׂרָאֵל, עָלָיו: כְּלוֹמַר, יִשְׁתַּאֲרוּן כֻּלְּהוּ עָלָיו.

122. "And confess over him all the iniquities" (Ibid.) is similar to "that he shall confess that he has sinned in that thing (lit. 'over her')" (Vayikra 5:5). We established that "over her" means that the person becomes cleansed and that sin rests on her, ON THE SHEEP. So also here "and confess over him," implies that after the priest makes a confession on behalf of Yisrael over him, ALL THE SINS will rest "over him."

123. א״ל ר' אַבָּא, אִי הָכִי וְהָא כְּתִיב וְלֹא יִזְבְּחוּ עוֹד אֶת זִבְחֵיהֶם לַשְּׂעִירִים, אָמַר לֵיהּ שָׁאנֵי הָכָא, דְּהָתָם לַשְּׂעִירִים הֲווֹ קְרֵבִין קָרְבְּנָא, וּבְג״כ לָא כְּתִיב וְלֹא יִזְבְּחוּ עוֹד אֶת זִבְחֵיהֶם שְׂעִירִים, אֶלָּא לַשְּׂעִירִים, דְּהָתָם לַשְּׂעִירִים הֲווֹ עַבְדֵי פּוּלְחָנָא, וְשׁוּלְטָנוּתָא. וְהָכָא וְנָשָׂא הַשָּׂעִיר עָלָיו אֶת כָּל עֲוֹנוֹתָם, וְקָרְבְּנָא לָא אִתְעֲבֵיד אֶלָּא לְקוּדְשָׁא בְּרִיךְ הוּא. ת״ח, דִּבְגִינֵי קָרְבְּנָא מִתְבַּסְּמָן עִלָּאִין וְתַתָּאִין, וְדִינָא לָא שַׁרְיָא וְשַׁלְטָא עָלַיְיהוּ דְיִשְׂרָאֵל.

123. Rabbi Aba said to him: If so, behold it is written, "And they shall no more offer their sacrifices to the demons (also: 'goats')" (Vayikra 17:7), SO HOW CAN YOU SAY THAT THE GOAT OF AZAZEL CORRESPONDS WITH THE GOAT ABOVE? He answered him: Here things are different as there they used to offer sacrifices to goats, as it is not written: 'And they shall no more offer their sacrifices goats', but rather "to the goats" as they worshipped goats AND GAVE THEM authority. Here ONLY "and the goat shall bear upon it all their iniquities" (Vayikra 16:22), and the sacrifice was made only for the Holy One, blessed be He. Come and see: as a result of this sacrifice, those on high and those below are perfumed, and Judgment neither dwells nor rules upon Yisrael.

20. An appointed man

A Synopsis

We learn that certain people are prepared for certain things, so that one man is fit for achieving blessings while another is fit for curses. Bilaam was ready for evil but not prepared for good; even when he blessed his blessings were not fulfilled, but his curses always prevailed. There was a man who was recognizably fit to be the one to take the goat to the mountain and push it off. The goat is purchased with money from the whole congregation so that it atones for everyone.

124. תָּאנָא, וְשִׁלַּח בְּיַד אִישׁ עִתִּי הַמִּדְבָּרָה. מַהוּ אִישׁ עִתִּי. אֶלָּא רָזָא דְמִלָּה הָכִי הוּא בְּכָל מַה דְּאִתְעָבֵיד, בָּעֵי ב"נ זַמִּין לְהַהִיא מִלָּה. אִית ב"נ דְּבִרְכְתָא אִתְקַיִּים עַל יְדֵיהּ יַתִּיר מֵאַחֲרָא. ת"ח, מַה כְּתִיב בֵּיהּ בְּכַהֲנָא, טוֹב עַיִן הוּא יְבוֹרָךְ, אַל תִּקְרֵי יְבוֹרָךְ, אֶלָּא יְבָרֵךְ, בְּגִין דְּהוּא זַמִּין דְּיִתְקַיִּים בִּרְכָתָא עַל יְדֵיהּ בְּהַאי.

124. We have learned about "and shall send him away by the hand of an appointed man into the wilderness" (Vayikra 16:21). What is meant by appointed? HE ANSWERS: The secret of the matter is as follows. Whatever needs to be done, THE DOER needs to be ready to do it. There are people through whom the blessing comes true more than through others. THE REASON IS DUE TO HIS PREPARATION FOR THE MATTER. Come and see what is written about the priest. "He that has a good eye shall be blessed" (Mishlei 22:9). Do not read 'shall be blessed', but rather 'He shall bless'. As a result of his good eye, he is ready so that the blessing will thus prevail through him.

125. וְאִית ב"נ דְּהוּא זַמִּין לְאִתְקַיְּימָא לְוָוטִין עַל יְדֵיהּ, וּבְכָל מַה דְּיַשְׁגַּח לֵיתֵי לְוָוטַיָּיא וּמְאֵרָה וּבְעֵיתָא כְּגוֹן בִּלְעָם, דְּאִקְרֵי רַע עַיִן, דַּהֲוָה זַמִּין בְּכָל בִּישׁ, וְלָא הֲוָה זַמִּין לְטָב. וְאַף עַל גַּב דְּבָרֵךְ, בִּרְכָתֵיהּ לָא בִּרְכָתָא, וְלָא אִתְקַיִּים. וְכַד הֲוָה לָיִיט, כָּל מַאן דְּלָיִיט אִתְקַיִּים, וַאֲפִילוּ בְּרִגְעָא חֲדָא, וְעַל דָּא כְּתִיב, שְׁתֻם הָעָיִן. בְּכָל אֲתַר דְּעֵינֵיהּ שַׁלְטָא אִתְלַטְיָיא.

-251-

125. There is a man who is fit for curses to occur through him. Wherever he looks, there would be curses, anathemas and confusions. For example, Bilaam was called evil-eyed, as he was ready for every evil but not prepared for good. Even when he blessed, his blessing was no blessing and it was not fulfilled. But when he cursed, it prevailed; even in one instance IT WOULD COME TO BE. Therefore, it is written, "Whose eyes are open," (Bemidbar 24:3). Every place his eye had seen was cursed.

126. ת״ח מַה כְּתִיב. וַיָּשֶׁת אֶל הַמִּדְבָּר פָּנָיו, בְּגִין דְּיִתְעַר מֵהַהוּא סִטְרָא הַהוּא דְּשַׁלְטָא תַּמָּן, וְיֵיתֵי בְּדַלְטוֹרְיָא עָלַיְיהוּ דְיִשְׂרָאֵל. מַה כְּתִיב בְּהוּ בְּכַהֲנֵי, טוֹב עַיִן הוּא יְבוֹרָךְ, דְּהוּא הֲוָה זַמִּין בְּהַאי, וְשָׁארֵי בִּרְכָתָא בְּאַשְׁגָּחוּתָא דִילֵיהּ. וְעַ״ד תָּנֵינָן, יִסְטֵי ב״נ אֲפִילוּ מִמֵּאָה אָרְחִין, וְלָא יִאְרַע בב״נ דְּאִית לֵיהּ עֵינָא בִּישָׁא.

126. Come and see what is written, "But he set his face toward the wilderness" (Ibid. 1) for the purpose of arousing the force that rules there, NAMELY THE OTHER SIDE, so it should come slandering and denouncing Yisrael. It is written of the priests, "He that has a good eye shall be blessed," as he is ready for this and the blessing prevails where he aims his eyes. As a result, we have learned that a person should turn away even from one hundred ways and avoid meeting someone who has an evil eye.

127. אוּף הָכָא וְשִׁלַּח בְּיַד אִישׁ עִתִּי, דְּהוּא זַמִּין לְהַאי. וְרָשִׁים לְהַאי, וְכַהֲנָא הֲוָה אִשְׁתְּמוֹדַע בֵּיהּ, חַד עֵינָא יַתִּיר מֵאָחֳרָא פּוּרְתָא. סוּרְטָא דְּעַל עֵינָא אִתְחַפְיָא בְּשַׂעֲרִין סַגִּיאִין. מִכְחָלָא עֵינָא, וְלָא מִסְתָּכַּל בְּמֵישָׁר. הַאי הוּא ב״נ זַמִּין לְהַאי, וְכַדְקָא חֲזֵי לֵיהּ. וְעַ״ד כְּתִיב בְּיַד אִישׁ עִתִּי.

127. Also here, "And shall send him away by the hand of an appointed man," MEANING THAT he is ready for this and marked for it. The priest recognized him, because one eye was slightly larger than the other, the skin above the eye, NAMELY THE EYELIDS, was covered by large hairs and the eye was blue-colored and looked squintingly. This is the person appointed for this matter, TO SEND THE GOAT TO AZAZEL, and he is fitting for this. Therefore, it is written, "By the hand of an appointed man."

128. בְּגוּשׁ חֲלָבָא הֲוָה ב״נ, דִּבְכָל אֲתָר דְּמָחֵי בִּידוֹי, הֲוָה מִית, וְלָא הֲווֹ בְּנֵי נָשָׁא מְקָרְבִין בַּהֲדֵיהּ. בְּסוּרְיָא הֲוָה ב״נ, דִּבְכָל אֲתָר דְּאִסְתְּכַּל אֲפִילוּ לְטָב, כֹּלָּא אִתְהַפַּךְ לְבִישׁ. יוֹמָא חַד הֲוָה בַּר נָשׁ אָזִיל בְּשׁוּקָא, וַהֲווֹ אַנְפּוֹי נְהִירִין. אָתָא הַהוּא בַּר נָשׁ וְאִסְתְּכַּל בֵּיהּ, וְאִתְבְּקַע עֵינֵיהּ. בְּג״כ, בְּכֹלָּא הֲוָה ב״נ זַמִּין, לְהַאי וּלְהַאי. וְעַל דָּא כְּתִיב טוֹב עַיִן הוּא יְבוֹרָךְ, אַל תִּקְרֵי יְבוֹרָךְ אֶלָּא יְבָרֵךְ.

128. In Gush Chalav, there was a person that would kill wherever he struck with his hand, and people would not approach him. In Syria, there was a person that wherever he looked, even if he meant well, everything would turn to bad. One day, there was a person going to the market and his face was aglow, so that person came and stared at him and his eye burst. Hence, in all THINGS, EITHER GOOD OR BAD, there is someone fit for either the one or the other. Consequently, the verse says, "He that has a good eye shall be blessed." Do not pronounce it: 'shall be blessed', but 'shall bless'.

129. וְתָאנָא, הַאי ב״נ דַּהֲוָה אָזִיל לְמַדְבְּרָא, כַּד מָטָא בֵּיהּ בְּהַהוּא שְׂעִירָא הֲוָה סָלִיק לְטוּרָא, וְדָחֵי לֵיהּ בִּתְרֵין יְדוֹי. וְלָא הֲוָה נָחִית לְפַלְגוּת טוּרָא, עַד דְּאִתְעֲבֵיד שַׁיְיפִין שַׁיְיפִין. וְהַהוּא ב״נ הֲוָה אָמַר, כָּךְ יִמָּחוּ עֲוֹנוֹת עַמָּךְ וְגוֹ׳. וּבְגִין דְּסָלִיק הַהוּא קַטֵיגוֹרְיָא וְאִתְעֲבֵיד סַנֵיגוֹרְיָא דְּיִשְׂרָאֵל, כְּדֵין קוּדְשָׁא בְּרִיךְ הוּא, כָּל חוֹבַיְיהוּ דְּיִשְׂרָאֵל, וְכָל מַה דִּכְתִיב בְּאִינוּן פִּתְקִין דִּלְעֵילָא, לְאַדְכְּרָא חוֹבַיְיהוּ דִּבְנֵי נָשָׁא, נָטִיל לוֹן וְרָמֵי לוֹן כְּהַאי גַּוְונָא, לַאֲתָר דְּאִתְקְרֵי מְצוּלוֹת יָם. הה״ד, וְתַשְׁלִיךְ בִּמְצוּלוֹת יָם כָּל חַטֹּאתָם.

129. We have learned this person would go WITH THE GOAT to the desert. When he arrived there with the goat, he would ascend the mountains, push the goat off with both hands and it would not even reach halfway through the mountain when its limbs would fall apart. That man would say: So may be blotted all the sins of Your people. THROUGH THIS, the prosecutors would turn to defend Yisrael. Then would the Holy One, blessed be He, take all sins of Yisrael, and all that is written with the verdicts on high, which mention the sins of men. And He would cast them out in this manner, AS

THE GOAT WAS CAST OFF FROM THE MOUNTAIN, to a place called the depths of the sea, WHICH IS THE SECRET OF A PLACE OF DARKNESS AND OF THE JUDGMENTS OF THE LEFT THAT IS BENEATH MALCHUT THAT IS CALLED SEA. This is the meaning of the verse, "And You will cast all their sins into the depths of the sea" (Michah 7:19).

130. תָּאנָא, וּמֵאֵת עֲדַת בְּנֵי יִשְׂרָאֵל יִקַּח שְׁנֵי שְׂעִירֵי עִזִּים לְחַטָּאת, וּמֵאֵת עֲדַת, בְּגִין דְּיְהֵא מִכֻּלְּהוּ, וְיִתְכַּפֵּר לְכֻלְּהוּ. דְּהָא כָּל חוֹבַיְיהוּ דִּבְנֵי יִשְׂרָאֵל הָכָא תַּלְיָין, וְכֻלְּהוּ מִתְכַּפְּרֵי בְּדָא. וְלָא סַגִּי מב"ן חַד. וּמֵאָן אֲתָר אִתְנְסִיבוּ מֵאִינוּן קוּפִּין דְּבַעֲזָרָה נַטְלִין אַגְרָא, וְאַיְיתֵי לְהוּ מֵאִינוּן דְּמֵי דַּהֲווֹ מִכֻּלְּהוּ.

130. We have learned that "And he shall take from the congregation, of the children of Yisrael two kids of the goats for a sin offering" (Vayikra 16:5). THE VERSE SAYS, "from the congregation." THIS IS TO TEACH that they should buy it with everyone's MONEY, and atonement will thus come to all, as all sins of Yisrael are impending here and all will attain atonement from this act. THEREFORE, it is not enough TO TAKE MONEY from one person. From where is it taken? The money is taken from the public fund boxes in the sanctuary, and they bring THE GOATS with this money, which is the contributed property of everyone.

131. וְהַהוּא שְׂעִירָא אָחֳרָא, דַּהֲוָה אִשְׁתְּאַר לְקוּדְשָׁא בְּרִיךְ הוּא, עַבְדִּין לֵיהּ חַטָּאת בְּקַדְמֵיתָא. וְהָא אוּקִימְנָא בְּאָן אֲתָר הֲוָה מִתְקַשְּׁרָא. וּלְבָתַר דָּא מִתְקָרְבִין הָנֵי, וּמִתְבַּסְּמִין כֹּלָּא, וְאִשְׁתְּאָרוּ יִשְׂרָאֵל זַכָּאִין קַמֵּי קוּדְשָׁא בְּרִיךְ הוּא, מִכָּל חוֹבִין דְּעָבְדוּ וְחָבוּ קַמֵּיהּ. הה"ד כִּי בַיּוֹם הַזֶּה יְכַפֵּר עֲלֵיכֶם וְגוֹ'.

131. They make from the outset a sin offering of the other goat that remained before the Holy One, blessed be He, and we have already established to which place it is attached. Afterwards, they are sacrificed and all things become better, and Yisrael remain in the clear before the Holy One, blessed be He, from all sins committed. This is the essence of the verse, "For on that day will He forgive you..." (Vayikra 16:29).

21. The two goats

A Synopsis

We learn that the two goats were parted and one remained for the portion of God. On that day the priest offered sacrifices for his own sins and then for the sins of all the people.

132. תּוּ אָמַר ר' שִׁמְעוֹן, וַיֹּאמֶר יַעֲקֹב אֶל רִבְקָה אִמּוֹ הֵן עֵשָׂו אָחִי אִישׁ שָׂעִיר וְאָנֹכִי אִישׁ חָלָק. מַאי קָא רְמִיזָא, אֶלָּא וַדַּאי עֵשָׂו אִישׁ שָׂעִיר, הוּא מֵהַהוּא דְּאִקְרֵי שָׂעִיר, דְּהָא מֵהַהוּא סִטְרָא אָתֵי. וְאָנֹכִי אִישׁ חָלָק: גְּבַר מֵהַהוּא דְּפָלִיג לְכָל שְׁאָר עַמִּין רַבְרְבִין מְמָנָן. דִּכְתִּיב אֲשֶׁר חָלַק יְיָ' אֱלֹהֶיךָ אוֹתָם, וּכְתִיב כִּי חֵלֶק יְיָ' עַמּוֹ וְגוֹ'. תּוּ אִישׁ חָלָק, מִתְּרֵי שְׂעִירִים וְאִשְׁתְּאַר חֲדָא. דְּכַהֲנָא פָּלִיג לֵהּ, חַד לְחוּלְקֵיהּ, וְחַד לְקוּדְשָׁא בְּרִיךְ הוּא. אֲמַאי. בְּגִין דְּיַטְעִין עַל כַּתְפוֹי כָּל חוֹבוֹי דְּיַעֲקֹב, דִּכְתִּיב וְנָשָׂא הַשָּׂעִיר עָלָיו אֶת כָּל עֲוֹנוֹתָם, עֲוֹנוֹת תָּם.

132. Rabbi Shimon said, "And Jacob said to Rivkah his mother, Behold, Esau my brother is a hairy man, and I am a smooth man" (Beresheet 27:11). What is this statement hinting at? Surely, Esau was a hairy (Heb. *sa'ir*) man, of him that is called goat (Heb. *seir*), WHICH IS THE OTHER SIDE, as it comes from the same aspect. "And I am a smooth (Heb. *chalak*) man," MEANING a man WHO WAS GIVEN (HEB. *NECHELAK*) from what He allotted (Heb. *chalak*) to the ministers of the other nations, as it is written, "Which Hashem your Elohim has allotted to all the nations" (Devarim 4:19) and, "For Hashem's portion (Hbe. *chelek*) is His people" (Devarim 32:9). Furthermore, "a smooth man" MEANS the two goats WERE PARTED and there remained one PORTION, which the priest divided (Heb. *chilek*). One went to the portion OF JACOB and one for the Holy One, blessed be He. Why? In order that THE GOAT carry upon its shoulders all Jacob's sins, as written, "And the goat shall bear upon it all their iniquities (Heb. *avonotam*)" (Vaykira 16:22). THESE COMPRISE THE LETTERS, Avonot (Eng. 'sins') tam (lit. 'a perfect man'), REFERRING TO THE SINS OF JACOB KNOWN AS THE PERFECT MAN.

133. תָּאנָא, בְּהַהוּא יוֹמָא כַּמָה פְּתִיחִין פְּתִיחָן לְקַבְּלֵיהוֹן דְּיִשְׂרָאֵל לְקַבְּלָא צְלוֹתֵיהוֹן. זַכָּאָה חוּלְקֵיהוֹן דְּיִשְׂרָאֵל, דְּהָא קוּדְשָׁא בְּרִיךְ הוּא

בָּעָא לְזַכָּאָה לוֹן, וּלְדַכְּאָה לוֹן, הה"ד כִּי בַיוֹם הַזֶּה יְכַפֵּר וְגוֹ'. בְּהַאי
יוֹמָא אִתְעֲטַּר כַּהֲנָא בְּכַמָּה עִטְרִין. בְּהַאי יוֹמָא פּוּלְחָנָא דְּכַהֲנָא יַקִּירָא
וְרַב מִכָּל פּוּלְחָנִין. לְכֹלָּא יָהַב חוּלָקָא בְּאִינּוּן קָרְבְּנִין דְּקוּדְשָׁא בְּרִיךְ
הוּא. בְּהַאי יוֹמָא אִתְעֲטַּר חֶסֶד בְּעָלְמָא עַל יְדָא דְּכַהֲנָא, מִקָרֵב קָרְבְּנִין
עַל חוֹבֵיהוֹן דְּעַמָּא. עַל חוֹבֵיה בְּקַדְמֵיתָא, וּלְבָתַר עַל חוֹבֵיהוֹן דְּעַמָּא.
מִקָרֵב עִלָּוָן עֲלֵיה וְעַל עַמָּא וְהָא אוֹקִימְנָא מִלֵּי.

133. We have learned that numerous doors opened before Yisrael on this day to receive their prayers. How fortunate is the lot of Yisrael that the Holy One, blessed be He, wishes to give them merit and to purify them. This is what the verse says, "For on that day will He forgive you..." On this day, the priest is bedecked with numerous crowns. On this day, the service of the priest is full of glory and far greater than on any other service. Everyone was given a share of these sacrifices to the Holy One, blessed be He. On this day Chesed is crowned in the world by the priest, who offers sacrifices for the sins of the people. First, HE OFFERED for his own sins and afterward for the sins of the people. He offered burnt offerings for himself and the nation. We have already established these matters.

22. A goat to Azazel

A Synopsis

The goat is dispatched to Azazel so that the Other Side will be separated from Yisrael and will not testify against Yisrael before God. We are told that every single thing in the world, whether good or bad, is needed, even the Angel of Death. The entire remedy depends on this, not to arouse the secret of judgment on high and thus intensify this judgment to annihilate mankind. That judgment is aroused through the sins of mankind.

רעיא מהימנא

134. פְּקוּדָא דָּא, לְמִפְלַח כַּהֲנָא רַבָּא פּוּלְחָנָא דְּהַהוּא יוֹמָא כְּמָה דְּאִצְטְרִיךְ, וּלְמִשְׁלַח שָׂעִיר לַעֲזָאזֵל. רָזָא דָּא כד"א, בְּגִין לְאִתְפָּרְשָׁא מֵעַמָּא קַדִּישָׁא, וְלָא יִתְבַּע חוֹבַיְיהוּ קַמֵּי מַלְכָּא. וְלָא יְקַטְרֵג עָלַיְיהוּ, דְּהָא לֵית לֵיה תְּקִיפוּ וְשׁוּלְטָנוּ, בַּר כַּד אִתְּקַף רוּגְזָא מִלְעֵילָא, וּבְהַהוּא דּוֹרוֹנָא אִתְהַפָּךְ לְבָתַר אַפּוֹטְרוֹפּוֹסָא עָלַיְיהוּ, וְעַל דָּא אִתְדַּחְיָיא מִקַּמֵּי מַלְכָּא. וְהָא אוֹקִימְנָא, בְּגִין דְּאִיהוּ קֵץ כָּל בָּשָׂר.

Ra'aya Meheimna (the Faithful Shepherd)

134. It is commanded that the High Priest should perform the service of that day as need be, and should dispatch the goat to Azazel. The secret is as you said, in order THAT THE OTHER SIDE be separated from the holy nation and not make demands for their sins before the King. He should not accuse them, as he has neither strength nor authority but when anger is intensified above. With this gift OF THE GOAT TO AZAZEL, he is then converted to be their guardian. As a result he is banished from before the King. We established that this is so, because he represents the end of all flesh.

135. וְעַמָּא קַדִּישָׁא יָהֲבִין לֵיהּ כְּמָה דְּאִצְטְרִיךְ לֵיהּ שָׂעִיר, וְרָזָא דָּא הֵן עֵשָׂו אֲחִי אִישׁ שָׂעִיר. כְּמָה דְּאִיהוּ בְּסִטְרָא דִּקְדוּשָׁה דְּכַר וְנוּקְבָא, אוּף הָכִי בְּסִטְרָא מְסָאֲבוּ דְּכַר וְנוּקְבָא. מַתְלָא אָמְרֵי, לְכַלְבָּא אַרְמֵי לֵיהּ גַּרְמָא, יְלַחֵךְ עַפְרָא דְּרַגְלָךְ.

135. The holy nation gives to him what is needed for him, NAMELY a goat (Heb. *seir*). This is the secret of "Behold, Esau my brother is a hairy (Heb. *sa'ir*) man" (Beresheet 27:11), AS HE IS AN ASPECT OF THE OTHER SIDE. IT CONTAINS MALE AND FEMALE CHARACTERISTICS, and just as in the side of holiness there is male and female, so too in the side of defilement there exist a male and female. A popular saying goes like this: Throw a bone to a dog and he will lick the dust off your feet; HERE ALSO, WE GIVE TO THE OTHER SIDE A GOAT AND HE IS CONVERTED TO BE A DEFENDER.

136. שָׁאֵלוּ לְבֶן זוֹמָא, מַהוּ לְסָרוּסֵי כַּלְבָּא. אָמַר לָהֶם, וּבְאַרְצְכֶם לֹא תַעֲשׂוּ, כָּל שֶׁבְּאַרְצְכֶם לֹא תַעֲשׂוּ. כְּמָה דְּאִצְטְרִיךְ עָלְמָא לְהַאי, הָכִי אִצְטְרִיךְ עָלְמָא לְהַאי. וְעַל דָּא אִתְּמַר, וְהִנֵּה טוֹב מְאֹד דָּא מַלְאָךְ הַמָּוֶת. לֵית לְבַטְּלָא לֵיהּ מִן עָלְמָא, עָלְמָא אִצְטְרִיךְ לֵיהּ, אע״ג דִּכְתִּיב בֵּיהּ, וְהַכְּלָבִים עַזֵּי נֶפֶשׁ לֹא יָדְעוּ שָׂבְעָה וְגוֹ', לָא יִתְבַּטְּלוּן מִן עָלְמָא. כֹּלָּא אִצְטְרִיךְ טוֹב וָרָע.

136. They ask ben Zoma: Is it permissible FOR US to emasculate a dog? He replies, "Neither shall you do thus in your land" (Vayikra 22:24). THE MEANING IS, you shall not do thus to anything in your land, EVEN TO A DOG, for as the world needs one thing, it needs another, MEANING THERE IS NOTHING IN THE WORLD THAT IS NOT NEEDED. Therefore, we learned that "and, behold, it was very good" (Beresheet 1:31) refers to the Angel of Death that he should not be blotted from the world, BECAUSE the world needs him. Even though it is written about him, THE ANGEL OF DEATH, "Yea, the dogs are greedy, they never have enough..." (Yeshayah 56:11). IT IS NOT GOOD that they should become extinct from the world. Everything is needed, BOTH good and bad.

137. וּבְגִינֵי כַּךְ אִית לָן בְּיוֹמָא דָּא לְמִרְמֵי לֵיהּ גַּרְמָא לְכַלְבָּא, עַד דְּאִיהוּ גָּרִיר, יֵיעוּל מַאן דְּיֵיעוּל לְגַבֵּי הֵיכָלָא דְּמַלְכָּא, וְלֵית מַאן דְּיִמְחֵי בִּידוֹי. לְבָתַר יְכַשְׁכֵּשׁ לֵיהּ בִּזְנָבֵיהּ.

137 Hence, we need on this day to throw a bone to the dog, MEANING THE GOAT OF AZAZEL. While he is dragging THE BONE, people may enter the palace of the King and no one dares to stop them, FOR THE ACCUSER IS

PREOCCUPIED WITH HIS GIFT. Afterwards, he will still be wagging his tail,
MEANING HE WILL BECOME A DEFENDER.

138. מַה כְּתִיב וְהִתְוַדָּה עָלָיו אֶת כָּל עֲוֹנֹת בְּנֵי יִשְׂרָאֵל, וּכְתִיב וְנָשָׂא
הַשָּׂעִיר עָלָיו אֶת כָּל עֲוֹנֹתָם. כֵּיוָן דְּאִיהוּ חָמֵי הַאי שָׂעִיר. תִּיאוּבְתֵּיה
לְגַבֵּיה, וּלְאִשְׁתַּכְלָלָא בַּהֲדֵיה, וְלָא יָדַע מֵאִינּוּן חוֹבִין דְּקָא נָטִיל שָׂעִיר.
תָּב לְגַבַּיְיהוּ דְּיִשְׂרָאֵל, חָמֵי לוֹן בְּלָא חוֹבִין, בְּלָא פְּשָׁעִין, דְּהָא כֻּלְּהוּ
שַׁרְיָאן בְּרֵישָׁא דְּשָׂעִיר, סָלִיק לְעֵילָא, וְשַׁבַּח לוֹן קָמֵי קוּדְשָׁא בְּרִיךְ
הוּא. וְקוּדְשָׁא בְּרִיךְ הוּא חָמֵי סַהֲדוּתָא דְּהַהוּא מְקַטְרְגָא, וְהוֹאִיל
וְתִיאוּבְתֵּיה לְרַחֲמָא עַל עַמֵּיה, אע"ג דְּאִיהוּ יָדַע כָּל עוֹבָדָא, חָס
עֲלַיְיהוּ דְּיִשְׂרָאֵל.

138. It is written, "And confess over him all the iniquities of the children of
Yisrael" (Vayikra 16:21) and "the goat shall bear upon it all their iniquities"
(Ibid. 22). When THE OTHER SIDE sees this goat, his desire towards it IS
AROUSED to be with it, and he does not know which of the sins the goat
took upon himself. He then returns to Yisrael and sees that they are free and
clear of sins and blemishes, as all sins are upon the head of the goat. He
ascends and praises them before the Holy One, blessed be He. The Holy
One, blessed be He, pays attention to the testimony of the accuser and, since
His desire is to have mercy on His people, He extends mercy to Yisrael even
though He is aware of all that transpired.

139. וְכֹלָּא שַׁרְיָא בְּדָא, בְּגִין דְּלָא יִתְעַר רָזָא דְּדִינָא מִלְּעֵילָא, וְיִתְתַּקַּף
הַאי וְיִשְׁתֵּצוּן בְּנֵי עָלְמָא, דְּהָא דָּא מִסִּטְרָא דְּדִינָא קַשְׁיָא קָא אָתֵי. וְאִי
יִתְעַר הַאי, בְּחוֹבֵי בְּנֵי אִינָשָׁא אִתְעַר. דְּהָא לֵית לֵיה אִתְעָרוּ לְסַלְּקָא
לְעֵילָא לְאִתְעָרָא דִּינָא קַשְׁיָא בַּר בְּדִיל חוֹבֵי בְּנֵי נָשָׁא. דְּהָא בְּשַׁעֲתָא
דב"נ עָבֵיד חוֹבָא, אִתְכְּנַשׁ הַאי, וְכַמָּה אֶלֶף סַיְיעָן דִּילֵיה, וּמִתְכַּנְפֵי
תַּמָּן, וְנַטְלֵי לֵיה, וְסַלְּקִי לְעֵילָא רַחֲמָנָא לִישֵׁזְבָן. וְעַל כֹּלָּא יָהַב קוּדְשָׁא
בְּרִיךְ הוּא עֵיטָא לְיִשְׂרָאֵל לְאִשְׁתְּזָבָא מִכָּל סִטְרִין. וְעַ"ד כְּתִיב, אַשְׁרֵי
הָעָם שֶׁכָּכָה לוֹ אַשְׁרֵי הָעָם שֶׁיְיָ' אֱלֹהָיו.

עַ"כ רַעְיָא מְהֵימְנָא

139. The entire REMEDY depends upon this, not to arouse the secret of the Judgment on high and thus intensify this Judgment to annihilate mankind. All this can come from harsh Judgment. If this JUDGMENT is awakened, it is awakened by the sins of mankind, since it is aroused to ascend high up to instigate the harsh Judgment only if it is as a result of the sins of mankind. When a person commits a sin, it gathers and joins other thousands who assist it. They assemble there and take it so as to bring it up. May the Merciful One protect us. For all of this, The Holy One, blessed be He, gave counsel to Yisrael to be save in every aspect, as written: "Happy is the people, that is in such a case: Happy is that people, whose Elohim is Hashem" (Tehilim 144:15).

End of Ra'aya Meheimna (the Faithful Shepherd)

23. "As cold water to a thirsty soul"

A Synopsis

As the rabbis are praying in a field, a fiery cloud descends and surrounds them. Rabbi Shimon tells them that Solomon gave three books to the world, Shir Hashirim, Kohelet and Mishlei, and that these correspond to Chochmah, Binah and Da'at. He says every verse speaks about two subjects, the Left and Right Columns, and thus they equate to the Central Column. Rabbi Shimon then examines the verse "A cold water to a thirsty soul" and "good news from a far country."

140. עַד דַּהֲווֹ אָזְלֵי, יָתְבוּ בְּחַד חֲקַל, וְצַלּוּ. נַחַת חַד עֲנָנָא דְּאֶשָּׁא, וְאַסְחַר לוֹן. א״ר שִׁמְעוֹן, הָא חֲמֵינָא דְּקוּדְשָׁא בְּרִיךְ הוּא רְעוּתָא דִּילֵיהּ הָכָא. נֵיתִיב. יָתְבוּ וַהֲווֹ אַמְרֵי מִלֵּי דְּאוֹרַיְיתָא. פָּתַח וְאָמַר, מַיִם קָרִים עַל נֶפֶשׁ עֲיֵפָה וּשְׁמוּעָה טוֹבָה מֵאֶרֶץ מֶרְחָק, הָא אִסְתַּכַּלְנָא בְּמִלּוֹי דִּשְׁלֹמֹה מַלְכָּא, וְכֻלְּהוּ בְּחָכְמָה אַמְרָן.

140. As they were going, they stayed in a field and prayed. A fiery cloud descended and surrounded them. Rabbi Shimon said: I believe that the wish of the Holy One, blessed be He, is here. Let us sit down. They sat and discussed words of Torah. He said, "As cold water to a thirsty soul, so is good news from a far country" (Mishlei 25:25). I examined the words of King Solomon and found that they were said with wisdom.

141. ת״ח ג' סִפְרִין דְּחָכְמְתָא אַפִּיק שְׁלֹמֹה לְעָלְמָא, וְכֻלְּהוּ בְּחָכְמְתָא עִלָּאָה. שִׁיר הַשִּׁירִים חָכְמָה, קֹהֶלֶת תְּבוּנָה, וּמִשְׁלֵי דַעַת. לָקֳבֵל ג' אִלֵּין, עָבַד ג' סְפָרִים. שִׁיר הַשִּׁירִים כְּנֶגֶד חָכְמָה הֲכֵי הֲוָא. קֹהֶלֶת לָקֳבֵל תְּבוּנָה, הֲכֵי הֲוָא. מִשְׁלֵי לָקֳבֵל דַעַת. בְּמַאי אִתְחֲזֵי. אֶלָּא כָל אִינּוּן קְרָאֵי בִּתְרֵי גְּווֹנֵי אִינּוּן, רֵישָׁא וְסֵיפָא תְּרֵי גְּווֹנֵי אִתְחַזְיָיא. וְכַד מִסְתַּכְּלֵי קְרָאֵי, דָּא כָּלִיל בְּדָא, וְדָא כָּלִיל בְּדָא, בְּג״כ שָׁקִיל לָקֳבְלֵיהּ דְּדַעַת.

141. Come and see that Solomon did present to the world three books of wisdom and all contain heavenly wisdom. Shir Hashirim represents wisdom,

Kohelet represents understanding and Mishlei represents knowledge. Corresponding to these three, NAMELY CHOCHMAH, BINAH AND DA'AT, he formulated these books – Shir Hashirim corresponds to Chochmah, Kohelet to Tevunah, and Mishlei to Da'at. THIS IS THE SECRET OF THE THREE COLUMNS. How is this shown? HE ANSWERS: All these verses appear in two styles. The beginning OF THE VERSE and the end OF THE VERSE appear as two distinct styles, MEANING IT SPEAKS ABOUT TWO SUBJECTS, THE ASPECTS OF THE TWO COLUMNS, RIGHT AND LEFT. When you examine the verses, you find that they are each comprised in the other, THAT THE TWO SUBJECTS IN THE VERSE ARE INCLUDED ONE IN THE OTHER. For this reason, it is equivalent to Da'at, THE SECRET OF THE CENTRAL COLUMN THAT INCLUDES RIGHT AND LEFT TOGETHER. FROM HERE, WE DERIVE THAT ALL HIS WORDS APPEAR IN THE SECRET OF THE THREE COLUMNS AND SO HIS BOOKS ARE DIVIDED INTO THREE COLUMNS, NAMELY CHOCHMAH, BINAH AND DA'AT.

142. הַאי קְרָא לָאו רֵישֵׁיה סֵיפֵיה וְלָאו סֵיפֵיה רֵישֵׁיה. וְכַד אִסְתַּכַּלְנָא בֵּיה, כֹּלָּא כָּלִיל חַד בְּחַד, בֵּין מִסֵּיפֵיה לְרֵישֵׁיה, בֵּין מֵרֵישֵׁיה לְסֵיפֵיה. שְׁמוּעָה טוֹבָה מֵאֶרֶץ מֶרְחָק מַיִם קָרִים עַל נֶפֶשׁ עֲיֵפָה. מַיִם קָרִים עַל נֶפֶשׁ עֲיֵפָה וּשְׁמוּעָה טוֹבָה מֵאֶרֶץ מֶרְחָק, וְדָא וְדָא נַיְיחָא דְרוּחָא, כְּמָה דְּהַאי נַיְיחָא דְרוּחָא, כָּךְ הַאי נַיְיחָא דְרוּחָא.

142. HE EXPLAINS HIS WORDS: In this verse, its beginning is not its end, nor does its end match up with its beginning, MEANING THEY ARE TWO DIFFERENT IDEAS. But when I examine them closely, I see common characteristics included from one to the other, both for its beginning to its end or vice versa. IT IS WRITTEN, "good news from a far country" and "As cold water to a thirsty soul," IN WHICH "as cold water to a thirsty soul" IS ONE CONCEPT and "good news from a far country" IS A SEPARATE CONCEPT. YET THEY ARE RELATED ONE TO THE OTHER, as both speak of satisfaction; just as the one gives satisfaction, so does the other give satisfaction. THIS IS THE CENTRAL COLUMN INCLUDING BOTH CONCEPTS, AS WE SAID.

143. עַד דַּהֲווֹ יַתְבֵי, אָתָא חַד בַּר נָשׁ, אָמַר, אִנְתּוּ דְּרִבִּי שִׁמְעוֹן אִתְּסִיאַת מִמַּרְעָהָא. וְחַבְרַיָּיא שָׁמְעוּ קָלָא, דְּקוּדְשָׁא בְּרִיךְ הוּא שָׁבַק

לְאִינּוּן חוֹבֵי דְּדָרָא. א"ר שִׁמְעוֹן, הָא אִתְקַיָּים הָכָא קְרָא, וּשְׁמוּעָה
טוֹבָה מֵאֶרֶץ מֶרְחָק, הָכִי הוּא נַיְיחָא דְּרוּחָא, כְּמוֹ מַיִם קָרִים עַל נֶפֶשׁ
עֲיֵפָה. אָמַר לְהוּ נְקוּם וְנֵזִיל דְּקוּדְשָׁא בְּרִיךְ הוּא אַרְחִישׁ לָן בְּנִסִּין.

143. As they were sitting, someone arrived and said that the wife of Rabbi
Shimon was healed from her illness. The friends heard a proclamation that
the Holy One, blessed be He, forgave the sins of the generation. Rabbi
Shimon said: Now was fulfilled the verse, "good news from a far country"
which gives satisfaction "as cold water to a thirsty soul." He said to them:
Let us rise and go as the Holy One, blessed be He, is performing for us
miracles.

144. פָּתַח וְאָמַר, מַיִם קָרִים עַל נֶפֶשׁ עֲיֵפָה, דָּא אוֹרַיְיתָא. דְּכָל מַאן
דְּזָכֵי לְמִלְעֵי בְּאוֹרַיְיתָא, וּמְרַוֵּי נַפְשָׁא מִנָּהּ, מַה כְּתִיב וּשְׁמוּעָה טוֹבָה
מֵאֶרֶץ מֶרְחָק קוּדְשָׁא בְּרִיךְ הוּא אַכְרִיז עָלֵיהּ כַּמָּה טָבָאן לְאוֹטָבָא לֵיהּ
בְּעָלְמָא דֵּין וּבְעָלְמָא דְּאָתֵי. הה"ד, וּשְׁמוּעָה טוֹבָה, מַאן אֲתַר מֵאֶרֶץ
מֶרְחָק, מֵאֲתַר דְּקוּדְשָׁא בְּרִיךְ הוּא הֲוָה רָחִיק מִנֵּיהּ בְּקַדְמֵיתָא, מֵאֲתַר
דַּהֲוָה ב"נ בִּדְבָבוּ עִמֵּיהּ בְּקַדְמֵיתָא, דִּכְתִּיב וְאֶרֶץ מִתְקוֹמְמָה לוֹ,
מֵהַהוּא אֲתַר מַקְדִּימִין לֵיהּ שְׁלָם, הה"ד, מֵאֶרֶץ מֶרְחָק. וּכְתִיב מֵרָחוֹק
יְיָ' נִרְאָה לִי וְאָהַבְתָּ עוֹלָם אֲהַבְתִּיךְ עַל כֵּן מְשַׁכְתִּיךְ חָסֶד.

144. He opened the discussion saying, "Cold water to a thirsty soul" is
referring to Torah. Of all those who merit to toil in Torah and satiate their
souls from it, it is written, "good news from a far country." The Holy One,
blessed be He, announces about many favors for him in this world and in the
World to Come. This is the meaning of "good news." Whence do they come
TO BE GOOD? "From a far country," MEANING from the place in which the
Holy One, blessed be He, was far off from him at the beginning, MEANING
where He was in enmity with him at first, as it is written, "And the earth
shall rise up against him" (Iyov 20:27). From this place, they welcome him
with peace. This is the meaning of, "A far country." It is also written,
"Hashem appeared to me from afar, saying, I have loved you with an
everlasting love: therefore I have remained true to you" (Yirmeyah 31:2).
THE END OF THE ARTICLE IS MISSING.

24. The singers Heiman, Yedutun and Asaf

A Synopsis

Rabbi Yehuda says there are thousands of singers that sing to God with the first light of day, and thousands more with the first light of the moon, and thousands more at twilight. Rabbi Yosi elaborates on this by saying that with the first light of day judgment is stilled, so they all say words of praise. The morning is of Abraham, Chesed. Rabbi Yosi goes on to tell about what happens at twilight when Isaac judges the wicked and what happens after midnight. Additional information is given about the rulers who awaken above and below, Heiman and Yedutun. With the arrival of night everything is stilled and the opening in the door is not to be found. After midnight, Asaf is appointed above and below. When morning comes, Metatron arises, and this is a time of goodwill when Zeir Anpin talks with the Queen. Then Zeir Anpin extends a thread of blessing over her and over all who study the Torah.

145. וְיָצָא אֶל הַמִּזְבֵּחַ אֲשֶׁר לִפְנֵי יְיָ' וְכִפֶּר עָלָיו. ר' יְהוּדָה פָּתַח וְאָמַר, מִזְמוֹר לְאָסָף אֵל אֱלֹהִים יְיָ' דִּבֶּר וַיִּקְרָא אָרֶץ מִמִּזְרַח שֶׁמֶשׁ עַד מְבוֹאוֹ. תָּאנָא, אֶלֶף וַחֲמֵשׁ מֵאָה וְחַמְשִׁין רִבּוֹא מָארֵי שִׁירָתָא, מְזַמְּרִין לְקוּדְשָׁא בְּרִיךְ הוּא, כַּד נָהִיר יְמָמָא. וַאֲלֶף וַחֲמֵשׁ מֵאָה וְאַרְבְּעִין וּתְמַנְיָא בְּסִיהֲרָא. וַאֲלֶף וַחֲמֵשׁ מֵאָה וְתִשְׁעִין אֶלֶף רִבּוֹא בְּהַהִיא שַׁעֲתָא דְּאִקְרֵי בֵּין הָעַרְבַּיִם.

145. "And he shall go out to the altar that is before Hashem, and make atonement for it" (Vayikra 16:18). Rabbi Yehuda opened the discussion saying, "A psalm of Asaf. El, Elohim, Hashem, has spoken, and called the earth from the rising of the sun to the going down thereof" (Tehilim 50:1). We have learned that 1,550 tens of thousands of singers sing to the Holy One, blessed be He, with the first light of day, and 1,548 with the FIRST LIGHT OF moon, MEANING NIGHT. Another 1,590 tens of thousands SING PRAISE at the time of twilight.

146. ר' יוֹסֵי אָמַר, כַּד נָהִיר יְמָמָא, כָּל אִינוּן מָארֵי דִיבָבָא, מְשַׁבְּחָן בְּמִלֵּי תּוּשְׁבְּחָן, לְקַבְּלֵיהּ דְּהַאי בֹקֶר. דְּכַד אִתְּעַר הַאי בֹקֶר, כֻּלְּהוּ מִתְבַּסְּמִין, וְדִינָא אִשְׁתְּכִיךְ, וְאָמְרִין תּוּשְׁבְּחָן. הַה"ד, בְּרָן יַחַד כֹּכְבֵי

בֹקֶר וַיָּרִיעוּ כָּל בְּנֵי אֱלֹהִים. וְהַהוּא זִמְנָא, חֶדְוָותָא וּבִרְכָּאן מִשְׁתַּכְּחִין בְּעָלְמָא, וְקוּדְשָׁא בְּרִיךְ הוּא אִתְּעַר לְאַבְרָהָם לְאַחֲיָיא לֵיהּ, וְאִשְׁתַּעֲשַׁע בֵּיהּ, וְאַשְׁלְטֵיהּ בְּעָלְמָא. וּמְנָא לָן דְּהַאי בֹקֶר דְּאַבְרָהָם הוּא. דִּכְתִיב וַיַּשְׁכֵּם אַבְרָהָם בַּבֹקֶר.

146. Rabbi Yosi EXPLAINS THE WORDS OF RABBI YEHUDA, saying that with the light of day, all those who wail, MEANING THOSE DRAWN FROM THE LEFT COLUMN, SINCE FROM WHERE JUDGMENTS ARE DRAWN THEY WAIL CONSTANTLY. AND they praise with words of praise towards this morning, WHICH IS THE LIGHT OF CHASSADIM, because with the stirring of this morning, they all find fragrance, and Judgment is stilled. Thus they say words of praise. This is what is written, "When the morning stars sang together, and all the sons of Elohim shouted for joy" (Iyov 38:7). At this time, joy and blessings are found in the world when the Holy One, blessed be He, stirs Abraham, FOR HE IS THE SECRET OF CHESED, to revive him, and take pleasure in him and make him ruler over the world. THIS IS THE SECRET OF THE RULE BY DAY. How do we know that this morning is of Abraham, NAMELY CHESED? From the verse, "And Abraham rose up early in the morning" (Beresheet 22:3).

147. בְּהַהוּא זִמְנָא דְּבֵין הָעַרְבַּיִם, כָּל אִינוּן אֶלֶף וַחֲמֵשׁ מְאָה וְתִשְׁעִין אֶלֶף רִבּוֹא מָארֵי דִּילָלָה אִקְרוּן, וּמְזַמְּרִין בְּהַהִיא שַׁעֲתָא, וּקְטָטוּתָא שַׁרְיָא בְּעָלְמָא, וְהַהִיא שַׁעֲתָא אִתְּעָרוּתָא דְּאִתְּעַר קוּדְשָׁא בְּרִיךְ הוּא לְיִצְחָק, וְקָם וְדָאִין לְחַיָּיבַיָּא דְּעַבְרִין עַל פִּתְגָּמֵי אוֹרַיְיתָא, וְשִׁבְעָה נַהֲרֵי אֶשָׁא נַגְדִּין וְנָפְקִין וְחָלִין עַל רֵישֵׁיהוֹן דְּרַשִׁיעַיָּא, וְשַׁלְהוֹבֵי גוּמְרִין דְּנוּרָא מִתְעָרִין מֵעֵילָא לְתַתָּא, וּכְדֵין תָּב אַבְרָהָם לְאַתְרֵיהּ. כד"א, וְאַבְרָהָם שָׁב לִמְקוֹמוֹ. וְיוֹמָא אִתְפְּנֵי, וְחַיָּיבֵי גֵּיהִנָּם צַוְוחִין וְאָמְרִין אוֹי לָנוּ כִּי פָנָה הַיּוֹם כִּי יִנָּטוּ צִלְלֵי עָרֶב. וְהַהִיא שַׁעֲתָא, בָּעֵי ב"נ לְאִזְדַּהֲרָא, בִּצְלוֹתָא דְּמִנְחָה.

147. At twilight, all of these 1,590 tens of thousands THAT ARE DRAWN THERE, ARE called those who lament. They sing at that time and dissent is then dominant in the world. That hour is when the Holy One, blessed be He, awakens Isaac, REPRESENTING THE LEFT COLUMN OF ZEIR ANPIN. He

rises and judges the wicked that violate the words of the Torah. Seven rivers of fire – CORRESPONDING TO CHESED, GVURAH, TIFERET, NETZACH, HOD, YESOD AND MALCHUT – are drawn out and hover over the heads of the wicked, and a flame of fiery coals stirs from above downward. Then Abraham, THE SECRET OF CHESED, returns to his position, MEANING THAT CHESED RETURNS TO ITS SOURCE AND DISAPPEARS FROM THE ONES BELOW, as the verse says, "And Abraham returned to his place" (Beresheet 18:33). The day departs and the wicked in Gehenom cry out and say, "Woe to us! For the day declines, for the shadows of the evening are lengthened" (Yirmeyah 6:4). At that time, one should be prudent with the Minchah prayer.

148. בְּזִמְנָא דְּמָטֵי לֵילְיָא אִינּוּן אֶלֶף וְה׳ מְאָה וְאַרְבְּעִין וּתְמַנְיָא, אִקְרוּן מִבָּרָא לְפָרוֹכְתָּא, וְאָמְרִין שִׁירָתָא כְּדֵין דִּינִין דִּלְתַתָּא מִתְעָרִין, וְאַזְלִין וְשָׁאטִין בְּעָלְמָא, וְאִלֵּין אַמְרִין שִׁירָתָא עַד דְּיִתְפְּלִיג לֵילְיָא מִשְׁמָרָה וּפַלְגָּא. בָּתַר דְּיִתְפְּלִיג לֵילְיָא מִזְדַּמְּנֵי כֻּלְּהוּ אַחֲרִינֵי כַּחֲדָא, וְאַמְרֵי תְּהִלּוֹת, כד״א וּתְהִלּוֹת יְיָ׳ יְבַשֵּׂרוּ. ר׳ יְהוּדָה אָמַר כַּד רַעֲוָא אִשְׁתְּכַח בְּצַפְרָא, תְּהִלּוֹת יְיָ׳ מְבַשְּׂרִין.

148. With the arrival of night, these 1,548 tens of thousands THAT ARE THEN DRAWN are called outside of the curtain, where they recite songs. Then all the Judgments from below, MEANING THE JUDGMENTS OF MALCHUT, are stirred and go and wander through the world. These recite songs until the middle of the night, MEANING one watch and a half WATCH. After midnight, all the others come together, MEANING THOSE OF THE WATCH AND THE HALF WATCH FOLLOWING MIDNIGHT, and say praise, such as, "And they shall proclaim the praises of Hashem" (Yeshayah 60:6). Rabbi Yehuda said: When goodwill is present in the morning, the praise of Hashem will be recounted, BUT NOT AT NIGHT.

149. רִבִּי יוֹסֵי אָמַר, בָּתַר דְּרוּחָא דְּצָפוֹן אִתְּעַר בְּפַלְגוּת לֵילְיָא וְאָזִיל לֵיהּ, תְּהִלּוֹת מְבַשְּׂרֵי, עַד דְּיֵיתֵי צַפְרָא, וְאִתְּעַר הַאי בֹּקֶר, כְּדֵין חֶדְוָותָא וּבִרְכָאן אִשְׁתְּכַח בְּעָלְמָא.

149. Rabbi Yosi said: After the north wind is stirred at midnight and then moves on, BEING THE SECRET OF THE ILLUMINATION OF CHOCHMAH OF

THE LEFT SIDE CALLED THE NORTH WIND, THEN the praises can be proclaimed until the advent of morning. When this morning is stirred, WHICH IS THE LIGHT OF CHASSADIM, joy and blessings are prevalent on the world, WHICH ARE NOT CALLED 'PRAISES' AS DESCRIBED IN THE ADJACENT PARAGRAPH.

150. תָּאנָא, א"ר אַבָּא, כֻּלְהוּ הָכִי, וְעֵילָא מִנְּהוֹן סַרְכִין תְּלָתָא. בְּהַהִיא שַׁעֲתָא דְּאִתְּעַר הַאי בֹּקֶר, וּמִתְעָרִין תּוּשְׁבְּחָן, כָּל אִינּוּן אֶלֶף וַחֲמֵשׁ מְאָה וְחַמְשִׁין רִבּוֹא, אִתְמָנָא עָלַיְיהוּ חַד מְמָנָא, וְהֵימָן שְׁמֵיהּ לְקַבְלֵיהּ דִּלְתַתָּא, וּתְחוֹת יְדֵיהּ סַרְכִין מְמָנָן עָלַיְיהוּ לְאַתְקְנָא שִׁירָתָא

150. We have learned that Rabbi Aba said: EVERYTHING THAT RABBI YEHUDA AND RABBI YOSI SAID is so. Above them are three Chiefs. HE EXPLAINS: At that time, when this morning is awakened and the praises are roused of all the 1,550 tens of thousands, there is appointed upon them one chief by the name of Heiman who counters HEIMAN of below, WHO IS MENTIONED IN TEHILIM. Under his offlicialdom, officers are appointed over them to set up the hymns. HEIMAN EQUALS THE LETTERS IN YEMIN (LIT. 'RIGHT'), AS HE DRAWS HIS STRENGTH FROM THE RIGHT.

151. בְּהַהִיא שַׁעֲתָא דְּאִתְּעַר זִמְנָא דְּבֵין הָעַרְבַּיִם, וְזַמְרִין כָּל אִינּוּן אֶלֶף וַחֲמֵשׁ מְאָה וְתִשְׁעִין אֶלֶף רִבּוֹא מָארֵי דִּילָלָה, אִתְמָנָא עָלַיְיהוּ חַד מְמָנָא וִידוּתוּן שְׁמֵיהּ, לְקַבְלֵיהּ דִּלְתַתָּא, וּתְחוֹת יְדֵיהּ סַרְכִין מְמָנָן עָלַיְיהוּ, לְאַתְקְנָא הַהוּא זִמְרָא, כד"א זְמִיר עָרִיצִים.

151. When the period of twilight is activated and all 1,590 tens of thousands of lamenters are singing praise, there is appointed upon them one chief named Yedutun, who counters YEDUTUN from below MENTIONED IN TEHILIM. Beneath him chief officials are appointed to improve that song, as the verse states, "The song of tyrants" (Yeshayah 25:5), WHICH REFERS TO THE DESTRUCTION OF THE WICKED, AS EVEN THEIR MELODIES DEVASTATE THE WICKED. IN YEDUTUN ARE THE LETTERS OF YAD (ENG. 'HAND') AND YADUN (ENG. 'HE WILL JUDGE'), WHICH INDICATES THAT HE IS FROM THE LEFT HAND AND THAT JUDGMENTS STEM FROM HIM.

152. בְּהַהִיא שַׁעֲתָא דְּמָטֵי לֵילְיָא, מִתְעָרִין כָּל אִינּוּן דְּמִבְּרָא

לְפָרוֹכְתָּא, כְּדֵין שָׁכִיךְ כֹּלָּא, וּפִטְרָא לָא אִשְׁתְּכַח, וְדִינִין דִּלְתַתָּא מִתְעָרִין, כֻּלְּהוּ אִתְמְנָן כַּחֲדָא, אִלֵּין עַל אִלֵּין, עַד דְּאִתְפְּלִיג לֵילְיָא. בָּתַר דְּאִתְפְּלִיג לֵילְיָא, וּמִתְכַּנְּשֵׁי כֻּלְּהוּ, אִתְמְנָא עָלַיְיהוּ חַד מְמָנָא וְכָנִישׁ לְכָל מַשִׁרְיָין, כד"א מְאַסֵּף לְכָל הַמַּחֲנוֹת וְגוֹ', וְאָסָף שְׁמֵיהּ, לְקַבְלֵיהּ דִּלְתַתָּא, וּתְחוֹת יְדֵיהּ כָּל אִינּוּן סַרְכִין מְמָנָן, וּמְבַשְּׂרֵי תְּהִלּוֹת.

152. With the arrival of night, all these ANGELS who are outside of the veil stir MEANING THOSE THAT ARE DRAWN FROM THE BACK OF MALCHUT AND FROM HER EXTERNAL PART. Then, everything is stilled and there is no opening IN THE DOOR. The Judgments from below, THOSE OF MALCHUT – THE LOWEST OF ALL SFIROT – are all aroused, MEANING ALL THE JUDGMENTS are assigned together, these over those until midnight. After the assembly of all THE ANGELS THAT ARE DRAWN FROM THE CENTRAL COLUMN after midnight, one minister is appointed over them; he gathers all the camps, as the verse says, "The rearward (Heb. me'asef) of all camps" (Bemidbar 10:25). His name is Asaf (Eng. 'he gathered'), and he corresponds to ASAF down below, WHO IS MENTIONED IN TEHILIM. All appointed ministers and heralds of praise are under his tutelage.

153. עַד דְּאָתֵי צַפְרָא, כֵּיוָן דְּאָתֵי צַפְרָא, קָם הַהוּא נַע"ר, יוֹנֵק מִשָׁדֵי אִמֵּיהּ, לְדַכְאָה לְהוּ, וְעָאל לְשַׁמְּשָׁא. כַּד אִתְּעַר בֹּקֶר, כְּדֵין הִיא שַׁעֲתָא דְּרַעֲוָא, דְּאִשְׁתְּעֵי מַטְרוֹנִיתָא בְּמַלְכָּא, וּמַלְכָּא מָשִׁיךְ מִנֵּיהּ חַד חוּטָא דְּבִרְכָּאן וּפָרִיס עַל מַטְרוֹנִיתָא, וְעַל אִינּוּן דְּמִזְדַּוְוגֵי לֵהּ. מַאן אִינּוּן דְּמִזְדַּוְוגֵי עִמָּהּ. אִינּוּן דְּמִשְׁתַּדְּלֵי בְּאוֹרַיְיתָא בְּלֵילְיָא, כַּד אִתְפְּלַג.

153. This goes on until morning. When morning arrives, the youth rises, METATRON, who is nurtured at the breast of his mother, MALCHUT, to cleanse them, NAMELY THE ANGELS OF THE NIGHT, and he comes in to serve. The early morning is a period of goodwill when the Queen talks with the King, NAMELY ZEIR ANPIN. The King extends from Himself a single thread of blessings, NAMELY CHASSADIM, and spreads over the Queen and those allied with her, NAMELY those that toil in Torah at midnight.

154. ר' שִׁמְעוֹן אָמַר, זַכָּאָה חוּלָקֵיהּ מַאן דְּאָתֵי עִם מַטְרוֹנִיתָא,

בְּשַׁעֲתָא דְּאָתַת לְקַבְּלָא אַנְפֵּי מַלְכָּא, לְאִשְׁתָּעֵי בֵּיהּ. וְאִשְׁתְּכַח עִמָּהּ. בְּשַׁעֲתָא דְּאוֹשִׁיט מַלְכָּא יְמִינָא, לְקַבְּלָא לְמַטְרוֹנִיתָא. הה"ד אֶשָּׂא כַנְפֵי שַׁחַר אֶשְׁכְּנָה בְּאַחֲרִית יָם. מַאי אַחֲרִית יָם. הַהִיא שַׁעֲתָא אַחֲרִית דְּהַהוּא יָם הוּא. דְּכַד אִתְפְּלַג, שֵׁירוּתָא הֲוָה, וְדִינָא הֲוָה, וְהַשְׁתָּא אַחֲרִית הוּא דִּילָהּ, דְּמִסְתַּלְּקִין דִּינָהָא. וְעָאלַת בְּגַדְפּוֹי דְּמַלְכָּא, הִיא וְכָל אִינוּן דְּמִזְדַּוְּוגִין לֵהּ, הה"ד אֶשְׁכְּנָה בְּאַחֲרִית יָם.

154. Rabbi Shimon said: How fortunate is the share of he who comes with the Queen when she welcomes the King, ZEIR ANPIN, to talk with Him, for he is with her at the time when the King extends His right hand, DENOTING THE LIGHTS OF CHASSADIM, to receive the Queen, as it is written, "If I take the wings of dawn, and dwell in the uttermost parts of the sea" (Tehilim 139:9). What is "uttermost parts of the sea"? This is the hour OF MORNING WHEN SHE WELCOMES ZEIR ANPIN, the uttermost parts of the sea, MALCHUT. The middle OF THE NIGHT is then her beginning, AS THEN SHE BEGINS TO SHINE, and it pertains to Judgment, AS LONG AS NIGHT PREVAILS, DUE TO LACK OF CHASSADIM TO CLOTHE HER CHOCHMAH. WITH THE ARRIVAL OF MORNING, it is her "uttermost parts," as her Judgments end and she enters beneath the wings of the King, DENOTING ZEIR ANPIN, AS IF TO SAY SHE IS CLOTHING HERSELF WITH HIS CHASSADIM, she and all those RIGHTEOUS PEOPLE joined with her. The verse states, "And dwell in the uttermost parts of the sea."

155. וְתָאנָא, כָּל אִינוּן דְּמִשְׁתַּדְּלֵי בְּאוֹרַיְיתָא בְּשַׁעֲתָא דְּאִתְפְּלִיג לֵילְיָא. אִשְׁתַּתַּף בִּשְׁכִינְתָּא. וְכַד אָתֵי צַפְרָא, וּמַטְרוֹנִיתָא אִתְחַבְּרַת עִם מַלְכָּא, הוּא אִשְׁתְּכַח עִמָּהּ עִם מַלְכָּא. וּמַלְכָּא פָּרֵיס עַל כֻּלְּהוּ גַּדְפּוֹי, הה"ד יוֹמָם יְצַוֶּה יְיָ' חַסְדּוֹ וּבַלַּיְלָה שִׁירֹה עִמִּי וְגוֹ'.

155. We have learned that all those toiling in Torah in the middle of the night join with the Shechinah. When the morning arrives and the Queen, NAMELY THE SHECHINAH, joins with the King, ZEIR ANPIN, they too are with the King, and the King spreads His wings over all of them. This is the meaning of, "Yet Hashem will command His steadfast love in the daytime, and in the night His song shall be with me" (Tehilim 42:9).

156. תָּאנָא, בְּהַהִיא שַׁעֲתָא, אֲבָהָן מִזְדַּמְּנִין בְּמַטְרוֹנִיתָא, וְקַדְמִין לְאִשְׁתְּעֵי בַּהֲדָה, וּלְאִתְחַבְּרָא עִמָּה. וְקוּדְשָׁא בְּרִיךְ הוּא מַלִּיל עִמָּה בְּהוּ. וְהוּא קָאֵרִי לָהּ לְפָרְסָא לָהּ גַּדְפוֹי, הה"ד מִזְמוֹר לְאָסָף אֵל אֱלֹהִים יְיָ' דִּבֶּר וַיִּקְרָא אָרֶץ וְגוֹ'. אֵל: דָּא נְהִירוּ דְחָכְמְתָא, וְאִקְרֵי חֶסֶד. אֱלֹהִים: דָּא גְבוּרָה. יְדֹו"ד: דָּא שְׁלִימוּ דְכַלָּא, רַחֲמֵי. וְעַל דָּא, דִּבֶּר וַיִּקְרָא אֶרֶץ וְגוֹ'.

156. We have learned that at that hour, THE ARRIVAL OF MORNING, the Patriarchs – NAMELY CHESED, GVURAH, TIFERET OF ZEIR ANPIN – meet with the Queen and proceed to speak with her and join us with her. The Holy One, blessed be He, ZEIR ANPIN, speaks with her through them, and He calls her to spread His wings upon her. This is the meaning of the verse, "A psalm of Asaf. El, Elohim, Hashem, has spoken, and called the earth from the rising of the sun to the going down thereof." El refers to light of Chochmah and is called Chesed, NAMELY THE RIGHT COLUMN, DENOTING CHESED THAT RISES TO BECOME CHOCHMAH. Elohim denotes Gvurah, REFERRING TO THE LEFT COLUMN. Hashem refers to total perfection, to mercy, NAMELY THE CENTRAL COLUMN THAT BRINGS TOGETHER RIGHT TO LEFT. Therefore, THE CENTRAL COLUMN "has spoken and called the earth," DENOTING MALCHUT, AND IN THAT IT PERFECTS MALCHUT.

25. Yud Hei Vav Hei with the vowelization of Elohim

A Synopsis

Rabbi Elazar asks his father why, when Elohim always denotes judgment, Yud Hei Vav Hei should ever be pronounced with the vowels of Elohim. Rabbi Shimon says that he knows that there may sometimes be judgment where there is mercy, and vice versa, and when the wicked convert mercy to judgment then it is read 'Elohim'. We are told in detail of the three grades that are called with names of judgment, Binah, Gvurah and Malchut. The level of Binah is called Yud Hei Vav Hei with the vowelization of Elohim; the level of Gvurah is pronounced also with the lettering of Elohim; and the level of Malchut is pronounced Adonai, within which are the letters of judgment, *Din*.

157. רִבִּי אֶלְעָזָר הֲוָה יָתִיב קַמֵּיהּ דר"ש אֲבוֹי, אָמַר לֵיהּ, הָא תָּנֵינָן אֱלֹהִים בְּכָל אֲתַר דִּינָא הוּא. יוֹ"ד הֵ"א וָא"ו הֵ"א. אִית אֲתַר דְּאִקְרֵי אֱלֹהִים, כְּגוֹן אֲדֹנָ"י יֱהֹוִ"ה. אֲמַאי אִקְרֵי אֱלֹהִים, וְהָא אַתְוָון רַחֲמֵי אִינּוּן בְּכָל אֲתַר.

157. Rabbi Elazar was sitting before Rabbi Shimon, his father. He said to him: We have learned that THE NAME Elohim always denotes Judgment. The name Yud Hei Vav Hei is sometimes pronounced Elohim, MEANING WHEN IT IS WITH THE VOWELS OF ELOHIM, such as "Adonai Yud Hei Vav Hei" (Beresheet 15:8), PRONOUNCED WITH THE PUNCTUATION OF ELOHIM. HE QUESTIONS: Why pronounce it "Elohim" when its letters, NAMELY YUD HEI VAV HEI, always denote Mercy?

158. אָמַר לֵיהּ, הָכִי הוּא כְּתִיב בַּקְרָא, דִּכְתִיב וְיָדַעְתָּ הַיּוֹם וַהֲשֵׁבֹתָ אֶל לְבָבֶךָ כִּי יְיָ' הוּא הָאֱלֹהִים, וּכְתִיב יְיָ' הוּא הָאֱלֹהִים. אָמַר לֵיהּ מִלָּה דָּא יְדַעְנָא, דְּבַאֲתַר דְּאִית דִּינָא, אִית רַחֲמֵי. וּלְזִמְנָא, בַּאֲתַר דְּאִית רַחֲמֵי, אִית דִּינָא, א"ל תָּא חֲזֵי דְּהָכִי הוּא, יְדֹו"ד בְּכָל אֲתַר רַחֲמֵי. וּבְשַׁעֲתָא דִּמְהַפְּכֵי חַיָּיבַיָּא רַחֲמֵי לְדִינָא, כְּדֵין כְּתִיב יֱהֹוִ"ה, וְקָרֵינָן לֵיהּ אֱלֹהִים.

158. He said to him that it is written in the scripture, "Know therefore this day, and consider it in your heart, that Hashem He is Elohim" (Devarim

4:39). It is also written, "Hashem He is the Elohim" (I Melachim 18:39). He said to him: I know that where there is Judgment, there can be Mercy and sometimes where there is Mercy, there may be Judgment. THEREFORE, THE VERSE STATES "HASHEM HE IS THE ELOHIM." He continued: See that it is so, Yud Hei Vav Hei always stands for Mercy. But when the wicked convert Mercy to Judgment, the verse is written, "Yud Hei Vav Hei," but it is read "Elohim."

159. אֲבָל ת״ח רָזָא דְמִלָּה, ג׳ דַרְגִּין אִינּוּן, וְכָל דַרְגָּא וְדַרְגָּא בִּלְחוֹדוֹי, וְאע״ג דְכֹלָּא חַד, וּמִתְקַשְּׁרֵי בְּחַד, וְלָא מִתְפָּרְשֵׁי דָא מִן דָא. ת״ח, כֻּלְהוּ נְטִיעָן, וְכָל אִינּוּן בּוּצִינִין כֻּלְהוּ נְהִירִין וּמִתְלַהֲטָן וּמִשְׁתַּקְיָין וּמִתְבָּרְכָאן, מֵהַהוּא נַהֲרָא דְנָגִיד וְנָפִיק, דְכֹלָּא כָּלִיל בֵּיהּ, וּכְלָלָא דְכֹלָּא בֵּיהּ.

159. Come and analyze the secret of the matter. There are three degrees, yet each degree is independent even though they are one, connected into one and do not separate one from the other. Come and see: All the plants – NAMELY THE SFIROT – and all these candles – NAMELY THE SFIROT OF MALCHUT KNOWN AS THE FIERY LIGHTS – shine and blaze. All are watered and blessed from that river that continually flows, NAMELY BINAH, in which everything is included, AS ALL MOCHIN STEM FROM IT, and the sum of everything is within it.

160. וְהַאי נַהֲרָא אִתְקְרֵי אֵ״ם לְגִנְתָּא, וְעֵילָא מִגִּנְתָּא, בְּגִין דְּעֵדֶן מִשְׁתַּתֵּף בַּהֲדָהּ, וְלָא פָּרִישׁ מִנָּהּ. וּבְגִין כָּךְ, כָּל מַבּוּעִין נָפְקִין וְנַגְדִּין וְאִשְׁתַּקְיָין לְכָל עִיבָר. וּפַתְחִין בָּהּ פְּתִיחָן, וְעַל דָּא רַחֲמֵי מִנָּהּ מִשְׁתַּכְּחִין, וְרַחֲמִין פְּתִיחִין בָּהּ.

160. This river is called the mother of the Garden of Eden, DENOTING MALCHUT, AS BINAH IS REFERRED TO AS MOTHER (HEB. EM, ALEPH MEM), AS IT IS WRITTEN, "IF (HEB. IM, ALEPH MEM) YOU CRY AFTER BINAH" (MISHLEI 2:3), being higher than the Garden. IT IS CALLED MOTHER, because Eden, DENOTING CHOCHMAH, joins with it and does not leave it. For this reason, all the springs OF MOCHIN come out, draw FROM IT and water all sides, BOTH TO THE RIGHT OR TO THE LEFT, and open

doors within it. Hence, there is Mercy coming from it, DENOTING THE
CENTRAL COLUMN and Mercy opened in it AS THE BEGINNING OF THE
OPENING OF THE CENTRAL COLUMN, WHICH RECONCILES AND JOINS
RIGHT WITH LEFT BEING THE PERFECTION OF EVERYTHING, STARTS AT
BINAH.

161. וּבְגִין דְּקַרֵינָן לָהּ אֵם, נוּקְבָּא גְּבוּרָה, וְדִינָא מִנָּהּ נָפִיק. אִקְרֵי
רַחֲמֵי בִּלְחוֹדָהָא, הָא מִסִּטְרָהָא דִּינִין מִתְעָרִין. וּבְגִין כָּךְ כְּתִיב בְּרַחֲמֵי,
וְנָקוּד בְּדִינָא. אַתְוָון בְּרַחֲמֵי, וְאִתְנְגִיד דִּינָא מִסִּטְרָהָא, כְּגַוְונָא דָּא
יְהֶ"וֹה, הַאי דַּרְגָּא חַד.

161. For this reason, they call BINAH mother, DENOTING Nukva and
Gvurah, and Judgment comes forth from it. HENCE, it is referred to as
Mercy on its own, ITS OWN QUALITY. However, from its aspect, the
Judgments are aroused and THE NAME BINAH is written with Mercy,
MEANING WITH THE LETTERS YUD HEI VAV HEI, WHICH INDICATES
MERCY. Its vowels are of Judgment, MEANING THAT HER FOUR LETTERS
OF YUD HEI VAV HEI ARE VOWELED AS IN THE NAME OF ELOHIM.
THUS, the letters OF THE NAME ARE of Mercy, yet Judgments are drawn
from its aspect, AS HINTED IN THE VOWELIZATION OF THE NAME as
YeHeVoH. This is one grade.

162. דַּרְגָּא תִּנְיָינָא, מִסִּטְרָא דְּהַאי קַדְמָאָה, נָפִיק וְאִתְּעַר דַּרְגָּא אָחֳרָא
אִקְרֵי גְּבוּרָה, וְהַאי אִקְרֵי אֱלֹהִים, בְּאִלֵּין אַתְוָון מַמָּשׁ. וְשֵׁירוּתָא מִזְּעֵיר
אַנְפִּין הוּא, וּבֵיהּ אִתְאֲחִיד. וּבְגִין דְּאִתְאֲחִיד בְּהַאי, כְּתִיב יְיָ' הָאֱלֹהִים,
כִּי יְיָ' הוּא הָאֱלֹהִים, בְּאִלֵּין אַתְוָון, וְהוּא חַד, וְדָא הוּא דַּרְגָּא תִּנְיָינָא.

162. The second grade: From the aspect of the first GRADE, WHICH IS
BINAH, another grade named Gvurah, WHICH IS THE LEFT COLUMN OF
ZEIR ANPIN, comes out and is stirred. It is pronounced Elohim, NOT
MERELY IN ITS VOWELS, AS IN BINAH, BUT with its actual letters. Its
origin is Zeir Anpin, MEANING CHESED OF ZEIR ANPIN, WHENCE STEMS
GVURAH that is included in it, AS THE LEFT COLUMN OF ZEIR ANPIN IS
INCLUDED IN THE RIGHT COLUMN OF ZEIR ANPIN, WHICH IS CHESED.
Since it is included in CHESED, it is THEREFORE written, "Hashem He is

the Elohim" as Yud Hei Vav Hei – DENOTING CHESED – is the Elohim – DENOTING GVURAH. And here, IT DOES NOT MERELY HAVE THE VOWELS OF ELOHIM, AS IN BINAH, BUT IT IS INCLUDED in the letters OF ELOHIM, and they become one, JOINED ONE WITH THE OTHER. This is the second grade.

163. דַּרְגָּא תְּלִיתָאָה, צֶדֶק. כִּתְרָא בַּתְרָאָה, הַאי בֵּי דִינָא דְמַלְכָּא. וְתָאנָא אֲדֹנָ"י הָכִי כְּתִיב, וְהָכִי אִקְרֵי, וכ"י בְּהַאי שְׁמָא אִתְקְרֵי. וְהַאי שְׁמָא בַּאֲתַר דָּא אִשְׁתְּלִים. וְאִלֵּין אִינוּן ג' דַּרְגִּין, דְּאִקְרוּן בִּשְׁמַהוֹן דְּדִינָא. וְכֹלָּא מִתְקַשָּׁר חַד בְּחַד בְּלָא פֵּרוּדָא, כְּמָה דְּאוֹקִימְנָא.

163. The third grade is righteousness, DENOTING MALCHUT, which is the last Sfirah. This becomes the court of the King, OF ZEIR ANPIN. We have learned THAT THE NAME Adonai is thus spelled and thus pronounced. The Congregation of Yisrael, REFERRING TO MALCHUT, is called by this name. HOWEVER, THE NAME OF ZEIR ANPIN IS WRITTEN YUD HEI VAV HEI AND IS PRONOUNCED ADONAI. This name is completed in this place, MALCHUT. These are three levels called with names of Judgment, AS THE LEVEL OF BINAH IS CALLED YUD HEI VAV HEI WITH THE VOWELIZATION OF ELOHIM. THE LEVEL OF GVURAH IS PRONOUNCED ALSO WITH THE LETTERING OF ELOHIM AND THE LEVEL OF MALCHUT IS PRONOUNCED ADONAI. THESE ARE THE THREE NAMES OF JUDGMENT, AS WE DISCUSS HERE THE LEFT COLUMN, WHICH IS JUDGMENT, WHOSE SOURCE IS BINAH. THEREFORE, IT IS ONLY HINTED AT WITH THE VOWELIZATION OF ELOHIM, AND FROM THERE, IT IS DRAWN TO THE LEFT COLUMN OF ZEIR ANPIN. THERE IT IS ACTUAL YET INCLUDED IN THE RIGHT; HENCE, THE SECRET OF ELOHIM IS ALSO IN ITS LETTERING. FROM HERE IT MOVES TO MALCHUT, WHICH IS ENTIRELY BUILT FROM THE LEFT COLUMN AND IS THEREFORE PRONOUNCED ADONAI (ALEPH DALET NUN YUD), WHICH CONTAINS THE LETTERS OF JUDGMENT (DIN, DALET YUD NUN) EXPLICITLY. All join one with the other without separation as we have established.

26. Eheyeh Asher Eheyeh

A Synopsis

Rabbi Elazar does not understand the title verse, that means "I will ever be what I now am," and his father says that the name "Eheyeh" comprises everything, and is completely concealed. "Asher Eheyeh" means "I will draw, and give birth to all" – Ima/Binah is impregnated and ready to give forth all the details and to reveal the exalted name Yud Hei Vav Hei. God had explained the secret of the Holy Name to Moses, and Rabbi Shimon found in King Solomon's book that "Asher" means that the chamber, Binah, is in connection with Eden, Chochmah, when in the exalted knot. "Asher" is derived from happy and "Eheyeh" means prepared to give birth. At the time of birth it is not written "Asher" because the heavenly pair is separated, but rather "Eheyeh" which means that now it will produce and give birth, and all will be corrected. After the birth of Zeir Anpin, those other names were forsaken and it says Yud Hei Vav Hei.

164. אָמַר לֵיהּ, אִי נִיחָא קַמֵּיהּ דְּאַבָּא, הָא שְׁמַעֲנָא בְּהַאי, דִּכְתִיב אֶהְיֶה אֲשֶׁר אֶהְיֶה, וְלָא קַיְימָא בֵּיהּ. א"ל אֶלְעָזָר בְּרִי, הָא אוּקְמוּהָ חַבְרַיָּיא, וְהַשְׁתָּא בְּחַד מִלָּה אִתְקְשַׁר כֹּלָּא.

164. He said to him: If it is pleasing before my father, I heard that it is written about this, "I will ever be what I now am" (Heb. *eheyeh asher eheyeh*) (Shemot 3:14) and I do not understand it; NAMELY, I DO NOT UNDERSTAND ITS EXPLANATION. He replied: Elazar, my son, the friends have established it, and now it all connects to the same matter.

165. וְרָזָא דְּמִלָּה הָכִי הוּא. אֶהְיֶה, הָא כְּלָלָא דְּכֹלָּא. דְּכַד שְׁבִילִין סְתִימִין וְלָא מִתְפָּרְשָׁן, וּכְלִילָן בְּחַד אֲתַר. כְּדֵין אִקְרֵי אֶהְיֶה, כְּלָלָא כֹּלָּא, סָתִים וְלָא אִתְגַּלְיָיא.

165. The secret of the matter is this. THE NAME "Eheyeh" comprises everything, BEING THE SUPERNAL ABA AND IMA WHO ARE THE THREE FIRST SFIROT OF BINAH, ALWAYS IN THE SECRET OF THE VERSE, "HE DELIGHTS IN MERCY (HEB. *CHESED*)" (MICHAH 7:18) AND NEVER RECEIVE CHOCHMAH, AS when the paths are blocked and not clear, and are

all included in one place. Then they are called Eheyeh, which includes all. It is concealed and does not become revealed.

166. בָּתַר דְּנָפַק מְנֵּיהּ שֵׁירוּתָא, וְהַהוּא נָהָר אִתְעַבַּר לְאַמְשָׁכָא כֹּלָּא, כְּדֵין אִקְרֵי אֲשֶׁר אֶהְיֶה. כְּלוֹמַר, ע"כ אֶהְיֶה, אֶהְיֶה זַמִּין לְאַמְשָׁכָא וּלְאוֹלָדָא כֹּלָּא. אֶהְיֶה: כְּלוֹמַר, הַשְׁתָּא אֲנָא הוּא כְּלַל כֹּלָּא, כְּלָלָא דְּכָל פְּרָטָא. אֲשֶׁר אֶהְיֶה: דְּאִתְעַבְּרַת אִימָּא, וְזַמִּינַת לְאַפָּקָא פְּרָטִין כֻּלְּהוּ, וּלְאִתְגַּלְיָיא שְׁמָא עִלָּאָה.

166. After the beginnings OF the REVELATION OF MOCHIN emerges from it, and that river WHICH IS YISRAEL–SABA AND TEVUNAH, becomes pregnant, WITH MALE AND FEMALE, in order to draw everything, the beginnings is called "Asher Eheyeh." IT MEANS, I will draw, and give birth to all. "Eheyeh" means that now I include everything, the inclusion of every detail, MEANING EACH AND EVERY GRADE. "Asher Eheyeh" MEANS that Ima, WHICH IS BINAH, is impregnated and ready to give forth all the details and to reveal the exalted Name YUD HEI VAV HEI.

167. לְבָתַר בָּעָא מֹשֶׁה לְמִנְדַּע פְּרָטָא דְּמִלָּה מַאן הוּא, עַד דְּפָרִישׁ וְאָמַר אֶהְיֶה, דָּא הוּא פְּרָטָא, וְהָכָא לָא כְּתִיב אֲשֶׁר אֶהְיֶה. וְאַשְׁכַּחְנָא בְּסִפְרָא דִּשְׁלֹמֹה מַלְכָּא, אֲשֶׁר: בְּקִיטוּרָא דְּעֵדוּנָא קַסְטִירָא בְּחַבְרוּתָא עִלָּאָה אִשְׁתְּכַח. כד"א, בְּאָשְׁרִי כִּי אִשְּׁרוּנִי בָּנוֹת, אֶהְיֶה זַמִּינָא לְאוֹלָדָא.

167. Afterwards, Moses wanted to know the details of the matter. Then THE HOLY ONE, BLESSED BE HE, explained it to him, "THUS SHALL YOU SAY TO THE CHILDREN OF YISRAEL, Eheyeh" (Shemot 3:14). THIS NAME is specific TO YISRAEL–SABA AND TEVUNAH. Therefore, it is not written here: 'Asher Eheyeh'. I have found in the book of King Solomon that "Asher" MEANS the chamber, BINAH, is in connection with Eden, DENOTING CHOCHMAH, when in the exalted knot, as it is written, "Happy am I (Heb. *oshri*), for the daughters will call me blessed" (Beresheet 30:13). ALSO HERE, "ASHER" IS DERIVED FROM HAPPY, "Eheyeh" MEANS prepared to give birth.

168. ת״ח הֵיךְ נָחִית מִדַּרְגָּא לְדַרְגָּא, לְאוֹדָעָא רָזָא דִּשְׁמָא קַדִּישָׁא לְמֹשֶׁה. בְּקַדְמֵיתָא אֶהְיֶה, כְּלָלָא דְּכֹלָּא, סָתִים דְּלָא אִתְגַּלְיָיא כְּלָל, כְּמָה דַּאֲמֵינָא. וְסִימָן, וָאֶהְיֶה אֶצְלוֹ אָמוֹן וְגוֹ', וּכְתִיב לֹא יָדַע אֱנוֹשׁ עֶרְכָּהּ וְגוֹ'. לְבָתַר אַפִּיק הַהוּא נַהֲרָא, אִמָּא עִלָּאָה, אִתְעַבְּרַת, וְזַמִּינָא לְאוֹלָדָא. וְאָמַר אֲשֶׁר אֶהְיֶה, זְמִינָא לְאוֹלָדָא, וּלְתַקְּנָא כֹּלָּא. לְבָתַר שָׁארֵי לְאוֹלָדָא, וְלָא כְּתִיב אֲשֶׁר, אֶלָּא אֶהְיֶה: כְּלוֹמַר, הַשְׁתָּא יָפִיק וְיִתְתַּקַן כֹּלָּא.

168. Come and see how it came down from level to level in order to tell the secret of the Holy Name to Moses. At first there was "Eheyeh," which comprises everything in general. It is hidden and not revealed at all, BEING SUPERNAL ABA AND IMA as I have said. This is understood from, "Then I was (Eheyeh) by Him as a nursling" (Mishlei 8:30), and, "Man cannot know its price" (Iyov 28:13). FOR CHOCHMAH, BEING THE SECRET OF THE SUPERNAL ABA AND IMA, ARE CONCEALED AND IT IS WRITTEN ABOUT THEM, "MAN CANNOT KNOW ITS PRICE," AS CHOCHMAH IS HIDDEN WITHIN THEM AND NOT KNOWN AT ALL. Afterwards, SUPERNAL ABA AND IMA caused the river, which is supernal Ima, to emanate, and it became pregnant and was about to give birth. Then the verse says, "Asher Eheyeh," MEANING I am prepared to give birth and correct everything. Following this, she begins to give birth. THEN, it is not written: 'Asher', BECAUSE AT THE TIME OF BIRTH THE HEAVENLY PAIR IS SEPARATED AS MENTIONED, but "Eheyeh" which means that now it will produce and give birth and everything will be corrected.

169. בָּתַר דְּנָפִיק כֹּלָּא, וְאִתְתַּקַן כָּל חַד וְחַד בְּאַתְרֵיהּ, שָׁבַק כֹּלָּא, וְאָמַר יְהֹוָ״ה. דָּא פְּרָטָא, וְדָא קִיּוּמָא. וּבְהַהִיא שַׁעֲתָא יָדַע מֹשֶׁה, רָזָא דִּשְׁמָא קַדִּישָׁא, סָתִים וְגַלְיָא וְאִתְדַּבַּק מַה דְּלָא אִתְדַּבְּקוּ שְׁאָר בְּנֵי עָלְמָא, זַכָּאָה חוּלָקֵיהּ. אָתָא ר' אֶלְעָזָר וְנָשִׁיק יְדוֹי.

169. After everything had emerged and each one was established in its proper place, MEANING AFTER ZEIR ANPIN WAS BORN AND CAME BELOW TO ITS PLACE, He forsook everything, MEANING ALL THE ABOVE MENTIONED NAMES, and said Yud Hei Vav Hei. This is a detail, MEANING

THE SPECIFIC GRADE OF ZEIR ANPIN UNCONNECTED TO IMA. This is sustenance, MEANING ZEIR ANPIN THAT MOCHIN REFERRED TO AS SUSTENANCE. At that moment, Moses became aware of the secret of the Holy Name, the concealed and the revealed. He became attached as no other human LIKE HIM had. How fortunate is his lot. Rabbi Elazar approached and kissed his hands.

27. The proper order of writing the Name Yud Hei Vav Hei

A Synopsis
Rabbi Shimon tells his son that it is critical to write the Holy Name properly. He reiterates the information in the previous section by reference to the individual letters of Yud Hei Vav Hei.

170. א״ל, אֶלְעָזָר בְּרִי, מִכָּאן וּלְהָלְאָה, אִזְדְּהַר דְּלָא לְמִכְתַּב שְׁמָא קַדִּישָׁא, אֶלָּא כַּדְקָא יֵאוֹת. דְּכָל מַאן דְּלָא יָדַע לְמִכְתַּב שְׁמָא קַדִּישָׁא כַּדְקָא יֵאוֹת, וּלְקַשְׁרָא קִשְׁרָא דִּמְהֵימְנוּתָא קִשְׁרָא דְּחַד בְּחַד, בְּגִין לְיַחֲדָא שְׁמָא קַדִּישָׁא. עָלֵיהּ כְּתִיב, כִּי דְבַר יְיָ׳ בָּזָה וְאֶת מִצְוָתוֹ הֵפַר הִכָּרֵת תִּכָּרֵת וְגוֹ׳. אֲפִילוּ דְּגָרַע חַד דַּרְגָּא, אוֹ חַד קִשְׁרָא, מֵאַת חַד מִנַּיְיהוּ.

170. He said to him: Elazar, my son, be careful not to write the Holy Name improperly from now on. For of him who does not know to write the Holy Name properly and to tie the bond of Faith, the bond of one and one, OF ZEIR ANPIN AND MALCHUT, ACCORDING TO THE SECRET OF THE VERSE, "HASHEM SHALL BE ONE, AND HIS NAME ONE" (ZECHARYAH 14:9), so as to unify the Holy Name, it is written, "Because he has despised the word of Hashem, and has broken His commandment, that soul shall utterly be cut off" (Bemidbar 15:31). This is even if he causes a degradation of one level or one unity from just one letter among them.

171. ת״ח, י׳ בְּקַדְמֵיתָא, כְּלָלָא דְּכֹלָּא, סָתִים מִכָּל סִטְרִין, שְׁבִילִין לָא מִתְפַּתְּחִין, כְּלָלָא דִּדְכַר וְנוּקְבָּא. קוֹצָא דְּיו״ד דִּלְעֵילָּא, רְמִיזָא לְאַיִן. לְבָתַר, י׳ דְּאָפִיק הַהוּא נַהֲרָא דְּנָגִיד וְנָפִיק מִנֵּיהּ, וּלְאִתְעַבְּרָא מִנֵּיהּ ה׳, בְּהַאי כְּתִיב וְנָהָר יוֹצֵא מֵעֵדֶן. יוֹצֵא וְלָא יָצָא. בְּג״כ לָא בַּעְיָא לְאִתְפָּרְשָׁא מִנֵּיהּ. וּבְג״כ כְּתִיב רְעִיתִי.

171. Come and see that the Yud ' at the beginning OF THE NAME, YUD HEI VAV HEI, includes it all. It is concealed on all sides, and no paths open WITHIN IT. It encompasses male and female, NAMELY THE SUPERNAL ABA AND IMA, AS THE YUD IS THE SECRET OF ABA AND TWO LETTERS OF

THE YUD FULLY SPELLED – NAMELY VAV AND DALET – ARE IMA. THEY ARE CONCEALED AND UNOPENED. The tip at the top of the Yud hints at naught, MEANING KETER CALLED SO, SINCE THERE IS NO CONCEIVING IT. Afterwards, the Yud, THE SECRET OF EDEN, issued from itself that river that continually flows out, NAMELY BINAH. From it, Hei will conceive WITH A SON AND A DAUGHTER, WHICH ARE VAV AND DALET. ITS SHAPE HINTS AT ZEIR ANPIN AND MALCHUT AS EMBRYOS WITHIN IT, IN THE SHAPE OF DALET AND VAV. Of this HEI, it is written, "And a river went (lit. 'goes') out of Eden" (Beresheet 2:10). IT IS WRITTEN "goes out," MEANING CONTINUOUSLY FLOWING, not 'went out', IN THE PAST TENSE. For this reason, THE HEI need not part FROM THE YUD. As a result, it is written, "my love" (Shir Hashirim 4:1) IN RELATION TO HEI, WHICH IS WITH YUD AS TWO FRIENDS THAT NEVER PART FROM ONE ANOTHER.

172. וְאִי תֵּימָא נָהָר כְּתִיב, מַשְׁמַע חַד, וְהָא הָכָא ג'. הָכִי הוּא וַדַּאי, י' אַפִּיק תְּלָתָא, וּבִתְלָתָא אִתְכְּלָל כֹּלָּא. י' אַפִּיק לְקַמֵּיה הַהוּא נָהָר, וּתְרֵין בְּנִין דְּיַנְקָא לְהוּ אִימָא, וְאִתְעַבְּרַת מִנַּיְיהוּ, וְאַפִּיק לוֹן לְבָתַר. ה': כְּגַוְונָא דָא ה', וְאִינוּן בְּנִין תְּחוֹת אַבָּא וְאִימָא.

172. You may ask why "a river" is written indicating one, but in reality there are three; NAMELY BINAH, THAT IS PREGNANT WITH ZEIR ANPIN AND MALCHUT, AS DISCUSSED. HE ANSWERS: This is for sure that the Yud produced three. All are included in the three. This Yud issued this river before it, NAMELY BINAH, and two offspring with which Ima (Eng. 'mother') nurses and is impregnated and bears them afterwards. The Hei has this form: DALET WITHIN WHICH THERE IS THE VAV, WHICH IS THE CUT LEG WITHIN THE HEI, and these, DALET AND VAV, are the offsprings that are below Aba and Ima, WITH WHICH IMA IS PREGNANT, AS DISCUSSED.

173. בָּתַר דְּאוֹלִידַת, אֲפִיקַת בֵּן דְּכַר, וְשַׁוְּויֵיהּ לְקַמָּהּ, וּבָעֵי לְמִכְתַּב ו', וְהָאי יָרִית אַחֲסַנְתָּא דְּאַבָּא וְאִימָא, וְיָרִית תְּרֵין חוּלָקִין, וּמִנֵּיהּ אִתְזָן בְּרַתָּא. וְעַל דָּא, בָּעֵי לְמִכְתַּב לְבָתַר, ו"ה כַּחֲדָא כְּמָה דְהֵ"א קַדְמָאָה י"ה כַּחֲדָא, וְלָא בָּעֵי לְאַפְרְשָׁא לוֹן, אוּף הָכָא ו"ה כַּחֲדָא, וְלָא בָּעֵי לְאַפְרְשָׁא לוֹן. וְהָא אוֹקִימְנָא מִלֵּי. וְלָאַתַר אָחֳרָא סַלְּקִין הָנֵי מִלֵּי. זַכָּאָה חוּלָקֵיהוֹן דְּצַדִּיקַיָּיא, דְּיַדְעִין רָזִין עִלָּאִין דְּמַלְכָּא קַדִּישָׁא,

וְיִתְחֲזוּן לְאוֹדָאָה לֵיהּ, הה״ד אַךְ צַדִּיקִים יוֹדוּ לִשְׁמֶךָ יֵשְׁבוּ יְשָׁרִים אֶת פָּנֶיךָ.

173. After BINAH gave birth, she produced a male child, placed him before her, NAMELY ZEIR ANPIN, and there is a need to write Vav, WHICH HINTS ABOUT THE SON; NAMELY, ZEIR ANPIN AFTER HE WAS BORN AND CAME FORTH TO HIS PLACE. This one, THE SON, inherits Aba and Ima. AND ZEIR ANPIN inherits two portions, ONE FOR HIMSELF AND ONE FOR MALCHUT. From him is nurtured the daughter. Therefore, it is necessary to write afterwards Vav-Hei together, ONE AFTER ANOTHER, just as the first Hei IS JOINED together WITH THE YUD, MEANING Yud Hei. There must be no separation between them. Also here Vav Hei are together and there is no need to separate them. We already established these matters. These matters here are also taken up to another place. Fortunate is the portion of the righteous, who understand supernal secrets of the Holy King and are worthy to be thankful before Him. Thus, it is written, "Surely the righeous shall give thanks to Your name: the upright shall dwell in Your presence" (Tehilim 140:14).

174. תָּאנָא א״ר יְהוּדָה, אֵל אֱלֹהִים יְיָ' דִּבֶּר וַיִּקְרָא אָרֶץ. שְׁלִימוּ דְּכֹלָּא, שְׁלִימוּ דַּאֲבָהָן קַדִּישֵׁי. דִּבֶּר וַיִּקְרָא אָרֶץ, לְאִשְׁתַּכְּחָא בכ״י בִּשְׁלִימוּ בְּחֶדְוֹוָתָא. וּמֵאָן אֲתַר הוּא אִשְׁתְּכַח עִמָּהּ. הָדָר וְאָמַר, מִצִּיּוֹן מִכְלַל יוֹפִי אֱלֹהִים הוֹפִיעַ.

174. We have learned that Rabbi Yehuda said, "El Elohim, Hashem, has spoken, and called the earth" (Tehilim 50:1). "EL, ELOHIM AND YUD HEI VAV HEI" REFER TO CHESED, GVURAH AND TIFERET, WHICH ARE perfection of all, the perfection of the holy Patriarchs – NAMELY CHESED, GVURAH AND TIFERET. "Has spoken and called the earth": SPOKEN MEANS POURING AND EARTH REFERS TO MALCHUT in order to be in the Congregation of Yisrael in perfection and in joy. From what place is He with her? He repeated, "Out of Zion, the perfection of beauty, Elohim has shown forth" (Ibid. 2), MEANING FROM YESOD OF MALCHUT KNOWN AS ZION.

28. As is done below so is done above

A Synopsis

Rabbi Shimon explains how Jerusalem and Zion were established by God because He wanted to create the lower world similar to the upper world. Rabbi Yehuda says that there is no service of worship above until the priest performs his service below. When Yisrael stop their service below then it also stops above, and thousands of hosts above that are connected to the children of Yisrael hold up their service. Yet for all this God does not abandon Yisrael even when they sin. Rabbi Elazar deduces that perfection above and below depend on the priest, who makes atonement for himself and for everyone else. Lastly we hear from Rabbi Yitzchak that when Yisrael are in exile it is as if God is with them since the Shechinah never leaves them.

175. תָּאנָא כַּד בָּעָא קוּדְשָׁא בְּרִיךְ הוּא לְמִבְרֵי עָלְמָא דִלְתַתָּא, כֹּלָא כְּגַוְונָא דִלְעֵילָא עֲבַד לֵיהּ. עֲבַד יְרוּשָׁלֵים, אֶמְצָעִיתָא דְּכָל אַרְעָא. וַאֲתַר חַד דְּאִקְרֵי צִיּוֹן, עָלֵהּ. וּמֵהַאי אֲתַר מִתְבָּרְכָא. וּבְהַאי אֲתַר דְּצִיּוֹן שָׁארֵי עָלְמָא לְאִתְבַּנְאָה, וּמִנֵּיהּ אִתְבְּנֵי. הַהֲ"ד, אֵל אֱלֹהִים יְיָ' דִּבֵּר וַיִּקְרָא אָרֶץ מִמִּזְרַח שֶׁמֶשׁ עַד מְבוֹאוֹ. וּמֵאָן אֲתַר. מִצִּיּוֹן מִכְלַל יוֹפִי אֱלֹהִים הוֹפִיעַ. כְּלוֹמַר, מִצִּיּוֹן דְּהוּא שְׁלִימוּ דְיוֹפִי דְעָלְמָא, אֱלֹהִים הוֹפִיעַ. תָּ"ח, לָא אִתְבָּרְכָא יְרוּשְׁלֵם, אֶלָּא מִצִּיּוֹן. וְצִיּוֹן מֵעֵילָא, וְכֹלָא חַד בְּחַד אִתְקְשַׁר.

175. We have learned that when the Holy One, blessed be He, wanted to create the lower world, He made it all similar to the upper. He made Jerusalem the center of the entire earth, and one place above it called Zion, WHOSE SECRET IS YESOD. It receives blessings from this place. Through this place of Zion, the earth started to be built, and through it the world was built. This is what the verse says, "El Elohim, Hashem, has spoken, and called the earth from the rising of the sun to the going down thereof" (Tehilim 50:1). From which place? "Out of Zion, the perfection of beauty, Elohim has shown forth" (Ibid. 2), meaning Elohim did appear from Zion, which is the ultimate beauty of the world. Come and see that Jerusalem, WHICH IS MALCHUT, was blessed only from Zion, WHICH IS YESOD, and Zion WAS BLESSED from above, MEANING ZEIR ANPIN. Everything is one,

one bonded into one, AS ZEIR ANPIN AND MALCHUT, THE SECRET OF ONE ON ONE, ARE JOINED BY ZION.

176. תָּאנָא, אָמַר רִבִּי יְהוּדָה, וְיָצָא אֶל הַמִּזְבֵּחַ אֲשֶׁר לִפְנֵי יְיָ׳ וְכִפֶּר עָלָיו. אֶל הַמִּזְבֵּחַ סְתָם. כְּמָה דְאִתְעֲבֵיד לְתַתָּא, אִתְעֲבֵיד לְעֵילָא, וְכֹלָּא אִתְקְשַׁר חַד בְּחַד. וְתָאנָא, כְּמָה דִּבְהַאי יוֹמָא מְכַפֵּר כַּהֲנָא לְתַתָּא, הָכִי נָמֵי לְעֵילָא. וְכַד כַּהֲנָא דִלְתַתָּא מְסַדֵּר פּוּלְחָנֵיהּ, כַּהֲנָא דִּלְעֵילָא הָכִי נָמֵי, לָא אִשְׁתְּכַח לְעֵילָא, עַד דְּאִשְׁתְּכַח לְתַתָּא. וּמִתַּתָּא שָׁארֵי לְסַלְּקָא קְדוּשָׁה דְּמַלְכָּא עִלָּאָה, וּמִשְׁתַּכְּחִין כֻּלְּהוּ עָלְמִין חַד קַמֵּיהּ דְקוּדְשָׁא בְּרִיךְ הוּא.

176. Rabbi Yehuda said that it is written, "And he shall go out to the altar that is before Hashem, and make atonement for it" (Vayikra 16:18). "To the altar" is WRITTEN without further qualification, HINTING AT THE CELESTIAL ALTAR, NAMELY THE SECRET OF YESOD OF MALCHUT. As it is done below, so it is done above. All is intertwined one with one THROUGH THE ALTAR THAT IS YESOD OF MALCHUT. We have learned that just as on this day the priest procures forgiveness here below, IN THE TEMPLE, so it is above. When the priest here performs his service, so does the celestial priest, REPRESENTING CHESED OF ZEIR ANPIN THAT POURS ABUNDANCE TO MALCHUT. There is no SERVICE above, WHICH IS THE SECRET OF CHESED POURING TO MALCHUT, until there is SERVICE OF THE PRIEST below, since the holiness of the supernal King starts to rise from below. All worlds are in one unity before the Holy One, blessed be He.

177. א״ר יְהוּדָה, אִלְמָלֵא הֲווֹ יַדְעֵי יִשְׂרָאֵל אֲמַאי קוּדְשָׁא בְּרִיךְ הוּא פָּקִיד עֲלַיְיהוּ דְּיִשְׂרָאֵל, לְאוֹכָחָא לְהוּ יַתִּיר מִכָּל שְׁאָר עַמִּין, יִנְדְּעוּן דְּהָא קוּדְשָׁא בְּרִיךְ הוּא שָׁבִיק דִּידֵיהּ, וְלָא גָּבֵי מִנְּהוֹן חַד מִמֵּאָה. תָּאנָא, קוּדְשָׁא בְּרִיךְ הוּא כַּמָּה רְתִיכִין, כַּמָּה חַיָּילִין אִית לֵיהּ, כַּמָּה שׁוּלְטָנִין מְמָנָן מִשְׁתַּכְּחִין בְּפוּלְחָנֵיהּ, כַּד זַמִּין לְהוּ לְיִשְׂרָאֵל בְּהַאי עָלְמָא, אַכְתַּר לוֹן בְּכִתְרִין קַדִּישִׁין כְּגַוְונָא דִּלְעֵילָא, אַשְׁרֵי לוֹן בְּאַרְעָא קַדִּישָׁא, בְּגִין דְּיִשְׁתַּכְּחוּ בְּפוּלְחָנֵיהּ, קָשִׁיר לְכֻלְּהוּ עָלָאֵי בְּהוּ בְּיִשְׂרָאֵל.

177. Rabbi Yehuda said: If Yisrael knew why the Holy One, blessed be He, visited to punish them more than all other nations, they would be aware that the Holy One, blessed be He, overlooks and forgives His own and does not punish them even one percent. We have learned how many Chariots and how many hosts are possessed by the Holy One, blessed be He, and how many rulers and appointees are in His service. When He designated Yisrael in this world, He crowned them with holy crowns similar to those above and caused them to dwell in the Holy Land, WHICH CORRESPONDS TO MALCHUT, in order that they should worship Him. And He connected all the exalted beings with Yisrael.

178. וְחֶדְוָון לָא עַאֲלִין קַמֵּיה, וּפוּלְחָנָא לָא אִתְעָבֵיד קַמֵּיה לְעֵילָא, עַד דְּיִשְׂרָאֵל עַבְדִּין לְתַתָּא. כָּל זִמְנָא דְיִשְׂרָאֵל מִשְׁתַּכְּחִין בְּפוּלְחָנֵיה דְּמָארֵיהוֹן לְתַתָּא, הָכִי נָמֵי לְעֵילָא. בְּזִמְנָא דְיִשְׂרָאֵל בְּטֵלֵי פוּלְחָנָא לְתַתָּא. בְּטֵלֵי לְעֵילָא, וּפוּלְחָנָא לָא אִשְׁתְּכַח לָא לְעֵילָא וְלָא לְתַתָּא. וְעַל דְּיִשְׂרָאֵל בַּטְלוּ פוּלְחָנָא דְקוּדְשָׁא בְּרִיךְ הוּא כַּד שָׁארָן בְּאַרְעָא, הָכִי נָמֵי לְעֵילָא, כ"ש לְבָתַר.

178. No joy enters before Him, and the service is not performed before Him above until Yisrael perform below. As long as they are found below in the service of their Master, so it is above. But when Yisrael stop the service below, it stops above also, so no service is performed above or below. Since Yisrael voided the service of the Holy One, blessed be He, when they dwelt in the land of Yisrael it was likewise so above, and certainly later IN EXILE.

179. אָמַר קוּדְשָׁא בְּרִיךְ הוּא, יִשְׂרָאֵל אִי אַתּוּן יַדְעִין, כַּמָה אוּכְלוּסִין, כַּמָה חַיָּילִין, מִתְעַכְּבִין בְּגִינַיְיכוּ, תִּנְדְּעוּן דְּלֵית אַתּוּן כְּדַאי לְמֵיקָם בְּעָלְמָא, אֲפִילוּ שַׁעֲתָא חֲדָא. ועכ"ד מַה כְּתִיב, וְאַף גַּם זֹאת בִּהְיוֹתָם בְּאֶרֶץ אוֹיְבֵיהֶם לֹא מְאַסְתִּים וְגוֹ', וְיֵצֵא אֶל הַמִּזְבֵּחַ, אֶל הַמִּזְבֵּחַ סְתָם, אֲשֶׁר לִפְנֵי יְיָ' סְתָם. וְכִפֶּר עָלָיו לְבָתַר, וְיֵצֵא וְעָשָׂה אֶת עֹלָתוֹ וְאֶת עוֹלַת הָעָם וְגוֹ'. וְכִפֶּר עָלָיו מַאי קָא מַיְירֵי. א"ר יוֹסֵי, לְאַתְעָרָא חֶסֶד בְּעָלְמָא בְּקַדְמֵיתָא.

179. The Holy One, blessed be He, said, 'O Yisrael, if you would only know how many troops, how many hosts hold up THEIR SERVICE because of you ABOVE, you would have realized that you do not deserve to be in this world even one instant.' In spite of this, it is written, "And yet for all that, when they are in the land of their enemies, I will not cast them away..." (Vayikra 26:44). THEREFORE, in "And he shall go out to the altar," "the altar" is written unspecified AND DOES NOT NECESSARILY INDICATE THE LOWER ALTAR IN THE TEMPLE. ALSO, "that is before Hashem," is again unqualified, NOT NECESSARILY IN THE TEMPLE. YET THE ALTAR ALLUDES TO THE SUPERNAL ALTAR, WHICH IS MALCHUT THAT IS BEFORE HASHEM, ZEIR ANPIN. Afterwards, it reads, "And make atonement for it," then "offer his burnt offering, and the burnt offering of the people..." (Vayikra 16:24). HE ASKS: IF THE ALLUSION IS TO MALCHUT, then what is the meaning of, "And make atonement for it"? IS ATONEMENT APPLICABLE ABOVE? Rabbi Yosi said, "AND MAKE ATONEMENT FOR IT" MEANS to awaken Chesed in the world first.

180. תָּאנָא, כְּתִיב וְכִפֶּר עַל הַקֹּדֶשׁ מִטֻּמְאוֹת בְּנֵי יִשְׂרָאֵל. מַאי וְכִפֶּר עַל הַקֹּדֶשׁ. אֶלָּא א"ר אֶלְעָזָר, הָא תָּנֵינָן, חַיָּיבַיָּא עַבְדִין פְּגִימוּתָא לְעֵילָא, וּמִתְעָרִין דִּינִין, וְגַרְמִין לְאִסְתַּאֲבָא מַקְדְּשָׁא. וְחִוְיָא תַּקִּיפָא שָׁארֵי לְאִתְגַּלָּאָה. וּכְדֵין דִּינִין מִתְעָרִין בְּעָלְמָא, וּבְהַאי יוֹמָא, בָּעֵי כַּהֲנָא לְדַכְּאָה כֹּלָּא, וּלְאִתְעַטְּרָא כִּתְרָא קַדִּישָׁא דִּילֵיהּ, דְּהִיא רֵישָׁא דְּמַלְכָּא. בְּגִין דְּיֵיתֵי מַלְכָּא לְאַשְׁרָאָה בְּמַטְרוֹנִיתָא, וְכַד רֵישָׁא דְּמַלְכָּא נָטִיל, כֹּלָּא נָטִיל, וְיֵיתֵי לְאִזְדַּוְּוגָא בְּמַטְרוֹנִיתָא וּלְאַתְעָרָא חֵידוּ וּבִרְכָּאן בְּעָלְמָא.

180. We have learned that it is written, "And he shall make atonement for the holy place, because of the uncleanness of the children of Yisrael" (Ibid. 16). HE QUESTIONS: What is meant by "and he shall make atonement for the holy place"? However, Rabbi Elazar said: Behold, we learned that the wicked cause a defect above and awaken Judgments. They cause the sanctuary to become unclean and the mighty snake begins to reveal itself. At that point, Judgments are awakened in the world. On this day, the priest needs to bring purification to all and to crown His holy Sfirah, NAMELY CHESED OF ZEIR ANPIN, which is the head of the King, AS CHESED IS HIS FIRST SFIRAH, in order that the King come to dwell with the Queen,

NAMELY MALCHUT. As the head of the King travels, all move along, MEANING ALL HIS SFIROT, to join with the Queen and instill joy and blessings in the world.

181. אִשְׁתְּכַח דְּכָל שְׁלִימוּ דְּעֵילָּא וְתַתָּא, בְּכַהֲנָא תַּלְיָיא. דְּאִי אִתְּעַר כִּתְרָא דִּילֵיהּ, כֹּלָּא אִתְּעַר וְכֹלָּא בִּשְׁלִימוּ אִשְׁתְּכַח. וְעַ״ד כְּתִיב וְכִפֶּר עַל הַקֹּדֶשׁ. בְּקַדְמֵיתָא וְכִפֶּר עַל הַקֹּדֶשׁ. לְאַסְגָּאָה שְׁלָמָא בְּעָלְמָא, וּלְאַסְגָּאָה חֵידוּ בְּעָלְמָא. וְכַד חֵידוּ דְזִוּוּגָא אִשְׁתְּכַח בְּמַלְכָּא וּבְמַטְרוֹנִיתָא, כָּל שַׁמָּשִׁין, וְכָל בְּנֵי הֵיכָלָא, כֻּלְּהוּ אִשְׁתְּכָחוּ בְּחֵידוּ. וְכָל חוֹבִין דְּחָבוּ קָמֵי מַלְכָּא, אִתְכַּפָּר לְהוּ. הַה״ד, מִכֹּל חַטֹּאתֵיכֶם לִפְנֵי יְיָ׳ תִּטְהָרוּ. וּבְגִ״כ כְּתִיב וְכָל אָדָם לֹא יִהְיֶה בְּאֹהֶל מוֹעֵד בְּבֹאוֹ לְכַפֵּר בַּקֹּדֶשׁ עַד צֵאתוֹ. בְּשַׁעֲתָא דְּעָאל לְזַוּוּגָא לְהוּ, וּבְשַׁעֲתָא דְּמִזְדַּוּוּגִין מַלְכָּא וּמַטְרוֹנִיתָא, הַהִיא שַׁעֲתָא וְכִפֶּר בַּעֲדוֹ וּבְעַד בֵּיתוֹ.

181. It is apparent that perfection above and below depend on the priest. If his Sfirah is awakened, all are awakened and perfection is present. Therefore, it is written, "And he shall make atonement for the holy place." At first, "he shall make atonement for the holy place," MEANING to increase peace in the world and multiply joy in the world. When there is the joy of the joining of the King and Queen, all courtiers of the palace and all that serve show joy. All sins done before the King are atoned for, as it is written, "That you may be clean from all your sins before Hashem" (Ibid. 30). For this reason, it is written, "And there shall be no man in the Tent of Meeting when he goes in to make atonement in the holy place, until he comes out" (Ibid. 17). This is at the time when he enters to join them. At that hour, when the King and Queen are joined, he will "have made atonement for himself, and for his household" (Ibid.).

182. תָּאנָא, וְכָל אָדָם לֹא יִהְיֶה בְּאֹהֶל מוֹעֵד, רִבִּי יִצְחָק פָּתַח, וְזָכַרְתִּי אֶת בְּרִיתִי יַעֲקוֹב וְאַף אֶת בְּרִיתִי יִצְחָק וְגו׳, וְהַאי קְרָא אוּקְמוּהָ. תָּא חֲזֵי, בְּשַׁעֲתָא דְּיִשְׂרָאֵל בְּגָלוּתָא, כִּבְיָכוֹל קוּדְשָׁא בְּרִיךְ הוּא עִמְּהוֹן בְּגָלוּתָא, דְּהָא שְׁכִינְתָּא לָא אִתְעֲדֵי מִנַּיְיהוּ לְעָלְמִין. ת״ח, בְּזִמְנָא דְיִשְׂרָאֵל אִשְׁתְּכָחוּ בְּגָלוּתָא דְּבָבֶל, שְׁכִינְתָּא בֵּינַיְיהוּ שַׁרְיָא, וְתָאבַת

עִמְּהוֹן מִן גָּלוּתָא. וּבִזְכוּת אִינּוּן צַדִּיקַיָּיא דְּאִשְׁתָּאָרוּ בְּאַרְעָא, שְׁאֲרַת
בְּאַרְעָא, וְלָא אַעֲדֵי מִנַּיְיהוּ לְעָלְמִין. א"ר יְהוּדָה, דְּאִתְהַדְּרַת
מַטְרוֹנִיתָא בְּמַלְכָּא, וְאִתְהַדָּר כֹּלָּא בְּהִלוּלָא דְמַלְכָּא, בְּג"כ אִקְרוּן
אַנְשֵׁי כנה"ג, כנה"ג וַדַּאי.

182. "And there shall be no man in the Tent of Meeting." Rabbi Yitzchak said, "Then will I remember My covenant with Jacob, and also My covenant with Isaac..." (Vayikra 26:42). This verse has been explained. Come and see: When Yisrael are in exile, it is as if the Holy One, blessed be He, is with them in exile, as the Shechinah never forsakes them. When Yisrael were in exile in Babylon, the Shechinah resided among them and returned with them from exile. In the merits of these righteous people who remained in the land, She resided in the land and never left them. Rabbi Yehuda said: Then the Queen returned to the King and all returned TO BE IN the banquet of joy of the king. For this, they are called the men of the Great Assembly. The Great Assembly surely, AS MALCHUT CALLED ASSEMBLY RETURNED FROM ITS DIMINISHED STATUS DURING THE EXILE TO REGAIN HER PROMINENCE.

29. "Then will I remember My covenant with Jacob"

A Synopsis

Rabbi Yehuda says that whenever the children of Yisrael are in exile, God brings them out of exile if they are found worthy, but even if they are not worthy He does not forget them. We learn why Jacob is mentioned first in the title verse.

183. תָּאנָא, בְּכָל זִמְנָא דְיִשְׂרָאֵל בְּגָלוּתָא, אִי אִינּוּן זַכָּאִין, קוּדְשָׁא בְּרִיךְ הוּא אַקְדִּים לְרַחֲמָא עָלַיְיהוּ, וּלְאַפָּקָא לוֹן מִגָּלוּתָא. וְאִי אִינּוּן לָא זַכָּאִין, מְעַכֵּב לוֹן בְּגָלוּתָא, עַד הַהוּא זִמְנָא דְּאִתְגְּזַר. וְכַד מָטָא זִמְנָא, וְאִינּוּן לָא אִתְחֲזְיָין, קוּדְשָׁא בְּרִיךְ הוּא אַשְׁגַּח לִיקָרָא דִּשְׁמַיָא, וְלָא אַנְשֵׁי לְהוּ בְּגָלוּתָא, הה"ד וְזָכַרְתִּי אֶת בְּרִיתִי יַעֲקֹב וְגוֹ'. אִלֵּין אֲבָהָן דְּכֹלָּא, רָזָא דִּשְׁמָא קַדִּישָׁא.

183. We have learned that whenever Yisrael are in exile and are found worthy, the Holy One, blessed be He, hastens His mercy for them and draws them out from exile. If they are not found worthy, He keeps them in exile until the time He originally decreed. If that time arrives yet they are not worthy OF REDEMPTION, the Holy One, blessed be He, is mindful of the glory of His Name, and does not forget them in exile. This is the meaning of the verse, "Then will I remember My covenant with Jacob..." (Vayikra 26:42). For they are everyone's Patriarchs, REFERRING TO CHESED, GVURAH AND TIFERET, the secret of the Holy Name, YUD HEI VAV HEI, AS HE IS MINDFUL OF THE GLORY OF HIS NAME.

184. רְבִּי חִיָּיא אָמַר, מַאי טַעֲמָא יַעֲקֹב קַדְמָאָה הָכָא. אֶלָּא, בְּגִין דְּיַעֲקֹב כְּלָלָא דַּאֲבָהָן, וְהוּא אִילָנָא קַדִּישָׁא. בְּג"כ, ו' דִּשְׁמָא קַדִּישָׁא בֵּיהּ אֲחִידָא, וְהָכִי קָרֵינָן יַעֲקֹב בּוֹ'. ר' יִצְחָק, אָמַר וָא"ו בְּאַתְוֹוי י"ג מְכִילָן, דְּיָרִית יְרוּתָא דִי"ג מַבּוּעִין דְּמַבּוּעָא סְתִימָא קַדִּישָׁא.

184. Rabbi Chiya said: What is the reason that Jacob is MENTIONED first in the verse, AS IT READS, "THEN WILL I REMEMBER MY COVENANT WITH JACOB" AND LATER ISAAC AND LATER ABRAHAM? HE ANSWERS: Jacob, TIFERET, is the principal of the fathers, AS TIFERET ABSORBS WITHIN IT

CHESED AND GVURAH, ALSO KNOWN AS ABRAHAM AND ISAAC. He is the holy tree, MEANING ZEIR ANPIN THAT INCLUDES ALL SIX ENDS. As such, the Vav of the Holy Name YUD HEI VAV HEI holds to him, so we pronounce Jacob with a Vav. Rabbi Yitzchak said: Vav FULLY SPELLED with all its letters HAS THE NUMERICAL VALUE OF THIRTEEN, NAMELY the thirteen attributes OF MERCY, AS JACOB, BEING ZEIR ANPIN, inherits the inheritance of the thirteen springs of the Holy sealed spring KNOWN AS ARICH ANPIN. FROM HIS BEARD ARE DRAWN THIRTEEN CORRECTIONS TO ZEIR ANPIN CALLED JACOB AND FOR THIS REASON, JACOB IS SPELLED WITH VAV.

30. The Vav has a silent Aleph in it

A Synopsis
We learn the inner meaning of the Aleph in the pronunciation of
Vav as Vav Aleph Vav. Similar inferences can be drawn from the
pronunciation of Nun as Nun Vav Nun and from the open and
closed Mem of Mem. We are reminded again of the importance of
the priest in his role of awakening peace above and below.

185. ר' אַבָּא אָמַר, וָא"ו אֲמַאי כָּלִיל ו' א' ו'. אֶלָּא, ו' דְּיָתִיב עַל
כּוּרְסְיָיא, כד"א וְעַל דְּמוּת הַכִּסֵּא דְּמוּת כְּמַרְאֵה אָדָם עָלָיו מִלְמָעְלָה.
א' סָתִים בְּגַוֵּיה וְלָא אִתְגַּלְיָיא, וְדָא הוּא דִּכְתִיב בִּי נִשְׁבַּעְתִּי נְאָם יְיָ,
בְּג"כ כְּתִיב, וְלָא אִקְרֵי, בַּתְרָאָה, כְּלָלָא דְּקַדְמָאָה. בַּתְרָאָה, הָא
אוּקִימְנָא דָּא יְסוֹד, דְּאִיהוּ סִיּוּמָא דְּגוּפָא, וּכְלָלָא דִּילֵיה. וְעַ"ד כְּלִילָן
אַתְוָון דָּא בְּדָא, וָא"ו, רֵישָׁא וְסִיּוּמָא, כְּמָה דְּאוּקִימְנָא.

185. Rabbi Aba said: Why does the letter Vav contain Vav-Aleph-Vav וָא"ו
IN THIS PRONUNCIATION? HE ANSWERS: Vav, MEANING ZEIR ANPIN, sits
on the throne, REFERRING TO MALCHUT CALLED THRONE, as the verse
reads, "And upon the likeness of the throne was the likeness as the
appearance of a man above upon it" (Yechezkel 1:26), REFERRING TO ZEIR
ANPIN. The Aleph is silent within VAV and is not revealed, AS THE ALEPH
REPRESENTS ARICH ANPIN, CLOTHED FROM THE CENTER DOWNWARD
WITH ZEIR ANPIN, AND IS NOT REVEALED OUTSIDE OF ZEIR ANPIN. This
is what is written, "'By Myself have I sworn', says Hashem" (Beresheet
22:16), AS ZEIR ANPIN SWORE BY ARICH ANPIN WHO IS CLOTHED
WITHIN HIM. For this reason, THE ALEPH is written but not pronounced,
MEANING WHEN WE READ THE VAV, THE ALEPH IS SILENT AND IS NOT
HEARD IN ITS PRONUNCIATION, AS IT HINTS AT ARICH ANPIN WHO IS
CONCEALED AND INCOMPREHENSIBLE. The last VAV comprises the first
and we have established that THE LAST VAV is Yesod, the ending of the
body, TIFERET, and comprises it all, AS IT IS PART OF THE BODY.
Therefore, the letters are connected one with the other, Vav-Aleph-Vav
being the beginning and end, MEANING TIFERET AND YESOD THAT ARE
ONE, AND THE ALEPH REPRESENTS ARICH ANPIN CLOTHED IN TIFERET,
as we have explained.

186. וְתָאנָא, תְּרֵין אַתְוָון אִינּוּן, כְּהַאי גַּוְונָא וְא"ו דַּאֲמֵינָא, נו"ן אוּף הָכִי. וְאע"ג דְּאוּקְמוּהָ מִלָּה, נו"ן הָכִי מִתְפָּרְשָׁא: נ' כְּפוּפָה, דָּא מַטְרוֹנִיתָא. וּסְמִיכָא לָהּ ו', דְּאִיהוּ יְסוֹד, בְּגִין לְאִתְבָּרְכָא מִנֵּיהּ. ן' פְּשׁוּטָה, אִתְפַּשְּׁטוּתָא דְּתִפְאֶרֶת. וְע"ד כְּלִילָן אַתְוָון, וּמִתְאַחֲדָן דָּא בְּדָא. וְאִי תֵּימָא, אֲמַאי אַהֲדָר ו' אַנְפּוֹי מִנּו"ן כְּפוּפָה, וְאַהֲדָר אַנְפּוֹי לְגַבֵּי ן' פְּשׁוּטָה. אֶלָּא בְּגִין יְקָרָא דְּמַלְכָּא, אַהֲדָר אַנְפּוֹי לְקַבְלֵיהּ דְּמַלְכָּא.

186. We have learned in relation to these two letters that the same thing I said about the Vav is true about the Nun נון. Even though they have established this matter IN ANOTHER WAY, the Nun can be explained so. The bent Nun נ refers to the Queen, and next to it is Vav ו, which is Yesod, so that MALCHUT attains blessing from it. The straight final Nun ן is the expansion of Tiferet, so the letters are brought together and united one with the other. AS TIFERET, WHICH IS THE STRAIGHT NUN, REACHES OUT TO INSPIRE YESOD, WHICH IS VAV; AND YESOD REACHES OUT TO INFLUENCE MALCHUT, WHICH IS THE BENT NUN. If you ask why does the Vav turn its face away from the bent Nun and show its face to the straight final Nun? This is done to show honor to the King, WHO IS THE STRAIGHT NUN, MEANING TIFERET AS MENTIONED. THEREFORE, YESOD turns its face towards the King, MEANING THAT YESOD AND TIFERET ARE ALWAYS AS ONE AS IT APPEARS IN THE ADJACENT PARAGRAPH.

187. וְתָאנָא, מֵ"ם לָא כָּלִיל בְּגַוֵּיהּ אָת אָחֳרָא, אֶלָּא מ' פְּתוּחָה, ם' סְתוּמָה. מ' פְּתוּחָה: דְּהוּא כַּד דְּכַר אִתְחַבַּר עִמָּהּ. ם' סְתוּמָה: יוֹבְלָא. דְּהָא סְתִימִין אָרְחָהָא וְאע"ג דְּמִתְפַּשְּׁטִין לְזִמְנִין, וְאִית דְּמַתְנֵי בְּהַאי כד"א גַּן נָעוּל אֲחוֹתִי כַלָּה גַּל נָעוּל מַעְיָן חָתוּם.

187. We have learned that the Mem מ does not include within it any other letter, AS THE LETTER IN THE FULL SPELLING IS ALSO MEM, but Mem is open מ and final Mem is closed ם. The open Mem INDICATES MALCHUT

WHEN the male joins with her AND IT IS OPEN IN ORDER TO RECEIVE THE
ABUNDANCE. The closed Mem POINTS TO Jubilee, MEANING BINAH,
WHOSE WAYS ARE CONCEALED. THEREFORE, THE FINAL MEM IS ALSO
CLOSED FROM ALL SIDES AND, even though THAT BINAH spreads out AT
times, IT IS CONSIDERED CLOSED MEM. Some learn about this matter,
from, "A garden enclosed is my sister, my bride; a spring shut up, a fountain
sealed" (Shir Hashirim 4:12), NAMELY THAT ALSO THE CLOSED FINAL
MEM HINTS AT MALCHUT, WHEN IT IS CALLED A SEALED FOUNTAIN.

188. אָמַר ר' יִצְחָק, בְּשַׁעֲתָא דְמַלְכָּא קַדִּישָׁא אַדְכַּר לְהוּ לְיִשְׂרָאֵל בְּגִין
שְׁמֵיהּ, וְאַהֲדָרַת מַטְרוֹנִיתָא לְאַתְרָהָא, כְּתִיב, וְכָל אָדָם לֹא יִהְיֶה
בְּאֹהֶל מוֹעֵד בְּבֹאוֹ לְכַפֵּר בַּקֹּדֶשׁ. כַּךְ כַּהֲנָא, בְּשַׁעֲתָא דְעָאל לְיַחֲדָא
שְׁמָא קַדִּישָׁא, וּלְכַפְּרָא בְּקוּדְשָׁא, לְזַוְוגָא לְמַלְכָּא בְּמַטְרוֹנִיתָא. כְּתִיב
וְכָל אָדָם לֹא יִהְיֶה בְּאֹהֶל מוֹעֵד וְגו'.

188. Rabbi Yitzchak said: When the Holy King remembers Yisrael for His
Name's sake and returns the Queen to her position, it is written, "And there
shall be no man in the Tent of Meeting when he goes in to make atonement
in the holy place" (Vayikra 16:17). At the time the priest enters to unify the
Holy Name and makes atonement in the holy place to join the King with the
Queen, it is then written, "And there shall be no man in the Tent of
Meeting..."

189. תָּאנָא, ר' יְהוּדָה אָמַר, כַּהֲנָא אִתְּעַר שְׁלָמָא בְּעָלְמָא, לְעֵילָא
וְתַתָּא. וְתָנְיָא עָאל בְּדַרְגָּא חַד, אַסְחֵי גוּפֵיהּ. נָפִיק מֵהַאי דַרְגָּא,
לְדַרְגָּא אָחֳרָא אַסְחֵי גוּפֵיהּ. אָחִיד שְׁלָמָא בְּהַאי וּבְהַאי, קָדֵשׁ יְדוֹי,
וּמִתְבָּרְכָאן כַּחֲדָא. וּבְכֹלָּא בָּעֵי לְאַחֲזָאָה עוֹבָדָא, וּבָעֵי לְאַחֲזָאָה
לְבוּשׁוֹי, דְּיִתְלַבַּשׁ כְּגַוְונָא דְּעוֹבָדָא דְּיִתְכַּוֵּון, עַד דְּיִסְדַּר כֹּלָּא כְּמָה
דְּאִצְטְרִיךְ, וְיִתְבָּרְכוּן עֶלָאֵי וְתַתָּאֵי.

189. We have learned that Rabbi Yehuda said: The priest awakens peace in
the world above and below. We have learned that he enters the first level OF
MALCHUT and washes his body. He departs this level to the next, OF ZEIR
ANPIN, washes his body and extends peace to this one and that one, ZEIR

ANPIN AND MALCHUT. He sanctifies his hands and they are blessed together. In everything, he needs to show action BELOW IN ORDER TO TRIGGER ITS COUNTERPART ABOVE. He needs to show that the garments he wears should be in line with his actions and he should aim to organize everything as needed. Then the upper and lower beings will be blessed.

31. The Yud with its engravings

A Synopsis
Rabbi Shimon explains the movement and meaning of the letters in
the Holy Name.

190. תָּאנָא ר' שִׁמְעוֹן, פָּתַח יוֹ"ד בְּגִלּוּפוֹי, אַתְוָון בְּסִטְרִין, אִתְקַשְׁרָן
בְּיוֹ"ד. יוֹ"ד אָזִיל לְיוֹ"ד יוֹ"ד סָלִיק בְּיוֹ"ד. יוֹ"ד אָזִיל לְוָי"ו, מִתְכַּנְשֵׁי
בה'. וּמְכַוֵּון דַּעְתָּא, אִתְחַבָּר ה' בְּוָא"ו.

190. Rabbi Shimon taught, the Yud makes an opening with its engraving,
and the letters SPREAD to the sides, MEANING EACH LETTER FROM THE
NAME YUD HEI VAV HEI SPREADS IN THREE COLUMNS and joins up with
the Yud. EACH OF THE COLUMNS IS TIED TO YUD, DENOTING
CHOCHMAH AND THE RIGHT COLUMN. The Yud moves towards the Yud;
THAT IS, CHOCHMAH, THE FIRST YUD OF THE NAME YUD ALEPH HEI
DALET VAV NUN HEI YUD, MOVES TO MALCHUT, ITS LAST YUD. The
Yud, MALCHUT, rises to the Yud, CHOCHMAH. LATER, the Yud OF
CHOCHMAH moves to Vav, WHICH IS ZEIR ANPIN. BUT FIRST, THE LIGHT
OF CHOCHMAH assembles inside the Hei, BINAH, which then directs Da'at,
AS DA'AT IS PLACED BETWEEN CHOCHMAH AND BINAH. AND LATER, the
Hei joins with the Vav.

191. ה' עִלָּאָה אָחִיד תַּרְעוֹי בְּגִלּוּפֵי תַכְסִיסִין, אַחֲדָא בִּנְהִירוּ אֶלַף
וַחֲמֵשׁ מְאָה וְשַׁבְעִין אַכְסַדְרִין סְתִימִין. סָלִיק ה', וְאִתְעַטָּר חַמְשִׁין
זִמְנִין, לָן' תַּרְעִין קַיְימִין דְּקַיְימִין, כַּד אִתְגְּלַף בְּעִטְרוֹי, נַהֲרִין אַנְפִּין
דְּמַלְכָּא, וָא"ו אִתְפְּשַׁט לְע"ב גְּלִיפִין.

191. HE SAYS: The upper Hei OF THE NAME YUD HEI VAV HEI, NAMELY
BINAH, maintains its gates, MEANING THE FIFTY GATES OF BINAH, in its
design and arrangement, MEANING ITS ORDERLY DESIGN. THEN, it grasps
the glow of 1,570 covered parlors. ONE THOUSAND IS THE SECRET OF
CHOCHMAH AND THE RIGHT COLUMN, FIVE HUNDRED IS THE SECRET
OF BINAH AND THE LEFT COLUMN AND SEVENTY IS THE SECRET OF
DA'AT, THE CENTRAL COLUMN. Then the Hei, NAMELY BINAH, rises to be

crowned fifty times for its fifty gates OF BINAH, which maintain whatever is maintaining. When BINAH is designed with her crowns – MEANING HER TWO CROWNS, WHICH IS THE SECRET OF HER DA'AT – the face of the King, ZEIR ANPIN, glows FROM HERE. The Vav spreads to 22 engravings, NAMELY THE NAME OF AYIN BET.

192. מְעַטֵּר ה' לוֹ', בְּעֶ' אֶלֶף וְה' מְאָה כִּתְרִין, דְּמִתְעַטְּרָן בְּחַד כִּתְרָא, הה"ד בַּעֲטָרָה, שֶׁעִטְּרָה לוֹ אִמּוֹ. ו' בִּתְרֵין רֵישִׁין, גְּלִיפָא רֵישָׁא, קוֹצָא חַד לְעֵילָא, וְקוֹצָא חַד לְתַתָּא, וְי' נָחִית לוֹ', גְּלִיפָא דְּגִלּוּפִין בְּגַוַּיְיהוּ, שַׁבְעִין אַנְפִּין דְּעִטְּרִין מֵעֵילָא לְתַתָּא. בֵּיהּ טָאסִין גְּבִיעִין וּפַרְחִין, דָּא סָלִיק, וְדָא נָחִית מִתְגַּלְּפִין חַד בְּחַד.

192. The Hei adorns the Vav with 70,500 crowns – THE SECRET OF CHESED, GVURAH, TIFERET, NETZACH, HOD AND YESOD OF CHOCHMAH, THE SECRET OF SEVENTY THOUSAND, WHICH IS THE RIGHT COLUMN. CHESED, GVURAH, TIFERET, NETZACH, HOD AND YESOD OF BINAH ARE THE SECRET OF FIVE HUNDRED, THE LEFT COLUMN, which are adorned with one crown, BEING THE SECRET OF DA'AT THAT UNIFIES AND INCLUDES THEM. This is the essence of the verse, "With the crown with which his mother crowned him" (Shir Hashirim 3:11). BINAH IS CONSIDERED THE MOTHER OF VAV THAT IS ZEIR ANPIN. IT TURNS OUT THAT the Vav's top is engraved with two tops, NAMELY CHOCHMAH AND BINAH. THEREFORE, THERE ARE TWO TIPS WRITTEN AT THE TOP OF THE VAV, one tip higher, HINTING AT CHOCHMAH, and one tip lower, HINTING AT BINAH. The Yud, NAMELY CHOCHMAH, lowers then on to the Vav, MEANING THAT THE VAV IS JOINED WITH THE YUD LIKE THE HEI. The main impression of all the engravings, MEANING THE CENTRAL COLUMN, between THE TWO TOPS, IS the seventy faces adorned from above downwards. Goblets and flowers hover in it. This one rises, NAMELY FLOWERS, the other descends and they are engraved one in the other.

193. אִתְקְשַׁר י' בְּה', ה' בּו', ו' בְּה'. דָּא אָחִיד בְּדָא, כְּמָה דְּאַתְּ אָמַר, וַתֵּשֶׁב בְּאֵיתָן קַשְׁתּוֹ וַיָּפֹזּוּ זְרוֹעֵי יָדָיו מִידֵי אֲבִיר יַעֲקֹב. וּכְתִיב, אֵיתָן מוֹשָׁבֶךָ וְשִׂים בַּסֶּלַע קִנֶּךָ. כְּדֵין אִתְקְשַׁר כֹּלָּא חַד בְּחַד, דָּא בְּדָא, נְהִירִין מִפִתְחָן, וְנַהֲרִין אַנְפִּין כֻּלְּהוּ, כְּדֵין כֻּלְּהוּ נַפְלִין עַל אַנְפַּיְיהוּ,

וּמִזְדַּעְזְעָן, וְאָמְרֵי בְּרִיךְ שְׁמָא יְקָרָא מַלְכוּתֵיהּ לְעָלַם וּלְעָלְמֵי עָלְמִין.

193. The Yud is tied to the Hei ה, the Hei with the Vav and the Vav with the Hei. One is tied with the other, MEANING THAT THE VAV, WHICH IS ZEIR ANPIN, IS CONNECTED WITH THE HEI, WHICH IS MALCHUT. Just as you say in the verse, "But his bow abode in strength, and the arms of his hands were made supple by the hands of the mighty One of Jacob" (Beresheet 49:24), IN WHICH "STRENGTH" IS YESOD AND "HIS BOW" IS MALCHUT. THUS YESOD OF ZEIR ANPIN IS ATTACHED TO MALCHUT, and "Strong is your dwelling place, and you put your nest in a rock" (Bemidbar 24:21), WHEREBY "STRONG" REFERS TO YESOD AND "ROCK" IS MALCHUT. They are tied together, one with another, and the keys are aglow WITH THE ILLUMINATION OF CHOCHMAH. All faces are illuminated, WHICH IS THE SECRET OF SEVENTY FACES MENTIONED EARLIER. Then they all prostrate and tremble AS A RESULT OF THE JUDGMENTS REVEALED WITH THE ILLUMINATION OF CHOCHMAH, and they say: 'Blessed is the name of the glory of His kingdom forever and ever'.

32. "From all your sins before Hashem, that you may be clean"

A Synopsis
We learn that the high priest is capable of bringing atonement on the people because he is a chariot to Zeir Anpin; he is the voice of Zeir Anpin. We read about God's forgiveness of sins. We read about the high priest when he enters the Holy of Holies and hears the sounds of the cherubs' wings. As a result of his actions, there is joy above and below.

194. קָלָא מִתְקַשָּׁר עֲמֵיה דְּכַהֲנָא, וְהוּא אָתִיב לְגַבַּיְיהוּ. וְאָמַר תִּטְהָרוּ. תִּטְהָרוּ לָא אַמְרִין שְׁאַר כַּהֲנֵי וְעַמָּא, בַּר כַּהֲנָא רַבָּא, כַּד אִתְקְשַׁר בֵּיה הַהוּא קָלָא.

194. The voice, NAMELY ZEIR ANPIN, THE CENTRAL COLUMN, joins with the priest, MEANING THE PRIEST BECOMES A CHARIOT TO ZEIR ANPIN. He says to them, "That you may be clean" (Vayikra 16:30). BEING A CHARIOT TO THE CENTRAL COLUMN, HE CAN BRING ON THEM THE ILLUMINATION OF CHOCHMAH THAT BRINGS FORGIVENESS OF SINS AND CLEANSING. Neither the people nor any other priest say, "That you may be clean," except the High Priest when the voice is attached to him, MEANING ZEIR ANPIN. THEN HE IS CAPABLE OF BRINGING ATONEMENT ON THEM AND HE PROCLAIMS "THAT YOU MAY BE CLEAN."

195. תָּאנָא, מִכֹּל חַטֹּאתֵיכֶם לִפְנֵי יְיָ', כֵּיוָן דִּכְתִיב מִכֹּל חַטֹּאתֵיכֶם, אֲמַאי לִפְנֵי יְיָ'. אֶלָּא א"ר יִצְחָק, לִפְנֵי יְיָ' מַמָּשׁ.

195. We have learned "from all your sins before Hashem" (Ibid.). HE QUESTIONS: If he already wrote, "TO CLEANSE YOU from all your sins," why WRITE "before Hashem THAT YOU MAY BE CLEAN"? Rabbi Yitzchak said, "THAT YOU MAY BE CLEAN...before (lit. 'in the face of') Hashem," MEANING THE ILLUMINATION OF THE FACE OF HASHEM. AS THE ILLUMINATION OF HASHEM'S FACE IS THE SECRET OF THE ILLUMINATION OF CHOCHMAH, ACCORDING TO THE SECRET MEANING OF THE VERSE, "A MAN'S WISDOM MAKES HIS FACE TO SHINE" (KOHELET 8:1). IT ATONES FOR SINS AND BRINGS CLEANSING.

196. דְּתַנְיָא, מֵרֵישָׁא דְּיַרְחָא סַפְרִין פְּתִיחִין, וְדַיְינֵי דַיְינִין. בְּכָל יוֹמָא

וְיוֹמָא בָּתֵי דִינִין אִתְמַסְרָן, לְאִתְפַּתְּחָא בְּדִינָא, עַד הַהוּא יוֹמָא דְּאִקְרֵי תִּשְׁעָה לְיַרְחָא. בְּהַהוּא יוֹמָא, סַלְקִין דִּינִין כֻּלְּהוּ לְמָארֵי דְּדִינָא, וּמְתַקְּנֵי כֻּרְסְיָיא עִלָּאָה דְּרַחֲמֵי, לְמַלְכָּא קַדִּישָׁא. בְּהַהוּא יוֹמָא בָּעָאן יִשְׂרָאֵל לְתַתָּא, לְמֶחֱדֵי בְּחֶדְוָותָא לְקַדְמוּת מָארֵיהוֹן, דְּזַמִּין לְיוֹמָא אָחֳרָא, לְמֵיתַב עָלַיְיהוּ בְּכוּרְסְיָיא קַדִּישָׁא דְּרַחֲמֵי, בְּכוּרְסְיָיא דְּוַותְּרָנוּתָא.

196. We have learned that from the new moon, MEANING ROSH HASHANAH (THE JEWISH NEW YEAR), the books are opened and the judges judge. The courts start to judge daily until that day known as the ninth day of the month. On that day, all judicial decisions go up to the judge. They prepare a supernal throne of Mercy for the Holy King. On this day, Yisrael need to rejoice in joy before their Master who will on the second day be sitting on His throne of Mercy for them, His throne of absolution MEANING FORGIVENESS OF SINS.

197. וְכָל אִינּוּן סִפְרִין דִּפְתִיחִין קַמֵּיה, וּכְתִיבִין קַמֵּיה כָּל אִינּוּן חוֹבִין, הוּא מְזַכֵּי לוֹן, וּמַדְכֵּי לוֹן מִכֻּלְּהוּ, הה"ד מִכֹּל חַטֹאתֵיכֶם לִפְנֵי יְיָ' תִּטְהָרוּ. לִפְנֵי יְיָ' מַמָּשׁ, אִינּוּן דְּאַמְרֵי קְרָא, עַד הָכָא אַמְרִין, וְלָא יַתִּיר. וְלֵית רְשׁוּ לְאָחֳרָא דִּילְמָא תִּטְהָרוּ, אֶלָּא כַּהֲנָא רַבָּא, דְּפָלַח פּוּלְחָנָא, וְקָשַׁר שְׁמָא קַדִּישָׁא בְּפוּמֵיה, וְכַד הֲוָה אִתְקְשַׁר וּמִתְבָּרֵךְ בְּפוּמֵיה, הַהוּא קָלָא נָחִית וּבָטַשׁ בֵּיה, וְאִתְנְהִיר מִלָּה בְּפוּמֵיה דְּכַהֲנָא, וְאוֹמֵר תִּטְהָרוּ. פָּלַח פּוּלְחָנָא, וּמִתְבָּרְכִין כָּל אִינּוּן עִלָּאִין דְּאִשְׁתָּארוּ.

197. All these books are open before Him and are recorded before Him all these sins. He credits them and cleanses them from all sins. This is the essence of the verse, "From all your sins before Hashem, that you may be clean." "Before Hashem" literally; THIS REFERS TO THE ILLUMINATION OF THE FACE OF HASHEM, THE SECRET OF THE ILLUMINATION OF CHOCHMAH WHICH FORGIVES ALL SIN. Those that recite this verse only to this point are permitted to do so, NAMELY UNTIL "BEFORE HASHEM" but no more, as no one else is permitted to announce "that you may be clean" but the High Priest ALONE, who performs the service and unifies the Holy

Name. When he unifies THE HOLY NAME and the blessing is in his mouth, that voice, NAMELY ZEIR ANPIN, comes down, strikes him and causes the word to glow in the mouth of the priest, and he says, "That you may be clean." He performs his service and thus the rest of the supernal beings are blessed.

198. וּלְבָתַר אַסְחֵי גוּפֵיה, וְקִדֵּשׁ יְדוֹי, לְאַעֲלָא בְּפוּלְחָנָא אָחֳרָא קַדִּישָׁא. עַד דְּיִתְכַּוֵּון לְמֵיעַל לַאֲתַר אָחֳרָא עִלָּאָה, קַדִּישָׁא מִכֹּלָּא. ג' שׁוּרִין סָחֲרִין לֵיה, כַּהֲנֵי אָחוֹי, וְלֵיוָאֵי, וּמִכָּל שְׁאָר עַמָּא כֻּלְּהוּ. זַקְפִין יְדִין עָלֵיה בִּצְלוֹתָא וְקִטְרָא דְּדַהֲבָא זַקְפָּא בְּרַגְלֵיה.

198. Afterwards, he washes his body and sanctifies his hands to enter into another holy service. Then he aims to enter another most holy, lofty place; NAMELY, THE HOLY OF HOLIES. Three rows surround THE HIGH PRIEST-his colleague priests, Levite and the rest of the people. THEY REPRESENT THE THREE COLUMNS, PRIEST AND LEVITE REPRESENT RIGHT AND LEFT AND YISRAEL REPRESENT THE SECRET OF THE CENTRAL COLUMN. They raise their hands towards him in prayer. A knot OF ROPE of gold hangs from his leg, FROM FEAR PERHAPS HE WOULD DIE IN THE HOLY OF HOLIES, AND THEY WOULD NEED TO PULL HIM OUT WITH THIS ROPE.

199. נָטִיל ג' פְּסִיעָן, וְכֻלְּהוּ קַיְימִין בְּקִיוּמַיְיהוּ, וְלָא נַטְלִין בַּתְרֵיה נָטִיל ג' פְּסִיעָן אָחֳרָן, אַסְחַר לְדוּכְתֵּיה. נָטִיל ג' פְּסִיעָן, אַסְתִּים עַיְינִין, וְאִתְקְשַׁר לְעֵילָא. עָאל לַאֲתַר דְּעָאל, שָׁמַע קוֹל גַּדְפֵּי דִּכְרוּבַיָּיא מְזַמְּרִין, וְאָקִישָׁן גַּדְפִין פְּרִישָׁאן לְעֵילָא. הֲוָה אַקְטִיר קְטוֹרֶת, מִשְׁתַּכְּכָא קוֹל גַּדְפַּיְיהוּ וּבִלְחִישׁוּ אִתְדַּבְּקָן.

199. He takes three steps, but the others remain where they are and do not follow. He takes another three steps and returns to his place. He walks three paces, closes his eyes, connects to that which is above and enters that certain place, NAMELY THE HOLY OF HOLIES. He hears the sound of wings of the Cherubs, singing and fanning their wings that are stretched upward. When he would offer the incense, the sound of their wings quieted and they were silently clasped together.

200. אִי כַּהֲנָא זָכֵי, דְּהָא לְעֵילָּא בְּחֶדְוּוּ אִשְׁתְּכַח, אוּף הָכָא בְּהַהִיא שַׁעֲתָא נָפִיק רַעֲוָא דִּנְהוֹרָא, מִתְבַּסְּמָא מֵרֵיחִין דְּטוּרֵי אֲפַרְסְמוֹנָא דַּכְיָא דִּלְעֵילָּא, וְאַזְלָא בְּכָל הַהוּא אֲתַר, אָעֵיל רֵיחָא בִּתְרֵי נוּקְבֵי דְּחוֹטְמֵיה, וְאִתְיַישְׁבָא לִבָּא. כְּדֵין כֹּלָּא הוּא בִּלְחִישׁוּ, וּפְטָרָא לָא אִשְׁתְּכַח תַּמָּן. פָּתַח כַּהֲנָא פּוּמֵיה בִּצְלוֹתָא בִּרְעוּתָא בְּחֶדְוָותָא, וְצַלֵּי צְלוֹתֵיה.

200. Since joy prevails above, if the priest merits it here too, BELOW, at that time the goodwill of light is manifested and scented with the fragrance of mountains of the pure supernal balsam, which fragrance spreads throughout that place. It enters the two nostrils of the priest and his heart is satisfied. Then there is silence with no fault to be found. The priest opens his mouth in prayer willingly and with joy, and he utters his prayer.

201. בָּתַר דְּסַיֵּים, זַקְפִין כְּרוּבַיָּיא כְּמִלְּקַדְמִין גַּדְפַּיְיהוּ, וּמְזַמְּרִין. כְּדֵין יָדַע כַּהֲנָא דִּרְעוּתָא הֲוָו, וְעִידָּן חֶדְוָותָא לְכֹלָּא, וְעַמָּא יַדְעִין דְּאִתְקַבֵּל צְלוֹתֵיה, כְּמָה דִכְתִיב אִם יִהְיוּ חֲטָאֵיכֶם כַּשָּׁנִים כַּשֶּׁלֶג יַלְבִּינוּ. וְהוּא תָּב לַאֲחוֹרֵיה, וְצַלֵּי צְלוֹתֵיה. זַכָּאָה חוּלְקֵיה דְּכַהֲנָא, דְּהָא עַל יְדוֹי חֵידוּ עַל חֵידוּ אִשְׁתְּכַח הַהוּא יוֹמָא לְעֵילָּא וְתַתָּא, עַל הַהִיא שַׁעֲתָא כְּתִיב, אַשְׁרֵי הָעָם שֶׁכָּכָה לּוֹ, אַשְׁרֵי הָעָם שֶׁיְיָ' אֱלֹהָיו.

201. After he completes HIS PRAYER, the Cherubs raise their wings as before and sing. At that point, the priest realizes that goodwill prevails, a time of joy for all. The people know that his prayer was accepted, as the verse reads, "Though your sins be like scarlet, they shall be as white as snow" (Yeshayah 1:18). THE PRIEST steps back and utters his prayer. How fortunate is the share of the priest. As a result of him, there is joy upon joy that day on high and low. Concerning that hour, it is written, "Happy is that people, that is in such a case: happy is that people, whose Elohim is Hashem" (Tehilim 144:15).

33. "With my soul have I desired You in the night"

A Synopsis
Rabbi Shimon tells Rabbi Chiya that God is the spirit and soul of everyone, so that everyone desires to cling to Him. We hear different explanations of the title verse.

202. וְהָיְתָה לָכֶם לְחֻקַּת עוֹלָם בַּחֹדֶשׁ הַשְּׁבִיעִי בֶּעָשׂוֹר לַחֹדֶשׁ תְּעַנּוּ אֶת נַפְשׁוֹתֵיכֶם וְגוֹ'. רְבִּי חִיָּיא פָּתַח, נַפְשִׁי אִוִּיתִיךָ בַּלַּיְלָה אַף רוּחִי בְקִרְבִּי אֲשַׁחֲרֶךָ וְגוֹ'. נַפְשִׁי אִוִּיתִיךָ בַּלַּיְלָה. נַפְשִׁי בַּלַּיְלָה מִבָּעֵי לֵיהּ, מַאי נַפְשִׁי אִוִּיתִיךָ. אַף רוּחִי בְקִרְבִּי אֲשַׁחֲרֶךָ, יְשַׁחֲרֶךָ מִבָּעֵי לֵיהּ. אֶלָּא הָכִי תָּאנָא, קוּדְשָׁא בְּרִיךְ הוּא רוּחָא וְנַפְשָׁא דְכֹלָּא, וְיִשְׂרָאֵל אַמְרֵי נַפְשִׁי וְרוּחִי אַנְתְּ. בְּגִין כַּךְ אִוִּיתִיךָ לְאַדְבְּקָא בָּךְ, וַאֲשַׁחֲרֶךָ לְאַשְׁכְּחָא רְעוּתָךְ.

202. "And this shall be a statute for ever to you: that in the seventh month, on the tenth day of the month, you shall afflict your souls..." (Vayikra 16:29). Rabbi Chiya said, "With my soul have I desired You in the night; with my spirit within me I seek You..." (Yeshayah 26:9). HE QUESTIONS, "With my soul have I desired You in the night": It should simply read: 'My soul at night'. What does it mean, "With my soul have I desired You in the night"? ALSO, "with my spirit within me I seek You" should have said: 'It seeks You'. HE ANSWERS: We have learned that the Holy One, blessed be He, is the spirit and soul of all, so Yisrael are saying, "You are my soul and spirit." For this reason, I have desired You, to cling to You. "I seek You" to find Your goodwill.

203. ר' יוֹסֵי אָמַר, בְּשַׁעֲתָא דְּב"נ נָאִים בְּעַרְסֵיהּ. נָפְקָא נַפְשֵׁיהּ, סַלְקָא וְאַסְהִידַת בֵּיהּ בב"נ, עַל כָּל מַה דַּעֲבַד בְּכָל יוֹמָא. גוּפָא אָמַר לְנַפְשָׁא, נַפְשִׁי אִוִּיתִיךָ בַּלַּיְלָה, אַף רוּחִי בְקִרְבִּי אֲשַׁחֲרֶךָ.

203. Rabbi Yosi said: At the time one sleeps in his bed, his soul departs, ascends and testifies about him concerning that person's activities of that entire day. THEREFORE, the body says to the soul, "My soul, have I desired you in the night," WHEN YOU GO OUT OF ME, "my spirit within me, I seek you."

204. ד"א נַפְשִׁי אִוִּיתִיךָ, אָמְרָה כְּנֶסֶת יִשְׂרָאֵל קָמֵי קוּדְשָׁא בְּרִיךְ הוּא, נַפְשִׁי אִוִּיתִיךָ בַּלַּיְלָה, בְּעוֹד דַּאֲנָא בְּגָלוּתָא בֵּינֵי עֲמַמְיָא, וּמְנִיעָא נַפְשִׁי מִכָּל בִּישָׁתָא דְּקוּטְרָא בְּנֵי עֲמַמְיָא, נַפְשִׁי אִוִּיתִיךָ, בְּגִין לְאָתָבָא לְאַתְרִי. אַף רוּחִי בְקִרְבִּי אֲשַׁחֲרֶךָּ, כְּלוֹמַר, אע"ג דְּאִינּוּן מְשַׁעְבְּדִין לִבְנַי, בְּכָל שִׁעְבּוּדָא, רוּחָא קַדִּישָׁא לָא אִתְעֲדֵי מִנַּאי, בְּגִין לְמִשְׁחַר לָךְ, וּלְמֶעְבַּד פִּקּוּדֶיךָ.

204. Another explanation for, "With my soul have I desired You in the night..." The Congregation of Yisrael said before the Holy One, blessed be He, "With my soul have I desired You in the night," MEANING so long as I find myself in exile among other nations and withhold my soul from all evil that is connected with the nations. "With my soul have I desired You" in order to return to my place. "With my spirit within me I seek You," meaning even though they subject my children to every kind of oppression, the Holy Spirit does not depart from them in order that they should seek You and perform Your commandments.

205. ר' יִצְחָק אָמַר, אָמְרוּ יִשְׂרָאֵל קָמֵי קוּדְשָׁא בְּרִיךְ הוּא, בְּעוֹד דְּנַפְשִׁי בִּי, אִוִּיתִיךָ בַּלַּיְלָה. מַאי טַעְמָא בַּלַּיְלָה, אֶלָּא בְּגִין דְּהַאי נֶפֶשׁ בְּהַאי שַׁעְתָּא, אִצְטְרִיךְ לְחַמְדָּא לָךְ. אַף רוּחִי בְקִרְבִּי אֲשַׁחֲרֶךָּ, כַּד אִתְעַר בִּי רוּחָא קַדִּישָׁא, אֲשַׁחֲרֶךָ בְּאִתְעֲרוּתָא לְמֶעְבַּד רְעוּתָךְ. כִּי כַּאֲשֶׁר מִשְׁפָּטֶיךָ לָאָרֶץ בְּזִמְנָא דְּמִשְׁפָּט נָחִית בְּאַרְעָא, לְבַסְמָא עָלְמָא, כְּדֵין צֶדֶק לָמְדוּ יוֹשְׁבֵי תֵבֵל. כְּלוֹמַר יַכְלִין לְמִסְבַּל דִּינָא דְּצֶדֶק, וְלָא יִשְׁתְּצֵי עָלְמָא מִנֵּיהּ. אֵימָתַי צֶדֶק לָמְדוּ יוֹשְׁבֵי תֵבֵל, כַּאֲשֶׁר מִשְׁפָּטֶיךָ לָאָרֶץ רִבִּי חִזְקִיָּה אָמַר, נַפְשִׁי אִוִּיתִיךָ בַּלַּיְלָה, דָּא כְּנֶסֶת יִשְׂרָאֵל. אַף רוּחִי בְקִרְבִּי אֲשַׁחֲרֶךָּ, דָּא קוּדְשָׁא בְּרִיךְ הוּא.

205. Rabbi Yitzchak said: Yisrael said before the Holy One, blessed be He, so long as my soul is within me "have I desired You in the night." Wherefore "in the night"? It is because the Nefesh at that time needs to covet You. "With my spirit within me I seek You," MEANING when the Holy Spirit stirs within me, I seek You with excitement in order to do Your will. "For when Your sentences are on the earth," MEANS at the time when

justice, MEANING ZEIR ANPIN, comes down to earth, MEANING to bring fragrance to the world, TO MALCHUT. Then "the inhabitants of the world learn righteousness" (Ibid.), which means that they are capable of tolerating the Judgments of righteousness and mankind should not perish as a result of it. When will "the inhabitants of the world learn righteousness"? "When Your sentences are on the earth." Rabbi Chizkiyah said, "With my soul (*Nefesh*) have I desired You in the night" refers to the Congregation of Yisrael, NAMELY MALCHUT, while "with my spirit (*Ruach*) within me I seek You" refers to the Holy One, blessed be He. MALCHUT IS THE SECRET OF NEFESH AND THE HOLY ONE, BLESSED BE HE, IS THE SECRET OF RUACH.

34. "As the hart pants"

A Synopsis

Rabbi Shimon says that all those who take pleasure in the Torah need have no fear, as the Torah is called 'delights'; the righteous take great delight in God and He in them. The Congregation of Yisrael deeply desires to be watered from Elohim in this world and in the World to Come, and that flow is enabled by the righteous.

206. רִבִּי אַבָּא הֲוָה יָתִיב קָמֵיהּ דְּרִבִּי שִׁמְעוֹן, קָם ר' שִׁמְעוֹן בְּפַלְגּוּ לֵילְיָא, לְמִלְעֵי בְּאוֹרַיְיתָא. קָמוּ ר' אֶלְעָזָר וְרִבִּי אַבָּא עִמֵּיהּ. פָּתַח ר' שִׁמְעוֹן וְאָמַר, כְּאַיִּל תַּעֲרוֹג עַל אֲפִיקֵי מָיִם כֵּן נַפְשִׁי תַעֲרוֹג אֵלֶיךָ אֱלֹהִים. הַאי קְרָא אוּקְמוּהָ חַבְרַיָּיא, זַכָּאִין אִינּוּן יִשְׂרָאֵל מִכָּל עַמִּין, דְּקוּדְשָׁא בְּרִיךְ הוּא יָהַב לוֹן אוֹרַיְיתָא קַדִּישָׁא, וְאוֹרִית לוֹן נִשְׁמָתִין קַדִּישִׁין מֵאֲתַר קַדִּישָׁא, בְּגִין לְמֶעְבַּד פִּקּוּדוֹי, וּלְאִשְׁתַּעֲשְׁעָא בְּאוֹרַיְיתָא, דְּכָל מַאן דְּאִשְׁתַּעֲשַׁע בְּאוֹרַיְיתָא, לָא דָּחִיל מִכֹּלָּא. דִּכְתִיב לוּלֵי תוֹרָתְךָ שַׁעֲשׁוּעָי אָז אָבַדְתִּי בְעָנְיִי.

206. Rabbi Aba was staying with Rabbi Shimon. Rabbi Shimon rose at midnight to study Torah, and Rabbi Elazar and Rabbi Aba rose with him. Rabbi Shimon opened the discussion saying, "As the hart pants after the water brooks, so my soul pants for You, Elohim" (Tehilim 42:2). The friends have established this verse. Fortunate are Yisrael more than all nations that the Holy One, blessed be He, gave them the Holy Torah and bequeathed to them saintly souls from a holy source in order that they should observe His commandments and take pleasure with the Torah. All those who take pleasure in the Torah need not fear anything, as it is written, "Unless Your Torah had been my delights, I should have perished in my affliction" (Tehilim 119:92).

207. מַאן אִינּוּן שַׁעֲשׁוּעָי. אוֹרַיְיתָא דְּאוֹרַיְיתָא שַׁעֲשׁוּעִים אִקְרֵי, דִּכְתִיב וָאֶהְיֶה שַׁעֲשׁוּעִים יוֹם יוֹם. וְדָא הוּא דִּתְנֵינָן, קוּדְשָׁא בְּרִיךְ הוּא אָתֵי לְאִשְׁתַּעֲשְׁעָא עִם צַדִּיקַיָּיא בְּגִנְתָא דְּעֵדֶן. מַאי לְאִשְׁתַּעֲשְׁעָא. בְּגִין לְמֶחְדֵּי בְּהוּ. דִּתְנֵינָן, זַכָּאִין אִינּוּן צַדִּיקַיָּא, דִּכְתִיב בְּהוּ, אָז תִּתְעַנַּג עַל יְיָ', בְּגִין לְאִתְעַנְּגָא מֵהַהוּא שַׁקְיוּ דְּנַחֲלָא, כד"א וְהִשְׂבִּיעַ בְּצַחְצָחוֹת

נַפְשֶׁךָ. כִּבְיָכוֹל, קוּדְשָׁא בְּרִיךְ הוּא מִשְׁתַּעֲשַׁע בְּהוּ, מֵהַהוּא שַׁקְיוּ
דְּנַחֲלָא דְּמִתְעַנְּגֵי, בְּהוּ צַדִּיקַיָּא. וְעַל דָּא אָתֵי לְאִשְׁתַּעְשְׁעָא עִם
צַדִּיקַיָּא. וְכָל מַאן דְּאִשְׁתְּדַל בְּאוֹרַיְיתָא, זָכֵי לְאִשְׁתַּעְשְׁעָא עִם
צַדִּיקַיָּא, מֵהַהוּא שַׁקְיוּ דְּנַחֲלָא.

207. What are my delights? The Torah as the Torah is called delights, as it is written, "And I was daily His delight" (Mishlei 8:30). We have learned that the Holy One, blessed be He, comes to delight Himself with the righteous in the Garden of Eden. What is meant by 'delight Himself'? IT MEANS to rejoice in them. As we learned, fortunate are the righteous about whom it is written, "Then you shall delight yourself in Hashem" (Yeshayah 58:14), so as to take pleasure from the drink of the stream, MEANING BINAH, as is written, "And satisfy your soul in drought" (Ibid. 11). It is as if the Holy One, blessed be He, delights in them by means of that drink of the stream that the righteous take pleasure in, so He comes to have delight with the righteous. All those that toil in the Torah will merit to find delight in the righteous from that drink of the stream, MEANING BINAH.

208. תָּאנָא, כְּאַיָּל תַּעֲרוֹג עַל אֲפִיקֵי מָיִם, דָּא כְּנֶסֶת יִשְׂרָאֵל. כד"א, אֱיָלוּתִי לְעֶזְרָתִי חוּשָׁה. תַּעֲרוֹג עַל אֲפִיקֵי מָיִם, וַדַּאי לְאִשְׁתַּקְיָא מִשַּׁקְיוּ דְּמַבּוּעֵי דְּנַחֲלָא, ע"י דְּצַדִּיק. תַּעֲרוֹג: כד"א, לַעֲרוּגַת הַבּוֹשֶׂם, כֵּן נַפְשִׁי תַעֲרוֹג אֵלֶיךָ אֱלֹהִים. לְאִשְׁתַּקְיָא מִנָּךְ, בְּעָלְמָא דֵּין וּבְעָלְמָא דְּאָתֵי.

208. We have learned that "as the hart (Heb. *ayal*) pants after the water brooks" refers to the Congregation of Yisrael, NAMELY MALCHUT, as the verse says, "O my strength (Heb. *eyal*), haste You to help me" (Tehilim 22:20). "MY STRENGTH" REFERS TO MALCHUT. "Pants after the water brooks," MEANING to be watered by the water of the spring, REFERRING TO BINAH, through the aid of the Righteous, NAMELY YESOD. "Pants (Heb. *ta'arog*)" as the verse says, "To the beds (Heb. *arugot*) of spices" (Shir Hashirim 6:2). "So my soul pants for You, Elohim," MEANING to be watered from You in this world and the World to Come.

209. מַבּוּעֵי נַחֲלָא מַאן אִינּוּן. מַבּוּעָא חַד לְעֵילָּא, דִּכְתִּיב וְנָהָר יוֹצֵא מֵעֵדֶן לְהַשְׁקוֹת אֶת הַגָּן וְגוֹ'. וּמִתַּמָּן נָגִיד וְנָפִיק, וּמַשְׁקֵי גִּנְתָּא, וְכָל

אִינּוּן נַחֲלִין, נַגְדִּין וְנָפְקִין וּמִתְכַּנְּשִׁין בִּתְרֵי מַבּוּעִין, דְּאִקְרוּן נֶצַח וְהוֹד,
וְאִלֵּין אִקְרוּן אֲפִיקֵי מַיִם, בְּהַהוּא דַּרְגָּא דְּצַדִּיק, דְּמִנֵּיהּ נָגִיד וְנָפִיק
וּמִשְׁתַּקְיָא גִּנְתָּא. בְּגִין כָּךְ אַיָּל וּצְבִי כַּחֲדָא מִשְׁתַּכְחֵי, צֶדֶק וְצַדִּיק.

209. HE QUESTIONS: What are the sources of the spring? HE ANSWERS: THERE IS one spring above, NAMELY BINAH, as it is written, "And a river went out of Eden to water the Garden..." (Beresheet 2:10). It flows on from there and waters the Garden, NAMELY MALCHUT. All these streams, NAMELY THE SFIROT OF ZEIR ANPIN THAT RECEIVE FROM THE RIVER, flow out and join in the two springs known as Netzach and Hod OF ZEIR ANPIN. These are called water brooks AND POUR in that level called Righteous, MEANING YESOD OF ZEIR ANPIN, from which it continues and goes out; and the Garden is watered, NAMELY MALCHUT. For this reason, the hart and the deer are together, REFERRING TO righteousness and the Righteous, NAMELY YESOD AND MALCHUT THAT ARE TOGETHER. HART STANDS FOR MALCHUT AND DEER FOR YESOD.

35. "The voice of Hashem makes the hinds to calve"

A Synopsis
We hear several explanations of the title verse, all having to do with the fact that Zeir Anpin strengthens and nurtures his warriors.

210. תָּאנָא, כְּתִיב קוֹל יְיָ' יְחוֹלֵל אַיָּלוֹת, אַיָּלוֹת, אַיֶּלֶת כְּתִיב חֲסֵר, דָּא אַיֶּלֶת הַשַּׁחַר. ד"א אַיְלוֹת הַשָּׂדֶה, דְּתַנְיָא, בְּפַלְגוּת לֵילְיָא, בְּשַׁעֲתָא דְּקוּדְשָׁא בְּרִיךְ הוּא עָאל לְגִנְתָּא דְּעֵדֶן לְאִשְׁתַּעְשְׁעָא עִם צַדִּיקַיָּיא, הַאי קוֹל נָפִיק, וְכָאִיב כָּל אִינּוּן אַיַּלְתָּא דְּסַחֲרָנֵי כּוּרְסְיָיא יַקִּירָא קַדִּישָׁא, הה"ד שִׁשִּׁים גִּבּוֹרִים סָבִיב לָהּ. ד"א יְחוֹלֵל אַיָּלוֹת, כד"א חוֹלְלָה יָדוֹ נָחָשׁ בָּרִיחַ. וַיֶּחֱשׂוֹף יְעָרוֹת כד"א. בְּיַעֲרַת הַדְּבָשׁ, וּכְתִיב אָכַלְתִּי יַעְרִי עִם דִּבְשִׁי, וְיָנָקָא לְהוּ כְּאִמָּא דְיָנָקָא לִבְנִין.

210. We have learned that it is written, "The voice of Hashem makes (lit. 'frightens') the hinds (Heb. *ayalot*) to calve" (Tehilim 29:9). IT IS PRONOUNCED "*ayalot*," yet spelled without Vav. This is the gazelle (Heb. *ayelet*) of dawn, REFERRING TO MALCHUT. Another explanation of the wild hinds: We have learned that at midnight, when the Holy One, blessed be He, enters the Garden of Eden to delight in the righteous, this voice, NAMELY ZEIR ANPIN, goes out and strikes pain to all those hinds that surround the holy throne of glory, NAMELY MALCHUT. This is what is written, "Sixty valiant men are round about it..." (Shir Hashirim 3:7). Another explanation, "Makes (Heb. *yecholel*) the hinds to calve" as it says "his hand slew (Heb. *cholelah*, also: 'created') the slant serpent" (Iyov 26:13), WITH CHOLELAH MEANING THAT HE CREATED AND STRENGTHENED. ALSO, "*YECHOLEL*" MEANS HE STRENGTHENS THE HINDS THAT ARE THE SIXTY WARRIORS. "And strips the forests bare" (Tehilim 29:9), as the verse says, "honeycomb (lit. 'forest of honey')" (I Shmuel 14:27),and, "I had eaten my honeycomb with my honey" (Shir Hashirim 5:1), MEANING THAT ZEIR ANPIN, WHICH IS THE SECRET OF THE VOICE OF HASHEM, nurtures those SIXTY VALIANT MEN CALLED HINDS as a mother nurtures her children. THEREFORE, IT IS WRITTEN, "THE VOICE OF HASHEM MAKES THE HINDS TO CALVE," MEANING IT NURTURES AND MAINTAINS THEM.

36. The seventy sounds of a woman in labor

A Synopsis

The Faithful Shepherd, Moses, says that at the time before the coming of Messiah, the sages of Kabbalah will have a time of hardship; they will be in distress, sadness and poverty like the pains of the one who has given birth, the Shechinah. At that time she will open to give birth to the two Messiahs, due to the pain of those people who are so good and kind and truthful, who love and fear God.

רעיא מהימנא

211. אָמַר רַעְיָא מְהֵימָנָא, בְּהַהוּא זְמְנָא, אַלֵּין מָארֵי מַתְנִיתִין מָארֵי חָכְמְתָא עִלָּאָה, מָארֵי קַבָּלָה, מָארֵי רָזֵי תּוֹרָה, שַׁעֲתָא דְּחִיקַת לוֹן. וְהַאי אִיהוּ דְּאָמַר כְּאַיָּל תַּעְרוֹג עַל אֲפִיקֵי מָיִם, דְּאִינּוּן אֲפִיקֵי מַיִם דְּאוֹרַיְיתָא לְגַבֵּי שְׁכִינְתָּא. וְלֵית תּוֹרָה, אֶלָּא עַמּוּדָא דְּאֶמְצָעִיתָא. דִּיהוֹן אַלֵּין אֲפִיקֵי מַיִם, בְּצַעֲרָא בִּיגוֹנָא בְּעַנְיוּתָא, וְאַלֵּין אִינּוּן חֲבָלִים צִירִין דְּיוֹלֵדָה, דְּאִיהִי שְׁכִינְתָּא, דְּאִתְּמַר בָּה, וְתָגֵל יוֹלַדְתֶּךָ. וּבְאִינּוּן חֲבָלִים, תְּהֵא בְּצַעֲרָא דִּלְהוֹן.

Ra'aya Meheimna (the Faithful Shepherd)

211. The Faithful Shepherd, NAMELY THE SOUL OF MOSES, said, at that time, BEFORE THE COMING OF MESSIAH, the Mishnah scholars, sages of supernal wisdom, scholars of Kabbalah, scholars of the secrets in the Torah, will have a time of hardship, AS THEY HAVE NOTHING TO SUPPORT THEM. This is the meaning of, "As the hart (Heb. *ayal*) pants after the water brooks" (Tehilim 42:2) as they, NAMELY THE SAGES MENTIONED EARLIER, are springs of water of Torah flowing to the Shechinah, AS TORAH IS REFERRED TO AS WATER. Torah is the central pillar, MEANING ZEIR ANPIN, THE CENTRAL COLUMN. These springs of water, NAMELY THE SAGES MENTIONED EARLIER FROM WHICH COMES FORTH TORAH MEANING WATER, are in distress, in sadness and in poverty. These are the pains and distresses of the one who has given birth, namely the Shechinah, as it is written in regard to Her, "And let her who bore you rejoice" (Mishlei 23:25). She will be in those labor pains, MEANING with their distress OF

-308-

THE SCHOLARS OF WISDOM AND TORAH, AS MENTIONED, AS THEIR
AGONY IS CONSIDERED AS THE LABOR PAINS OF THE SHECHINAH.

212. וּבְאִינּוּן חֲבָלִים דְּצַוְוחַת בְּהוֹן, אִתְּעָרַת שַׁבְעִין סַנְהֶדְרִין דִּלְעֵילָא,
עַד דְּיִתְּעַר קוֹל דִּילָהּ עַד יְהֹנַ"ה, וּמִיַּד קוֹל יְיָ' יְחוֹלֵל אַיָּלוֹת, דְּאִינּוּן
מָארֵי מַתְנִיתִין, בְּתוּלוֹת אַחֲרֶיהָ רֵעוֹתֶיהָ, כֻּלְּהוֹן יֶהֱוֹן לוֹן חִיל כַּיּוֹלֵדָה
מַמָּשׁ, בְּדַחֲקִין, דְּדַחֲקָא לוֹן שַׁעֲתָא, בְּכַמָּה נְשִׁיכִין דְּיֵצֶר הָרָע, דְּחִוְיָא
דְּנָשִׁיךְ לוֹן בְּכַמָּה דַּחֲקִין.

212. The seventy members of the heavenly Sandhedrin are alerted with
these pains of birth that She cries, until Her voice reaches Yud Hei Vav Hei.
Immediately, "the voice of Hashem makes the hinds to calve" (Tehilim
29:9). This refers to the ABOVE MENTIONED masters of the Mishnah THAT
ARE THE SECRET MEANING OF "the virgins, her companions that follow
her" (Tehilim 45:15). All of them will be trembling as the one who gives
birth, literally with distress, as the time presses upon them with many bites
of the Evil Inclination, which is the snake that bites at them with various
TYPES OF distress.

213. בְּהַהוּא זִמְנָא אִתְפַּתְּחַת לְאוֹלָדָא מְשִׁיחָא, בְּגִין חֲבָלִים וְדוֹחֲקִים
דְּצַדִּיקִים, וּמָארֵי מִדּוֹת, וּמָארֵי רָזִין דְּאוֹרַיְיתָא, מָארֵי בּוֹשֶׁת וַעֲנָוָה,
מָארֵי יִרְאָה וְאַהֲבָה, מָארֵי חֶסֶד, אַנְשֵׁי חַיִל יִרְאֵי אֱלֹהִים, אַנְשֵׁי אֱמֶת,
שׂוֹנְאֵי בָצַע, דְּדַחֲקָא לוֹן שַׁעֲתָא. וְהַאי הוּא דְּאוּקְמוּהָ מָארֵי מַתְנִיתִין,
דּוֹר שֶׁבֶּן דָּוִד בָּא, אַנְשֵׁי חַיִל יְסוֹבְבוּ מֵעִיר לָעִיר וְלָא יְחוֹנָנוּ, וְיִרְאֵי
חֵטְא יִמָּאֵסוּ, וְחָכְמַת סוֹפְרִים תִּסְרַח, וּתְהִי הָאֱמֶת נֶעְדֶּרֶת, וְהַגֶּפֶן תִּתֵּן
פִּרְיָהּ, וְהַיַּיִן בְּיוֹקֶר.

213. At that time, She is opened to give birth to Messiah. This is owing to
the pain and distress of the pious, men of good qualities, sages of secrets of
the Torah, people of humility and shame, of fear and love, of kindness, men
of valor, fearing Elohim, truthful men, who despise bribes, for whom it is a
time of poverty. This is what the sages of the Mishnah have explained. In
the times in which the son of David will come, a valiant men will go
circulating from city to city but will not be shown favor. Those that fear sin

will be despised and the wisdom of scribes will be sullied. Truth will be absent and the vine will give its fruit but wine will be expensive.

214. וּמֵאִינּוּן קָלִין דְּיָהֵיבַת, דְּאִינּוּן שַׁבְעִין, לָקֳבֵל שַׁבְעִין תֵּיבִין דְּיַעֲנָךְ יְיָ' בְּיוֹם צָרָה, אִתְפַּתְּחַת רַחְמָה, דְּאִיהִי ב', כְּלִילָא מִתְּרֵין בֵּיתִין, לְאוֹלָדָא ב' מְשִׁיחִין, וְאָעִילַת רֵישָׁה בֵּין בִּרְכָּהָא, דְּאִיהוּ רֵישָׁא דִּילָהּ, עַמּוּדָא דְּאֶמְצָעִיתָא. תְּרֵין שׁוֹקָהָא, נֶצַח וְהוֹד, תְּרֵין נְבִיאִים. מִתַּמָּן אוֹלִידַת תְּרֵין מְשִׁיחִין. בְּהַהִיא זִמְנָא וַיֶּחֱשֹׂף יְעָרוֹת, יִתְעֲבָר נָחָשׁ מֵעָלְמָא.

ע"כ רעיא מהימנא

214. From these sounds that She cries, the seventy SOUNDS equaling the seventy words IN THE PSALM, "May Hashem hear you in the day of trouble" (Tehilim 20), Her womb is opened. This refers to the letter Bet (=two) MEANING CHAMBER OF (HEB. *BEIT*) THE WOMB, encompassing two chambers in order to give birth FROM THEM to two Messiahs – MESSIAH, SON OF DAVID AND MESSIAH, SON OF JOSEPH. She brings her head between her knees. Her head is the central pillar, MEANING ZEIR ANPIN. HER KNEES ARE two thighs, Netzach and Hod, which are the two prophets. From there are born two Messiahs, AS MENTIONED. At that time, He "strips the forests bare," MEANING CHOCHMAH WILL BE REVEALED. The serpent will be removed from the world, AS THE ILLUMINATION OF CHOCHMAH WILL DO AWAY WITH ALL KLIPOT.

End of Ra'aya Meheimna (the Faithful Shepherd)

37. Nefesh and Ruach

A Synopsis

Rabbi Shimon tells Rabbi Aba that just as the Nefesh and Ruach cling to the body who loves them, man must love God and cling to Him, as the love of the soul and spirit. Men who rise every night to study the Torah will be blessed with God's love. The righteous ones, whose spirits and souls cling to God with the proper love, will rule on the earth below, and what they decree for the world will happen. We learn that when the holy souls come from above and the righteous of the world draw them through mating, there are very few that merit it. From the very beginning the souls of the great righteous ones have stood before God who watches them until it is time for them to come into a body; they deserve to ascend to heaven while they are still alive, like Elijah and Enoch. The levels of the souls of the righteous are greater than the angels, and they come down in every generation, in the future God will renew the world with them.

215. אָ"ל ר' אַבָּא, נַפְשִׁי אִוִּיתִיךְ בַּלַּיְלָה אַף רוּחִי בְקִרְבִּי אֲשַׁחֲרֶךָ, נַפְשִׁי בַּלַּיְלָה מִבָּעֵי לֵיהּ. אֲשַׁחֲרֶךָ, יְשַׁחֲרֶךְ מִבָּעֵי לֵיהּ. אָ"ל הָא אוּקְמוּהָ, כד"א אֲשֶׁר בְּיָדוֹ נֶפֶשׁ כָּל חָי וְרוּחַ כָּל בְּשַׂר אִישׁ.

215. Rabbi Aba said to him, "With my soul (Nefesh) have I desired You in the night; with my spirit (Ruach) within me I seek You..." (Yeshayah 26:9). HE QUESTIONS: It should simply state "my Nefesh in the night," MEANING IT SHOULD SAY, 'MY SOUL IN THE NIGHT; WITH MY SPIRIT WITHIN ME I SEEK YOU.' Why write also "I seek You," when it should say, 'it seeks You', AS IT REFERS TO HIS SPIRIT. He answered: We have established? that it resembles "in whose hand is the soul of every living thing, and the breath (lit. 'Ruach') of all mankind" (Iyov 12:10), MEANING THAT MY NEFESH AND MY RUACH ARE NOT HIS OWN NAMES, BUT ARE TWO LIGHTS – RUACH AND NEFESH – CLAD IN A BODY, AS EXPLAINED FURTHER.

216. ת"ח נַפְשָׁא וְרוּחָא אִשְׁתַּתְּפֵי כַּחֲדָא לְעָלְמִין. תָּנָא פּוּלְחָנָא שְׁלֵימָתָא דְּבָעֵי בַּר נָשׁ לְמִפְלַח לְקוּדְשָׁא בְּרִיךְ הוּא, כְּמָה דְּתָנֵינָן וְאָהַבְתָּ אֶת יְיָ' אֱלֹהֶיךָ וְגוֹ'. דְּיִרְחִים לֵיהּ לְקוּדְשָׁא בְּרִיךְ הוּא רְחִימוּתָא דְּנֶפֶשׁ מַמָּשׁ, וְדָא הוּא רְחִימוּתָא שְׁלֵימָתָא, רְחִימוּתָא דְּנַפְשֵׁיהּ וְרוּחֵיהּ.

כְּמָה דְּאִתְדְּבָּקוּ אִלֵּין בְּגוּפָא, וְגוּפָא רָחִים לוֹן. כַּךְ יִתְדְבָּק ב"נ לְרַחֲמָא
לֵיהּ לְקוּדְשָׁא בְּרִיךְ הוּא, רְחִימוּתָא דְּנַפְשֵׁיהּ וְרוּחֵיהּ, לְאַדְבְּקָא בֵּיהּ.
הה"ד נַפְשִׁי אִוִּיתִיךָ בַּלַּיְלָה נַפְשִׁי מַמָּשׁ.

216. Come and see that the Nefesh and Ruach always exist jointly in the world. We have learned the total service that man must serve the Holy One, blessed be He, is as we have learned, "And you shall love Hashem, your Elohim..." (Devarim 6:5). He needs to love the Holy One, blessed be He, with his very soul. This is referred to as an utter love, the love of his Nefesh and Ruach. Just as these NEFESH AND RUACH cling to the body and the body loves them, so must man love the Holy One, blessed be He, and cling to Him, as the love of the Nefesh and Ruach. This is in essence the verse, "With my soul have I desired You in the night," MEANING my very soul THAT IS CLAD IN MY BODY.

217. אַף רוּחִי בְקִרְבִּי אֲשַׁחֲרֶךָּ, אִתְדְּבְּקָא בָּךְ בִּרְחִימוּתָא סַגִּיאָה,
בַּלַּיְלָה. דְּבָעֵי בַּר נָשׁ מֵרְחִימוּתָא דְקוּדְשָׁא בְּרִיךְ הוּא, לְמֵיקַם בְּכָל
לֵילְיָא, לְאִשְׁתַּדְּלָא בְּפוּלְחָנֵיהּ, עַד דְּיִתְעַר צַפְרָא, וְיִתְמְשַׁךְ עָלֵיהּ חוּטָא
דְחֶסֶד. דְּתַנְיָא, זַכָּאָה חוּלָקֵיהּ דְּהַהוּא ב"נ דִּרְחִימוּתָא דָא רָחִים לֵיהּ
לְקוּדְשָׁא בְּרִיךְ הוּא, וְהָנֵי זַכָּאֵי קְשׁוֹט דִּמְרַחֲמִין לֵיהּ לְקוּדְשָׁא בְּרִיךְ
הוּא הָכִי, עָלְמָא מִתְקַיְּימָא בְּגִינֵיהוֹן, וְשַׁלְטִין עַל כָּל גְּזֵירִין קָשִׁין
דִּלְעֵילָא וְתַתָּא.

217. "With my spirit within me I seek You," MEANING I will cling to You with much love at night. Man needs to rise every night out of love for the Holy One, blessed be He, to toil with His service until morning rises, so there will be drawn upon him a thread of grace. We have learned that fortunate is the portion of man that loves the Holy One, blessed be He, with this love. The world survives thanks to these truly righteous ones who so love the Holy One, blessed be He, and they have sway over all harmful edicts that appear above and below.

218. תָּאנָא, הַהוּא זַכָּאָה דְּאִתְדַּבַּק בְּרוּחֵיהּ וְנַפְשֵׁיהּ לְעֵילָא, בְּמַלְכָּא
קַדִּישָׁא, בִּרְחִימוּתָא כַּדְקָא יָאוֹת. שַׁלִּיט בְּאַרְעָא דִּלְתַתָּא, וְכָל מַה

דְּגָזַר עַל עָלְמָא אִתְקַיָּים. מְנָ"ל, מֵאֵלִיָּהוּ. דִּכְתִּיב חַי יְיָ' אֲשֶׁר עָמַדְתִּי לְפָנָיו אִם יִהְיֶה הַשָּׁנִים הָאֵלֶּה טַל וּמָטָר כִּי אִם לְפִי דְבָרִי.

218. We have learned that the pious one, whose Ruach and Nefesh cling to the above, to the Holy King, with the proper love, will rule upon the earth below and what he decrees for the world will come to pass. How do we know this? From Elijah, as it is written, "As Hashem the Elohim of Yisrael lives, before whom I stood, there shall not be dew or rain these years, but acording to my word" (I Melachim 17:1).

219. תָּא חֲזֵי, בְּשַׁעֲתָא דְּאַתְיָין נִשְׁמָתִין קַדִּישִׁין מֵעֵילָּא לְתַתָּא, וְאִינּוּן זַכָּאֵי עָלְמָא, מְשַׁלְּפֵי לְהוּ מִמַּלְכָּא וּמַטְרוֹנִיתָא, זְעִירִין אִינּוּן, דְּבַהֲהוּא שַׁעֲתָא דְּנָחֲתִין, קַיְימָא קָמֵי מַלְכָּא, וּרְעוּתָא דְּמַלְכָּא לְאִסְתַּכְּלָא בָּהּ, כְּמָה דְּאוֹקִימְנָא, בְּשַׁעֲתָא דְּנָשַׁב קוּדְשָׁא בְּרִיךְ הוּא רוּחָא בְּכָל חֵילָא וְחֵילָא דִּשְׁמַיָּא, כֻּלְּהוּ חַיָּילִין אִתְעֲבִידוּ, וְקַיְימֵי בְּקִיּוּמַיְיהוּ, הה"ד וּבְרוּחַ פִּיו כָּל צְבָאָם. וּמִנַּיְיהוּ אִתְעַכְּבוּ עַד דְּקוּדְשָׁא בְּרִיךְ הוּא אָחִית לְהוּ לְתַתָּא.

219. Come and see: When the holy souls come from above downwards and the pious of the world draw them from the King and the Queen, NAMELY FROM THE UNION OF MALE AND FEMALE, there are few THAT MERIT it, that at the precise moment when they descend TO EARTH, they are standing AND SERVING before the King, who pleases to look at it. AFTERWARDS, IT DESCENDS INTO THE WORLD. When the Holy One, blessed be He, blew the breath INTO EVERY SINGLE SOUL AND into every angel in Heaven, all the hosts were created and stood complete, as we have established. This is what the verse says, "And all the hosts of them by the breath of His mouth" (Tehilim 33:6). Among THE SOULS, there are those that remain STANDING BEFORE THE HOLY ONE, BLESSED BE HE, AS MENTIONED, until the Holy One, blessed be He, causes them to descend.

220. וְתָאנָא, מִיּוֹמָא דְּאִתְבְּרֵי עָלְמָא, קַיְימֵי קַמֵּיהּ דְּקוּדְשָׁא בְּרִיךְ הוּא, וְאִתְעַכְּבוּ עַד דְּמָטָא זִמְנָא לְאַחֲתָא לוֹן בְּאַרְעָא, וְאִלֵּין שְׁלִיטוּ לְעֵילָּא וְתַתָּא, הה"ד חַי יְיָ' אֲשֶׁר עָמַדְתִּי לְפָנָיו, אֲשֶׁר אֲנִי עוֹמֵד לָא כְּתִיב,

אֶלָּא אֲשֶׁר עָמַדְתִּי. לְבָתַר אַהֲדָר לְאַתְרֵיהּ, וְסָלִיק לְאִדָּרֵיהּ, וְאִינּוּן אַחֲרָנִין לָא סַלְּקִין עַד דִּימוּתוּן. בְּגִין דְּלָא קַיְימוּ קוֹדֶם לָכֵן כְּאִינּוּן אַחֲרָנִין. וּבְגִין כַּךְ אֵלִיָּהוּ אִתְעָבֵיד שְׁלִיחָא, מַלְאָכָא לְעֵילָּא, וְאִלֵּין דְּמִתְדַּבְּקָן יַתִּיר לְמַלְכָּא.

220. We have learned that from the day the world was created, THE SOULS OF THE GREAT PIOUS ONES have stood before the Holy One, blessed be He, held back IN HIS PRESENCE. THE HOLY ONE, BLESSED BE HE, WATCHES THEM until the time arrives to send them below, MEANING TO BECOME CLOTHED WITH A BODY, and they rule above and below. Thus the verse, "As Hashem the Elohim of Yisrael lives, before whom I stood." It doesn't say, 'I stand', but "I stood," MEANING BEFORE DESCENDING TO THIS WORLD. Afterwards, he returned to his place IN HEAVEN and entered his chamber. Other SOULS do not ASCEND TO THEIR PLACE until they die. This is because they never stood earlier BEFORE THE HOLY ONE, BLESSED BE HE, ON THAT LEVEL of the others, NAMELY ENOCH AND ELIJAH THAT MERITED TO ASCEND TO THEIR PLACE WHEN STILL ALIVE. For this reason, Elijah became a messenger and angel above, AND ENOCH TOO. And these were those that clung most to the King, MEANING MORE THAN AN ANGEL.

221. אַשְׁכַּחְנָא בְּסִפְרָא דְּאָדָם קַדְמָאָה דְּכָל רוּחִין קַדִּישִׁין דִּלְעֵילָּא, עָבְדִין שְׁלִיחוּתָא, וְכֻלְּהוּ אַתְיָין מֵאֲתַר חַד. דְּנִשְׁמָתְהוֹן דְּצַדִּיקַיָּיא מִתְּרֵי דַּרְגִּין דְּכְלִילָן בְּחַד, וּבְגִין כַּךְ סַלְּקִין יַתִּיר, וְדַרְגֵּיהוֹן יַתִּיר, וְהָכִי הוּא. וְכָל אִינּוּן דַּהֲווֹ טְמִירִין תַּמָּן, נַחְתּוּ וּסְלִיקוּ בְּחַיֵּיהוֹן, כְּגוֹן חֲנוֹךְ דְּלָא אִשְׁתְּכַח בֵּיהּ מִיתָה. וְהָא אוֹקִימְנָא מִלָּה דָּא, בַּחֲנוֹךְ וְאֵלִיָּהוּ.

221. I found in the book of Adam that all Holy Spirits above, MEANING ANGELS, do the mission OF THE HOLY ONE, BLESSED BE HE, and all come from one place. The souls of the righteous COME from two levels joined into one. Therefore, they ascend higher THAN ANGELS and their levels are greater THAN ANGELS. This is so. All those that were hidden there went down and up during their lifetime, such as Enoch, who did not die. We have already established this matter regarding Enoch and Elijah.

222. וְתָאנָא מְאָה וְעֶשְׂרִין וַחֲמֵשׁ אֶלֶף דַּרְגִּין לְנִשְׁמָתְהוֹן דְּצַדִּיקַיָּיא, סְלִיקוּ בִּרְעוּתָא, עַד לָא אִתְבְּרֵי עָלְמָא, דְּקוּדְשָׁא בְּרִיךְ הוּא מְזַמְּנָא לְהוּ בְּעָלְמָא דֵּין, בְּכָל דָּרָא וְדָרָא, וְסַלְקִין וְטָאסִין עָלְמָא, וּמִתְקַשְּׁרֵי בִּצְרוֹרָא דְחַיֵּי, וְזַמִּין קוּדְשָׁא בְּרִיךְ הוּא לְחַדְתָּא עָלְמָא בְּהוּ, עָלַיְיהוּ כְּתִיב, כִּי כַאֲשֶׁר הַשָּׁמַיִם הַחֲדָשִׁים וְהָאָרֶץ הַחֲדָשָׁה וְגוֹ'.

222. We have learned that 125,000 levels of the pious souls arose in the desire OF THE HOLY ONE, BLESSED BE HE, before the world was created. The Holy One, blessed be He, designated them for this world in every generation. They ascend, fly in the world, and join in the bundle of life, MEANING MALCHUT. In the future, the Holy One, blessed be He, will renew the world with them. About them, it is written, "For as the new heavens and the new Earth..." (Yeshayah 66:22).

223. תְּעַנּוּ אֶת נַפְשׁוֹתֵיכֶם, נַפְשׁוֹתֵיכֶם קָאֲמַר, בְּגִין דְּיִשְׂרָאֵל מִשְׁתַּכְחִין קָמֵי מַלְכָּא קַדִּישָׁא זַכָּאִין, וִיהֵא רְעוּתָא דִּלְהוֹן לְגַבֵּי קוּדְשָׁא בְּרִיךְ הוּא, וּלְאִתְדַּבְּקָא בֵּיהּ, בְּגִין דְּיִתְכַּפֵּר לְהוּ חוֹבַיְיהוּ. וְעַל דָּא, מַאן דְּאָכַל וְשָׁתֵי בִּתְשִׁיעָאָה, וּמְעַנַּג נַפְשֵׁיהּ בְּמֵיכְלָא וּמִשְׁתְּיָיא, אִשְׁתְּכַח בַּעֲשִׂירָאָה עִנּוּיָא דְּנַפְשָׁא בִּתְרֵין חוּלְקִין, וְאִשְׁתְּכַח כְּאִלּוּ אִתְעַנֵּי תְּשִׁיעָאָה וַעֲשִׂירָאָה. אֶת נַפְשׁוֹתֵיכֶם: לְאַכְלְלָא כֹּלָא, גּוּפָא וְנַפְשָׁא, וּלְאִתְכַּנְעָא בְּהַאי יוֹמָא, לְאִתְכַּפְּרָא עַל חוֹבֵיהוֹן.

223. "You shall afflict your souls..." (Vayikra 16:29). It says "your souls" in order that Yisrael be found meritorious before the Holy King, and meet with the goodwill of the Holy One, blessed be He. They must cling to Him in order that all their sins may be forgiven. Therefore, whoever eats and drinks on the ninth day and pleasures his soul with food and drink will find himself with the affliction on the tenth day doubled, and it will be considered as if he fasted on the ninth and tenth. "Your souls" includes all, body and soul, to surrender on this day in order to have atonement for sins.

224. תָּאנָא כִּי בַיּוֹם הַזֶּה יְכַפֵּר עֲלֵיכֶם. בַּיּוֹם הַזֶּה. הַיּוֹם הַזֶּה מִבָּעֵי לֵיהּ. אֶלָּא בַּיּוֹם הַזֶּה דַּיְיקָא, דְּבֵיהּ אִתְגְּלֵי עַתִּיקָא קַדִּישָׁא, לְכַפְּרָא עַל

חוֹבֵיהוֹן דְּכֹלָּא.

224. We have learned that "for on that day will He forgive you" (Ibid.). HE ASKS: IT SAYS, "on that day," but it should read 'that day'. HE ANSWERS, "On that day" is precise, as Atika Kadisha, MEANING KETER, is revealed in it to forgive everyone's sins.

38. "A little city"

A Synopsis

Rabbi Aba talks about the verse, "There was a little city, and few men within it," saying that there are few who deserve to live there, and that God comes to join with them and live there and protect it. There is a wise man who lives there, and he is wise because he studies the Torah and keeps its precepts. But his wisdom is despised, as people do not want to pay attention to the Torah.

225. ד"א תְּעַנּוּ אֶת נַפְשׁוֹתֵיכֶם. ר' אַבָּא פָּתַח וְאָמַר, עִיר קְטַנָּה וַאֲנָשִׁים בָּהּ מְעָט וְגוֹ', עִיר קְטַנָּה, הָא אוּקְמוּהָ. אֲבָל עִיר קְטַנָּה, כד"א, עִיר עָז לָנוּ יְשׁוּעָה יָשִׁית וְגוֹ'. וּכְתִיב וְלֹא אָבֹא בְּעִיר. עִיר קְטַנָּה, זְעֵירָא הִיא, דְּהִיא בַּתְרָאָה מִכְּלָּא, תַּתָּאָה מִכְּלָּא, שׁוּרוֹי רַבְרְבִין, תַּקִּיפִין, קַדִּישִׁין, עִיר הַקֹּדֶשׁ אִקְרֵי. וַאֲנָשִׁים בָּהּ מְעָט, זְעֵירִין אִינּוּן דְּזַכָּאן לְסַלְּקָא לְגַוָּוהּ, וּלְמִשְׁרֵי בָּהּ, כד"א מִי יַעֲלֶה בְהַר יְיָ' וּמִי יָקוּם בִּמְקוֹם קָדְשׁוֹ וְגוֹ'. וְעַ"ד אֲנָשִׁים בָּהּ מְעָט.

225. Another explanation for, "You shall afflict your souls" (Vayikra 16:29): Rabbi Aba opened the discussion saying, "There was a little city, and few men within it" (Kohelet 9:14). "A little city" has been explained. Yet the little city is as in, "We have a strong city; He sets up salvation..." (Yeshayah 26:1) and, "And I will not come as an enemy (also: 'in a city')" (Hoshea 11:9), WHERE CITY REFERS TO MALCHUT. "A little city" is small, because it is the last of all SFIROT and the lowest of them all. Its walls are large, strong and holy, and it is called a holy city. "And few men within it": Few are those who merit to enter within and dwell there, as the verse says, "Who shall ascend into the mountain of Hashem? or who shall stand in His holy place?..." (Tehilim 24:3). Therefore, "and few men within it."

226. וּבָא אֵלֶיהָ מֶלֶךְ גָּדוֹל, דָּא קוּדְשָׁא בְּרִיךְ הוּא. לְאִזְדַּוְּוגָא בָּהּ, וּלְמִשְׁרֵי בָּהּ, וְסָבַב אוֹתָהּ, כד"א וַאֲנִי אֶהְיֶה לָהּ נְאֻם יְיָ' חוֹמַת אֵשׁ סָבִיב וְגוֹ'. וּבָנָה עָלֶיהָ מְצוֹדִים גְּדוֹלִים, דְּבָנָה שׁוּרוֹי, רַבְרְבִין תַּקִּיפִין יָאֵיאָן וְשַׁפִּירִין קַדִּישִׁין. עִיר הַקֹּדֶשׁ אִקְרֵי, וְכָל יְקָרָא דְּמַלְכָּא עַיֵּיל בְּגַוָּוהּ. ובג"כ, הִיא בִּלְחוֹדָהָא כְּלִילָא מִכָּל עַטְרֵי דְּמַלְכָּא, וְכָל עַטְרֵי
-317-

מַלְכָּא בָּה מִתְעַטְּרִין. בְּג"כ, וַאֲנָשִים בָּה מְעָט כְּתִיב.

226. "And there came a great King against (or: 'to') it" (Kohelet 9:14). This refers to the Holy One, blessed be He, who comes to join with it and reside in it. "And besieged (or: 'circled') it" as the verse says, "'For I', says Hashem, 'will be to her a wall of fire round about...'" (Zecharyah 2:9). "And built great siegeworks against it" (Kohelet 9:14) means that He builds its big, strong, fine, beautiful and holy walls, MEANING THE PROTECTION THAT EXTERNAL FORCES WILL NOT BE NURTURED FROM IT. It is called the holy city. All the majesty of the King He brought within. Therefore, it alone comprises all crowns of the King, BEING THE MOCHIN OF ZEIR ANPIN, ACCORDING TO THE SECRET OF THE VERSE, "A VIRTUOUS WOMAN IS A CROWN TO HER HUSBAND" (MISHLEI 12:4). ZEIR ANPIN IS NOT CROWNED WITH THE ILLUMINATION OF CHOCHMAH, SAVE WHEN HE IS UNITED WITH MALCHUT, SINCE CHOCHMAH IS REVEALED IN MALCHUT ONLY, and all crowns of the King are decorated with it. For this reason, there are "few men within it," AS NOT ALL PEOPLE MERIT IT.

227. וּמָצָא בָה אִיש מִסְכֵּן וְחָכָם, הה"ד נְקִי כַפַּיִם וּבַר לֵבָב. מִסְכֵּן: כד"א וַיִּבֶן עָרֵי מִסְכְּנוֹת לְפַרְעֹה, מִתְעַטָּר בְּעִטְרִין תַּקִּיפִין, בְּעִטְרֵי אוֹרַיְיתָא, בְּעִטְרֵי פִּקּוּדֵי אוֹרַיְיתָא דְּמַלְכָּא. וְחָכָם, דְּזָכֵי בָּה בְּהַאי חָכְמָה. וְחָכָם, דְּהוּא חַכִּים יַתִּיר מִכֹּלָּא לְעַיְּינָא בְּפוּלְחָנָא דְּמָארֵיה, בְּגִין לְמִזְכֵּי בָּה, וּלְאַעֲלָא בָּה. הֲדָא הוּא דִּכְתִיב, וּמִלַּט הוּא אֶת הָעִיר בְּחָכְמָתוֹ. וּמִלַּט: כְּמוֹ אִמַּלְטָה נָא וְאֶרְאֶה אֶת אֶחָי, אִמַּלְטָה נָא שָמָּה. אוּף הָכָא וּמִלַּט הוּא אֶת הָעִיר בְּחָכְמָתוֹ.

227. "Now there was found in it a poor (Heb. misken) wise man" (Kohelet 9:15). This resembles what is written, "He that has clean hands, and a pure heart" (Tehilim 24:4). HE IS CALLED "Misken" in accordance with the words, "And they built for Pharaoh treasure (Heb. miskenot) cities" (Shemot 1:11), MEANING he is crowned with crowns of strength, with the crowns of Torah and with the crowns of the Torah precepts of the King. He is called wise, because he merits wisdom, AS MALCHUT IS CALLED THE LOWER CHOCHMAH BECAUSE IN HER CHOCHMAH REVEALED, AS MENTIONED. ALSO, HE IS CALLED wise, because he is wiser than all PEOPLE to contemplate the service of his Master, so he may gain enough merit to enter

that service. This is the idea of the verse, "And he by his wisdom saved the city" and "saved" is to be understood as, "Let me go away, I pray you, and see my brothers" (I Shmuel 20:29). Also, "let me escape there" (Beresheet 19:20) SPEAKS ABOUT RESCUE. Here also, "And he by his wisdom saved the city": THROUGH HIS MEDITATION, HE SAVED IT FROM THE EXTERNAL FORCES FEEDING UPON IT.

228. וְאָדָם לֹא זָכַר אֶת הָאִישׁ הַמִּסְכֵּן הַהוּא, וְאָדָם לָא זָכַר, לְמֶעְבַּד פִּקּוּדֵי אוֹרַיְיתָא, לְאִשְׁתַּדְּלָא בְּאוֹרַיְיתָא, כְּהַהוּא גְּבַר מִסְכְּנָא דְּאִתְחַבַּר בְּכֹלָּא, בְּגִין לְמִזְכֵּי בָּהּ. וְאָמַרְתִּי אֲנִי טוֹבָה חָכְמָה מִגְּבוּרָה. דְּהָא בְּהַהוּא עָלְמָא, לָא יָהֲבִין רְשׁוּ לְמֵיעַל, בַּר הָנֵי זַכָּאֵי קְשׁוֹט, הָנֵי דְּמִשְׁתַּדְּלֵי בָּהּ בְּאוֹרַיְיתָא יוֹמָא וְלֵילֵי, וּמִתְעַטְּרֵי בְּפִקּוּדֵי אוֹרַיְיתָא בְּהַאי עָלְמָא, לְמֵיעַל בְּהוּ לְעָלְמָא דְּאָתֵי.

228. "Yet no man remembered that poor man" (Kohelet 9:15) MEANING THAT no one remembered to perform the commandment of the Torah and to toil in the Torah as that poor man that joined to everything in order to merit it. "Then said I, wisdom is better than strength" (Kohelet 9:16), MEANING permission to enter that world is given only to truly righteous men, to those who toil in Torah day and night, as well as crown themselves with the commandments of the Torah in this world to arrive with them in the World to Come.

229. וְחָכְמַת הַמִּסְכֵּן בְּזוּיָה וּדְבָרָיו אֵינָם נִשְׁמָעִים. דְּהָא בְּנֵי נָשָׁא לָא מִסְתַּכְּלִין בֵּיהּ, וְלָא בָּעָאן לְאִתְחַבְּרָא בֵּיהּ, וּלְאַצִית לְמִלּוֹי. דְּתָנָא, כָּל מַאן דְּאָצִית לְמִלּוֹי דְּאוֹרַיְיתָא, זַכָּאָה הוּא בְּהַאי עָלְמָא, וּכְאִלּוּ קַבִּיל תּוֹרָה מִסִּינַי. וַאֲפִילוּ מִכָּל בַּר נָשׁ נָמֵי בָּעֵי לְמִשְׁמַע מִלּוֹי דְּאוֹרַיְיתָא. וּמַאן דְּאַרְכִין אוּדְנֵיהּ לְקַבְּלֵיהּ, יָהִיב יְקָרָא לְמַלְכָּא קַדִּישָׁא, וְיָהִיב יְקָרָא לְאוֹרַיְיתָא. עֲלֵיהּ כְּתִיב, הַיּוֹם הַזֶּה נִהְיֵיתָ לְעָם לַיְיָ' אֱלֹהֶיךָ.

229. "Nevertheless the poor man's wisdom is despised, and his words are not heard" (Ibid.). As people do not WISH TO look at him, they do not want to be with him and pay attention to his words. We have learned that all who pay attention to the words of Torah are fortunate in this world. It is as if

they have received the Torah from Sinai. One should even listen to words of the Torah from anyone. One who lends an ear to him gives honor to the Holy King and glory to the Torah, and about him is written, "This day you are become the people of Hashem your Elohim" (Devarim 27:9).

39. "Just and victorious"

A Synopsis

Rabbi Shimon says that the nations of the Other Side have taken the abundance that should have belonged to Yisrael. But the righteous will eventually be victorious and the queen, Malchut, will return to them. We learn about the seven pillars that the world rests on, and the one pillar, the Righteous, or Yesod, that they rest on. Lastly Rabbi Shimon talks about the everlasting statute that God has made for Yisrael.

230. תָּאנָא, יוֹמָא חַד הֲווֹ אַזְלֵי חַבְרַיָּיא עִמֵּיהּ דְּרַבִּי שִׁמְעוֹן, אָמַר ר"ש, חֲמֵינָא אִלֵּין עַמִּין כֻּלְּהוּ עִלָּאֵי, וְיִשְׂרָאֵל תַּתָּאֵי מִכֻּלְּהוּ, מַאי טַעֲמָא. בְּגִין דְּמַלְכָּא אַשְׁדַּר מַטְרוֹנִיתָא מִנֵּיהּ, וְאָעִיל אֲמָהוּ בְּאַתְרָהָא. כד"א, תַּחַת שָׁלֹשׁ רָגְזָה אֶרֶץ וְגו'. תַּחַת עֶבֶד כִּי יִמְלוֹךְ וְגו'. וְשִׁפְחָה כִּי תִירַשׁ גְּבִירְתָּהּ. מַאן שִׁפְחָה. הִיא כְּתְרָא נוּכְרָאָה, דְּקָטַל קוּדְשָׁא בְּרִיךְ הוּא בּוּכְרָא דִּלְהוֹן בְּמִצְרַיִם. דִּכְתִיב עַד בְּכוֹר הַשִּׁפְחָה אֲשֶׁר אַחַר הָרֵחַיִם. אֲחַר הָרֵחַיִם הֲוַת יָתְבָא בְּקַדְמֵיתָא, וְהַשְׁתָּא, הַאי שִׁפְחָה תִּירַשׁ גְּבִירְתָּהּ.

230. We have learned that one day the friends were walking with Rabbi Shimon. Rabbi Shimon said, I see all nations are higher above and Yisrael are below all. Why? It is because the King has dismissed the Queen from Him, and invited a maid in her stead, as the verse says, "For three things the earth is disquieted...for a slave when he becomes king...and a handmaid that is heir to her mistress" (Mishlei 30:21-23). Who is this handmaid? She is the foreign kingdom OF THE OTHER SIDE, whose firstborn Hashem smote in Egypt, as is written, "Even to the firstborn of the maidservant that is behind the mill" (Shemot 11:5). At first, she used to sit behind the millstone, but now she is "a handmaid that is heir to her mistress." INSTEAD OF EXTENDING HER ABUNDANCE TO HOLY MALCHUT, THIS MAID OF THE OTHER SIDE TAKES ALL THE ABUNDANCE AND EXTENDS IT TO THE NATIONS THAT ARE FROM HER SIDE.

231. בָּכָה ר"ש וְאָמַר, מַלְכָּא בְּלָא מַטְרוֹנִיתָא, לָא אִקְרֵי מַלְכָּא. מַלְכָּא דְּאִתְדַּבַּק בְּשִׁפְחָה בְּאַמָהוּ דְּמַטְרוֹנִיתָא, אָן הוּא יְקָרָא דִּילֵיהּ. וּזְמִינָא

קָלָא לְבַשְׂרָא לְמַטְרוֹנִיתָא, וְלֵימָא גִּילִי מְאֹד בַּת צִיּוֹן הָרִיעִי בַּת יְרוּשָׁלַם הִנֵּה מַלְכֵּךְ יָבֹא לָךְ צַדִּיק וְנוֹשָׁע הוּא. כְּלוֹמַר, צַדִּיק הוּא נוֹשָׁע, בְּגִין דַּהֲוָה רָכִיב עַד הַשְׁתָּא בַּאֲתַר דְּלָאו דִּילֵיהּ, בַּאֲתַר נוּכְרָאָה, וְיָנִיק לֵיהּ.

231. Rabbi Shimon wept and said: A king without a queen is not considered a king, so a king who clings to a maid who is the servant of the queen, where is his honor? A voice will inform the Queen saying, "Rejoice greatly, O daughter of Zion; shout, O daughter of Jerusalem: behold your king comes to you: he is just and victorious" (Zecharyah 9:9). The Righteous, YESOD, is victorious, because until now he rode in a place that is not his, in a strange place, NAMELY THE MAID, and nurtured it. NOW THE QUEEN RETURNS TO HIM.

232. וְעַל דָּא כְּתִיב עָנִי וְרוֹכֵב עַל חֲמוֹר, עָנִי הֲוָה בְּקַדְמֵיתָא, וְרוֹכֵב עַל חֲמוֹר, כְּמָה דְּאוּקִימְנָא, אִינּוּן כִּתְרִין תַּתָּאִין דְּעַמִּין עכ״ו, דְּקָטִיל קוּדְשָׁא בְּרִיךְ הוּא בּוּכְרָא דִּלְהוֹן בְּמִצְרַיִם, הה״ד וְכָל בְּכוֹר בִּבְהֵמָה, וְהָא אוּקִימְנָא מִלֵּי. כְּבִיכוֹל צַדִּיק וְנוֹשָׁע הוּא, הוּא וַדַּאי יַתִּיר מִכֹּלָּא. בְּגִין דְּעַד הַשְׁתָּא שָׁארֵי צַדִּיק בְּלָא צֶדֶק. וְהַשְׁתָּא דְּיִזְדַּוְּוגוּן כַּחֲדָא, צַדִּיק וְנוֹשָׁע הוּא, דְּהָא לָא יָתִיב בְּסִטְרָא אַחֲרָא. תָּאנָא, הַצַּדִּיק אָבַד וְאֵין אִישׁ שָׂם עַל לֵב וְגוֹ', הַאי קְרָא קַשְׁיָא, הַצַּדִּיק אָבַד, נֶאֱבַד מִבָּעֵי לֵיהּ, מַהוּ אָבַד. אֶלָּא אָבַד מַמָּשׁ, וּמַאי אָבַד. אָבַד לְמַטְרוֹנִיתָא, וְאִתְדַּבַּק בַּאֲתַר אַחֲרָא, דְּאִקְרֵי שִׁפְחָה.

232. About this, it is written, "Humble, and riding upon an donkey" (Ibid.), as he was poor at first "and riding upon an donkey." As we have established, it refers to the lower crowns of the idolatrous nations, the firstborn of which Hashem killed in Egypt, AS THEY ARE CONSIDERED "AN DONKEY." This is the meaning of, "And all the firstborn of cattle" (Shemot 11:5). We have established this matter so to speak with "just and victorious" MEANING that he is more VICTORIOUS than anyone. Until now, the Righteous, NAMELY YESOD, resided without righteousness, DENOTING MALCHUT. Now that THE RIGHTEOUS AND RIGHTEOUSNESS are joined, he is "just and victorious," because he NO LONGER dwells in the Other Side.

We have learned that "the righteous perishes (lit. 'is lost'), and no man lays it to heart" (Yeshayah 57:1). This verse is complicated. IT READS "lost" when it should be written 'is lost'. So what is the meaning of "lost"? HE ANSWERS: He really lost. What did he lose? The Queen – and he joined another place called maid.

233. א"ר יִצְחָק לְר' שִׁמְעוֹן, אִי נִיחָא קַמֵּי דְּמֹר, הָא דִּתְנֵינָן, דִּכְתִיב
וְצַדִּיק יְסוֹד עוֹלָם, מַאן דְּאָמַר, דְּעַל שִׁבְעָה קַיְימִין קַיְימָא עָלְמָא.
וּמַאן דְּאָמַר, עַל חַד קַיְימָא עָלְמָא, הֵיךְ מִתְיַישְׁבָן מִלֵּי. אָמַר לֵיהּ,
כֹּלָּא מִלָּה חַד הוּא, דְּהָא ז' אִינּוּן וּבְהוּ אִית חַד קַיְימָא, דְּאִקְרֵי צַדִּיק,
וְקַיְימֵי עָלֵיהּ, וְעָלְמָא בְּהַאי אִתְקַיְּימָא. וְכַד אִתְקַיְּימָא עָלְמָא עָלֵיהּ,
כְּאִלּוּ אִתְקַיַּים עַל כֻּלְּהוּ שִׁבְעָה. וְעַ"ד כְּתִיב, וְצַדִּיק יְסוֹד עוֹלָם. וְהָא
אוֹקִימְנָא מִלֵּי בְּכַמָּה אֲתַר.

233. Rabbi Yitzchak said to Rabbi Shimon: If it pleases my master, we have learned "but the righteous is an everlasting foundation" (Mishlei 10:25). Some explain that the world rests upon seven pillars, but some say the world rests on one pillar, NAMELY YESOD, AS THE VERSE SAYS, "BUT THE RIGHTEOUS IS AN EVERLASTING FOUNDATION." How do we reconcile these words SO THAT THEY DON'T CONFLICT? He answered: They all pertain to the same idea. There are seven – THE SEVEN SFIROT, CHESED, GVURAH, TIFERET, NETZACH, HOD, YESOD AND MALCHUT – and among them, there is one pillar called Righteous, WHO IS YESOD. THE SEVEN rest upon it and the world is sustained upon it. As it rests upon it, it is as if it rests upon all the seven, SINCE YESOD CONSISTS OF SEVEN SFIROT – CHESED, GVURAH, TIFERET, NETZACH, HOD, YESOD AND MALCHUT. Therefore, it is written, "But the righteous is an everlasting foundation (Heb. Yesod)" and we have several times established these matters.

234. וְתָאנָא, הַאי שִׁפְחָה זְמִינָא לְשַׁלְטָאָה בְּאַרְעָא קַדִּישָׁא דִּלְתַתָּא,
כְּמָה דַּהֲוַת מַטְרוֹנִיתָא שַׁלְטָא בְּקַדְמֵיתָא, דִּכְתִיב צֶדֶק יָלִין בָּהּ,
וְהַשְׁתָּא שִׁפְחָה כִּי תִירַשׁ גְּבִירְתָּהּ בְּכֹלָּא. וְזַמִּין קוּדְשָׁא בְּרִיךְ הוּא,
לְאָתָבָא לְמַטְרוֹנִיתָא לְאַתְרָהָא כְּקַדְמֵיתָא, וּכְדֵין מִמַּאן הוּא חֶדְוָותָא,
הֲוֵי אֵימָא חֶדְוָותָא דְּמַלְכָּא, וְחֶדְוָותָא דְּמַטְרוֹנִיתָא. חֶדְוָותָא דְּמַלְכָּא,

בְּגִין דְּיֵתוֹב לָהּ וְיִתְפְּרַשׁ מִשִּׁפְחָה, כַּדְקָא אֲמֵינָא. וְחֶדְוָותָא דְּמַטְרוֹנִיתָא, בְּגִין דְּתֵיתוֹב לְאִזְדַּוְּוגָא בְּמַלְכָּא, הה״ד גִּילִי מְאֹד בַּת צִיּוֹן וְגוֹ'.

234. We have learned that this maid would eventually rule the Holy Land below, just as the Queen ruled at first, as it says, "Righteousness lodged in it" (Yeshayah 1:21), REFERRING TO MALCHUT CALLED RIGHTEOUSNESS, but now "a handmaid that is heir to her mistress" in every respect, BOTH ABOVE AND BELOW. However, the Holy One, blessed be He, will in the future return the Queen to her original position and then whose joy will it be? One says: The joy of the King and Queen. It is the joy of the King for returning to her and casting off the maid as we said. It is the joy of the Queen, because she has returned to join the King. This is the essence of, "Rejoice greatly, O daughter of Zion."

235. תָּא חֲזֵי, כְּתִיב וְהָיְתָה זֹאת לָכֶם לְחֻקַּת עוֹלָם. וְהָיְתָה לָכֶם מִבָּעֵי לֵיהּ, מַאי זֹאת. הָא דְּאֲמָרָן, לְחֻקַּת עוֹלָם. בְּכָל אֲתַר וְאֲתַר חֻקַּת עוֹלָם אִתְקְרֵי, גְּזֵרָה דְּמַלְכָּא, דְּעַיֵּיל כָּל נִמּוּסוֹי בַּאֲתַר דָּא, וְאַסְתִּים לוֹן, כְּמָאן דְּסָתִים כֹּלָּא, בְּאַסְקוֹפָא חֲדָא. חֻקַּת עוֹלָם וַדַּאי. בְּהַאי זֹאת רָשִׁים וְחָקַק כָּל גְּנִיזִין דִּילֵיהּ, וְכָל טְמִירִין דִּילֵיהּ.

235. Come and see that it is written, "And this (Heb. zot fem.) shall be an everlasting statute to you" (Vayikra 16:34). HE QUESTIONS: It should read, 'It shall be...to you'. Wherefore the word zot? HE ANSWERS: THE EXPLANATION OF THE VERSE IS as we said. It is an everlasting statute, WHICH IS MALCHUT, which is always referred to as "an everlasting statute," WHICH MEANS the decree of the King, as He placed all His laws in this place, MALCHUT, and sealed them as one seals everything in a storehouse. IT IS assuredly "an everlasting statute." In this "zot" DENOTING MALCHUT, He marks and engraves all His storehouses and hidden things.

40. "You shall afflict your souls"

A Synopsis
Rabbi Shimon tells us that one should eat and drink on the ninth of the month more than any other day. On the tenth day, the judgments cause wisdom to be revealed. We read that the children of Yisrael were only exiled because they renounced God, and He forgives them on the Day of Atonement.

236. בַּחֹדֶשׁ הַשְּׁבִיעִי בֶּעָשׂוֹר לַחֹדֶשׁ. בֶּעָשׂוֹר דַּיְיקָא, כְּמָה דְּאוֹקִימְנָא. תְּעַנּוּ אֶת נַפְשׁוֹתֵיכֶם, וַדַּאי הָכִי הוּא, וְהָא אִתְּמַר נַפְשׁוֹתֵיכֶם וַדַּאי. דְּהָא בְּנַפְשָׁא תַּלְיָא מִלְּתָא, וּבְגִין כָּךְ, אֲכִילָה וּשְׁתִיָּה מִתְּשִׁיעָאָה, יַתִּיר מִיּוֹמָא אָחֳרָא. וְאע"ג דְּהַאי מִלָּה אִתְּמַר בְּגַוְונָא אָחֳרָא, וְכֹלָּא שַׁפִּיר, וְהַאי וְהַאי מִלָּה חֲדָא, וְכָל חַד בְּאַתְרֵיה, וְהָכִי הוּא.

236. "In the seventh month, on the tenth day of the month" (Vayikra 16:29). Tenth is exact as we have learned THAT TENTH DENOTES MALCHUT. "You shall afflict your souls" (Ibid.): This is exact. We have learned "your souls (Nefashot)" indeed, as it all depends upon Nefesh, AS THE LIGHT OF MALCHUT IS CALLED NEFESH AND NEFESH ALWAYS DENOTES MALCHUT. For this reason, one should eat and drink from the ninth of the month, DENOTING YESOD, more than any other day. Even though we learned this in another manner, it is all very well. They amount to the same thing and each thing is in its own place. This is how it should be.

237. וְתָאנָא, בְּהַאי יוֹמָא, כָּל חֵידוּ, וְכָל נְהִירוּ, וְכָל וַתְרָנוּתָא דְּעָלְמִין, כֻּלְּהוּ תַּלְיָין בְּאִימָּא עִלָּאָה, דְּכָל מַבּוּעִין נַגְדִּין וְנָפְקִין מִנָּהּ. וּכְדֵין נְהִירִין כָּל אִינּוּן בּוֹצִינִין, וְנַהֲרִין בִּנְהִירוּ בְּחֶדְוְותָא, עַד דְּמִתְבַּסַּם כֹּלָּא. וּכְדֵין כָּל אִינּוּן דִּינִין אִשְׁתְּכָחוּ בִּנְהִירוּ, וְדִינָא לָא אִתְעֲבֵיד, וְעַל דָּא תְּעַנּוּ אֶת נַפְשׁוֹתֵיכֶם.

237. We have learned that on that day, all joy and every light and every indulgence in the worlds, NAMELY FORGIVENESS OF SINS, all depend on supernal Ima. All springs are drawn and flow from it, MEANING BOTH THE ILLUMINATION OF CHOCHMAH AND THE ILLUMINATION OF CHASSADIM.

Then all these candles glow, BEING THE SECRET OF THE LIGHTS OF THE FIRE WITHIN MALCHUT, and they glow with light and joy until everything becomes fragrant. At that point, all Judgments are within the glow, AS THOSE JUDGMENTS DRAWN FROM THE FIVE AFFLICTIONS CAUSE CHOCHMAH TO SHINE FORTH. IF NOT FOR THEM, THE CHOCHMAH WOULD NOT BECOME REVEALED AS MENTIONED. The Judgment is not being carried out, BUT IS MERELY IMPENDING. This is the meaning of, "You shall afflict your souls," TO ENABLE THE ILLUMINATION OF CHOCHMAH.

238. אָמַר רַבִּי אַבָּא, הָא אוֹקִים לָהּ מַר, מִן גּוּפָא דְּמַתְנִיתָא, לָא גָּלוּ יִשְׂרָאֵל מֵאַרְצָם, עַד שֶׁכָּפְרוּ בְּקוּדְשָׁא בְּרִיךְ הוּא. דִּכְתִּיב, אֵין לָנוּ חֵלֶק בְּדָוִד וְלֹא נַחֲלָה בְּבֶן יִשָׁי, וְהָא אִתְּמַר. קְרָא אַחֲרִינָא אַשְׁכַּחְנָא בְּהַאי, דִּכְתִּיב, רְאֵה בֵיתְךָ דָוִד. א"ל, הָכִי הוּא וַדַּאי, בֵּית דָּוִד אִקְרֵי, כְּמָה דִּכְתִּיב בֵּית יַעֲקֹב לְכוּ וְנֵלְכָה בְּאוֹר יְיָ'. בֵּית יַעֲקֹב, כד"א וּבֵית תִּפְאַרְתִּי אֲפָאֵר. לְכוּ וְנֵלְכָה בְּאוֹר יְיָ', דִּכְתִּיב וְנָהָר יוֹצֵא מֵעֵדֶן לְהַשְׁקוֹת אֶת הַגָּן, וְנָטַע הַאי גָּן לְאִשְׁתַּעְשָׁעָא בֵּיהּ עִם צַדִּיקַיָּיא, דְּבֵיהּ שַׁרְיָין.

238. Rabbi Aba said: My master has told us from the text of the Mishnah that Yisrael were only exiled from their land for renouncing the Holy One, blessed be He, as it is written, "We have no part in David, neither have we inheritance in the son of Yishai" (II Samuel 20:1). DAVID DENOTES MALCHUT, SO THEY WERE SAYING, "WE HAVE NO PART IN MALCHUT." I have found another verse on this. It is written, "Now see to your own house, David" (I Melachim 12:16). HE QUESTIONS: DOES THE HOUSE OF DAVID ALSO DENOTE MALCHUT? He replied: Certainly MALCHUT is referred to as the house of David, as it is written, "O house of Jacob, come, and let us walk in the light of Hashem" (Yeshayah 2:5). The house of Jacob is similar to that which is written in, "And I will glorify My house of glory (*Tiferet*)" (Yeshayah 60:7), SINCE JACOB IS TIFERET AND THE HOUSE OF TIFERET IS MALCHUT. IN THE SAME MANNER, THE HOUSE OF DAVID POINTS TO MALCHUT. THE EXPLANATION OF THE VERSE, "O HOUSE OF JACOB, come, and let us walk in the light of Hashem": IT HAS THE SAME MEANING as in, "And a river went out of Eden to water the garden" (Beresheet 2:10). RIVER REFERS TO ZEIR ANPIN THAT WATERS THE GARDEN THAT IS

MALCHUT. He planted the Garden to enjoy himself there with the pious ones who dwell within. THEREFORE, IT IS SAID, "O HOUSE OF JACOB," DENOTING MALCHUT, "COME, AND LET US WALK IN THE LIGHT OF HASHEM," WHICH IS ZEIR ANPIN THAT WATERS MALCHUT.

239. תָּאנָא, כְּתִיב אַךְ בֶּעָשׂוֹר לַחֹדֶשׁ הַשְּׁבִיעִי הַזֶּה יוֹם הַכִּפּוּרִים הוּא וְגוֹ' וְעִנִּיתֶם אֶת נַפְשׁוֹתֵיכֶם. וּכְתִיב וְהָיְתָה לָכֶם לְחֻקַּת עוֹלָם בַּחֹדֶשׁ הַשְּׁבִיעִי וְגוֹ'. אַךְ דִּכְתִּיב מַאי קָא בָּעֵי הָכָא. אָ"ל, לְמְעוּטָא קָא אַתְיָא. דְּכֵיוָן דְּאָמַר וְעִנִּיתֶם אֶת נַפְשׁוֹתֵיכֶם בְּתִשְׁעָה לַחֹדֶשׁ, אָמַר לְבָתַר אַךְ בֶּעָשׂוֹר. אַךְ עָשׂוֹר מִבָּעֵי לֵיהּ, דְּבֶעָשׂוֹר תַּלְיָא מִלְּתָא.

239. We have learned that it is written, "Also (lit. 'but') on the tenth day of this seventh month there shall be a day of atonement...and you shall afflict your souls" (Vayikra 23:27). It is also written, "And this shall be a statute for ever to you: that in the seventh month, on the tenth day of the month, you shall afflict your souls" (Vayikra 16:29). IN THE LATTER IT DOES NOT SAY, "BUT ON THE TENTH." What is meant by "but ON THE TENTH" that is written in this verse? He replied to him: It comes to exclude, FOR WHEREVER THE WORD "BUT (HEB. ACH)" IS WRITTEN, ITS PURPOSE IS TO EXCLUDE. Since it is written, "And you shall afflict your souls: on the ninth day of the month" (Vayikra 23:32), so it says later "but on the tenth day." It should merely say, 'but tenth day', ONLY IT TEACHES US that with the tenth rests the whole matter OF "YOU SHALL AFFLICT YOUR SOULS," YET NOT ON THE NINTH DAY OF THE MONTH.

240. אָ"ל אִי הָכִי, אַךְ בַּיּוֹם הָרִאשׁוֹן תַּשְׁבִּיתוּ שְּׂאוֹר מִבָּתֵּיכֶם, וְתָנֵינָן אַךְ חִלֵּק, חֶצְיוֹ אָסוּר בַּאֲכִילַת חָמֵץ, וְחֶצְיוֹ מוּתָּר. אוּף הָכָא אַךְ בֶּעָשׂוֹר לַחֹדֶשׁ, אֵימָא דְּחֶצְיוֹ אָסוּר בַּאֲכִילָה, וְחֶצְיוֹ מוּתָּר. אָ"ל אוּף הָכָא בְּוְעִנִּיתֶם אֶת נַפְשׁוֹתֵיכֶם תַּלְיָא, דְּהָא עִנּוּי לָא אִשְׁתְּכַח אֶלָּא מִפַּלְגּוּת יוֹמָא וּלְהָלְאָה, וְשַׁפִּיר הוּא אַךְ בְּוְעִנִּיתֶם אֶת נַפְשׁוֹתֵיכֶם.

240. He said to him: If so, "but on the first day you shall have put away leaven out of your houses" (Shemot 12:15). We have learned "but" sets a dividing line, meaning for a half day the eating of leaven is prohibited and

for a half day it is permitted. It is also written here, "But on the tenth day of the month," meaning a half time forbidden to eat and a half time permitted. So He said to him here also, "And you shall afflict your souls." There is a separation, in that affliction takes place from midday onward, MEANING AFTER THE TIME ALLOTTED TO EATING. Thus "but" divides. This applies to "and you shall afflict your souls" as well.

241. אָמַר רַבִּי אֶלְעָזָר, כְּתִיב, כִּי בַיּוֹם הַזֶּה יְכַפֵּר עֲלֵיכֶם וְגו'. אֲכַפֵּר עֲלֵיכֶם מִבָּעֵי לֵיהּ. אֶלָּא יְכַפֵּר עֲלֵיכֶם, לְאַכְלְלָא יוֹבְלָא, דְּנָגִיד מַבּוּעֵי לְאַשְׁקָאָה בְּהַאי יוֹמָא לְכָל עִיבָר, לְאַרְוָאָה כֹּלָּא, וּלְאַשְׁקָאָה כֹּלָּא. וְדָא עֲלֵיכֶם, כְּלוֹמַר, בְּגִינֵיכוֹן לְדַכְּאָה לְכוֹן בְּהַאי יוֹמָא, דִּכְתִיב לִפְנֵי יְיָ' תִּטְהָרוּ. וְלָא יִשְׁלוֹט עֲלַיְיכוּ דִּינָא.

241. Rabbi Elazar said: It is written, "For on that day will He forgive you..." (Vayikra 16:30). It should say, 'will I forgive you', AS IF SOMEONE IS SPEAKING FOR HIMSELF. HE ANSWERS, "Will He forgive you" SPOKEN IN THIRD PERSON includes Jubilee, DENOTING BINAH, from which springs flow, MEANING THE ILLUMINATION OF CHOCHMAH, to water on this day all sides and to water and satiate everything. This is the meaning of "you," namely "for you," in order to cleanse you this day, as it says, "that you may be clean of all your sins before Hashem" (Ibid.). Harsh Judgment will not affect you.

242. רַבִּי יְהוּדָה, אָמַר זַכָּאִין אִינּוּן יִשְׂרָאֵל, דְּקוּדְשָׁא בְּרִיךְ הוּא אִתְרְעֵי בְּהוּ, וּבָעֵי לְדַכְּאָה לְהוּ, דְּלָא יִשְׁתְּכַח בְּהוּ חוֹבָה, בְּגִין דִּיהוֹן בְּנֵי הֵיכָלֵיהּ, וִידוּרוּן בְּהֵיכָלֵיהּ. וּלְזִמְנָא דְּאָתֵי כְּתִיב, וְזָרַקְתִּי עֲלֵיכֶם מַיִם טְהוֹרִים וְגו'.

242. Rabbi Yehuda said: How lucky were Yisrael that the Holy One, blessed be He, craved them and wished to cleanse them, so that no sin would be found with them, in order that they could be members of His chamber and dwell in His palace. Regarding the future, it is written, "Then will I sprinkle clean water upon you..." (Yechezkel 36:25).

41. "Out of the depths I have cried to You, Hashem"

A Synopsis
Rabbi Yehuda says that when God wanted to create the world He consulted the Torah, who said that if He did create man, man would sin and make Him angry. The Torah warned God that if he reacted to man's sinful actions the world would not survive. Therefore God did not create the world until He created repentance, and repentance is always available for mankind so people can be cleansed from their sins.

243. רִבִּי יְהוּדָה פָּתַח, שִׁיר הַמַּעֲלוֹת מִמַּעֲמַקִּים קְרָאתִיךְ יְיָ'. תָּנֵינָן, בְּשַׁעֲתָא דְּבָרָא קוּדְשָׁא בְּרִיךְ הוּא עָלְמָא, בָּעָא לְמִבְרֵי בַּר נָשׁ, אַמְלִיךְ בְּאוֹרַיְיתָא, אָמְרָה קַמֵּיהּ, תִּבְעֵי לְמִבְרֵי הַאי בַּר נָשׁ, זַמִּין הוּא לְמֶחֱטֵי קַמָּךְ, זַמִּין הוּא לְאַרְגָּזָא קַמָּךְ. אִי תַּעֲבִיד לֵיהּ כְּעוֹבָדוֹי, הָא עָלְמָא לָא יָכִיל לְמֵיקַם קַמָּךְ, כ"שׁ הַהוּא בַּר נָשׁ. א"ל, וְכִי לְמַגָּנָא אִתְקְרֵינָא, אֵל רַחוּם וְחַנּוּן אֶרֶךְ אַפַּיִם.

243. Rabbi Yehuda opened the discussion saying, "A song of ascent. Out of the depths I have cried to You, Hashem" (Tehilim 130:1). We have learned that when the Holy One, blessed be He, created the world, He wanted to create man. He took counsel in the Torah. She said before Him: You wish to create this man, he will sin before you. He will anger You and, if You react to him according to his deeds, the world then will not survive before You, certainly not man. THE HOLY ONE, BLESSED BE HE, said to her, "Am I for no reason called an "El, merciful and gracious longsuffering" (Shemot 34:6).

244. וְעַד לָא בָּרָא קוּדְשָׁא בְּרִיךְ הוּא עָלְמָא, בָּרָא תְּשׁוּבָה, אָמַר לָהּ לִתְשׁוּבָה, אֲנָא בָּעֵינָא לְמִבְרֵי בַּר נָשׁ בְּעָלְמָא, עַל מְנָת דְּכַד יְתוּבוּן לָךְ מֵחוֹבֵיהוֹן, דְּתֶהֱוֵי זְמִינָא לְמִשְׁבַּק חוֹבֵיהוֹן, וּלְכַפְּרָא עֲלַיְיהוּ. וּבְכָל שַׁעֲתָא וְשַׁעֲתָא תְּשׁוּבָה זְמִינָא לְגַבֵּי בְּנֵי נָשָׁא, וְכַד בְּנֵי נָשָׁא תַּיְיבִין מֵחוֹבַיְיהוּ, הַאי תְּשׁוּבָה תָּבַת לְגַבֵּי קוּדְשָׁא בְּרִיךְ הוּא, וְכַפֵּר עַל כֹּלָּא, וְדִינִין אִתְכַּפְיָין, וּמִתְבַּסְּמָן כֻּלְּהוּ, וּבַר נָשׁ אִתְדְּכֵי מֵחוֹבֵיהּ.

244. Before He created the world He created repentance. The Holy One, blessed be He, said to repentance, WHICH IS THE SECRET OF BINAH CALLED REPENTANCE: 'I wish to create man in the world on the condition if they turn to you from their sins, you will be ready to forgive their sins and render atonement.' At every hour, repentance is available for mankind. When mankind repents from their iniquities, this repentance, NAMELY BINAH, returns to the Holy One, blessed be He, MEANING EXTENDS MOCHIN TO ZEIR ANPIN and atones for all. The Judgments are all subdued and mitigated, and man is purified of his sins.

245. אֵימָתַי אִתְדְּכֵי ב״נ מֵחוֹבֵיה בְּשַׁעֲתָא דְעָאל בְּהַאי תְּשׁוּבָה כַּדְקָא חֲזֵי. ר' יִצְחָק אָמַר, דְּתָב קָמֵי מַלְכָּא עִלָּאָה, וְצַלֵּי צְלוֹתָא מֵעוּמְקָא דְּלִבָּא, הה״ד מִמַּעֲמַקִּים קְרָאתִיךָ יְיָ.

245. HE QUESTIONS: When is he cleansed from his sin? HE ANSWERS: When he properly enters repentance. Rabbi Yitzchak said: When he returns before the supernal King and prays from the depths of the heart, as the verse states, "Out of the depths I have cried to You, Hashem."

246. רִבִּי אַבָּא אָמַר, מִמַּעֲמַקִּים קְרָאתִיךָ יְיָ, אֲתַר גְּנִיז הוּא לְעֵילָּא, וְהוּא עֲמִיקָא דְבֵירָא, וּמֵהַאי נָפְקִין נַחֲלִין וּמַבּוּעִין לְכָל עִיבַר, וְהַהוּא עֲמִיקָא דַעֲמִיקָתָא אִקְרֵי תְּשׁוּבָה. וּמַאן דְּבָעֵי לְאָתָבָא וּלְאִתְדַּכְּאָה מֵחוֹבוֹי, בְּהַאי עוּמְקָא אִצְטְרִיךְ לְמִקְרֵי לְקוּדְשָׁא בְּרִיךְ הוּא, הה״ד מִמַּעֲמַקִּים קְרָאתִיךָ יְיָ.

246. Rabbi Aba said, "Out of the depths I have cried to You, Hashem" MEANS there is a hidden spot above. It is the depth of the well, DENOTING BINAH. From here flow streams and springs in every direction and the deepest part is called repentance. One who wishes to return and cleanse oneself from sins in this depth needs to call upon the Holy One, blessed be He, as the verse says, "Out of the depths I have cried to You, Hashem."

247. תָּאנָא, בְּשַׁעֲתָא דַּהֲוָה ב״נ חָב קָמֵי מָארֵיה, וְקָרִיב קָרְבָּנֵיה עַל מַדְבְּחָא, וְכַהֲנָא מְכַפֵּר עֲלֵיה, וּבָעֵי בְּעוּתֵיה עֲלֵיה, מִתְעָרִין רַחֲמֵי,

-330-

וְדִינִין מִתְבַּסְּמָן, וּתְשׁוּבָה אָרִיק בִּרְכָאן, בְּמַבּוּעִין דְּנַגְדִּין וְנָפְקִין,
וּמִתְבָּרְכִין כֻּלְּהוּ בּוּצִינִין כַּחֲדָא, וּבַר נָשׁ אִתְדְּכֵי מֵחוֹבֵיהּ.

247. We have studied that when one sins before his Master, Mercy is awakened if he offers his sacrifice on the altar and the priest attains forgiveness for him and prays his prayer for him. The Judgments are mitigated and repentance, NAMELY BINAH, pours out blessings in the springs that emerge and flow. All candles are blessed together, NAMELY THE SFIROT OF MALCHUT, and one is cleansed from his sin.

42. Ten types of Chochmah

A Synopsis

We read how God (Ein Sof) produced ten Sfirot, and we are told that He is they and they are He, like a flame attached to a burning coal. We also read of the unholy Chochmot, or wisdoms, that are Klipot. These contain all types of sorcery like the kind that the Egyptians used, and Yisrael learned these erroneous ways from the Egyptians. We learn why Isaac blessed Jacob with both Chassadim and Chochmah.

248. תָּא חֲזֵי, קוּדְשָׁא בְּרִיךְ הוּא, אַפִּיק עֶשֶׂר כִּתְרִין, עִטְרִין קַדִּישִׁין לְעֵילָא, דְּאִתְעַטָּר בְּהוּ, וּמִתְלַבָּשׁ בְּהוּ, וְהוּא אִינּוּן, וְאִינּוּן הוּא, כְּשַׁלְהוֹבָא דַּאֲחִידָא בְּגוּמְרָא, וְלֵית תַּמָן פֵּרוּדָא. לָקֳבֵיל דְּנָא, אִית עֶשֶׂר כִּתְרִין דְּלָא קַדִּישִׁין לְתַתָּא, וְאִינּוּן אֲחִידָן בְּזוּהֲמָא דְּטוּפְרָא דְּחַד עִטְרָא קַדִּישָׁא, דְּאִקְרֵי חָכְמָה. וְעַל דָּא אִקְרוּן חָכְמוֹת.

248. Come and see: The Holy One, blessed be He, THE SECRET OF THE ENDLESS LIGHT, produced ten Sfirot, holy lofty crowns, with which He is crowned and clothed. He is they and they are He, as a flame attached to a burning coal. There is no separation BETWEEN THE ENDLESS LIGHT, BLESSED BE HE, AND THE SFIROT THAT CLOTHE HIM. Correspondingly, there are ten Sfirot that are not holy below, held by the filth of the nails of one holy Sfirah called Chochmah, DENOTING MALCHUT CALLED THE LOWER CHOCHMAH. THE ILLUMINATING LIGHTS AT HER BACK PARTS ARE CALLED NAILS AND WITHIN THEIR REFUSE, CALLED THE FILTH OF THE NAILS, THE KLIPOT ARE ATTACHED. Therefore, they are called Chochmot (lit. 'wisdom' plural).

249. וְתָאנָא, עֲשָׂרָה זִינֵי חָכְמוֹת אִלֵּין נַחְתּוּ לְעָלְמָא. וְכֻלְּהוּ אִסְתְּאָבוּ בְּמִצְרַיִם, בַּר מֵחַד דְּאִתְפְּשַׁט בְּעָלְמָא, וְכֻלְּהוּ זִינֵי חֲרָשֵׁי אִינּוּן, וּמִנַּיְיהוּ יַדְעֵי מִצְרַיִם חֲרָשִׁין, עַל כָּל בְּנֵי עָלְמָא. וְכַד מִצְרָאֵי בָּעָאן לְמֶעְבַּד כְּנוּפְיָיא בְּחַרְשַׁיְיהוּ לְעוֹבָדֵיהוֹן, הֲווֹ נַפְקֵי לְחַקְלָא לְטוּרֵי רָמָאי, וְדָבְחִין דְּבָחִין, וְעַבְדִין גּוּמִין בְּאַרְעָא, וְסַחֲרִין הַהוּא דָּמָא סוֹחֲרָנֵיהּ דְּהָנֵי גוּמִין, וּשְׁאָר דָּמָא מִתְכַּנְפֵי בְּהַנְהוּ גוּמִין, וּבִשְׂרָא שַׁוְּין עֲלַיְיהוּ. וּקַרְבִין

-332-

קָרְבְּנֵיהוֹן, לְאִינּוּן זִינִין בִּישִׁין, וְאִינּוּן זִינִין בִּישִׁין מִתְכַּנְּשִׁין וּמִתְקָרְבִין כַּחֲדָא, וּמִתְפַּיְּיסִין בַּהֲדַיְיהוּ בְּהַהוּא טוּרָא.

249. We have learned that ten types of these Chochmot, OF KLIPOT, descended to the world and all WERE GIVEN TO and became unclean in Egypt, except for one that spread THROUGHOUT THE WORLD EXCEPT EGYPT. They consisted of all types of sorcery, and from them the Egyptians knew sorcery more than the rest of mankind. When the Egyptians wished to gather kinds of sorceries for their purposes, they used to go out into the field to the high mountains and offer sacrifices. They made diggings in the ground and surrounded the diggings with blood while the rest of the blood gathered within the diggings. They placed upon it flesh. They offered the sacrifice to evil beings. And these evil beings gathered and approached together, and were appeased by them on that mountain.

250. יִשְׂרָאֵל דַּהֲווֹ בְּשִׁעְבּוּדֵיהוֹן, הֲווֹ מִתְקָרְבִין לְהוֹן, וְאוֹלְפוּ מִנַּיְיהוּ, וַהֲווֹ טָעָאן בַּתְרַיְיהוּ, וְהַיְינוּ דִּכְתִיב כְּמַעֲשֵׂה אֶרֶץ מִצְרַיִם אֲשֶׁר יְשַׁבְתֶּם בָּהּ לֹא תַעֲשׂוּ וּכְמַעֲשֵׂה אֶרֶץ כְּנַעַן וְגוֹ', וּכְתִיב וְלֹא יִזְבְּחוּ עוֹד אֶת זִבְחֵיהֶם לַשְּׂעִירִים וְגוֹ'. תָּאנָא, בְּשַׁעֲתָא דַּהֲווֹ מְקָרְבִין לְהוֹן עַל גַּבֵּי חַקְלָא, וַהֲווֹ מְזַמְּנֵי הַהוּא דָּמָא, וּמְקָרְבֵי קָרְבְּנַיְיהוּ, הֲווֹ מִתְכַּנְּפֵי כָּל אִינּוּן זִינִין בִּישִׁין, וְחָמָאן לְהוֹן כְּגַוְונָא דִשְׂעִירִים, כֻּלְּהוּ מַלְיָין שַׂעֲרָא, וּמוֹדָעֵי לְהוּ מַה דְּאִינּוּן בַּעְיָין.

250. Yisrael, who were subjugated by the Egyptians, approached them, learned from them, followed their erroneous ways, as the verse says, "After the doings of the land of Egypt, in which you dwelt, shall you not do: and after the doings of the land of Canaan..." (Vayikra 18:3). It is also written, "And they shall no more offer their sacrifice to demons..." (Vayikra 17:7). We have learned that when they were offering before them upon the field and preparing the blood and offering their sacrifices, all these evil types assembled and they saw them as demons, as they were full of hair and they told them what they wanted.

251. ת"ח, יִצְחָק מַה כְּתִיב בֵּיהּ, וַיִּגַּשׁ יַעֲקֹב אֶל יִצְחָק אָבִיו וַיְמֻשֵׁהוּ, אָמַר, דָּא לָא אִתְעֲדֵי, אֶלָּא מַטְּלָא דִשְׁמַיָּא דְּנָגִיד עַל אַרְעָא. אָמַר רִבִּי

יוֹסֵי, וּמִשְׁמַנֵּי הָאָרֶץ, בְּכֹלָּא בְּרָכֵיה. מ"ט. בְּגִין דְּחָמָא לֵיה בְּשַׂעֲרָא, אָמַר לְמֶעְבַּד דָּא, וּמִשְׁמַנֵּי הָאָרֶץ אִצְטְרִיךְ, וְלָא זוּהֲמָא דְּאַרְעָא, דְּהַאי זוּהֲמָא הוּא דְּאַרְעָא, וְכַד טַלָּא דִּשְׁמַיָּא וּמִגְדָּא דְּאַרְעָא מִתְחַבְּרָאן אִתְעֲבַר הַאי זוּהֲמָא.

251. Come and see what is written concerning Isaac, "And Jacob went near to Isaac his father; and he felt him" (Beresheet 27:22). He said: He is lacking only the dew from heaven that flowed upon the earth, MEANING THAT HE LACKS ONLY THE BOUNTY OF ZEIR ANPIN CALLED HEAVEN, THE LIGHT OF CHASSADIM, AS HE IS A CHARIOT FOR ZEIR ANPIN. BUT HE DOES NOT NEED THE ILLUMINATION OF CHOCHMAH. Rabbi Yosi spoke, "And the fatness of the earth" (Ibid. 28) IS ALSO WRITTEN DENOTING THE ILLUMINATION OF CHOCHMAH, and he blessed him with everything, BOTH CHASSIDIM AND CHOCHMAH. Why DID HE BLESS HIM WITH THE ILLUMINATION OF CHOCHMAH? When he saw him with hair, DENOTING JUDGMENTS, he said, in order to remove this FROM HIM, he needs "the fatness of the earth" DENOTING THE ILLUMINATION OF CHOCHMAH, but not the filth of the earth, LIKE THE OTHER SIDE THAT FEEDS UPON THE FILTH OF THE NAILS. This filth comes from the earth, DENOTING MALCHUT. When the dew of Heaven and the fine fruit of the earth join, DENOTING ZEIR ANPIN AND MALCHUT, that filth passes.

43. "One who inquires of the dead"

A Synopsis
The rabbis discuss the last of the lower unholy Sfirot, Malchut of the Other Side. They say that the souls of evildoers who died are the demons of the world, and while they are punished part of the time in Gehenom they also hover over the world and mislead wicked people. The souls mourn for their bodies which are being eaten by worms, and the sorcerers perform their witchcraft at the graves.

252. אָמַר ר' חִיָּיא, בַּתְרַיְיתָא דְּאִינּוּן כְּתְרִין תַּתָּאִין דְּלָא קַדִּישִׁין, הַאי הוּא הה"ד וְדוֹרֵשׁ אֶל הַמֵּתִים, וְדָא הוּא עֲשִׂירָאָה דְּכֹלָּא. דְּתַנְיָא א"ר יִצְחָק אָמַר רִבִּי יְהוּדָה, נַפְשָׁתָא דְּרַשִׁיעַיָּיא אָלֵין אִינּוּן מַזִּיקִין דְּעָלְמָא.

252. Rabbi Chiya said the last of these lower unholy Sfirot is that which is mentioned in the verse, "Or one who inquires of the dead" (Devarim 18:11). This is the tenth of all THE SFIROT, NAMELY MALCHUT OF OTHER SIDE. THERE ARE TEN TYPES OF SORCERY IN THE VERSE CORRESPONDING TO THE TEN SFIROT OF THE OTHER SIDE. According to what we have learned, Rabbi Yitzchak said: The souls of evildoers THAT DIED are the demons of the world, AND ABOUT THEM, THE VERSE DESCRIBES "WHO INQUIRES OF THE DEAD."

253. אָמַר רִבִּי יוֹסֵי, אִי הָכִי טַב לְהוּ לְחַיָּיבַיָּא דְּאִתְעַבְדִין מַזִּיקִין בְּעָלְמָא, אָן הוּא עוֹנְשָׁא דְּגֵיהִנָּם. אָן הוּא בִּישָׁא דִּזְמִינָא לְהוֹן בְּהַהוּא עָלְמָא. אָמַר רִבִּי חִיָּיא, הָכִי תָּנֵינָן, וְהָא אוֹקִימְנָא מִלֵּי, נַפְשָׁתָא דְּרַשִׁיעַיָּיא בְּשַׁעֲתָא דְּנָפְקִין מֵעָלְמָא, כַּמָה גַּרְדִּינֵי נְמוּסִין מִזְדַּמְּנֵי לְקַבְּלָא לְהוּ, וּלְאַעֲלָאָה לְהוּ לְגֵיהִנָּם, וְעָאלִין לְהוּ בִּתְלַת דִּינִין בְּכָל יוֹמָא, בַּגֵּיהִנָּם. לְבָתַר מִזְדַּוְּוגֵי בְּהוּ, וְאַזְלִין וְשָׁאטִין בְּעָלְמָא, וּמַטְעָן לְהוּ לְרַשִׁיעַיָּיא, לְאִינּוּן דְּקָא אַסְתִּים תְּשׁוּבָה מִקַּמַּיְיהוּ. לְבָתַר תַּיְיבִין לְהוּ לְגֵיהִנָּם, וְאִתְדָּנוּן תַּמָּן, וְכַךְ בְּכָל יוֹמָא.

253. Rabbi Yosi said: If so, it is pleasing to the wicked to become harming forces in the world. Where is the punishment of Gehenom and where is the bad that awaits them in that world? Rabbi Chiya replied: We have learned

and established that many prosecutors are ready to receive the souls of the wicked at the time they depart the world and deliver them to Gehenom. They receive three punishments daily in Gehenom. Later, DEMONS join them and the souls go, hover over the world and mislead the wicked people against whom repentance has been closed. Then they are returned to Gehenom to be punished there – and this continues daily.

254. לְבָתַר דְּאַזְלִין בְּהוּ, וְשָׁאטִין בְּהוּ בְּעָלְמָא, מְהַדְּרִין לְקִבְרַיְיהוּ, וְחַמָּן תּוֹלַעְתָּא דְּגוּפָא מְנַקְּרֵי בִּשְׂרָא וּמִתְאַבְּלָן עָלַיְיהוּ, וְאִינּוּן חַרְשִׁין הֲווֹ אַזְלֵי לְבֵי קִבְרֵי, וְחַרְשֵׁי בְּחַרְשַׁיְיהוּ, וְעַבְדִין חַד צַלְמָא דְּבַר נָשׁ, וְדַבְחִין קַמֵּיהּ חַד צְפִירָא. לְבָתַר עָאלִין לְהַהוּא צְפִירָא, בְּהַהוּא קִבְרָא, וְהַהוּא צַלְמָא מְתַּבְּרִין לֵיהּ לְאַרְבַּע סִטְרִין, וּמַעֲלִין לֵיהּ לְאַרְבַּע זִיוְוָיָין דְּקִבְרָא. כְּדֵין מְחָרְשֵׁי בְּחַרְשַׁיְיהוּ, וּמִתְכַּנְּפֵי אִינּוּן כְּנוּפֵי, וְאִינּוּן זִינִין בִּישִׁין, וּמַיְיתִין הַהִיא נַפְשָׁתָא, וְעָאל בְּקִבְרָא וּמִשְׁתָּעֵי בַּהֲדַיְיהוּ.

254. After THE DEMONS go with them through the world, they return them to their graves and they see body worms picking at THEIR flesh. THE SOULS mourn for them, FOR THE BODIES. These sorcerers go to the cemeteries and perform their sorcery, make an image of a human form and slaughter before it a goat. Later, they bring that goat to that grave and that image they shatter to four directions and raise it to the four corners of the grave. Then they perform their sorcery. All these groups assemble with evil kinds and bring this soul, which enters the grave, and speaks with them.

44. Nefesh, Ruach, Neshamah

A Synopsis

We read about the three levels of soul of a righteous person, Nefesh, Ruach and Neshamah. If he deserves the spiritual soul, he is given the Ruach, and then there is awakened in him a higher desire to learn about God. Then he deserves the highest level, the Neshamah. We are told how the Nefashot of the righteous who died are in this world to protect living people; the deceased are aware of distress in the world. The Ruach of the righteous dead go to the earthly Garden of Eden, and the Neshamah go to the supernal Garden of Eden, called the Bond of Life. We learn how the levels of soul communicate with one another to draw God's mercy to the world.

255. א״ר יִצְחָק, זַכָּאִין אִינּוּן צַדִּיקַיָּיא בְּעָלְמָא דֵין, וּבְעָלְמָא דְּאָתֵי, דְּהָא כֻּלְּהוּ קַדִּישִׁין. גּוּפָא דִּלְהוֹן קַדִּישָׁא. נַפְשָׁא דִּלְהוֹן קַדִּישָׁא. רוּחָא דִּלְהוֹן קַדִּישָׁא. נִשְׁמָתָא דִּלְהוֹן קֹדֶשׁ קָדָשִׁים. תְּלַת דַּרְגִּין אִינּוּן, כְּגַוְונָא דִּלְעֵילָא. דְּתַנְיָא א״ר יְהוּדָה, כְּתִיב תּוֹצֵא הָאָרֶץ נֶפֶשׁ חַיָּה, דָּא הִיא נִשְׁמָתָא דְּאָדָם קַדְמָאָה. תָּא חֲזֵי, תְּלַת דַּרְגִּין אִינּוּן, וְאִתְדַּבָּקוּ כְּחַד, נֶפֶשׁ, רוּחַ, נְשָׁמָה. וְעִלָּאָה מִנַּיְיהוּ, נִשְׁמָה.

255. Rabbi Yitzchak said: How fortunate are the pious in this world and the World to Come, as they are all holy. Their bodies are holy and their Nefesh is holy. Their Ruach is holy and their Neshamah is the Holy of Holies. There are three levels – NEFESH, RUACH AND NESHAMAH – just like above, reflecting MALCHUT, TIFERET AND BINAH OF ABOVE. As Rabbi Yehuda has taught, it is written, "Let the earth bring forth living creatures (Heb. 'nefesh')" (Beresheet 1:24), which refers to the soul of Adam. Come and see: These three levels – Nefesh, Ruach and Neshamah – join together, and the superior one is Neshamah.

256. דא״ר יוֹסֵי, בְּכֻלְּהוּ בְּנֵי נָשָׁא אִית נֶפֶשׁ, וְאִית נֶפֶשׁ עִלָּאָה מִנֶּפֶשׁ. זָכָה ב״נ בְּהַאי נֶפֶשׁ, מְרִיקִין עָלֵיהּ עִטְרָא חַד, דְּאִקְרֵי רוּחַ. הה״ד, עַד יֵעָרֶה עָלֵינוּ רוּחַ מִמָּרוֹם. כְּדֵין אִתְּעַר ב״נ בְּאִתְעֲרוּתָא אָחֳרָא עִלָּאָה, לְאִסְתַּכְּלָא בְּנִמּוּסֵי מַלְכָּא קַדִּישָׁא. זָכָה בַּר נָשׁ בֵּיהּ בְּהַהוּא רוּחָא,

מְעַטְּרִין לֵיהּ בְּכִתְרָא קַדִּישָׁא עִלָּאָה, דְּכָלִיל כֹּלָא, דְּאִקְרֵי נְשָׁמָה. דְּאִתְקְרֵי נִשְׁמַת אֱלוֹהַּ.

256. As Rabbi Yosi said, every person has a Nefesh, an ANIMALISTIC NEFESH and he has a supernal Nefesh, DENOTING a SPIRITUAL Nefesh. If man merits that soul, he is given a crown called Ruach, as the verse says, "Until a spirit be poured upon us from on high" (Yeshayah 32:15). Then there awakens in man a different supernal awakening to search the ways of the Holy King. When man merits the Ruach, he is crowned with a heavenly, holy, all – inclusive Sfirah called Neshamah, called the Neshamah of Eloha.

257. וְתָאנָא בְּרָזָא דְּרָזִין, בְּגוֹ רָזִין דְּסִפְרָא דִּשְׁלֹמֹה מַלְכָּא, הַאי קְרָא, דִּכְתִיב וְשַׁבֵּחַ אֲנִי אֶת הַמֵּתִים שֶׁכְּבָר מֵתוּ, כֵּיוָן דִּכְתִיב וְשַׁבֵּחַ אֲנִי אֶת הַמֵּתִים, אֲמַאי שֶׁכְּבָר מֵתוּ. אֶלָּא שֶׁכְּבָר מֵתוּ בְּהַאי עָלְמָא בְּפוּלְחָנָא דְּמָארֵיהוֹן.

257. We studied in the greatest secret, among the mysteries of the book of King Solomon, this verse that states, "So I praised the dead that are already dead" (Kohelet 4:2). If it is written, "So I praised the dead," why CONTINUE "that are already dead"? HE ANSWERS: THIS REFERS TO those that already died in this world doing the service of their Master, THEY RENOUNCE THE WORLD (LIT. 'DIE') FOR THE SERVICE OF THEIR MASTER, AS TORAH IS SUSTAINED ONLY BY THOSE WHO GIVE THEMSELVES UP FOR IT.

258. וְתַמָּן כְּתִיב, תְּלָת מָדוֹרִין עֲבַד קוּדְשָׁא בְּרִיךְ הוּא לְצַדִּיקַיָּיא, חַד לְנַפְשָׁאן דְּאִינּוּן צַדִּיקַיָּיא, דְּלָא אִסְתַּלְּקוּ מֵהַאי עָלְמָא, וּשְׁכִיחִין בְּהַאי עָלְמָא. וְכַד אִצְטְרִיךְ עָלְמָא רַחֲמִין, וְאִינּוּן חַיִּין יַתְבִין בְּצַעֲרָא, אִינּוּן מְצַלּוּ צְלוֹתָא עָלַיְיהוּ, וְאַזְלִין וּמוֹדְעִין מִלָּה לְאִינּוּן דְּמִיכִין דְּחֶבְרוֹן, וּמִתְעָרִין, וְעַאלִין לג"ע דְּאַרְעָא, דְּתַמָּן רוּחֵיהוֹן דְּצַדִּיקַיָּיא, מִתְלַבְּשָׁן בְּעִטְרִין דִּנְהוֹרָא, וְאִתְיַיעֲטוּ בְּהוּ, וְגַזְרִין גְּזֵרָה, וְקוּדְשָׁא בְּרִיךְ הוּא עָבֵיד רְעוּתָא דִּלְהוֹן, וְחָס עַל עָלְמָא.

258. IN THE BOOK OF KING SOLOMON, it is written that the Holy One, blessed be He, made three dwellings for righteous people, FOR THEIR

NEFESH, RUACH AND NESHAMAH AFTER THEIR DEMISE. One is for the Nefashot (Heb. plural) of the righteous that did not depart this world and are still in this world, AS THE NEFESH OF THE DECEASED DOES NOT DEPART THIS WORLD. When the world needs mercy and living PEOPLE are in distress, the Nefashot pray for them. They go and tell this to those who slumber in Hebron, MEANING THE PATRIARCHS, who awaken and go to the earthly Garden of Eden, where the Ruach of the righteous are clothed with crowns of light, take counsel with them and make a decree. And the Holy One, blessed be He, fulfills their wish and shows mercy to the world.

259. וְאִינּוּן נַפְשָׁן דְּצַדִּיקַיָּיא, מִשְׁתַּכְּחִין בְּהַאי עָלְמָא, לְאַגָּנָא עַל חַיָּיא, וְהַאי אִקְרֵי נֶפֶשׁ, וְדָא לָא אִסְתַּלְּקָא מֵהַאי עָלְמָא, וּשְׁכִיחָא בְּהַאי עָלְמָא, לְאַסְתַּכְּלָא וּלְמִנְדַּע וּלְאַגָּנָא עַל דָּרָא. וְהַאי הוּא דְּאָמְרוּ חַבְרַיָּיא, דְּמֵתֵי יַדְעֵי בְּצַעֲרָא דְּעָלְמָא. וְעוֹנָשָׁא דְּחַיָּיבִין דִּי בְּאַרְעָא, בְּהַאי הוּא, דִּכְתִיב וְנִכְרְתָה הַנֶּפֶשׁ הַהִיא מֵעַמֶּיהָ.

259. These Nefashot of the righteous are in this world to protect living PEOPLE. This is known as Nefesh. It does not depart this world and is present in this world to watch and know about and to protect the generation. The friends say that the deceased are aware of distress in the world and the punishment of the wicked in the land is by that NEFESH, as it is written, "That Nefesh shall be cut off from his people" (Vayikra 7:20).

260. וּמָדוֹרָא תִּנְיָינָא הוּא ג"ע דִּי בְּאַרְעָא. בֵּיהּ עָבֵד קוּדְשָׁא בְּרִיךְ הוּא מָדוֹרִין עִלָּאִין יַקִּירִין, כְּגַוְונָא דְּהַאי עָלְמָא, וּכְגַוְונָא דְּעָלְמָא עִלָּאָה. וְהֵיכָלִין בִּתְרֵין גְּוָונִין, דְּלֵית לְהוֹן חוּשְׁבְּנָא, וְאִילָנִין וַעֲשָׂבִין וְרֵיחִין דְּסַלְּקִין בְּכָל יוֹמָא. וּבְהַאי אֲתַר שָׁארֵי הַהוּא דְּאִקְרֵי רוּחַ דְּאִינּוּן צַדִּיקַיָּיא, וּמָדוֹרָא דְּהַהוּא רוּחָא בֵּיהּ שָׁארֵי. וְכָל רוּחַ וְרוּחַ מִתְלַבְּשָׁא בִּלְבוּשׁ יַקִּירָא, כְּגַוְונָא דְּהַאי עָלְמָא, וּכְגַוְונָא דְּהַהוּא עָלְמָא עִלָּאָה.

260. The second dwelling is the earthly Garden of Eden. In it, the Holy One, blessed be He, made upper precious dwellings that are similar to this world and similar to the supernal world, MEANING THEY ARE INCLUDED WITH ASPECTS OF MALCHUT AND ASPECTS OF BINAH. THE GARDEN IS THE

SECRET OF MALCHUT AND EDEN IS THE SECRET OF BINAH. The chambers are ALSO of two types LIKE THE DWELLING without number, and trees and grasses and fragrances rise daily. In that place rests that which is called Ruach of these righteous. This is the dwelling in which Ruach dwells. Each Ruach is clothed with precious garments of the likeness of this world and the supernal world.

261. מָדוֹרָא תְּלִיתָאָה, הַהוּא מָדוֹרָא עִלָּאָה קַדִּישָׁא, דְּאִתְקְרֵי צְרוֹרָא דְּחַיֵּי. דְּתַמָּן מִתְעַדְּנָא הַהוּא דַּרְגָּא עִלָּאָה קַדִּישָׁא, דְּאִקְרֵי נִשְׁמָה. וְהַאי אִתְדְּבַק לְאִתְעַנְּגָא בְּעִדּוּנָא עִלָּאָה. עֲלֵיהּ כְּתִיב, אָז תִּתְעַנַּג עַל יְיָ׳ וְהִרְכַּבְתִּיךָ וְגוֹ׳.

261. The third dwelling is the holy dwelling on high called the bundle of Life, MEANING THE GARDEN OF EDEN ON HIGH. There, the highest, holy level called Neshamah has pleasure. It clings to find pleasure in the most high Eden and it is written, "Then you shall delight yourself in Hashem; and I will cause you to ride..." (Yeshayah 58:14). THE GARDEN OF EDEN ON HIGH IS CALLED THE HIGH PLACES OF THE EARTH.

262. וְתָאנָא, בְּשַׁעֲתָא דְּאִצְטְרִיךְ עָלְמָא רַחֲמֵי, וְאִינּוּן צַדִּיקַיָּיא זַכָּאִין. הַהוּא נֶפֶשׁ דְּאִשְׁתַּכְּחָא בְּעָלְמָא, לְאַגָּנָא עַל עָלְמָא. נֶפֶשׁ סָלִיק וְאָזִיל וְשָׁאט בְּעָלְמָא, וּמוֹדַע לְרוּחַ. וְרוּחַ סָלִיק וְאִתְעַטָּר, וּמוֹדַע לַנְשָׁמָה. וּנְשָׁמָה לְקוּדְשָׁא בְּרִיךְ הוּא. וּכְדֵין חָס קוּדְשָׁא בְּרִיךְ הוּא עַל עָלְמָא. כְּדֵין נַחְתָּא מֵעֵילָּא לְתַתָּא, נְשָׁמָה אוֹדַע לְרוּחַ, וְרוּחַ אוֹדַע לְנַפְשָׁא.

262. We have learned that when the world needs Mercy, THEN the Nefesh of these meritorious righteous men, which is in this world in order to defend the world, rises, flies across the world and alerts the Ruach. The Ruach rises, adorns itself and alerts the Neshamah. The Neshamah alerts the Holy One, blessed be He, and then He has mercy on the world. Then He descends from above downwards, the Neshamah informs the Ruach and the Ruach informs the Nefesh.

263. וּבְכָל שַׁבְּתָא וְשַׁבְּתָא, וְרֵישׁ יַרְחָא, כֻּלְּהוּ, מִתְחַבְּרָן וּמִתְעַטְּרָן

כְּחַד, עַד דְּאִזְדַּוְּוגוּ לְמֵיתֵי לְסַגְדָּא לְמַלְכָּא עִלָּאָה. וּלְבָתַר תַּיְיבִין לְאַתְרַיְיהוּ. הה"ד וְהָיָה מִדֵּי חֹדֶשׁ בְּחָדְשׁוֹ, וּמִדֵּי שַׁבָּת בְּשַׁבַּתּוֹ יָבֹא כָל בָּשָׂר וְגוֹ'.

263. Every Shabbat and new Moon, NEFESH, RUACH, AND NESHAMAH join and clothe themselves together until they are united to come forth and bow before the most high King. Afterwards, they return to their positions. This is the essence of the verse, "And it shall come to pass, that every new moon, and every Shabbat, shall all flesh come..." (Yeshayah 66:23).

264. וּבְשַׁעֲתָא דְּאִצְטְרִיךְ עָלְמָא רַחֲמֵי, וְחַיָּיא אַזְלֵי וּמוֹדָעֵי לְהוּ לְנַפְשַׁיְיהוּ, דְּצַדִּיקַיָּיא, וּבָכָאן עַל קִבְרַיְיהוּ, אִינּוּן דְּאִתְחָזוּ לְאוֹדָעָא לְהוּ. מ"ט. דְּשַׁוְּויָין רְעוּתָא דִּלְהוֹן לְאִתְדַּבְּקָא נַפְשָׁא בְּנַפְשָׁא, כְּדֵין אִתְעָרִין נַפְשַׁיְיהוּ דְּצַדִּיקַיָּיא, וּמִתְכַּנְפֵי וְאַזְלִין וְשָׁאטִין לִדְמִיכֵי חֶבְרוֹן, וּמוֹדִיעֵי לְהוּ צַעֲרָא דְּעָלְמָא. וְכֻלְּהוּ עָאלִין בְּהַהוּא פִּתְחָא דג"ע, וּמוֹדִיעֵי לְרוּחַ. וְאִינּוּן רוּחִין דְּמִתְעַטְּרָן בג"ע, מַלְאֲכֵי עִלָּאִין אַזְלֵי בֵּינַיְיהוּ. וְכֻלְּהוּ מוֹדִיעִין לַנְשָׁמָה. וּנְשָׁמָה אוֹדָעַת לְקוּדְשָׁא בְּרִיךְ הוּא, וְכֻלְּהוּ בָּעָאן רַחֲמֵי עַל חַיִּין, וְחָס קוּדְשָׁא בְּרִיךְ הוּא עַל עָלְמָא בְּגִינֵיהוֹן. וְעַל דָּא אָמַר שְׁלֹמֹה, וְשַׁבֵּחַ אֲנִי אֶת הַמֵּתִים שֶׁכְּבָר מֵתוּ וְגוֹ'.

264. When the world needs mercy, the living go and inform the Nefashot (Heb. plural) of the righteous, and weep on their graves. Those who are worthy to inform the righteous men: what is the reason THEY ARE WORTHY? BECAUSE they concentrate on clinging to Nefesh with Nefesh; then the Nefashot of the righteous awaken, assemble, fly to the slumberers of Hebron, inform them of the distress of the world, and they all ascend to the door of the Garden of Eden to inform the Ruach. These Ruchot (Heb. plural) that are adorned in the Garden of Eden, with celestial angels going among them, all inform the Neshamah, the Neshamah informs the Holy One, blessed be He, and all beg for mercy for the living. And the Holy One, blessed be He, shows Mercy to the world on their behalf. This is what Solomon meant in, "So I praised the dead that are already dead."

45. "One who inquires of the dead," part two

A Synopsis

Rabbi Aba tells how people can take a scroll of Torah to the gravesites of righteous men, which awakens their souls, and the dead then realize that the world is in distress but there is no one who knows how to inform the dead about the problem. The rabbis talk about the importance of repentance and fasting, and about how critical it is to never change a single letter of the Torah. They say that when there are no more righteous men in the world, the world will survive only by the merits of the deceased. We learn that when a righteous person leaves this world he is then found in all three worlds, Briyah, Yetzirah and Asiyah. He shields the world during his lifetime and even more after death.

265. אָמַר ר' חִיָּיא, תַּווהְנָא אִי אִית מַאן דְּיָדַע לְאוֹדְעָא לְהוּ לְמֵתַיָּיא, בַּר אֲנָן. אָמַר רִבִּי אַבָּא, צַעֲרָא מוֹדְעָא לְהוּ. אוֹרַיְיתָא מוֹדְעָא לְהוּ. דְּהָא בְּשַׁעֲתָא דְּלֵית מַאן דְּיָדַע בְּהַאי, אַפְקֵי אוֹרַיְיתָא סָמוּךְ לְקִבְרֵי, וְאִינּוּן מִתְעָרֵי, עַל אוֹרַיְיתָא עַל מַה אִתְגַּלְיָיא לְהַהוּא אֲתַר, כְּדֵין דּוּמָה אוֹדַע לְהוֹן.

265. Rabbi Chiya said: I wonder if anyone knows how to notify the deceased besides us. Rabbi Aba replied: The pain THAT PEOPLE SUFFER, informs them. The Torah informs them. At the time when no one has knowledge, NAMELY HOW TO ALERT THE SOULS OF THE RIGHTEOUS MEN, they bring out a scroll of Torah near the graves and the souls are awakened wondering as to what reason the Torah appears exiled at this place. Then THE ANGEL Dumah informs them.

266. אָמַר ר' יוֹסֵי, וְאִינּוּן יַדְעֵי דְּהָא עָלְמָא בְּצַעֲרָא, וְחִיָּיא לָא אִתְחֲזוּן, וְלָא יַדְעֵי לְאוֹדְעָא לְהוּ. בֵּיהּ שַׁעֲתָא כֻּלְּהוּ צַוְוחִין עַל אוֹרַיְיתָא דְּאִתְקַלְנָא וְאִתְגַּלְיָיא לְהַהוּא אֲתַר. אִי בְּנֵי נָשָׁא תַּיְיבִין וּבְכָאן בְּלִבָּא שְׁלִים, וְתַיְיבִין קָמֵי קוּדְשָׁא בְּרִיךְ הוּא, כֻּלְּהוּ מִתְכַּנְּשֵׁי, וּבְעָאן רַחֲמֵי, וּמוֹדִיעִין לְאִינּוּן דְּמִיכֵי חֶבְרוֹן, וְעָאלִין וּמוֹדְעִין לְרוּחַ דבג"ע, כְּמָה דְּאַמְרָן.

266. Rabbi Yosi said: they realize that the world is in distress, and the living people are neither worthy of nor know how to inform them. At that very time everyone wails the Torah – we have failed and the Torah has been exiled to this place. If people return WITH REPENTANCE and cry with a complete heart, they then return to the Holy One, blessed be He. All assemble and seek mercy, and inform the slumberers of Hebron, and enter and inform the Ruach in the Garden of Eden, as we have mentioned.

267. וְאִי אִינּוּן לָא תַּיְיבִין בְּלִבָּא שְׁלִים לְמִבָּעֵי וּלְמִבְכֵּי עַל צַעֲרָא דְעָלְמָא. וַוי לְהוֹן, דְּכֻלְּהוּ מִתְכַּנְּפֵי לְרֵיקָא אַמְרֵי מַאן גָּרַם לְאוֹרַיְיתָא קַדִּישָׁא דְּאִתְגַּלְיָיא עַל יְדַיְיהוּ בְּלָא תְּשׁוּבָה. וְכֻלְּהוּ אָתָאן לְאַדְכְּרָא חוֹבַיְיהוּ בְּגִינֵי כַּךְ לָא יַהֲכוּן תַּמָּן בְּלָא תְּשׁוּבָה וּבְלָא תַּעֲנִיתָא לְמִבָּעֵי בָּעוּתָא קַמַּיְיהוּ. ר׳ אַבָּא אָמַר, בְּלָא תְּלַת תַּעֲנִיתָא. רַבִּי יוֹסֵי אָמַר, אֲפִילוּ חַד, וּבְהַהוּא יוֹמָא, וּבִלְבַד דְּעָלְמָא יָתִיב בְּצַעֲרָא טְפֵי, כְּדֵין כֻּלְּהוּ מִזְדַּוְּוגֵי לְמִבָּעֵי רַחֲמִין עַל עָלְמָא.

267. If they do not repent whole heartedly, entreating and crying for the distress of the world, woe to them, in that they assembled for nothing. They say: Who caused the Holy Torah to be exiled because of them who failed to do repentance. Then they come to list their sins. Therefore, none should go there without repenting or without fasting to seek requests. Rabbi Aba said: Not without three fasts. Rabbi Yosi says: Even one FAST SUFFICES, but it must be on that same day as long as the multitudes sit in great distress. Then they would come together, MEANING NEFESH, RUACH AND NESHAMAH, seeking mercy upon the world.

268. תָּאנָא, אָמַר רַבִּי יְהוּדָה, יוֹמָא חַד הֲוֹו אַזְלֵי רַבִּי חִזְקִיָּה וְר׳ יֵיסָא בְּאוֹרְחָא, עָרְעוּ בְּגוּשׁ חָלָב, וַהֲוָה חָרִיב, יָתְבוּ סָמִיךְ לְבֵי קִבְרֵי, וְר׳ יֵיסָא הֲוָה בִּידֵיהּ חַד קִיטְרָא דס״ת דְּאִקְרַע, עַד דְּיָתְבוּ אִתְרְגִישׁ חַד קִבְרָא קַמַּיְיהוּ, וְצָוְוחַ וַוי וַוי, דְּהָא עָלְמָא בְּצַעֲרָא שְׁכִיחַ, הָא אוֹרַיְיתָא הָכָא דְּאִתְגַּלְיָיא, אוֹ חַיָּיא אָתוּ לְחַיְּיכָא עֲלָן, וּלְכַסְּפָא בְּכִסּוּפָא עֲלָן בְּאוֹרַיְיתַיְיהוּ. אִזְדַּעֲזָעוּ רַבִּי חִזְקִיָּה וְר׳ יֵיסָא.

268. We have learned that Rabbi Yehuda said: One day, Rabbi Chizkiyah and Rabbi Yesa were going along the road and they encountered A PLACE

CALLED Gush Chalav. It was in a state of destruction. They sat adjacent to the cemetery. Rabbi Yesa had in his possession one portion of a ripped scroll of Torah, MEANING HE HAD IN HIS HAND A PORTION OF A RIPPED SCROLL OF THE TORAH WITH A COLUMN WITHIN IT. As they were sitting, one grave quivered before them, and cried: Woe, Woe, the world is in distress as the Torah has been exiled here, or maybe the living have come to mock and to shame us with their Torah. Rabbi Chizkiyah and Rabbi Yesa quivered.

269. אָמַר ר' חִזְקִיָּה מַאן אַתְּ. אָמַר לֵיהּ מֵיתָא אֲנָא, וְהָא אִתְּעַרְנָא לְגַבֵּי ס"ת. דְּזִמְנָא חֲדָא הֲוָה יָתִיב עָלְמָא בְּצַעֲרָא, וְאָתוּ חַיָּיא הָכָא, לְאַתְעָרָא לָן בְּסֵפֶר תּוֹרָה, וַאֲנָא וְחַבְרָאי אַקְדִּימְנָא לְגַבֵּי דְּמִיכֵי חֶבְרוֹן, וְכַד אִתְחַבְּרוּ בְּגַן עֵדֶן בְּרוּחֵיהוֹן דְּצַדִּיקַיָּיא, אִשְׁתְּכַח קַמַּיְיהוּ, דְּהַהוּא ס"ת דְּאַיְיתוּ לְקַמָּן אִינּוּן חַיָּיא הֲוָה פָּסוּל וּמְשַׁקֵּר בִּשְׁמָא דְּמַלְכָּא, עַל דְּאִשְׁתְּכַח וָא"ו יַתִּיר בְּהַהוּא קְרָא דְּוְשׁוֹסַעַת שֶׁסַע שְׁתֵּי פְרָסוֹת, וְאָמְרוּ דְּהוֹאִיל וְשַׁקְרוּ בִּשְׁמָא דְּמַלְכָּא דְּלָא יְתוּבוּן לְגַבֵּיהוֹן, וְדָחוּ לִי וּלְחַבְרָאי בְּהַהִיא שַׁעֲתָא מִבֵּי מְתִיבְתָּא.

269. Rabbi Chizkiyah said TO THE GRAVE: Who are you? He answered: I am dead. I was just awakened for the sake of the Torah scroll. Once the world was in distress and the living came here with a Torah scroll to awaken us. My associates and I hurried to the slumberers at Hebron and, when they joined the spirits of the righteous in the Garden of Eden, it was found that the Torah scroll brought before us by the living was unfit. They were false to the name of the King, because an extra Vav was found in the Torah in the verse, "Whatever parts the hoof, and is clovenfooted" (Vayikra 11:3), WHICH WAS SPELLED WITH A REDUNDANT VAV. They said that since they were false to the name of the King, AS THE TORAH IS THE NAME OF THE KING, they would not return to them TO LET THEM KNOW IF THEIR PRAYER WAS ACCEPTED. They then dismissed me and my associates from the Yeshivah.

270. עַד דְּחַד סָבָא דַּהֲוָה בֵּינַיְיהוּ, אֲזַל וְאַיְיתֵי סַפְרָא דְּרַב הַמְנוּנָא סָבָא, וּכְדֵין אִתְּעַר רַבִּי אֶלְעָזָר בר"ש, דַּהֲוָה קָבִיר עִמָּנָא, וְאָזַל וּבָעָא בג"ע עָלַיְיהוּ, וְאִתְּסֵי עָלְמָא, כְּדֵין שָׁארוּ לָן, וּמִן הַהוּא יוֹמָא דְּסַלִּיקוּ

לֵיהּ לר״א מִבֵּי קִבְרָא דָא, וְאִתְיְיהִיב לְגַבֵּי אֲבוּהָ, לֵית מַאן דְּאִתְּעַר
לְמֵיקָם קַמַּיְיהוּ דִּדְמִיכֵי חֶבְרוֹן, דְּמִסְתַּפֵּינָא מִן הַהוּא יוֹמָא דְּדָחוּ לִי
וְלַחֲבֵרַי. וְהַשְׁתָּא אֲתֵיתוּן לְגַבָּן, וְסֵפֶר תּוֹרָה גַּבֵּיכוֹן, אֲמֵינָא דְּהָא
עָלְמָא בְּצַעֲרָא אִשְׁתְּכַח. וְעַ״ד אִזְדַּעֲזַעְנָא, דְּאֲמֵינָא מַאן יַקְדִּים
לְאוֹדָעָא לְאִינּוּן זַכָּאֵי קְשׁוֹט דְּמִיכֵי חֶבְרוֹן, אִשְׁתְּמִיט ר׳ יֵיסָא בְּהַהוּא
קִיטְרָא דְּסֵפֶר תּוֹרָה. אָמַר ר׳ חִזְקִיָּה, חַס וְשָׁלוֹם לֵית עָלְמָא בְּצַעֲרָא,
וַאֲנָן לָא אֲתֵינָן לְהַאי.

270. Until one elder man who was among them went and brought the Torah scroll of Rav Hamnuna Saba (the elder). Then the son of Rabbi Shimon, Rabbi Elazar, who was buried with us, was awakened. He went and prayed in the Garden of Eden for them and the world was healed. Then they allowed us TO RETURN TO THE YESHIVAH. From the time they took Rabbi Elazar from this cemetery IN GUSH CHALAV and placed him near his father IN MERON, there is no one who will awaken to rise before the slumberers of Hebron, for we are afraid to do so since the day when they dismissed me and my friends FROM THE YESHIVAH. Now, you have come to us with your Torah scroll. Therefore, I am shaken up as I say: Who will hasten to notify these genuine righteous men slumbering in Hebron. Rabbi Yesa slipped away AND WENT OFF with that remnant of the Torah scroll. Rabbi Chizkiyah said: Heaven forbid, the world is not in distress and we did not come for this reason.

271. קָמוּ רִבִּי חִזְקִיָּה וְר׳ יֵיסָא וְאַזְלוּ. אַמְרֵי, וַדַּאי בְּשַׁעֲתָא דְּזַכָּאִין לָא
אִשְׁתְּכָחוּ בְּעָלְמָא, עָלְמָא לָא מִתְקַיְּימָא אֶלָּא בְּגִינֵיהוֹן דְּמֵתַיָּיא. אָמַר
ר׳ יֵיסָא, בְּשַׁעֲתָא דְּאִצְטְרִיךְ עָלְמָא לְמִטְרָא, אֲמַאי אַזְלֵינָן לְגַבֵּיהוֹן
דְּמֵתַיָּיא, וְהָא כְּתִיב וְדוֹרֵשׁ אֶל הַמֵּתִים וְאָסִיר. א״ל עַד כָּאן לָא
חֲמֵיתָא גַּדְפָּא דְּצִפֳּרָא דְּעֵדֶן. וְדוֹרֵשׁ אֶל הַמֵּתִים, אֶל הַמֵּתִים דַּיְיקָא.
דְּאִינּוּן חַיָּיבֵי עָלְמָא, דְּאִינּוּן מְעַמִּין עע״ז, דְּאִשְׁתְּכָחוּ תָּדִיר מֵתִים.
אֲבָל יִשְׂרָאֵל דְּאִינּוּן זַכָּאֵי קְשׁוֹט, שְׁלֹמֹה קָרָא עָלַיְיהוּ וְשַׁבֵּחַ אֲנִי אֶת
הַמֵּתִים שֶׁכְּבָר מֵתוּ, בְּזִמְנָא אַחֲרָא וְלָא הַשְׁתָּא. שֶׁכְּבָר מֵתוּ, וְהַשְׁתָּא
אִינּוּן חַיִּין.

271. Rabbi Chizkiyah and Rabbi Yesa left. They said surely when there are no righteous men in the world, the world will survive only by the merits of the deceased. Rabbi Yesa said: When the world needs rain, why do people go to the deceased TO PRAY? Does it not say about "one who inquires of the dead" that it is prohibited? He replied: You have not perceived the wing of the bird in Eden, REFERRING TO THE SECRET OF BINAH, MEANING YOU HAVE NOT ATTAINED THE LEVEL OF BINAH, SINCE THE VERSE "one who inquires of the dead" literally means the dead, denoting the world's evildoers from the idolatrous nations that are always dead, AS THE WICKED EVEN DURING THEIR LIFETIME ARE CALLED DEAD. But about Yisrael, who are truly righteous, Solomon said, "So I praised the dead that are already dead" (Kohelet 4:2), those that have already died at a different time, MEANING THEY GAVE THEMSELVES FOR THE TORAH, but not this time. They have already died, and now they are alive.

272. וְעוֹד, דִּשְׁאָר עַמִּין כַּד אָתָאן לִמְתֵיהוֹן, אַתְיָין בְּחַרְשִׁין, לְאִתְעָרָא עָלַיְיהוּ זִינִין בִּישִׁין. וְכַד יִשְׂרָאֵל אָתָאן לִמְתֵיהוֹן, אַתְיָין בְּכַמָּה תְּשׁוּבָה לְקַמֵּי קוּדְשָׁא בְּרִיךְ הוּא. בִּתְבִירוּ דְלִבָּא, בְּתַעֲנִיתָא לְקָבְלֵיהּ, וְכֹלָּא בְּגִין דְּנִשְׁמָתִין קַדִּישִׁין יִבְעוּן רַחֲמֵי לְקַמֵּי קוּדְשָׁא בְּרִיךְ הוּא עָלַיְיהוּ, וְקוּדְשָׁא בְּרִיךְ הוּא חָיֵיס עַל עָלְמָא בְּגִינֵיהוֹן.

272. Furthermore, when other nations come before their deceased, they come with sorcery to awaken kinds of evil beings. When Yisrael come to their deceased, they come in great repentance before the Holy One, blessed be He, with a broken heart and fasting. All this is done so that the holy souls will ask for mercy for their sake before the Holy One, blessed be He. And the Holy One, blessed be He, shows mercy to the world on their behalf.

273. וְעַל דָּא תָּנֵינָן, צַדִּיקָא אע"ג דְּאִתְפְּטַר מֵהַאי עָלְמָא, לָא אִסְתַּלָּק וְלָא אִתְאֲבִיד מִכָּלְהוּ עָלְמִין, דְּהָא בְּכֻלְּהוּ עָלְמִין אִשְׁתְּכַח יַתִּיר מֵחַיְּיוֹי. דִּבְחַיְּיוֹי אִשְׁתְּכַח בְּהַאי עָלְמָא בִּלְחוֹדוֹי, וּלְבָתַר אִשְׁתְּכַח בִּתְלַת עָלְמִין, וְזַמִּין לְגַבַּיְיהוּ, דִּכְתִיב עֲלָמוֹת אֲהֵבוּךְ, אַל תִּקְרֵי עֲלָמוֹת, אֶלָּא עוֹלָמוֹת. זַכָּאָה חוּלְקֵיהוֹן.

273. Therefore, we have learned that the righteous are not gone or lost from all worlds, even when he has departed this world. He is to be found in all the

worlds even more than during his lifetime, as he was located only in this world during his lifetime. Afterwards, he is in three worlds – NAMELY BRIYAH, YETZIRAH AND ASIYAH – and he is in them all, as it is written, "Therefore do the virgins (Heb. *alamot*) love you" (Shir Hashirim 1:3). Do not pronounce it *alamot* but *olamot* (lit. 'worlds'). Blessed is their share.

274. תָּאנָא, כְּתִיב וְהָיְתָה נֶפֶשׁ אֲדוֹנִי צְרוּרָה בִּצְרוֹר הַחַיִּים, וְהָיְתָה נֶפֶשׁ אֲדוֹנִי, נִשְׁמַת אֲדוֹנִי מִבָּעֵי לֵיהּ. אֶלָּא כְּמָה דְּאַמְרָן, דְּזַכָּאָה חוּלְקֵיהוֹן דְּצַדִּיקַיָּיא דְּכֹלָּא אִתְקְשַׁר דָּא בְּדָא, נֶפֶשׁ בְּרוּחַ וְרוּחַ בִּנְשָׁמָה, וּנְשָׁמָה בְּקוּדְשָׁא בְּרִיךְ הוּא. אִשְׁתְּכַח דְּנֶפֶשׁ צְרוּרָה בִּצְרוֹר הַחַיִּים.

274. We have learned that it is written, "Yet the soul (*Nefesh*) of my master shall be bound in the bond of life" (I Samuel 25:29). HE QUESTIONS: It says "the Nefesh of my Master," but it should read 'the Neshamah of my master', BECAUSE NEFESH REMAINS IN THIS WORLD AND ONLY NESHAMAH RISES TO THE BUNDLE OF LIFE. HE ANSWERS: As we said, fortunate is the share of the righteous men that everything is tied one to another – Nefesh with Ruach, Ruach with Neshamah and Neshamah with the Holy One, blessed be He. The result is that Nefesh is tied to the bond of life, AS IT IS CONNECTED TO NESHAMAH, WHICH IS THE BUNDLE OF LIFE.

275. א"ר אֶלְעָזָר, הַאי דְּאָמְרוּ חַבְרַיָּיא, גְּלוּתָא דס"ת אֲפִילוּ מִבֵּי כְּנִישְׁתָּא לְבֵי כְּנִישְׁתָּא אָחֳרָא אָסִיר. וכ"ש לְבֵי רְחוֹב, אֲמַאי לְבֵי רְחוֹב. א"ר יְהוּדָה, כְּמָה דְּאַמְרָן, בְּגִין דְּיִתְעָרוּן עָלֵיהּ וְיִתְבְּעוּן רַחֲמֵי עַל עָלְמָא. אָמַר ר' אַבָּא, שְׁכִינְתָּא כַּד אִתְגַּלְיָיא הָכִי נָמֵי מֵאֲתַר לַאֲתַר, עַד דְּאָמְרָה מִי יִתְּנֵנִי בַּמִּדְבָּר מְלוֹן אוֹרְחִים וְגוֹ' אוּף הָכָא בְּקַדְמֵיתָא מִבֵּי כְּנִישְׁתָּא לְבֵי כְּנִישְׁתָּא, לְבָתַר לְבֵי רְחוֹב, לְבָתַר בַּמִּדְבָּר מְלוֹן אוֹרְחִים. א"ר יְהוּדָה, בְּנֵי בָּבֶל מִסְתָּפוּ וְלָא קָא עַבְרֵי אֲפִילוּ מִבֵּי כְּנִישְׁתָּא לְבֵי כְּנִישְׁתָּא, כ"ש הַאי.

275. Rabbi Elazar said: Regarding that which the friends have said, it is forbidden to exile a Torah scroll even to be taken from one synagogue to another and certainly into the street. If so, why DO WE TAKE IT OUT into the street? Rabbi Yehuda replied: So it will awaken them to seek mercy for the

world. Rabbi Aba said that when the Shechinah went into exile, it also moved from place to place until She said, "Oh, that I were in the wilderness, in a lodging place of wayfaring men..." (Yirmeyah 9:1). Here too, at first the Torah is exiled from one synagogue to another and later into the street. Afterwards it is "in the wilderness, in a lodging place of wayfaring men." Rabbi Yehuda said: The Babylonians are reverent and do not pass the Torah scroll even from synagogue to synagogue and certainly not there, INTO THE STREET.

276. תַּנְיָא, אָמַר לְהוּ ר"ש לְחַבְרַיָּא, בְּיוֹמַאי לָא יִצְטָרְכוּן בְּנֵי עָלְמָא לְהַאי. אָ"ל רִבִּי יוֹסֵי, צַדִּיקַיָּיא מְגִינִּין עַל עָלְמָא בְּחַיֵּיהוֹן, וּבְמִיתָתְהוֹן יוֹתֵר מֵחַיֵּיהוֹן. הה"ד וְגַנּוֹתִי עַל הָעִיר הַזֹּאת לְהוֹשִׁיעָהּ לְמַעֲנִי וּלְמַעַן דָּוִד עַבְדִּי, וְאִילּוּ בְּחַיֵּיוֹהִי לָא כְּתִיב. א"ר יְהוּדָה מַאי שְׁנָא הָכָא דִּכְתִּיב לְמַעֲנִי וּלְמַעַן דָּוִד עַבְדִּי, דְּשָׁקִיל הַאי לְגַבֵּי הַאי. אֶלָּא, בְּגִין דְּדָוִד זָכָה לְאִתְקַשְּׁרָא בִּרְתִיכָא קַדִּישָׁא דַּאֲבָהָתָא, ובג"כ כֹּלָּא חַד, בְּרִיךְ הוּא לְעָלַם וּלְעָלְמֵי עָלְמַיָּא.

276. We have learned that Rabbi Shimon said to the friends: In my day, there will not be a need for mankind to do this, TO BRING OUT A TORAH SCROLL INTO THE STREET. Rabbi Yosi said to him: The righteous shield the world during their lifetime and even more so after their death, as it is written, "For I will defend this city to save it for My own sake, and for the sake of David My servant" (Yeshayah 37:35). Yet during the lifetime OF DAVID, it was not expressed. Rabbi Yehuda said, Why is this verse different, saying, "For My own sake, and for the sake of David My servant," giving the two equal importance? HE ANSWERS: The reason is that David merited to be joined to the holy Chariot of the Patriarchs, AS HE IS FOURTH TO THEM, THE SECRET OF MALCHUT. For this reason, everything is one. Blessed is He for ever and ever.

46. Tamar

A Synopsis

Rabbi Yitzchak says that the Holy Name is both concealed and revealed, that the Torah is both concealed and revealed, and that every verse and portion of the Torah is both concealed and revealed, there is always both a literal explanation and its mystery. The rabbis talk about Tamar, and Rabbi Aba wonders about "the entrance of eyes" spoken of in scripture. Rabbi Shimon explains that it has to do with the door or entrance by which one can see God. He interprets the story of Tamar as told in Beresheet, and it is obvious that there are both literal and esoteric explanations. Rabbi Aba says that the concealed matters of the Torah are given to saintly people, while the revealed, or obvious, matters are given to the rest of the people.

277. כְּמַעֲשֵׂה אֶרֶץ מִצְרַיִם אֲשֶׁר יְשַׁבְתֶּם בָּהּ לֹא תַעֲשׂוּ, ר' יִצְחָק פָּתַח, לְסַפֵּר בְּצִיּוֹן שֵׁם יְיָ' וּתְהִלָּתוֹ בִּירוּשָׁלָם. תַּמָּן תָּנֵינָן, שְׁמָא קַדִּישָׁא סָתִים וְגַלְיָא. וְאוֹרַיְיתָא דְּהִיא שְׁמָא קַדִּישָׁא עִלָּאָה, סָתִים וְגַלְיָא. וְכָל קְרָא דִּבְאוֹרַיְיתָא, וְכָל פַּרְשָׁתָא דְּאוֹרַיְיתָא, סָתִים וְגַלְיָא.

277. "After the doings of the land of Egypt, in which you dwelt, shall you not do" (Vayikra 18:3). Rabbi Yitzchak opened the discussion saying, "That men may declare the name of Hashem in Zion, and His praise in Jerusalem" (Tehilim 102:22). From there, we learned that the Holy Name is both concealed and revealed. THE CONCEALED IS YUD HEI VAV HEI AND THE REVEALED IS ADONAI. The Torah, which is the Holy Name on high OF ZEIR ANPIN, is concealed and revealed. Every verse in the Torah, every portion of Torah is concealed and revealed, MEANING THERE IS A LITERAL EXPLANATION AND ITS MYSTERY.

278. דְּתַנְיָא א"ר יְהוּדָה, מֵחֲצִיפוּתָא דְּצִדְקַת חֲדָא, נַפְקָן כְּמָה טָבָאן לְעָלְמָא. וּמַאן הִיא. תָּמָר. דִּכְתִּיב וַתֵּשֶׁב בְּפֶתַח עֵינַיִם. אָמַר רִבִּי אַבָּא, פַּרְשָׁתָא דָא מוֹכַח, דְּאוֹרַיְיתָא סָתִים וְגַלְיָא. וְהָא אִסְתַּכַּלְנָא בְּאוֹרַיְיתָא כֻּלָּא, וְלָא אַשְׁכַּחְנָא אֲתַר דְּאִקְרֵי פֶּתַח עֵינַיִם, אֶלָּא כֹּלָּא סָתִים, וְרָזָא דִּרְזִין הוּא.

278. We have learned that Rabbi Yehuda said: From the boldness of one righteous woman, many good things came to the world. Who is She? It is Tamar, as it is written, "And sat by the entrance of Enayim (lit. 'eyes')" (Beresheet 38:14). Rabbi Aba said: This portion proves TO US that Torah is both concealed and revealed, AND IT CONTAINS REVEALED MATTERS AND HIDDEN. I have looked through the entire Torah and I have not found anywhere a place called the entrance of eyes. This is because it is all concealed, mysteries among mysteries.

279. וְתָנֵינָא, מַאי חָמָאת צַדֶּקֶת זוֹ לְעוֹבָדָא דָא. אֶלָּא יַדְעַת בְּבֵיתָא דַּחֲמוֹהִי אָרְחוֹי דְּקוּדְשָׁא בְּרִיךְ הוּא, הֵיךְ מַדְבַּר הַאי עָלְמָא עִם בְּנֵי נָשָׁא. וּבְגִין דְּהִיא יַדְעַת, קוּדְשָׁא בְּרִיךְ הוּא אוֹקִים מִלָּה עַל יְדָהָא. וְאַזְלָא הָא כְּמָה דְּתָנֵינָן, אִזְדַּמְּנַת הֲוַת בַּת שֶׁבַע מוּ' יְמֵי בְּרֵאשִׁית לְמֶהֱוֵי אִמֵּיהּ דִּשְׁלֹמֹה מַלְכָּא. אוּף הָכָא אִזְדַּמְּנַת הֲוַת תָּמָר לְדָא, מִיּוֹמָא דְּאִתְבְּרֵי עָלְמָא.

279. We have learned, what did this pious woman contemplate that she did such a thing? HE ANSWERS: She understood from being in the house of her father-in-law the ways of the Holy One, blessed be He, NAMELY how He conducts this world with its human beings. Because she knew this, the Holy One, blessed be He, set up this matter to happen through her. This matter goes along the same line, as we have learned. Batsheba was designated FOR DAVID from the six days of Creation to be the mother of King Solomon. Here too, Tamar was designated for this from the creation of the world.

280. וַתֵּשֶׁב בְּפֶתַח עֵינַיִם, מַאן פֶּתַח עֵינַיִם כְּמָה דְּאַתְּ אָמֵר, וְהוּא יוֹשֵׁב פֶּתַח הָאֹהֶל. וּכְתִיב, וּפָסַח יְיָ' עַל הַפֶּתַח. וּכְתִיב פִּתְחוּ לִי שַׁעֲרֵי צֶדֶק וְגוֹ'. עֵינַיִם: דְּכָל עַיְינִין דְּעָלְמָא לְהַאי פִּתְחָא מְצַפָּאן. אֲשֶׁר עַל דֶּרֶךְ תִּמְנָתָה, מַאי תִּמְנָתָה. כד"א וּתְמוּנַת יְיָ' יַבִּיט. וְהָכִי אוֹקִימְנָא, תָּמָר אוֹקִימַת מִלָּה לְתַתָּא, וּפַרְחַת פַּרְחִין, וְאָנִיצַת עַנְפִין בְּרָזָא דִמְהֵימְנוּתָא.

280. "And sat by the entrance of Enayim": HE QUESTIONS: What is "the entrance of Enayim"? HE ANSWERS: It is as it says, "As he sat by the tent door" (Beresheet 18:1), "Hashem will pass over the door" (Shemot 12:23)

and, "Open to me the gates of righteousness" (Tehilim 118:19). "Enayim (lit. 'eyes')": The eyes of the whole world look to this door "which is by the way to Timna" (Beresheet 38:14). What is Timna? The verse reads, "And the similitude (heb. *tmunah*) of Hashem does he behold" (Bemidbar 12:8). So we explained that Tamar carried this out below, flowers appeared and branches sprouted in the secret of the Faith.

281. וִיהוּדָה עוֹד רָד עִם אֵל וְעִם קְדוֹשִׁים נֶאֱמָן. וַיִּרְאָהָ יְהוּדָה וַיַּחְשְׁבֶהָ לְזוֹנָה וְגוֹ'. כד"א, כֵּן דֶּרֶךְ אִשָּׁה מְנָאָפֶת. כִּי כִסְּתָה פָּנֶיהָ, וְאוֹקִימְנָא כִּי כִסְּתָה פָּנֶיהָ, כד"א, אָכְלָה וּמָחֲתָה פִיהָ, אוֹקִידַת עָלְמָא בְּשַׁלְהוֹבוֹי, וְאָמְרָה לֹא פָעַלְתִּי אָוֶן. מ"ט. בְּגִין כִּי כִסְּתָה פָּנֶיהָ, וְלֵית מַאן דְּיָדַע אוֹרְחָהָא, לְאִשְׁתְּזָבָא מִנַּהּ. וַיֵּט אֵלֶיהָ אֶל הַדֶּרֶךְ, אֶל הַדֶּרֶךְ מַמָּשׁ, לְאִתְחַבְּרָא חִוָּרָא בְּסוּמְקָא. וַיֹּאמֶר הָבָה נָא אָבֹא אֵלַיִךְ וְגוֹ', הָא אוֹקִימְנָא הָבָה בְּכָל אֲתַר.

281. "But Judah still rules with El, and is faithful with holy ones" (Hoshea 12:1). "When Judah saw her, he thought her to be a harlot..." (Beresheet 38:15) as the verse states, "Likewise the way of an adulterous woman" (Mishlei 30:20). "Because she had covered her face" (Beresheet 38:15): We have learned that "she had covered her face," MEANING similar to what you say, "She eats, and wipes her mouth" (Mishlei 30:20). She torched the world with her flames, "and says, I have done nothing wrong" (Ibid.). What is the reason? It is "because she had covered her face" and no one knows her ways in order to save themselves from her. "And he turned to her by the way" (Beresheet 38:16), to the way literally, to make white join with red. "And said, I pray you, let me come in to you..." (Ibid.). We established THAT "let me" always MEANS INVITATION.

282. כִּי לֹא יָדַע כִּי כַלָּתוֹ הִיא. כִּי כַלָּתוֹ הִיא דְּעָלְמָא, מְתַרְגְּמִינָן אֲרֵי שֵׁצָיַיתָא דְּעָלְמָא הִיא. מַאי טַעֲמָא לָא יָדַע. בְּגִין דְּהָא מְנַהֲרָן אַנְפָּהָא, לְקַבְּלָא מִנֵּיהּ, וְאִזְדַּמְּנָא לְאִתְבַּסְּמָא וּלְרַחֲמָא עָלְמָא ד"א כִּי כַלָּתוֹ הִיא, דָּא כַּלָּה מַמָּשׁ, דִּכְתִיב אִתִּי מִלְּבָנוֹן כַּלָּה.

282. "For he knew not that she was his daughter in law (Heb. *kalah*)" (Ibid.), MEANING the destruction (Heb. *kelayah*) of the world, as translated

-351-

into Aramaic, WHICH MEANS THAT HE DID NOT KNOW SHE WAS
DESTROYING THE WORLD, as *kalah* is derived from *kelayah*. Why did he
not know? Because she welcomed him so as to receive from him. She came
there to be alleviate and bestow mercy upon the world. ANOTHER
EXPLANATION FOR, "She was his daughter in law" is literally a bride (Heb.
kalah), as is written, "My bride (Heb. *kalah*), with me from Lebanon" (Shir
Hashirim 4:8).

283. וַתֹּאמֶר מַה תִּתֶּן לִי כִּי כִּי תָבֹא אֵלָי. הַשְׁתָּא כַּלָּה בַּעְיָא תַּכְשִׁיטָהָא.
וַיֹּאמֶר אָנֹכִי אֲשַׁלַּח גְּדִי עִזִּים מִן הַצֹּאן. לְמַלְכָּא דַּהֲוָה לֵיהּ בְּרָא
מֵאֲמָהוּ חֲדָא, וְאָזִיל בְּהֵיכָלָא, בָּעָא מַלְכָּא לְאִתְנַסְּבָא בְּמַטְרוֹנִיתָא
עִלָּאָה, וּלְאַעֲלָאָה בְּהֵיכָלֵיהּ. אָמְרָה מַאן יָהִיב לֵיהּ לְדֵין בְּהֵיכָלֵיהּ
דְּמַלְכָּא. אָמַר מַלְכָּא, מִכָּאן וּלְהָלְאָה אֲשַׁדַּר וְאַתְרִיךְ לִבְרָא דְּאָמַהוּ
מֵהֵיכָלָא דִּילִי.

283. "And she said, What will you give me, that you may come in to me?"
(Beresheet 38:16). Now the bride needs jewels. "And he said, I will send
you a kid from the flock" (Ibid. 17). THIS IS LIKE a king who had a son born
to him from a maidservant who used to walk about the palace. The king
wanted to marry a lady from high nobility and bring her to the palace. So
she said: Who allowed this one in the king's palace? The king said: From
now on, I will expel the son of the maidservant from my palace.

284. כַּךְ נָמֵי הָכָא, אָנֹכִי אֲשַׁלַּח גְּדִי עִזִּים מִן הַצֹּאן. וְהָא אוֹקִימְנָא,
בְּלָא תְבַשֵּׁל גְּדִי. וְכָל אִינּוּן בְּסִטְרָא דִּבְכוֹר בְּהֶמָה קָא אָתוּ. וְעַל דָּא
לָא כְּתִיב אָנֹכִי אֶתֵּן, אֶלָּא אָנֹכִי אֲשַׁלַּח, אַתְרִיךְ וְאַשְׁדָּר לֵיהּ, דְּלָא
יִשְׁתְּכַח בְּהֵיכָלִי.

284. Also here, "I will send you a kid from the flock." We established WHAT
IS MEANT BY A KID IN, "You shall not boil a kid" (Shemot 34:26). IT
REFERS TO THE OTHER SIDE THAT NURSES FROM MALCHUT BEFORE
SHE IS PURIFIED, and all these stem from the firstborn of cattle. Therefore,
it is not written: 'I will give', but "I will send," MEANING I will expel and
send it away so it shall not be in my palace.

285(1). וַתֹּאמֶר אִם תִּתֵּן עֵרָבוֹן עַד שָׁלְחֶךָ. אִלֵּין אִינוּן סִימָנִין
דְּמַטְרוֹנִיתָא, דְּאִתְבָּרְכָא מִן מַלְכָּא בְּזִוּוּגָהָא. וַיֹּאמֶר מַה הָעֵרָבוֹן אֲשֶׁר
אֶתֶּן לָךְ, וַתֹּאמֶר חוֹתָמְךָ וּפְתִילֶךָ וּמַטֶּךָ. אִלֵּין אִינוּן קִטְרֵי עִלָּאֵי,
תַּכְשִׁיטָהָא דְּכַלָּה אִתְבָּרְכָא מִתְּלָתָא אִלֵּין, נֶצַח הוֹד יְסוֹד, וְכֹלָּא
אִשְׁתְּכַח בִּתְלָתָא אִלֵּין וְכַלָּה מֵהָכָא מִתְבָּרְכָא. מִיַּד וַיִּתֶּן לָהּ וַיָּבֹא
אֵלֶיהָ וַתַּהַר לוֹ.

285a. "And she said, Will you give me a pledge, till you send it?"
(Beresheet 38:17) These are the marks of a Queen blessed by the King
during her nuptials. And he said: What pledge shall I give you? And she
said: Your signet, and your cord, and your staff (Ibid. 18). These are the
heavenly bonds, the jewels of the Bride who is blessed by these three –
NAMELY Netzach, Hod and Yesod. Everything is contained within these
three. The Bride is blessed from this. Immediately, "he gave it her, and
came in to her, and she conceived by him" (Ibid.).

285(2). וַיְהִי כְּמִשְׁלֹשׁ חֲדָשִׁים. מַאן מִשְׁלֹשׁ חֲדָשִׁים. בָּתַר דְּיִתְלָתוּן
יַרְחַיָּא, וְהָא ג' יַרְחִין אוּקִימְנָא. וְהָכָא כְּמִשְׁלֹשׁ חֲדָשִׁים, דְּשָׁארֵי יַרְחָא
רְבִיעָאָה לְאִתְעָרָא דִּינִין בְּעָלְמָא בְּחוֹבֵי בְּנֵי נָשָׁא, וְהִיא יַנְקָא מִסִּטְרָא
אַחֲרָא. כְּדֵין, וַיֻּגַּד לִיהוּדָה לֵאמֹר זָנְתָה תָּמָר כַּלָּתֶךָ, הָא כַּלָּה בְּסִטְרָא
אַחֲרָא אִשְׁתְּכַחַת. מַה כְּתִיב, הוֹצִיאוּהָ. כְּמָה דִּכְתִיב, הִשְׁלִיךְ מִשָּׁמַיִם
אֶרֶץ תִּפְאֶרֶת יִשְׂרָאֵל. וְתִשָּׂרֵף, בְּשַׁלְהוֹבֵי טִיהֲרָא בְּגָלוּתָא.

285b. "And it came to pass about three months after" (Ibid. 24). HE
QUESTIONS: What is meant by three months? HE ANSWERS: After a tripled
month. The three months ARE CHESED, GVURAH AND TIFERET, as we
have established. HERE IT IS WRITTEN, "About three months," MEANING as
the fourth month began, DENOTING MALCHUT, to stir up the Judgments in
the world due to the sins of mankind and to nurture from the Other Side.
Then, "it was told Judah, saying, Tamar your daughter in law has played the
harlot" (Ibid.), so the bride is found on the Other Side. It is written, "Bring
her out" (Ibid.) as the verse says, "And cast down from heaven (to) earth the
beauty of Yisrael" (Eichah 2:1). "And let her be burnt" (Beresheet 38:24)
with a flaming fire in exile.

285(3). מַה כְּתִיב, הִיא מוּצֵאת, לְאִתְמַשְׁכָא בְּגָלוּתָא. וְהִיא שָׁלְחָה אֶל חָמִיהָ לֵאמֹר לְאִישׁ אֲשֶׁר אֵלֶּה לּוֹ. לְאִישׁ אֲשֶׁר אֵלֶּה מִמֶּנּוּ לָא כְּתִיב, אֶלָּא לְאִישׁ אֲשֶׁר אֵלֶּה לּוֹ. דִּילֵיהּ סִימָנִין אִלֵּין מִשְׁתַּכְּחִין, אָנֹכִי הָרָה. מִיָּד וַיַּכֵּר יְהוּדָה וַיֹּאמֶר צָדְקָה מִמֶּנִּי. צָדְקָה וַדַּאי, וּשְׁמָא גְּרִים. מַאן גְּרִים לָהּ, שְׁמָא דָּא. הֲדָר וְאָמַר מִמֶּנִּי, דִּכְתִיב כִּי צַדִּיק יְיָ' צְדָקוֹת אָהֵב יָשָׁר יֶחֱזוּ פָּנֵימוֹ. צְדָקָה: צֶדֶק ה', דְּמִמֶּנִּי נַטְלַת שְׁמָא דָּא. מִמֶּנִּי יָרְתָא, מִמֶּנִּי אִשְׁתְּכַחַת.

285c. It is written, "When she was brought forth" to be drawn into the exile, "She sent to her father-in-law, saying, By the man whose these are, I AM WITH CHILD" (Ibid. 25). It is not written: 'from whom these are', but "whose these are," WHICH MEANS these items are proof of him by whom I am with child. THESE WERE BRIDAL ORNAMENTS AND THEY HAD ALREADY BECOME HERS, AS EARLIER MENTIONED, BUT ONLY HE GAVE THEM. Immediately, "And Judah acknowledged them, and said, She has been more righteous (Heb. *tzedakah*) than I" (Ibid. 26). Assuredly she is righteous, for this was brought about by that name, FOR SO IS MALCHUT CALLED. What brought upon her this name? He continued, "than I (also: 'from me')," as it is written, "For Hashem is righteous, He loves righteousness (Heb. *tzedakah*); the upright shall behold His face" (Tehilim 11:7). This is because *tzedakah* is justice (Heb. *tzedek*) and Hei, and she received that name from me. She inherited IT from me and all this is come from me.

286. א"ר יוֹסֵי, מ"ט חָמִיהָ כְּתִיב בְּאֲתַר חַד, יְהוּדָה בַּאֲתַר אָחֳרָא. אָ"ל, כֹּלָּא אִתְקְטַר דָּא בְּדָא. חָמִיהָ, בְּאֲתַר עִלָּאָה תַּלְיָ.

286. Rabbi Yosi said: What is the reason that in one place it states, "her father-in-law" and in another place it states, "And Judah"? He replied: Everything is intertwined. "Her father-in-law" refers to a subliminal meaning.

287. א"ר אֶלְעָזָר, פַּרְשָׁתָא דָּא אוּקִימְנָא בְּרָזָא עִלָּאָה, בְּכַמָּה גַּוְונִין. כַּד יִסְתַּכְּלוּן מִלֵּי, מִינָהּ יִשְׁתְּמַע רָזִין דְּאוֹרְחוֹי דְקוּדְשָׁא בְּרִיךְ הוּא,

וְדִינוֹי בְּכָל אֲתַר. וְהִיא יַדְעַת וְאַקְדִימַת גַּרְמָאָה לְמִלָּה דָּא, לְאַשְׁלָמָא אוֹרְחוֹי דְּקוּדְשָׁא בְּרִיךְ הוּא, בְּגִין דְּיִנְפְּקוּ מִינָהּ מַלְכִין שַׁלִּיטִין, וּזְמִינִין לְשַׁלְטָאָה עַל עָלְמָא. וְרוּת כְּהַאי גַּוְונָא עַבְדַּת.

287. Rabbi Elazar said: We have established this portion in esoteric terms in several ways. When we look into these words, we hear from it the secrets of the ways of the Holy One, blessed be He, and His Judgments everywhere, AS WE EARLIER EXPLAINED. TAMAR knew ALL THIS and she prepared herself for this to complement the ways of the Holy One, blessed be He, in order that kings and rulers would descend from He who will rule the world. Ruth did the same thing; ALSO RUTH IMPLORED BOAZ FOR A LEVIRATE MARRIAGE LIKE TAMAR.

288. א"ר אַבָּא, פַּרְשְׁתָּא דָּא בְּרָזָא דְּחָכְמְתָא דְּאוֹרַיְיתָא אִתְקַשְׁרָא, וְכֹלָּא סָתִים וְגַלְיָא. וְאוֹרַיְיתָא כֹּלָּא כְּהַאי גַּוְונָא אִשְׁתְּכַחַת. וְלֵית לָךְ מִלָּה בְּאוֹרַיְיתָא, דְּלָא רָשִׁים בָּהּ שְׁמָא קַדִּישָׁא עִלָּאָה, דְּסָתִים וְגַלְיָא. בְּגִינֵי כַּךְ, סְתִימֵי דְּאוֹרַיְיתָא, קַדִּישֵׁי עֶלְיוֹנִין יָרְתִין לָהּ, וְאִתְגַּלְיָא בִּשְׁאָר בְּנֵי עָלְמָא. כְּגַוְונָא דָּא כְּתִיב, לְסַפֵּר בְּצִיּוֹן שֵׁם יְיָ' וּתְהִלָּתוֹ בִּירוּשָׁלָם, דְּהָא בְּצִיּוֹן בְּמַקְדְּשָׁא, שָׁרֵי לְאַדְכְּרָא שְׁמָא קַדִּישָׁא כַּדְקָא חֲזֵי. וּלְבַר בְּכִינּוּיוֹ. וְעַל דָּא כֹּלָּא סָתִים וְגַלְיָא. תָּאנָא, כָּל מַאן דְּגָרַע אֶת חַד מֵאוֹרַיְיתָא. אוֹ יוֹסִיף אֶת חַד בְּאוֹרַיְיתָא, כְּמַאן דִּמְשַׁקֵּר בִּשְׁמָא קַדִּישָׁא עִלָּאָה דְּמַלְכָּא.

288. Rabbi Aba said: This portion is tied to esoteric wisdom of the Torah. It is all concealed yet revealed, MEANING THERE IS IN IT ESOTERIC AND LITERAL EXPLANATIONS. The entire Torah is similar this way, IN HIDDEN SUBLIME MEANINGS AND THE LITERAL EXPLANATIONS. There is not a matter of Torah in which the Holy subliminal Name is not impressed, which is both concealed and revealed. The concealed matters of Torah are bequeathed to the highly saintly ones and THE REVEALED MATTERS are revealed to the rest of the people. In relation to this, it is written, "That men may declare the name of Hashem in Zion, and His praise in Jerusalem" (Tehilim 102:22). "In Zion" refers to the Temple, where it is permitted to pronounce the Holy Name, YUD HEI VAV HEI, in the proper fashion.

However, outside THE TEMPLE, only the appelation can be mentioned, NAMELY ADONAI, BUT NOT THE WAY IT IS WRITTEN. Everything is concealed and yet revealed, AS THE NAME, YUD HEI VAV HEI, WHICH ONE IS FORBIDDEN TO MENTION, IS CONCEALED, BUT THE NAME ADONAI WHICH WE MENTION IS REVEALED. ALL MATTERS ARE IN THIS WAY. We have learned that anyone who deducts one letter from the Torah or adds one letter is like one who is false to the supernal Holy Name of the King.

47. The practices of Egypt

A Synopsis
Rabbi Yitzchak talks about the idolatry of the Egyptians, and Rabbi Chiya says that in the future God will cleanse His land from all the idolatrous nations.

289. א"ר יִצְחָק, עוֹבָדָא דְּמִצְרַיִם פַּלְחִין לְשִׁפְחָה, כְּמָה דְאוֹקִימְנָא. עוֹבָדָא דִּכְנַעַן, פַּלְחִין לְהַהוּא דְּאִקְרֵי שְׁבִי אֲשֶׁר בְּבֵית הַבּוֹר. וְעַל דָּא כְּתִיב, אָרוּר כְּנָעַן עֶבֶד עֲבָדִים יִהְיֶה לְאֶחָיו. בְּג"כ כֻּלְּהוּ מְכַדְּבִין בְּמִלִּין קַדִּישִׁין, וְעַבְדִּין עוֹבָדִין בְּכֹלָּא. בְּגִינֵי כָּךְ כְּמַעֲשֵׂה אֶרֶץ מִצְרַיִם אֲשֶׁר יְשַׁבְתֶּם בָּהּ וְגו'. ר' יְהוּדָה אָמַר, דְּעַבְדִּין דִּינִין בִּישִׁין לְשַׁלְטָא עַל אַרְעָא, כד"א וְלֹא תְטַמֵּא אֶת אַדְמָתְךָ. וּכְתִיב וַתִּטְמָא הָאָרֶץ.

289. Rabbi Yitzchak said: IT WAS the practices of Egypt THAT THEY USED to worship the maidservant, MEANING THE KLIPAH CALLED MAIDSERVANT, as we have explained. The practice of Canaan WAS TO worship THAT PLACE called "the captive that was in the dungeon" (Shemot 12:29). Therefore, it is written, "Cursed be Canaan; a servant of servants shall he be to his brethren" (Beresheet 9:25). For this reason, they all falsified in matters of holiness and everything practiced IDOLATRY. For this reason, IT IS WRITTEN, "After the doings of the land of Egypt, in which you dwelt..." (Vayikra 18:3). Rabbi Yehuda said: They created evil Judgments that will rule over the land, NAMELY MALCHUT, as the verse says, "That your land be not defiled" (Devarim 21:23) and, "And the land is defiled" (Vayikra 18:27).

290. כְּמַעֲשֵׂה אֶרֶץ מִצְרַיִם וְגו', רַבִּי חִיָּיא פָּתַח, לְאֶחוֹז בְּכַנְפוֹת הָאָרֶץ וְגו', תָּאנָא, זַמִּין קוּדְשָׁא בְּרִיךְ הוּא לְדַכְּאָה לְאַרְעֵיהּ, מִכָּל מְסָאֲבוּתָא דְּעַמִּין עע"ז, דְּסָאִיבוּ לָהּ. כְּהַאי מַאן דְּאָחִיד בְּטַלִּיתֵיהּ, וְאַנְעַר טְנוּפָא מִנֵּיהּ. וְכָל אִינוּן דְּאִתְקְבָרוּ בְּאַרְעָא קַדִּישָׁא, לְמִשְׁדֵּי לוֹן לְבַר, וּלְדַכְּאָה אַרְעָא קַדִּישָׁא מִסִּטְרָא אָחֳרָא, כִּבְיָכוֹל דַּהֲוָה מַתְזְנָא לִשְׁאַר רַבְרְבֵי עַמִּין, וּלְקַבְּלָא מְסָאֲבוּתָא דִּלְהוֹן, וּלְדַבְּרָא לוֹן. וְזַמִּין לְדַכְּאָה לָהּ לְאַעֲבָרָא לוֹן לְבַר.

290. "After the doings of the land of Egypt": Rabbi Chiya said, "That it might take hold of the ends of the earth, that the wicked might be shaken out of it" (Iyov 38:13). We have learned that the Holy One, blessed be He, in the future will cleanse His land, MALCHUT, from all the defilement of the idolatrous nations that defiled it, just as one takes hold of a garment and shakes out from it all the filth, referring to all THE WICKED buried in the Holy Land. SO HE WILL SHAKE OUT THE LAND in order to cast them out and IN ORDER to purify the Holy Land, DENOTING MALCHUT, from the Other Side. It is as if it was sustaining the other ministers of the nations, from whom it received defilement in order to guide them. And He will cleanse it and remove THE MINISTERS OF THE NATIONS to the outside.

48. "But when you entered, you defiled My land"

A Synopsis
Rabbi Yehuda tells us how fortunate people are who live in the Holy Land, and how they will deserve later to live in the higher Holy land. He speaks about the consequences of dying in the Holy Land and dying elsewhere.

291. ר' שִׁמְעוֹן הֲוָה מַדְכֵּי שׁוּקֵי דִּטְבֶרְיָא, וְכָל דַּהֲוָה תַּמָּן מִית, הֲוָה סָלִיק לֵיהּ, וּמְדַכֵּי אַרְעָא. תָּאנָא, כְּתִיב וַתָּבֹאוּ וַתְּטַמְּאוּ אֶת אַרְצִי וְגוֹ', אָמַר רִבִּי יְהוּדָה זַכָּאָה חוּלָקֵיהּ מַאן דְּזָכֵי בְּחַיָּיוֹי לְמִשְׁרֵי מָדוֹרָא בְּאַרְעָא קַדִּישָׁא. דְּכָל מַאן דְּזָכֵי לָהּ, זָכֵי לְאַנְגָּדָא מִטַּלָּא דִּשְׁמַיָּא דִּלְעֵילָּא, דְּנָחִית עַל אַרְעָא. וְכָל מַאן דְּזָכֵי לְאִתְקַשְׁרָא בְּחַיָּיוֹי בְּהַאי אַרְעָא קַדִּישָׁא, זָכֵי לְאִתְקַשְׁרָא לְבָתַר בְּאַרְעָא קַדִּישָׁא עִלָּאָה.

291. Rabbi Shimon was cleansing the marketplaces of Tiberias. He dug out all the dead that were there, and cleansed the land. We have learned that it is written, "But when you entered, you defiled My land" (Yirmeyah 2:7). Rabbi Yehuda said: Fortunate is the portion of he who deserves during his lifetime to make his dwelling in the Holy Land. All who merit it will cause the dew of the heaven above to continue to descend upon the earth, so all who deserve the Holy Land in this lifetime will later deserve the higher Holy Land, MALCHUT.

292. וְכָל מַאן דְּלָא זָכֵי בְּחַיָּיוֹי, וּמַיְיתִין לֵיהּ לְאִתְקַבְּרָא תַּמָּן, עֲלֵיהּ כְּתִיב, וְנַחֲלָתִי שַׂמְתֶּם לְתוֹעֵבָה. רוּחֵיהּ נָפִיק בִּרְשׁוּתָא נוּכְרָאָה אָחֳרָא, וְגוּפֵיהּ אָתֵי תְּחוֹת רְשׁוּתָא דְּאַרְעָא קַדִּישָׁא כְּבִיכוֹל, עָבֵיד קֹדֶשׁ חוֹל, וְחוֹל קֹדֶשׁ. וְכָל מַאן דְּזָכֵי לְמֵיפַק נִשְׁמָתֵיהּ בְּאַרְעָא קַדִּישָׁא, אִתְכַּפָּרוּ חוֹבוֹי, וְזָכֵי לְאִתְקַשְׁרָא תְּחוֹת גַּדְפּוֹי דִּשְׁכִינְתָּא, דִּכְתִיב וְכִפֶּר אַדְמָתוֹ עַמּוֹ. וְלֹא עוֹד אֶלָּא אִי זָכֵי בְּחַיָּיוֹי, זָכֵי לְאִתְמַשְּׁכָא עֲלֵיהּ רוּחָא קַדִּישָׁא תָּדִיר, וְכָל מַאן דְּיָתִיב בִּרְשׁוּתָא אָחֳרָא, אִתְמְשַׁךְ עֲלֵיהּ רוּחָא אָחֳרָא נוּכְרָאָה.

292. About all those who did not merit during their lifetime TO BE IN THE HOLY LAND and are brought there later to be buried, it is written, "And made My heritage an abomination" (Ibid.). His spirit expired under another, strange dominion and his body came under the dominion of the Holy Land, so he made, so to speak, the sacred profane and the profane sacred. Those who deserve that their souls expire in the Holy Land will have their sins forgiven and will merit to be bound under the wings of the Shechinah, as it is written, "And will forgive His land" (Devarim 32:43). Moreover, if he merits during his lifetime TO BE IN THE HOLY LAND, he will merit to have drawn upon him consistently the Holy Spirit. Those who dwell under another dominion, MEANING OUTSIDE THE HOLY LAND, will have drawn upon them a foreign spirit.

293. תָּאנָא, כַּד סָלִיק רַב הַמְנוּנָא סָבָא לְהָתָם, הֲווֹ עִמֵּיהּ תְּרֵיסַר בְּנֵי מְתִיבְתָּא דִּילֵיהּ, אָמַר לוֹן, אִי אֲנָא אָזִיל לְאָרְחָא דָא, לָאו עַל דִּידִי קָא עֲבִידְנָא, אֶלָּא לְאָתָבָא פִּקְדוֹנָא לְמָארֵיהּ. תָּנֵינָן כָּל אִינוּן דְּלָא זָכוּ לְהַאי בְּחַיֵּיוֹי, אָתִיבִין פִּקְדוֹנָא דְּמָארֵיהוֹן לְאָחֳרָא.

293. We have learned that when Rav Hamnuna Saba (the elder) ascended there, THE HOLY LAND, he had with him twelve members of his Yeshiva students. He said to them: If I go this way, it is not for my own sake that I do so but to return the pledge to its owner. We have learned that all those who did not merit this, TO LIVE IN THE HOLY LAND, during their lifetime must return the Master's pledge to another, NAMELY THE SOUL THAT WAS GIVEN TO THEM, TO THE OTHER SIDE.

294. א"ר יִצְחָק, בְּגִינֵי כַּךְ, כָּל מַאן דְּאַעְבָּר מֵאִינוּן זִינִין בִּישִׁין, אוֹ רְשׁוּתָא אָחֳרָא בְּאַרְעָא, אַרְעָא אִסְתְּאָבַת, וַוי לֵיהּ לְהַהוּא גְּבַר, וַוי לְנַפְשֵׁיהּ, דְּהָא אַרְעָא קַדִּישָׁא לָא מְקַבְּלָא לֵיהּ לְבָתַר. עֲלֵיהּ כְּתִיב, יִתַּמּוּ חַטָּאִים מִן הָאָרֶץ, בעה"ז, ובעה"ב, וּרְשָׁעִים עוֹד אֵינָם, בִּתְחִיַּית הַמֵּתִים, כְּדֵין בָּרְכִי נַפְשִׁי אֶת יְיָ' הַלְלוּיָהּ.

294. Rabbi Yitzchak said: Because of this, whoever brings into the land any of the evil beings or other domains defiles the land. Woe is to him, woe to his soul, as the Holy Land will not receive him after that. Of him, it is

written, "The sinners will be consumed out of the earth" (Tehilim 104:35) in this world and the World to Come. Then, "the wicked will be no more" (Ibid.) during the resurrection of the dead. Then "Bless you Hashem, my soul, Haleluyah" (Ibid.).

49. The Holy One, blessed be He, the Torah and Yisrael

A Synopsis

Rabbi Aba says that because of the holy covenant, Yisrael are fortunate that God has given them truthful statutes and planted them with the Tree of Life and placed the Shechinah among them. Rabbi Shimon says there are three levels intertwined with each other, meaning God, the Torah and Yisrael; each of them has a hidden level and a revealed level. All who are circumcised are given the revealed words of the Torah and are given the strict commandments, and only those who are of higher levels are given the supernal meanings of the Torah.

295. אֶת מִשְׁפָּטַי תַּעֲשׂוּ וְאֶת חֻקֹתַי תִּשְׁמְרוּ לָלֶכֶת בָּהֶם וְגוֹ', רְבִּי אַבָּא אָמַר, זַכָּאָה חוּלָקָא דְיִשְׂרָאֵל, דְקוּדְשָׁא בְּרִיךְ הוּא אִתְרְעֵי בְּהוּ מִכָּל עַמִּין עע"ז, וּבְגִין רְחִימוּתָא דִילֵיהּ עָלַיְיהוּ, יָהִיב לוֹן נִימוּסִין דִקְשׁוֹט, נָטַע בְּהוּ אִילָנָא דְחַיֵּי, אַשְׁרֵי שְׁכִינְתָּא בֵּינַיְיהוּ. מ"ט. בְּגִין דְיִשְׂרָאֵל רְשִׁימִין בִּרְשִׁימָא קַדִישָׁא בְּבִשְׂרַיְיהוֹן. וְאִשְׁתְּמוֹדְעָן דְאִינְהוּ דִילֵיהּ, מִבְּנֵי הֵיכָלֵיהּ.

295. "You shall do My Judgments, and keep My ordinances, to walk in them..." (Vayikra 18:4). Rabbi Aba said: Fortunate is the lot of Yisrael that the Holy One, blessed be He, desires them above all the idolatrous nations. As a result of His love for them, He gave them truthful statutes, planted with them the Tree of Life, ZEIR ANPIN, and caused the Shechinah to dwell in their midst. What is the reason? It is because Yisrael are marked with the holy impression in their flesh and so are recognized as His and members of His temple.

296. וּבְגִינֵי כָּךְ, כָּל אִינּוּן דְלָא רְשִׁימִין בִּרְשִׁימוּ קַדִישָׁא בְּבִשְׂרַיְיהוֹן לָאו אִינּוּן דִילֵיהּ, וְאִשְׁתְּמוֹדְעָן דְכֻלְהוּ מִסִּטְרָא דִמְסָאֲבוּתָא אַתְיָין, וְאָסִיר לְאִתְחַבְּרָא בְּהוּ, וּלְאִשְׁתָּעֵי בַּהֲדַיְיהוּ, בְּמִלּוֹי דְקוּדְשָׁא בְּרִיךְ הוּא וְאָסִיר לְאוֹדְעָא לְהוּ מִלֵּי דְאוֹרַיְיתָא, בְּגִין דְאוֹרַיְיתָא כֻּלָּא שְׁמָא דְקוּדְשָׁא בְּרִיךְ הוּא, וְכָל אָת דְאוֹרַיְיתָא, מִתְקַשְׁרָא בִּשְׁמָא קַדִישָׁא. וְכָל מַאן דְלָא אִתְרְשִׁים בִּרְשִׁימָא קַדִישָׁא בְּבִשְׂרֵיהּ, אָסִיר לְאוֹדְעָא

לֵיהּ מִלָּה דְּאוֹרַיְיתָא. וכ"ש לְאִשְׁתַּדְּלָא בֵּיהּ.

296. Because of this, all those that are not marked in their flesh with the holy impression, MEANING THEY ARE NOT CIRCUMCISED, are not His people. They are not OF THE HOLY ONE, BLESSED BE HE. It is apparent that they stem from the direction of impurity and it is prohibited to fraternize with them and speak with them regarding matters of the Holy One, blessed be He. It is prohibited to relate words of Torah to them, as the entire Torah is the name of the Holy One, blessed be He. Every letter of the Torah is connected with the Holy Name; THEREFORE, ANYONE whose flesh is not marked with the holy impression must not be informed of Torah words, and one must not study with him.

297. ר"ש פָּתַח, זֹאת חֻקַּת הַפֶּסַח כָּל בֶּן נֵכָר לֹא יֹאכַל בּוֹ, וּכְתִיב וְכָל עֶבֶד אִישׁ וְגוֹ'. וּכְתִיב תּוֹשָׁב וְשָׂכִיר לֹא יֹאכַל בּוֹ. וּמַה פִּסְחָא דְּאִיהוּ בִּשְׂרָא לְמֵיכְלָא, עַל דְּאִתְרְמִיז בְּמִלָּה קַדִּישָׁא, אָסִיר לְכָל הָנֵי לְמֵיכַל בֵּיהּ, וּלְמֵיהַב לְהוּ לְמֵיכַל, עַד דְּאִתְגְּזָרוּ. אוֹרַיְיתָא דְּהִיא קֹדֶשׁ קָדָשִׁים שְׁמָא עִלָּאָה דְּקוּדְשָׁא בְּרִיךְ הוּא, עאכ"ו.

297. Rabbi Shimon opened the discussion saying, "This is the ordinance of the Pesach: no stranger shall eat of it" (Shemot 12:43). It is also written, "But every man's servant..." (Ibid. 44) and "a foreign and a hired servant shall not eat of it" (Ibid. 45). If something like eating the pascal lamb is forbidden to the uncircumcised just because it hints at a holy matter – MEANING BECAUSE "HASHEM WILL PASS OVER THE DOOR..." (IBID. 23) – then how much more should the Torah, which is the Holy of Holies, the sublime name of the Holy One, blessed be He, be forbidden to them.

298. רִבִּי אֶלְעָזָר שָׁאִיל לְרִבִּי שִׁמְעוֹן אֲבוּהִי, א"ל, הָא תָּנֵינָן אָסוּר לְלַמֵּד תּוֹרָה לְעכו"ם, וְשַׁפִּיר אִתְּעֲרוּ חַבְרַיָּיא דְּבָבֶל, דִּכְתִּיב לֹא עָשָׂה כֵן לְכָל גּוֹי, אֲבָל כֵּיוָן דְּאָמַר מַגִּיד דְּבָרָיו לְיַעֲקֹב, אֲמַאי חֻקָּיו וּמִשְׁפָּטָיו לְיִשְׂרָאֵל. א"ל, אֶלְעָזָר ת"ח, זַכָּאִין אִינּוּן יִשְׂרָאֵל, דְּחוּלָקָא עִלָּאָה קַדִּישָׁא דָּא נָטַע בְּהוּ קוּדְשָׁא בְּרִיךְ הוּא, דִּכְתִּיב כִּי לֶקַח טוֹב נָתַתִּי לָכֶם, לָכֶם, וְלָא לְעַמִּין עע"ז.

298. Rabbi Elazar asked of Rabbi Shimon his father: We learned that it is prohibited to teach Torah to idolaters and very beautifully did the Babylonian scholars explain that which is written, "He has not dealt so with any other nation" (Tehilim 147:20). But ONE COULD ASK since it is written, "He declares His word to Jacob" (Ibid. 19), so why write again, "His statutes and His Judgments (lit. 'justices') to Yisrael"? IT IS A REDUNDANT EXPRESSION. He replied: Elazar. Come and see how fortunate are Yisrael within whom this supernal portion was planted by the Holy One, blessed be He, as it is written, "For I give you a good doctrine" (Mishlei 4:2) – to you and not to the idolatrous nations.

299. וּבְגִין דְּאִיהִי גְּנִיזָא עִלָּאָה יַקִּירָא, שְׁמֵיהּ מַמָּשׁ, אוֹרַיְיתָא כֹּלָּא סָתִים וְגַלְיָא, בְּרָזָא דִשְׁמֵיהּ. וְעַל דָּא, יִשְׂרָאֵל בִּתְרֵין דַּרְגִּין אִינוּן, סָתִים וְגַלְיָא, דְּתָנֵינָן תְּלַת דַּרְגִּין אִינּוּן מִתְקַשְׁרָן דָּא בְּדָא, קוּדְשָׁא בְּרִיךְ הוּא, אוֹרַיְיתָא, וְיִשְׂרָאֵל. וְכָל חַד, דַּרְגָּא עַל דַּרְגָּא, סָתִים וְגַלְיָא. קוּדְשָׁא בְּרִיךְ הוּא דַּרְגָּא עַל דַּרְגָּא, סָתִים וְגַלְיָא. אוֹרַיְיתָא הָכִי נָמֵי סָתִים וְגַלְיָא. יִשְׂרָאֵל הָכִי נָמֵי דַּרְגָּא עַל דַּרְגָּא, הֲדָא הוּא דִכְתִּיב, מַגִּיד דְּבָרָיו לְיַעֲקֹב חֻקָּיו וּמִשְׁפָּטָיו לְיִשְׂרָאֵל. תְּרֵי דַּרְגִּין אִינוּן, יַעֲקֹב וְיִשְׂרָאֵל, חַד גַּלְיָא, וְחַד סָתִים.

299. Because she is supernal, precious and hidden, His very name in the entire Torah is both concealed and revealed, AS IT CONTAINS THE ESOTERIC AND LITERAL MEANING in the secret of His name. Hence, Yisrael find themselves on two levels, MEANING concealed and revealed, as we learned there are three levels intertwined with each other, MEANING the Holy One, blessed be He, the Torah and Yisrael. Each OF THEM has one level above another, MEANING a hidden and a revealed one. As the Holy One, blessed be He, is a level upon level, concealed and revealed, the Torah is also concealed and revealing. Yisrael too is a level upon a level. This is what is written, "He declares His word to Jacob, His statutes and His Judgments (lit. 'justices') to Yisrael." Here are two levels, Jacob and Yisrael, one revealing, THE LEVEL OF JACOB, and one concealed, THE LEVEL OF YISRAEL.

300. מַאי קָא מַיְירֵי. אֶלָּא כָּל מָאן דְּאִתְגְּזַר וְאִתְרְשִׁים בִּשְׁמָא קַדִּישָׁא, יָהֲבִין לֵיהּ בְּאִינּוּן מִלִּין דְּאִתְגַּלְיָין בְּאוֹרַיְיתָא, כְּלוֹמַר, מוֹדִיעִין לֵיהּ

בְּרֵישֵׁי אַתְוָון, בְּרֵישֵׁי פִּרְקִין, יָהֲבִין עֲלֵיהּ חוּמְרָא דְּפִקּוּדֵי אוֹרַיְיתָא,
וְלָא יַתִּיר, עַד דְּיִסְתַּלַּק בְּדַרְגָּא אָחֳרָא, הה"ד מַגִּיד דְּבָרָיו לְיַעֲקֹב. אֲבָל
חֻקָּיו וּמִשְׁפָּטָיו לְיִשְׂרָאֵל, דְּאִיהוּ בְּדַרְגָּא עִלָּאָה יַתִּיר. וּכְתִיב לֹא יִקָּרֵא
שִׁמְךָ עוֹד יַעֲקֹב וְגוֹ'. חֻקָּיו וּמִשְׁפָּטָיו לְיִשְׂרָאֵל, אִלֵּין רָזֵי אוֹרַיְיתָא
וְנִמּוּסֵי אוֹרַיְיתָא, וְסִתְרֵי אוֹרַיְיתָא, דְּלָא יִצְטָרְכוּן לְגַלָּאָה אֶלָּא לְמַאן
דְּאִיהוּ בְּדַרְגָּא עִלָּאָה יַתִּיר כַּדְקָא חֲזֵי.

300. HE QUESTIONS: What does the verse mean IN THE WORDS, "HIS STATUTES AND HIS JUDGMENTS (LIT. 'JUSTICES') TO YISRAEL"? HE ANSWERED: everyone who is circumcised and marked with the Holy Name is passed on with the revealed words of the Torah. He is informed generally of basic matters in brief, and has placed upon him the very strict CARE of the commandments of the Torah, and not more until he is elevated to another level. This is what the verse says, "He declares His word to Jacob," but "His statutes and His Judgments (lit. 'justices') to Yisrael" is a higher level, as it is written, "Your name shall not be called any more Jacob..." (Beresheet 35:10). THUS, ISRAEL IS MORE ESTEEMED THAN JACOB. THEREFORE, it is written, "His statutes and His Judgments (lit. 'justices') to Israel." These are the secrets of the Torah, the statutes of the Torah and the hidden parts of the Torah, which are not revealed except to one who finds himself to be on a more lofty level, as is proper.

50. It is prohibited to teach the Torah to the uncircumcised

A Synopsis

We read that the Torah must be taught only to the circumcised, and that even some of them are considered idolaters if they do not follow the commandments of the Torah. We learn of the supernal meaning of the alphabet, and most particularly of the letter Aleph.

301. וּמַה לְיִשְׂרָאֵל הַאי, לְעַמִּין עע"ז עאכ"ו, וְכָל מַאן דְּלָא אִתְגְּזַר וְיָהֲבִין לֵיהּ אֲפִילוּ אָת זְעֵירָא דְּאוֹרַיְיתָא, כְּאִלוּ חָרִיב עָלְמָא, וּמְשַׁקֵּר בִּשְׁמָא דְּקוּדְשָׁא בְּרִיךְ הוּא, דְּכֹלָא בְּהַאי תַּלְיָא, וְדָא אִתְקְשַׁר, דִּכְתִיב אִם לֹא בְרִיתִי יוֹמָם וָלַיְלָה חֻקּוֹת שָׁמַיִם וָאָרֶץ לֹא שָׂמְתִּי.

301. If it is so to Yisrael, THAT TORAH IS NOT TO BE REVEALED BUT TO ONE WHO IS IN THE UPPER LEVEL, it is all the more so with the idolatrous nations. If one gives to all those who are uncircumcised even a single letter of the Torah, it is considered as if he devastated the world and was false to the name of the Holy One, blessed be He. It is all dependent upon this, CIRCUMCISION. One is bound to the other, TORAH IS CONNECTED TO CIRCUMCISION, as it is written, "If My covenant be not day and night, it were as if I had not appointed the ordinances of heaven and earth" (Yirmeyah 33:25).

302. תָּא חֲזֵי, כְּתִיב וְזֹאת הַתּוֹרָה אֲשֶׁר שָׂם מֹשֶׁה לִפְנֵי בְּנֵי יִשְׂרָאֵל. לִפְנֵי בְּנֵי יִשְׂרָאֵל שָׂם, אֲבָל לִשְׁאָר עַמִּין לָא שָׂם. בְּג"כ דַּבֵּר אֶל בְּנֵי יִשְׂרָאֵל. וְאֶל בְּנֵי יִשְׂרָאֵל תֹּאמַר. וְכֵן כֻּלְּהוּ. יְנוּחוּן אֲבָהָן דְּעָלְמָא, אִינּוּן הִלֵּל וְשַׁמָּאי, דְּהָכִי אָמְרוּ לְאוּנְקְלוּס, וְלָא אוֹדְעוּ לֵיהּ מִלָּה דְּאוֹרַיְיתָא עַד דְּאִתְגְּזַר.

302. Come and see: It is written, "And this is the Torah which Moses set before the children of Yisrael" (Devarim 4:44). "Before the children of Yisrael" he set it, but not before the other nations, so for this reason, speak to the children of Yisrael. "You shall say to the children of Yisrael" (Vayikra 20:2), and it is so in all places, ONLY TO YISRAEL. May they rest, the fathers of the world, Hillel and Shamai, who spoke so to Onkelos, but they did not reveal Torah topics to him until he was circumcised.

303. וְתָא חֲזֵי, מִלָּה קַדְמָאָה דְּאוֹרַיְיתָא, דְּיָהֲבִין לֵינוֹקֵי, אָלֶ"ף בֵּי"ת, דָּא מִלָּה דְּלָא יַכְלִין בְּנֵי עָלְמָא לְאַדְבְּקָא בְּסוּכְלְתָנוּ, וּלְסַלְקָא לֵיהּ בִּרְעוּתָא, וכ"ש לְמַלְּלָא בְּפוּמֵיהוֹן. וַאֲפִילוּ מַלְאֲכֵי עִלָּאֵי, וְעִלָּאֵי דְּעִלָּאֵי, לָא יַכְלִין לְאַדְבְּקָא, בְּגִין דְּאִינּוּן סְתִימִין דִּשְׁמָא קַדִּישָׁא. וְאַלֶף וְאַרְבַּע מְאָה וַחֲמֵשׁ רִבְבָן דְּעָלְמִין, כֻּלְּהוּ תַּלְיָין בְּקוֹצָא דְּאַלֶ"ף, וְשַׁבְעִין וּתְרֵין שְׁמָהָן קַדִּישִׁין גְּלִיפִין בְּאַתְווֹי רְשִׁימִין, דְּקַיְימוּ בְּהוּ עִלָּאֵי וְתַתָּאֵי, שְׁמַיָּא וְאַרְעָא, וְכוּרְסַיָּיא יְקָרָא דְּמַלְכָּא, תַּלְיָין מִסִּטְרָא חֲדָא לְסִטְרָא חֲדָא, דִּפְשִׁיטוּתָא דְּאַלֶף, קִיוּמָא דְּעָלְמִין כֻּלְּהוּ, וְסַמְכִין דְּעִלָּאִין וְתַתָּאִין בְּרָזָא דְּחָכְמְתָא.

303. Come and see: The first subject of the Torah we give to children is the Alphabet. This is a matter that mankind cannot comprehend, nor can it rise in their minds, not to mention saying it with their mouths. Even supernal angels and the most sublime can not comprehend it, as these matters are the mysteries of the Holy Name. There are 14,050,000 worlds dependent upon the stroke of the Aleph א, MEANING THE STROKE OF THE UPPER YUD OF THE ALEPH, and 72 holy names are engraved in the impressed letters in them. The high and low beings; heaven, earth and the seat of glory of the King – are hanging from one side to the other side, MEANING FROM THE UPPER STROKE TO THE LOWER STROKE of the expansion of the Aleph. They sustain all the worlds and are the supports of the upper and lower beings within the secret of wisdom.

304. וּשְׁבִילִין סְתִימִין, וְנַהֲרִין עֲמִיקִין, וְעֶשֶׂר אֲמִירָן, כֻּלְּהוּ נָפְקִין מֵהַהוּא קוֹצָא תַּתָּאָה דִּתְחוֹת אַלֶף. מִכָּאן וּלְהָלְאָה שָׁארֵי לְאִתְפַּשְּׁטָא אַלֶף בְּבֵית. וְלֵית חוּשְׁבָּן לְחָכְמְתָא דְּהָכָא אִתְגְּלִיף.

304. Concealed paths, THE SECRET OF THE 32 PATHS OF CHOCHMAH, and deep rivers, THE SECRET OF THE SFIROT OF BINAH, ten sayings, THE SECRET OF THE TEN SFIROT OF DA'AT THAT UNIFIES CHOCHMAH AND BINAH, DENOTING THE SECRET OF CHOCHMAH, BINAH AND DA'AT OF ZEIR ANPIN, all come out AND FLOW INTO THE WORLDS from the lower tip underneath the Aleph. FOR THE LOWER YUD OF THE ALEPH IS THE

SECRET OF MALE AND FEMALE, AS MENTIONED, WHOSE LIGHTS FLOW
THROUGH THE LOWER TIP OF THE YUD. THEREFORE, IT IS COLLECTIVE,
AS ALL ARE COLLECTED WITHIN THE ALEPH. From here on begin THE
LIGHTS OF Aleph to spread to the Bet. One can not keep track of the
wisdom that is engraved here.

305. בְּגִינֵי כַּךְ, אוֹרַיְיתָא קִיוּמָא דְּכֹלָּא, וּמְהֵימְנוּתָא דְּכֹלָּא, לְקַשְׁרָא
קִשְׁרָא דִּמְהֵימְנוּתָא דָּא בְּדָא כַּדְקָא חֲזֵי. וּמַאן דְּאִתְגְּזַר, אִתְקַשַּׁר
בְּהַהוּא קִשְׁרָא דִּמְהֵימְנוּתָא. וּמַאן דְּלָא אִתְגְּזַר, וְלָא אִתְקַשַּׁר בֵּיהּ,
כְּתִיב בֵּיהּ, וְכָל זָר לֹא יֹאכַל קֹדֶשׁ. וְכָל עָרֵל לֹא יֹאכַל בּוֹ. דְּהָא אִתְּעַר
רוּחַ מִסְאֲבָא דִּמְסִטְרֵיהּ, וְאָתֵי לְאִתְעָרְבָא בִּקְדוּשָׁה. בְּרִיךְ רַחֲמָנָא,
דְּפָרִישׁ לְיִשְׂרָאֵל בְּנוֹי, רְשִׁימִין בִּרְשִׁימָא קַדִּישָׁא, מִנַּיְיהוּ וּמִזּוּהֲמָא
דִּלְהוֹן. עֲלַיְיהוּ כְּתִיב, וְאָנֹכִי נְטַעְתִּיךְ שׂוֹרֵק כֻּלֹּה זֶרַע אֱמֶת. וּבְגִינֵי כַּךְ,
תִּתֵּן אֱמֶת לְיַעֲקֹב, וְלָא לְאָחֳרָא. תּוֹרַת אֱמֶת, לְזֶרַע אֱמֶת. אָתָא רִבִּי
אֶלְעָזָר וּנְשָׁקֵיהּ עַל יְדוֹי.

305. For this reason, the Torah, THE SECRET OF ZEIR ANPIN, is the
sustenance of everything and the Faith of all to bind the bond of Faith,
NAMELY MALCHUT, one with another properly. He who is circumcised is
bound with that bond of Faith, but he who is not circumcised is not bound
with it, as it is written, "No stranger shall eat of the holy thing" (Vayikra
22:10) and "for no uncircumcised man shall eat of it" (Shemot 12:48). The
spirit of defilement is stirred up from him and it comes to intermingle with
holiness. Blessed is the Merciful One who set apart His children, Yisrael,
who are marked with the holy impression, from them and their filth. About
them, it is written, "And I had planted you a noble vine, an entirely right
seed" (Yirmeyah 2:21). For this reason, IT IS WRITTEN, "You will show
truth to Jacob" (Michah 7:20) and to no one else, a true Torah to a true seed.
Rabbi Elazar approached and kissed him on his hands.

306. רִבִּי חִזְקִיָּה אָמַר, כְּתִיב כִּי לֹא יִטּוֹשׁ יְיָ' אֶת עַמּוֹ בַּעֲבוּר שְׁמוֹ וְגוֹ',
כִּי לֹא יִטּוֹשׁ יְיָ' אֶת עַמּוֹ, מ"ט בַּעֲבוּר שְׁמוֹ הַגָּדוֹל. בְּגִין דְּכֹלָּא אִתְקַשַּׁר
דָּא בְּדָא, וּבַמֶּה אִתְקַשָּׁרוּ יִשְׂרָאֵל בְּקוּדְשָׁא בְּרִיךְ הוּא. בְּהַהוּא רְשִׁימָא
קַדִּישָׁא דְּאִתְרְשִׁים בְּבִשְׂרַיְיהוֹן. וּבְגִינֵי כַּךְ, לֹא יִטּוֹשׁ יְיָ' אֶת עַמּוֹ. וְלָמָּה.

בַּעֲבוּר שְׁמוֹ הַגָּדוֹל דְּאִתְרְשִׁים בְּהוּ.

306. Rabbi Chizkiyah said: It is written, "For Hashem will not abandon His people for His great name's sake..." (I Samuel 12:22). "Hashem will not abandon His people" for what reason? "for His great name's sake" as everything is interconnected. With what are Yisrael connected to the Holy One, blessed be He? It is with that holy impression marked in their flesh. For this reason, Hashem will not abandon His people. And why? IT IS DUE to His great Name marked on them.

307. תָּאנָא, אוֹרַיְיתָא אִקְרֵי בְּרִית, וְקוּדְשָׁא בְּרִיךְ הוּא אִקְרֵי בְּרִית.
וְהַאי רְשִׁימָא קַדִּישָׁא אִקְרֵי בְּרִית. וְעַל דָּא כֹּלָּא אִתְקְשַׁר דָּא בְּדָא, וְלָא
אִתְפְּרַשׁ דָּא מִן דָּא. א"ל ר' יֵיסָא, אוֹרַיְיתָא וְיִשְׂרָאֵל שַׁפִּיר אֲבָל
קוּדְשָׁא בְּרִיךְ הוּא מְנָלָן דְּאִקְרֵי בְּרִית. א"ל דִּכְתִיב וַיִּזְכּוֹר לָהֶם בְּרִיתוֹ,
וְהָא אִתְיְידַע, וְהָא אִתְּמַר.

307. We have learned that the Torah is called "covenant." The Holy One, blessed be He, is called covenant and this holy mark, MEANING CIRCUMCISION, is called "covenant." So they are all intertwined and not apart one from another. Rabbi Yesa said to him that Torah and Yisrael ARE CALLED COVENANT, and that is fine. But how do we know that the Holy One, blessed be He, is called covenant? He replied: Because it is written, "And He remembered for them His covenant" (Tehilim 106:45) and it is well known THAT THE SECRET OF IT IS YESOD, as we have learned.

308. וְאֶת חֻקֹּתַי תִּשְׁמְרוּ, חֻקּוֹתַי: אִלֵּין אִינּוּן נְמוּסֵי מַלְכָּא. מִשְׁפָּטַי:
אִלֵּין אִינּוּן גְּזֵרֵי אוֹרַיְיתָא, רַבִּי יְהוּדָה אָמַר, כָּל אִינּוּן נְמוּסִין מֵאֲתַר
דְּאִקְרֵי צֶדֶק, אִקְרוּן חֻקּוֹתַי, וְאִינּוּן גְּזֵרַת מַלְכָּא. וּבְכָל אֲתָר דְּאִקְרֵי
מִשְׁפָּט אִקְרוּן דִּינָא דְּמַלְכָּא, דְּאִיהוּ מַלְכָּא קַדִּישָׁא, קוּדְשָׁא בְּרִיךְ הוּא,
מַלְכָּא דִּשְׁלָמָא כֹּלָּא דִּילֵיהּ. הוּא דְּהוּא מַלְכָּא קַדִּישָׁא, בַּאֲתַר דִּתְרֵין
חוּלָקִין אֲחִידָן דָּא בְּדָא. וְעַל דָּא כְּתִיב, צֶדֶק וּמִשְׁפָּט מְכוֹן כִּסְאָךְ,
וְאִינּוּן דִּינָא וְרַחֲמֵי. וּבְגִינֵי כַּךְ חֹק וּמִשְׁפָּט. וְע"ד כְּתִיב חֻקָּיו וּמִשְׁפָּטָיו
לְיִשְׂרָאֵל. לְיִשְׂרָאֵל וְלָא לִשְׁאָר עַמִּין.

308. "And keep My ordinances" (Vayikra 18:4): "My ordinances" are the customs of the King, NAMELY ZEIR ANPIN. "My Judgments (lit. 'justices')" (Ibid.) are the decrees of the Torah. Rabbi Yehuda said: All these customs stem from the place called righteousness, DENOTING MALCHUT. They are called "My ordinances" and are Royal decrees. Wherever something is called Justice, it refers to Royal Laws of the Holy King, the Holy One, blessed be He, the King to whom all peace is His, being the Holy King in a place where two portions are held one with another, MEANING Judgment and Mercy. Therefore, it is written, "Righteousness and justice are the foundation of Your throne" (Tehilim 89:15) and they are Judgment and Mercy. For this reason, THEY ARE ordinance and Judgment. Of this, it is written, "His statutes and His Judgments (lit. 'justices') to Yisrael" (Tehilim 147:19) to Yisrael, but not to any other nation.

309. בַּתְרֵיהּ מַה כְּתִיב, לֹא עָשָׂה כֵן לְכָל גּוֹי. וְתָנֵינָן, אע"ג דְּאִתְגְּזַר וְלָא עָבֵיד פִּקּוּדֵי אוֹרַיְיתָא, הֲרֵי הוּא כְּגוֹי בְּכֹלָּא, וְאָסִיר לְמֵילַף לֵיהּ פִּתְגָּמֵי אוֹרַיְיתָא. וְעַ"ד תָּנֵינָן מִזְבַּח אֲבָנִים, דָּא מִזְבַּח אֲבָנִים מַמָּשׁ. וְהָא קַשְׁיוּ דִּלְבֵּיהּ בְּאַתְרֵיהּ קַיְּימָא, וְזוּהֲמָא לָא אִתְפְּסַק מִנֵּיהּ. בְּגִינֵי כָּךְ, לָא סָלִיק בִּידֵיהּ הַהוּא גְּזִירוּ, וְלָא מְהַנְיָא לֵיהּ. וְעַ"ד כְּתִיב, כִּי חַרְבְּךָ הֵנַפְתָּ עָלֶיהָ וַתְּחַלְלֶהָ.

309. It is later written, "He has not dealt so with any other nation" (Ibid. 20). We have learned that even though he was circumcised, if he does not perform the commandments of the Torah he is to be considered an idolater throughout. It is thus forbidden to teach him the words of the Torah. We have learned that "you will make Me an altar of stone" (Shemot 20:22). This, CIRCUMCISION, is considered literally an altar of stone, MEANING IT SOFTENS HIS STONE HEART, but for he WHO IS CIRCUMCISED YET DOES NOT OBSERVE THE COMMANDMENTS OF THE TORAH, the hardness of his heart remains as is and the filth does not cease from him. For this reason, the circumcision did not succeed nor did it help him. Therefore, it is written, "For if you lift up your tool upon it, you have defiled it" (Ibid.). THIS MEANS THAT EVEN THOUGH YOU RAISED YOUR SWORD UPON IT, MEANING IF ONE IS CIRCUMCISED, YET DOES NOT OBSERVE THE COMMANDMENTS, "YOU HAVE DEFILED IT" – THE CIRCUMCISION BECOMES DEFILED AND IS TO NO AVAIL. THUS, IT IS PROHIBITED TO TEACH HIM TORAH.

310. בְּגִינֵי כַּךְ, לֹא עָשָׂה כֵן לְכָל גּוֹי סְתָם. וּמִשְׁפָּטִים בַּל יְדָעוּם לְעָלַם וּלְעָלְמֵי עָלְמִין. מִלָּה אָחֳרָא, לָא יַהֲבִינָן לְהוּ, כ"ש רָזֵי אוֹרַיְיתָא, וְנִמּוּסִין דְּאוֹרַיְיתָא. וּכְתִיב, כִּי חֵלֶק יְיָ' עַמּוֹ יַעֲקֹב חֶבֶל נַחֲלָתוֹ, אַשְׁרֵי הָעָם שֶׁכָּכָה לּוֹ אַשְׁרֵי הָעָם שֶׁיְיָ' אֱלֹהָיו.

310. For this reason, "He has not dealt so with any other nation." "NATION," is unspecified, INCLUDING ALSO HIM THAT IS CIRCUMCISED YET DOES NOT PERFORM THE PRECEPTS. "And as for His ordinances they have not known them" forever and ever. Another interpretation, MEANING ACCORDING TO THE LITERAL MEANING OF THE TORAH AND THE PRECEPTS, we do not hand to them, and surely not the esoteric explanations of Torah and the ordinances of Torah. It is written, "For Hashem's portion is His people; Jacob is the lot of His inheritance" (Devarim 32:9) and "Happy is that people, that is in such a case: happy is that people, whose Elohim is Hashem" (Tehilim 144:15).

51. Four keys

A Synopsis
We learn what the Mishnah says about the ways of the lights, and about the four keys of different colors that were made for the directions of the world. Many supernal secrets are spoken of, with the number four being the link between them. We read of the sixty warriors who are led by a strong youth, and of the swords they wield.

311. מַתְנִיתִין, בְּנִמּוּסֵי טְהִירִין. אַרְבַּע מַפְתְּחָן שָׁוְיָין, לְאַרְבַּע סִטְרֵי עָלְמָא. בְּזִוְיָיתְהוֹן אִשְׁתְּכָחוּ. חַד לִסְטַר אַרְבַּע, וְאַרְבַּע לִסְטַר חַד. אִתְגַּלְּפָן בְּחַד גַּוְונָא. בְּהַהוּא גַּוְונָא, תְּכֵלָא, וְאַרְגְּוָונָא וְצֶבַע זְהוֹרִי, וְחִוָּורָא, וְסוּמָקָא. דָּא עָיֵיל בְּגַוְונָא דְּחַבְרֵיהּ, וְדִידֵיהּ בֵּיהּ רָשִׁים.

311. We have learned in the Mishnah about the ways of the lights. Four keys were made for the directions of the world, and there is one KEY for the four directions in their corners. There are four DIRECTIONS for each direction and they are engraved with one color. In the color ARE MIXED blue, purple, scarlet, white and red. One blends into the color of the other and ITS COLOR, MEANING THAT OF ITS NEIGHBOR, is found in it.

312. אַרְבַּע רֵישִׁין כַּחֲדָא אִסְתְּלִיקוּ, וּבְחַד דִּיּוּקְנָא מִתְדַּבְּקָן. חַד רֵישָׁא אִסְתְּלִיק, מִגּוֹ סַחֲיוּ דְּאִסְתְּחֵי. תְּרֵי אַיַּילְתָּא קְצִיבִין בְּשִׁיעוּרָא חַד, סַלְקָן מֵהַהוּא סַחֲיוּתָא, דִּכְתִּיב כְּעֵדֶר הַקְּצוּבוֹת שֶׁעָלוּ מִן הָרַחְצָה. בְּשַׂעֲרָא דִּלְהוֹן, חֵיזוּ דְּאֶבֶן טָבָא דְּאַרְבַּע גַּוְונִין.

312. Four heads rose together joined as one form. One head arose from the washing, where it was washed. Two gazelles of equal size rose from that washing, as it is written, "Like a flock of shorn (also: 'measured') ewes, which came up from the washing" (Shir Hashirim 4:2). Within their hair is the appearance of a precious stone of four colors.

313. אַרְבַּע גַּדְפִּין דְּכַסְיָין עַל גּוּפָא, וִידִין זְעִירִין תְּחוֹת גַּדְפַּיְיהוּ. וְחָמֵשׁ בְּחָמֵשׁ גְּלִיפָן. טָאסִין לְעֵילָּא לְעֵילָּא מֵהֵיכָלָא, דִּשַׁפִּירָא בְּרֵיוָוא וְיָאֶה לְמֶחֱזֵי.

313. Four wings cover the body with small hands beneath their wings, each engraved with five. They fly high above the chamber that is beautiful in form and handsome in appearance.

314. חַד עוּלֵים רַבְיָא, נָפִיק שְׁנָן חַרְבָּא, דְּמִתְהַפְּכָא לְגוּבְרִין לְנוּקְבִין. נַטְלִין לְמָשִׁיחָא דְּאֵיפָה בֵּין שְׁמַיָּא וּבֵין אַרְעָא. לְזִמְנִין נַטְלִין לָהּ בְּכָל עָלְמָא, וְכָל מְשִׁיחִין בָּהּ מָשִׁיחִין, דִּכְתִיב אֵיפַת צֶדֶק וְגוֹ'.

314. One strong youth came out with a sharp sword that turns into males and females, who carry the measuring of an efa between heaven and earth, sometimes carrying it throughout the world. All are measured by it, as is written, "A just efa" (Vayikra 19:36).

315. חַד חֵיזוּ דִּבְדוֹלְחָא, קַיְימָא עַל חַרְבָּא חַד, בְּרֵישָׁא דְּהַהוּא חַרְבָּא מְלַהֲטָא סוּמָקָא מִגּוֹ בְּדוֹלְחָא. תְּרֵין סִטְרִין מֵהַאי גִּיסָא וּמֵהַאי גִּיסָא, אִתְחֲזֵי הַהוּא חַרְבָּא, בִּרְשִׁימִין עֲמִיקִין, חַד גְּבַר תַּקִּיף, עוֹלְמָא דְּקַיְּימָא בי״ג עָלְמִין. חֲגִיר הַהוּא חַרְבָּא, לְמֶעְבַּד נוּקְמִין. עִמֵּיהּ חֲגִירִין שִׁתִּין אָחֳרָנִין, כֻּלְּהוּ מִתְיַילְפֵי נַצְחִין קְרָבָא, הה״ד חֲגוֹר חַרְבְּךָ עַל יָרֵךְ גִּבּוֹר הוֹדְךָ וַהֲדָרֶךָ. וּכְתִיב כֻּלָם אֲחוּזֵי חֶרֶב מְלוּמְדֵי מִלְחָמָה וְגוֹ'. בְּכַמָּה גַּוְונִין מִתְהַפְּכִין אַנְפַּיְיהוּ, לֵית דְּיָדַע לוֹן, בַּר חַד תּוֹלַעְתָּא דְּשָׁאט בֵּין נוּנֵי יַמָּא, כָּל אֲבָנִין דְּאַעְבַּר עֲלַיְיהוּ מִתְבַּקְעִין.

315. There is a crystal mirror on one sword. On the top of that sword glistens the color of red in the midst of the crystal. From the two sides very deep impressions appear in that sword. One strong warrior, a youth standing in thirteen worlds, is girded with that sword to do vengeance. With him are sixty other mighty warriors girded with swords, all trained to be victorious in war. This is the meaning of the verse, "Gird your sword upon your thigh, O mighty warrior: your glory and your majesty" (Tehilim 45:4). It is also written, "All girt with swords, and expert in war..." (Shir Hashirim 3:8). They turn forward in several ways, and no one knows them except one worm that swims among the fish of the sea. All rocks that pass over them break up.

316. בְּהַהוּא זִמְנָא, קָלָא דְּנָפִיק מֵאִינוּן דַּחֲגִירֵי חַרְבָּא, מִבְקַע תְּמָנֵיסָר

טוּרִין רַבְרְבִין, וְלֵית מָאן דְּיַרְכִּין אוּדְנֵיהּ. כֻּלְּהוּ עָלְמָא סְתִימִין עַיְינִין,
אֲטִימִין לִבָּא, לֵית מָאן דְּיַשְׁגַּח דְּהָא בִּנְיָינָא לִסְתּוֹר כַּד עֲבָדִין עוֹבָדָן
דְּלָא מִתְכַּשְׁרָן, סָאטִין מֵאָרְחָא דְּתַקָּנָא, יְמִינָא אַעְדֵּי, וּשְׂמָאלָא
שַׁלְטָא, כְּדֵין עֶרְיָין אִשְׁתְּכָחוּ. וַוי לְחַיָּיבַיָּא דְּגַרְמִין דָּא בְּעָלְמָא, דְּהָא
לָא מִתְבָּרְכִין לְעֵילָא, עַד דְּיִשְׁתְּצוּן אִינּוּן לְתַתָּא. הה"ד וּרְשָׁעִים עוֹד
אֵינָם בָּרְכִי נַפְשִׁי אֶת יְיָ' הַלְלוּיָהּ. (ע"כ..

316. At that time, the sound that is emitted from those girded with swords, NAMELY THE SIXTY WARRIORS, breaks eighteen large mountains. No one lends his ear, everyone is blind and has a closed heart. There is no one to see that this construction is about to shatter. When unseemly deeds are done and people turn away from the correct way, the right is removed, DENOTING THE ILLUMINATION OF CHASSADIM, and the left rules WITHOUT THE RIGHT. Then there is nakedness. Woe to the wicked who bring it upon the world, as there is no blessing above before these EVILDOERS are vanquished here below. This is what the verse says, "And the wicked will be no more. Bless You Hashem, O my soul, Haleluyah" (Tehilim 104:35).

52. An apple tree and a rose

A Synopsis
Rabbi Chiya says that the Congregation of Yisrael praises God with the image of an apple. From Rabbi Shimon we learn that is because it includes color, fragrance and taste, and because the apple is a cure-all. He says that God praises the Congregation of Israel with the image of a rose because of the fragrance of their good deeds.

317. עֶרְוַת אָבִיךָ וְעֶרְוַת אִמְּךָ לֹא תְגַלֵּה רִבִּי חִיָּיא פָּתַח. כְּתַפּוּחַ בַּעֲצֵי הַיַּעַר כֵּן דּוֹדִי בֵּין הַבָּנִים וְגוֹ'. הַאי קְרָא אוּקְמוּהָ חַבְרַיָּיא, אֲבָל כַּמָה חֲבִיבָה כְּנֶסֶת יִשְׂרָאֵל קָמֵי קוּדְשָׁא בְּרִיךְ הוּא. דְּהִיא מְשַׁבַּחַת לֵיהּ בְּהַאי. הָכָא אִית לְאִסְתַּכְּלָא, אֲמַאי מְשַׁבַּחַת לֵיהּ בְּתַפּוּחַ, וְלָא בְּמִלָּה אָחֳרָא, אוֹ בִּגְוָונִין אוֹ בְּרֵיחָא אוֹ בְּטַעֲמָא.

317. "The nakedness of your father, or the nakedness of your mother, shall you not uncover" (Vayikra 18:7). Rabbi Chiyah opened the discussion saying, "Like the apple tree among the trees of the wood, so is my beloved among the sons..." (Shir Hashirim 2:3). This verse has been expounded by the friends. Yet, how beloved is the Congregation of Yisrael before the Holy One, blessed be He, that she lauds Him in this VERSE. We should look into this. Why does she laud Him through the apple and not with something else or with something THAT HAS color, or fragrance or taste.

318. אֲבָל הוֹאִיל וּכְתִיב תַּפּוּחַ, בְּכֹלָּא הִיא מְשַׁבַּחַת לֵיהּ, בִּגְוָונִין, בְּרֵיחָא, וּבְטַעֲמָא. מַה תַּפּוּחַ הוּא אַסְוּותָא לְכֹלָּא, אוּף קוּדְשָׁא בְּרִיךְ הוּא אַסְוּותָא לְכֹלָּא. מַה תַּפּוּחַ אִשְׁתְּכַח בִּגְוָונֵי, כְּמָה דְּאוֹקִימְנָא, אוּף קוּדְשָׁא בְּרִיךְ הוּא אִשְׁתְּכַח בִּגְוָונִין עִלָּאִין. מַה תַּפּוּחַ אִית בֵּיהּ רוּחָא דָקִיק מִכָּל שְׁאָר אִילָנֵי, אוּף קוּדְשָׁא בְּרִיךְ הוּא כְּתִיב בֵּיהּ וְרֵיחַ לוֹ כַּלְּבָנוֹן. מַה תַּפּוּחַ טַעֲמֵיהּ מְתִיקָא, אוּף קוּדְשָׁא בְּרִיךְ הוּא כְּתִיב בֵּיהּ חִכּוֹ מַמְתַקִּים.

318. HE ANSWERS: Since it is written "apple tree," IT TURNS OUT she is lauding him in every manner, with color, fragrance and with taste. Just as

the apple is a cure-all also the Holy One, blessed be He, is a cure for all. Just as apple appears in colors – as we established, IT HAS WHITE, RED, GREEN – so does the Holy One, blessed be He, appear in supernal colors – NAMELY CHESED, GVURAH AND TIFERET THAT ARE THE SECRET OF WHITE, RED AND GREEN. As the apple tree has a fine fragrance MORE than other trees, so about the Holy One, blessed be He, it is written, "And His fragrance like the Lebanon" (Hoshea 14:7). Just as the apple's taste is sweet, so also is the Holy One's, blessed be He, as it is written, "His mouth is most sweet" (Shir Hashirim 5:16).

319. וְקוּדְשָׁא בְּרִיךְ הוּא מְשַׁבַּח לָהּ לכ״י כְּשׁוֹשַׁנָּה, וְהָא אוֹקִימְנָא מִלֵּי, אֲמַאי כְּשׁוֹשַׁנָּה, וְהָא אִתְּמַר. ר׳ יְהוּדָה אָמַר, בְּשַׁעֲתָא דְּאַסְגִּיאוּ זַכָּאֵי בְּעָלְמָא, כְּנֶסֶת יִשְׂרָאֵל סַלְקָא רֵיחִין טָבִין, וּמִתְבָּרְכָא מִמַּלְכָּא קַדִּישָׁא, וְאַנְפָּהָא נְהִירִין. וּבְזִמְנָא דְּאַסְגִּיאוּ חַיָּיבִין בְּעָלְמָא, כִּבְיָכוֹל כ״י לָא סַלְקָא רֵיחִין טָבִין, וְאִטְעֲמַת מִסִּטְרָא אָחֳרָא מְרִירָא. כְּדֵין, כְּתִיב הִשְׁלִיךְ מִשָּׁמַיִם אֶרֶץ וְגוֹ׳, וְאַנְפָּהָא חֲשׁוֹכָן.

319. And the Holy One, blessed be He, praises the Congregation of Yisrael like a rose, and we have already explained why HE PRAISED HER as a rose. Rabbi Yehuda said: When righteous men increase in the world, the Congregation of Yisrael, DENOTING MALCHUT, raises good fragrance BEING THE SECRET OF THE ILLUMINATION OF CHOCHMAH THAT SHINES FROM BELOW UPWARD AS FRAGRANCE, and is blessed WITH CHASSADIM from the Holy King, and her face shines. But when the wicked increase in the world, it is as if the Congregation of Yisrael does not raise up the good fragrance, and tastes from the bitter FEEDING of the Other Side. Then it is written, "And cast down from heaven (to) earth..." (Eichah 2:1), MEANING THE COUPLING OF ZEIR ANPIN CALLED HEAVEN AND MALCHUT CALLED EARTH HAS BEEN DISBANDED, and her face is dark.

320. רִבִּי יוֹסֵי אָמַר, בְּשַׁעֲתָא דְּאַסְגִּיאוּ זַכָּאִין בְּעָלְמָא, כְּתִיב שְׂמֹאלוֹ תַּחַת לְרֹאשִׁי וִימִינוֹ תְּחַבְּקֵנִי. וּבְזִמְנָא דְּאַסְגִּיאוּ חַיָּיבִין בְּעָלְמָא, כְּתִיב הֵשִׁיב אָחוֹר יְמִינוֹ. רִבִּי חִזְקִיָּה אָמַר מֵהָכָא, וְנִרְגָּן מַפְרִיד אַלּוּף, כְּלוֹמַר פָּרִישׁ מַלְכָּא מִן מַטְרוֹנִיתָא, הַהַ״ד עֶרְוַת אָבִיךָ וְעֶרְוַת אִמְּךָ לֹא תְגַלֵּה.

320. Rabbi Yosi said, when righteous men multiply in the world, it is written, "His left hand is under my head, and his right hand embraces me" (Shir Hashirim 2:6), MEANING THE RIGHT AND THE LEFT JOIN IN UNITY, ONE WITH ANOTHER. When the wicked multiply in the world, it is written, "He has drawn back His right hand from before the enemy" (Eichah 2:3), AND THE LEFT RULES WITHOUT THE RIGHT. THEN ALL JUDGMENTS ARE POURED DOWN FROM IT. Rabbi Chizkiyah said, We understand it from here, WHERE IT IS WRITTEN, "and a whisperer separates close friends" (Mishlei 16.28), meaning that the King separates from the Queen, BECAUSE OF THE EVIL MAN CALLED WHISPERER. This is the meaning of the verse, "The nakedness of your father, or the nakedness of your mother, shall you not uncover" MEANING YOU SHOULD NOT CAUSE THE UNCOVERING OF JUDGMENTS ABOVE TO THE NURTURING OF THE OTHER SIDE THROUGH WHICH A SPLIT IN THE HOLY UNION WILL OCCUR.

53. "That his mother taught him"

A Synopsis

Rabbi Shimon tells his son that as long as the children of Yisrael obey the will of God, He stays with them, but when they disobey Him he leaves them, yet still the Shechinah stays with them and thus she is separated from God. Because she produced Solomon, her wise son, there was great rejoicing when Solomon attained wisdom and recited Shir Hashirim; then God made his residence with her. At that time all the children of Yisrael merited the higher levels, and there was joy above and below.

321. רִבִּי אֶלְעָזָר הֲוָה יָתִיב קָמֵי אֲבוֹי, אָמַר לֵיהּ, אִי פְּרַקְלִיטָא בְּעָלְמָא בְּמַטְרוֹנִיתָא אִשְׁתְּכַח, וְאִי קַטִיגוֹרְיָא בְּעָלְמָא, בְּמַטְרוֹנִיתָא אִשְׁתְּכַח, אֲמַאי. אָמַר לֵיהּ, לְמַלְכָּא דַּהֲוָה לֵיהּ בַּר מִמַּטְרוֹנִיתָא, כָּל זִמְנָא דְּהַהוּא בְּרָא עָבֵיד רְעוּתָא דְּמַלְכָּא, מַלְכָּא עָבֵיד מָדוֹרֵיהּ בְּמַטְרוֹנִיתָא. וְכָל זִמְנָא דְּלָא הֲוָה הַהוּא בַּר עָבֵיד רְעוּתָא דְּמַלְכָּא, מַלְכָּא פָּרִישׁ מָדוֹרֵיהּ מִמַּטְרוֹנִיתָא.

321. Rabbi Elazar was sitting before his father. He said to him. If there is an advocate in the world, he goes to the Queen, if there is an accuser, he goes to the Queen, BUT NOT HIGHER THEN MALCHUT. HE ASKS, why IS THIS SO? He replied IT IS SIMILAR to a king who had a son with the queen; as long as the son carries through the wishes of the king, the king will maintain his residence with the queen. If the son does not obey the king, the king removes his residence from the queen.

322. כַּךְ קוּדְשָׁא בְּרִיךְ הוּא וכ"י, כָּל זִמְנָא דְּיִשְׂרָאֵל עַבְדִּין רְעוּתָא דְּקוּדְשָׁא בְּרִיךְ הוּא, קוּדְשָׁא בְּרִיךְ הוּא שַׁוֵּי מָדוֹרֵיהּ בִּכְנֶסֶת יִשְׂרָאֵל. וְכָל זִמְנָא דְּיִשְׂרָאֵל לָא עַבְדִּין רְעוּתָא דְּקוּדְשָׁא בְּרִיךְ הוּא, קוּדְשָׁא בְּרִיךְ הוּא לָא שַׁוֵּי מָדוֹרֵיהּ בכ"י. מ"ט. בְּגִין דְּיִשְׂרָאֵל הוּא בְּרָא בּוּכְרָא דְּקוּדְשָׁא בְּרִיךְ הוּא, דִּכְתִיב בְּנִי בְכוֹרִי יִשְׂרָאֵל. אִמָּא, דָּא הִיא כְּנֶסֶת יִשְׂרָאֵל דִּכְתִיב וְאַל תִּטּוֹשׁ תּוֹרַת אִמֶּךָ.

322. It is so with the Holy One, blessed be He, and the Congregation of Yisrael. As long as Yisrael obey the will of the Holy One, blessed be He, He

installs His residence with the Congregation of Yisrael. When Yisrael disobey His will, the Holy One, blessed be He, no longer places His residence with the Congregation of Yisrael. Why? It is because Yisrael are firstborn of the Holy One, blessed be He, as it is written, "Yisrael is My son, My firstborn" (Shemot 4:22). The Congregation of Yisrael is the mother of Yisrael, as it is written, "And do not forsake the Torah of your mother" (Mishlei 1:8).

323. ת״ח, כָּל זִמְנָא דְיִשְׂרָאֵל רְחָקִין מֵהֵיכָלָא דְמַלְכָּא, כִּבְיָכוֹל מַטְרוֹנִיתָא אִתְרַחֲקַת עִמְּהוֹן. מ״ט. בְּגִין דְמַטְרוֹנִיתָא לָא אַקְדִּימַת קִיסְטָא לְהַאי בַּר, לְאַלְקָאָה לֵיהּ, לְמֵיהַךְ בְּאוֹרַח מֵישָׁר. בְּגִין דְמַלְכָּא לָא אַלְקֵי לִבְרֵיהּ לְעָלְמִין. אֶלָּא שָׁבֵיק כֹּלָּא בִּידָא דְמַטְרוֹנִיתָא, לְאַנְהָגָא הֵיכָלָא, וּלְאַלְקָאָה בְּרָהּ, וּלְדַבְּרָא לֵיהּ בְּאוֹרַח קְשׁוֹט, לְקָבְלֵיהּ דְמַלְכָּא.

323. Come and see: As long as Yisrael are distant from the King's palace, so to speak, the Queen distances herself with them FROM THE KING. What is the reason? It is because the Queen did not whip that son before, so he should walk in the right path. For the King never strikes his son, but leaves it to the hand of the Queen; she should manage the palace, punish her son, and guide him in the truthful way before the King.

324. וְרָזָא דְמִלָּה דִכְתִיב דִּבְרֵי לְמוֹאֵל מֶלֶךְ מַשָּׂא אֲשֶׁר יִסְּרַתּוּ אִמּוֹ, דָּא בַּת שֶׁבַע, וְהָא אִתְּמַר כְּתִיב, מִשְׁלֵי שְׁלֹמֹה בֵּן חָכָם יְשַׂמַּח אָב וּבֵן כְּסִיל תּוּגַת אִמּוֹ. תּוּגַת אִמּוֹ וַדַּאי. חֲמֵי מַה כְּתִיב, בֵּן חָכָם יְשַׂמַּח אָב, בְּעוֹד דְּהַאי בַּר אָזִיל בְּאוֹרַח מֵישָׁר, וְהוּא חַכִּימָא, יְשַׂמַּח אָב, דָּא מַלְכָּא קַדִּישָׁא לְעֵילָּא. יְשַׂמַּח אָב סְתָם. אִשְׁתְּכַח הַאי בַּר בְּאוֹרְחָא תְּקָלָא, מַה כְּתִיב וּבֵן כְּסִיל תּוּגַת אִמּוֹ. תּוּגַת אִמּוֹ וַדַּאי, דָּא כְּנֶסֶת יִשְׂרָאֵל. וְרָזָא דְמִלָּה כְּתִיב, וּבְפִשְׁעֲכֶם שֻׁלְּחָה אִמְּכֶם.

324. The secret of the matter, it is written, "The words of King Lemuel, the prophecy, that his mother taught him" (Mishlei 31:1). His mother is Batsheba, NAMELY, THE SECRET OF MALCHUT CALLED BATSHEBA (LIT.

'DAUGHTER OF SEVEN'). We have learned that it is written, "The proverbs
of Solomon. A wise son makes a glad father: but a foolish son is the grief of
his mother" (Mishlei 10:1). Assuredly he is the grief of his mother. See
what is written, "A wise son makes a glad father," MEANING so long as the
son walks in a straight path, and he is wise, he "makes a glad father." This
refers to the Holy King above, MEANING ZEIR ANPIN, as it is written,
"Makes a glad father" without specifying, WHICH POINTS TO THE FATHER
ABOVE. AND IF this son is on a stumbling manner, it is written, "But a
foolish son is the grief of his mother." For sure it is the grief of his mother,
referring to the Congregation of Yisrael, DENOTING MALCHUT. The secret
of the matter is the words, "And for your transgressions was your mother
put away" (Yeshayah 50:1), WHO IS MALCHUT.

325. ת"ח, לָא אִשְׁתְּכַח חֶדְוָותָא קַמֵּי קוּדְשָׁא בְּרִיךְ הוּא, כְּיוֹמָא דְּסָלִיק
שְׁלֹמֹה לְחָכְמְתָא, וְאָמַר שִׁיר הַשִּׁירִים. כְּדֵין נְהִירוּ אַנְפּוֹי דְּמַטְרוֹנִיתָא,
וְאָתֵי מַלְכָּא לְמִשְׁרֵי מָדוֹרֵיה עִמָּה. הה"ד, וַתֵּרֶב חָכְמַת שְׁלֹמֹה וְגוֹ'.
מַאי וַתֵּרֶב. דְּסַלְקָא שְׁפִירוּ דְּמַטְרוֹנִיתָא, וְאִתְרַבִּיאַת בְּדַרְגָּהָא עַל כָּל
שְׁאַר דַּרְגִּין, בְּגִין דְּמַלְכָּא שַׁוֵּי מָדוֹרֵיה בָּה. וְכָל כַּךְ לָמָה. בְּגִין
דְּאַפִּיקַת בְּרָא חַכִּימָא דָא לְעָלְמָא.

325. Come and see: There was not such joy before the Holy One, blessed be
He, as on the day that Solomon attained wisdom and recited Shir Hashirim.
Then the face of the Queen shone, the King placed His residence with her,
as it is written, "And Solomon's wisdom excelled..." (I Melachim 5:10).
What is meant by "excelled"? IT MEANS THAT the beauty of the Queen
increased, and her levels grew above all other levels SHE HAD EVER HAD,
because the King put His residence with her. And why is all that? Because
she produced this wise son.

326. וְכַד אַפִּיקַת לֵיה לִשְׁלֹמֹה, לְכָל יִשְׂרָאֵל אַפִּיקַת, וְכֻלְּהוּ הֲווֹ
בְּדַרְגִּין עִלָּאִין זַכָּאִין כִּשְׁלֹמֹה. דְּקוּדְשָׁא בְּרִיךְ הוּא חַדֵּי בְּהוּ, וְאִינּוּן
בֵּיה. וּבְיוֹמָא דְּשַׁכְלֵל שְׁלֹמֹה בֵּיתָא לְתַתָּא, אַתְקִינַת מַטְרוֹנִיתָא בֵּיתָא
לְמַלְכָּא. וְשַׁווּ מָדוֹרֵיהוֹן כַּחֲדָא, וּנְהִירוּ אַנְפָּהָא בְּחֶדְוָה שְׁלִימוּ. כְּדֵין
אִשְׁתְּכַח חֶדְוָותָא לְכֹלָּא, לְעֵילָּא וְתַתָּא. וְכָל כַּךְ לָמָה. בְּגִין דִּכְתִּיב,

מַשָּׁא אֲשֶׁר יִסְּרַתּוּ אִמּוֹ, דְּדַבְּרַת לֵיהּ לִרְעוּתָא דְּמַלְכָּא.

326. When she produced Solomon, MEANING SHE INSPIRED HIM WITH HER WISDOM, she produced all Yisrael. All merited the high levels as Solomon, as the Holy One, blessed be He, rejoiced with them and they with Him. On the day that Solomon constructed the Temple below, the Queen prepared the house for the King, they placed their residence together, her face glowed with total joy. Then there was joy for all, above and below. Why so? Because it is written, "That his mother taught him," as she guided according to the King's wishes.

327. וְכַד הַאי בַּר כְּמָה דַּאֲמֵינָא, לָא אִתְדְּבַּר לִרְעוּתֵיהּ דְּמַלְכָּא. כְּדֵין הִיא עֶרְיָיתָא דְּכֹלָּא, עֶרְיָיתָא דְּכָל סִטְרִין דְּהָא מַלְכָּא פָּרִישׁ מִמַּטְרוֹנִיתָא, וּמַטְרוֹנִיתָא אִתְרַחֲקַת מֵהֵיכָלֵיהּ, ובג"כ עֶרְיָיתָא הִיא דְּכֹלָּא. וְכִי לָא עֶרְיָיתָא הוּא, מַלְכָּא בְּלָא מַטְרוֹנִיתָא, וּמַטְרוֹנִיתָא בְּלָא מַלְכָּא. וְעַ"ד כְּתִיב, עֶרְוַת אָבִיךְ וְעֶרְוַת אִמְּךָ לֹא תְגַלֵּה אִמְּךָ הִיא. אִמְּךָ הִיא וַדַּאי, וְשַׁרְיָא עִמָּךְ, בְּגִינֵי כַּךְ לֹא תְגַלֶּה עֶרְוָתָהּ.

327. When this son, as I said, does not conduct himself to the satisfaction of the King, then there is nakedness everywhere, CAUSING THE REVELATION OF JUDGMENTS IN MALCHUT, THE SECRET OF THE UNCOVERING OF NAKEDNESS, nakedness on all sides, BOTH RIGHT AND LEFT. For the King now moves apart from the Queen, the Queen is distanced from His palace, so there is nakedness everywhere. Is this not nakedness if the King is not with the Queen, and the Queen without the King? Therefore, it is written, "The nakedness of your father, or the nakedness of your mother, shall you not uncover: she is your mother" (Vayikra 18:7), surely, DENOTING MALCHUT, and she dwells with you. Therefore, "you shall not uncover her nakedness."

54. "He shall mightily roar because of His habitation"

A Synopsis

Rabbi Shimon reveals the secret that when the lower Hei is withheld from receiving blessings, the upper Hei withholds blessings from every level. This happens when Zeir Anpin and Nukva are separated, and the source of the spring of blessings stops. Therefore from the day that the Temple was destroyed there has not been a day without curses or a day when blessings are found in the world. When people do not repent, the day eventually comes that the rulers of other nations are given permission to rule over Yisrael, and the upper Hei pours its blessings to the Other Side.

328. ר"ש אָקִישׁ יְדוֹי וּבָכָה, וְאָמַר וַוי אִי אֵימָא וְגַלֵּינָא רָזָא, וַוי אִי לָא אֵימָא, דְּיֵיבְדּוּן חַבְרַיָּיא מִלָּה. אֲהָהּ יְיָ׳ אֱלֹהִים כָּלָה אַתָּה עוֹשֶׂה אֶת שְׁאֵרִית יִשְׂרָאֵל. מַאי אֲהָהּ. וּמַאי כָּלָה אַתָּה עוֹשֶׂה. אֶלָּא רָזָא דְמִלָּה, בְּזִמְנָא דְהֵ׳ תַּתָּאָה אִתְתַּרְכַת מֵהֵיכָלָא דְמַלְכָּא, ה׳ אָחֳרָא עִלָּאָה בְּגִינָהּ מַנְעַת בִּרְכָתָא. וּכְדֵין כְּתִיב, אֲהָהּ כָּלָה אַתָּה עוֹשֶׂה. בְּגִין דְּכַד אִיהִי אִתְמַנְעַת מִבִּרְכָאן, ה׳ אָחֳרָא מַנְעַת לוֹן מִכֹּלָּא. מַאי טַעֲמָא. בְּגִין דְּבִרְכָאן לָא מִשְׁתַּכְּחֵי, אֶלָּא בַּאֲתַר דְּשַׁרְיָין דְּכַר וְנוּקְבָּא.

328. Rabbi Shimon clasped his hands and wept. He cried: Woe if I do speak and reveal the secret, woe if I do not and the friends lose THIS matter. Ah Hashem Elohim! Will You make a full end of the remnant of Yisrael?" (Yechezkel 11:13). What is meant by "Ah" and what is meant by "Will You make a full end"? HE ANSWERS: The secret of the matter is, that when the lower Hei OF YUD HEI VAV HEI, WHICH IS MALCHUT, is expelled from the chamber of the King, the other upper Hei OF YUD HEI VAV HEI, DENOTING BINAH, withholds the blessings for its sake. Then is written, "Ah (Aleph Hei Hei)...Will You make a full end," BECAUSE THE IMPAIRMENT REACHES BOTH HEIS OF YUD HEI VAV HEI, BINAH AND MALCHUT, because when THE LOWER HEI IS WITHHELD from receiving blessings, the other UPPER Hei withholds BLESSINGS from all, NOT SPREADING EVEN TO ZEIR ANPIN. What is the reason? It is because blessings are to be found only where there are Male and a Female, AND SINCE MALCHUT IS EXPELLED FROM ZEIR ANPIN, THERE ARE NO BLESSINGS IN ZEIR ANPIN BECAUSE OF HIS BEING WITHOUT THE FEMALE.

-382-

329. וְעַל דָּא כְּתִיב, יְיָ' מִמָּרוֹם יִשְׁאָג וּמִמְּעוֹן קָדְשׁוֹ יִתֵּן קוֹלוֹ שָׁאֹג יִשְׁאַג עַל נָוֵהוּ עַל נָוֵהוּ מַמָּשׁ. דָּא מַטְרוֹנִיתָא, וְדָא הוּא וַדַּאי. וּמַאי אוֹמֵר. אוֹי שֶׁהֶחֱרַבְתִּי אֶת בֵּיתִי וְכוּ'. בֵּיתִי זִוּוּגָא דְּמַטְרוֹנִיתָא. וְדָא הוּא וַדַּאי, עֶרְוַת אָבִיךָ וְעֶרְוַת אִמְּךָ לֹא תְגַלֵּה. דְּהָא מִכָּל סִטְרִין עֶרְיָיתָא הוּא. וּכְדֵין, לָבְשׁוּ שָׁמַיִם קַדְרוּת וְשַׂק הוּשַׂם כְּסוּתָם דְּהָא אֲתַר אַחֲסָנַת בִּרְכָאן דְּמַבּוּעֵין דְּנַחֲלִין דַּהֲווֹ נְגִידִין וְשַׁקְיָין כַּדְקָא חֲזוּ, אִתְמְנָעוּ.

329. So it is written, "Hashem shall roar from on high, and utter His voice from His holy habitation; He shall mightily roar because of His habitation" (Yirmeyah 25:30), because of His actual habitation, namely the Queen, WHO IS GONE. It is surely so THAT HE ROARS. What does He say? THUS: woe that I have demolished My house. "My house" MEANS the union with the Queen. This is surely the meaning of, "The nakedness of your father, or the nakedness of your mother, shall you not uncover." From all directions there is nakedness, NAMELY BLEMISH. FOR WHEN MALCHUT, YOUR MOTHER, PARTED DUE TO THE SIN OF THE LOWER BEINGS, THEN THE LIGHTS DEPARTED FROM ZEIR ANPIN AS WELL. THUS, ZEIR ANPIN, YOUR FATHER, WAS DAMAGED. Then "I clothe the heavens with blackness, and I make sackcloth their covering" (Yeshayah 50:3), MEANING ZEIR ANPIN REFERRED TO AS HEAVEN, as the place of the reception of blessings of the springs' sources, WHICH ARE IN BINAH which were flowing and watering ZEIR ANPIN properly, withdrew AND STOPPED.

330. תָּנֵינָן, כַּד אִתְפְּרַשׁ מַלְכָּא מִמַּטְרוֹנִיתָא, וּבִרְכָּאן לָא מִשְׁתַּכְּחָן, כְּדֵין אִקְרֵי ו"י. מ"ט ו"י. דְּתַנְיָא, רֵישָׁא דִּיסוֹד י', דְּהָא יְסוֹד ו' זְעֵירָא הוּא, וְקוּדְשָׁא בְּרִיךְ הוּא ו' רַבְרְבָא עִלָּאָה. וְעַ"ד כְּתִיב וָ"ו תְּרֵין וָוִין כַּחֲדָא, וְרֵישָׁא דְּהַאי יְסוֹד י' הוּא. וְכַד אִתְרַחֲקַת מַטְרוֹנִיתָא מִמַּלְכָּא, וּבִרְכָּאן אִתְמְנָעוּ מִמַּלְכָּא, וְזִוּוּגָא לָא אִשְׁתְּכַח בְּרֵישָׁא דִּיסוֹד, נָטִיל ו' עִלָּאָה לְהַאי רֵישָׁא דִּיסוֹד דְּהוּא י', וְנָגִיד לֵיהּ לְגַבֵּיהּ, כְּדֵין הוּא ו"י, ו"י לְכֹלָּא, לְעִלָּאִין וְתַתָּאִין.

330. We have learned that when the King parted from the Queen and there were no blessings, ZEIR ANPIN is called 'woe (Vav Yud)', MEANING WOE

IS TO ME. Why IS IT CALLED "woe"? IT IS as we learned that the head of
Yesod is the Yud, as Yesod ITSELF is a small Vav, and the Holy one blessed
be He, MEANING ZEIR ANPIN, is a large higher Vav. Therefore, Vav is fully
spelled with two Vav's together, POINTING TO ZEIR ANPIN AND YESOD.
The top of this Yesod is Yud. When the Queen is separated from the King
and the blessings are withheld from the King, DENOTING ZEIR ANPIN, and
there is no coupling at the head of Yesod, THEN the upper Vav, NAMELY
ZEIR ANPIN, takes the head of Yesod, namely Yud, and draws it to itself.
Then THE COMBINATION becomes Vai (woe), MEANING "woe" to all, the
upper and the lower; SINCE THE LOWER BEINGS DO NOT RECEIVE, THE
UPPER DO NOT RECEIVE SO AS TO POUR UPON THEM, AS MENTIONED.

331. וְעַ"ד תָּנֵינָן, מִיּוֹמָא דְאִתְחֲרִיב יְרוּשָׁלַם, בִּרְכָאן לָא אִשְׁתְּכָחוּ
בְּעָלְמָא, וְלֵית לָךְ יוֹם דְּלָא אִשְׁתְּכַח בֵּיה לְוָוטִין, דְּהָא בִּרְכָאן אִתְמְנָעוּ
בְּכָל יוֹם. אָמַר לֵיה, אוֹ הָכִי, אוֹ"י אוֹ הוֹ"י, מַהוּ.

331. Therefore, we learned from the day that the Temple was destroyed,
blessings are not to be found in the world, and there is not a day in which
there are no curses, as the blessings THAT ARE SUPPOSED TO COME daily
are withheld, AND INSTEAD BECOME CURSES. He replied, if so, If it was
written: Oy or Hoy, AND NOT VAI what is THEIR EXPLANATION?

332. אָמַר לֵיה, כַּד מִלָּה תַּלְיָא בִּתְשׁוּבָה, וְלָא תַּיְיבִין, כְּדֵין ה' עִלָּאָה
נָטִיל לוֹן, וְאַנְגִּיד לְוָאו וְי', לְגַבֵּהּ, בְּגִין דְּלָא תַּיְיבִין, כְּדֵין אִקְרֵי הוֹי.
הוֹי כַּד אִסְתַּלָּק מַלְכָּא לְעֵילָּא לְעֵילָּא, וְצַוְוחִין בְּנֵי נָשָׁא וְלָא אַשְׁגַּח
בְּהוּ. וְהַהוּא עִלָּאָה אֶהְיֶה טְמִירָא, סָלִיק לוֹ', וְי' לְגַבֵּיה, בְּגִין דְּלָא
אִתְקְבִּיל צְלוֹתֵיהּ, כְּדֵין אִקְרֵי אוֹי, דְּהָא א' סָלִיק לְגַבֵּיה הוּ' וְי'. וּכְדֵין
תְּשׁוּבָה לָא אִשְׁתְּכַח. וְעַ"ד אִסְתַּלָּק מֵאִלֵּין אַתְוָון ה', דְּהָא בִּתְשׁוּבָה
לָא תַּלְיָיא.

332. He said to him: When things depend upon repentance and people do
not repent, the sublime Hei OF YUD HEI VAV HEI, BEING BINAH, takes
and attracts the Vav and the Yud to itself, as they are not repenting. It then
BECOMES A COMBINATION OF HEI-VAV-YUD called Hoy, MEANING Hoy

(lit. 'ah'), when the King, ZEIR ANPIN, departs higher and higher TO BINAH. People cry but no one pays attention. SOMETIMES, that supernal concealed NAME, EHEYEH, DENOTING KETER, raises the Vav, ZEIR ANPIN, and the Yud, BEING THE HEAD OF YESOD, to itself, because one's prayer is not accepted, AND IT BECOMES THE COMBINATION OY (ALEPH VAV YUD). Then it is called Oy, as the Aleph THAT IS EHEYEH brings up to it the Vav and the Yud. Then repentance is not available, so the Hei departs from these letters, as it is no longer dependent on repentance, WHICH IS THE SECRET OF BINAH CALLED HEI.

333. וַדַּאי כַּד אַסְגִּיאוּ חוֹבֵי עָלְמָא טְפֵי, וּתְשׁוּבָה הֲוָה תַּלְיָא בְּקַדְמֵיתָא, וְלָא בָּעוּ, כְּדֵין אִסְתַּלָּק ה', וא' סָלִיק לוֹ' יוֹ"ד לְגַבֵּיהּ, וְאִקְרֵי אוֹי. וְכַד חָרִיב בֵּי מַקְדְּשָׁא, וּתְשׁוּבָה אִסְתַּלָּקַת, כְּדֵין צָוְוחוּ וְאָמְרוּ, אוֹי לָנוּ כִּי פָנָה הַיּוֹם. מַאי כִּי פָנָה הַיּוֹם. דָּא הוּא יוֹמָא עִלָּאָה, דְּאִקְרֵי תְּשׁוּבָה, דְּאִסְתַּלָּק וְאִתְעֲבַר, וְלָא שְׁכִיחַ. הַהוּא יוֹמָא דְּאִשְׁתְּמוֹדַע, לְפַשְׁטָא יְמִינָא לְקַבְּלָא חַיָּיבִין, וְהָא אִתְפְּנֵי מִכֹּלָּא, וְלָא אִשְׁתְּכַח, וְעַל דָּא אָמְרוּ אוֹי, וְלָא הוֹי. כִּי יִנָּטוּ צִלְלֵי עָרֶב, דְּהָא אִתְיְיהִיב רְשׁוּ לְרַבְרְבֵי מְמָנָן דִּשְׁאָר עַמִּין, לְמִשְׁלַט עֲלַיְיהוּ.

333. Surely this is when sins in the world multiply excessively. At first, repentance was available but they did not want TO REPENT, then the Hei takes off, BEING BINAH, THE SECRET OF REPENTANCE and the Aleph, BEING KETER, raises the Vav Yud to it, so it is now called Oy. When the Temple was destroyed and repentance was gone, then they cried and said, "Woe (Oy) to us! For the day declines" (Yirmeyah 6:4). What is meant by "For the day declines"? It refers to the supernal day, MEANING BINAH called repentance, which departed and is not available. This is that specific day that extends its right hand to welcome evildoers. It has departed from all and is not available. Therefore, they say Oy instead of Hoy "for the shadows of the evening are lengthened" (Ibid.), MEANING PERMISSION has been granted to the rulers over other nations to rule over YISRAEL.

334. תָּאנָא, סָלִיק ו' לְעֵילָא לְעֵילָא, וְהֵיכָלָא אִתּוֹקַד, וְעַמָּא אִתְגְּלֵי, וּמַטְרוֹנִיתָא אִתְתָּרְכַת, וּבֵיתָא אִתְחֲרָבַת. לְבָתַר כַּד נָחִית וו' לְאַתְרֵיהּ,

אַשְׁגַּח בְּבֵיתֵיהּ וְהָא אִתְחֲרִיב, בָּעֵי לְמַטְרוֹנִיתָא, וְהָא אִתְרַחֲקַת וְאַזְלַת. חָמָא לְהֵיכָלֵיהּ, וְהָא אִתּוֹקַד. בָּעָא לְעַמָּא, וְהָא אִתְגְּלֵי. חָמָא לְבִרְכָּאן דְּנַחֲלִין עֲמִיקִין דַּהֲווֹ נַגְדִּין, וְהָא אִתְמְנָעוּ. כְּדֵין כְּתִיב, וַיִּקְרָא יְיָ' אֱלֹהִים צְבָאוֹת בַּיּוֹם הַהוּא לִבְכִי וּלְמִסְפֵּד וּלְקָרְחָה וְלַחֲגוֹר שָׂק. וּכְדֵין לָבְשׁוּ שָׁמַיִם קַדְרוּת.

334. We have learned that the Vav, DENOTING ZEIR ANPIN, ascended high up TO KETER, BEING THE SECRET OF ALEPH, AS MENTIONED. The sanctuary was consumed, the people exiled, the Queen expelled, and the Temple was in ruins. Later, as the Vav returned to its position, it took notice of the Temple and found it in ruins. It sought the Queen , but she moved far away. It saw its sanctuary, but it was consumed by fire, and it looked for the people but they were exiled. It saw the blessings of the deep streams FROM BINAH that were flowing, but now ceased. Then it is written, "And on that day did Adonai Elohim Tzevaot call to weeping, and to mourning, and to baldness, and to girding with sackcloth" (Yeshayah 22:12). Then, "I clothe the heavens, ZEIR ANPIN, with blackness."

335. כְּדֵין ו' י' אִתְנְגִיד חַד לָקֳבֵיל חַד. וְהֵ' עִלָּאָה, נָגִיד מַבּוּעֵי לְסִטְרָא אָחֳרָא, וּבִרְכָּאן לָא מִשְׁתַּכְּחָן. דְּהָא דְּכַר וְנוּקְבָּא לָא אִשְׁתְּכָחוּ, וְלָא שַׁרְיָין כַּחֲדָא. כְּדֵין שָׁאַג יִשְׁאַג עַל נָוֵהוּ. בָּכָה ר"ש, וּבָכָה ר' אֶלְעָזָר, אָמַר ר' אֶלְעָזָר, בְּכִיָּה תְּקִיעָא בְּלִבָּאי מִסִּטְרָא חֲדָא, וְחֶדְוָותָא בְּלִבָּאי מִסִּטְרָא אָחֳרָא. דְּהָא שְׁמַעְנָא מִלִּין, דְּלָא שְׁמַעְנָא עַד הַשְׁתָּא, זַכָּאָה חוּלָקִי.

335. Then the Vav and Yud draw one towards the other. THE YUD, BEING THE HEAD OF YESOD, IS DRAWN TO THE VAV, ZEIR ANPIN, AND SEPARATES FROM MALCHUT. The upper Hei OF YUD HEI VAV HEI, BEING BINAH, pours its sources to the Other Side, and no blessings abound, because no Male and Female are present, ZEIR ANPIN AND MALCHUT, and they do not dwell together. Then "He shall mightily roar because of His habitation" (Yirmeyah 25:30), MALCHUT. Rabbi Shimon wept and Rabbi Elazar wept. Rabbi Elazar said: There is a lament placed in my heart on one side and a joy in my heart on the other, as I have heard words that I never heard until now. How blessed is my lot.

55. "The nakedness of your father's wife shall you not uncover"

A Synopsis

Rabbi Shimon says that there is concealed knowledge in the words of the title verse. He says that "your father's wife" is the wife of Zeir Anpin who is in exile with Yisrael and who is far from Him. When she is called "your mother" she is with the King, and the command is to be careful not to separate them through sinning. Even when she is in exile a man must be careful not to alienate her so that she will not cease to stand guard over him.

336. עֶרְוַת אֵשֶׁת אָבִיךְ לֹא תְגַלֵּה, מַאן אֵשֶׁת אָבִיךְ. אר"ש, הָא תָּנֵינָן, כָּל מִלּוֹי דְּאוֹרַיְיתָא סָתִים וְגַלְיָא, כְּמָה דִּשְׁמָא קַדִּישָׁא סָתִים וְגַלְיָא, אוֹרַיְיתָא דְּהִיא שְׁמָא קַדִּישָׁא, הָכִי נָמֵי סָתִים וְגַלְיָא. הָכָא כֹּלָּא בְּאִתְגַּלְיָיא, יְדִיעָא סָתִים כְּמָה דְּאוֹקִימְנָא.

336. "The nakedness of your father's wife shall you not uncover" (Vayikra 18:8). HE QUESTIONS: Who is your father's wife? Rabbi Shimon said: We learned that all the words of the Torah are concealed yet revealed, just as the Holy Name is concealed yet revealed. IT IS WRITTEN YUD HEI VAV HEI AND READ ADONAI. The Torah, which is the Holy Name, is also concealed and revealed. Here IN THIS VERSE, all is openly manifest, MEANING ACCORDING TO THE LITERAL MEANING THE VERSE IS SPEAKING ABOUT THE WIFE OF THE FATHER. BUT THERE IS IN IT concealed knowledge, as we have established.

337. וְהַאי קְרָא הָכִי הוּא, אֵשֶׁת אָבִיךְ תָּאנָא, כָּל זִמְנָא דְּמַטְרוֹנִיתָא אִשְׁתְּכַחַת בְּמַלְכָּא, וְיַנְקָא לָךְ, אִקְרֵי אִמָּךְ. הַשְׁתָּא דְּאִתְגַּלְיָא עִמָּךְ וְאִתְרָחֲקַת מִן מַלְכָּא, אֵשֶׁת אָבִיךְ אִתְקְרֵי. אִנְתּוּ הִיא דְּמַלְכָּא קַדִּישָׁא לָא אִתְפְּטָרַת בְּתֵרוּכִין מִינֵּהּ, אִנְתְּתֵיהּ הִיא וַדַּאי. כְּמָה דִכְתִיב, כֹּה אָמַר יְיָ' אֵי זֶה סֵפֶר כְּרִיתוּת אִמְּכֶם אֲשֶׁר שִׁלַּחְתִּיהָ. אֶלָּא וַדַּאי אִנְתּוּ הִיא דְּמַלְכָּא, אע"ג דְּאִתְגַּלְיָיא.

337. This verse is such, "Your father's wife" we have learned. As long as the Queen is with the King and she nurtures you, FROM HER ABUNDANCE, she is called your mother. Now, IN EXILE, she has been exiled with you and

-387-

is far from the King, so she is called "your father's wife." She is the wife of the Holy King, ZEIR ANPIN, as she was never set free with a divorce. She is surely His wife, as it is written, "Thus says Hashem, Where is the bill of your mother's divorcement, with which I have put her away?" (Yeshayah 50:1). Surely she is the wife of the King even though she was exiled.

338. וְעַ"ד פָּקִיד עָלָה תְּרֵי זִמְנֵי, כַּד יָתְבָא בְּמַלְכָּא בְּזִוּוּגָא חַד, וְאִתְקְרֵי אִמָּךְ, דִּכְתִיב עֶרְוַת אִמְּךָ לֹא תְגַלֵּה, לָא תַּעֲבִיד דְּיִתְרַחֲקוּן דָּא מִן דָּא, וְתִשְׁתְּלַח עַל חוֹבָךְ, כְּמָה דִכְתִיב וּבְפִשְׁעֲכֶם שֻׁלְחָה אִמְּכֶם. וְחַד, כַּד הִיא בְּגָלוּתָא עִמָּךְ, וְאִתְגַּלְיָיא מֵהֵיכָלָא דְמַלְכָּא, וְאִתְקְרֵי אִנְתּוּ דְמַלְכָּא. אע"ג דְּאִתְרַחֲקַת מִנֵּיהּ לָא תַּעֲבִיד בְּגִין דְּתַעְדֵּי מִבֵּינָךְ, וְיִשְׁלְטוּן בָּךְ שַׂנְאָךְ, וְלָא תִּסְתַּמַּר עֲלָךְ בְּגָלוּתָא. הה"ד עֶרְוַת אֵשֶׁת אָבִיךָ לֹא תְגַלֵּה. מַאי טַעְמָא. בְּגִין כִּי עֶרְוַת אָבִיךָ הוּא. אע"ג דְּאִתְרַחֲקַת מִן מַלְכָּא, אַשְׁגָּחוּתָא דְמַלְכָּא בָּהּ תְּדִירָא, וּבָעֲיָא לְאִסְתַּמְּרָא לְקָבְלָה יַתִּיר, וְלָא תֵּיחוּב לְגַבָּהּ.

338. Therefore, He commanded about her twice, once when she sits united with the King and is called "your mother," as written, "The nakedness of your mother, shall you not uncover," MEANING do not cause them to separate from each other, or her to be sent away because of your sin, as it is written, "And for your transgressions was your mother put away" (Ibid.). The other was when she is in exile with you, exiled from the palace of the King, called THEN wife of the King. Even though she was distanced from THE KING, do not cause her to turn away from you, and thus your enemies will gain control over you and she will not guard you in exile. This is what is written, "The nakedness of your father's wife shall you not uncover." What is the reason? Because she is "your father's nakedness." Although she was distanced from the King, the King's supervision is still upon her constantly, so one needs to watch himself more carefully in relation to her, so as not to sin against her.

56. "That He see no unclean thing in you"

A Synopsis
Rabbi Shimon begins speaking about the Shechinah and how she protects Yisrael, especially when they are in exile, from the other nations. Only when they sin is her power to protect them weakened. We learn that the children of Yisrael are detained in exile for three reasons: because they treated the Shechinah with contempt, because they turned their faces away from her, and because they defiled themselves.

339. רָבִּי שִׁמְעוֹן פָּתַח, כִּי יְיָ' אֱלֹהֶיךָ מִתְהַלֵּךְ בְּקֶרֶב מַחֲנֶךָ לְהַצִּילְךָ וְגוֹ'. כִּי יְיָ' אֱלֹהֶיךָ: דָּא שְׁכִינְתָּא, דְּאִשְׁתְּכָחַת בְּהוּ בְּיִשְׂרָאֵל, וְכ"ש בְּגָלוּתָא, לְאַגָּנָא עָלַיְיהוּ תְּדִירָא מִכָּל סִטְרִין, וּמִכָּל שְׁאָר עַמִּין, דְּלָא יְשֵׁיצוּן לְהוּ לְיִשְׂרָאֵל.

339. Rabbi Shimon opened the discussion saying, "For Hashem your Elohim walks in the midst of your camp, to deliver you..." (Devarim 23:15). "For Hashem your Elohim" refers to the Shechinah prevailing in Yisrael, all the more so in exile, to shield them always from all sides and from all other nations so that they cannot destroy Yisrael.

340. דְּתַנְיָא, לָא יַכְלִין שַׂנְאֵיהוֹן דְּיִשְׂרָאֵל לְאַבְאָשָׁא לְהוּ, עַד דְּיִשְׂרָאֵל מַחֲלִישִׁין חֵילָא דִּשְׁכִינְתָּא מִקַּמֵּי רַבְרְבֵי מְמָנָן דִּשְׁאָר עַמִּין. כְּדֵין יַכְלִין לְהוֹן שַׂנְאֵיהוֹן דְּיִשְׂרָאֵל, וְשַׁלְטִין עָלַיְיהוּ, וְגָזְרִין עָלַיְיהוּ כַּמָּה גְּזֵירִין בִּישִׁין. וְכַד אִינּוּן תַּיְיבִין לְקַבְלָהּ, הִיא מִתַבְּרַת חֵילָא וְתוּקְפָּא דְּכָל אִינּוּן מְמָנָן רַבְרְבִין, וְתַבְרַת חֵילָא וְתוּקְפָּא דְּשַׂנְאֵיהוֹן דְּיִשְׂרָאֵל, וְאִתְפְּרָעָא לְהוּ מִכֹּלָּא.

340. We have learned that the foes of Yisrael are not capable of harming them until Yisrael weaken the power of the Shechinah before the appointed ministers of other nations. Only then can the enemies of Yisrael overcome them, rule them and decree many harsh decrees regarding them. When Yisrael return towards Her WITH REPENTANCE, THE SHECHINAH smashes the power and strength of these appointed chiefs, breaks the power and strength of the enemies of Yisrael and takes revenge against them all.

341. וְעַל דָּא וְהָיָה מַחֲנֶיךָ קָדוֹשׁ, דְּבָעֵי ב״נ דְּלָא יִסְתְּאַב בְּחוֹבוֹי, וְיַעֲבָר עַל פִּתְגָּמֵי אוֹרַיְיתָא. דְּאִי עָבֵיד הָכֵי, מְסָאֲבִין לֵיהּ, כְּמָה דִּכְתִּיב וְנִטְמֵתֶם בָּם, בְּלָא א׳. וְתָאנָא, מָאתָן וּתְמַנְיָא וְאַרְבְּעִין שַׁיְיפִין בְּגוּפָא, וְכֻלְּהוּ אִסְתַּאֲבָן, כַּד אִיהוּ אִסְתָּאַב. כְּלוֹמַר, כַּד בָּעֵי לְאִסְתַּאֲבָא. וְעַ״ד, וְהָיָה מַחֲנֶיךָ קָדוֹשׁ. מַאי מַחֲנֶיךָ, אִלֵּין אִינּוּן שַׁיְיפֵי גוּפָא. וְלֹא יִרְאֶה בְךָ עֶרְוַת דָּבָר, מַאי עֶרְוַת דָּבָר. עֶרְיְיתָא נוּכְרָאָה לְהַאי דָּבָר רְמַז, כְּמָה דְּאוֹקִימְנָא. דְּאִי הָכִי, וְשָׁב מֵאַחֲרֶיךָ וַדַּאי. וְעַל דָּא עֶרְוַת אֵשֶׁת אָבִיךָ לֹא תְגַלֵּה. מ״ט. בְּגִין דִּכְתִּיב עֶרְוַת אָבִיךָ הוּא, כְּמָה דְּאוֹקִימְנָא.

341. Therefore, "shall your camp be holy" (Ibid.). One must SEE that he does not become defiled through his sins and through transgressing the words of Torah. If he does so, they defile him, as it is written, "That you should be defiled (Heb. *venitmetem*) by them" (Vayikra 11:43). The word "*Venitmetem*" is written without Aleph, POINTING TO AN EXTRA MEASURE OF DEFILEMENT. We have learned that there are 248 limbs in the body and all become defiled when one becomes defiled, meaning as soon as he wants to become defiled, it IMMEDIATELY ACQUIRES DEFILEMENT. "Therefore shall your camp be holy." What is meant by "your camp"? This refers to the limbs of the body. "That He see no unclean (lit. 'nakedness of') thing in you" (Devarim 23:15). What is a "nakedness of thing"? This is an allusion THAT YOU MUST NOT BRING a strange nakedness to come to this thing, FOR IT IS STRANGE TO MALCHUT CALLED 'THING', as we have established. If YOU DO so, He will surely "turn away from you" (Ibid.). Therefore "your father's wife shall you not uncover" (Vayikra 18:8). What is the reason? It is because it is written, "It is your father's nakedness" (Ibid.), as we have established.

342. תָּאנָא, עַל ג׳ מִלִּין מִתְעַכְּבִין יִשְׂרָאֵל בְּגָלוּתָא. עַל דְּעַבְדִין קְלָנָא בִּשְׁכִינְתָּא בְּגָלוּתָא. וּמֵהַדְרֵי אַנְפַּיְיהוּ מִן שְׁכִינְתָּא, וְעַל דִּמְסָאֲבֵי גַרְמַיְיהוּ קָמֵי שְׁכִינְתָּא. וְכֻלְּהוּ אוֹקִימְנָא בְּמַתְנִיתָא דִּילָן.

342. We have learned that Yisrael are detained in exile for three things: For treating the Shechinah with contempt in exile; for turning away their face from the Shechinah, AS IT IS WRITTEN, "FOR THEY HAVE TURNED THEIR BACK TO ME, AND NOT THEIR FACE" (YIRMEYAH 2:27). Finally, for

defiling themselves before the Shechinah, WITHOUT CONSIDERING THAT THE SHECHINAH IS WITH THEM IN EXILE. We explained them all in our Mishnah.

57. A man who had a mark on his face

A Synopsis

The rabbis encounter a man with a mark on his face, and they deduce that he has transgressed the Torah through some kind of incest. The man confesses that he did lay with his sister, after which he intervened in an argument and was struck on the forehead. A doctor saved him by giving him spiritual healing, and the doctor was Rabbi Samlai. Because the man repents, Rabbi Aba cures his mark on the spot. The man promises to toil day and night in the Torah from now on. Another time, we hear that same man lecturing on the Torah, saying that evil people are rewarded in this world but that God will obliterate them in the World to Come, where they will be dust under the feet of the righteous. Anyone who transgresses the Torah is marked by the Torah so that the eyes of Hashem recognize him and warn others to stay away from him.

343. רְבִּי אַבָּא, הֲוָה אָזִיל לְקַפּוֹטְקִיָּא, וַהֲוָה עִמֵּיהּ רְבִּי יוֹסֵי. עַד דַּהֲווֹ אָזְלֵי, חָמוּ חַד בַּר נָשׁ, דַּהֲוָה אָתֵי, וּרְשִׁימָא חַד בְּאַנְפּוֹי. א"ר אַבָּא, נִסְטֵי מֵהַאי אוֹרְחָא, דְּהָא אַנְפּוֹי דְּדֵין אַסְהִידוּ עֲלֵיהּ, דְּעָבַר בַּעֲרָיָיתָא דְּאוֹרַיְיתָא, בְּגִינֵי כַּךְ אִתְרְשִׁים בְּאַנְפּוֹי. א"ל רְבִּי יוֹסֵי, אִי הַאי רְשִׁימָא הֲוָה לֵיהּ כַּד הֲוָה יְנוּקָא, מַאי עֲרָיָיתָא אִשְׁתְּכַח בֵּיהּ. א"ל, אֲנָא חֲמֵינָא בְּאַנְפּוֹי, דְּאַסְהִידוּ בַּעֲרָיָיתָא דְּאוֹרַיְיתָא.

343. Rabbi Aba was going to Cappadocia with Rabbi Yosi. As they were going, they saw a man approaching there who had a mark on his face. Rabbi Aba said: Let us leave this road as this man's face testifies that he transgressed the rules of incest in the Torah. Therefore, his face is marked. Rabbi Yosi replied: If he had this mark since childhood, what incest would be then with him? He replied: I see his face testifying that he transgressed on a sexual misconduct mentioned in the Torah.

344. קָרָא לֵיהּ רְבִּי אַבָּא, א"ל אֵימָא מִלָּה, הַאי רְשִׁימָא דְּאַנְפָּךְ, מַה הוּא. אָמַר לוֹן, בְּמָטוּתָא מִנַּיְיכוּ, לָא תַּעַנְשׁוּ יַתִּיר לְהַהוּא בַּר נָשׁ, דְּהָא חוֹבוֹי קָא גָּרְמוּ לֵיהּ. אָמַר רְבִּי אַבָּא מַהוּ אָמַר לֵיהּ. יוֹמָא חַד הֲוֵינָא אָזִיל בְּאָרְחָא אֲנִי וַאֲחוֹתִי, שָׁרֵינָא בְּחַד אוֹשְׁפִּיזָא, וְרָוֵינָא חַמְרָא, וְכָל

הַהוּא לֵילְיָא אֲחִידְנָא בַּאֲחָתִי. בְּצַפְרָא קַמְנָא, וְאוֹשְׁפִּיזָאי קָטַט בְּחַד
גַּבְרָא, עָיֵילְנָא בֵּינַיְיהוּ, וְקַטְרוּ לִי דָא מֵהַאי גִּיסָא, וְדָא מֵהַאי גִּיסָא,
וּרְשִׁימָא דָא הֲוָה עָיֵיל לְבֵי מוֹחָא, וְאִשְׁתְּזַבְנָא עַל יְדָא דְּחַד אַסְיָיא
דְּאִית בְּגַוָון.

344. Rabbi Aba called him. He said to him, Tell me this, what is this mark
on your face? He replied: Please do not punish anymore this man, as his sins
caused this mark. Rabbi Aba said: What happened? He answered: One day
my sister and I were traveling, we stayed in one inn and we become
intoxicated. All night, I held my sister. In the morning, I awoke and found
the innkeeper arguing with another man. I intervened IN ORDER TO
SEPARATE THEM. They struck me, one from one side and the other from the
other side. This mark has remained on my forehead. I was saved by a doctor
who was among us.

345. אָמַר לֵיה, מַאן הוּא אַסְיָיא. אָמַר לֵיה, רִבִּי שַׂמְלָאי הוּא. א"ל
מַאי אַסְווּתָא יָהַב לָךְ. א"ל אַסְווּתָא דְּנַפְשָׁא. וּמֵהַהוּא יוֹמָא אַהֲדַרְנָא
בִּתְשׁוּבָה. וּבְכָל יוֹמָא חֲזֵינָא אַנְפָּאי בְּחַד חֵיזוּ, וּבָכֵינָא קַמֵי קוּדְשָׁא
בְּרִיךְ הוּא, דְּהוּא רִבּוֹן עָלְמִין עַל הַהוּא חוֹבָה. וּמֵאִינּוּן דִּמְעִין אַסְחֵינָא
אַנְפָּאי. אָמַר רִבִּי אַבָּא, אִי לָאו דְּאִתְמְנַע מִנָךְ תְּשׁוּבָה, אַעֲבַרְנָא
מֵאַנְפָּךְ הַהוּא רְשִׁימָא. אֲבָל קָרֵינָא עָלָיךְ, וְסָר עֲוֹנֶךְ וְחַטָּאתְךְ תְּכוּפָּר.
אָמַר לֵיה, ג' זִמְנִין אֵימָא. אָמַר לֵיה ג' זִמְנִין, וְאִתְעֲבַר רְשִׁימָא.

345. He said to him: Who is the doctor? He replied: He is Rabbi Samlai. He
asked: What cure did he give you? He replied: Spiritual healing. From that
day, I returned with repentance. Every day I see my face in the mirror,
WITHOUT ANY CHANGE. I have wept before the Holy One, blessed be He, עם
דו the Master of the world for that sin. With these tears, I have washed my
face. Rabbi Aba said: If repentance would not have been withheld from you,
I would have removed the impression on your face, but I will announce
upon you, "And your iniquity is taken away, and your sin is purged"
(Yeshayah 6:7). He told him to repeat this three times. He said it three times
and the mark disappeared.

346. אָמַר ר' אַבָּא, וַדַּאי מָארָךְ הָא בָּעָא לְאַעְבְּרָא מִנָךְ, דְּוַדַּאי

בְּתְשׁוּבָה אִשְׁתְּכַחַת. אָמַר לֵיהּ, נָדַרְנָא מֵהַאי יוֹמָא לְאִתְעַסְּקָא
בְּאוֹרַיְיתָא יְמָמָא וְלֵילְיָא. אָמַר לֵיהּ, מַה שְׁמָךְ. אָמַר לֵיהּ אֶלְעָזָר. אָמַר
לֵיהּ אֵל עָזַר, וַדַּאי שְׁמָא גָרִים, דֵּאֱלָהָךְ סִיַּיעָךְ, וַהֲוָה בְּסַעֲדָךְ, שַׁדְרֵיהּ
רִבִּי אַבָּא וּבַרְכֵיהּ.

346. Rabbi Aba said: Surely your Master wished to remove THE MARK from
you, as you were in a state of repentance. He said to him: I vow from this
day ONWARD to toil in Torah day and night. He said to him: What is your
name? He replied: Elazar. He responded: El Azar, (lit. 'God helped'), surely
the name has some bearing, as your Elohim helped you and was with you.
Rabbi Aba sent him off and blessed him.

347. לְזִמְנָא אָחֳרָא, הֲוָה רִבִּי אַבָּא אָזִיל לְגַבֵּי ר"ש, עָאל בְּמָאתֵיהּ,
אַשְׁכְּחֵיהּ דַּהֲוָה יָתִיב וְדָרִישׁ, אִישׁ בַּעַר לֹא יֵדַע וּכְסִיל לֹא יָבִין אֶת
זֹאת. אִישׁ בַּעַר לֹא יֵדַע וְגוֹ', כַּמָּה טִפְּשִׁין אִינוּן בְּנֵי עָלְמָא, דְּלָא
מַשְׁגִּיחִין וְלָא יַדְעִין וְלָא מִסְתַּכְּלִין לְמִנְדַע אוֹרְחוֹי דְּקוּדְשָׁא בְּרִיךְ הוּא,
עַל מַה קַיְימִין בְּעָלְמָא. מַאן מְעַכֵּב לְהוּ לְמִנְדַע טִפְּשׁוּתָא דִּלְהוֹן. בְּגִין
דְּלָא מִשְׁתַּדְלֵי בְּאוֹרַיְיתָא, דְּאִילוּ הֲווֹ מִשְׁתַּדְלֵי בְּאוֹרַיְיתָא יִנְדְעוּן
אוֹרְחוֹי דְּקוּדְשָׁא בְּרִיךְ הוּא.

347. Another time, Rabbi Aba went to Rabbi Shimon. He entered his city
and found THAT VERY SAME PERSON WHO PREVIOUSLY HAD THE MARK
sitting and lecturing, "A brutish man does not know; nor does a fool
understand this" (Tehilim 92:7). "A brutish man does not know..." Look
how foolish people are, for they do not pay attention, know, nor examine in
order to know the ways of the Holy One, blessed be He, for what purpose
they are in the world. What blocks them from perceiving their own
stupidity? It must be due to their not toiling in the Torah, for if these people
would toil in Torah, they would comprehend the ways of the Holy One,
blessed be He.

348. וּכְסִיל לֹא יָבִין אֶת זֹאת, דְּלָא מִסְתַּכַּל וְלָא יָדַע נִימוּסֵי דְּזֹאת
בְּעָלְמָא. דְּע"ג דְּדָאִין עָלְמָא בְּדִינוֹי וְחַמָאן לְדִינוֹי דְּהַאי זֹאת, דְּמָטָאן

עַל בְּנֵי נָשָׁא דְּאִינּוּן זַכָּאִין, וְלָא מָטָאן עַל רַשִׁיעַיָּא, חַיָּיבִין, דְּעַבְרִין
עַל פִּתְגָּמֵי אוֹרַיְיתָא, דִּכְתִיב בִּפְרוֹחַ רְשָׁעִים כְּמוֹ עֵשֶׂב וְגוֹ'. דְּהַאי
עָלְמָא יָרְתִין לֵיהּ בְּכָל סִטְרוֹי, וְדִינִין לָא מָטוּן עָלוֹי בְּהַאי עָלְמָא.
וְאִלְמָלֵא דְּדָוִד מַלְכָּא אוֹדְעֵיהּ בְּסוֹפֵיהּ דִּקְרָא, לָא יַדְעֵינָן, דִּכְתִיב
לְהִשָּׁמְדָם עֲדֵי עַד, לְשֵׁיצָאָה לְהוֹן מֵהַהוּא עָלְמָא, וּלְמֶהֱוֵי עַפְרָא תְּחוֹת
רַגְלֵיהוֹן דְּצַדִּיקַיָּיא, דִּכְתִיב וְעַסּוֹתֶם רְשָׁעִים כִּי יִהְיוּ אֵפֶר תַּחַת כַּפּוֹת
רַגְלֵיכֶם.

348. "Nor does a fool understand this (Heb. *zot*)," MEANING they do not look into nor know the practices of "zot," MEANING MALCHUT REFERRED TO AS *ZOT,* in the world. Even though THE HOLY ONE, BLESSED BE HE, judges the world with His Judgments and PEOPLE see the Judgments of *Zot,* they come upon the righteous people and do not affect the guilty evildoers who transgress the words of Torah, as it is written, "When the wicked spring like grass..." (Ibid. 8). They inherit this world in all aspects and harsh penalties do not affect them, YET PEOPLE DO NOT KNOW WHY. Unless King David revealed this at the end of the verse, they would not know, as it is said, "That they shall be destroyed forever" (Ibid). HE PAYS THEM REWARD FOR THEIR GOOD DEEDS IN THIS WORLD in order to obliterate them from the World to Come. They will be THERE dust under the feet of the righteous, as it is written, "And you shall tread down the wicked; for they shall be ashes under the soles of your feet" (Malachi 3:21).

349. תּוּ פָּתַח וְאָמַר, וַיָּקָם בִּי כַחֲשִׁי בְּפָנַי יַעֲנֶה. בְּמַאי קָא מַיְירֵי. אֶלָּא,
זַכָּאָה חוּלָקֵיהּ דְּב"נ דְּאִשְׁתָּדַּל בְּאוֹרַיְיתָא, לְמִנְדַּע אוֹרְחוֹי דְּקוּדְשָׁא
בְּרִיךְ הוּא. דְּכָל מַאן דְּאִשְׁתָּדַּל בְּאוֹרַיְיתָא, כְּאִלּוּ אִשְׁתָּדַּל בִּשְׁמֵיהּ
מַמָּשׁ. מַה שְׁמֵיהּ דְּקוּדְשָׁא בְּרִיךְ הוּא עָבֵיד נִימוּסִין. אוּף אוֹרַיְיתָא הָכִי
נָמֵי. ת"ח, הַאי מַאן דְּעָבַר עַל פִּתְגָּמֵי אוֹרַיְיתָא, אוֹרַיְיתָא סַלְקָא
וְנַחְתָּא וְעָבְדָא בֵּיהּ בב"נ רְשִׁימִין בְּאַנְפּוֹי, בְּגִין דְּיִסְתַּכְּלוּן בֵּיהּ עִלָּאֵי
וְתַתָּאֵי, וְכֻלְּהוּ אוֹשְׁדָן לְוָוטִין עַל רֵישֵׁיהּ.

349. Furthermore, He began to say, "And my leanness rising up against me bears witness to my face" (Iyov 16:8). HE QUESTIONS: What is the verse

speaking about? HE ANSWERS: Fortunate is the man who toils in Torah in order to recognize the ways of the Holy One, blessed be He, for whoever toils in the Torah, it is as if he deals in His actual Name. Just as the Name of the Holy One, blessed be He, creates laws IN THE WORLD, so does the Torah. Come and see: One who infringes with matters of Torah, the Torah rises and then descends to make impressions on the face of that person in order that those on high and those below see him. All send their curses upon his head, AND THIS IS THE ESSENCE OF THE VERSE, "AND MY LEANNESS RISING UP AGAINST ME BEARS WITNESS TO MY FACE," MEANING THE MARKS THE TORAH MADE IN HIS FACE.

350. וְתָאנָא, כָּל אִינּוּן עֵינֵי יְיָ', דְּאַזְלִין וְשָׁאטִין בְּעָלְמָא לְמִנְדַּע אוֹרְחוֹי דִּבְנֵי נָשָׁא, כֻּלְּהוֹן זַקְפִין עַיְינִין, וּמִסְתַּכְּלִין בְּאַנְפּוֹי דְּהַהוּא ב״נ, וְחָמָאן לְהוּ, וְכֻלְּהוּ פַּתְחִין עֲלֵיהּ וַוי׳ וַוי. וַוי לֵיהּ בְּהַאי עָלְמָא, וַוי לֵיהּ בְּעָלְמָא דְּאָתֵי. אִסְתְּלָקוּ מִסּוֹחֲרָנֵיהּ דִּפְלַנְיָא, דְּהָא סַהֲדוּתָא בְּאַנְפּוֹי, וְרוּחָא דִּמְסָאֲבָא שַׁרְיָא עֲלוֹי. וְכָל אִינּוּן יוֹמִין דְּאִשְׁתְּכַח רְשִׁימוּ בְּאַנְפּוֹי לְסַהֲדוּתָא, אִי אוֹלִיד בַּר, אַשְׁלִיף לֵיהּ רוּחָא מִסִּטְרָא דִּמְסָאֲבָא. וְאִלֵּין אִינּוּן חַיָּיבֵי דָּרָא, תַּקִּיפֵי אַנְפִּין, דְּמָארֵיהוֹן שָׁבִיק לוֹן בְּהַאי עָלְמָא, לְשֵׁיצָאָה לְהוּ בְּעָלְמָא דְּאָתֵי.

350. We have learned that all these eyes of Hashem, THE ANGELS OF PROVIDENCE, go and roam throughout the world to learn of the actions of men. They raise their eyes and all look at the face of that person, see him, and open their mouths: Woe, woe, woe to him in this world and woe to him in the World to Come. Remove yourselves from around him, as his face testifies that the spirit of defilement rests upon him. THIS IS THE ESSENCE OF THE VERSE, "BEARS WITNESS TO MY FACE," AS THE LEANNESS TESTIFIES TO HIS FACE. All these days, that mark testifies on his face. If he begets a son, he draws upon him the spirit of defilement. Such are the evildoers of the world, insolent people, whose Master allows them to stay in this world in order to vanquish them in the World to Come.

351. תָּנֵינָן, הַאי צַדִּיקָא זַכָּאָה דְּאִשְׁתְּדַּל בְּאוֹרַיְיתָא יְמָמָא וְלֵילְיָא, קוּדְשָׁא בְּרִיךְ הוּא מָשִׁיךְ עֲלֵיהּ חַד חוּטָא דְּחֶסֶד. וְאִתְרְשִׁים לֵיהּ בְּאַנְפּוֹי, וּמֵהַהוּא רְשִׁימָא דַּחֲלֵי עִלָּאֵי וְתַתָּאֵי. הָכִי נָמֵי מַאן דְּעָבַר עַל

פִּתְגָּמֵי אוֹרַיְיתָא, מַשְׁכָאן עֲלֵיה רוּחָא דִמְסָאֲבָא, וְאִתְרְשִׁים לֵיה
בְּאַנְפּוֹי, וּמִנֵּיה עָרְקִין עִלָּאֵי וְתַתָּאֵי. וְכֻלָּא מַכְרְזֵי עֲלֵיה, אִסְתְּלָקוּ
מִסַחֲרָנֵיה דִּפְלַנְיָא, דְּעָבַר עַל פִּתְגָּמֵי אוֹרַיְיתָא, וְעַל פִּקּוּדֵי דְּמָארֵיה,
וַוי לֵיה, וַוי לְנַפְשֵׁיה. הַאי אַשְׁלִיף רוּחָא דִמְסָאֲבָא, דְּאִשְׁתְּכַח עִמֵּיה,
וְאוֹרִית לֵיה לִבְרֵיה, וְהַאי הוּא דְּקוּדְשָׁא בְּרִיךְ הוּא לֵית לֵיה בֵּיה
חוּלָקָא, וְשָׁבִיק לֵיה, לְשֵׁיצָאָה לֵיה לְעָלְמָא דְּאָתֵי.

351. We have learned that the righteous who toils in Torah day and night, the Holy One, blessed be He, draws upon him a thread of grace, which is marked on his face. From that mark, both those on high and those below have fear. Likewise, whoever violates the words of Torah, a spirit of defilement is drawn upon him, which is marked on his face and causes those high and low to flee from before him. They all proclaim: Leave the vicinity of he, who violated the Torah and the commandments of his Master. Woe to him and to his soul, and this person draws the spirit of defilement that is with him and transmits it to his son. In such a man the Holy One, blessed be He has no part, and He spares him in order to destroy him in the World to Come.

352. אָמַר לֵיה ר׳ אַבָּא, שַׁפִּיר קָאמְרַת, מְנָא לָךְ הַאי. אָמַר לֵיה הָכִי
אוֹלִיפְנָא. וְאוֹלִיפְנָא, דְּהַאי יְרוּתָא בִּישָׁא, אַחֲסִינוּן כֻּלְּהוּ בְּנוֹי, אִי לָא
יְתוּבוּן, דְּהָא לֵית מִלָּה קַיְּימָא קָמֵי תְּשׁוּבָה. וַאֲנָא הָכִי אוֹלִיפְנָא,
דְּאַסְווּתָא דָּא יָהֲבוּ לִי זִמְנָא חֲדָא, דַּהֲוֵינָא רְשִׁים בְּאַנְפָּאי, וְיוֹמָא חַד
הֲוֵינָא אָזִיל בְּאוֹרְחָא, וְאִעְרַעְנָא בְּחַד זַכָּאָה, וְעַל יְדוֹי אִתְעֲבַר מִנַּאי
הַהוּא רְשִׁימָא. אָמַר לִי, מַה שְׁמָךְ. א"ל אֶלְעָזָר, וְקָרֵי עֲלַי אֶלְעָזָר
אָחֳרָא. א"ל, בְּרִיךְ רַחֲמָנָא, דַּחֲמֵינָא לָךְ, וְזָכֵינָא לְמֶחֱמֵי לָךְ בְּהַאי.
זַכָּאָה חוּלָקָךְ בְּעָלְמָא דֵּין וּבְעָלְמָא דְּאָתֵי, אֲנָא הוּא דְּאִעְרַעְנָא לָךְ.

352. Rabbi Aba said to him: You have spoken well. Where did you acquire this? He replied: I studied this. I also learned that this evil inheritance OF THE SPIRIT OF DEFILEMENT is acquired by all his children if they do not turn to penance, as nothing can stand in the way before repentance. So have I learned. This cure, NAMELY REPENTANCE, was given me once upon a

time, when my face was marked. One day, I was walking and met one meritorious person, and through him was the mark removed from my face. He asked me my name. I replied Elazar. He announced me to be a different Elazar. RABBI ABA said to him: Blessed is the Merciful One that I have met you and deserved to see you accomplishing this. Blessed is your share in this world and the World to Come. It was I who met you.

58. Batsheba

A Synopsis

The formerly marked man, Elazar, tells Rabbi Aba of a time when a passerby told him that his red cow is called Bathsheba, mother of Solomon, as long as he merits forgiveness. Rabbi Aba explains to him that it was because everything referring to the cow is in sevens, and all pertain to sacrifice and cleansing.

353. אִשְׁתְּטַח קַמֵּיהּ, אַיְיתֵיהּ לְבֵיתֵיהּ, אַתְקִין קַמֵּיהּ טְרַטִיסָאֵי דְּנַהֲמָא, וּבִשְׂרָא דְּעֶגְלָא תְּלִיתָאָה. בָּתַר דְּאָכְלוּ, א״ל הַהוּא גַּבְרָא, ר׳, אֵימָא לִי חַד מִלָּה, חֲדָא תּוֹרְתָא סוּמָקָא אִית לִי, אִימָּא דְּעֶגְלָא דְּבִשְׂרָא דָּא דַּאֲכִילְנָא, וְיוֹמָא חַד עַד לָא אִתְעַבְּרַת וְאוֹלִידַת, אֲזִילְנָא בַּתְרָאָהּ לְמַרְעָא לְמַדְבְּרָא, עַד דִּדְבָּרְנָא לָהּ אַעֲבַּר קַמַּאי חַד גַּבְרָא, א״ל, מַה שְּׁמָהּ דְּתוֹרְתָא דָּא. אֲמֵינָא, מִן יוֹמָא דְּאִתְיְילִידַת לָא קָרֵינָא לָהּ בִּשְׁמָא. א״ל, בַּת שֶׁבַע אֵם שְׁלֹמֹה אִתְקְרֵי, אִי תִּזְכֶּה לְכַפָּרָה. וַאֲנָא בְּעוֹד דְּאָהֲדַרְנָא רֵישַׁאי, לָא חֲמֵינָא לֵיהּ, וְחַיִּיכְנָא מֵהַהוּא מִלָּה.

353. THIS MAN ELAZAR prostrated himself before him. He brought him home, prepared three measures of bread and a three year old calf. After eating, the man said to him: Rabbi, tell me one thing. I had a red cow, the mother of this calf whose flesh we are eating. One day, before she became pregnant and gave birth, I followed her to her pasture in the desert. As I led her, a man came by and asked me for the name of the cow. I replied that from the day she was born, I never called her by name. He said to me: Batsheba, mother of Solomon, is she called if you merit forgiveness FOR YOUR SINS. When I turned around, I saw him no more. I laughed at this thing.

354. וְהַשְׁתָּא דְּזָכִינָא בְּאוֹרַיְיתָא, אִתְעָרְנָא עַל הַהִיא מִלָּה, וּמִן יוֹמָא דְּאִתְפְּטַר ר׳ שַׁמְלַאי מֵהָכָא, לָא הֲוָה ב״נ דְּיַנְהִיר לָן בְּאוֹרַיְיתָא כְּוָותֵיהּ. וַאֲנָא דְּחִילְנָא לְמֵימַר מִלָּה דְּאוֹרַיְיתָא דְּלָא אוֹלִיפְנָא. וּמִלָּה דָּא דְּאִסְתַּכַּלְנָא דְּמִלָּה דְּחָכְמְתָא הִיא, וְלָא יְדַעְנָא. א״ל, וַדַּאי מִלָּה דְּחָכְמְתָא הִיא, וּרְמִיזָא עִלָּאָה הִיא לְעֵילָּא וּלְתַתָּא.

354. Now that I have merited Torah, I have been rushed up again about that matter. From the day Rabbi Samlai departed from here, there was no one who could shed light on Torah as he. I fear to state words of Torah that I have not learned. The thing THAT MAN TOLD ME, I have realized it to be a matter of wisdom, but I do not understand it. He replied: It surely is a matter of wisdom, being a supernal hint above and below.

355. אֲבָל תָּ"ח, בַּת שֶׁבַע אִתְקְרֵי מַמָּשׁ בְּרָזָא דְּחָכְמְתָא. בְּגַ"כ כְּתִיב בָּהּ כֹּלָּא בְּשֶׁבַע. ז' פָּרוֹת. ז' שְׂרֵפוֹת. ז' הַזָּאוֹת. ז' כְּבוּסִים. ז' טְמֵאִים. ז' טְהוֹרִים. ז' כֹּהֲנִים. וּמֹשֶׁה וְאַהֲרֹן בְּחוּשְׁבְּנָא דְּהָא כְּתִיב, וַיְדַבֵּר יְיָ' אֶל מֹשֶׁה וְאַהֲרֹן וְגוֹ'. וְשַׁפִּיר קָאָמַר הַהוּא גַּבְרָא, דְּאָמַר בַּת שֶׁבַע, וְכֹלָּא רָזָא דְחָכְמְתָא הִיא.

355. Come and see: SHE, THE RED COW, is actually called Batsheba according to the secret of wisdom, DENOTING MALCHUT NAMED COW FROM HER LEFT ASPECT, AS THE MALE IS CALLED AN OX AND THE FEMALE A COW. SHE IS RED DUE TO GVUROT. That is why everything referring to her is in sevens, FOR IN THE CHAPTER THERE IS MENTION OF cow seven TIMES; ALSO, seven burnings, seven sprinkles, seven washings, seven unclean, seven clean and seven priests with Moses and Aaron included in the count of seven. THEY ARE ALSO CALLED PRIESTS, as it is written IN THE CHAPTER, "And Hashem spoke to Moses and Aaron..." (Bemidbar 19:2). That man that spoke of Batsheba (lit. 'daughter of seven') spoke very well. All this pertains to the secret of wisdom.

356. אָ"ל, בְּרִיךְ רַחֲמָנָא דִּשְׁמַעְנָא מִלָּה דָא. בְּרִיךְ הוּא דְּהָא אַקְדִּים לִי שְׁלָם בְּקַדְמֵיתָא, לְמִזְכֵּי לְהַאי. דִּכְתִיב שָׁלוֹם שָׁלוֹם לָרָחוֹק וְלַקָּרוֹב אָמַר יְיָ'. אֲנָא כַּד הֲוֵינָא רָחוֹק, קוּדְשָׁא בְּרִיךְ הוּא אַקְדִּים לִי שְׁלָם לְמֶהֱוֵי קָרוֹב. קָרָא עֲלֵיהּ ר' אַבָּא, אַתָּה שָׁלוֹם וּבֵיתְךָ שָׁלוֹם וְכֹל אֲשֶׁר לְךָ שָׁלוֹם.

356. He said to him: Blessed is the Merciful One that I was able to hear this thing. Blessed is he who offered me first a greeting of peace, in order to merit this, as it is written, "'Peace, peace, both for far and near', says

Hashem" (Yeshayah 57:19). When I was far off, the Holy One, blessed be He, greeted me first in peace, MEANING HE INVITED ME to be near. Rabbi Aba announced about him, "Peace be both to you, and peace to your house, and peace to all that you have" (I Shmuel 25:6).

59. Two female spirits

A Synopsis
We learn that after Cain killed Abel, Adam lived apart from his wife for 130 years, not wanting to produce more children that would be destroyed. Female spirits used to couple with him at that time, and they produced demons or plagues. Cain had been born from the filth of the serpent, and from that line all the evildoers of the world have come. For this reason, all spirits and demons in the world are partly of people below and partly of angels.

357. עֶרְוַת אֲחוֹת אָבִיךָ לֹא תְגַלֵּה. רַבִּי חִיָּיא פָּתַח, וְאִישׁ אֲשֶׁר יִקַּח אֶת אֲחוֹתוֹ בַּת אָבִיו אוֹ בַת אִמּוֹ וְרָאָה אֶת עֶרְוָתָהּ וְגוֹ'. תַּמָּן תָּנֵינָן, מֵאָה וּתְלָתִין שְׁנִין, אִתְפְּרַשׁ אָדָם מֵאִתְּתֵיהּ, וְלָא הֲוָה אוֹלִיד. מִדְּקָטַל קַיִן לְהֶבֶל, לָא בָּעָא אָדָם לְאִזְדַּוְּוגָא בְּאִתְּתֵיהּ. רַבִּי יוֹסֵי אָמַר, מִשַּׁעֲתָא דְּאִתְגְּזַר עָלֵיהּ וְעַל כָּל עָלְמָא מִיתָה, אָמַר, אֲמַאי אֲנָא אוֹלִיד לְבַעֲתוּתָא. מִיַּד אִתְפְּרַשׁ מֵאִתְּתֵיהּ.

357. "You shall not uncover the nakedness of your father's sister..." (Vayikra 18:12). Rabbi Chiya opened the discussion saying, "And if a man shall take his sister, his father's daughter, or his mother's daughter, and see her nakedness..." (Vayikra 20:17). We have learned that Adam lived apart from his wife for 130 years and did not beget children, since Adam did not want to copulate with his wife after Cain slew Abel. Rabbi Yosi taught that from the time death was decreed for him and all mankind, he has said, why should I beget children that will be destroyed? He immediately separated from his wife.

358. וּתְרֵין רוּחִין נוּקְבִין, הֲווֹ אַתְיָין וְאִזְדַּוְּוגָן עִמֵּיהּ, וְאוֹלִידוּ. וְאִינּוּן דְּאוֹלִידוּ הֲווֹ מַזִּיקִין דְּעָלְמָא, וְאִקְרוּן נִגְעֵי בְּנֵי אָדָם. וְאִלֵּין סָאטָן לִבְנֵי אָדָם, וְשַׁרְיָין בְּפִתְחָא דְּבֵיתָא, וּבְבֵירָאֵי, וּבְבָתֵּי כִּסָּאֵי. וְעַ"ד ב"נ, דְּאִשְׁתְּכַח בְּפִתְחָא דְּבֵיתֵיהּ שְׁמָא קַדִּישָׁא שַׁדַּי בְּכִתְרִין עִלָּאִין, כֻּלְּהוּ עָרְקָאן וְאִתְרַחֲקָן מִנֵּיהּ, הה"ד וְנֶגַע לֹא יִקְרַב בְּאָהֳלֶךָ. מַאי וְנֶגַע לֹא יִקְרַב. אִלֵּין נִגְעֵי בְּנֵי אָדָם.

358. Two female spirits used to come and couple with him and they gave birth. They gave birth to demons called the plagues of mankind. They would fly to people and rest at their doors, wells and restrooms. Therefore all DEMONS flee and distance themselves from people who have on their door posts the holy name Shadai of the supernal Sfirot. This is the essence of the verse, "Nor shall any plague come near your dwelling" (Tehilim 91:10). What is meant by "nor shall any plague come near"? It is the MENTIONED plagues of people.

359. וְתָאנָא, בְּשַׁעֲתָא דְּנָחַת אָדָם בְּדִיּוּקְנָא עִלָּאָה, בְּדִיּוּקְנָא קַדִּישָׁא, וְחָמוּ לֵיהּ עִלָּאֵי וְתַתָּאֵי, כֻּלְּהוּ קְרִיבוּ גַּבֵּיהּ, וְאַמְלִכוּהוּ עַל הַאי עָלְמָא. בָּתַר דְּאָתָא חִוְיָא עַל חַוָּה, וְאָטִיל בָּהּ זוּהֲמָא, לְבָתַר אוֹלִידַת קַיִן. מִתַּמָּן נִתְיַיחֲסוּ כָּל דָּרִין חַיָּיבִין דְּעָלְמָא. וּמָדוֹרָא דְּשֵׁדִין וְרוּחִין, מִתַּמָּן אִשְׁתְּכָחוּ, וּמִסִּטְרוֹי. וּבְגִינֵי כַּךְ כָּל רוּחִין וְשֵׁדִין, פְּלָגוּתָא אִית בְּהוּ מִבְּנֵי נָשָׁא דִּלְתַתָּא, וּפְלָגוּתָא מִמַּלְאֲכֵי עִלָּאֵי דִּלְעֵילָּא. וְכֵן כַּד אִתְיְילִידוּ מֵאָדָם אִינּוּן אָחֳרָנִין, כֻּלְּהוּ אִשְׁתְּכָחוּ כְּהַאי גַּוְונָא, פַּלְגּוּ מִתַּתָּאֵי, וּפַלְגּוּ מֵעִלָּאֵי.

359. We have learned that when Adam descended with the supernal image, a holy form, and those on high and below saw him, they approached him and crowned him ruler over this world. Later, when the serpent came upon Eve, it injected its filth in her. Following this, she gave birth to Cain; SHE DELIVERED CAIN FROM THE FILTH OF THE SERPENT. From that genealogy were the subsequent generations of the world's evildoers and the habitations of demons and spirits come from there and his side. For this reason, all spirits and demons in the world are partly of people below and partly of the angels on high, AS THEY ARE BORN HALF FROM THE FILTH OF THE SERPENT, UPON IT WHICH THE ANGEL SAMAEL RODE. THEREFORE, HALF STEM FROM THE ANGELS. THEIR OTHER HALF IS HUMAN, BECAUSE THEY WERE BORN FROM CAIN WHO WAS HUMAN. These other DEMONS born from Adam THROUGH TWO FEMALE SPIRITS, AS MENTIONED ABOVE, are all similar as they stem half from below and half from above.

60. Lilit and Na'amah

A Synopsis

We are told that Adam also had daughters that were beautiful, and we hear about Tubal Cain and Na'amah, about the demons and spirits, and about the role of Lilit. If a man is holy God sends three angels to guard him and his house. Asmodeus, the king of the demons, told Solomon about the many kinds of impurity that people contract if they are not saved through the Torah.

360. בָּתַר דְּאִתְיְלִידוּ מֵאָדָם, אוֹלִיד מֵאִינּוּן רוּחֵי בְּנָתָן, דְּדַמְיָן לִשְׁפִּירוּ דִּלְעֵילָא, וּלִשְׁפִּירוּ דְּתַתָּאֵי. וְעַ"ד כְּתִיב, וַיִּרְאוּ בְנֵי הָאֱלֹהִים אֶת בְּנוֹת הָאָדָם כִּי טוֹבוֹת הֵנָּה וְגוֹ', וְטָעָן כֹּלָּא בַּתְרַיְיהוּ. וְחַד דְּכוּרָא אִשְׁתְּכַח, דְּאָתָא לְעָלְמָא מֵרוּחֵיה דְּסִטְרָא דְקַיִן, וְקָרוֹן לֵיהּ תּוּבַל קַיִן. וַחֲדָא נוּקְבָּא נָפְקַת עִמֵּיה, וַהֲווֹ בִּרְיָין וְטָעָאן בַּתְרָאָה, וְאִתְקְרֵי נַעֲמָ"ה. מִינָּהּ נַפְקוּ רוּחִין וְשֵׁדִין אָחֳרָנִין. וְאִינּוּן תַּלְיָין בַּאֲוִירָא, וְאוֹדְעִין מִלִּין לְאִינּוּן אָחֳרָנִין דְּשְׁכִיחִין לְתַתָּא.

360. After THE DEMONS were born to Adam, he had daughters from these spirits that were similar in beauty to those on high and those below. Therefore, it is written, "The sons of Elohim saw that the daughters of men were fair" (Beresheet 6:2). All were going astray after them. There was one male, who was born to the spirit from the aspect of Cain, and he was named Tuval Cain. A female was born with him. People were going astray after her, and she was called Na'amah. From her came other spirits and demons. They were hovering in the air, revealing matters to the others who were below, IN THE WORLD.

361. וְדָא תּוּבַל קַיִן, אַפִּיק זַיְינֵי קְטוּלָא לְעָלְמָא. וְדָא נַעֲמָה אִתְרְגִישַׁת בְּרִיגְשָׁתָא, וְאִתְדַּבְּקַת בְּסִטְרָהָא. וְעַד כְּעַן הִיא קַיְימָא, וּמְדוֹרָהָא בֵּין רִיגְשֵׁי יַמָּא רַבָּא, וְנַפְקַת וְחַיֶּיכַת בִּבְנֵי נָשָׁא, וְאִתְחַמְּמַת מִנַּיְיהוּ בְּחֶלְמָא, בְּהַהוּא תִּיאוּבְתָּא דִּב"נ, וְאִתְדַּבְּקַת בֵּיה. תִּיאוּבְתָּא נַטְלַת וְלָא יַתִּיר. וּמֵהַהוּא תִּיאוּבְתָּא אִתְעַבְּרַת, וְאַפִּיקַת זַיְינִין אָחֳרָנִין לְעָלְמָא.

361. This Tuval Cain introduced weaponry to the world, AS HE SHARPENED ALL EARTHENWARE, COPPER AND IRON. While attached to her aspect, this

Na'amah used to be in a state of great commotion. She still lives, dwelling among the roars of the great sea. She comes out, sports with people, warms herself by them in a man's dream by his lust, and attaches herself to him. She takes FROM HIM that passion, but not more. From that lust, she becomes pregnant and produces many species OF DEMON in the world.

362. וְאִלֵּין בְּנִין דְּאוֹלִידַת מִבְּנֵי נָשָׁא, מִשְׁתַּכְּחִין לְקַבְּלֵי נוּקְבֵי בְּנֵי נָשָׁא, וּמִתְעַבְּרָן מִנַּיְיהוּ, וְאוֹלִידָן רוּחִין, וְכֻלְּהוּ אַזְלִין לְלִילִית קַדְמֵיתָא, וְהִיא מְגַדֶּלֶת לוֹן. וְהִיא נַפְקַת לְעָלְמָא, וּבָעְיָא רַבְיָיהָא, וְחָמַת רַבְיֵי בְּנֵי נָשָׁא, וְאִתְדַּבְּקַת בְּהוּ, לְקַטְלָא לְהוּ, וּלְאִשְׁתְּאֲבָא בְּרוּחַיְיהוּ דְּרַבְיֵי בְּנֵי נָשָׁא וְהִיא אַזְלַת בְּהַהוּא רוּחָא, וְאִזְדַּמְּנָן תַּמָּן ג׳ רוּחִין קַדִּישִׁין, וְטָאסִין קַמָּהּ, וְנַטְלִין הַהוּא רוּחָא מִנָּהּ, וּמַנִּיחִין לֵיהּ קַמֵּי קוּדְשָׁא בְּרִיךְ הוּא, וְתַמָּן מִתְאַלְּפֵי קַמֵּיהּ.

362. These children, NAMELY DEMONS AND SPIRITS, that she bore to humans are SEEN IN DREAMS to human females who conceive from them and bear spirits. They go to the primordial Lilit and she rears them. She goes out into the world, seeks children, sees human children and attaches herself to them in order to kill them. Then she joins with the spirits of the children and goes with that spirit. Three holy spirits come. They fly before her, take from her that spirit, place it before the Holy one, blessed be He. There they study before Him.

363. בְּגִינֵי כַּךְ אוֹרַיְיתָא אַזְהֲרַת לְהוּ לִבְנֵי נָשָׁא, וְהִתְקַדִּשְׁתֶּם וִהְיִיתֶם קְדוֹשִׁים וַדַּאי. אִי אִשְׁתְּכַח ב״נ קַדִּישָׁא, לָא מִסְתָּפֵי מִינָּהּ, דִּכְדֵין זַמִּין קוּדְשָׁא בְּרִיךְ הוּא לְאִלֵּין ג׳ מַלְאָכִין קַדִּישִׁין דְּאֲמָרָן, וְנַטְרִין לֵיהּ לְהַהוּא רַבְיָיא, וְהִיא לָא יַכְלָא לְאַבְאָשָׁא לֵיהּ, הה״ד לֹא תְאֻנֶּה אֵלֶיךָ רָעָה וְנֶגַע לֹא יִקְרַב בְּאָהֳלֶךָ. מַאי טַעֲמָא לֹא תְאֻנֶּה אֵלֶיךָ רָעָה. בְּגִין כִּי מַלְאָכָיו יְצַוֶּה לָּךְ, וּכְתִיב כִּי בִי חָשַׁק וַאֲפַלְּטֵהוּ.

363. For this reason, the Torah warns people, "You shall therefore sanctify yourselves, and you shall be holy" (Vayikra 11:44). Surely, if a man is holy, he need not fear LILIT. Then the Holy One, blessed be He, designates these

three holy angels which we spoke about, and they guard that child, so she cannot harm him. This is the meaning of the verse, "No evil shall befall you, nor shall any come near your dwelling" (Tehilim 91:10). For what reason is it that "no evil shall befall you"? "For He shall give His angels charge over you" (Ibid. 11) and, "Because he has set his delight upon Me, therefore will I deliver him" (Ibid. 14).

364. דְּאִי ב"נ לָא אִשְׁתְּכַח קַדִּישָׁא, וְאַשְׁלִיף רוּחָא מִסְטְרָא דִמְסָאֲבָא, כְּדֵין הִיא אַתְיָא וְחַיְיכַת בֵּיה בְּהַהוּא רַבְיָא. וְאִי קַטִילַת לֵיה, אִשְׁתְּאֲבַת בְּהַהוּא רוּחָא, וְלָא תַּעְדֵּי מִנֵּיה לְעָלְמִין. וְאִי תֵּימָא אִינּוּן אָחֳרָנִין, דְּקַטִּילַת לוֹן, וְאִזְדַּמְנוּ קַמַּה אִינּוּן תְּלָתָא קַדִּישִׁין, וְנַטְלִין מִנַּהּ הַהוּא רוּחָא, הָא לָא בְּסִטְרָא דִמְסָאֲבָא אִשְׁתְּכָחוּ, אֲמַאי שַׁלְטָא לְקַטְלָא לְהוּ. אֶלָּא, הַאי כַּד ב"נ לָא אִתְקַדָּשׁ, אֲבָל לָא אִתְכַּוְּון לְאִסְתַּאֲבָא וְלָא אִסְתְּאַב, בְּגִין כַּךְ יָכְלָא לְשַׁלְטָאָה בְּגוּפָא, וְלָא בְּרוּחָא.

364. If a person is not holy, but draws a spirit from the side of defilement, then LILIT comes and plays with the child. If she kills him, she clings to the spirit OF THE CHILD and never lets go. If you ask, What about the others THAT DID NOT DRAW SPIRIT FROM DEFILEMENT? She kills them and there appear before her these three holy SPIRITS who take away his spirit. Behold, these people were never in the side of defilement, so why does she have the ability to kill them? HE ANSWERS: This is so when they are not sanctified; THEREFORE, SHE CAN KILL THEM. They never had any intention to become unclean and they did not become unclean. Therefore, she only has control over his body, TO KILL HIM but not the spirit, AS THE SPIRIT IS BROUGHT BEFORE THE HOLY ONE, BLESSED BE HE.

365. וְזִמְנִין אִשְׁתְּכַח דְּנָפְקַת נַעֲמָה לְעָלְמָא, לְאִתְחַמְמָא מִבְּנֵי נָשָׁא, וְאִשְׁתְּכַח ב"נ בְּקִשּׁוּרָא דְּתִיאוּבְתָּא עִמָּה, וְאִתְעַר מִשְׁנָתֵיה, וְאָחִיד בְּאַנְתְּתֵיה, וְשָׁכִיב עִמָּה, וּרְעוּתָא דִילֵיה בְּהַהוּא תִּיאוּבְתָּא דַּהֲוָה לֵיה בְּחֶלְמֵיה, כְּדֵין הַהוּא בַּר דְּאוֹלִיד, מִסִּטְרָא דְּנַעֲמָה קָא אַתְיָא, דְּהָא בְּתִיאוּבְתָּא דִילָהּ אִשְׁתְּכַח הַאי, כַּד נַפְקָא לִילִי"ת וְחָמָאת לֵיה, יָדְעַת

מִלָּה, וְהִיא אִתְקְטָרַת בֵּיהּ, וּמַגְדְּלַת לֵיהּ כְּאִינּוּן אֲחֲרָנִין בְּנוֹי דְּנַעֲמָ"ה, וְאִשְׁתְּכְחַת עִמֵיהּ זִמְנִין סַגִּיאִין, וְלָא קַטְלָא לֵיהּ.

365. Sometimes it happens that Na'amah goes out into the world to heat herself against people, and a man would find himself bound to her with desire. He awakens from his sleep, joins and lies with his wife, but his thoughts are STILL with the desire he had in his dream. Then the child born stems from Na'amah, because all this happened while he had a desire for her. When Lilit comes out and sees the child, she understands the situation THAT HE STEMS FROM NA'AMAH. She clings to him and raises him like the other children of Na'amah. Also, she stays with him a long time, but does not kill him, AS HE PERTAINS TO HER SIDE.

366. הַאי הוּא ב"נ, דְּבְכָל סִיהֲרָא וְסִיהֲרָא אִתְפְּגִים, וְלָא אִתְיָאֲשָׁא מִנֵּיהּ לְעָלְמִין, דְּהָא בְּכָל סִיהֲרָא וְסִיהֲרָא כַּד אִתְחַדְּשָׁא בְּעָלְמָא, לִילִי"ת נָפְקָא, וּפַקְדָּא עַל כֻּלְּהוּ דְּהִיא מַגְדְּלַת, וְחַיְיכָא בְּהוּ, וּכְדֵין הַהוּא ב"נ פָּגִים בְּהַהוּא זִמְנָא, זַכָּאִין אִינּוּן צַדִּיקַיָּיא, דְּמִתְקַדְּשֵׁי בִּקְדוּשָׁה דְּמַלְכָּא, עֲלַיְיהוּ כְּתִיב וְהָיָה מִדֵּי חֹדֶשׁ בְּחָדְשׁוֹ וּמִדֵּי שַׁבָּת בְּשַׁבַּתּוֹ וְגוֹ'.

366. Such a man, with every NEW moon, becomes defective and she never gives up with him. With the renewal of the moon, NAMELY THE START OF THE NEW MONTH, Lilit goes out, visits all THE CHILDREN in her care and jests with them. That person is then defective at that time. Fortunate are the just, who sanctify themselves with the sanctity of the King. About them, it is written, "And it shall come to pass, that every new moon, and every Shabbat..." (Yeshayah 66:23).

367. כְּמִלִּין אִלֵּין גַּלֵּי שְׁלֹמֹה מַלְכָּא, בְּסִפְרָא דְּאַשְׁמְדָאי מַלְכָּא, וְאַשְׁכַּחְנָא בֵּיהּ אֶלֶף וְאַרְבַּע מְאָה וַחֲמֵשׁ זִינֵי מְסָאֲבוּתָא, דְּמִסְתַּאֲבֵי בְּהוּ בְּנֵי נָשָׁא. דְּגַלֵּי דָּא אַשְׁמְדָאי לִשְׁלֹמֹה מַלְכָּא.

367. King Solomon revealed these things in his book about Asmodeus, king OF THE DEMONS. I found in it 1,405 kinds of impurity that people contract. This was revealed by Asmodeus to Solomon, the king.

368. וַוי לְהוּ לִבְנֵי נָשָׁא, דְּכֻלְּהוּ אֲטִימִין וּסְתִימִין עַיְינִין, וְלָא יַדְעִין,
וְלָא שַׁמְעִין, וְלָא מַשְׁגִּיחִין, הֵיךְ קַיְימִין בְּעָלְמָא. וְהָא עֵיטָא וְאַסְוּותָא
קַמַיְיהוּ, וְלָא מִסְתַּכְּלִין. דְּהָא לָא יַכְלִין בְּנֵי נָשָׁא לְאִשְׁתְּזָבָא, אֶלָּא
בְּעֵיטָא דְאוֹרַיְיתָא. דִּכְתִּיב, כִּי יִהְיֶה בְךָ אִישׁ אֲשֶׁר לֹא יִהְיֶה טָהוֹר
מִקְּרֵה לָיְלָה אֲשֶׁר לֹא יִהְיֶה טָהוֹר דַּיְיקָא, מִקְּרֵה לָיְלָה דַּיְיקָא, וְהָא
אוֹקִימְנָא מִלֵּי, בְּעֵיטָא דְאוֹרַיְיתָא קַדִּישָׁא. דְּהָכִי כְּתִיב בְּאוֹרַיְיתָא
קַדִּישָׁא, וְהִתְקַדִּשְׁתֶּם וִהְיִיתֶם קְדוֹשִׁים כִּי אֲנִי יְיָ' אֱלֹהֵיכֶם.

368. Woe to those people who are all obtuse and blind and neither know, listen nor pay attention to the reason they are in the world. Advice and cure are before them, but they do not see, for people cannot be saved, except with the guidance of Torah, as it is written, "If there be among you any man, that is not clean by reason of uncleanness that chances by night" (Devarim 23:11). "That is not clean" is precise, MEANING THAT HIS BIRTH WAS COME THROUGH THE SPIRIT OF DEFILEMENT, AS MENTIONED. "Uncleanness that chances by night" exactly, MEANING AT SLEEP WHEN DREAMING. We have already established these matters with the counsel of the holy Torah, as it is written in the Torah, "You shall therefore sanctify yourselves, and you shall be holy, for I am Hashem your Elohim" (Vayikra 20:7); THEN NO EVIL WILL BEFALL YOU.

61. Seth

A Synopsis
This section tells us that all the righteous in the world come from the lineage of Seth, who was born after Cain and Abel died. God increased Chesed in the world, and with each male a female was born to populate the world.

369. תָּאנָא, בָּתַר דְּאִסְתָּלָקוּ קַיִן וְהֶבֶל, אִתְהֲדָר אָדָם לְאִנְתְּתֵיה, וְאִתְלָבַּשׁ בְּרוּחָא אָחֳרָא, וְאוֹלִיד לְשֵׁת. מִכָּאן אִתְיַיחֲסוּ דָּרֵי דְצַדִּיקַיָּיא בְּעָלְמָא. וְאַסְגֵּי קוּדְשָׁא בְּרִיךְ הוּא חֶסֶד בְּעָלְמָא, וּבְכָל חַד אִתְיְילִידַת נוּקְבָּא עִמֵּיה, לְאִתְיַישְׁבָא עָלְמָא. כְּגַוְונָא דִּלְעֵילָּא. וְהָא אוּקְמוּהָ חַבְרַיָּיא בִּסְתִּימָאָה דְּמַתְנִיתִין, דִּכְתִּיב וְאִישׁ אֲשֶׁר יִקַּח אֶת אֲחוֹתוֹ בַּת אָבִיו אוֹ בַת אִמּוֹ וְגוֹ', חֶסֶד הוּא. חֶסֶד הוּא וַדַּאי, וּבָתַר דְּשָׁארֵי חֶסֶד, גִּזְעִין וְשָׁרְשִׁין נָפְקִין מִתְּחוֹת לְעֵילָּא, וְאִתְפָּרְשָׁן עַנְפִּין, וְקָרִיב אִתְרְחַק. כְּדֵין עַנְפָּא אַסְגֵּי, וְאָתֵי לְאִתְחַבְּרָא בְּזִוּוּגָא חַד בְּאִילָנָא. הַאי בְּקַדְמֵיתָא, הַאי בִּסְתִּימָא דְּעָלְמָא. בְּגִין דִּכְתִּיב אָמַרְתִּי עוֹלָם חֶסֶד יִבָּנֶה. אֲבָל מִכָּאן וּלְהָלְאָה בְּנֵי נָשָׁא דְּיִשְׁתַּכְחוּן בֵּיהּ, וְנִכְרְתוּ לְעֵינֵי בְּנֵי עַמָּם.

369. We have learned that after the passing of Cain and Abel, Adam returned to his wife. A different spirit enveloped him and he begot Seth. From this lineage, the righteous trace their line in the world. The Holy One, blessed be He, increased Chesed in the world, and with each was also born a female to populate the world, just as above, AS ZEIR ANPIN AND MALCHUT WERE BROTHER AND SISTER. The friends have established in the general Mishnah that it is written ABOUT THEM, "And if a man shall take his sister, his father's daughter, or his mother's daughter, and see her nakedness... It is a disgraceful (Heb. *chesed,* it is confusing but the word chesed can mean disgraceful or kindness) deed" (Vayikra 20:17). Assuredly it is Chesed, for after Chesed rests, offspring and roots come out underneath upwards, and branches spread, MEANING ZEIR ANPIN AND MALCHUT. What was near moved away. Then the branches grew, ZEIR ANPIN AND MALCHUT, and came to join into one in a tree. This was in the beginning, in the concealed state of the world. It is written, "For I have said, the world is built by love

(*chesed*)" (Tehilim 89:3). THEREFORE, from now on, people in this situation THAT MARRY THEIR SISTER "shall be cut off in the sight of their people" (Vayikra 20:17).

370. תָּאנָא עֶרְוַת אֲחוֹת אָבִיךָ, כְּמָה דְּאִתְגַּלְיָיא בְּסְתִּימָא. כְּתִיב, כִּי יְשָׁרִים דַּרְכֵי יְיָ' וְצַדִּיקִים יֵלְכוּ בָם וְגוֹ', זַכָּאָה חוּלָקֵיהוֹן דְּצַדִּיקַיָּיא, דְּיַדְעֵי אָרְחוֹי דְּקוּדְשָׁא בְּרִיךְ הוּא, וְאָזְלִין בְּהוּ, וְאִשְׁתְּמוֹדְעָן גַּבַּיְיהוּ. זַכָּאָה חוּלָקֵיהוֹן.

370. We have learned that "the nakedness of your father's sister" is TO BE EXPLAINED as revealing in that which is hidden. It is written, "For the ways of Hashem are right, and the just do walk in them..." (Hoshea 14:10). How blessed is the lot of the just that know the ways of the Holy One, blessed be He, and walk in them. They are made known to them. Blessed is their share.

62. Chesed came and separated them

A Synopsis

We read about the movement of the letters Yud Hei Vav Hei in the
Holy Name, and how Chesed causes the mating of Malchut with
Zeir Anpin. We learn also that Chochmah and Binah are never
parted, for their union does not depend on Chesed.

371. תָּאנָא, אִתְעַבְּרַת הֵ"א עִלָּאָה בִּרְחִימוּתָא וַחֲבִיבוּתָא דְּלָא
מִתְפְּרַשׁ מִנָּהּ יוֹ"ד לְעָלְמִין. אִתְעַבְּרַת וְאַפִּיקַת וָא"ו, לְבָתַר קָאֵים קַמָּהּ,
וְיַנְקָא לֵיהּ. וְדָא וָא"ו כַּד נָפְקָא, בַּת זוּגוֹ נַפְקָא עִמֵּיהּ. אַתְיָא חֶסֶד
אִתְּעַר גַּבֵּיהּ, וּפָרִישׁ לוֹן, וְנַפְקוּ גִּזְעִין מִתְּחוֹת לְעֵילָא, וְאִתְפַּשְׁטוּ עַנְפִין,
וְאַסְגִּיאוּ, וְאִתְעֲבִידַת הֵ"א תַּתָּאָה. וְאִתְרַבִּיאַת בְּעַנְפָּהָא לְעֵילָא לְעֵילָא,
עַד דְּאִזְדַּוְוגַת בְּאִילָנָא עִלָּאָה, וְאִתְחַבָּרוּ וָא"ו עִם הֵ"א, מַאן גָּרִים לוֹן.
חֶסֶד הוּא. חֶסֶד הוּא וַדַּאי. דְּחַבַּר לוֹן כַּחֲדָא.

371. We have learned that the upper Hei, BINAH, became pregnant lovingly
and fondly, for the Yud, CHOCHMAH, never parts from it (her). She
conceived and delivered Vav, BEING ZEIR ANPIN, WHICH IS THE SECRET
OF VAV IN THE HEI. Afterwards, it stands before her, MEANING THE VAV
THAT IS AFTER THE YUD HEI IN THE NAME OF YUD HEI VAV HEI, and
she nurses it. This Vav when departing FROM BINAH, its pair MALCHUT
comes out with it, Chesed rouses itself towards him, ZEIR ANPIN, separates
them ONE FROM THE OTHER, and stems shoot forth from bottom to top.
The branches spread, ZEIR ANPIN AND MALCHUT, and grow. The lower Hei
is formed. Its branches grow higher and higher until MALCHUT pairs with
the supernal tree, BEING ZEIR ANPIN, and Vav then joins, BEING ZEIR
ANPIN, with the Hei, DENOTING MALCHUT, AS SAID EARLIER. Who
brought this about? "It is a disgraceful (Heb. 'chesed') deed." Chesed
certainly joins them together.

372. יוֹ"ד עִם הֵ"א עִלָּאָה. לָא תַּלְיָא חִבּוּרָא דִּלְהוֹן בְּחֶסֶד, אֶלָּא
בְּמַזָּלָא תַּלְיָיא חִבּוּרָא דִּלְהוֹן, וַחֲבִיבוּתָא דִּלְהוֹן, דְּלָא מִתְפָּרְשָׁן
לְעָלְמִין. יוֹ"ד אִתְקְשַׁר בְּהֵ"א, וְהֵ"א אִתְקְשַׁר בְּוָא"ו, וָא"ו אִתְקְשַׁר
בְּהֵ"א, וְהֵ"א אִתְקְשַׁר בְּכֹלָּא. וְכֹלָּא חַד קְשׁוּרָא הוּא, וְחַד מִלָּה. לָא

אִתְפְּרָשׁוּ דָא מִן דָא לְעָלְמִין. כְּבִיָכוֹל, מַאן דְּגָרִים פְּרוּדָא, כְּאִלּוּ חָרִיב עָלְמָא, וְאִקְרֵי עֶרְיָיתָא דְּכֹלָּא.

372. The joining of Yud with supernal Hei, CHOCHMAH WITH BINAH, is not dependent on Chesed, AS ARE ZEIR ANPIN AND MALCHUT, but their joining and attachment and dependent on Mazal, BEING THE BEARD OF ARICH ANPIN WHO JOINS CHOCHMAH WITH BINAH, for they never separate. The Yud is tied with the Hei and the Hei is tied to the Vav. The Vav is tied to the LAST Hei and the Hei is tied to all, YUD-HEI-VAV. All is considered one knot, and one thing; they never separates from each other, so to speak. If one causes division, it is considered as if he is destroying the world. This is referred to as the nakedness of all.

63. "Hashem shall be one, and His name One"

A Synopsis

We are told that Hashem is not One now because Zeir Anpin and Malchut are parted, and at present the flow from Binah does not sustain Zeir Anpin. In the future, however, God will return the Shechinah to her position and everything will find itself in one unity. Before that final unity, the kingdom of Esau will be judged.

373. וּלְזִמְנָא דְּאָתֵי, זַמִּין קוּדְשָׁא בְּרִיךְ הוּא לְאֲתָבָא שְׁכִינְתָּא לְאַתְרָהָא, וּלְאִשְׁתַּכְּחָא כֹּלָּא בְּזִוּוּגָא חַד דִּכְתִּיב בַּיוֹם הַהוּא יִהְיֶה יְיָ׳ אֶחָד וְגוֹ׳. וְאִי תֵּימָא הַשְׁתָּא לָאו הוּא אֶחָד. לָא, דְּהָא הַשְׁתָּא חַיָּיבֵי עָלְמָא גָּרְמוּ, דְּלָא אִשְׁתְּכַח חַד. דְּהָא מַטְרוֹנִיתָא אִתְרְחֲקַת מִן מַלְכָּא, וְלָא מִשְׁתַּכְּחֵי בְּזִוּוּגָא. אִמָּא עִלָּאָה אִתְרְחֲקַת מִן מַלְכָּא וְלָא יַנְקָא לֵיהּ.

373. In the future, the Holy One, blessed be He, will return the Shechinah to Her position, as everything will find itself in one unity, as it is written, "On that day Hashem shall be one, and His name One" (Zecharyah 14:9). If you ask: So now, He is not one? No, as now the evildoers cause ZEIR ANPIN AND MALCHUT not to be as one, as the Queen distances herself from the King, and they do not find themselves joined. Supernal Ima, BEING BINAH, distances herself from the King and does not nourish Him.

374. בְּגִין דְּמַלְכָּא בְּלָא מַטְרוֹנִיתָא, לָא מִתְעַטֵּר בְּעִטְרוֹי דְּאִמָּא, כְּמָה בְּקַדְמֵיתָא כַּד אִתְחַבַּר בְּמַטְרוֹנִיתָא, דְּעֲטָרָא לֵיהּ, בְּכַמָּה עִטְרִין, בְּכַמָּה זְהִירִין בְּעִטְרִין קַדִּישִׁין עִלָּאִין. דִּכְתִּיב צְאֶינָה וּרְאֶינָה בְּנוֹת צִיּוֹן בַּמֶּלֶךְ שְׁלֹמֹה וְגוֹ׳, דְּאִזְדְּוַוג בְּמַטְרוֹנִיתָא, כְּדֵין עַטְרָא לֵיהּ אִימָּא עִלָּאָה כַּדְקָא יָאוֹת. וְהַשְׁתָּא דְּלָא אִשְׁתְּכַח מַלְכָּא בְּמַטְרוֹנִיתָא, כְּדֵין אִימָּא עִלָּאָה נָטְלַת עִטְרָאָה וּמָנָעַת מִנֵּיהּ מַבּוּעֵי דְּנַחֲלִין, וְלָא אִשְׁתְּכַח בְּקִשּׁוּרָא חַד. כִּבְיָכוֹל לָא אִשְׁתְּכַח חַד.

374. BINAH DOES NOT SUSTAIN ZEIR ANPIN, because the King without the Queen is not crowned with the crowns of Ima, as He used to be in the beginning when He was joined with the Queen, WHEN IMA USED TO ADORN HIM with several crowns, numerous lights, with supernal holy

crowns, as it is written, "Go forth, daughters of Zion, and behold King Solomon with the crown with which his mother crowned him..." (Shir Hashirim 3:11). When He joined with the Queen, supernal Ima crowned Him properly. Now that the King is not with the Queen, the supernal Ima takes back her crowns, withholds from Him the sources of the streams and He is not part of the one connection. CONSEQUENTLY, He is not found to be one, so to speak.

375. וּבְזִמְנָא דְּתֵיתוּב מַטְרוֹנִיתָא לַאֲתַר הֵיכָלָא, וּמַלְכָּא יִזְדַּוֵּוג עִמָּהּ בְּזִוּוּגָא חַד. כְּדֵין, יִתְחַבַּר כֹּלָּא כַּחֲדָא, בְּלָא פֵּרוּדָא, וְעַל דָּא כְּתִיב, בַּיּוֹם הַהוּא יִהְיֶה יְיָ' אֶחָד וּשְׁמוֹ אֶחָד. בַּיּוֹם הַהוּא: בְּזִמְנָא דִּיתוּב מַטְרוֹנִיתָא לְהֵיכָלָא, כְּדֵין כֹּלָּא אִשְׁתְּכַח חַד בְּלָא פֵּרוּדָא. וּכְדֵין וְעָלוּ מוֹשִׁיעִים בְּהַר צִיּוֹן לִשְׁפּוֹט וְגוֹ'.

375. At the time when the Queen returns to the chamber, the King will rejoin her in one mating, and everything will join together without division. Therefore, it is written, "On that day Hashem will be one, and His name one." "On that day," MEANING when the Queen will return to the palace, everything will be one without division. Then "liberators shall ascend upon Mount Zion to judge the mountain of Esau" (Ovadyah 1:21).

376. דְּתָנֵינָא, אָמַר ר' שִׁמְעוֹן, לָא תֵּיעוּל מַטְרוֹנִיתָא בְּחֶדְוָותָא בְּהֵיכָלֵיהּ עַד דְּיִתְדָּן מַלְכוּתָא דְּעֵשָׂו, וְתִיסַב מִנֵּיהּ נוּקְמִין דְּגָרְמָא כָּל הַאי. לְבָתַר תִּזְדַּוֵּוג בְּמַלְכָּא, וִיהֵא חֶדּוּ שְׁלִים, הה"ד, וְעָלוּ מוֹשִׁיעִים בְּהַר צִיּוֹן לִשְׁפּוֹט אֶת הַר עֵשָׂו בְּקַדְמֵיתָא, וּלְבָתַר וְהָיְתָה לַיְיָ' הַמְּלוּכָה. מַאן מְלוּכָה, דָּא מַטְרוֹנִיתָא. הה"ד, וְהָיְתָה לַיְיָ' הַמְּלוּכָה. וּלְבָתַר דְּיִזְדַּוְּוגָן כַּחֲדָא, מַה כְּתִיב. וְהָיָה יְיָ' לְמֶלֶךְ עַל כָּל הָאָרֶץ בַּיּוֹם הַהוּא יִהְיֶה יְיָ' אֶחָד וּשְׁמוֹ אֶחָד.

376. We have learned that Rabbi Shimon said: The Queen will not enter in joy in His palace until the kingdom of Esau will be judged, and she will have her vengeance for causing all this. Then she will join with the King and joy will be complete. This is the meaning of the verse, "And liberators

shall ascend upon Mount Zion to judge the mountain of Esau" at first, then "and the kingdom shall be Hashem's" (Ibid.). What is meant by kingdom? It refers to the Queen. This is the meaning of, "And the kingdom shall be Hashem's." After they rejoin, it is written, "And Hashem shall be the King over all the earth: on that day Hashem shall be one, and His name One."

64. Supernal Ima is a friend, lower Ima a bride

A Synopsis
Rabbi Yehuda interprets "You shall not uncover the nakedness of your father's brother...your mother's sister" to mean that through the sins of Yisrael Jerusalem below is destroyed. Malchut is from Aba and Ima together, from Chochmah and Binah together.

377. עֶרְוַת אֲחִי אָבִיךָ לֹא תְגַלֵּה. תָּאנֵי רַבִּי יְהוּדָה, דָּא יִשְׂרָאֵל לְתַתָּא. וַאֲחוֹת אִמְּךָ: דָּא יְרוּשָׁלֵם דִּלְתַתָּא. דִּבְחוֹבִין אִלֵּין, יִגְלוּן יִשְׂרָאֵל בֵּינֵי עַמְמַיָּא, וְיִתְחֲרִיב יְרוּשָׁלֵם לְתַתָּא. וְעַ״ד תָּנֵינָן, רְחִימוּתָא דְּקוּדְשָׁא בְּרִיךְ הוּא דְּקָרָא לְיִשְׂרָאֵל אַחִים, שֶׁנֶּאֱמַר לְמַעַן אַחַי וְרֵעָי אֲדַבְּרָה נָא וְגוֹ'.

377. "You shall not uncover the nakedness of your father's brother" (Vayikra 18:14): Rabbi Yehuda said that this verse speaks of Yisrael below, AS YISRAEL ARE THE BROTHERS OF ZEIR ANPIN, WHO IS YOUR FATHER. "Your mother's sister" (Ibid. 13) is Jerusalem on earth, THE SISTER OF MALCHUT ABOVE, YOUR MOTHER. Through these sins IS UNCOVERED THE NAKEDNESS OF YISRAEL, MEANING Yisrael will be in exile among the nations. THE NAKEDNESS OF JERUSALEM IS UNCOVERED, MEANING Jerusalem below will be destroyed. About this, we learned of the love of the Holy One, blessed be He, in that He called Yisrael brothers, as it is written, "For my brethren and friends' sake, I will now say..." (Tehilim 122:8). THEREFORE, THE VERSE SAYS ABOUT THEM, "THE NAKEDNESS OF YOUR FATHER'S BROTHER."

378. א״ר יְהוּדָה, אִי אַחַי לָמָּה רֵעָי, וְאִי רֵעָי לָמָּה אַחַי. אֶלָּא תָּאנָא, הַהוּא מִלָּה דְּלָא אִתְעֲדֵי לְעָלְמִין, אִקְרֵי רֵעַ, כד״א רֵעֲךָ וְרֵעַ אָבִיךָ אַל תַּעֲזוֹב. וְהַאי רָזָא דְּמִלָּה דְּאָמַר ר״ש, אִימָא עִלָּאָה, רַעְיָא אִקְרֵי, בְּגִין דְּלָא אִתְעֲדֵי רְחִימוּתָא דְּאַבָּא מִנָּה לְעָלְמִין. וְאִימָא תַּתָּאָה כַּלָּה אִקְרֵי, וְאִקְרֵי אֲחוֹת, כְּמָה דְּאוֹקִימְנָא אֲחוֹת לָנוּ קְטַנָּה.

378. Rabbi Yehuda said: If it says "brethren," why IS WRITTEN "friends" and if "friends," why WRITE "brethren"? HE ANSWERS: We have learned

that something that is never interrupted is called a friend, as it is said, "Do not forsake your own friend, and your father's friend" (Mishlei 27:10). This is the secret of what Rabbi Shimon said: Supernal Ima, NAMELY BINAH, is called "friend," because the love of Aba never ceases from her. The Ima below, MEANING MALCHUT, is called bride and is called sister, as we have explained the verse, "We have a little sister" (Shir Hashirim 8:8), DENOTING MALCHUT.

379. וְהַיְינוּ סְתָם מַתְנִיתָא דִּילָן, דִּכְתִיב הָכָא, עֶרְוַת אֲחוֹתְךָ בַת אָבִיךָ אוֹ בַת אִמֶּךָ, כֵּיוָן דְּאָמַר בַּת אָבִיךָ, מַאי אוֹ בַת אִמֶּךָ. אֶלָּא, אִי מִסִּטְרָא דְּאַבָּא אִשְׁתְּכַחַת, חָכְמָה אִתְקְרֵי. וְאִי מִסִּטְרָא דְּאִימָא, בִּינָה אִתְקְרֵי. וְעַכ"פ בֵּין הַאי וּבֵין הַאי, מֵאִימָא וְאַבָּא אִשְׁתְּכַחַת. דְּהָא יוֹ"ד לָא אִתְעָדֵי מִן ה' לְעָלְמִין. וְדָא הוּא רָזָא דְּמִלָּה, מוֹלֶדֶת בַּיִת: מִסִּטְרָא דְּאַבָּא. אוֹ מוֹלֶדֶת חוּץ: מִסִּטְרָא דְּאִימָא.

379. This is like the Mishnah that is unspecific, MEANING THAT WITH WHAT WAS MENTIONED THAT ABA AND IMA ARE NEVER SEPARATED, THE GENERAL WORDS OF THE MISHNAH WILL BE UNDERSTOOD. It is written here, "The nakedness of your sister, the daughter of your father, or daughter of your mother" (Vayikra 18:9). Since it is said, "the daughter of your father," what is "or daughter of your mother"? HE ANSWERS: If she is from the side of Aba, MEANING THE SIDE OF ABA IS DOMINANT IN HER, MALCHUT is named Chochmah. If she is from the side of Ima, MEANING THAT THE SIDE OF IMA IS DOMINANT IN HER, she is called Binah. At any rate, whether from here or there, she is from Aba and Ima TOGETHER, for the Yud, WHICH IS ABA, never parts from the Hei, NAMELY IMA. This is the secret in the verse, "Whether she is born at home" (Ibid.) WHEN SHE IS from the side of Aba and "or born abroad" (Ibid.) WHEN SHE IS from the side of Ima, AS IMA IS THE EXTERNAL PART OF ABA. THE END OF THE VERSE EXPLAINS ITS BEGINNING.

380. רִבִּי אַבָּא אָמַר, בְּחָכְמָה יִבָּנֶה בָּיִת, מַאן הוּא בַּיִת דְּאִתְבְּנֵי בְּחָכְמָה. הֲוֵי אֵימָא דָּא נָהָר דְּנָפִיק מֵעֵדֶן, בְּגִינֵי כָּךְ מוֹלֶדֶת בַּיִת. אוֹ מוֹלֶדֶת חוּץ. כַּד נַפְקַת מִן ו', כְּמָה דִכְתִיב, עֶצֶם מֵעֲצָמַי וּבָשָׂר מִבְּשָׂרִי. וּכְתִיב וַיִּקַּח אַחַת מִצַּלְעוֹתָיו, וְדָא הוּא מוֹלֶדֶת חוּץ, מֵאֲתַר דִּזְעֵיר

אַנְפִּין אִשְׁתְּכַח, כְּמָה דְּאִתְּמַר.

380. Rabbi Aba said, "Through wisdom a house is built" (Mishlei 24:3). What is a house built with Chochmah? Some say it is the river flowing from Eden, MEANING BINAH. For this reason it is WRITTEN, "born at home," MEANING MALCHUT BORN FROM BINAH CONSIDERED A HOUSE FOR CHOCHMAH. "Or born abroad," MEANING when MALCHUT comes out of the Vav, BEING ZEIR ANPIN, as it is written WHEN ADAM, ZEIR ANPIN, SAID ABOUT EVE, MALCHUT, "Bone of my bones, and flesh of my flesh" (Beresheet 2:23). It is also written, "And He took one of his sides" (Ibid. 21), SO MALCHUT IS COMING OUT FROM ZEIR ANPIN. This is "born abroad," from the place where Zeir Anpin is, WHICH IS CONSIDERED ON THE OUTSIDE OF IMA, as we have learned.

the secret of the matter. They will meditate with their hearts with a complete wish, and the offspring they produce are called children of the King. If these cause a flaw down below, it is as if they cause harm to the bride on high, NAMELY MALCHUT. Then we find written, "You shall not uncover the nakedness of your daughter in law (Heb. *kalah*, also: 'bride')." This EXPLANATION is for those who comprehend Torah ways. For the rest of the people, THE EXPLANATION IS the revealed one, MEANING literally your actual daughter-in-law, THE WIFE OF HIS SON. Because of this sin, the Shechinah departs from them, NAMELY, HE ALSO HINTS THAT THE BRIDE ON HIGH DEPARTS BECAUSE OF THIS DEFECT BELOW.

ואוֹת לְבֵית דָּוִד, לְאַחֲסָנָא מַלְכוּתָא קַדִּישָׁא הוּא

א שִׁירָתָא דְּאָמַר דָּוִד עַל מַלְכוּ עִלָּאָה קַדִּישָׁא.

382. Rabbi Yitzchak said, "There the tribes used (Ibid. 4). Who are the tribes? HE ANSWERS: boundaries that spread from that large and strong BEING THE SECRET OF FOUR SFIROT – CHES AND MALCHUT. EACH HAS THREE COLUMNS BOUNDARIES. FROM ZEIR ANPIN, THEY ARE WHERE THEY ARE CALLED BY THE NAME OF T inherited from Aba and Ima. This is what is writt MEANING from the good testimony that the holy s "The tribes of Yah, an appointed practice (lit. 'test THE TWELVE BOUNDARIES ARE THE SECRET MEANING THE ILLUMINATION OF EDEN (CHOCHM rivers flowing from Yah (Yud Hei), WHICH ARE AE the purpose "to give thanks to the name of Hashem" "for there are set thrones of Judgment, the thrones (Ibid. 5), in order to bequeath the Holy Kingdom generations. This is the poem recited by David conce kingdom.

, כֹּלָּא בְּרָזָא עִלָּאָה הוּא, לְאַחֲזָאָה דְּמַאן דְּפָגִים
עֶרְוַת כַּלָּתְךָ לֹא תְגַלֵּה, דְּתָנֵינָן עוֹנָתָן שֶׁל ת"ח
דִּיַדְעִין רָזָא דְּמִלָּה, וִיכַוְּונוּן לִבָּא, וְיִשְׁתְּכַח
ן דְּאוֹלִידוּ אִקְרוּן בְּנִין דְּמַלְכָּא. וְאִי אִלֵּין פְּגִימוּ
פְּגִמִין אִינוּן בְּכַלָּה דִּלְעֵילָּא, כְּדֵין כְּתִיב עֶרְוַת
בְּגִין אִינוּן דְּיַדְעִין אוֹרְחִין דְּאוֹרַיְיתָא. שְׁאָר עַמָּא
ֶלָּתְךָ מַמָּשׁ, וּבְחוֹבָא דָּא שְׁכִינְתָּא אִסְתְּלָקַת

383. Rabbi Chizkiyah said: All is according to the su that one who causes a defect below causes a defect a uncover the nakedness of your daughter in law" (Vay learned that the marital visits of the scholars are on Sh

381
bles
belo
"Jer
ME
TOC
that
Kin
Kin
ME

ִילָּא
ֲרֵי,
ְמַאי
ִטְרֵי
ְּרָה

ֵלִין
ְלוֹן
ְֵיד
ִין,
ְמֶה

5. Yisrael are brothers to the Holy One, blessed be He

A Synopsis

bbi Yehuda says that the children of Yisrael are brothers to God cause His love for them has never been interrupted. Rabbi tzchak talks about "the tribes of Yah" and the twelve boundaries at spread from Zeir Anpin, the Tree. Rabbi Chizkiyah concludes at all their discussion shows that anyone who causes a defect low causes one above, although the explanation given to most ople of the scripture "you shall not uncover the nakedness..." is e obvious one, that one should not lay with those who are related them. Because of this sin, the Shechinah leaves them.

381. וְעַ"ד א"ר יְהוּדָה, יִשְׂרָאֵל אָחִין אִקְרוּן לְקוּדְשָׁא בְּרִיךְ הו אַעֲדֵי רְחִימוּתָא דִּלְהוֹן לְעָלְמִין. יְרוּשְׁלֵם דִּלְתַתָּא אָחוֹת אִמְּךָ כְּמָה דִּכְתִיב יְרוּשָׁלַם הַבְּנוּיָה כְּעִיר שֶׁחוּבְּרָה לָה יַחְדָּיו וְ שֶׁחוּבְּרָה לָה יַחְדָּיו. בְּגִין דְּאִזְדַּוּוֹג בָּה מַלְכָּא מְשִׁית סִטְרִין, בְּ מַלְכָּא, בְּדַרְגָּא דְּצַדִּיק, וְכָל כִּתְרֵי מַלְכָּא כְּלִילָן בֵּיהּ. וְהַיְינוּ לָה יַחְדָּיו.

bbi Yehuda continued: Yisrael are called brothers to the Holy One, be He, as His love for them has never been interrupted. Jerusalem s called "your mother's sister" (Vayikra 18:13), as it is written, m, built as a city that is compact together..." (Tehilim 122:3), G THAT JERUSALEM BELOW IS LIKE THE CITY THAT IS COMPACT HER, MALCHUT. What is meant by "compact together"? It means King joined, in the six ends, ZEIR ANPIN, with all aspects of the with the grade of the Righteous, YESOD, in which all Sfirot of the re included. This is the meaning of, "that is compact together," G TOGETHER WITH ALL SFIROT OF ZEIR ANPIN.

382. רִבִּי יִצְחָק אָמַר, שָׁשָׁם עָלוּ שְׁבָטִים שִׁבְטֵי יָהּ. מַאן שְׁבָטִים תְּרֵיסַר תְּחוּמִין, דְּמִתְפָּרְשָׁן מֵהַהוּא אִילָנָא רַבָּא וְתַקִּיף, דְּאַחִכ מִסִּטְרָא דְּאַבָּא וְאִמָּא. הה"ד שִׁבְטֵי יָהּ, מִסְפַּר סַהֲדוּתָא, דִּ בְּרָא קַדִּישָׁא דִּכְתִיב שִׁבְטֵי יָהּ עֵדוּת לְיִשְׂרָאֵל, וְאִינוּן נַהֲרִין עַ דְּנַגְדִּין וְאִתְמַשְּׁכָן מִן יָהּ. וְכָל כַּךְ לָמָּה. לְהוֹדוֹת לְשֵׁם יְיָ'. כִּ

66. The Holy Name is engraved in certain ways

A Synopsis

We learn how the Holy Name is engraved with the 22 letters, and what this has to do with the flow from above. The section talks about the secret of seventy and 72, and about how the letters of the name Ayin-Bet ascended in ways known only to truly righteous men. Whoever wishes to know and understand the permutations of the Holy Names needs to know the letters marked in every individual Sfirah, and then he will know and have power in everything. Moses was able to stand among the holy angels because he knew the Holy Names that the angels did not.

384. תָּאנָא, אִתְגְּלִיף שְׁמָא קַדִּישָׁא בְּסִטְרִין יְדִיעָן, בְּאַתְוּון רְשִׁימִין דְּעֶשְׂרִין וּתְרֵין י' בָּא' א' בְּי' י' בְּב', ב' בְּי' י' בְּד', ד', בְּי'. י' בְּה'. י' בְּג'. ה' בְּי'. ג' בְּי'. בְּי'. כֻּלְּהוּ מִתְגַּלְּפֵי בְּיו"ד יו"ד סָלִיק לוֹן.

384. We have learned that the Holy Name is engraved in certain ways, with the letters of the 22 letters imprinted: Yud in Aleph, Aleph in Yud, Yud in Bet, Bet in Yud, Yud in Dalet, Dalet in Yud, Yud in Hei, Yud in Gimel, Hei in Yud, Gimel in Yud, Vav in Yud. So they are all engraved in the Yud. The Yud lifts them AS IT LIFTS ALL 22 LETTERS.

385. ה"א כָּלִיל בְּיו"ד, מִנֵּיהּ נָפְקַת, כְּדֵין מְעַטְּרִין לַאֲבָהָן. אִתְפְּתְּחַת ה"א בְּנַחֲלוֹי, וְאִעֲטַּר לְרֵישָׁא דְּו', דְּתַמָּן שַׁרְיָין אֲבָהָן.

385. The Hei OF THE NAME YUD HEI VAV HEI, BEING BINAH, is included in the Yud OF YUD HEI VAV HEI. It emerges from it, AS BINAH EMANATES FROM CHOCHMAH. Then CHOCHMAH AND BINAH, WHICH ARE YUD HEI OF YUD HEI VAV HEI crown the Patriarchs, MEANING CHESED, GVURAH AND TIFERET OF ZEIR ANPIN CALLED ABRAHAM, ISAAC AND JACOB. The Hei is opened with its streams, MEANING WITH THE FIFTY GATES OF BINAH IN IT, and crowns the head of the Vav, MEANING IT SUPPLIES THE FIRST THREE SFIROT TO ZEIR ANPIN, THE SECRET OF VAV OF YUD HEI VAV HEI, where the Patriarchs dwell. THIS MEANS THAT THE PATRIARCHS, CHESED, supernal GVURAH AND TIFERET, RISE AND BECOME HEAD — MEANING CHOCHMAH, BINAH AND DA'AT — THROUGH THE ILLUMINATION OF THE FIFTY GATES OF BINAH.

386. ו' כָּלִיל שִׁית אַתְוָון, וְכֻלְּהוּ כָּלִיל יוֹ"ד. יוֹ"ד אִתְגְּלִיף בְּגְלוּפוֹי,
וְסָלִיק לְאִתְעַטְּרָא בִּתְרֵיסַר אַתְוָון אָחֳרָנִין, מִנֵּיהּ נָפְקוּ עֲשַׂר אֲמִירָן
בִּגְלוּפוֹי, וְכֻלְּהוּ שְׁבִילִין דְּאוֹרְחָא עִלָּאָה, יַקִּירָא דְּכֹלָּא. כְּדֵין ה"א
אָחֳרָא אִתְכְּלִילַת מִן כֻּלְּהוּ, גְּלִיפָא מִסִּטְרָא מְתִיחָא טְמִירָא, לְאוֹלָדָא
לְתַתָּא.

386. HE SAYS: Vav consists of six letters, MEANING IT IS MADE UP OF SIX
LETTERS FROM ALEPH TO VAV THAT PRECEDE IT. The Yud includes them
all, AS THE YUD CONTAINS ALL NINE LETTERS THAT PRECEDE IT, AMONG
WHICH IS THE VAV AND THE SIX LETTERS INCLUDED THEREIN. THIS IS
THE YUD THAT IS ABOVE THE VAV, AS MENTIONED. This Yud is engraved
with marks, MEANING WITH THE INCLUSION OF THE NINE LETTERS THAT
PRECEDE IT, and ascends TO THE YUD OF YUD HEI VAV HEI, THAT
INCLUDES ALL 22 LETTERS to be crowned with the twelve other letters
FROM YUD TO TAV. THEN IT IS ALSO PART OF THE 22 LETTERS LIKE THE
YUD OF YUD HEI VAV HEI. THEN ten engraved sayings, MEANING TEN
SFIROT, come out of it, and all of the paths of the supernal most precious
way. Then the other Hei OF YUD HEI VAV HEI, MALCHUT, contains them
all, MEANING, IT RECEIVES FROM ALL LIGHTS AS MENTIONED, carved
from the part of the concealed peg, YESOD OF ZEIR ANPIN, to give birth
below, MEANING TO BE WORTHY TO BEAR SOULS.

387. אִתְגְּלִיפוּ כֻּלְּהוּ בְּאַרְבְּעִין וּתְרֵין אַתְוָון, וְכֻלְּהוּ פְּרִישְׁנָא בְּמַתְנִיתָא
דִּידָן, וְכֻלְּהוּ סַלְקָן בְּרֵישָׁא דְּמַלְכָּא.

387. All THE LIGHTS THAT WERE IN YUD, WHICH IS ATOP THE VAV – THE
FIRST THREE SFIROT OF ZEIR ANPIN – are marked by the 42 letters, as we
have explained in our Mishnah. All ascend to the head of the King,
MEANING THE FIRST THREE SFIROT OF ZEIR ANPIN, AS EARLIER
DISCUSSED.

388. שֶׁבַע שַׁבָּתִין שְׁלֵימִין, מִתְפָּרְשִׁין בְּשַׁבְעִין אַתְוָון. שַׁבְעִין וּתְרֵין
אִסְתְּלָקוּ, וְאִסְתְּלָקוּ בְּאוֹת ו', רְשִׁימָן בפ' וַיְהִי בְּשַׁלַּח פַּרְעֹה בְּקְרָא
וַיִּסַּע וַיָּבֹא וַיֵּט. כַּד נַטְלַת שְׁכִינְתָּא, וְז' רְשִׁימִין אִתְרְשִׁימוּ בֵּיהּ, שַׁבְעִין

אִסְתַּלָּקוּ מִנֵּיהּ, בְּאַתְוָון רְשִׁימִין. תָּאנָא, אִסְתַּלָּקוּ אַתְוָון בִּרְשִׁימִין יְדִיעָן, וְאָרְחִין סְתִימִין, בַּר לְזַכָּאֵי קְשׁוֹט, סַמְכֵי עָלְמָא.

388. Seven complete weeks, MEANING SEVEN SFIROT OF MALCHUT THAT IS CALLED SHABBAT, WHEN THEY ARE COMPLETED, are expressed by seventy letters OF THE NAME OF AYIN-BET (72). THE MAIN BODY IS SEVENTY, AND TWO EXTRA ARE THE SECRET OF WITNESSES OR SCRIBES. HE EXPLAINS HIS WORDS: When the 72 ascended, they ascended by the letters Vav, DENOTING ZEIR ANPIN, IN ITS CHESED, GVURAH AND TIFERET, which are listed in the portion of Beshalach in the verses, "And the angel...removed...and it came... And Moses stretched out" (Shemot 14:19-21). When the Shechinah receives FROM ZEIR ANPIN and the seven impressions are stamped on Her BY HIM, NAMELY SEVEN COMPLETE SFIROT, THEN seventy imprinted letters OF THE NAME AYIN-BET rise from Her. We have learned that the letters OF THE NAME AYIN-BET ascended through certain marks and hidden ways KNOWN only to truly righteous men, pillars of the world.

389. אָמַר רִבִּי שִׁמְעוֹן לְר׳ אֶלְעָזָר, ת״ח, הָנֵי עֶשְׂרִין וּתְרֵין אַתְוָון דִּגְלִיפִין בְּאוֹרַיְיתָא, כֻּלְּהוּ מִתְפָּרְשָׁן בְּהָנֵי עֲשַׂר אֲמִירָן. כָּל אֲמִירָה וַאֲמִירָה מֵאִלֵּין עֲשַׂר, דְּאִינּוּן כִּתְרֵי מַלְכָּא כֻּלְּהוּ גְּלִיפִין בְּאַתְוָון יְדִיעָן, בְּגִינֵי כַּךְ שְׁמָא קַדִּישָׁא אִתְכַּסְיָיא בְּאַתְוָון אָחֳרָנִין, וְכָל אֲמִירָה, אוֹזִיף לַאֲמִירָה עִלָּאָה מִנָּהּ אַתְוֹוי, בְּגִין דְּאִתְכְּלִיל הַאי בְּהַאי. וְעַ״ד שְׁמָא קַדִּישָׁא, גְּלִיפְנָא לֵיהּ בְּאַתְוָון אָחֳרָנִין, בְּגִין דְּאִתְכַּסְיָין דָּא בְּדָא, וְדָא בְּדָא, עַד דְּמִתְקַשְּׁרָן כֻּלְּהוּ כַּחֲדָא.

389. Rabbi Shimon said to Rabbi Elazar: Come and see that these 22 letters engraved in the Torah are all explained in the ten sayings, THE TEN SFIROT – KETER, CHOCHMAH, BINAH, CHESED, GVURAH, TIFERET, NETZACH, HOD, YESOD AND MALCHUT. Each and every saying of these ten, the Sfirot of the King, are engraved by certain letters, IN AS MUCH AS THE LETTERS ARE THE SECRET OF THE VESSELS OF THE SFIROT AND EACH SFIRAH HAS ITS OWN SPECIAL VESSELS. For this reason, the Holy Name, YUD HEI VAV HEI, is enveloped with other letters, MEANING WITH ADONAI, AS THE VESSELS OF ZEIR ANPIN, THE SECRET OF YUD HEI

VAV HEI, ARE CLOTHED AND ENVELOPED WITH THE VESSELS OF
MALCHUT, THE SECRET OF ADONAI. Each saying lends letters to the
saying above it, as one is included in the other. Therefore, we pronounce the
Holy Name YUD HEI VAV HEI with the other letters OF ADONAI, as they
are covered AND DRESSED one with the other until they are connected
together.

390. וּמַאן דְּבָעֵי לְמִנְדַּע צֵרוּפֵי שְׁמָהָן קַדִּישִׁין, לִינְדַע אִינּוּן אַתְוָון
דִּרְשִׁימִין בְּכָל כִּתְרָא וְכִתְרָא, וּכְדֵין לִינְדַע וְיִתְקַיַּים בְּכֹלָּא. וְהָא
גְּלִיפְנָא לוֹן, בְּכָל אִינּוּן אַתְוָון דִּרְשִׁימָן וִידִיעָן בְּכָל כִּתְרָא וְכִתְרָא,
מִסִּפְרָא עִלָּאָה דִּשְׁלֹמֹה. וְהָכִי סָלִיק בִּידָן, וְחַבְרַיָּיא גְּלִיפִין לוֹן, וְשַׁפִּיר
הוּא, דְּהָא כָּל כִּתְרָא וְכִתְרָא אוֹזִיף לְחַבְרֵיהּ אַתְוֹוי, כְּמָה דְּאוֹקִימְנָא,
וּלְזִמְנִין דְּלָא אִצְטְרִיךְ אֶלָּא, בְּאַתְוֹוי אִינּוּן דִּרְשִׁימִין בֵּיהּ. וְכֻלְּהוּ יְדִיעָן
לְגַבֵּי חַבְרַיָּיא וְהָא אוֹקִימְנָא לוֹן.

390. He who wishes to know AND TO UNDERSTAND the permutations of the
Holy Names NEEDS to know these letters marked in every individual Sfirah;
then he will know and have power in everything. We copied them with the
letters written in and specific to every Sfirah from the supernal book of
Solomon. We succeeded in this and the friends wrote them. It is well THAT
THEY WROTE THEM, as every Sfirah lends letters, WHICH ARE NECESSARY
TO KNOW AND REMEMBER, to its neighbor, as we established IN THE
ADJACENT PARAGRAPH. Sometimes it is only necessary TO KNOW those
letters listed in THE SFIRAH itself, BUT NOT THE LETTERS LENT TO IT. The
friends know this and we have established this.

391. זַכָּאִין אִינּוּן צַדִּיקַיָּיא בְּעָלְמָא דֵּין וּבְעָלְמָא דְּאָתֵי, דְּקוּדְשָׁא בְּרִיךְ
הוּא בָּעֵי בִּיקָרֵיהוֹן, וּמְגַלֵּי לְהוֹן רָזִין עִלָּאִין דִּשְׁמֵיהּ קַדִּישָׁא, דְּלָא גַּלֵּי
לְעִלָּאִין קַדִּישִׁין, וְעַ״ד יָכִיל מֹשֶׁה, לְאִתְעַטְּרָא בֵּינֵי קַדִּישִׁין, וְכֻלְּהוּ לָא
יַכְלֵי לְמִקְרַב בַּהֲדֵיהּ, כְּנוּרָא יָקִידְתָּא, וְגוֹמְרֵי דְּאֶשָׁא. דְּאִי לָאו הָכִי,
מַאן הֲוָה לֵיהּ לְמֹשֶׁה, לְמֵיקַם בֵּינַיְיהוּ. אֶלָּא זַכָּאָה חוּלָקָא דְּמֹשֶׁה,
דְּהָא כַּד שָׁארֵי לְמַלָּלָא עִמֵּיהּ קוּדְשָׁא בְּרִיךְ הוּא, בָּעָא לְמִנְדַּע שְׁמֵיהּ
קַדִּישָׁא, סָתִים וְגַלְיָא, בְּכָל חַד וְחַד כַּדְקָא חֲזֵי, וּכְדֵין אַדְבַּק וְיָדַע יַתִּיר

מִכָּל בְּנֵי עָלְמָא.

391. Happy are the righteous in both this world and the World to Come, as the Holy One, blessed be He, desires to honor them and reveals to them esoteric matters concerning His Holy Name that He did not even reveal to holy supernal ANGELS. Therefore, Moses was able to be adorned even among the holy ANGELS, and they were unable to approach him as if he were a burning fire and flaming hot coals. THE REASON WAS THAT HE MENTIONED THE HOLY NAMES THAT THE ANGELS DID NOT KNOW. Were it not for that, what did Moses have THAT HE WOULD BE ABLE to stand among them? Blessed was Moses' lot that when the Holy One, blessed be He, began to speak with him, he wanted to know His Holy Name, both the concealed and revealed, each one properly. Then he united and knew more than all mankind.

392. תָּא חֲזֵי, בְּשַׁעֲתָא דְּסָלִיק מֹשֶׁה גּוֹ עֲנָנָא יַקִּירָא, עָאל בֵּינֵי קַדִּישִׁין. פָּגַע בֵּיהּ חַד מַלְאָכָא בְּשַׁלְהוֹבֵי נוּרָא, בְּעַיְינִין מְלַהֲטָן, וְגַדְפּוֹי מוֹקְדָן, בָּעָא לְשַׁאֲפָא לֵיהּ בְּגַוְוֵיהּ. וְהַהוּא מַלְאָכָא קְמוּא"ל שְׁמֵיהּ, כְּדֵין אַדְכַּר מֹשֶׁה חַד שְׁמָא קַדִּישָׁא. דַּהֲוָה גָּלִיף בִּתְרֵיסַר אַתְוָון, וְאִזְדַּעְזַע וְאִתְרְגַשׁ, עַד דְּסָלִיק מֹשֶׁה בֵּינַיְיהוּ. וְכֵן לְכָל חַד וְחַד, זַכָּאָה חוּלָקֵיהּ וְהָא אוֹקִימְנָא מִלֵּי.

392. Come and see: At the time Moses ascended the cloud and entered among the holy ANGELS, one angel, by the name Kemuel, came to him in a flame of fire with burning eyes and flaming wings, and wanted to swallow him. Then Moses mentioned one Holy Name which was engraven with twelve letters. He trembled and shook, and Moses was thus able to ascend among them. So happened with each one. Blessed is his lot. We discussed this earlier.

67. The nakedness of a woman and her daughter

A Synopsis

We are reminded of the laws against incest. Rabbi Yosi says that repentance brings good results as long as the one who repents also stops sinning. He says that David did not sin in his relationship with Bathsheba, because she was destined for him from the Day of Creation, but he did sin by causing Uriah's death.

393. עֶרְוַת אִשָּׁה, וּבִתָּה לֹא תְגַלֵּה. תָּאנָא, בְּתִקּוּנֵי מַטְרוֹנִיתָא אוֹקִימְנָא אִלֵּין עֶרְיָין, אע"ג דְּאִינּוּן בְּאִתְגַּלְיָיא וּבִסְתִּימָא, וְתַמָּן בַּת בְּנָהּ וּבַת בִּתָּהּ. דְּהָא עָלְמָא אִצְטְרִיךְ לוֹן, וְאִינּוּן יְשׁוּבָא דְּעָלְמָא, כְּמָה דְּאוֹקִימְנָא. וּמַאן דְּגַלֵּי חַד עֶרְיָיתָא מִנַּיְיהוּ, וַוי לֵיהּ, וַוי לְנַפְשֵׁיהּ, דְּהָא גַלֵּי בְּגִין דָּא עֶרְיָין אַחֲרָנִין.

393. "You shall not uncover the nakedness of mother and daughter" (Vayikra 18:17). We have learned that these kinds of incest are among the laws of the Queen, even though they are both revealed and hidden. There are listed "her son's daughter, or her daughter's daughter" (Ibid.), for the world needs them to populate the world, as we have learned. One who reveals one nakedness of these, woe to him and woe to his soul, as because of this he will uncover other nakednesses.

394. וְתַנְיָא מִלָּה בַּתְרָאָה דַּעֲשַׂר אֲמִרָן דְּאוֹרַיְיתָא, לֹא תַחְמוֹד אֵשֶׁת רֵעֶךָ, בְּגִין דְּהַאי כְּלָלָא דְּכֹלְהוּ. וּמַאן דְּחָמִיד אִתְּתָא אָחֳרָא, כְּאִלּוּ אַעֲבָר עַל אוֹרַיְיתָא כֻּלָּא. בְּרַם לָא אִית מִלָּה דְּקַיְּימָא קַמֵּי תְּשׁוּבָה. וכ"ש אִי קַבִּיל עוֹנָשֵׁיהּ כְּדָוִד מַלְכָּא. אָמַר רַבִּי יוֹסֵי, תָּנֵינָן, כָּל מַאן דְּחָב וְאִתְפְּרַשׁ מֵהַהוּא חוֹבָא, תְּשׁוּבָה קָא מְעַלְּיָיא לֵיהּ טְפֵי. וְאִי לָאו, לָא סָלִיק בִּידֵיהּ תְּשׁוּבָה, וְלָא מְעַלְּיָיא לֵיהּ. אִי הָכִי, דָּוִד הֵיךְ לָא אִתְפְּרַשׁ מִבַּת שֶׁבַע לְבָתַר. אָמַר לֵיהּ, בַּת שֶׁבַע דִּידֵיהּ הֲוַת, וְדִידֵיהּ נָטִיל, דְּהָא מִית בַּעְלָהּ.

394. We have learned the last statement of the Ten Commandments of the Torah, reads, "You shall not covet your neighbor's wife" (Shemot 20:14), as

this generally represents the whole of them. He who covets another woman is considered transgressing the entire Torah. However, nothing stands before repentance, all the more so if he is willing to accept upon himself his penalty like King David. Rabbi Yosi said: We have learned that repentance does much good to whoever has sinned and then parted from the sin. If he does not PART FROM IT, repentance does not help and is to no avail. HE QUESTIONS: How was it that David did not part from Batsheba afterwards? He replied: Batsheba was his. He took what was his, as her husband had died.

395. דְּתַנְיָא, אִזְדַּמְּנַת הֲוַת בַּת שֶׁבַע לְדָוִד, מִיּוֹמָא דְּאִתְבְּרֵי עָלְמָא, וּמָה עַכְּבָא לֵיהּ. דְּנָטַל בְּרַתֵּיהּ דְּשָׁאוּל מַלְכָּא, וְהַהוּא יוֹמָא נָטַל לָהּ אוּרִיָּה בְּרַחֲמֵי, אַף עַל גַּב דְּלָא הֲוַת דִּילֵיהּ. לְבָתַר אָתָא דָּוִד, וְנָטִיל דִּילֵיהּ, וְעַל דְּדָוִד דָּחִיק שַׁעֲתָא קַמֵּי קוּדְשָׁא בְּרִיךְ הוּא לְקַטְלָא לְאוּרִיָּה וּלְמֶעְבַּד הָכִי. אַבְאִישׁ קַמֵּיהּ, וְאַעֲנַשׁ לֵיהּ לְדָוִד, דְּהָא קוּדְשָׁא בְּרִיךְ הוּא בָּעָא לְאָתָבָא לֵיהּ לְדָוִד, לְקַיְּימָא לֵיהּ מַלְכוּתָא קַדִּישָׁא עִלָּאָה. וְכַד תָּאַב, לְדִידֵיהּ תָּאַב.

395. We have learned that Batsheba was chosen for David from the day of Creation. What had delayed HIS TAKING HER was because he took the daughter of King Saul. That day, Uriah took her mercifully even though she was not to be his. Later, David came and took what was his. Since David forced time before the Holy One, blessed be He, to kill Uriah and behave in this way, he sinned before Him. So He punished David, because the Holy One, blessed be He, wanted to return BATSHEBA to David in order to sustain for his sake the holy supernal kingdom, AS BATSHEBA WAS THE CHARIOT OF MALCHUT. So what he yearned for was really his.

396. תָּאנָא, א"ר יוֹסֵי, מַאי דִּכְתִּיב אֲנִי יְיָ'. אֲנִי יְיָ': עָתִיד לִיתֵּן שָׂכָר טוֹב לַצַּדִּיקִים לֶעָתִיד לָבֹא. אֲנִי יְיָ' עָתִיד לְהִפָּרַע מִן הָרְשָׁעִים לֶעָתִיד לָבֹא. אִינּוּן דִּכְתִּיב בְּהוֹ הַפּוֹשְׁעִים בִּי. כְּתִיב אֲנִי יְיָ', וּכְתִיב אֲנִי אָמִית וַאֲחַיֶּה. אע"פי שֶׁאֲנִי בְּמִדַּת הָרַחֲמִים, הָרְשָׁעִים הוֹפְכִים אוֹתִי לְמִדַּת הַדִּין. דְּתַנְיָא, שֵׁם מָלֵא: יְיָ' אֱלֹהִים. זָכוּ יְיָ', וְאִי לָאו אֱלֹהִים. א"ר שִׁמְעוֹן, חַיָּיבִין עַבְדֵי פְּגִימוּתָא לְעֵילָּא. מַאי פְּגִימוּתָא כְּמָה דְּאוֹקִימְנָא

פְּגִימוּתָא מַמָּשׁ, וְהָא אִתְּמַר.

396. We have learned that Rabbi Yosi said: It is written, "I am Hashem" (Vayikra 18:30), MEANING I am Hashem, who will give good reward for the righteous in the World to Come. I am Hashem who will take revenge upon the wicked in the World to Come, MEANING upon those about whom it is written, "That have rebelled against Me" (Yeshayah 66:24). HE QUESTIONS: It is written, "I am Hashem," WHICH POINTS TO THE QUALITY OF MERCY and it is written, "I kill, and I make alive" (Devarim 32:39), WHICH POINTS TO THE QUALITY OF JUDGMENT. HE ANSWERS: Even though I have the quality of Mercy, the evildoers convert Me to the quality of Judgment. We have learned that Yud Hei Vav Hei Elohim is a full name. YUD HEI VAV HEI STANDS FOR MERCY AND ELOHIM FOR JUDGMENT, MEANING if they merit it, then it is Yud Hei Vav Hei. If they do not merit, it is Elohim. Rabbi Shimon said, The evildoers cause a defect above. What is the defect? It is, as we established, a real defect as explained EARLIER.

68. "A woman in the impurity of her menstrual flow"

A Synopsis

Rabbi Yehuda taught that because Rabbi Shimon's generation were righteous, it was all right for secrets to be revealed, but in other generations they will be hidden.

397. תָּאנָא כְּתִיב וְאֶל אִשָּׁה בְּנִדַּת טוּמְאָתָה לֹא תִקְרַב לְגַלּוֹת עֶרְוָתָה, תָּנֵי רִבִּי יְהוּדָה, דָּרָא דרשב"י שָׁארֵי בְּגַוֵּיהּ, כֻּלְּהוּ זַכָּאִין, חֲסִידִין, כֻּלְּהוּ דַחֲלֵי חַטָאָה נִינְהוּ. שְׁכִינְתָּא שַׁרְיָא בֵּינַיְיהוּ, מַה דְּלֵית כֵּן בְּדָרִין אָחֳרָנִין. בְּגִינֵי כַּךְ מִילִין אִינוּן מִתְפָּרְשָׁן, וְלָא אִתְטַמְּרָן בְּדָרִין אָחֳרָנִין לָאו הָכִי, וּמִלִּין דְּרָזֵי עִלָּאָה לָא יַכְלִין לְגַלָּאָה, וְאִינוּן דְּיַדְעֵי מִסְתָּפוּ. דר"ש כַּד הֲוָה אָמַר רָזָא דְּהַאי קְרָא, חַבְרַיָּיא כֻּלְּהוּ עֵינֵיהוֹן נַבְעִין דִּמְעִין, וְכֻלְּהוּ מִילִין דְּאָמַר הֲווֹ בְּעֵינַיְיהוּ גַּלְיָין, כְּמָה דִּכְתִיב פֶּה אֶל פֶּה אֲדַבֶּר בּוֹ וּמַרְאֶה וְלֹא בְחִידֹת.

397. We have learned it is written, "Also you shall not approach to a woman in the impurity of her menstrual flow, to uncover her nakedness" (Vayikra 18:19). Rabbi Yehuda taught, the generation in which Rabbi Shimon bar Yochai dwells are all meritorious, all pious, all sin fearing, the Shechinah dwelling in their midst. Not so in other generations. For this reason, these things are expounded and not concealed, IN HIS GENERATION. In other generations it is not so, and supernal secrets can not be revealed. And those who do know them are afraid TO REVEAL. When Rabbi Shimon would relate the secret of this verse among all the friends, their eyes would flow with tears. All the words he said were being revealed before their very eyes, as the verse says, "With him I speak mouth to mouth, manifestly, and not in dark speeches" (Bemidbar 12:8).

69. A true egg

A Synopsis
The rabbis consider the secrets of the higher levels and wonder
how it is possible to reveal them, because they seem so mysterious.
They are told not to try to reveal them, for it is not time to bring
the higher wisdom down to the lower levels.

398. דְּיוֹמָא חַד שָׁאִיל ר' יֵיסָא אָמַר, בֵּיעָא דְּקוּשְׁטָא, דְּנָפְקָא מֵעוֹפָא
דְּשַׁרְיָא בְּנוּרָא, וְאִתְבְּקַע לְאַרְבַּע סִטְרִין. תְּרֵין סַלְקִין מִנַּיְיהוּ, וְחַד
מָאִיךְ, וְחַד רְבִיע בְּרְבִיעָא דְּיַמָּא רַבָּא. א"ר אַבָּא, עַבְדַת קַמֵּיהּ דר"ש,
קֹדֶשׁ חוֹל, דְּהָא כְּתִיב פֶּה אֶל פֶּה אֲדַבֶּר בּוֹ. א"ל ר"ש, עַד לָא יִתְבְּקַע
בֵּיעָא, תִּסְתָּלַק מֵעָלְמָא. וְכָךְ הֲוָה בְּאִדְרָא דר"ש.

398. One day, Rabbi Yesa asked about the following. He said: A true egg
that laid the bird who dwells in fire breaks up into four sides. Two rise from
them, one is lowered and one squats by the great sea. Rabbi Aba said: Are
you making before Rabbi Shimon the holy into profane, about whom it is
written, "With him I speak mouth to mouth" (Bemidbar 12:8)? Rabbi
Shimon said to him: BEFORE the time of the egg to split, you will depart
from this world. This happened in the gathering of Rabbi Shimon.

399. תָּאנָא, בְּיוֹמוֹי דר"ש הֲוָה אָמַר בַּר נָשׁ לְחַבְרֵיהּ, פְּתַח פִּיךְ וְיָאִירוּ
דְּבָרֶיךְ. בָּתַר דְּשָׁכִיב ר"ש, הֲווֹ אַמְרֵי אַל תִּתֵּן אֶת פִּיךְ לַחֲטִיא אֶת
בְּשָׂרֶךְ.

399. We have learned that during the days of Rabbi Shimon a person would
say to his friend: Open your mouth and let your words shine forth. After the
demise of Rabbi Shimon, they would say, "Do not let your mouth cause
your flesh to sin" (Kohelet 5:5), MEANING DO NOT REVEAL SECRETS.

70. "A woman in the impurity of her menstrual flow," part two

A Synopsis
Rabbi Shimon taught that if people would read the Torah they would not make God angry. We learn that as a result of people's sins the serpent above was awakened and injected his poison in the female; therefore the male left her since she was unclean. The world will be in woe if he joins with her when she is unclean.

400. תַּנְיָא אר״ש, אִי בְּנֵי עָלְמָא מִסְתַּכְּלָן בְּמָה דִּכְתִיב בְּאוֹרַיְיתָא, לָא יֵיתוּן לְאַרְגְּזָא קֵמֵי מָארֵיהוֹן. תָּאנָא, כַּד מִתְעָרִין דִּינִין קַשְׁיָין לְאַחֲתָא בְּעָלְמָא, וְאֶל אִשָּׁה בְּנִדַּת טוּמְאָתָהּ וְגוֹ', הָכָא כְּתִיב סוֹד יְיָ' לִירֵאָיו, וּבְאִדְּרָא קַדִּישָׁא אִתְּמַר, הָכָא אִצְטְרִיכְנָא לְגַלָּאָה, דְּהָא לַאֲתַר דָּא אִסְתַּלָּק.

400. We have learned Rabbi Shimon said that if people would look at what is written in the Torah, they would not come to anger their Master. We have learned when harsh Judgments are stirred to descend to the world, IT IS then WRITTEN, "To a woman in the impurity of her menstrual flow..." (Vayikra 18:19). About this, it is written, "The secret of Hashem is with them that fear Him" (Tehilim 25:14). We have learned this in the Holy gathering and here I wish to reveal this secret. Here it is proper to do, MEANING HERE IS THE PLACE TO REVEAL IT.

401. דְּתָנֵינָן, בְּשַׁעֲתָא דְּחִוְיָא תַּקִּיפָא דִּלְעֵילָא אִתְּעַר, בְּגִין חוֹבֵי עָלְמָא, שָׁארֵי וְאִתְחַבָּר עִם נוּקְבָא, וְאָטִיל בָּהּ זוּהֲמָא, אִתְפְּרַשׁ דְּכוּרָא מִינָהּ, בְּגִין דְּהָא אִסְתָּאֲבַת, וְאִתְקְרִיאַת מְסָאֲבָא, וְלָא אִתְחֲזֵי לִדְכוּרָא לְמִקְרַב בַּהֲדָהּ, דְּווי אִי אִסְתָּאַב הוּא בַּהֲדָהּ, בְּזִמְנָא דְּאִיהִי אִסְתָּאֲבַת.

401. We have learned that when the strong serpent from above was awakened as a result of earth's sins, he dwelt and joined the female and injected his poison in her. Then the male departed from her because she was unclean, and she was called unclean. Then it would not be proper for the male to approach her. Woe TO THE WORLD, if he would become unclean with her when she was unclean.

71. Kinds of impurity

A Synopsis

We learn of the many kinds of impurity that descended with the serpent and how some of them clung to the female; when she is defiled harsh judgments circulate in the world. When the woman wants to be purified she must cut her hair and her nails.

402. וְתָאנָא, מְאָה וְעֶשְׂרִין וַחֲמֵשׁ זִינֵי מְסָאֲבוּתָא נַחְתּוּ לְעָלְמָא, דְּמִתְאַחֲדָן מִסִּטְרָא דְּחִוְיָא תַּקִּיפָא, וְשִׁבְעָה וְעֶשְׂרִין רַבְרְבִין מִנַּיְיהוּ, מִתְאַחֲדָן בְּנוּקְבֵי, וְאִתְדַּבְּקָן בְּהוּ. וַוי לְמַאן דְּיִקְרַב בַּהֲדָהּ בְּהַהוּא זִמְנָא, דְּמַאן דְּיִקְרַב בַּהֲדָהּ, אַחֲזֵי פְּגִימוּתָא לְעֵילָא, דְּהָא בְּחוֹבָא דָא, אִתְּעַר חִוְיָא תַּקִּיפָא לְעֵילָא, וְאַשְׁדֵּי זוּהֲמָא בַּאֲתַר דְּלָא אִצְטְרִיךְ, וְאִתְחַבָּר בְּנוּקְבָּא, וְאִתְרַבֵּי שַׂעֲרֵיהּ לִדְכוּרָא, בְּנוּקְבָּא אִסְתְּאָבַת, וְשַׂעֲרָהָא רַבָּא, וְטוּפְרָהָא סַגִּיאוּ, וּכְדֵין דִּינִין שַׁרְיָין לְאִתְּעָרָא בְּעָלְמָא, וְיִסְתַּאֲבוּן כֹּלָּא. הה"ד, כִּי אֶת מִקְדַּשׁ יְיָ' טִמֵּא, מִקְדַּשׁ יְיָ' אִסְתְּאַב, בְּחוֹבַיְיהוּ דִּבְנֵי נָשָׁא.

402. We have learned that 125 kinds of impurity descended to earth joined AND HELD BY the side of the mighty serpent, and the greater 27 of them hold to the female to join with her. Woe to anyone approaching her at this time, for one who does approach her points to a defect above. With this sin, the mighty serpent above is awakened to spew poison in places where he should not, and he joins the female. The hairs of the male grow and the female is defiled. Her hair grows and her nails grow. Then harsh Judgments begin circulating in the world and everything becomes defiled. This is the essence of the verse, "Because he has defiled the sanctuary of Hashem" (Bemidbar 19:20). The sanctuary of Hashem was defiled due to sins of mankind.

403. תָּאנָא, מַאי דִּכְתִּיב וְאֵיבָה אָשִׁית בֵּינְךָ וּבֵין הָאִשָּׁה, אַרְבָּעָה וְעֶשְׂרִים זִינֵי מְסָאֲבוּתָא אָטִיל חִוְיָא בְּנוּקְבָּא, כַּד אִתְחַבָּר עִמָּהּ, כְּחוּשְׁבָּן וְאֵיבָה, וְעֶשְׂרִין וד' זִינִין מִתְעָרִין לְעֵילָא, וְעֶשְׂרִין וְאַרְבַּע לְתַתָּא. וְשַׂעֲרָא רַבָּא, וְטוּפְרִין סַגִּיאוּ, וּכְדֵין דִּינִין מִתְעָרִין בְּכֹלָּא.

וְתָאנָא כַּד בָּעַת אִתְּתָא לְאִתְדַכְּאָה, בַּעְיָא לְסַפְּרָא הַהוּא שַׂעֲרָא דְרַבֵּי
בְּיוֹמָא דְּאִיהִי מְסָאֲבָא, וּלְסַפְּרָא טוּפְרָהָא, וְכָל הַהוּא זוּהֲמָא דִי בְּהוֹן.

403. We have learned that which is written, "And I will put enmity (Heb. *ve'eivah*) between you and the woman" (Beresheet 3:15). The serpent placed 24 types of defilement in the female when he joined with her, according to the numerical value of *"ve'eivah,"* 24 types stir above and 24 below. The hairs grow and nails grow, then Judgments are awakened in the world. We have learned that when a woman wishes to purify, she needs to cut THE AMOUNT OF hair that grew from the time she became unclean and needs to cut her nails and all the filth within them.

72. The filth of the nails

A Synopsis

We are told that one who eradicates his nails entirely has awakened kindness in the world, because many bad spirits are aroused by the filth in the nails. Sorcerers can perform witchcraft with them, and a person can be harmed if someone steps on their nails.

404. דְּתָאנָא בְּרָזֵי דִּמְסָאֲבוּתָא, זוּהֲמָא דְּטוּפְרִין, יִתְּעַר זוּהֲמָא אָחֳרָא, וּבְגִינֵי כָּךְ, בַּעְיָין גְּנִיזָא, וּמַאן דְּאַעְבָּר לוֹן לְגַמְרֵי, כְּאִלּוּ אִתְּעַר חֶסֶד בְּעָלְמָא. דְּתָנְיָא לָא לִבְעֵי לֵיהּ לְאִינִישׁ לְמֵיהַב דּוּכְרָנָא לְזִינִין בִּישִׁין. דְּתָנֵינָן אֶלֶף וְאַרְבַּע מְאָה וְה' זִינִין בִּישִׁין, מִתְאַחֲדָן בְּהַהוּא זוּהֲמָא, דְּאָטִיל חִוְיָא תַּקִּיפָא, וְכֻלְּהוּ מִתְעָרִין בְּהַהוּא זוּהֲמָא דְּטוּפְרִין.

404. We have learned that in the secrets of defilement, the filth of the nails stir other filth, MEANING THE FILTH OF THE SERPENT. For this reason, it is necessary to hide them. One who eradicates them entirely, BY BURNING THEM, is considered as having awakened Chesed in the world. We have learned that man does not need to leave a memorial for those evil kinds. As we have learned, 1,405 bad types are caught up in the filth that the mighty serpent spews. All are roused by that filth in the nails.

405. וַאֲפִילּוּ מַאן דְּבָעֵי, יַעֲבִיד בְּהוּ חַרְשִׁין לִבְנֵי נָשָׁא, מִשּׁוּם אִינּוּן דְּתַלְיָין בְּהוּ, וּמַאן דְּאַעְבָּר לוֹן, כְּאִלּוּ אַסְגֵּי חֶסֶד בְּעָלְמָא, וְדִינִין בִּישִׁין לָא מִשְׁתַּכְּחִין. וְיַעֲבַר הַהוּא זוּהֲמָא וְטוּפְרָהָא דְּרָשִׁים בֵּיהּ. דְּתַנְיָא, מַאן דְּדָרִיךְ בְּרַגְלֵיהּ, אוֹ בִּמְסָאנֵיהּ עֲלַיְיהוּ, יָכִיל לְאִתְזְקָא. וּמַה בְּהַאי שִׁיּוּרֵי דְּשִׁיּוּרֵי דְּזוּהֲמָא דִּלְעֵילָּא כָּךְ, אִתְּתָא דִּמְקַבְּלָא וְאִתְחַבְּרַת בְּחִוְיָא, וְאָטִיל בָּהּ זוּהֲמָא, עאכ"ו. וַוי לְעָלְמָא דִּמְקַבְּלָא מִינָּהּ מֵהַהוּא זוּהֲמָא, בְּגִינֵי כָּךְ וְאֶל אִשָּׁה בְּנִדַּת טוּמְאָתָהּ לֹא תִקְרַב.

405. Anyone who wants to, can perform witchcraft with them on people, due to these DEMONS that derive from them. He who eradicates them, MEANING BURNS THEM, is considered as if he multiplies kindness in the world so that evil Judgments are not present, and that filth will be annulled,

and its nails that are marked by it, BY THAT FILTH. We have learned that one who steps by foot or shoes on the nails might be harmed. If it is so with the remnants of what was left of the refuse above, then howmuch more so the woman that welcomes and joins with the serpent in whom he injected his refuse. Woe to the world who will receive from her AT THIS TIME, SINCE IT RECEIVES from that refuse. "Also you shall not approach to a woman in the impurity of her menstrual flow" (Vayikra 18:19), MEANING NOT TO RECEIVE FROM MALCHUT AT THE TIME THE SERPENT JOINS HER, BECAUSE OF THE SIN OF LOWER BEINGS, AND INJECTS FILTH INTO HER.

73. Bring before Me atonement

A Synopsis

Rabbi Shimon says that God said: 'Bring before Me atonement on the New Moon,' and he describes what this means. He says that God asks this in order that Malchut will become fragrant and the serpent will pass away from her.

406. אָמַר רִבִּי שִׁמְעוֹן, אָמַר קוּדְשָׁא בְּרִיךְ הוּא, הָבִיאוּ עָלַי כַּפָּרָה בְּר"ח. עָלַי וַדַּאי, בְּגִין דְּיִתְעַבָּר הַהוּא חִוְיָא, וְיִתְבַּסַּם מַאן דְּבַעְיָא. עָלַי: כְּמָה דִכְתִיב שְׂרָפִים עוֹמְדִים מִמַּעַל לוֹ. וְעַ"ד כְּתִיב בְּקֹרַח, הַנּוֹעָדִים עַל יְיָ', דִּבְגִינֵיהוֹן אַתְּעַר מַאן דְּאַתְּעַר דְּאָתֵי מִסִּטְרַיְיהוּ. אוּף הָכִי הָבִיאוּ עָלַי כַּפָּרָה, עָלַי מַמָּשׁ. בְּגִין דְּיִתְבַּסַּם וְיִתְעַבָּר וְלָא אִשְׁתְּכַח חִוְיָא בַּאֲתַר דְּשָׁארֵי. וְכָ"כ לָמָה. עַל שֶׁמִעַטְתִּי אֶת הַיָּרֵחַ, וְשַׁלְטָא בָּהּ מַאן דְּלָא אִצְטְרִיךְ. ובַג"כ כְּתִיב וְאֶל אִשָּׁה בְּנִדַּת טוּמְאָתָהּ לֹא תִקְרַב.

406. Rabbi Shimon said: The Holy One, blessed be He, said, 'Bring atonement before Me on the New Moon', BECAUSE I HAVE REDUCED THE MOON, MALCHUT. "Before Me" surely MEANS ON MY BEHALF, in order to remove the serpent FROM NURSING FROM MALCHUT, and to perfume the one who needs to, NAMELY MALCHUT. "Before (lit. 'upon') Me" TO BE EXPLAINED, as "Serafim stood above him" (Yeshayah 6:2), WHICH DOES NOT MEAN OVER HIM, HEAVEN FORBID, BUT FOR HIS SAKE AND FOR HIS GLORY. HERE TOO, "UPON ME" IS TO BE EXPLAINED AS 'FOR MY SAKE'. Therefore, it is written regarding Korah, "Who are gathered together are against (lit. 'upon') Hashem" (Bemidbar 16:11), WHICH ALSO MEANS "FOR HASHEM," MEANING for them, BECAUSE OF THE SIN OF KORAH AND HIS CONGREGATION, someone was awakened from their side, MEANING THE OTHER SIDE, TO BLEMISH HASHEM. Also here, "Bring before Me your atonement" upon Me literally, MEANING FOR MY SAKE AND FOR ME, in order that MALCHUT will have fragrance and the serpent will pass from her and not be found where it dwelt, MEANING IN A PLACE OF LACK DUE TO THE DIMINISHED MOON. What is all this for? Because I reduced the moon, NAMELY MALCHUT, and he who should not has sway over her. Hence, "also you shall not approach to a woman in the impurity of her menstrual flow" (Vayikra 18:19), AS IN THE ADJACENT PARAGRAPH.

407. זַכָּאָה דָּרָא, דר"ש בֶּן יוֹחָאי שָׁארֵי בְּגַוֵּיה. זַכָּאָה עַדְבֵיה בֵּין עִלָּאִין וְתַתָּאִין. עָלֵיה כְּתִיב, אַשְׁרֵיךְ אֶרֶץ שֶׁמַּלְכֵּךְ בֶּן חוֹרִין. מַהוּ בֶּן חוֹרִין. דְּזָקִיף רֵישָׁא לְגַלָאָה, וּלְפָרְשָׁא מִלִּין וְלָא דָחִיל. כְּהַאי דְּאִיהוּ בֶּן חוֹרִין, וְיֵימָא מַאי דְּבַעְיָא וְלָא דָחִיל. מַהוּ מַלְכֵּךְ. דָּא הוּא רשב"י, מָארֵיה דְּאוֹרַיְיתָא, מָארֵיה דְּחָכְמְתָא. דְּכַד הֲוָה ר' אַבָּא וְחַבְרַיָּיא חָמָאן לְר' שִׁמְעוֹן, הֲווֹ רַהֲטֵי אֲבַתְרֵיה, וְאַמְרֵי, אַחֲרֵי יְיָ' יֵלְכוּ כְּאַרְיֵה יִשְׁאָג.

407. Happy is the generation that Rabbi Shimon dwells therein. Happy is his lot among the higher and lower beings. Regarding him, it is written, "Happy are you, O land, when your king is free" (Kohelet 10:17). What is meant by "free"? His head stands straight and he states matters without fear, as one who is free. He says what he wants and fears not. Who is "your king"? This refers to Rabbi Shimon bar Yochai, master of Torah, master of wisdom. When Rabbi Aba and the sages would see Rabbi Shimon, they would run after him saying, "They shall walk after Hashem, who shall roar like a lion" (Hoshea 11:10).

74. "And it shall come to pass, that every new moon"

A Synopsis

Rabbi Shimon talks about "every new moon, and every Shabbat," saying that they all pertain to one level. There is universal joy when Atika Kadisha, Keter, is revealed to them. He talks about the festival of the New Moon, and how the sun glows with the joy of the light of Atika above.

408. אָמַר ר' שִׁמְעוֹן, כְּתִיב וְהָיָה מִדֵּי חֹדֶשׁ בְּחָדְשׁוֹ וּמִדֵּי שַׁבָּת בְּשַׁבַּתּוֹ, אֲמַאי שָׁקִיל דָּא בְּדָא. אֶלָּא כֹּלָּא בְּחַד דַּרְגָּא סְלִיקוּ, דָּא אִזְדַּוַּוג בְּדָא. וְחֶדְוָותָא דְּדָא בְּדָא לָא אִשְׁתְּכַח, אֶלָּא כַּד אִתְגְּלֵי עַתִּיקָא קַדִּישָׁא, וּכְדֵין חֶדְוָותָא דְּכֹלָּא. וְתָנֵינָן, כְּתִיב מִזְמוֹר שִׁיר לְיוֹם הַשַּׁבָּת, לְיוֹם הַשַּׁבָּת מַמָּשׁ. שְׁבָחָא דְּקָא מְשַׁבַּח קוּדְשָׁא בְּרִיךְ הוּא. כְּדֵין חֶדְוָותָא אִשְׁתְּכַח, וְנִשְׁמְתָא אִתּוֹסְפַת. דְּהָא עַתִּיקָא אִתְגְּלֵי וְזִוּוּגָא יִזְדַּמַּן.

408. Rabbi Shimon said: It is written, "And it shall come to pass, that every new moon, and every Shabbat..." (Yeshayah 66:23). HE QUESTIONS: Why are they compared, MEANING WHY ARE BOTH CONSIDERED TOGETHER IN THE VERSE? HE ANSWERS: All pertain to one level and the one is united with the other. SHABBAT, BEING ZEIR ANPIN, IS UNITED WITH THE NEW MOON, DENOTING MALCHUT. There is no joy of one in the other, WHEN THEY ARE NOT UNITED. Only when Atika Kadisha, KETER, is revealed TO THEM, is there universal joy. We have learned that it is written, "A psalm, a poem for the Shabbat day" (Tehilim 92:1). It is expressly for the Shabbat day, ZEIR ANPIN, THE SECRET OF THE SHABBAT DAY, denoting the praise which the Holy One, blessed be He, recites. Then is found joy and an additional soul, due to the fact that Atika was revealed and the union OF ZEIR ANPIN AND MALCHUT is occurring.

409. אוּף הָכִי בְּחֶדְוָותֵי סִיהֲרָא, דְּהָא נָהִיר לָהּ שִׁמְשָׁא בְּחֶדְוָותָא דִּנְהִירוּ דְּעַתִּיקָא לְעֵילָּא. בְּגִינֵי כַּךְ הַאי קָרְבְּנָא הוּא לְעֵילָּא, בְּגִין דְּיִתְבְּסַם כֹּלָּא, וְיִשְׁתְּכַח חֶדְוָותָא בְּעָלְמָא, וְעַ"ד הָבִיאוּ עָלַי כַּפָּרָה, דַּיְיקָא מִלָּה.

409. It is the same with the renewal of the moon, MEANING AT THE NEW MOON. The sun, DENOTING ZEIR ANPIN, shines on it with the joy of the light of Atika above. For this reason, the sacrifice of the New Moon is above in order to bring fragrance to all, and joy should be prevalent in the world. Therefore, 'bring atonement before Me'. This wording is literal IN ORDER TO AWAKEN THE UNION.

410. תָּאנָא, כְּתִיב עוֹלַת שַׁבַּת בְּשַׁבַּתּוֹ עַל עוֹלַת הַתָּמִיד, דְּבָעֵי לְכַוְּונָא לְבָּא לְעֵילָא לְעֵילָא, יַתִּיר מִשְּׁאָר יוֹמִין. וְעַ"ד עַל עוֹלַת הַתָּמִיד דַּיְיקָא. תַּנְיָא, כְּתִיב בְּחַנָּה וַתִּתְפַּלֵל עַל יְיָ', עַל דַּיְיקָא, בְּגִין דְּבָנִין בְּמַזָּלָא קַדִישָׁא תַּלְיָין, כְּמָה דְּאוּקִימְנָא וְלֵית לָךְ מִלָּה בְּאוֹרַיְיתָא, אוֹ אָת זְעֵירָא בְּאוֹרַיְיתָא. דְּלָא רְמִיזָא בְּחָכְמְתָא עִלָּאָה, וְתַלְיָין מִנֵּיהּ תָּלֵי תָּלִין רָזִין דְּחָכְמְתָא עִלָּאָה, הַה"ד קְוּוצוֹתָיו תַּלְתַּלִים, וְהָא אִתְּמַר.

410. We have learned that it is written, "This is the burnt offering of every Shabbat, beside (lit. 'over') the continual burnt offering" (Bemidbar 28:10), MEANING one needs to aim his heart much higher this day than other days. Therefore, "over the continual burnt offering" is to be understood literally, AS "OVER" IS TO BE EXPLAINED ABOVE THE CONTINUAL OFFERING. We have learned that it is written concerning Hannah, "And prayed to (lit. 'over') Hashem" (I Shmuel 1:10). "Over" literally, MEANING ABOVE HASHEM, ZEIR ANPIN, as children are dependent on the holy Mazal, THE BEARD OF ARICH ANPIN. We have established this TO BE HIGHER THAN ZEIR ANPIN. Not a single thing in the Torah, or small letter in the Torah, does not hint at the supernal wisdom. Mounds and mounds (Heb. *tilim*) of supernal wisdom depend upon it. This is the meaning of, "His locks (Heb. *taltalim*) are wavy" (Shir Hashirim 5:11), as we have already learned.

75. "Cast your burden upon Hashem"

A Synopsis

We learn that the title verse means 'above Hashem', namely Mazal, for this is a prayer for sustenance. The righteous are fortunate in this world and in the World to Come because they are able to draw that sustenance from a high place.

411. ר' יוֹסֵי אַשְׁכָּחֵיהּ לְר' אַבָּא, דַּהֲוָה יָתִיב וְקָאָרֵי, הַאי קְרָא דִּכְתִּיב, הַשְׁלֵךְ עַל יְיָ' יְהָבְךָ, עַל דַּיְיקָא, דְּהָא מְזוֹנֵי בְּמַזָּלָא תַּלְיָין. ר' יְהוּדָה הֲוָה קָאָרֵי, עַל זֹאת יִתְפַּלֵּל כָּל חָסִיד אֵלֶיךָ לְעֵת מְצֹא. עַל זֹאת וַדַּאי. לְעֵת מְצֹא, הָא אוּקִימְנָא, אֲבָל לְעֵת מְצֹא, כְּמָה דִּכְתִּיב דִּרְשׁוּ יְיָ' בְּהִמָּצְאוֹ קְרָאוּהוּ בִּהְיוֹתוֹ קָרוֹב. ד"א לְעֵת מְצֹא, בְּשַׁעֲתָא דְּנַהֲרִין נַגְדִּין וְאִתְמַשְּׁכָאן, וּמִסְתַּפְּקֵי אֲבָהָן, וּמִתְבָּרְכָאן כֹּלָּא. רַק לְשֵׁטֶף מַיִם רַבִּים, מַאן שֵׁטֶף מַיִם רַבִּים, דָּא עֲמִיקָא דְּמַבּוּעִין וְנַהֲרִין, דְּמַאן יִזְכֶּה לֵיהּ, וּמַאן יִזְכֶּה לְקָרְבָא וּלְסַלְּקָא תַּמָּן. הה"ד בֵּיהּ, רַק לְשֵׁטֶף מַיִם רַבִּים אֵלָיו לֹא יַגִּיעוּ דְּהָא לָא זַכָּאן, וְלָא יַכְלִין.

411. Rabbi Yosi found Rabbi Aba sitting and reading this verse, "Cast your burden upon Hashem" (Tehilim 55:23). "Upon" is precise, MEANING ABOVE HASHEM, ZEIR ANPIN. Sustenance is dependent on Mazal, THE BEARD OF ARICH ANPIN. Rabbi Yehuda used to read, "For (lit. 'upon') this (Heb. *zot* fem.) shall everyone that is godly pray to You in a time when You may be found" (Tehilim 32:6). "Upon *Zot*" surely, MEANING ABOVE MALCHUT CALLED *ZOT*, BEING TIFERET THAT IS ABOVE MALCHUT. "In a time...be found," we established that it REFERS TO A WOMAN. Yet "in a time...be found" is like the words, "Seek Hashem while He may be found, call upon Him while He is near" (Yeshayah 55:6), REFERRING TO THE TEN DAYS OF REPENTANCE. Another explanation for, "In a time...be found," MEANING when the rivers, THE LIGHTS OF BINAH, flow and are drawn continuously. The Patriarchs, BEING CHESED GVURAH TIFERET, receive and all are blessed, FOR EVERY PIOUS MAN SHOULD PRAY FOR THIS. What is meant by "the flood of great waters" (Tehilim 32:6)? HE ANSWERS: It is the depth of the springs and rivers, BEING ATIKA KADISHA, FROM WHICH ARE DRAWN THE LIGHTS AND SPRINGS TO BINAH. For who will merit it, and who will merit to come near and ascend there! This is what is meant by

the verse, "The flood of great waters shall not come near him." It is because they are not worthy and not capable OF RECEIVING FROM ATIKA.

412. רִבִּי יִצְחָק אָמַר, כְּתִיב אַחַת שָׁאַלְתִּי מֵאֵת יְיָ' אוֹתָהּ אֲבַקֵּשׁ וְגוֹ'. זַכָּאִין אִינּוּן צַדִּיקַיָּיא, דְּכַמָה גְּנִיזִין עִלָּאִין טְמִירִין לְהוּ בְּהַהוּא עָלְמָא, דְּקוּדְשָׁא בְּרִיךְ הוּא מִשְׁתַּעֲשַׁע בְּהוּ בְּאִינּוּן עָלְמִין, כְּמָה דְּאוֹקִימְנָא בְּנֹעַם יְיָ', וְהָא אִתְּמַר. ר' חִזְקִיָּה אָמַר מֵהָכָא, עַיִן לֹא רָאָתָה אֱלֹהִים זוּלָתְךָ יַעֲשֶׂה לִמְחַכֵּה לוֹ. יַעֲשֶׂה, תַּעֲשֶׂה מִבְּעֵי לֵיהּ. אֶלָּא יַעֲשֶׂה וַדַּאי, הַיְינוּ יוֹסִיף עַל יָמֶיךָ חֲמֵשׁ עֶשְׂרֵה שָׁנָה. וְהַיְינוּ הַשְׁלֵךְ עַל ה' יְהָבְךָ. וּכְתִיב וַתִּתְפַּלֵּל עַל יְיָ'. וְכֹלָּא חַד.

412. Rabbi Yitzchak said: It is written, "One thing have I desired of Hashem, that I will seek after...to behold the beauty of Hashem" (Tehilim 27:4). Blessed are the pious that numerous supernal treasures await them in that world, DENOTING BINAH, as the Holy One, blessed be He, delights in them in these worlds, as we have explained. FOR THEIR SAKE HE ASKED TO BEHOLD the beauty of Hashem. We have already learned THAT IT IS THE GLOW OF ATIKA THAT IS DRAWN IN BINAH. RABBI YITZCHAK DISPUTES WITH RABBI YEHUDA, WHO SAID THAT "THE FLOOD OF GREAT WATERS SHALL NOT COME NEAR HIM" REFERS TO THE LIGHTS OF ATIKA THAT CANNOT BE CONCEIVED. HOWEVER, THERE ARE SOME RIGHTEOUS WHO MERIT THIS TOO. Rabbi Chizkiyah says: From here, IT SEEMS THAT THERE ARE PIOUS WHO DO MERIT THE LIGHT OF ATIKA, as written, "Neither has the eye seen, that an Elohim, beside You, should do such a thing for him that waits for Him" (Yeshayah 64:3). HE ASKS, 'He should do': It should have said, 'You should do', SINCE IT WRITES "BESIDE YOU," A TERM OF SECOND PERSON. HE REPLIES: Rather, 'he should do' is precise, BECAUSE IT REFERS TO ATIKA. THEREFORE, HE SPEAKS IN TERMS OF THIRD PERSON. Similarly, "behold, I (lit. 'he') will add to your days fifteen years" (Yeshayah 38:5). IT SHOULD HAVE SAID, 'I WILL ADD', SINCE IT PRECEDES IT WITH "BEHOLD (LIT. 'HERE I AM')." IT IS ONLY BECAUSE IT ALLUDES TO ATIKA, WHO IS NOT CONCEIVED TO BE HERE. THEREFORE, HE SAYS IN THIRD PERSON, "HE WILL ADD." IT IS BECAUSE LIFE IS DRAWN FROM MAZAL, MEANING FROM THE BEARD OF ATIKA. Similarly, "Cast your burden upon Hashem" MEANS ABOVE HASHEM, NAMELY MAZAL, FOR THIS IS A PRAYER FOR SUSTENANCE. It is also written, "And

prayed to (lit. 'over') Hashem," ALSO REFERRING TO MAZAL THAT IS HIGHER ABOVE OF HASHEM, AS THIS PRAYER WAS FOR CHILDREN. Yet all is one, FOR IT IS ALL DRAWN FROM THE MAZAL, THE BEARD OF ATIKA KADISHA. THUS, IT IS POSSIBLE TO RECEIVE AND DRAW ABUNDANCE ALSO FROM ATIKA KADISHA, UNLIKE RABBI YEHUDA'S WORDS.

413. זַכָּאָה חוּלָקֵיהוֹן דְּצַדִּיקַיָּיא, בְּעָלְמָא דֵין וּבְעָלְמָא דְּאָתֵי, עֲלַיְיהוּ כְּתִיב וְיִשְׂמְחוּ כָל חוֹסֵי בָךְ לְעוֹלָם יְרַנֵּנוּ וְתָסֵךְ עָלֵימוֹ וְיַעְלְצוּ בְךָ אוֹהֲבֵי שְׁמֶךָ. וּכְתִיב אַךְ צַדִּיקִים יוֹדוּ לִשְׁמֶךָ יֵשְׁבוּ יְשָׁרִים אֶת פָּנֶיךָ. וּכְתִיב וְיִבְטְחוּ בְךָ יוֹדְעֵי שְׁמֶךָ כִּי לֹא עָזַבְתָּ דוֹרְשֶׁיךָ יְיָ'.

413. Fortunate is the portion of the righteous in this world and the World to Come. Regarding them, it is written, "But let all those that put their trust in You rejoice: let them ever shout for joy, because You do defend them: and let those who love Your name be joyful in You" (Tehilim 5:12). It is also written, "Surely the righteous shall give thanks to Your name: the upright shall dwell in Your presence" (Tehilim 140:14) and "They that know Your name will put their trust in You: for You, Hashem, have not forsaken those who seek You" (Tehilim 9:11).

בָּרוּךְ יְיָ' לְעוֹלָם אָמֵן וְאָמֵן. יִמְלוֹךְ יְיָ' לְעוֹלָם אָמֵן וְאָמֵן.

Blessed is Hashem forever. Amen and Amen. May Hashem reign forever. Amen and Amen.

NOTES